MANAGERIAL ECONOMICS

MANAGERIAL ECONOMICS

by

JOEL DEAN

GRADUATE SCHOOL OF BUSINESS
COLUMBIA UNIVERSITY

and

JOEL DEAN ASSOCIATES

PRENTICE-HALL, INC.

Englewood Cliffs, N. J.

Current printing (last digit):
25   24   23   22   21   20

PRINTED IN THE UNITED STATES OF AMERICA
54997—C

To
PHYLLIS, JOEL, GRETCHEN,
GILLIAN, *and* JURRIEN

Acknowledgments to Publishers

THE AUTHOR wishes to acknowledge his gratitude to the publishers who graciously permitted him to use parts of the following of his articles and monographs in this book:

ARTICLES

"Cost Structures of Enterprises and Break-even Charts," *American Economic Review,* May, 1948.

"When A Motor Vehicle Should Be Replaced," *Society of Automotive Engineers Quarterly Transactions,* October, 1948.

"Determination of Pricing Policy Under Competitive Conditions," *American Management Association,* 1949.

"Problems of Product-Line Pricing," *Journal of Marketing,* January, 1950.

"Product Line Policy," *Journal of Business,* October, 1950.

"Pricing Policies for New Products," *Harvard Business Review,* November, 1950.

"How Much to Spend on Advertising," *Harvard Business Review,* January, 1951.

"Cyclical Policy on the Advertising Appropriation," *Journal of Marketing,* January, 1951.

"Measuring Profits for Executive Decisions," *Accounting Review,* April, 1951.

"Capital Rationing and the Firm's Demand for Capital," *Zeitschrift für Ökonometrie,* 1951.

MONOGRAPHS

Statistical Determination of Costs, With Special Reference to Marginal Costs, University of Chicago Press, 1936.

Statistical Cost Functions of a Hosiery Mill, University of Chicago Press, 1941.

The Relation of Cost to Output for a Leather Belt Shop, National Bureau of Economic Research, 1941.

Long-Run Behavior of Costs in a Chain of Shoe Stores, University of Chicago Press, 1942, with R. Warren James.

Pricing from the Seller's Standpoint, Columbia University, 1949.

Capital Budgeting, Columbia University Press, 1951.

Preface

THE PURPOSE of this book is to show how economic analysis can be used in formulating business policies. It is therefore a departure from the main stream of economic writings on the theory of the firm, much of which is too simple in its assumptions and too complicated in its logical development to be managerially useful. The big gap between the problems of logic that intrigue economic theorists and the problems of policy that plague practical management needs to be bridged in order to give executives access to the practical contributions that economic thinking can make to top-management policies.

In developing an economic approach to executive decisions, this book draws upon economic analysis for the concepts of demand, cost, profit, competition, and so on, that are appropriate for the decision, and it draws upon modern methods of econometrics and market research for getting estimates of the relevant concept. For certain problems it was necessary to develop some extensions and reformulations of economic theory, in the light of what a businessman knows or can reasonably expect to guess. Although the book is preoccupied with concepts rather than detailed techniques of estimation, it concentrates on those concepts that can be measured and applied to management problems.

The book does not attempt to cover all aspects of either management or economics: it deals only with those phases of enterprise economics that strike me as particularly useful to the management of a large industrial corporation. Most of the analysis is an outgrowth of my consulting work, and I have learned much from my clients and from my consulting associates.

My greatest debt is to Stephen Taylor of Joel Dean Associates. He has been of major assistance at every stage of this undertaking: hammering out the ideas, criticizing, editing, and re-writing my drafts, revising galleys, and preparing exhibits. Philip Brooks, another associate, developed many of the ideas in the course of our work for clients. He also suggested important improvements in the chapters on "Profits," "Costs," "Advertising," and "Capital Budgeting." Melvin de Chazeau, of Cornell University, read the entire manuscript with discernment and made many helpful suggestions. James Bonbright and Carl Shoup of Columbia University have heartened and helped me throughout this undertaking; David Blank and Samuel Richmond have also been

kind enough to read much of the manuscript and make useful suggestions.   Ralph Cordiner of General Electric Company, Frederick
Donner of General Motors Corporation, John Kusik of the Chesa-
peake and Ohio Railway Company, and Albert Nickerson of Socony-
Vacuum Oil Company also read parts of the manuscript and helped
me with their comments.   Miss Mary Hudson typed the whole manuscript, cheerfully, competently, and in many versions.   It is a pleasure
to express my gratitude for all this assistance.

Yonkers   J. D.
January, 1951.

Table of Contents

Charts

Tables

TABLES

MANAGERIAL
ECONOMICS

Chapter 1

PROFITS

I. INTRODUCTION

II. NATURE OF PROFITS

WHAT TO EXCLUDE
TYPES OF PROFIT THEORY
Reward for Risk-taking
Frictions and Imperfections
Innovations
SUMMARY

III. PROFIT MEASUREMENT

CONCEPTUAL CONFLICT
SPECIFIC ISSUES
Depreciation
Treatment of Capital Gains and Losses
Current vs. Historical Costs
Contemporary-dollar profits
Constant-dollar profits
IMPACT ON BUSINESS DECISIONS
SUMMARY

IV. POLICIES ON PROFIT MAXIMIZATION

REASONS FOR LIMITING PROFITS
Competitive Considerations
Public Relations
Labor Relations
Customer Relations
Maintaining Control
Nonfinancial Amenities
STANDARDS OF REASONABLE PROFITS
Form of Standard
Setting the Standard
Capital-attracting rate of return
The "plow-back" rate
Normal earnings
Popular conceptions of reasonable earnings
Choosing a Standard
SUMMARY

V. PROFITS FOR CONTROL

Profits

I. INTRODUCTION

A BUSINESS FIRM is an organization designed to make prof its, and profits are the primary measure of its success. Social criteria of business performance usually relate to quality of products, rate of progress, and behavior of prices. But these are tests of the desirability of the whole profit system. Within that system, profits are the acid test of the individual firm's performance.

The first purpose of this chapter is to bring out what is meant by the economic concept of profit. The word "profit" has different meanings to businessmen, accountants, tax collectors, workers, and economists, and it is often used in a loose, polemical sense that buries its real significance and destroys the basis for discussion. In appraising a company, we must first understand how profits arise, before we can decide what is and is not a profit, and before we can improve the company's profit position.

The second purpose of this chapter is to consider a few managerial aspects of profits. We shall discuss three kinds of problems: (1) profit measurement, i.e., economic analysis of accounting data for policy-making; (2) policy decisions on profit standards and profit goals; and (3) the use of profits for control purposes in a complex business organization.[1]

II. NATURE OF PROFITS

In the theory of income distribution, economists classify all income of the economy into types, according to the nature of its

---

[1] There is a fourth kind of profit problem, which we will not take up in this chapter, namely, what to do with profits after they are made. This is a financial problem that involves a strategic choice between paying out profits in dividends as opposed to reinvesting them. This choice enters into capital budgeting and promotional outlays to increase sales and is discussed in Chapters 10 and 6. It also enters into decisions on cash budgeting, liquidity preferences, and short-term external investments—matters outside the scope of this book.

source. Wages are income from direct labor; interest is the income from letting other people use one's money; rent is the excess of the value produced by a productive factor over the payment needed to induce it to work; and profit is the excess of income over cost of production. Wages, interest, and rent have had a firm standing in theory for well over a century, but profit has always been a center of controversy. When does it appear? Who produces it? Who gets it? [2]

In a stationary economy, in which everything turns out as expected and people know exactly what their incomes will be, costs can be accurately imputed and the whole of the economic system can be distributed as wages, interest, and rent; so there remains no residual for profits. A firm can make agreements beforehand to pay as costs these incomes to the factors of production. But in the real world, incomes do not turn out as expected. Someone gets a bonus and someone else finds himself short. The resulting unexpected residuals could be shared equally by all factors of production through a profit-sharing plan, but they usually are not. Most people would rather be able to count on a limited income than depend on the uncertain chance of striking a bonanza. In practice, almost everyone gets a commitment from his employer to pay a definite income, and one or a few people (those who own the equity) agree to take what is left as profit.

Since profits are at the end of the line in the distribution of sales revenue, they are difficult to forecast accurately and therefore have a large element of risk. In this sense, they are something more than the net receipts of the firm in a stationary economy.

What To Exclude

As a simple starting point, profits, then, are the revenue that is left after costs. But what to include as costs has caused much argument. Outlays for material, for labor, and interest on borrowed money cause no contention but what about top executives' salaries? Some economists think wages of management, even when paid as salaries (rather than as dividends) should be included in costs; others think they are part of profits. But the

---

[2] For a summary of arguments, see R. A. Gordon, "Enterprise, Profits, and the Modern Corporation," in American Economic Association, *Readings in the Theory of Income Distribution*, Philadelphia, The Blakiston Company, 1946, pp. 558–570.

central issues concern non-cash items such as income that owners could earn if working elsewhere, and interest that their funds could command if lent to other firms. These opportunity costs do not appear on the books and hence are excluded from conventional accounting profits.

The economist may or may not include as a cost the value of the risk-taker's time spent on problems of the firm. If he does view it as a cost, then his concept of profit includes wages of management. The economist may or may not deduct as a cost interest on the risk-taker's capital in arriving at profits. If he does not deduct it, his concept of profits comes close to the concept of conventional accounting, i.e., the income that goes to owners of the stock.[3]

If he does deduct this interest, he must decide what interest rate to use: (1) the market rate on riskless investments,[4] such as government bonds; or (2) a rate that reflects risk and uncertainty, i.e., that allows for possibilities of earning more or less than the market rate on governments. When equity capital is costed at a "riskless" rate of interest, what remains as profit is the premium return on capital that is paid for the unpleasant task of assuming risk. When equity capital is costed at a rate that reflects risks, then presumably the remaining profit will be symmetrically distributed between positive or negative, i.e., all profit is windfall. These windfall profits do not pay for any specific economic service, but function as a lure, which presumably on balance costs society nothing.

In modern industry, an interest cost is not imputed for equity money. Hence, profits reported under accounting conventions lump interest return with reward for taking risks. Blanketing the interest cost on owners' funds into reported profits results in a substantial exaggeration of "pure" profits, since about three-quarters of the capital of corporate enterprise is composed of equi-

---

[3] Interest on income bonds is deducted in computing accounting profits, but dividends on preferred stock, which have the same economic significance, are not. Viewing profits as the income to common stock avoids this anomaly.

[4] "Riskless" only in the sense of maximum assurance of payment of interest and principal in money. Fluctuations in the purchasing power make even these risky. To remove this hazard, Remington Rand issued bonds whose interest and principal payments were adjusted by a price level index. During the inflation in Germany that followed World War I, kilowatt-hour bonds and rye bonds were issued.

ties.   Thus, what is, by accounting convention,[5] labeled net profits in the corporate income statement, is not profits as the economist typically views them.   Instead, it is a hybrid which includes elements of interest and perhaps wages and rent, as well as economic profits.[6]   To break this into its components would require extensive study of the history of capital structure and activities of the firm.

There is, however, a rough parallel to an interest cost of equity funds in a large and mature corporation which has scattered public ownership.   Dividends on common stock may approximate an interest cost of capital.   When there are thousands of passive and uninformed stockholders, ownership is far removed from the profit-creating function; hired management takes over.   Dividends are paid largely to keep stockholders passive and management enthroned and to maintain the company's reputation in the capital markets.   Consequently, cash dividend income to common stockholders takes on the nature of a generous, though somewhat uncertain interest return on capital.   The remaining accounting earnings, which are roughly analogous to "pure" profits, are retained for internal investment.   These plowed-back, "pure" profits are "received" by the owners only in the form of appreciation of the market value of their stock and the reduction of the uncertainty of the common dividend flow.

Types of Profit Theory

Economic theories on profits may be put in three broad groups: The first looks upon profits as the reward for bearing risks and uncertainties; the second views profits as the consequence of frictions and imperfections in the competitive adjustment of the economy to dynamic changes; the third sees profits as the reward for successful innovation.

---

[5] Accountants, of course, are not agreed in their concepts or methods of measuring profits.   They are at odds, for example, in the way in which inventory should be accounted for.   LIFO produces a different concept of profits than FIFO as discussed in Section III.   Different depreciation methods, moreover, yield different profit concepts.

[6] Reported accounting profits might be broken down in several ways: for example, (1) pure interest on riskless investments; (2) a compensation for risk and uncertainty; (3) a reward for high-level managerial labor; and (4) frictional and monopoly rewards (not necessary for keeping an economy going, but needed to induce innovation).

Reward for Risk-taking

According to some theories, profits are the factor payment for taking the risk—for agreeing to take what is left over after contractual outlays have been made. To an important degree this profit theory is based upon the notion that, although some people prefer riskiness (as is evidenced by the hopelessness of campaigns to suppress gambling) most people do not; at least they don't like it in making investments. Consequently, a higher reward is required as the risk increases. The tendency of the market price of a stock to fall when some development brings recognition of increased riskiness supports this basic assumption.

A distinction can be made between risk and uncertainty. Risk is a calculable (at least conceptually) actuarial probability. It has a "most probable" actuarial value and dispersion about it. The degree of riskiness is then measured by the amount of this dispersion. In contrast, uncertainty, in its pure form, does not make it possible to know either the most probable value or the amount of dispersion about it. This is much the same distinction that is sometimes made between insurable and non-insurable risks where the uncertainties attached to the latter are so imponderable that no insurance company is large enough to assume these hazards.[7]

One of the major uncertainties of a businessman, for example, comes from holding special purpose assets as opposed to holding general purchasing power. To be sure, there are price-level risks from holding cash or its equivalent, but there is an even greater risk in holding a resort hotel. Such hazards derive from dynamic shifts in tastes and technology that do not lend themselves to actuarial calculations.

Risks are, of course, not confined to owners who receive profits. Non-entrepreneurial risks are also important. One of these is the risk of vocational specialization. A worker who invests his time and money in an apprenticeship cannot be sure to get a return on that investment over his lifetime, since the craft may become obsolete. In addition, there are risks of unemployment

---

[7] With the advent of the government's full employment commitments, farm price supports, and guaranteed income for landlords, the nation as a whole has taken over many insurance functions of bearing both risks and uncertainties.

which, though recognized, and to some degree "insured," remain important.

Frictions and Imperfections

Instead of viewing profits as factor income for assuming risks, a second group of theories look upon profit as a result of frictions and imperfections in the adjustment of the economy to change.

Profits appear because the economy cannot adjust itself to changes in costs and demand immediately; that is, profits are the result of disequilibrium and imperfect competition. For example, when available production facilities failed to meet the postwar boom in durable goods demand, a profit bonanza resulted.[8] Every change in the value of land may be explained by this theory, since the supply of land is in general fixed, and its price should reflect foreseeable income from it. This concept further regards as profit the enhanced earnings of a permanent monopoly, where entry of competitors is estopped by legal barriers (such as patent protection), or by control of scarce resources or markets. In fact, according to this theory, profit occurs in every situation where the marginal product does not equal its marginal cost. It encompasses all imperfections of competition and thus goes far beyond the usual idea of profit as the return for some kind of entrepreneurial activity, be it only risk-taking.

Innovations

In the third type of profit theory, profits are viewed as a wage for the service of innovation. As in the risk theories, they are thus a functional income, but risk plays no essential part in the innovation theory. Profits in this theory are tied to dynamic development, the most prided feature of the American economy. More than any other theory of profits, this one gets at the meaning of "profits" as the word is commonly used today, for it is hard to deny that innovation has been the backbone of business success in this country.

Innovation refers broadly to any purposeful change in production methods or consumer tastes that increases national output

---

8 In some cases, e.g., steel and automobiles, the boom profits were foregone to some extent by the large producers, who restrained prices for reasons of long-run effects (see Section IV below). Much of the profit was taken by dealers in extras, bonuses, and used-car trade-ins, and other "gray-market" differentials.

more than it increases costs. The increase in net output is the profit that comes from innovation.[9]

In the pure theory of innovation profits [10] the key role is played by the entrepreneur (synonymous with innovator), who sees the value of a new idea and is able to organize and carry out the job of turning it into cash. (He is not the inventor who finds the idea; business genius rarely comes with intellectual genius.) Generically, the new idea is either a method to produce an existing product at less cost, to expand its sales at existing prices, or to make a new product that will sell at higher prices. When the economy functions as a free-enterprise system (and frequently in other types of system), the entrepreneur converts the idea into a net increase in national output by acting as organizer: he borrows capital at market interest rates, hires workers at current wage rates, and sets up the production and sales function into a going concern. Everyone employed is paid as much as he could earn elsewhere, and the entrepreneur pockets the surplus over these (opportunity) employment costs.

Risk and uncertainty are not necessary to this theory. Conceivably, innovation can strike (and shatter) a stationary economy, as conceived in economic theory. In this case the entrepreneur may be able to forecast what his gain will be while other firms are blissfully ignorant of the impending obsolescence hanging over them. But if there is risk, it is carried by the capitalist, not the enterpreneur, who stands to lose nothing but his reputation.

By this theory, then, profit is the reward for disrupting the status quo. It is neither capricious, as in friction theories, nor is it necessarily identified with invested capital, as in the important risk-bearing theories.

After the innovation hits the market, there is a long or short period of readjustment (see Chapter 7, "Basic Price," Section III) in which new firms climb onto the band wagon, labor shifts to the new industry, and obsolete products die out. If nothing else happens, things eventually reach equilibrium again, with

---

[9] Innovation and its profits are by no means limited to the business world or to a competitive system; they occur when the government builds a TVA, when the Russians discover oil in Siberia, or when Crusoe devises a bow and arrow. The essential distinction here among social systems is the way in which the new surplus is distributed.

[10] As stated by Schumpeter in *Theory of Economic Development*, Cambridge: Harvard University Press, 1934.

a new set of wages, prices, producers, and products.   By this time the profits have been eliminated, for innovation profits exist only in times of dynamic change.   If competition is complete, prices have again been battered down to cost levels.   But if, by patents or some such barrier, the entrepreneur has held off competition, his profits have turned into a monopoly revenue, which is not profit, but a rent.   The rental revenue can occasionally be expropriated by a monopoly factor of production, e.g., a tightly organized labor union.

Innovations are viewed here against a background of equilibrium, and profits arise in the transition from one equilibrium to another.   Equilibrium may be a dubious concept in a dynamic economy, since innovations not only overlap but are highly interrelated in their nature and timing.   But equilibrium is by no means essential to the argument.   The innovation theory drives at the historical fact (neglected by stationary analysis) that capitalism flourishes in a rapidly changing economic scene—that when development slows its pace, competitive enterprise develops hardening of the arteries, and the economy degenerates toward cartels, the corporate state, and nationalization of industry. Although this general notion is now familiar, a theory that incorporates it into a system gives it intellectual appeal and persuasiveness.   The innovation theory should be the keystone of social policy for sustaining our economic virility.   It has implications for tax laws, antitrust laws, patents, and the orientation of public education and research in maintaining incentives to create new ideas.

In this theory, profits become an objective measure of the social value of ideas.   Although individually we may have value judgments on good and bad innovations, most of us would hesitate to thrust our tastes onto everyone.   The national consensus is found in market performance.   (Subject, of course, to the usual qualifications about imperfect markets.)

The concept of innovation becomes very broad in this theory, since it includes not only new products such as plastics and economic theories, but new organizations (grocery chains), new markets (electric cooking), new promotion (singing commercials), and new raw materials (aluminum).   To an important degree, innovation has been built into the competitive system complete with research laboratories and advertising staffs.   In many industries everyone has to run fast to stay in the same place.   True innovation should be distinguished from style rivalry.   Credible evidence of true innovation is a high rate of company growth from plowed-back earnings.

In American industry, innovation profits take many forms. Consequently the theory should not be tested in solely financial terms.   A favorite paradox among political economists is that the mainspring of innovation is top corporate management, which works for a salary, while profits go to stockholders, who know nothing about the company's research efforts and are passive about hiring the men who do.   Our high rate of innovation shows that management has effective incentives, though they may be to a large degree intangible.

Aside from indirect financial rewards such as management bonus systems and stock ownership (see Chapter 10, "Capital Budgeting," Section III), there seems to be much psychic income in the form of prestige, control, and social glory in operating a growing firm.[11]

To evaluate the adequacy of management's incentives we need to combine a vast statistical study with first-hand experience and insight.   Though the investigation may be beyond the scope of the economist *per se*, the problem has great economic significance, for technologically there seems to be no limit to innovation possibilities, and the only restraints on further advance are ability and the incentives to use it.   The important product of this kind of study should be more knowledge of how, through innovation, executive talent can be stepped up by financial and non-financial rewards.[12]   An analysis of these rewards would give clues to the impact of taxation and equalization of income distribution on a strategic type of business incentive.

---

[11] Under psychic theories of management income, retained earnings go both to stockholders, as gains in market value of shares, and to management, as an increase in the size of their domain.   Retained earnings can be broadly conceived as the pure profits of the corporation, while dividends are the cost of capital (Chapter 10, Section III), provided they are limited to the amount needed to maintain a market rate of return on historical investment.   This conception corresponds to Schumpeter's original statement of the innovation theory, in which he considered profits the real source of the world's accumulated capital, whereas factor incomes, including interest on capital, were devoted entirely to consumption.

[12] These problems are discussed further in Section IV below, and in Chapter 10, "Capital Budgeting," Section III.   A valuable contribution in this field is R. A. Gordon, *Business Leadership in the Large Corporation,* Brookings Institution, Washington, 1945.

Summary

This section has indicated that concepts of profit are more varied than are the concepts of any other type of income. Although there is room for debate about how to measure wages, interest, and rent in economic terms, theorists are at least agreed on what kinds of functions generate these incomes. The profit concept presents, beside the measurement problems, the problem of choosing among a variety of points of view on the function that produces profit. Theories that ascribe profits to risk-bearing or chance when uncertainty exists can be fitted into advanced concepts of the stationary economy, but they have little relevance to an economy that is growing in size and developing new products and technology. For the dynamic manufacturing industries, which are the principal concern of this book, the most telling concept of profits depicts them as the gains in national income that are generated by the managerial drive for distinction through creative innovation.

III. PROFIT MEASUREMENT

We now turn from concepts of profits as pure surplus (unrelated to capital) to the more common notion of profits as earnings on stockholders' capital. This concept is more conventional in coverage as well as form, since it includes interest on investment and compensation for risks, in addition to rewards for somebody's innovation. This shift in meaning is made because we examine problems of measuring and forecasting profits from a managerial viewpoint, and management's job is laid out in terms of earnings on stockholders' capital.

Multiple meanings of the word "profits" have always been troublesome. Accountants have made an energetic effort in recent years to discard the word for their purposes and to refer to the conventional concept as "business income," a neutral term that avoids any overlap with economic theory. In this section we consider the economic problems of measuring business income.

Economists are unhappy about conventional accounting methods for measuring business income. Many think them inadequate and sometimes misleading for penetrating analysis, which often requires a complete reshaping of the conventional income statement. What are the specific economic objections to the standard rules of accounting procedure, and how does the economist intend to improve on the accountant's handiwork? In this section we shall sketch the broad outlines of this classic controversy and suggest the kinds of modifications of conventional income statements that are important to economists and appropriate for different managerial purposes.

The most important points of difference between the economist's and accountant's approaches center around: (1) the inclusiveness of costs, i.e., what should be subtracted from revenue to get profit; (2) the meaning of depreciation; (3) the treatment of capital gains and losses; and, perhaps most important, (4) the price-level basis for valuation of assets, i.e., current vs. historical costs.

The first of these controversies, i.e., what should be included in costs, was explored in our examination of the nature of profits in Section II. Before turning to the remaining three, we shall examine the basic concepts that underlie these disputes. We need such a conceptual framework to determine how each issue should be resolved for the particular managerial decisions at hand.

Conceptual Conflict

The role of futurity in economic values and in business decisions underlies all three of these issues in measuring profits. Economists look to the future as the basic source of value of today's assets, and the businessman recognizes that for his decisions the past is irrelevant, except as a forecaster of the future. But the accountant has a problem here. In an effort to maintain sound, conservative "standards of factuality," accountants want to report historical facts and eschew "speculation" about the future.

To an accountant, net income is essentially a historical record of the past. To an economist, net income is essentially a speculation about the future. Every person knows that his earnings will fluctuate over the years, rising in prosperity and as his abilities grow, and falling in recession and old age. He knows that he can borrow against his future peaks and that he has to save for his future troughs. These expectations govern the amount he can spend now. This amount may be regarded as his real-goods income. In economic terms, he finds the present capital value of his entire future earnings and spends as income this year one installment of a lifetime annuity on that capital value. For corporations, life is eternal, and net income can be measured as the maximum amount that can be distributed in dividends (theoretically from now into the indefinite future) without impairing the company's earning power. Hence, the concept aims at preservation of stockholders' real capital. To estimate income, then, requires a forecast of all future changes in demand, changes in production processes, cash outlays to operate the business, cash revenues, and price changes (to state cash flows in terms of constant purchasing power). That is, we need a cash budget (adjusted for purchasing power) which forecasts farther into the future than anyone can see. If this were available, a program could be planned for borrowing and investing cash so as to allow for an annual cash dividend payment that would be equivalent to the uniform consumption of real goods that we here conceive of as the index of the firm's income.

This concept of business income is an unattainable ideal, but it shows the importance of future flows in income measurement and it is the right arbiter in choosing the most proximate accounting treatment of specific costs and revenues. The accountant's concept of income, like this one, requires for its measurement a consolidation of dated transactions of cash outlays and cash receipts. But there is a basic difference: the accountant uses *past* transactions instead of *future*.[13]

Accountants measure income by finding the difference between net assets at the beginning of the year and net assets at the close of the year. Among the assets, they list cash outlays that were made for inventory, land, plant and equipment, and long-term investments, together with cash on hand, near-cash (marketable securities), and claims that will soon be cash (accounts receivable, accrued income) or goods and services (prepaid expenses). From the total they deduct some future cash outlays—the definite liabilities and, sometimes, contingent outlays. They also deduct part of the amount that had been spent for long-lasting plant and equipment, and say that that part represents the fraction of the original cost that has already been put into production of inventory and thence into cash. The total assets minus reserves and

----

[13] The economist says sunk costs are irrelevant; but sunk costs are not scorned by the accountant.

liabilities constitutes net worth, the year-to-year change in which is annual income.[14]

A balance sheet occasionally contains intangible assets such as good will or patent protection, which nominally are anticipation of the future. But their valuation on the books is not closely related to expectations. These accounts originate in purchases of trade names, markets, or patents, and reflect the amounts paid. For conservatism, accountants usually want to write them down as rapidly as profits permit. Good will on the balance sheet of a new corporation may represent promoter's profits or watered stock. As markets are established and profits come in, the good will is written off the books. Thus, the paper good will may be written off as the real good will builds up.

An economist's balance sheet has quite a different interpretation, since it is an attempt to aggregate the future earnings of the firm's properties now on hand. Each asset has earning power by itself. The value of this earning power is hard to compute, but it is certainly not less than the price the asset can bring in the current market. The value of the combined assets is in general greater than the value of the separate assets. This added value depends on the existence of a going organization, with trained personnel, established market connections, and effective leadership.[15] It may be called good will or "going-concern value," but it is entirely different from most kinds of good will in accounting. The important point is that an economic balance sheet derives entirely from income expectations, while an accounting balance sheet can be viewed as the basic tool for computing accounting income.

As we mentioned above, the uncertainties that crop up in every step of this approach make it suitable for only the broadest profit estimates, but it does provide a guide to "right" and "wrong" in accounting practices for income analysis.

Even though accountants and economists start from widely different viewpoints in measuring income, they could conceivably

---

[14] Thus, although accountants do not derive the income entirely from past costs, they do limit speculations on future cash receipts to the very certain; guesses on future outlays are sometimes more generous, as when they include contingency reserves.

[15] When the value of the parts exceeds that of the total, it is obviously time to liquidate.

come up with the same estimates, but this could occur only in a stationary economy, where prices were frozen and where competition insured that cost was a good measure of value. In the real world of business cycles, wars, and technological revolutions, estimates of business income made by accountants and economists are as different as their purposes and approaches. Both kinds of income measurement are important to management, but substituting one for the other is more misleading than is commonly supposed.

Specific Issues

Depreciation

Treatment of depreciation is an important instance of this basic conflict. Only in the last fifty years has depreciation been a generally accepted charge against income. As businessmen came to realize that some provision must be made for the future replacement of equipment, some kind of depreciation reserve accounting was needed. The accountants' insistence that the reserve be related to the original cost rather than to the cost of replacement—which is usually quite different—gives depreciation accounting full economic usefulness only under the simplest hypothetical conditions of stable prices and foreseeable obsolescence.

Accountants make periodic depreciation charges to income to recover the cost of equipment before its usefulness is exhausted. The procedure is to estimate the useful life in years and to make the annual charge just large enough to recover the original cost within that period.[16]

The objective of this procedure is to allocate the total cost of equipment to production during the period in which it will be used. The effect is to insure that revenues equal to original cost are not distributed as dividends, but are rather put back into assets, such as more equipment or cash. Whether the amount that is thus put out of reach of dividends will actually be enough for replacement is not considered part of this accounting problem.

---

[16] Rarely is the useful life of equipment as long as its possible physical life. When equipment is retired because it is out of date long before it is physically worn out, some firms make two charges: one for deterioration, which is determined by the estimated physical life, and one for obsolescence, which is determined by economic life and makes up the deficiencies in the charges for physical deterioration. Most firms do not distinguish charges for these two causes of retirement, but merely charge depreciation over the shorter period determined by "obsolescence life."

Replacement is viewed by accountants as having no bearing on measurement of profits.

For economists, there are two distinct kinds of depreciation charge. The first is the opportunity cost of equipment, that is, the most profitable alternative use of it that is foregone by putting it to its present use.[17] The alternative involved in using the asset for one year may be viewed as selling it at the beginning instead of the end of the year. The opportunity cost could then be measured by the fall in value of the equipment during the year. This shrinkage in disposal value, which measures the capital-wastage from postponing its disposal for one year, produces a depreciation cost estimate which is quite different from straight-line depreciation for an individual year. For example, it is common to charge as annual depreciation one-fifth of an automobile's original cost. Yet the decline in disposal value during the first year is normally nearer to 40 per cent than to 20 per cent of original cost. Inherently it has no relation to cost; disposal value rose during some postwar years, producing negative depreciation costs, from an economic viewpoint.

The opportunity-cost of depreciation depends upon the nature of the alternative. The alternative may be to keep the equipment idle and save it for later years. Or there may be no alternative uses in other places or times, and thus no real cost of using it in its present function. A hydro-electric dam is perhaps an illustration of this kind of specialized and immobile sunk investment. The economic cost of using the equipment for one year, in any case, has nothing to do with original cost and nothing to do with eventual disposal of the equipment—the two important factors in accountanting depreciation.

The second kind of depreciation cost is the exhaustion of a year's worth of limited valuable life. In the case of the dam, where there is no opportunity cost, the future useful life (which measures its unique value to the going concern) is nevertheless continually running out. To preserve owners' capital, enough of the dam's gross earnings must be saved and reinvested to shift capital out of the dam into equally profitable ventures, perhaps a replacement dam. The amount of this kind of economic de-

---

[17] This is sometimes called "user cost." For a description of several varieties of user cost, see W. A. Lewis, *Overhead Costs,* New York, Rinehart & Co. Inc., 1949, p. 4.

preciation is not determined by the historical cost of the equipment. It is better measured by replacement value of equipment that will produce comparable earnings. This kind of depreciation is not a cost; the cost was incurred when capital was originally frozen into the plant. Rather, it is an act of saving, and the amount to charge each year is a financial problem related to past, present, and future patterns of gross earnings, as well as to price level expectations.

Both of these economic concepts of depreciation are important to management. The first, opportunity cost, is needed for operating problems of profit-making, the second, replacement of eroded earnings ability, is needed for financial problems of preserving and administering capital. For neither, however, does original cost play any role in estimates.

Treatment of Capital Gains and Losses

Capital gains and losses, or "windfalls," as they are often called, may be defined loosely as unanticipated changes in the value of property relative to other real goods. That is, a windfall reflects a change in someone's anticipation of the property's earning power.[18] Fluctuations in stock market prices are almost all of this nature.

"Property" should be interpreted broadly here to include executive ability, organizational structure, brand names, and market connections. All the assets that comprise the value of the firm are vulnerable to windfall changes. For instance, the value of cash deteriorates in inflation; accounts receivable are hit by defaults not allowed for in bad debt reserves; inventory is subject to fire, flood, price drops, and substitute competition; the value of plant facilities is slashed when competitors install new, cost-cutting equipment; and patent protection can be made worthless by a court decision. The list of possibilities is endless.

These are capital losses, which, in a progressive society, are probably larger on balance than capital gains. Many of these risks can be diluted by insurance-type charges, such as surplus reserve

---

[18] This conception of capital gains as inherently unanticipated is not the tax definition. But definitions that are evidentiary, e.g., increases in market value, are essentially equivalent. It is hard to conceive in principle of a non-capricious capital gain, since capital value is based on foreseeable income. Similarly, capital losses are clearly windfalls, since nobody makes an investment in expectation of a loss.

appropriations or high depreciation rates. And when conservative managements actually over-insure, the excess eventually appears as capital gains.

A sound accounting policy to follow concerning windfalls is never to record them until they are turned into cash by a purchase or sale of assets, since it is never clear until then *exactly* how large they are in dollar terms.[19] Occasionally major write-downs are made when value has apparently been wiped out; but the chastening experience of 1929–1932 has virtually eliminated the practice of write-ups beyond original cost.

This accounting policy of not recognizing windfalls until they are cashed raises the problem of the proper accounting treatment for non-recurring cash items in the income statement. Many of these items relate to windfalls of preceding years. Accountants are not agreed on whether the validating cash transaction should be charged against income or against surplus. (For a discussion, see *Accounting Research Bulletin 32*, American Institute of Accountants.) But for some types of windfall, such as loss on sale of undepreciated machinery, it has been common to rewrite the former years' statements, allowing for the realized windfalls.

How the windfall is reported in financial statements is not a matter of interest to economists (as long as they are explained). They are concerned with the future, not the past. The important thing is that gains and losses usually can be foreseen for some time before they are realized in cash. A fact-minded management must have some sort of balance sheet, if only an estimated one, that realizes surprises long before they have become exact enough to be acceptable to accountants. For example, if prices are to be determined with the objective of producing a "reasonable" rate of return on the valuation of investment, they should reflect projectable windfalls even though not yet cashed. Otherwise, a target rate of return based on a historically "factual," but nevertheless fictitious capital value, may lead to later and unpleasant surprises from the resulting price policies.

---

[19] Exceptions to this cash-realization rule are (1) valuation of inventory at cost price or market price, whichever is lower—a conservative rule that calls for write-downs during deflation (when market price may fall below cost of inventory) but no write-ups during inflation; and (2) valuation of marketable securities at current market price, a figure that is easily found in the newspapers. But the apparent precision that seems to warrant these exceptions is often misleading as a measure of either liquidation value or earning power of the assets.

Current vs. Historical Costs

In measuring income, accountants typically state costs in terms of the price level at the time of the purchase, by recording the historical outlay, rather than in terms of the current price level. Various inconsistent reasons for this have been advanced by accountants: (1) because historical costs produce more accurate measurement of income; (2) because historical costs are less debatable (more objective) than the calculation of present replacement value; (3) because the function of the accountant is to record history whether or not history has relevance for future business or economic problems, but presumably in the hope that it has.[20]

Arguments on historical cost accounting have been going on for decades, but never was the debate more vigorous than during the 1941–1948 inflation. This was an extremely turbulent time: business was scrambling to fill postwar demand and was jockeying for new market positions; there was a rush to get new products on the market; capital expenditures were being made at a tremendous rate. The situation was rich with windfall gains and losses, resulting from the violent changes in demand, supply, and price structure. Management needed the best kind of information to keep track of conditions and to plan astutely. Inflation carried prices to nearly double their level of ten years before; a general revision of ideas was called for on the value of a dollar and the meaning of the older assets on the books. One of the significant by-products of inflation was a bitter controversy among accountants, lawyers, economists, and politicians on the truth or fiction of accounting practice in such a period. The argument was a cross-hatch of speculations on legal and moral obligations to investors, tax liabilities, established accounting traditions, future price levels, and political convenience. Out of the controversy came income statements with a rash of special reserves and footnote explanations, and some extraordinary depreciation treatments.[21]

---

20 The view that accounting is not essentially a process of valuation, but is the allocation of historical costs to current and succeeding periods, has recently had distinguished sponsorship. See *Accounting Review*, Vol. XI, No. 2 (June, 1936), p. 188. See also *Accounting Research Bulletin* No. 33, American Institute of Accountants, October 14, 1948.

21 Among the latter were U. S. Steel's increased rate of depreciation on original cost, and Chrysler's write-down of postwar plant acquisitions to prewar cost levels before starting depreciation charges.

The implied assumption of most depreciation policies was that we would eventually get back to prewar prices. This assumption seemed quite unreal and irrelevant to most economists, and it was clear that published income statements had only begun to recognize the basic change in the purchasing power of the dollar. With prices on a new high plateau, depreciation charges in terms of prewar prices were carrying only about half the load of financing postwar replacements, and it was almost impossible to determine what part of the capital investment boom was really adding to the nation's productive capacity.

Statistics of corporate earnings were probably gross overstatements of economic earnings,[22] although the amount of the distortion was difficult to estimate. In a period of inflation, cost of living goes up for corporations as well as for persons. The cost of refilling inventories, replacing worn equipment, and expanding capacity all go up. Yet accounting procedures generally fail to take adequate account of these increases. When inventories and depreciation are charged at original costs, rather than at the higher replacement cost, inventory and plant are revalued as they are turned over. Orthodox accounting vigilantly keeps ordinary revaluations from getting into the profit and loss account—by treating them as surplus adjustments. But when revaluations find their way into the accounts indirectly, by the process of turnover of assets during inflation, they *do* get into the earnings account. These revaluation profits are treated as ordinary business income and cannot in the books be distinguished from other income. Hence, accounting profit overstates real business income, not only during an inflation but for some time after prices have reached stability. It is clearly not enough to deflate the reported income figure by dividing money profits by some cost-of-living index after the manner in which real wages are found. Profits are a residual in a calculation that uses dollars of many different dates—today's cash dollars, last year's inventory dollars, and equipment dollars of many years of prosperity and depression. To measure real profits, all these assets must be stated in dollars of the same purchasing power. This is an elaborate operation, and the desirable data on prices, products, and dates are usually hard to estimate. With some expediting assumptions, however, usable approximations can be

---

[22] This view was widespread and was undoubtedly one of the factors that kept stock market prices low relative to current reported earnings.

made. In respect to price-level impacts, three kinds of earnings estimates may be distinguished: (1) jumbled-dollar profits; (2) contemporary-dollar profits; and (3) constant-dollar profits. The earnings reported by conventional accounting are, as we have seen, a jumble of dollars of different dates and usually of different purchasing power.

Contemporary-dollar profits. The second kind can be estimated by making price-level adjustments that would make the revenues and costs of a particular year reflect dollars of that year's purchasing power. This removes much of the distortion caused by scrambling dollars of different size in the same income statement. Profits estimates, based each year on contemporary dollars would be directly usable for several managerial purposes (e.g., appraising current executive performance). They would also serve as an intermediate step in approximating constant-dollar profits, since a simple deflation analogous to that of converting money wages into "real wages" would be legitimate for practical purposes.

Contemporary-dollar profits are analogous to those that would be shown by conventional accounting for a manufacturing corporation which had no tangible assets, not even inventories. It is assumed that the company buys materials hand-to-mouth at current market prices, and rents equipment at rentals that continuously reflect the current replacement cost of the equipment. The earnings that are estimated by approximating this no-asset situation would represent operating profits in contemporary dollars. This kind of adjustment segregates not only the illusory gains and losses from price-level fluctuations, but also reveals some of the more permanent capital gains and losses caused by changes in relative prices.

For many enterprises, contemporary-dollar profits can be approximated by a combination of replacement-value depreciation and LIFO costing of materials. Straight-line depreciation of replacement value does not, as we have seen, tackle directly the problem of reflecting economic depreciation in the sense of either user costs or of earning-power erosion.

But replacement-cost depreciation is good as far as it goes, even though it doesn't go all the way. It is preferable to original cost depreciation for most management decisions.

Last-in-first-out (LIFO) inventory accounting can, in periods of inflation, help approximate contemporary-dollar earnings. It is now widely used and can qualify as a legitimate method of costing materials for income tax purposes.   By the LIFO method, the last materials purchased are the first charged to cost of goods sold, and when the inventory turnover is slow, business income is measured on the basis of more recent prices of materials than under the first-in-first-out (FIFO) method.   When prices are rising, LIFO produces a lower income than FIFO, (since stated material costs are higher) and when prices are falling it shows a higher income. LIFO thus tends to wash out the paper profits that result from comparing a closing inventory with an equal opening inventory stated at different prices.

But the choice between LIFO and FIFO is still a choice between historical-cost accounting methods, and neither method fully meets the economist's request for a valuation at current market prices.   In a year such as 1946, when there was an upheaval in prices accompanied by physical expansion of inventories, LIFO could give closing inventory values and cost of goods sold with dollars of different purchasing power about as jumbled as those produced by FIFO.   Moreover, when inventories are being reduced, cost of goods sold and inventory levels begin to show increasingly ancient and irrelevant prices.   To attain the ideal of economic realism, a full restatement of inventory in constant prices is required.

An interesting estimate of the effect of contemporary-dollar profit deflation [23] was that the figure $50 billion for total corporate profits for 1946–1948 was 38 per cent fictitious.   Nineteen billion was actually inventory profits (i.e., increase in the dollar value of a constant physical inventory) plus underdepreciation (failure to charge enough depreciation for replacement purposes).

Constant-Dollar profits.   The MAPI study was actually an incomplete statement of the total distortion that had occurred, however, since it neglected the capital losses that inflation had produced in the purchasing power of cash assets.   That is, if prices rose 50 per cent between 1940 and 1947, a bank balance of $1 million in 1947 was worth only two-thirds of the same balance in 1940 in terms of what it could buy.[24]   This and other less important

---

[23] *Inflation and Postwar Profits,* Machinery and Allied Products Institute, May, 1949.

[24] It may be asked why holding cash during inflation is viewed as a loss, since it is also possible to say that the man who holds real assets makes a profit relative to the man who holds cash.   This is a relative matter, of course, and depends

effects should be included in a complete estimate of profit distortion during an inflation.

This kind of total deflation to real terms was tested by the author for three of the largest electrical manufacturers for the period 1935–1947. All assets were stated in terms of their 1935 price levels by deflating each major group of assets by means of an appropriate price index. Changes in the companies' total net assets from year-end to year-end, plus dividends, and minus new capital funds added (also stated in 1935 dollars), gave a measure of their real profits. This method of estimating real earnings eliminated from the accounts the reported profits caused by inflation of inventory dollar values that meant nothing in real terms; it eliminated the apparent expansion of facilities that merely reflected the high cost of equipment, and it brought out the loss in real value of cash assets.[25]

The results of the study are given in Chart 1–1, where the aggregate reported income is contrasted with the same income stated in dollars of constant purchasing power, and with the real profits derived by the complete deflation process. The contrast between the apparent and real course of events is striking; it is the result of a long and continuous rise in the price level. The surge of prices from June, 1946, through 1947 is reflected in the dramatic gap between reported and deflated income for 1947. The disparity varies among companies, according to varying policies on cash, inventory, and postwar plant expenditures; but for manufacturers of this general type, the pattern of profit behavior shown in Chart 1–1 is fairly typical.

It should be noted that this profit deflation is not a complete statement of the economic concept of income for these companies.

---

partly on the nature of the inflation. If inflation is caused by real deprivation, say, after an earthquake, the man who holds an undamaged house has profited relative to most people. But when inflation is the result of a wage-price spiral, nothing is destroyed but the value of cash, and this is most reasonably viewed as a loss relative to the ability of wage earners and real goods owners to buy consumption goods.

[25] Such an analysis raises many problems of methodology which it would be inappropriate to discuss in detail here. The most important of these are (1) the choice of appropriate price indices; (2) choice of a base period for the indices which reflects adequately the researcher's notion of a "normal" relation of prices among the various types; and (3) the degree of refinement that seems worth while in the separate deflation of asset accounts, considering the rough applicability of the price indices to the properties of a few selected companies. The three companies studied were General Electric Co., Westinghouse Electric and Mfg. Co., and Allis Chalmers Mfg. Co.

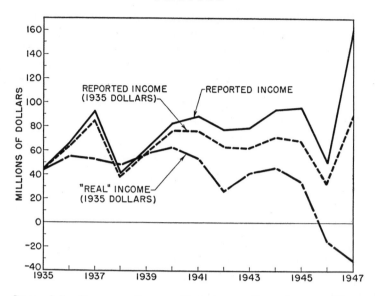

CHART 1–1. REPORTED INCOME COMPARED TO REAL INCOME: THREE
ELECTRICAL MANUFACTURERS—1935–1947. (Source: Annual reports
of the three companies, modified by our figures.)

It adjusts the accounting figures only for price-level changes, not
for capital gains and losses in terms of real-goods value.[26]

Impact on Business Decisions

The central role that profit estimates play in business decisions
gives point to the foregoing critique of accepted accounting
practices in measuring profits.[27] In general, the kind of profit
measurement needed for most business decisions comes closer to
the ideal of the economist than to the practice of the accountant.

[26] If shifts in the price structure of labor, materials, and equipment are assumed
to measure accurately shifts in the relative value of assets, a partial analysis of windfalls can be combined with this deflation by expressing all assets at reproduction
costs and deflating the totals for the period to constant-value dollars by a single
index of the price level. This contrasts with the method actually used, where
each asset group—cash, buildings, and so forth—was deflated by a special-purpose
index which reflected price changes for that group alone. For a study of real
income using a single price index, see R. A. Jones, "Effect of Inflation on Capital
and Profits: Record of Nine Steel Companies," Journal of Accountancy, Vol. 87
(Jan., 1949), p. 9.

[27] Accountants are by no means unaware of these problems. A statement of the
issues, with a plea for more flexible thinking by accountants in the face of major
price changes, is given in G. O. May, Business Income and Price Levels—An Accounting Study, American Institute of Accountants, July, 1949.

Without an understanding of these underlying conceptual conflicts between accounting conventions and economic analysis there is danger that accounting profits will influence business thinking in areas beyond their proper realm. Accounting is designed for special purposes of financial analysis and for codifying public regulation and tax administration. The legal consequences of accounting are so important that great uniformity and general agreement in practice are demanded.

But to carry these exacting requirements into fields of general economic analysis in shaping business policy is often to parody or obscure the real nature of a highly uncertain situation. It can easily confuse a management unsophisticated in the relations of accounting to economic reality.

Unquestionably the inability of accounting profits to measure economic conceptions of business income has distorted some management decisions. Many executives are contemptuous of economic modifications of conventional profits. Reasoning largely by epithet, they label them "visionary" and "academic." Others reject price-level adjustments because they believe the all-that-goes-up-must-come-down doctrine: the sins of illusory inflation profits will be washed whiter than snow by subsequent illusory losses. Some executives are aware of an economic reality behind the accounting facade. They realize, for example, that depreciation based on prewar cost is inadequate for postwar replacement. But such mental reservations and adjustments are not definitive enough for economically correct managerial' decisions. Moreover, even the perspicacious executive may be a victim of the accounting system: his performance and pay are likely judged on the basis of the profits the accounts *do* report, regardless of what they *should* report. Mistaken decisions of individual firms that are caused by jumbled-dollar profits may add up to important distortions in the functioning of the economy.

Summary

In the examination of the economic problems of measuring business income, profits are conceived not as a pure residual, but as earnings on stock-holders' capital, including interest and risk premium. Aside from this matter of what to include, the underlying conceptual conflict between economists and accountants concerns futurity. Economic ideas of income, assets, and net worth all look to the future for their meaning, while the corresponding financial accounts are all histories of past transactions. Although history is often a guide to the future, it is not a substitute for projections of the future. A thorough-going recasting of accounting records to strive to estimate the most sophisticated economic conception of profits is not a practical goal. For economists, profits are the embodiment of manifold conjectures about the future, which are bound to have such wide error ranges that they can be of little managerial usefulness. The main contribution of economic analysis is conceptual rather than metrical. It can serve as an arbiter of accounting fashions.

Economists have misgivings about straight-line, original-cost depreciation. For many executive decisions an opportunity-cost concept of depreciation has more meaning. The depreciation charge should also serve to preserve not the original dollar investment, but the earning power of the plant. Thus replacement-value depreciation, though it doesn't go far enough, is preferable to original cost.

During inflation, the jumbled-dollar profits obtained by conventional accounting procedures overstate real business income. A partial correction can be made by each year expressing all costs in dollars whose purchasing power is the same as that year's revenues. A combination of LIFO and current replacement-value depreciation will usually approximate these contemporary-dollar profits. A full correction of price-level distortions requires separate deflation of all assets each year to dollars of constant purchasing power. Price-level valuations are not the only differences between economists and accountants in measuring business income.

The disparities between scrambled-dollar profits calculated from historical-cost records and value expectations in constant dollars are always wide—surprisingly so in years of stability—and there is a need to measure real income.

Measurement of real income starts with financial accounts, trimmed down to dollars of constant size. But it also involves a mixture of economic analysis, executive judgment, and imagination. When these are combined in the right proportions, approximations that are usable for business decisions can be made. Management problems take innumerable forms, and an accounting system that would fit them all is hard to conceive. The accounts should instead be made a source of basic data that can be fitted in different ways to different particular needs.

IV. POLICIES ON PROFIT MAXIMIZATION

In Section II, we discussed the nature of profits in the theory of income and the purpose of profits in the economy in directing energies and materials into their most effective uses. This section deals with business attitudes and policies on profits in the present-day world. Economic theory makes a fundamental assumption that maximizing profits is the basic objective of every firm. But in recent years "profit maximization" has been extensively qualified by theorists to refer to the long run; to refer to management's rather than to owners' income; to include nonfinancial income such as increased leisure for highstrung executives and more congenial relations between executive levels within the firm; and to make allowance for special considerations such as restraining competition, maintaining management control, holding off wage demands, and forestalling antitrust suits. The concept has become so general and hazy that it seems to encompass most of man's aims in life.

This trend reflects a growing realization by theorists that many firms, and particularly the big ones, do not operate on the principle of profit maximizing in terms of marginal costs and revenues, but rather set standards or targets of reasonable profits. For instance, evidence of this kind of approach was found frequently in interviews with executives on pricing methods. (See Chapter 7, Section IV on Cost-plus Pricing.) Of course, it has never been clear whether these studies brought out the real thinking of businessmen, or just their pious utterances for public consumption. Nevertheless, profit planning can be seen in many other contexts, particularly in writings on control of business finances. Often it is a process of cutting and fitting cost and revenue forecasts to a desired profit margin on sales. The resulting return on investment then shows whether the plan is desirable or not.

The policy problems in setting profit standards arise only in imperfect, that is, real-world, competition. When competition is intense enough to approximate "pure-competition," prices have to be set close to the cost level, and only by trying to maximize profits can a firm stay solvent. But for many products a firm has a substantial monopoly position, either short-run or permanent, and has a range of discretion in pricing. Such firms must make crucial policy decisions on profit standards. The purpose of this section is to sketch out the conceptual groundwork for these decisions. The questions that will be considered are:

1. What are the reasons for aiming at limited, rather than maximum, profits?
2. What standards of "reasonable" profits are available?
3. How can these standards be applied?

Reasons for Limiting Profits

The reasons for limiting profits may be roughly classified as follows:

1. To discourage potential competitors.
2. To woo the voting public and restrain the zeal of anti-trusters.
3. To restrain wage demands of organized labor.
4. To maintain customer good will.
5. To keep control undiluted.
6. To maintain pleasant working conditions.

There is a basic difference to be emphasized between the first four reasons and the last two. The first four are reasons why the company as an entity wants to limit short-run profits in order to maximize profits in the long run (or more strictly, to maximize the present value of the enterprise). The last two are reasons why the executives, as distinguished from the company, want to limit profits in order to maximize their own benefits (of whatever kind). Management's financial interest in the modern corporation is typically small, and only one of many motives that keep executives going. Other motives which are just as important often run counter to the corporate financial interests, and thus distinguish management clearly from stockholders, in whose eyes the company is essentially a financial, as opposed to a social, organization.

Competitive Considerations

The rationale for profit restriction varies with the particular situation and with the way the executive thinks about the problem. An orthodox economic reason is to hold off the entry of competition in a weak monopoly situation. A "weak" monopoly is one that has no protective barriers around strategic resources or markets,

and that has little real patent protection.   Competitors can invade
the market as soon as they discover its profitability, find ways to
skirt the patents, and make the necessary development outlays in
product design, production plant, technique, and market penetration.   But as long as there is a significant cost in entry of the
market, the incumbent may be wise to forego his full short-run
profits and restrain prices to a level that leaves a less enticing profit
prospect to new entrants.   This intricate problem in price policy
is discussed more fully in Chapter 7.   In the context of this
section, such "stayout" pricing is a straightforward illustration of
subordinating short-run to long-run profit maximization.

Public Relations

Profit restraint is exercised nowadays with a sharp eye toward
public relations and political impact, since public standards are
framed more by ethical judgments than by the canons of classical
economics.

For instance, reported earnings are a standard for appraising a
company's pricing restraint in an inflationary period.   With an
eye on public relations as well as on economic welfare, many large
firms set prices below maximum-profit levels when a stigma attaches to charging what buyers will pay.   The very large amount
of advertising that was devoted to a defense of the postwar level
of the advertiser's profits attests to the importance attached to
this problem.   For many firms that are large and economically
pivotal, a goal of "reasonable" or "socially respectable" profits
makes a better policy than maximizing profits during such a
period.   Top management's problem is to decide what earnings
level is adequate and inconspicuous and to plan prices and promotion to attain this level.

Similarly, some firms are concerned about the effect of overly
large profits upon their relations with the federal government.
Profit-level data typically enters the Antitrust Division's major
Sherman Act complaints, to cite the clearest instance.   The steel
industry's price and production policies have become a political
football, and their price increase of December, 1949, produced
a Congressional investigation and report that hinted obscurely of
the "public utility" nature of the industry.[28]

---

[28] "December 1949 Steel Price Increases," Joint Committee on the Economic
Report, 81st Congress, 2nd Session, Report No. 1373 (March 27, 1940), p. 29.

Labor Relations

Profit restraint plays a strategic role in labor relations for leaders of important industries. The doctrine of ability to pay as a wage-rate criterion, popularized by Walter Reuther in 1945, has had a checkered career. It came into many major disputes during the inflation, particularly when fact-finding boards were used, since all parties had pious hopes of avoiding another price increase. During this period, profit restraint was essentially a defensive action, since it implies that any attempt to raise profits by raising prices would be frustrated by further wage increases. If wages are as sticky on the downward side as they appear to be, an industry puts itself in a vulnerable position for meeting a recession when it permits a wage-price spiral of this kind during a period of over-full employment.[29]

When there is demand for full-capacity output throughout the economy, and price is unimportant, a spiral in one industry relative to others hardly affects sales. But after the postwar rush has subsided and competition forces prices nearer to a cost level, there may appear a new structure of prices. Industries that restrained prices and wages may then be in a better competitive position than those that let them fly. But downward rigidity and industry differentials of wages is a keystone to this argument.

Customer Relations

Profit restraint is also important in maintaining customer good will. Buyers often think of a "fair" price in terms of cost of production and feel that they are being exploited when profits are high. This attitude of buyers, although not part of classical economic theory, is important because it is durable: the butcher who makes the most of an inelastic demand when meat is scarce may be boycotted when supply is restored. From the seller's standpoint, this profit restraint is in the interest of long-run profits. If he charges customers a markup related to some long-run demand elasticity, he can do it for longer and make a larger aggregate profit than he can by pricing for short-run elasticity.[30]

---

[29] The coal industry presents the clearest illustration of this process at present.

[30] But profit restraint for improving consumer relations is of course not merely a matter of long-run maximization; sellers have ethical norms of behavior—notions of "just price" and "fair profit"—which may conflict with even longsighted cupidity.

Maintaining Control

Another reason for limiting profits that has received some attention recently among theorists is management's desire to maintain control of the firm.[31] This limitation is manifested in a strong preference for liquidity, an abhorrence of debt, and a conservative attitude toward expansion. Since these are topics of capital budgeting, they are discussed in more detail in Chapter 10, Section III.

Cash is, of course, as much a working tool as the raw material inventory or the fuel supply, and a minimum balance is needed to meet everyday fluctuations in demand for it. But the size of the current ratio (ratio of current assets to current liabilities) and the net quick assets are probably the most closely watched items on most balance sheets. Although liquidity position can logically be viewed as underlying maintenance of control, it is probably often an independent managerial comfort which blunts sheer profit maximization. As a consequence of balance-sheet considerations, executives sometimes deliberately choose a less profitable but more liquid alternative, when as is common the two pull in opposing directions.[32]

As we pointed out above, control considerations are a qualification of profit maximization for the firm, but not necessarily for management. Maintenance of control is subsidiary to, and not necessarily in conflict with, maximizing the profits of management over a long period of time. Since management is not identical with the firm as a financial unit, there are many reasons why executives may not intend to maximize the company's financial earnings, but there is a *prima facie* assumption that they will act to maximize their own incomes. However, even this assumption needs some qualification.

Nonfinancial Amenities

The restraints on profits imposed for the sake of mutual respect, friendship, and good living within the firm, though subtle, are quite pervasive. Running a taut ship is a constant strain on all

---

[31] E.g., see M. W. Reder, "A Reconsideration of the Marginal Productivity Theory," *Journal of Political Economy*, Vol. 55, No. 5 (October, 1947).

[32] The possibility of developing a formal theory to reconcile these opposing forces is discussed by W. W. Cooper, "Revisions to the Theory of the Firm," *American Economic Review*, December, 1949, pp. 1204–1222.

hands, and in good times a monopoly can afford a great deal of slack for the sake of the good things in life. This is one of the important sources of cyclical cost flexibility that give the break-even point so much elasticity. (See Section V.)

Possibly the inadequacy of hired management's incentives to maximize profits has also tended to make the "public service" aspects of business leadership more interesting to executives. There appears to be growing preoccupation with the "social re-sponsibilities of management," i.e., increasing concern with the direct effects of management's decisions upon workers, consumers, and the business cycle. Whether such considerations deflect management's actions significantly from profit-making can prob-ably never be determined, since retreat to "long-run" profitability defies analysis. To an old-fashioned economic liberal, the fact that management has latitude to sacrifice profits to take care of its "social responsibilities" indicates a degree of imperfection in competition that blunts the sharp edge of the economy's efficiency. To him, maximizing profits is the chief social responsibility of management in a competitive economy.

Standards of Reasonable Profits

Assuming that, for some of these reasons, voluntary limitation of profits is desirable, what form of profit standard should be used, and how should "reasonable profits" be determined?

Form of Standard

Profit standards can be formulated in aggregate dollar terms, as a percentage of sales, or as a return on investment. They can be formulated for individual products or for the combined product line of the firm. Profit measurements for single products are somewhat illusory when common costs are allocated to them by some arbitrary method, but the alternative of using the gross or "contribution" profits, i.e., the spread over incremental costs for each product, is often difficult for the public to understand and appraise. Total net profits of the enterprise usually receive the greatest attention.

The form of profit standard that is appropriate depends on its uses. For the purpose of discouraging potential competitors, re-turn on investment is the relevant standard, if new entrants have similar costs. For soothing consumers or beating down suppliers, percentage margins over unit cost in relation to the dollars they spend is usually appropriate.   Thus, in the postwar inflation, public protest over high meat prices was countered by the packers with income statements showing profits at about 1½ per cent (1947) of sales.   But with sales equal to 10 times net worth, this thin margin still left them an adequate return of 15 per cent on equity capital.   An electric power company, on the other hand, with an annual revenue only one-fourth the size of invested capital might rather emphasize its 5 per cent return on investment than its 25 per cent margin over costs.

It is evident that ratios of profits to sales are an eccentric standard of profitability.   They vary widely among firms that have the same return on invested capital when there are differences in vertical integration of production processes, depth of mechanization, and capital structure and turnover.   Since conventional net profits are principally an investor's income, return on capital is the most important form of profit standard from the owners' viewpoint.

Setting the Standard

A problem more basic than the mere *form* of the profit standard is the question of suitable *criteria* for setting the level of the standard.   Several criteria merit consideration.
1. What it takes to attract outside capital.
2. What earnings are needed to finance the firm's development solely from retained profits (plus depreciation).
3. What the company or comparable firms have normally earned.
4. What the man in the street thinks is a "reasonable profit." The first two profit criteria are in terms of the earnings necessary for adequate capital formation, i.e., replacement and addition to buildings, equipment, and working capital.

The Capital-attracting Rate of Return.   A profit standard can be formulated in terms of the cost of new capital in the impersonal capital markets.   If stocks are being traded in the market at five times their current earnings, it is usually necessary to earn about 20 per cent on book investment in order to sell new stock at a price that "protects the equity" of present stockholders in the company (i.e., a price higher than book value).   This standard has an important role in the regulation of public utilities, where commissions are required to permit earnings sufficient to maintain investors' capital. It therefore has wide public acceptance. But clear though it may be in theory, such a "capital-attracting" rate of return requires many arbitrary decisions and approximations in practice.

The capital-attracting rate depends, for instance, on the company's capital structure—i.e., the proportion—of bonds, preferred stock, and common stock. Nowadays debt capital costs about 3 per cent, while equity capital costs much more. Suppose a dividend yield of 6 per cent is required on a good utility common stock, and that invested capital of 67 per cent debt securities and 33 per cent common stock is acceptable. Then the average cost of capital is about 4 per cent in cash outlay. If the capital structure should be two-thirds stock and one-third debt, the cost is 5 per cent. A capital structure with no debt costs 6 per cent. Moreover, a capital structure with a high debt ratio—over 75 per cent, for instance—increases the risks of common stock ownership and thus raises the cost of equity capital.

A second problem is to decide whether the earnings standard should be based on the current cost of capital, or some long-run average cost. The supply price of capital fluctuates widely over a period of years with the general bearishness and bullishness of the stock market, and with the state of the government bond market. Should earnings keep in line with the latest market conditions? Not necessarily, unless the company actually wants to sell some new securities soon. On the contrary, cyclical fluctuations in both earnings and capital costs make it expedient to use the long-run market rate as a target for long-run earnings when there are no immediate needs for new capital.

A third important problem with this standard is to find the relevant indicator in the market for the company's cost of capital. This is not simple, for capital costs vary widely among industries and among individual companies. Variations arise from differences in growth prospects, cyclical stability, capital structure, and opinions on management ability. Market prices of the company's own securities are *prima facie* the most direct indicators. But since they may reflect special momentary influences such as fluctuations in dividend policy, or closely held stock that has recently been distributed to the public, these market prices may not be as reliable as a well-constructed industry sample. Designing relevant samples and choosing a period for long-run averages that reflects cyclical highs and lows and is indicative of the future are important technical problems that must be faced, but they are beyond the scope of this brief discussion.

The "Plow-back" Rate. The second standard of the capital-needs approach is in terms of the aggregate profits that must be retained in the business to finance a desired rate of growth without resort to the capital markets. This standard is most relevant for companies that wish, for reasons that will be outlined in Chapter 10 ("Capital Budgeting"), Section III, to avoid outside financing. It must be used with discretion, however. A return high enough to provide from retained earnings the capital needed by a rapidly growing industry (e.g., petroleum, 1910–1950) would be a powerful inducement to entry by new competitors.

Furthermore, high plow-back rates do not have the public acceptance that the capital-attracting rate has. Ideally, from the social viewpoint, all earnings should be distributed to stockholders who themselves should choose whether or not to reinvest them, and, if so, in what industries and companies. Distributed earnings are subjected to the forces of competition in the capital markets, and are supposedly allocated to segments of the economy with the highest earnings prospects. Retained earnings, which are sheltered from these competitive forces, and are under management's exclusive control, may be, for private reasons, wasted on low-earning projects within the company. Whether or not market-allocation is actually superior depends on the relative abilities of management and outside investors to estimate earnings prospects. If capital is allocated inside the corporation on approximately the same principles that act in the capital markets (see Chapter 10, "Capital Budgeting"), there is at least a strong likelihood that within the scope of its operations management's appraisal of investment prospects within the firm can be a more accurate resource allocator than the outside investor's forecasts of average earnings.

The plow-back standard is highly individualistic, since it depends on a company's "needs," competition, stockholder politics, and public relations.

"Normal" Earnings. Another criterion of reasonable profits is normal earnings of the company or of an industry group, conceived in terms of some average level over a normal period. A strictly autonomous standard, such as the firm's own past earnings,

has, in some instances, more validity than might appear. If the past level of earnings has been sufficient to attract capital, and has not invited too much potential competition, and has kept stockholders reasonably happy, it may really embody the economic rationale for the other criteria of reasonable profits discussed above. But the company's own past earnings are defensible as a criterion only when they rest on some such rationale. A broader-gauge standard in terms of a group of companies with comparable products and risks is more likely to have a functional justification. Strictly applied, this would require careful selection of comparable companies. More loosely applied, broad averages for the entire industry, or for a broad sample of manufacturing companies, can be used.[33]

In addition to the problem of comparability of the group of companies whose earnings is averaged, there is the problem of determining the normal period.[34] Chart 1–2 shows the charac-

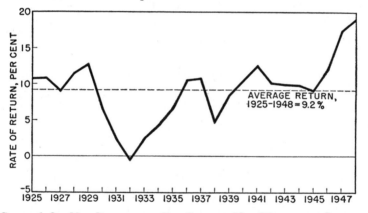

CHART 1–2. NET PROFIT AS A PER CENT OF NET WORTH FOR LEADING MANUFACTURING CORPORATIONS—1925–1948. (Source: National City Bank of N. Y.)

---

[33] Aggregate statistics of manufacturing corporation earnings can be found in the U. S. Statistics of Income (based on tax returns). The National City Bank publishes compilations of earnings of more than a thousand leading manufacturers based on annual reports to stockholders. Earnings data are also compiled by the SEC and the FTC. These sources provide an empirical approximation to this criterion of normal earnings.

[34] The excess profits statute of World War II was based on the presumption that the years 1936–1939 were normal, or at least that profits during that period were not caused by the war. The BIR has suggested that in contesting the normality of this period, companies use the period 1922–1939 as a criterion of normality for the company. For some uses to which an earnings standard is put, it is not an average over a period of years that is relevant, but rather the current level of earnings in comparable industries.

teristic volatility of corporate earnings that makes the choice of period an important factor in setting the standard.

Popular Conceptions of Reasonable Earnings. A standard of reasonable profits might be based on the results of surveys to find the public's idea of a fair profit. Such surveys evidently provide a generous profit standard. In a McGraw-Hill poll of factory workers, 60 per cent thought that a profit margin of 10 per cent or more on sales was reasonable, and 30 per cent said a 25 per cent margin or more was fair.[35]

Choosing a Standard

Which of these standards should a company use? They give widely varying target results, depending on market conditions, measuring methods, public attitudes, and investor optimism. Actually, different standards should be used for different purposes, since no one criterion of profits is acceptable to everyone who is interested in them. For instance:

1. *To keep out potential competition.* Logically, the capital-attracting rate should be used, but capital costs differ so among companies that this may be a treacherous standard to rely on. Perhaps normal earnings for a wide sector of industry is a more reliable guide.

2. *To maintain liquidity and avoid debt.* Earnings for this purpose must be expressed as a plow-back rate at the level that management chooses for a soft cushion of cash relative to growth rate.

3. *To keep the antitrusters happy.* Normal earnings of companies with similar risks in competitive industries provide a standard of competitive profits. A standard based on the company's long-term cost of capital goes all the way to a regulatory approach.

4. *To restrain wage pressures and price controls.* Normal earnings related to a long-term average may be acceptable to hold off these pressures, but this branch of dialectics is based on mysterious and unpredictable premises, and acceptable standards shift with the times.

5. *For long-term growth.* This depends on financing plans, but in general a capital-attracting standard relevant to forecast periods is needed.

---

[35] *Business Week,* October 15, 1949, p. 42.

6. *Departmental profit standards.* This is really a matter of capital budgeting, but such standards should not fall below the cost of capital.

7. *Bonus plans for management.* Profit standards for management bonuses depend on the purpose of the bonus. For maintenance of dividend rates, a normal-earnings standard may be enough, but growth companies need to set higher targets, related to plans for internal and external financing.

Summary

Profit standards are partly a product of political and emotional imperfections of the economy and partly a rational economic phenomenon in imperfect competition. They are established to maximize profits in subtle and devious ways that escape any clean analytical treatment in theory, and we therefore use the convenient idea that they are a denial of the profit maximization concept. The kinds of standards used are heterogeneous; choice of a standard depends on its purpose and its persuasive values. No one standard fits all uses, but a company may need a standard for only one use (e.g., to attract equity capital). "Fair profits" is an overused epithet in the verbal battle for slices of the economic pie. Different standards for different purposes help to clarify managerial thinking on this problem.

V. PROFITS FOR CONTROL

The use of the profit incentive and profit accounting in the measurement and control of executive performance in large business enterprises is another managerial aspect of profits. Perhaps the major internal threat to vitality in the big corporation is bureaucratic deviationism, the tendency for middle and lower management to think in terms of security and routine or personal ambitions that conflict with the company's profit-making objectives. When lower supervisory levels are rated in importance by simple size standards—sales volume, number of employees, production performance—they have no direct feel of the profit system, and no taste for the painful work of minimizing costs.

Keith Powlison [36] has pointed out three common deviationist tendencies that appear when the profit motive is attenuated: (1)

---

[36] "The Profit Motive Compromised," *Harvard Business Review,* March, 1950, p. 102.

More energy is spent in expanding sales volume and product lines than in raising profitability, the valid company objective. (2) Subordinates spend too much time and money doing jobs to perfection regardless of cost and usefulness—this is particularly common among staff men who don't understand or appreciate the insignificance of that last digit in their estimates and projections. (3) Lower management's insecurity feelings become barricaded by expensive overstocking and playing-safe tactics, since there is no reward for imaginative ventures that can possibly offset the perils of making a mistake.

Companies that have become concerned about this problem have sought methods of measuring and rewarding executive performance that will guard against this hardening of the profit-seeking arteries. Such plans have two characteristics in common. The first is realignment of the managerial organization to shift the basic breakdown of operating responsibility from a functional basis (e.g., marketing versus production versus finance) to a commodity basis. The effect is to break the company up into several integral operating units (divisions) and give the executive authority over all functions in his division, and make him responsible for profits. The autonomy of division managers is, of course, not complete. They operate under general supervision and have the benefit of "advice" from a general staff, often at a higher executive echelon. But within the framework of the rules of the game imposed by broad company policies, they have authority and responsibility.

The second common trait is reorientation of accounting reports to conform to the areas of executive responsibility. Each executive is given a profit goal for his operation and his performance is appraised on the basis of periodic profit and loss statements, as well as subordinate budgetary controls.

This kind of managerial decentralization and control-by-profits has important advantages for the big company. The number of centers of initiative that are geared to profit objectives is multiplied. Greater scope can be given to division managers to exercise their own ingenuity in solving problems which can be better understood at the operating unit level, and top management can economize routine supervision and have more time for planning and for broad policy. By testing many executives on the firing line of experience with full-fledged integral operations, a screening device is provided for finding fireballs in the lower ranks.[37]

This philosophy of managerial control raises many interesting economic issues that complicate its application to administrative problems.   These issues center around the methods for measuring divisional profits, and the levels at which profit goals are set. Here are two examples:

(1) Should profit goals be set in terms of total net profits for the division, or should they be confined to the contribution to total profits that is determined by the costs and revenues that divisional management can control?   Controllable profits are usually quite different from net profits of the division, since the latter get the impact of allocated overheads, such as the president's salary, costs of central-office staff work, and depreciation of equipment used jointly with other divisions.   The most appropriate profit standards of divisional performance are therefore set in terms of revenues minus the expenses that current management can do something about. Arbitrarily prorated costs controlled by higher echelons should not be charged against "controllable profits": each cost should be charged against the lowest executive who has total discretion over it.   Profits should be measured in aggregate dollars rather than as return on investment or profit margins. Investments made by previous managements are beyond the control of current management.   A profit standard set in terms of return on total investment makes new executives responsible for purchasing policies and capital expenditures that have been made before their time or above their level in the company.   Each executive would thus be given the widest discretion in pricing and promotion for reaching his profit goals and he would be freed from the sins of previous managements.

Some of the central office costs can be allocated to divisions by charging them for services rendered.   But in principle the division manager should then be empowered to buy as much or little of this staff service as he wishes.   This approach may be feasible for specialized staff work such as legal council, engineering advice, and some kinds of research.   But if divisional management lacks the vision and courage to exploit these purchased services to the hilt, the whole value of the large-scale multiple-

---

[37] An exposition of General Motors policy on decentralization and profit control is found in Peter Drucker, *The Concept of the Corporation*, New York, John Day Co., Inc., 1946.

product enterprise is stifled, and the company is a mere collection of small businesses. To avoid this condition requires intelligent divisional management, education programs by top management, and promotional selling of central-office staff functions.

(2) Should the company shoot at maximizing the profits of each autonomous unit, or are there strategic overtones of total company objectives that make this procedure wrong? This question becomes hard to answer when there is a long ladder of vertical integration, for many of the divisions are then created largely for standby, hedging, or control value. For instance, small mine and forest reserves may be bought as insurance against future supply shortages; or pilot-plant production may be maintained on parts that are largely bought outside, to keep checks on suppliers' costs.

With vertical integration, relative profitability of divisions may depend to a large extent on transfer prices—the prices charged by one division to another for transfer of products. Some companies require that divisions should purchase supplies from the cheapest source, whether this source is inside or outside the company. Such a requirement puts market pressures on all productive levels to minimize costs and maximize profits. This principle is sound, but encounters difficulties in practice, for several reasons. (1) It applies only to fairly standardized product components, such as spark plugs or steel sheets, or to products that are sold to outsiders as well as to other divisions. For special-design stampings, and so forth, there is no reasonable market price. (2) There are problems of quality differentials between outsiders' products and the company's own standards. (3) Small suppliers may offer discriminatory bargain prices just to get a foot in the door as a steady supplier. (4) When supplying divisions have excess capacity, top management sometimes puts pressure on buying divisions to trade inside the company at prices that give a decent return to supplying divisions.

When there is no ruling market price to use on interdivisional sales, transfer prices are set at levels to give goal rates of return to supplying divisions, but the use of arbitrary standards rules out a policy of maximizing divisional profits.[38] Arbitrary "transfer prices" destroy a useful criterion for the value of vertical or-

---

[38] E.g., transfers to marketing divisions may be set at prices to give x per cent margin on fair trade retail prices, or x per cent on marketing investment.

ganization, so that decisions about acquisitions and dispositions have to rest on more subjective strategic considerations.

These complications don't rule out the use of divisional profit accounting for control purposes, but they mean that profit standards must be set largely by managerial ukase, designed with discretion and wisdom.

Chapter 2

COMPETITION

45

Chapter 2

Competition

I. INTRODUCTION

BUSINESS DECISIONS are dominantly competitive in orientation. Consequently, the executive needs an understanding of the structure of competition in his industry. Although there is no substitute for the intimate knowledge of competitors' ways that is acquired by a battle-hardened executive, economic analysis of the anatomy of types of competition can shortcut the process of understanding an individual competitive framework, and can provide insight into probable behavior patterns.

Only in the last few decades has economic analysis systematically studied competitive structure. Collusion, restraint of trade, oligopoly, and giantism in industry have always been prominent social problems, and a whole body of law had been created to control them. But economic analysts before 1939 did not make serious attempts to incorporate phenomena of imperfect competition into general economic theory.

The development of systematic, full-fledged theories of imperfect competition in the early thirties [1] produced a new approach to industry studies and stimulated widespread empirical investigation of competitive structures.

Although it is inappropriate here to examine the theoretical issues that motivated and focused these studies, we can make use of the materials on competitive structure that have grown out of them. The fact that they are oriented toward problems of explaining economic behavior and tracing the consequences of structure on the functioning of the economy does not destroy their

---

[1] The two books that pulled together the fragmentary doctrines on the subject and developed it into a systematic feature of economic theory were Joan Robinson's *Economics of Imperfect Competition* (New York, Macmillan, 1933), and E. H. Chamberlin's *Theory of Monopolistic Competition* (Cambridge, Harvard University Press, 1938).

usefulness for managerial economics, for they present some of the broader aspects of a firm's competitive problems. Our discussion deals with types of competition, the problem of delimiting the scene of competitive action, methods of measuring competition, analyzing the results, and antitrust developments. A great many studies of competitive structures in various industries have been produced in recent years. We have selected those that combine the virtues of broad scope and succinct treatment.[2]

II. KINDS OF COMPETITIVE SITUATIONS

In the following article Clair Wilcox describes the most commonly known types of competition. They are not a uniform group in the sense of a spectrum of competitive intensities. Some of them consider different aspects—dimensions—of competition that may or may not coexist in the same market, such as oligopoly and cutthroat competition. Any classification of competitive structure must depend on the use to be made of it, and Wilcox's objective here was to relate the usual ideas of competition to an empirical study of its nature in American industry. He has nevertheless produced a convenient reference catalog on the terminology of competition.

THE NATURE OF COMPETITION [3]
By Clair Wilcox

Competition has many different meanings. The term always denotes the presence in a specific market of two or more sellers and two or more buyers of a definite commodity, each seller acting independently of every other seller and each buyer independently of every other buyer. But the term usually carries a further connotation. There is perfect competition, pure competition, imperfect competition, monopolistic competition, non-price competition, oligopolistic competition, cutthroat or destructive competition, predatory and discriminatory competition, unfair and fair competition, potential competition, and effective or workable competition. Each of these concepts will be examined in turn.

[2] For a recent bibliography of competition, see Joe Bain, "Price and Production Policies," in *Survey of Contemporary Economics,* H. Ellis, Editor, Philadelphia, Blakiston Co., 1948.

[3] Reprinted from *Competition and Monopoly in American Industry* (TNEC Monograph 21), 1941.

Perfect Competition

The requirements of perfect competition are five: First, the commodity dealt in must be supplied in quantity and each unit must be so like every other unit that buyers can shift quickly from one seller to another in order to obtain the advantage of a lower price. Second, the market in which the commodity is bought and sold must be well organized, trading must be continuous, and traders must be so well informed that every unit sold at the same time will sell at the same price. Third, sellers must be numerous, each seller must be small, and the quantity supplied by any one of them must be so insignificant a part of the total supply that no increase or decrease in his output can appreciably affect the market price. Buyers likewise must be numerous, each buyer must be small, and the quantity bought by any one of them must be so insignificant a part of the total demand that no increase or decrease in his purchases can appreciably affect the price. Under these circumstances, the seller who sets his price above the market level will sell nothing and the seller who sets his price below this level would get all of the business were it not for the fact that he lacks the capacity to handle it. No seller will be able to get more than the market price; no seller will need to take less, since he can sell at the prevailing figure whatever quantity he is equipped to produce. Each seller will therefore take the market price as given and adjust his output to it, carrying production up to the point where the cost of producing an additional unit will equal the income that can be derived from its sale. Similarly, since no buyer will be able to obtain a supply at a figure below the market price and no buyer will need to pay more than the market price to obtain whatever quantity he desires, each buyer will take the price as given and adjust his purchases to it. Fourth, there must be no restraint upon the independence of any seller or buyer, either by custom, contract, collusion, the fear of reprisals by competitors, or the imposition of public control. Each one must be free to act in his own interest without regard for the interests of any of the others. Fifth, the market price, uniform at any instant of time, must be flexible over a period of time, constantly rising and falling in response to the changing conditions of supply and demand. There must be no friction to impede the movement of capital from industry to industry, from product to product, or from firm to firm; investment must be speedily withdrawn from unsuccessful undertakings and transferred to those that promise a profit. There must be no barrier to entrance into the market; access must be granted to all sellers and all buyers at home and abroad. Finally, there must be no obstacle to elimination from the market; bankruptcy must be permitted to destroy those who lack the strength to survive.

Perfect competition, thus defined, probably does not exist, never has existed, and never can exist. The term denotes the extreme of freedom from control over price, just as the term monopoly, in its strictest definition, is used to denote the opposite extreme of unlimited control over price. Actual competition always departs, to a greater or lesser degree, from the ideal of perfection. Perfect competition is thus a mere concept, a standard by which to measure the varying degrees of imperfection that characterize the actual markets in which goods are bought and sold.

Pure Competition

Pure competition comes close to the ideal of perfection without completely attaining it. Under pure competition, information as to present and prospective conditions of supply and demand may be imperfect or unequally distributed; custom may restrain complete independence of action; friction may impede the movement of capital between industries, products, and firms; minor obstacles may limit access to and withdrawal from the field. But other of the conditions of perfect competition must be preserved; commodities must be standardized; sellers and buyers must be numerous and small; no one of them may control enough of the supply or the demand appreciably to affect the price; each of them must take price as given and adjust his output or purchases to it. Pure competition is said to characterize the organized commodities markets and the securities exchanges. But even here individual traders or groups of traders acting in concert have been known to control enough of the supply or the demand to manipulate the price. Pure competition undoubtedly does exist, but its occurrence is comparatively rare.

Imperfect Competition

Imperfect competition involves a more serious departure from one or more of the requirements of perfection. Information may be hidden from traders, the composition of commodities and the prices at which sales are made kept secret. Restrictive contracts, the conventions of the trade, or the fear of reprisals by competitors may inhibit freedom of action. Serious obstacles may check the mobility of capital, hinder entrance to the field, or delay elimination from it. The conditions requisite to pure, as well as to perfect, competition may likewise be lacking. The product sold by each seller, though essentially like that sold by every other, may be so differentiated that buyers will be unwilling to shift quickly from one to another. If one seller sets his price above the market level he will not lose all of his trade to the others; if he sets it below the market level he will not attract all of their trade to himself. He may fix his price, within limits, therefore, at any figure he chooses. Sellers, moreover, may be few in number and any one of them of such size that an increase or decrease in his output will appreciably affect the prospective price. In this case, the seller, instead of taking price as given and carrying production up to the point where the cost of an additional unit would equal the income derived from its sale, will consider the probable effect of variations in production upon the price and adjust his output accordingly. His production policy will therefore differ from that which would be followed by a seller under the conditions of perfect or pure competition. A comparable situation may obtain on the buyers' side of the market. Conditions such as these make for imperfection in competition. And since such conditions are present, to a greater or lesser extent, in many if not in most markets, it must be recognized that the occurrence of imperfect competition is common.

Monopolistic Competition

Monopolistic competition is the form of imperfect competition which results from the differentiation of products by sellers. Under monopolistic competition, sellers may be numerous and no one of them may control a major part of the supply of the common commodity which all of them are offering for sale. But each seller may so differentiate his portion of the supply of that commodity from the portions sold by others that buyers will hesitate to shift their purchases from his product to that of another in response to differences in price. Products serving a common purpose may be individualized by variations in their composition, in the sizes of the units in which they are sold, in the services which accompany the sale, in style, and in such superficial matters as packaging, brand names, and sales appeal. Such differentiation may enable one seller to charge more than another, and even to advance his price, without losing sales, always, however, within the limits set by the availability of products which may be readily substituted for his own. Monopolistic competition is thus monopolistic only up to the point where substitution takes place and competitive only beyond that point. It obtains in many markets; probably in a majority of the markets for manufactured consumers' goods in the United States.

Non-price Competition

Perfect and pure competition, since they require commodity standardization, pertain to competition in price alone. Imperfect and monopolistic competition, since they permit product differentiation, pertain also to sellers' competition in quality, in service, in style, and in advertising and salesmanship. Competition in quality and in service may be quite as effective in giving the buyer more for his money as is competition in price. Competition in service, however, may compel the buyer to pay for something he does not use or want as a condition of obtaining the commodity he desires. Competition in style may give satisfaction to the buyer, but it may also destroy the value of the goods he purchases by hastening their obsolescence. Competition in advertising and salesmanship are necessary concomitants of competition in quality, service, and style, but they may not, in themselves, give the buyer a value which is equal to their cost. Each of these forms of competition is a common feature of the markets for manufactured consumers' goods.

Oligopoly

Oligopoly is the form of imperfect competition which obtains when sellers are few in number and any one of them is of such size that an increase or decrease in his output will appreciably affect the market price. The commodity produced by the sellers may be standardized or differentiated; the size of each seller's output in relation to the total supply is the test. In such a situation, as has been said, the seller will consider the probable effect of variations in his output upon the price and adjust his production accordingly. He will consider, also, the probable reaction of his competitors to variations in his price, and may forego the expansion in sales which he might obtain by setting his price at a lower level if he believes that they will shortly meet or undercut it. Since there are many fields in which sellers are few in number, oligopolistic competition is of common occurrence. A comparable situation, oligopsony, may obtain on the buyers' side of the market.

Cutthroat or Destructive Competition

Competition is said to be cutthroat or destructive when the existence of idle capacity and the pressure of fixed charges lead sellers successively to cut prices to a point where no one of them can recover his costs and earn a fair return on his investment. Competition which threatens to produce this result is called price warfare. Price warfare could not occur under perfect or pure competition, since the output of each seller would be so small a part of the total supply that it would be unnecessary for him to cut his price in order to increase his sales. There can be no question, however, that price wars do occur under oligopoly; that, in a metaphorical sense, at least, the throats of business enterprises are cut; that these legal entities are injured or destroyed; and that investment values suffer in the process. The railroad rate wars of the sixties and the seventies of the nineteenth century are a case in point. The difficulty with the concept lies in the ease with which it lends itself to abuse. It cannot be said with certainty that a series of price cuts is destructive unless someone has made an impartial analysis of the costs of the price cutters, determined what rate of return it is fair for them to receive, and discovered that the cut prices will not cover the legitimate costs plus the fair return. The terms cutthroat and destructive, however, are frequently applied, in the absence of any such investigation, to ordinary competition in price. Thus employed, they can have no more weight than any other epithet.

Predatory and Discriminatory Competition

Competition is said to be predatory when one seller cuts his price for the sole purpose of eliminating another, discriminatory when he confines the cut to a portion of his sales that competes with those made by another.   He may cut prices uniformly, deliberately sacrificing present earnings in an effort to obtain future monopoly power and profit.   He may discriminate among localities, temporarily cutting his price in one area while he maintains it in others, raising it again when he has eliminated his local rivals.   He may discriminate among products, temporarily cutting his price on one brand while he maintains it on others, dropping the fighting brand when it has served its purpose.   There can be no question that such tactics have been frequently employed.   But this concept, too, presents difficulties. The test of predation is intent, but the price cutter's purpose is known only to himself, is only to be inferred by others.   In cases of flagrant discrimination the inference may be plain; in cases of general price reduction it is less so.   The competitor who finds it difficult to meet another's price may well believe that his rival intends to eliminate him, but this conviction cannot be taken as sufficient proof of such intent.   Every act of competition is designed to attract business to one competitor rather than another and, to that extent, to eliminate the latter from the market.   The line beyond which such activity is to be denounced as predatory is not an easy one to draw.

Unfair and Fair Competition

The concept of unfairness and fairness in competition has made its appearance in the opinion of the business community, in formal codes of business ethics, in common law, in the Federal Trade Commission Act, in the Commission's decisions, in the submittals presented to the Commission by trade practice conferences, in the National Industrial Recovery Act, in the codes approved by the National Recovery Administration, and in the unfair trade and fair trade laws recently enacted by the legislatures of a majority of the American States.   The concept is thus ethical and legal rather than economic. Its precise content is indeterminate, since opinions, codes, laws, and decisions differ one from another and each of them may be modified with the passage of time.   It would be possible in economics so to define unfair competition as to include within the concept all of those methods and only those methods which give one competitor an advantage or place another at a disadvantage which has nothing to do with their comparative efficiency in the production and distribution of goods.   But relevance to efficiency cannot be taken as the accepted test of fairness, since measures involving competition in efficiency have sometimes been condemned and measures unrelated to efficiency approved.   In fact, no such objective principle has been

employed to distinguish between those methods which are said to be
unfair and those which are said to be fair.

The fairness of many competitive practices has been, and remains,
in dispute. As to certain other practices, however, agreement is general. It is considered to be unfair to take customers away from a
competitor by misrepresenting the quality or the price of one's goods;
to interfere with the sales of a competitor by defaming him, dis-
paraging his products, harassing his salesmen, obstructing his deliv-
eries, damaging his goods, intimidating his customers, bribing their
purchasing agents, or inducing them to break their contracts with
him, by organizing boycotts against him, or by entering into restrictive contracts with distributors which are designed to exclude him
from the market; or otherwise to handicap a competitor by spying
on him, stealing his trade secrets, involving him in false litigation, or
inducing his employees to go out on strike, by persuading the producers of materials to discriminate against him, or by entering into
exclusive contracts with them in order to deprive him of a source of
supply. These and similar practices have been denounced by the
legislatures and the courts and forsworn by business itself. In general, they fall within the category of acts designed to give a competitor
an advantage unrelated to his productive efficiency.

In recent years the concept of unfairness has been applied to a
radically different sort of behavior. The codes of fair competition
approved by the N.R.A. condemned such acts as cutting a price
without first informing one's competitors and waiting for several
days in order to give them an opportunity to follow suit, selling at
a price below some average of the costs of all the firms in one's trade,
cutting a price indirectly by giving larger trade-in values, discounts,
premiums, or guaranties than those given by one's competitors, expanding one's productive capacity, operating one's machines beyond
a fixed number of hours, or producing a larger quantity of goods than
that allowed by a quota fixed in conference with one's competitors.
The unfair trade laws condemn the practice of selling goods at a
price below their cost plus a fixed mark-up. The fair trade laws
condemn the practice of selling goods at a price below that specified
by their producer in a contract with a single distributor. In specific
cases the recent employment of the concept has completely reversed its
previous application. The basing-point price practice in the steel
industry, condemned by the Federal Trade Commission, was required
by the code of fair competition approved by the N.R.A. Resale
price maintenance, repeatedly condemned by the Commission, is approved by the fair-trade laws of 44 States. The tendency appears to
be toward denouncing as unfair any effort to compete on the basis of
price. The effect is to rob the concept of unfairness of whatever
significance it may once have had.

The terms cutthroat, destructive, predatory, and unfair have been
applied almost exclusively to situations in which business units com-

pete as sellers. They might be applied with equal logic to situations in which such units compete as buyers. Producers who were few in number might conceivably bid the prices of raw materials up to a point where no one of them could cover his costs and earn a fair return. One producer might temporarily bid up such prices for the purpose of eliminating another. Any producer, in purchasing materials, might resort to practices which others would regard as unfair. Application of these concepts to competition in buying, however, would involve the same difficulties as does their application to competition in selling. The general failure to attempt such an application may be attributed to the fact that practices objectionable to competitors have made their appearance less frequently on the buyers' than on the sellers' side of the market.

Potential Competition

Potential competition, either as a supplement to actual competition or as a substitute for it, may restrain producers from overcharging those to whom they sell or underpaying those from whom they buy. The essential condition of potential competition is the preservation of freedom to enter or to leave the market. There must be no insuperable barrier, natural or artificial, to the importation or exportation of goods, to the expansion or removal of existing enterprises, or to the establishment of new ones. The exclusive ownership of scarce resources, the heavy investment required for entry into many fields, the fixed character of much existing equipment, high costs of transportation, restrictive tariffs, exclusive franchises, and patent rights constantly operate to destroy the threat of competition. Science, invention, and the development of technology constantly operate to keep this threat alive. Potential competition, insofar as the threat survives, may compensate in part for the imperfection characteristic of actual competition in the great majority of competitive markets.

Effective or Workable Competition

Competition among sellers, even though imperfect, may be regarded as effective or workable if it offers buyers real alternatives sufficient to enable them, by shifting their purchases from one seller to another, substantially to influence quality, service, and price. Competition, to be effective, need not involve the standardization of commodities; it does, however, require the ready substitution of one product for another; it may manifest itself in differences in quality and service as well as in price. Effective competition depends, also, upon the general availability of essential information; buyers cannot influence the behavior of sellers unless alternatives are known. It requires the presence in the market for several sellers, each of them possessing the capacity to survive and grow, and the preservation of conditions which keep alive the threat of potential competition from others. It cannot be expected to obtain in fields where sellers are so few in number, capital requirements so large, and the pressure of fixed charges so strong, that price warefare, or the threat of it, will lead almost inevitably to collusive understandings among the members of the trade. Effective competition requires substantial independence of action; each seller must be free to adopt his own policy governing production and price; each must be able and willing constantly to reconsider his policy and to modify it in the light of changing conditions of demand and supply. The test of effectiveness and workability in competition among sellers is thus to be found in the availability to buyers of genuine alternatives in policy among their sources of supply.

Effective or workable competition among buyers cannot obtain in the case of specialized products, produced on specialized equipment, to meet the particular specifications of a single buyer; it can appear only in connection with the exchange of goods which are in general demand. It depends upon the availability to sellers of information concerning the offers made by buyers. It requires the presence in the market of several buyers, each of them strong enough to survive and grow, and the preservation of conditions which permit new buyers to enter the market and enable sellers to make sales elsewhere. It requires substantial independence of action on the part of every buyer to the end that sellers may be afforded genuine alternatives in policy among their sources of demand.

The concept of effective or workable competition, though less definite, is more generally useful than that of perfect competition. It fulfills, in part, at least, many of the conditions requisite to perfection. It includes all of the area of pure competition and much of that of imperfect, monopolistic and non-price competition. It requires the preservation of the threat of potential competition. It may even exist under the conditions of oligopoly and oligopsony. It may be difficult to distinguish from cutthroat or destructive competition, but it is inconsistent, in general, with those forms of competition that may properly be defined as cutthroat, destructive, or predatory, and with many of the competitive practices that have usually been condemned as unfair. In brief, competition may be said to be effective or workable whenever it operates over time to afford buyers substantial protection against exploitation by sellers. For this is the social function which competition is supposed to perform.

The Instability of Competition and Monopoly

In those industries which appear normally to be competitive, competition is constantly breaking down. Competitors continually seek to limit competition and to obtain for themselves some measure of monopoly power. They enter into agreements governing prices and production. They set up associations to enforce such agreements.

They procure the enactment of restrictive legislation. For a time they may succeed in bring competition under control. But these arrangements, too, are constantly breaking down. Competitors violate the agreements. Associations lack the power to enforce them. New enterprises come into the field. Restrictive statutes are invalidated by the courts or repealed by the legislatures. The lines of control are repeatedly broken and reformed. The facts that describe the situation existing in such an industry today may not apply to the one in which it will find itself tomorrow.

In those industries that appear at any time to be monopolized, likewise, monopoly is constantly tending to break down. Human wants may be satisfied in many different ways. Shifts in consumer demand may rob the monopolist of his market. Invention may develop numerous substitutes for his product. In the words of Nourse and Drury:

> The man who today tries to fence in an industrial highway and exact an exorbitant toll from those who would travel this road to consumer satisfaction is in danger of defeating himself. Under modern conditions of technology, applied science is likely to find other means of progress. The chemist will build a detour around him, the physicist will drive a tunnel under him, or a biological overpass will be devised.

The monopolist may suffer, too, from the lack of the stimulus to efficiency which is afforded by active competition. His originality may give way to inertia, his energy to lethargy. He may be inclined to play safe and let well enough alone. He is likely to devote more attention to the conservation of investment values than he does to the improvement of materials, machines, processes, and products. In such a situation vigorous competitors may arise to dispute his exclusive occupancy of the field. Government, finally, may intervene. Legislation may forbid practices that were once allowed. Enforcement may catch up with violations of the law. For one or another of these reasons, few of the great trusts that were formed near the turn of the century now possess anything approaching absolute monopoly power. But few of the fields that were then monopolized have become effectively competitive. Combinations have been dissolved, new competitors have arisen, and competition has been restored, only to give way to a succession of devices designed for the purpose of dividing markets and maintaining prices. Here, again, the lines of control are repeatedly broken and repeatedly reformed.

III. DESTRUCTIVE COMPETITION

Lloyd Reynolds' empirical study of cutthroat competition in the cotton textile industry illustrates one of the market types discussed by Wilcox in the preceding section. Reynolds' study shows the kind of information that can be used to test the existence of this kind of competition. Note in particular the discussion of excess capacity as a relative concept in economics.

A contrast in remedies for a cutthroat situation is illustrated by the reaction of the British cotton mills to their interwar depression problem. Having no antitrust laws to inhibit them, they turned to intricate schemes for restricting production, controlling prices, and eliminating excess capacity by industry-wide levies. As in all such control schemes, their greatest problem was the maverick firms who preferred to exploit rather than to accept the cartel controls.[4]

CUTTHROAT COMPETITION [5]

By Lloyd G. Reynolds

I

Economists have long maintained that free competition tends to promote economic efficiency. Businessmen, however, have remained singularly unconvinced. In trade journals and at manufacturers' conventions competition is termed "ruinous," "unethical," "cutthroat," "destructive." The control of competition through patents, tariffs, mergers, trade associations and informal agreements has been a major objective of business policy.

The competitive practices condemned by business-men are of two quite separate types, which should be clearly distinguished. Cutthroat competition sometimes refers to false advertising, adulteration of goods, commercial bribery, defamation of competitors, and similar fraudulent practices.[6] It would be generally agreed that such practices are undesirable, and they therefore raise no major question of public policy.

Second, and perhaps more commonly, cutthroat competition refers to acts which tend directly or indirectly to lower the existing price structure.[7] It can scarcely be argued, however, that price reductions

---

[4] A. F. Lucas, *Industrial Reconstruction and the Control of Competition,* Toronto, Longmans, Green & Co., 1937, Ch. VII.

[5] Reprinted from *American Economic Review,* Vol. 30, pp. 736–744 (December, 1940).

[6] For a more complete list of such practices, see Leverett S. Lyon and others, *The National Recovery Administration,* Brookings Institution, Washington, 1935, especially chapters 22, 26, and 27.

[7] Most goods are sold at a wide variety of prices, which are not necessarily changed simultaneously or proportionately. It is therefore more correct to speak of the price structure being undermined than of the price being cut. The conventional term "price cutting" is used below, however, for reasons of convenience.

are always unjustified.   A price cut which reflects a reduction in raw material costs or an improvement in manufacturing technique is clearly reasonable.   Under what conditions, then, does price cutting become cutthroat?

Most of those who denounce price cutting are rather vague on this point.   Emphasis on the *motivation* of producers is reflected in such terms as "chiseler," "unfair," "unethical."   In other cases certain *techniques* of price reduction, such as secret rebates or fictitious advertising allowances, are condemned.   Neither of these criteria, however, provides a satisfactory basis for distinguishing cutthroat competition from competition in general.   It does not matter very much what a price concession is called—"rebate," "allowance," "discount," or plain "cut."   The important thing is that prices have been reduced. And they are probably reduced in most cases because some producers hope thereby to increase their short-run profits or bolster their cash reserves.   There is no reason to assume that producers who reduce prices are more malicious or more greedy than their rivals.

It seems more useful to say that competition becomes cutthroat when prices and profits fall below a specified level.   Cutthroat competition may be said to exist in an industry when the average rate of return on stockholders' investment remains for some time below the rate which would equalize the attractiveness of this industry and other industries to investors.[8]   The period considered must be long enough to include years of prosperity as well as years of depression.   The discussion which follows is concerned only with industries which experience subnormal earnings over at least one complete business cycle, and which therefore have some claim to the status of chronic problems.

Cutthroat competition, thus defined, can arise only where there is excess capacity of the fixed factors engaged in the industry.   Excess capacity may be said to exist when, if all plants in the industry were to be used to capacity,[9] the profit ratio of the industry would be below normal.   Under pure competition, subnormal profits indicate the presence of excess capacity, while profits above normal indicate a

---

[8] After allowance has been made for the relative riskiness of the industry under consideration, its earnings should correspond to the average earnings of all industries which are open to new producers. This definition is somewhat more general than the usual definition of "normal profits." It does not assume that total investment in all industries is constant, nor does it assume that pure competition prevails. It is quite legitimate to average the earnings of industries marked by differing degrees of monopoly, provided only that "closed" industries are not included.

The weakness of existing profits data, of course, limits the practical usefulness of this definition.   Only in the most obvious cases can we be certain that cutthroat competition exists.

[9] By the capacity of a plant is meant that rate of operation which would give the minimum average total cost. Capacity in this sense is not fixed, but will vary with changes in the costs of the factors of production. For a good discussion of the possible meanings of capacity and excess capacity, see J. M. Cassels, "Excess Capacity and Monopolistic Competition," *Quart. Jour. of Econ.*, May, 1937.

shortage of capacity. Under monopolistic competition, too, sub-normal profits are reliable evidence of excess capacity, but the reverse is not necessarily true, since it is possible for profits to be normal or above normal even though excess capacity exists.

The definition of excess capacity may be further clarified by contrasting it with unused capacity. While *excess* capacity can refer only to an industry, unused capacity may refer either to an industry or to an individual plant. The unused capacity of a plant or an industry is measured by the difference between actual output and capacity output over a given period. But the presence of unused capacity does not prove the existence of excess capacity, nor can a measurement of the former provide any indication of the extent of the latter. The excess capacity of an industry is the amount which, if withdrawn from production, would bring a rise in prices sufficient to restore normal profits. This cannot be ascertained without an analysis of all demand curves in the industry.

II

The view that cutthroat competition tends in time to correct itself is supported by the experience of the cotton textile industry.[10] The consequences of competition in this industry have been frequently lamented in trade journals and elsewhere. Excess capacity, as indicated by profit ratios, seems to have appeared about 1923, and has persisted almost to the present day. The consumption of cotton goods has increased very little over this period, due in part to the development and cheapening of rayon fabrics. At the same time the productive capacity of the industry has been increased by longer hours of plant operation and by the building of new plants in the southern states.

The possibility of spreading overhead affords a powerful incentive to longer hours of operation.[11] New England mills have traditionally

---

[10] It is impossible to consider the cotton textile industry as a unit because of the great variety of its products. The discussion which follows relates only to producers of the principal product—grey cotton print cloth. Most print cloth is sold in the grey, through New York selling agents, to "convertors" who have the cloth printed and resell it to garment manufacturers, wholesalers or retailers. Cloth is sold in a few standard grades, based on weight and closeness of weave, and trademarking and advertising are unknown. The convertor is necessarily an expert judge of cloth, and advertising appeals would have little effect on him. The number of print cloth producers is relatively large; and no firm produces more than a few per cent of the total output. This branch of the industry thus approximates the conditions of pure competition.

[11] Night operation, while it increasees unit labor costs, cuts unit overhead cost almost in half. R. E. Loper, a textile engineer, has estimated that double-shift operation reduces the cost of manufacturing print cloth by about 5 per cent (*Textile World*, Feb. 4, 1928, p. 119). This estimate assumes that night wages are 10 per cent higher than day wages and that efficiency is from 5 to 8 per cent lower at night. In an industry which operates on so small a profit margin as textiles, a saving of 5 per cent may make the difference between failure and good profits.

operated a single 8-hour shift.   In the South, however, a large reservoir of labor and the absence of laws regulating night work led to a steady growth of two- and even three-shift operation during the twenties. The NRA code for the industry limited each mill to 80 hours per week, but this had the effect of increasing rather than reducing the hours operated, since all producers then tended to operate the full 80 hours. The surviving New England producers were able to adopt this practice because of the widespread unemployment among New England textile workers.   In 1936 each active spindle operated on the average 3,926 hours or 75 hours per week, compared with 2,869 hours or 55 hours per week in 1923.   This evidently amounts to an increase of almost one-third in the capacity of the industry during this period.

In addition to increased capacity from this source there has been extensive building of new plants in the southern states.   The southern producer has a slight advantage in the cost of raw cotton, the cost of mill construction, and local tax rates, and a marked advantage in wage rates.   During the twenties hourly wage rates of textile operatives were about 50 per cent higher in New England than in the South. The differential in unit labor costs was undoubtedly less than this,[12] but it must still have been considerable.   No data are available concerning total unit costs in the two areas, but profits figures may serve as indirect evidence.   From 1925–29 a selected group of southern companies earned 5.8 per cent on stockholders' investment, while selected New England companies earned 1.5 per cent.   A more complete survey for the years 1933 and 1934 showed earnings of 7.1 per cent in the South, 0.33 per cent in New England (Table 1).   The relative profitableness of cotton textiles in the South caused plant capacity to increase from 16 million spindles in 1923 to 18.5 million spindles in 1937.[13]   These additional plants intensified the problem of excess capacity in the industry as a whole.

Frequent efforts have been made to bring excess capacity under control.   Leaders of the industry have advised restriction of output, and the Cotton Textile Institute has tried to secure agreement among

---

[12] Two things must be borne in mind here: (i) the efficiency of southern operatives may be lower than that of New England workers because of lack of training, climatic differences, and the like.   Union officials contend, on the other hand, that the efficiency of southern workers is sometimes higher because they have no preconceived ideas as to how many machines they should tend.   (ii) Many southern workers live in company towns, rent their houses from the company, buy at company stores and from company-owned utilities.   In this case wages may be either higher or lower than they appear to be, depending on whether the prices charged by the company are below or above the cost of providing the services. It is generally believed that these services are provided below cost and thus constitute an addition to nominal wages, though this too is denied by the union.

[13] C. T. Main, *Growth and Decline of Cotton Spindles in the United States,* Boston, 1938.   The number of spindles in Virginia and North Carolina reached a peak in 1930.   In South Carolina, Georgia and Alabama, however, the industry continued to grow until 1935.   There has been in recent years a tendency for Virginia and North Carolina to lose plants to the deep South in the same way that New England originally lost them to Virginia and North Carolina.

Table 2–1

Profits in Cotton Textiles and in All Manufacturing
Percentage to Capitalization

Year	All manufac- turing [1]	Cotton textiles		
		All [2]	Northern [3]	Southern [3]
1919	18.3	32.5		
20	12.3	12.1		
1	2.9	9.4		
2	10.2	11.4		
3	11.2	11.0		
4	10.0	1.3		
5	12.1	4.3	−1.6	5.2
6	12.4	3.2	−0.4	3.7
7	9.5	10.2	3.2	10.4
8	11.0	4.7	2.9	5.7
9			2.4	4.1
30				
1				
2				
3	0.7	6.6	3.8	10.2
4	3.0	1.3	−3.1	4.0
5	5.7	−1.0		
6	7.9	2.6		

[1] 1919–28: R. C. Epstein, *Industrial Profits in the United States,* National Bureau of Economic Research, New York, 1934, p. 242.

1933–36: W. L. Crum, "Cyclical Changes in Corporate Profits," *Rev. of Econ. Stat.,* May, 1939, pp. 49–61.

[2] 1919–28: R. C. Epstein, *op. cit.,* p. 254 ("cotton weaving").

1933–36: Federal Trade Commission, *Reports on the Textile Industries,* 1933–36.

[3] 1925–29: C. E. Fraser and G. F. Doriot, *Analyzing Our Industries,* McGraw-Hill, New York, 1932, p. 120.

1933–34: Cabinet Committee *Report on the Textile Industry,* 1934, p. 61. Federal Trade Commission, *op. cit.,* 1933–36.

All figures represent net income after charges as a percentage of stockholders' investment.

producers to this end. These efforts have been uniformily unsuccessful. An agreement among the sixty producers of print cloth would not only be difficult to secure and enforce, but it would necessarily receive considerable publicity and would be suspect under the Sherman act. Entrance to the industry, too, is relatively easy. Not only is the necessary investment small,[14] but support for new ventures has in the past been readily forthcoming from textile machinery manufacturers

[14] The average southern cotton mill has about 30,000 spindles. While some mills are much larger, it is doubtful whether expansion beyond 50,000 spindles brings any reduction in unit costs. The profits reports of the Federal Trade Com-

and local chambers of commerce. A restriction plan which increased textile profits materially would lead at once to fresh investment, and this would either break the plan or reduce its profitability. The most serious obstacle to agreement, however, has been the difference of viewpoint between southern and northern producers. New England producers have been inclined to welcome control, though even here the strong individualistic tradition of the industry has prevented complete agreement. Many southern producers, on the other hand, have failed to see why they should restrict their profitable operations in order to hold an umbrella over marginal New England mills.[15] On this rock of southern opposition all proposals for control have been broken.

Individual producers, of course, have frequently chosen to operate below capacity.[16] This voluntary restriction of output, however, has been insufficient to restore the former profitability of the industry. Mill margins declined steadily from 1923 to 1932, recovered sharply in the last half of 1933, but sagged again from the end of 1933 to the summer of 1936.[17] During this fourteen-year period, profits in cotton textiles appear to have been no more than half those of manufacturing industry generally (Table 2–1). While this is not conclusive proof, it is strong *prima facie* evidence of the existence of cutthroat competition.

It is desirable to distinguish in this regard between the northern and southern branches of the industry. During the years for which data are available (1925–29 and 1933–34), southern producers averaged more than 6 per cent on stockholders' investment. It is doubtful

---

mission seem to indicate that the earnings of small mills are at least as high as, and perhaps higher than, those of the largest producers. (See, for example, F.T.C., *Report on the Textile Industry,* Jan.–June, 1936.)

[15] There is an additional reason for southern opposition to production control. In a company town, the company must maintain utility and other services whether the workers are employed or not, and in addition must provide enough cash income to hold the working force together. Under these conditions labor becomes to a considerable extent a fixed cost, and any reduction in output raises unit costs considerably.

[16] It is impossible to measure exactly the amount of unused capacity in the industry because of the complications introduced by multiple-shift operation. If one assumes that all New England mills customarily worked one 8-hour shift and that one-half of the southern mills worked two 8-hour shifts, then the utilization of capacity (spindle-hours operated as a percentage of total possible spindle-hours) over the period 1924–36 was 75.8 per cent. These assumptions, however, which are those made by the Brookings Institution (E. G. Nourse, *America's Capacity to Produce,* Brookings Institution, Washington, 1934, pp. 194–202), almost certainly understate the customary working time of the industry and therefore understate the amount of unused capacity.

[17] "Mill margin" is the difference between the price of a pound of a specified grade of print cloth (in this case, 38.5 inches, 64 x 60, 5.35) and the cost of the cotton contained in the cloth. It indicates, in other words, the amount which the manufacturer receives to cover his operating expenses and yield a profit. The margin on the standard grade of cloth noted above fell from 22.5 cents per pound in 1923, to 18.0 cents in 1929, to 9.9 cents at the beginning of 1933. After recovering to 23 cents at the end of 1933 it fell off once more, and reached 14 cents in the spring of 1936.

whether this constitutes cutthroat competition, particularly in view of the fact that plant capacity in the South increased appreciably during the period.[18]   One can be quite certain, however, that competition has been ruinous to the New England branch of the industry.   Low or negative earnings have resulted in a steady liquidation of productive capacity.   The number of spindles in place in New England fell from 18 millions in 1923 to 8 millions in 1937.   Though a small number of spindles and looms have been moved south and reërected, most of this reduction represents actual scrapping of machinery, with buildings left vacant or rented to new users.

The experience of the industry during the past fifteen years may now be summarized.   The development of excess capacity in the early twenties brought low earnings, which could be increased only by controlling production or by reducing plant capacity.   For reasons already indicated, control proved impossible and events took the latter course.   Under the pressure of shrinking processors' margins, elimination of marginal mills went steadily forward.   The total number of spindles in place fell from a peak of 38 millions in 1925 to 27 millions in 1938.   Available estimates indicate that the process of liquidation is nearing its end; and that the capacity of the industry is now only slightly in excess of probable future sales.[19]   Competition has thus performed, though tardily and haphazardly, its traditional function of adjusting productive capacity to effective demand.   The process of adjustment, of course, has been painful for many of those connected with the industry.   The chief losers have not been the owners of New England mills, whose investments had in most cases been thoroughly amortized from previous earnings, but the New England textile workers.   The closing of the mills has thrown some 100,000 New England workers out of employment, and large numbers of these workers are still unemployed.[20]

---

[18] The fact that total investment increased, however, does not necessarily prove that profits were more than "normal."   In a family business such as cotton textiles, ownership of capital is closely associated with the possession of managerial skills. It is the return to the capitalist-plus-manager which must be maximized. A displaced New England cotton manufacturer might gain by building a new plant in the South, even if the return on capital alone were less than he could have obtained elsewhere.

[19] It has been estimated that, if the average consumption of cotton goods from 1915–36 be taken as "normal," this demand could be satisfied by 21 million spindles operating 80 hours per week. (C. T. Main, op. cit., pp. 9–13.)   Since the number of active spindles in March, 1938, was only 24 millions, and since some margin is required to care for seasonal and cyclical peaks, it would seem that excess capacity has been largely eliminated.

[20] In November, 1937, 36 per cent of all gainfully employable persons in Lowell, Massachusetts, were totally unemployed, 35 per cent in Fall River, 41 per cent in New Bedford.   The figure for Massachusetts as a whole was only 22 per cent. (Computed from returns of the 1937 unemployment census on the assumption that three-quarters of the totally unemployed filed returns, and that the number of gainfully employed in Massachusetts increased by 8 per cent between 1930 and 1937.)

IV. THE NATURE OF MONOPOLY AND OLIGOPOLY

Two important facts of most competitive situations are lucidly analyzed by Professor Robinson in the following excerpts from his discussion of monopoly. The first is the problem of defining commodities, industries, and monopolies. Robinson's treatment is a translation into words of the "cross elasticity of demand," which in mathematical form is used by Triffin in his classification of competition.[21] The second is the essentially insoluble problem of predicting competitive behavior in oligopoly—a market with few sellers. The treatment of oligopoly is basic to the discussion in following chapters, which is largely benched on the assumption that each seller knows his competitors individually in each market.

MONOPOLY AND QUASI-MONOPOLY
By E. A. G. Robinson [22]

The Difficulty of Defining Monopoly

The nineteenth century, we are often told, was an era of competition, the twentieth century is an era of monopoly. With the broad truth of this statement few would disagree. The last quarter of the earlier century, it is true, saw a transition, more marked in some countries, less marked in others, from the old order to the new. The powerful semi-monopolistic concerns familiar to-day began to emerge in the United States and in Germany, and to a somewhat less extent in Great Britain and in other countries. When we speak of monopoly in this way most of us have a fairly clear idea of what it is that we mean. But if we are to argue closely regarding the actions of monopolists we must attempt a somewhat more precise definition.

What then is a monopoly, and what is a monopolist? A monopolist, we might say, is one who is in the position of being the sole seller of some commodity. But that definition has only enabled us to escape from our present difficulties by plunging us into other and worse difficulties. What is a commodity? The unhappy truth is that there is and can be no comfortable, hard and fast, definition of a commodity.[23] There is no simple homogeneous commodity produced by the manufacturers of motor cars, or of wireless sets, or of chocolates, which we can count and calculate, and compute that so many will be bought if the uniform price is so much, or that so many can be produced at

21 *Monopolistic Competition and General Equilibrium Theory*, Cambridge, Harvard University Press, 1940, Ch. III.

22 Reprinted from *Monopoly*, London, James Nisbet & Co., Ltd., 1941, pp. 3–8, 23–30.

23 For the difficulties involved in any attempt to define a commodity, see *The Structure of Competitive Industry* (Cambridge Economic Handbooks), pp. 6–13.

an average cost of so much per unit.   There is rather an infinite series
of closely competing substitutes.   Sometimes, as when a fleet of
trawlers catch identical fish in the same waters and land them in the
same state of freshness, the products of one producer are a perfect
substitute for the products of any other, and no one producer can
charge more than the price ruling in the market without losing all his
customers.   But more often the products of one producer are not a
perfect substitute for those of another.   There is some quality, perhaps real, perhaps quite imaginary, which leads purchasers to take
different views, so that there are certain customers who prefer the
products of one manufacturer to those of his closest competitors, so
that he may charge a fractionally higher price for his products without
losing all his sales.   In the case of the trawlers the elasticity of demand
for the products of our single producer is infinite, and the competition
can be called "perfect"; in the more usual case it is less than infinite,
and the competition may be called "imperfect."

Now if we wish to be precise in our definition of monopoly we
should say that every manufacturer is in the nature of things a
monopolist of his own products.   He alone produces those particular
products and he alone sells them.   The interesting problem is not
who is, and who is not, in this sense a monopolist, but rather in what
circumstances a monopolist is strong and in what circumstances he is
weak.   The strength of a monopolist lies in his power to raise his
prices without frightening away all his customers.   How much he can
raise them depends on the elasticity of demand for his particular products.   This, in turn, depends on the extent to which substitutes for his
products are available.   In the widest sense of the word, everything
that we buy is a substitute for everything else.   Apart from a few
physical necessities for existence, such as salt or water, every use of
money competes with every other use.   There is some increased margin
of price which would induce each of us to forsake one method of
satisfying our wants and employ an alternative method.   The width
of this margin depends on the fixity of our habits and on our respect
for convention.   Some people will clearly be less willing than others
to make a change.   Some, again, because of their wealth can longer
resist it.   But sooner or later a point is reached at which any of us
will give up one way of spending and take to another.

Obviously there are some products which are more likely to tempt
us away from a given form of expenditure than others.   There are,
that is to say, closer and more distant substitutes.   The closest substitutes may be so nearly identical with the original object of expenditure that a comparatively small difference of price is sufficient to persuade me to substitute them.   A Morris Eight is a substitute for an
Austin Eight, or a Pye radio set for a Murphy in a much nearer sense
than are radio sets for cars.   The closer the substitutes, and the greater
the elasticity therefore of the demand for a given manufacturer's product, the less he can raise his price without frightening away his custom-

ers, until in the limiting case of perfect competition, substitutes are so close and so identical that no increase of price is possible at all without the disappearance of all customers.

Now substitutes do not always form a perfect graduation from the closest to the most distant. More often there is at some point a break in this chain of substitutes. Palm Olive soap is a fairly close substitute for Pears Soap. Any very considerable change of price of the one or the other will persuade us to forsake the black cake for the green one, or *vice versa*. But between soaps of all sorts and the next best alternative there is for most of us a wide gap. We would willingly pay far more than we do for our soap before we would copy the Romans and go to our baths with a scraper and a bottle of oil. Thus anyone who could control the price of all soaps might be able to exploit us considerably. It is the double condition, first, of a gap in the chain of substitutes, second, of the possibility of securing control of all the close substitutes, which makes a monopolist strong; which enables him, in other words, to advance his price considerably and to make large profits out of his consumers.

There are not only difficulties in defining "a commodity," there are difficulties also in defining what we mean by "the sole seller." It would clearly be ridiculous to assume that no seller is a monopolist unless he supplies 100 per cent of the commodity or service, or to say, for example, that the local electricity supply company is not in a monopolistic position, because one or two people have their own generating plants. It would be equally ridiculous to declare that a group of producers do not form a monopoly because from time to time, or in certain markets, they have been known to compete. This difficulty of deciding where to draw the line between what is, and what is not, monopoly is not a difficulty that is unique to this particular problem. It pervades the whole of economics, and indeed, of many other sciences. For the truth is that there is a continuous gradation between competition and monopoly, just as there is between light and darkness, or between health and sickness.

It should now be clear that any simple definition of the terms "monopoly" and "monopolist" is impossible. In some industries where goodwill is important and difficulties of entry are considerable, it may be legitimate to regard any one of a small number of firms engaged in substantially imperfect competition as a monopolist, in the sense that its power of raising price is appreciable. In other industries where substitutes are closer, and goodwill less important, it may serve no useful purpose to regard firms engaged in very slightly imperfect competition as monopolists, and combination of all firms within the limit set by a gap in the chain of substitutes, may be a necessary condition of any effective monopoly.

The Demand for the Output of a Single Producer

It is important before we go further to examine rather more closely the meaning of the schedule of demand and its elasticity, as seen from the angle of the individual firm.

Suppose a firm reduces its prices in order to attract more customers, the extent of its success will depend partly, of course, on the power of price differences to induce customers to change their habits, or of cheaper prices to bring in new purchasers, but to an even greatert extent its success will depend upon the way in which other firms respond to its action. Let us consider for the moment the increased quantity of home-grown mutton that one particular butcher will sell if he lowers his price. The increase in the quantity demanded from him will be different according as we assume, first, that the price of all meat sold by other butchers is reduced in the same proportion; second, that the price of all mutton sold by others is reduced, but that of all other meat remains unchanged; third, that the price of all home-grown mutton is similarly reduced, but all imported mutton and all other meat remains unchanged; fourth, that the price of home-grown mutton in all other shops, and of all other meat everywhere, remains unchanged. The elasticity of the demand for our butcher's mutton will vary from comparative inelasticity in the first case to extreme elasticity in the last. This example helps us to see that there is nothing absolute about the schedule of demand that causes the individual firm's decisions. The schedule is a series of hypotheses based upon supposed responses of other firms to the actions of the first. A variation of these supposed responses will alter materially the consequently estimated elasticity of the individual firm's demand, its expected marginal revenue at different prices, and therefore the price that it will decide to fix.

Cat and Mouse Monopoly

If, therefore, we are to understand monopolistic or semi-monopolistic price policies, we must delve rather deeper into these assumptions that a firm will make regarding its nearest rivals. If the firm is one of a considerable number of close competitors, so that the preferences for one rather than another are not great, and a small price difference will attract a large increment of sales, and if an increase of its sales makes an insignificant inroad into the sales of any one of the remainder, then the responding price changes of other firms are likely to be negligible. In these circumstances we can reasonably treat the prices of all substitutes as fixed, and the demand for the products of the individual firm as highly, perhaps infinitely, elastic. This fixity of other prices is the assumption that corresponds to the condition of perfect competition.

But if our firm is one of a comparatively small number of firms in an industry, and if fairly considerable price changes are necessary to break down the habits and the more purely economic resistance of customers, then we can no longer assume that the most probable action ɔf rival producers will be to leave their prices unchanged. We must draw up a demand schedule for the products of our individuaï firm on the basis of some more likely policy on the part of these rival undertakings.

There are, of course, various decisions which they may make, and the hypothetical demand schedule of the individual firm will vary according as they are regarded as making one decision or another. They may decide to proceed with a given manufacturing programme, and sell the predetermined output at whatever price in the new circumstances it will fetch. They may decide to adopt the policy which we have already considered, that of leaving their prices unchanged. They may decide to turn out whatever output will give them the best profits when allowance is made for the new policy of the firm we are considering. They may decide to make the same proportionate price-cut as the first firm has made. All these are possible decisions by rival firms, and a firm which is considering its own price policy must make what assumptions it considers most probable. But each different assumption will yield, it is important to remember, a different demand curve, a different elasticity and a different marginal revenue.

We cannot follow out in detail the consequences to price and output of all these alternative assumptions. But it will, perhaps, be profitable to examine more closely the results of the last of these assumptions, that other firms cut their prices to a similar extent. This is in many cases a very probable assumption for an individual producer to make. If he can be certain that a given cut on his part will be followed by an equal cut on the part of his rivals, the only outcome of it will be to leave him with the same proportionate share in the total trade at a smaller margin of profit per unit. In these circumstances, he is likely to refrain from cutting price, unless he believes that the expansion of total sales which will follow from that cut of price will recompense him for the reduction in the margin of profit, his share in the total trade remaining unchanged. Now the elasticity of the demand for his goods (and therefore the marginal revenue), which this one producer is assuming, is exactly equal at each price to that elasticity of the total demand which a monopolist combination of all the firms would take into account in determining price.[24] Thus, if a group of producers all assume that a cut of price is likely to result in equal cuts by their rivals, so that no orders can be stolen from them, something not very different from a monopoly price is likely to be established.

We have, so far, been considering only the probable assumptions of a few rival producers as regards cuts of price. Their probable assumptions as regards advances of price will be more likely to depart from

---

[24] If one producer turns out 100 units daily out of a total production of 500, and if he assumes that a 2½ per cent reduction of price, which would increase the total demand to 525, would enable him to sell 105 units, he assumes in effect that both the total elasticity of demand and his own are approximately 2.

those that an individual monopolist would make. For the individual firm is likely to assume, as regards advances of price, that an advance on its part will not necessarily be accompanied by an advance on the part of its rivals, but that they will prefer to steal its markets. This assumption would appear often to be made even in those circumstances where the rival firms could in fact increase their profits more by accepting the advance of price than by stealing their rivals' markets. The reason for the assumption is obvious. A firm which initiates a cut of price is more likely to increase its proportionate share in the total trade than to diminish it; on the other hand, a firm that initiates an advance of price is more likely to diminish its proportion of the total trade than to maintain it. But the advance of price is only in the interests of the individual firm if it maintains its proportionate share or only slightly diminishes it. Consequently each firm hesitates to be the first to raise prices. It would appear, therefore, that where a number of firms are watching each other closely, a sort of cat and mouse equilibrium may be established. Reductions of price are likely to be made only in those circumstances in which a monopolist would reduce price, but advances of prices may not be made in all those circumstances in which a monopolist would advance price. Profits may, nevertheless, be increased up towards the level of monopoly if improvements of technique increase the margin of profit, and through fear of competitive price cutting no firm reduces the selling price. It may even happen that, from fear that cuts of price once started will be carried too far, a margin of profit per unit too large, and a volume of sales too small to maximize the monopoly profit, will be accepted.

It will be seen that this cat and mouse monopoly depends upon the assumption by each firm that it cannot, by price reductions, increase its share in the total trade. The assumptions of perfect competition are, as we have seen, that by a small price reduction an individual firm can increase its share in the total trade with no limit other than that of the total trade and with no delay, friction or cost. It is evident that the assumption that an individual firm will in fact make is likely to fall somewhere between these two limits, and price will approximate more nearly to monopoly price or to competitive price, according to the assumptions made. These assumptions will be affected not only by estimates of the price cuts or advances which rival producers will make, but also by estimates of the effects of those price cuts or advances upon the long period competitive position of the firm. For a price cut which may be immediately unprofitable may in longer periods be highly profitable, if a larger proportion of the total trade may be expected gradually to accrue to the firm which initiates the price cut.

Moreover the circumstances in which it will be in the interest of one individual firm to cut prices will depend not only upon the assumptions which the firm makes concerning its rivals' price policies, but also upon the effect of an increased or decreased volume of output upon

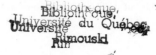

its own costs of production. A firm which can secure a considerable economy of manufacture from the consequent increased output will not reckon on so great a curtailment of its margin of profit through a given cut of price as a firm which expects no such economies. It will, therefore, regard a smaller increase of sales as sufficient justification for a cut in price. Unless, therefore, all the firms in the industry are in approximately the same stage of development and working to approximately the same proportion of their total capacity, they are unlikely to find that an equal price cut will benefit all equally, and one firm may be prepared to cut prices in circumstances in which the other firms would prefer to take no action. In this case, the cat and mouse monopoly is at an end, and a price closer to that which we may call the competitive price is likely to be established. But in many cases a cut in price is only profitable if it is sufficiently large to attract the attention of customers normally attached to a rival firm [25] and since a cut of this magnitude may be unprofitable, an equilibrium which would otherwise be apparently unstable may continue for long periods.

Two very important conclusions follow from the analysis with which we have just been concerned. First, monopoly price is fully as much a consequence of the attitude of a small number of firms to each other, of the assumptions that they make regarding each other, as of formal or informal agreements. We cannot assume that where there is no agreement, even of a tacit nature, competition exists. It all depends upon what one manufacturer thinks another manufacturer is going to do. It follows, therefore, that what we may call the detective story approach to the study of monopoly, the search for mysterious hidden agreements, is really a waste of time. Their existence may prove something, their non-existence proves nothing. Second, if we discover a condition of monopoly it is highly unlikely that we can with any certainty re-establish a condition of competition merely by breaking up that monopoly into a few constituent parts. It is very much more likely that we shall substitute the uncertainties of a cat and mouse monopoly for the certainties of an open one.

V. MARKET STRUCTURE AND COMPETITIVE BEHAVIOR

The market structure of an industry as a key to its competitive behavior has been emphasized by Mason, Wallace, and Bain. To them the goal of empirical industry studies is to establish "an objective classification of markets, each sub-category of which would contain industries with a uniform and distinctive type of

---

[25] I have been told that in one case the minimum significant cut is of the order of 10 per cent.

competitive behavior." [26] In particular, the many kinds of behavior found in markets with few sellers should be analyzed. However, even with the great number of such studies that have been made,[27]

> . . . there is really not enough accumulated information to permit the conclusive establishment of an explanatory classification which will account even on a qualitative level for observed differences in oligopolistic behavior, or, conversely, to support the conclusive rejection of the possibility of such a classification. And there are ample reasons for wondering if any such classification with demonstrable explanatory value can be developed in a world where the effects of dynamic change of and random uncertainty concerning the governing data may obliterate or obscure the virtual influence of basic environmental conditions. Nevertheless, various "scattered returns" have been drawn upon to formulate some tentative market classifications which go beyond those found in *a priori* theory.   Even though these classifications represent casually tested hypotheses rather than established findings, a mention of them may be deserved, in part because they have provided a basis for the experimental elaboration of the assumptions of *a priori* price theory. . . .

The penchant of this writer, after the suggestions of Mason and Wallace in their work at Harvard, would be to emphasize the following market characteristics as strategic in explaining observed differences in competitive and price behavior: the number and size distribution of sellers, the number and size distribution of buyers, whether a producer or consumer good (linked to product differentiation), the conditions of entry, the durability of the product, the time-trend of industry demand. From this could develop an abbreviated classification in the following form:

I. Many sellers, free entry.
- A. Consumers' goods, differentiated products, many buyers.
  1. Durable and style-varied goods.
  2. Non-durable goods.
- B. Producers' goods, unimportant product differentiation (not distinguished on basis of durability).
  1. Many buyers.
  2. Few buyers.
     (Further distinction possible on the basis of time-trend of demand.)

---

26 J. Bain, "Price and Production Policies," *Survey of Contemporary Economics,* H. Ellis, Ed., 1948, p. 158.
27 *Ibid.,* pp. 159–162.

II. Few sellers in general.
    A. Consumers' goods, differentiated products, many buyers.
        1. High concentration of output in hands of few sellers, very difficult entry.
            a. Durable goods, strong style elements.
            b. Non-durable goods.
        2. Moderate concentration, relatively easy entry (not distinguished on basis of durability).
    B. Producers' goods (not distinguished on basis of durability or product differentiation).
        1. High concentration, difficult entry.
            a. Many buyers.
            b. Few buyers.
        2. Moderate concentration, relatively easy entry.
            a. Many buyers.
            b. Few buyers.
    (Further distinction on the basis of time-trend of industry demand desirable.)

This classification, a revision of a basic model introduced by E. S. Mason about a decade ago, seems to the writer to establish sub-categories within each of which the available evidence . . . points to significant uniformities of behavior and among which there are systematic and significant differences, with respect to such matters as profit rates, ratio of selling to production cost, price behavior over time, product behavior over time, and so forth. . . . The problem of explanatory classification . . . remains open, and an explicit orientation of research toward its solution would be highly desirable. Experimentation with abstract price theory employing correspondingly elaborated assumptions, together with some realistic assumption concerning collusion, would also be desirable."

Professor Bain has made an intensive study of the Pacific Coast petroleum industry. The following extract, taken from the summary of Part II, illustrates the application of his approach.

PRICE BEHAVIOR AND COMPETITION
By Joe Bain [28]

Price Policies and Competition

The price policies of the major integrated companies were indeed the immediate origin of the observed price results, although these policies operated within limits set by the competition of producers and

---

[28] Reprinted from *Economics of Pacific Coast Petroleum Industry, Part II, Price Behavior and Competition*, Berkeley, University of California Press, 1945, pp. 349–357.

refiners in other areas and of independent refiners in the Pacific Coast area. What were the salient aspects of these policies?

Of primary importance was the closely concurrent action on price matters which the majors realized through their mutual acceptance of price leadership. Although isolated exceptions to relatively perfect major-company followership of the price leader were found in the depression period, when certain majors on occasion initiated independent price cuts, it is generally possible to refer to *the* price policy of the majors as a group.[29]

In its strictly pricing aspects, the following characteristics of the major policy stand out. The majors generally chose to set a purchase price for crude toward the upper limit which was established by the existing curtailment system and by the level of crude prices in other areas, and, as a corollary of the first choice, to discriminate between the domestic and export markets in the pricing of gasoline and other refined products, charging a relatively high domestic price and a necessarily lower export price. These were necessarily interrelated policies, and together they determined the general level of crude and refined product prices in the domestic market. Within the domestic market, the majors adopted a Los Angeles basing point for the pricing of both crude oil and refined products. This policy was the source of superior earnings to refining facilities situated in the San Francisco Bay area and in the San Joaquin Valley and of some virtual price discrimination in favor of Los Angeles. (The superior earnings, however, were enjoyed principally by only four major companies.)

Although these were the outlines of the broad price policy of the major firms, their total policy was complicated in its nonprice dimensions by their need for meeting and stabilizing the competition of minor refiners and distributive outlets and by their own internecine struggle for market volume. Two principal types of policy were employed, both separately and jointly, as a primary means of meeting minor competition in the Los Angeles area. First, extensive product differentiation policies, involving both the multiplication of the grades and prices of the gasoline sold under major brands and the promotion of secondary brands and outlets, were employed to maintain the prices of major "regular" grade and "premium" grade gasolines on a superior level. This policy was countered and in part neutralized by the minors and was not permanently successful. Second, the majors persistently endeavored to limit minor competition by assuming the surplus output of minors, who in turn limited their total production. This policy tended to establish a stable price structure, based on the

---

[29] On the other hand, the majors followed relatively independent courses in the nonprice aspects of their market policies, and no evidence of concerted action with respect to advertising, product development, or acquisition of distributive facilities, is apparent. At the same time, the independently adopted nonprice market policies of the majors were often similar enough that it is possible to characterize them collectively.

majors' quoted prices. But it again failed to provide an inherently stable solution to the competitive problem, because the uniform abstinence by all minor refiners from producing "excessive" outputs could not be insured under existing legal arrangements. Both of these major policies were buttressed by a third, which also served as the principal vehicle of competition within the major group. This was an extremely aggressive policy in the acquisition of distributive outlets by purchase, lease, and subsidy. All of the majors seem to have followed such an aggressive policy, and it was from it that the large investment in, and negligible return from, marketing facilities principally resulted.

The scope of the price policies of nonmajor companies was necessarily much more limited, including, in fact, little more than specific reactions to major-company policies. Independent crude producers were scarcely in a position to exercise any deliberate policy, being limited largely to deciding whether or not to accept proration quotas and whether or not to produce at the going price. Their defections from voluntary proration in the depression period had some significance, but otherwise they have not exercised any considerable influence on price behavior within the domestic market. Minor refiners are a heterogeneous lot, and their reactions to major policies have been various. Over a considerable period, however, their principal reactions were of two types. When unable to sell large amounts of gasoline to the majors, they tended to follow a low-price policy, selling at prices perceptibly below those of the majors in order to maintain and increase their market volumes. This policy tended to lead progressively to general domestic price instability. Their second major reaction was to accept the majors' offers to purchase their surplus gasoline, and to maintain prices and limit output so long as the majors purchased their limited outputs at favorable prices. The continuity of such arrangements was impaired, however, by the existence of "hold-out" minors who refused to concur in such action, by progressive defections from all such arrangements, and by legal prohibitions. In the net, the minor-refiner policy was one of imperfect and intermittent followership of the major lead, and its result was an imperfectly stable and intermittently unstable gasoline market. In this connection some importance may also be attached to price-cutting policies initiated by independent distributors in the Los Angeles area.

In sum, the price and market behavior observed in the Pacific Coast industry arose out of certain price policies adopted by the recognized major price leader, out of the close followership of the other majors, and out of the very imperfect followership of the bulk of the minor refiners. It arose also out of the vigorous nonprice competition among the majors and between the major and minor groups, which tended to replace price competition so far as the latter was checked by concurrent pricing action. It should be convenient in summary to evaluate the degree in which such policies were the natural outcome of the market structure from which they emerged.

Market Structure and Price Behavior

The connections at various market levels between market structure and price behavior were traced in some detail in preceding chapters, but it may be useful at this point to bring together the conclusions which were there developed. The market characteristic of broadest importance is the relationship of the location of Pacific Coast oil reserves and markets to those of other oil reserves and markets in the United States. Given this setting, several other aspects of market structure vie for principal importance. A good deal of significance attaches to the relative locations of crude-producing fields and markets within the Pacific Coast area. On one hand, the juxtaposition of the Los Angeles fields and the principal metropolitan market (in conjunction with the character of refining technique) made it highly probable that an independent, nonintegrated refining industry of many firms would play an important part in the Pacific Coast refined product market—the diseconomies of small scale were not prohibitive, and no great investment was required to deliver refined products to an adjacent market. On the other hand, the location of the remaining crude supply at some distance from any principal market made it probable that a few firms which were able to make large investments would secure most of this crude for refining. Furthermore, markets tributary to these crude supplies and other markets also dependent on long-distance transport facilities would probably be relatively closed to small-scale refiners and correspondingly reserved to large companies with ample pipe lines and tank ships. These probabilities, implicit in the market structure, seem to have been largely realized. The Los Angeles market has been strongly influenced by independent-refiner competition; the Valley and Coastal crude markets have been major-dominated; and the non-Los Angeles refined product markets have had a price behavior somewhat independent of the competitive forces which operated in Los Angeles. Geographical price discrimination against central and northern California markets has tended to persist, as an almost automatic outcome of the geographical relationship of crude reserves and markets.

Also important as aspects of market structure are the degrees of concentration which have existed at each of several levels within the industry, although these are, of course, in part the outcome of more basic structural considerations, including the geography of the market and the cost-scale characteristics of production and distribution. The relatively unconcentrated character of crude oil production has proved to be of minor significance since 1930 because of the imposition of central controls over crude oil production. The highly concentrated holdings of long-distance facilities for transporting both crude and refined products, however, has had considerable significance. The domination of such facilities by the majors (in conjunction with the aforementioned geography of crude reserves) made it effectively impossible for small refiners to enter non-Los Angeles markets with either plants or products in any important degree and thus set the stage for the existing variegated pattern of local competition. The concentration in the ownership of these facilities is in turn explained by their primary economic characteristic—that they involve a high unit cost and thus can be effectively acquired only by a few large companies. Their ability to bestow upon their owners substantial control of the markets which are dependent upon them in turn rests upon the character of the law, which makes it possible effectively to restrict them to private-carrier use. In sum, the highly concentrated control of transport facilities suggests probabilities with respect to price results and competition which have been largely fulfilled.

The pattern of concentration in refining, resting in turn upon geographical, transport, and other cost considerations, is also significant. The domination of the refinery market by an oligopoly of seven firms (a circumstance resting partly on the economies of large-scale refining but equally on the financial barriers to the acquisition of sufficient crude supplies) is the keystone to the understanding of numerous market results. First, it implies a buyers' oligopoly in crude oil and sets the stage for the exercise of deliberate pricing policies in the crude market by the seven major firms (an exercise facilitated by the control of crude transport facilities mentioned above). Second, it makes feasible the exercise, through a price-leadership, of related price policies in refined product markets. It is thus a necessary (although not a sufficient) condition for the emergence of domestic-export price discrimination and effective domestic cartelization. The counterpoint of concentration in refining is the existence of a considerable competitive fringe of small refineries, mostly in the Los Angeles area. This fringe has been the basis of chronic instability in the refined product markets and has established the probability of alternating periods of price wars and of artificial stabilization. It has also served as the basis for the clear emergence of a two-price market, with corresponding complications in the pattern of nonprice competition.

Another structural characteristic of great importance is the degree of integration of the principal productive stages of the industry within single firms. Integration of crude production with refining seems to have stemmed, from the standpoint of the refiner, from the desirability of securing a long-run supply of raw material and from the high profits of crude production; in general, the refining industry seems to have acquired producing properties whenever possible. The principal implications of this integration for price behavior have been twofold. First, it has endowed the dominant integrated refiners with the desire to maintain the price of nonintegrated crude at a relatively high level in order to maintain the value of their own reserves. Second, it has provided them with the relatively large profits of crude-producing investment and thus with a considerable reserve with which to finance nonprice (or even price) warfare in their refined product markets.

The integration of transportation facilities for bringing crude to the refinery or refined products to the market seems to have arisen rather naturally out of the specialized technical character of such facilities and out of the desire of large refiners to control such facilities in order to secure low-cost carriage for themselves and to deny it to small-scale competitors. This integration has been the basis of a strong major control of markets which are removed from crude-producing areas and of corresponding variations in price behavior. Integration of the facilities for marketing refined products has stemmed basically from the consumer-good character of the principal output, which makes sales promotion an attractive possibility, and from the ambitions of all refiners to expand their market volumes by exploiting such promotional possibilities. Its consequence (or that of the considerations which lead to its emergence) has been an extremely pervasive and expensive nonprice competition among refiners, which in turn has been manifested in high marketing costs and excess distributive capacity.

Product differentiation is often referred to as a significant characteristic in terms of which market situations may be distinguished. In an immediate sense it has been strategic in the refined product markets in question; differentiation has been the proximate basis of nonprice competition. If we take a dynamic rather than a static view, however, it is clear that any existing degree of differentiation is primarily the result of business policies which in turn arise out of more basic characteristics of market structure. In effect, it is the *differentiability* of gasoline and lubricants which has been basic to the explanation of market behavior. Given their potentiality for differentiation, sales policies of the general sort observed were extremely likely to emerge within the context of any imperfectly collusive market.[30]

A final category of market characteristics which is of great importance in the petroleum market includes the various aspects of the legal framework of the market. A necessary background of observed results is found in the general structure of property and business law, which makes possible, for example, the existing situation with respect to the ownership and leasing of oil-land rights, the effective private-carrier status of intrastate pipe lines, and the contractual control of nonowned distributive facilities. More specifically, however, two aspects of law stand out. First, the combination of federal and state law which serves as the basis for the so-called voluntary proration and curtailment of crude oil production has since 1930 been the main determinant of the general level of prices throughout the petroleum industry. The curtailment plan has roughly determined the annual output of crude oil in California and in other areas of the country. It has thus established the limits within which business price policies

---

[30] Particularly so far as integration of distributive facilities was feasible.

in the industry could fix crude and refined product prices, and has in this way determined the general level of the earnings of crude production and of the industry as a whole. To be sure, the curtailment policy has only established a range within which prices and earnings would fall, and the range has been wide enough so that the detailed investigation of the forces which determined exactly where they did fall is of great importance. But the existence of curtailment and the character of curtailment policy were the singly most important aspects of the market structure.

The second principal aspect of the legal framework has been the federal government policy toward business combinations and restraints of trade. During most of the period, the basis of this policy was the Sherman Act, as variously interpreted and enforced. The Act was important in several ways. First, it stood in the way of further combinations or merges involving property transfers and thus prevented a possibly inherent tendency toward substantial monopolization of refining and distribution by a few large companies. By the same token, it thus perpetuated an inherently unstable competitive situation and made it probable that the persistent combinative tendency would be relieved by buying programs designed to regulate output and stabilize price. Finally, it generally was the basis for attacking such buying programs as restraints of trade and resulted in their periodic abandonment and in the consequent reëmergence of price instability. In general, therefore, the Sherman Act stood in the way of tendencies which were strongly inherent in the market structure, and in preventing monopolization perpetuated or periodically revived a sort of quasi-competitive instability.

During the period from late 1933 until mid-1935, the Sherman Act policy was modified in favor of a sort of government-supervised industrial cartelization—N. R. A. Although imperfect in design and administration, the N. R. A. code system represented a radical shift from the Sherman Act policy. It temporarily legalized the fulfillment of the combinative tendency through loose-knit combinations, and it made possible a fuller degree of market control than was possible before or since. Because it began and ended in a relatively depressed business situation, however, the outcome of an N. R. A. plan in a normally prosperous economy can only be predicted.

Looking at the market structure as a whole, it is apparent that a very large proportion of the observed price results and competitive behavior in the California oil industry after 1930 can be fully rationalized in terms of this structure and of the profit-seeking propensity of private business. Within this market structure, in effect, profit-seeking enterprise seems very likely to produce a variety of results of the order observed and very unlikely to produce substantially different ones. In a quasi-oligopolistic market of the sort in question, there always remains a degree of basic uncertainty regarding what will happen, and we cannot legitimately suggest a unique association of market structure and price results.   Between the two, however, there exists an extremely high probability of systematic association, and it is suggested that the observed results tend to vindicate a law of probability.

Thus it may be suggested that the observed behavior emerged "naturally" from the given market structure, or, more precisely, from the more basic and inflexible elements of this structure.   It is not inferred, however, that the results are *natural* in any ethical sense.   They are only as natural as the various aspects of the market structure from which they arise, and it is evident that a number of the most strategic of these aspects are institutional or legal in character and potentially pliable to the application of the public will.   The legal framework of the market, in particular, is the expression of a governmental choice which can be modified or extended at will, and through its extension other aspects of market structure can be modified.   The curtailment policy might be revised in various ways, for example, or the carrier status of transport facilities modified, without introducing any more unnatural elements than are already present.   The current market structure has developed within the existing institutional framework, but it is no more the expression of the *natural* state of things than a number of other structures which can be conceived.   As we begin to appraise the social merits of the behavior of the industry in question, therefore, it is important not to confuse explanation with justification.   We have developed at least a partial explanation of behavior, but it must be justified or condemned on an entirely different set of grounds.

When conclusions have been drawn with respect to the social desirability of observed results, however, the essential utility of a knowledge of the relationship between market structure and behavior reëmerges. One of the primary avenues which public policy may follow in seeking to modify undesirable price results is that of deliberately modifying market structures.   As soon as the connection between the existing structure and behavior is understood, we may also appreciate the potentialities of various proposals for modifying market structure. Thus the alternatives of active enforcement or relaxation of the anti-trust laws, of further integration or partial or complete disintegration of the industry, of more liberal or more severe curtailment policies, of *laissez faire* or N. R. A., may be more clearly appraised.

VI. THE MONOPOLY PROBLEM

The antitrust laws add complications to collusion and monopoly in this country that are almost unknown in the rest of the world. British and continental writings on competition seem much too simplified in discussing combination and monopoly, since these are viewed as public, legal, and respectable restraints of competition. Although the antitrust laws often look weak and ineffectual, they have apparently made competition work better (judged against the European record) than we have any right to expect, considering the size of firms and the structure of our markets.

The impact of the antitrust laws on business decisions rises and declines with changes in the political climate, and their meaning undergoes constant mutation with the attitude of the courts and the development of the economy, and of economic theory. The fast turnover in policies produces a high rate of obsolescence in literature on the subject, but we are fortunate in having in Edward Mason's article an informed summary of the problems of size and collusion in relation to the Sherman Act.[31]

THE CURRENT STATUS OF THE MONOPOLY PROBLEM IN THE UNITED STATES [32]

By Edward S. Mason [33]

It is clearly an open question whether the people of the United States want competition and, if so, what kind of competition and in what areas. We apparently do not desire a competitive determination of farm prices and farm incomes. It is obvious from the Miller-Tydings Act and the fair trade laws now flourishing in forty-five states that we don't want price competition in a large section of retail trade. We have sought, and quite successfully, to "take wages out of competition." The action of the Texas Railroad Commission during the last few months in cutting back oil production by 750,000 barrels a day makes it clear that the "adjustment of supply to demand" in this area is not going to be accomplished exclusively by price competition. We don't want much disturbance of the channels of distribution from competitive sources and are apparently acquiescing in a reinterpretation of the Robinson-Patman Act "injury to competition" as injury to a competitor. Just recently I have become aware of the very cozy scheme worked out by the anthracite coal producers by means of which output is adjusted to sales.[34] Although, according to the producers, no consideration of price is allowed to intrude, John L. Lewis has indicated that the application of this system would be fine for the bituminous coal industry. One might extend considerably these examples of recent public action to soften the rigors of competition.

[31] The views of other economists may be found in "The Antitrust Laws: A Symposium," *American Economic Review*, Vol. 39, p. 689 (June, 1949), and in "Various Views on the Monopoly Problem," *Review of Economics and Statistics*, Vol. 31, No. 2 (May, 1949).

[32] An address delivered at the Centennial of the University of Wisconsin: Symposium on Law and the American Economy, May 6, 1949. Reprinted from *Harvard Law Review*, Vol. 62, No. 8 (June, 1949), pp. 1266–1285.

[33] Dean, Graduate School of Public Administration, Harvard University.

[34] N. Y. *Times*, April 19, 1949, p. 20, col. 2.

At the same time, and despite this course of events, we apparently do want competition in the industrial sector of the economy. The last ten years—particularly the last five—have witnessed the greatest flurry of antitrust activity since the passage of the Sherman Act. But the question can be raised, what kind of competition do we want?

Theories of Effective Competition

After the recent decision in the *Cement* case,[35] the Universal Atlas Cement Company issued the following statement: "Universal Atlas Cement Company is abandoning on July 7 next the method of selling cement which it has used continuously for more than forty years; namely, sales in the market served by it at delivered prices as low as those quoted by any competitor." [36]   The obvious implication of this announcement is that competition is being abandoned. On the other hand, quite a few people, including the Supreme Court of the United States, thought that what was being abandoned was a conspiracy to fix prices. Clearly competition means different things to different people.

There have always been at least two ways of looking at competition and of judging the effectiveness of competition in a particular market. In the first, competition is thought of as a type of market organization setting severe limits to the power or control exercised by the individual firm. This view stresses the limits, set principally by the number of his competitors, on the scope of action of a single seller or buyer. The other way of thinking about competition is in terms of the performance of firms in a market. Even pure competition—that plaything of economic theorists—can be thought of either in terms of market structure, large numbers of sellers and a standard product, or in terms of the performance which is supposed to result from these conditions, prices equal to marginal and to minimum average cost.

From the point of view of economic policy, competition is supposedly desirable, not as an end in itself, but for the results that are expected to follow from it.[37] These expected results may be paraphrased as efficient use of resources. Now under the technological and institutional conditions suited to pure competition—imagining such conditions to be found—it is possible to show that a competitive organization of resources will produce the results desired from competition—an efficient use of these resources. But if technological and institutional conditions are not compatible with pure competition and, at the same

---

35 FTC v. Cement Institute, 333 U. S. 683 (1948).

36 *The U. S. Steel Quarterly*, Aug., 1948, p. 7; Machlup, *The Basing Point System* (1949), p. 82.

37 On the other hand, an argument can be made on political grounds for competition conceived as a set of limits to the market position of firms, regardless of the relative efficiency of the business performance that results from this competition. Here we shall be concerned exclusively with the economic aspects of the problems.

time, are not deemed to be such as to justify a public utility regulation of the firms in question, there arises a problem of defining an acceptable kind of competition in terms of market structure such that it can normally be expected to be accompanied by the kind of performance considered acceptable in the use of resources.   This is in fact the core of the difficulty of devising standards of public action in the antitrust field.   None of the markets encountered meet the tests of pure competition; at the same time they fall short of a degree of monopoly justifying public utility regulation.[38]   What is a suitable test of effective competition?   Should it run in terms of market limitations on the scope of action of firms or in terms of standards of acceptable performance?   Is there, necessarily, any incompatibility between these objectives?   May not the conditions required of a competitive market structure be so defined as inevitably to produce desirable business performance?

Most of the recent literature on the subject of "workable competition" has stressed the conditions of market structure, the limitations on the market position or scope of action of firms, deemed necessary to the maintenance of effective competition.[39]   Such competition re-

---

[38] A few of the principal conditions that may "justify" the imposition of a public utility type of regulation could be spelled out fairly adequately. Lacking, however, the time and space to do so, I here limit myself to assertion.

[39] J. M. Clark was, to the best of my knowledge, the first writer to use the term "workable competition." He defines workable competition to mean a "rivalry in selling goods in which each selling unit normally seeks maximum net revenue, under conditions such that the price or prices each seller can charge are effectively limited by the free option of the buyer to buy from a rival seller or sellers of what we think of as 'the same' product, necessitating an effort by each seller to equal or exceed the attractiveness of the others' offerings to a sufficient number of buyers to accomplish the end in view." Clark, "Toward a Concept of Workable Competition," 30 *Am. Econ. Rev.* 241, 243 (1940).

Clair Wilcox defines workable competition as "the availability to buyers of genuine alternatives in policy among their sources of supply." Wilcox, "Competition and Monopoly in American Industry" 9 (TNEC Monograph 21, 1940).

George Stigler finds this conception "too loose." He prefers the following: "An industry is workably competitive when (1) there are a considerable number of firms selling closely related products in each important market area, (2) these firms are not in collusion, and (3) the long-run average cost curve for a new firm is not materially higher than that for an established firm." Stigler, "The Extent and Bases of Monopoly," 32 *Am. Econ. Rev.* 2–3 (Supp., June, 1942).

Corwin Edwards has developed the idea of workable competition in greatest detail.   In addition to numbers of sellers and buyers, absence of collusion and freedom of entry, he states a number of other conditions of which absence of a dominant trader among the number of buyers and sellers seems to be the most important.   Edwards, *Maintaining Competition* (1940) pp. 9–10.

These writers clearly think of workable competition in terms of market conditions imposing a set of limitations on the scope of action of the individual buyer or seller.   These limitations prevent the exploitation of buyers by sellers too few in number or in collusion with each other and prevent the exploitation of sellers by buyers.   There are an "adequate" number of alternatives from which to choose. Clark's conception of workable competition also emphasizes these limitations, but it appears from his discussion that limitations are not enough.

quires, to use the standard cliché, the availability to buyers of an adequate number of alternative independent sources of supply, and to sellers of an adequate number of independent customers. Workable competition is considered to require, principally, a fairly large number of sellers and buyers, no one of whom occupies a large share of the market, the absence of collusion among either group, and the possibility of market entry by new firms.

There has also been, on the other hand, a good deal of discussion of the kind of performance we should like to have from firms in the industrial sector of the economy. Among the kinds of business behavior emphasized as desirable have been the following: an unremitting pressure for product and process improvement, downward adjustment of prices concomitant with substantial reductions in costs, concentration of production in units of the most efficient size, neither larger nor smaller than those required for low-cost operation, an efficient adjustment of capacity to output, and the avoidance of a waste of resources in selling activities.

The question now arises whether workable competition, in terms of market structure, can be so defined that we may say, given these conditions, it is likely that business performance will meet the standards suggested above or, equally important, that if these conditions are not present, acceptable standards of business performance are unlikely to be attained. Alternatively we may raise the question whether business behavior lends itself to formulation of standards of acceptable performance such that a judgment of the appropriateness of antitrust action can be made independently of what we have here called market conditions.

Without attempting, at this point, a direct answer to these questions, it seems useful to call attention to certain possibilities of conflict between competitive standards formulated in terms of market conditions and standards of acceptable business performance. Space limitations prevent more than a summary indication of these possibilities.

1. The most familiar and one of the most bothersome possibilities of conflict has to do with the economies of scale in relation to the number of sellers or buyers required for most efficient operations. Costs in relation to size of plant can, in most industries, be well enough estimated to form a judgment on the minimum scale required for efficiency. The main difficulties arise in judging the economies of scale involved in the management of multi-plant properties, considering the functional complexity of management, and in disentangling the bargaining advantages of size from the advantages that pertain solely to the provisions of useful services. Is management a "technique for getting things done" [40] that carries with it significant economies

---

[40] See "The Public Responsibilities of Big Business," address delivered by Eugene Holman, President of Standard Oil Co. of N. J., at the Economic Club of Detroit on November 8, 1948. See also Drucker, *The Concept of the Corporation* (1946); Edwards, "Maintaining Competition" (1949) p. 116 n.37.

of scale?   The relation of size to the volume and quality of industrial research is another bothersome question that intrudes.

Enough has been said to indicate that a real possibility exists that the number of firms appropriate to efficiency, one aspect of desirable performance, may, in a number of industries, be too few to meet the market structure test of workable competition.   Nor does it necessarily follow that, under these conditions, regulation of the public utility type is called for.

2. A second possibility of conflict exists when all the market conditions of workable competition are fulfilled but the behavior of the firms involved follows a routine and standard pattern unvaried by enterprise of any sort.   Something like this seems to have characterized the system of retail distribution in the United States before the advent of chain stores and other mass distributors.   In a case like this, does one judge the effectiveness of competition from the market structure point of view favorable to traditional distributors or from the business performance point of view favorable to the innovating large-scale mass distributor? [41]

3. Suppose, to take a third possibility of conflict, that the market conditions required for workable competition lead, in an industry characterized by large cyclical variations in sales and by high overhead costs, to cut-throat competition which in periods of depression destroys efficient business organizations which, under average conditions, could survive.   This is the possibility, repeatedly emphasized by J. M. Clark, that apparently leads him to support a modified basing-point system in some industries having these characteristics.[42]   Without passing judgment on the frequency and importance of such situations, it is sufficient to indicate that the standards-of-business-performance approach might lead to a modification of the conditions thought to be required for workable competition.

4. Fourthly, one of the market conditions required for workable competition is the absence of collusion or agreement among the firms. But certain kinds of agreements clearly promote rather than restrain effective competition.   The agreement among traders to regulate marketing practices on the Chicago Board of Trade was considered by no less an authority than Justice Brandeis to promote competition.[43] Agreements to standardize classifications of products and terms of sale are frequently necessary to permit buyer comparisons of prices quoted from different sources of supply.   Under these and other circumstances the business performance that results from collusion must be considered to modify the application of standards drawn exclusively from market conditions.

---

[41] Cf. Adelman, "The A & P Case: A Study in Applied Economic Theory," 6̸ Q. J. Econ. 238 (1949).

[42] Most recently in Clark, "Law and Economics of Basing Points: Appraisals and Proposals," 39 Am. Econ. Rev. 430 (1949).

[43] Board of Trade of the City of Chicago v. United States, 246 U. S. 231 (1918).

5. Fifthly, it is possible that certain restraints of trade or a degree of market control incompatible with the market structure standard of workable competition may facilitate the introduction of desirable product and process innovations. This is an argument most effectively developed by J. A. Schumpeter.[44] His contention that the most effective kind of competition is that which derives from the introduction of new and improved products and from innovation in techniques of production has great merit. It is less clear, however, that industrial progressiveness stems mainly from firms of a size incompatible with the conditions of workable competition or necessitates arrangements among firms which violate these conditions. The relation of monopoly and competition to innovation is a relatively unknown area.

Other examples could be cited but perhaps enough has been said to indicate that antitrust action in a particular industry or industrial market may be thought appropriate on the basis of the business performance of firms in that market and inappropriate if judged by the presence or absence of the market conditions emphasized by the workable competition test.

Legal Criteria of Effective Competition

Business Performance and Market Structure in the Legal Definition of Monopoly

What considerations influence the courts in their decisions on antitrust action? Is effective competition conceived to be a set of market conditions or is it judged in terms of effective business performance? Some twelve years ago, under the title of "Monopoly in Law and Economics," I published an article designed to show that legal and economic ideas of monopoly were growing further apart.[45] In referring back to this ancient document, I am reminded of a statement of Justice Holmes, "It ought always to be remembered that historic continuity with the past is not a duty, it is only a necessity." [46] Although it is now a duty, I find it necessary to relate my present thinking on this question to what I thought earlier.

The argument of that article, simply stated, was that monopoly in the legal sense meant restrictive or abusive practices and, in the economic sense, control of the market; that the antithesis of legal monopoly was free competition, a state of affairs such that no actual or potential competitor was limited in his action either by agreement or the harassing tactics of large rivals, while the antithesis of economic monopoly was pure competition, a state of the market such that no buyer or seller could, by his own action, influence the price of the

---

44 Schumpeter, *Capitalism, Socialism, and Democracy* (2d ed. 1947) Chapters 7 and 8.

45 47 *Yale L. J.* 34 (1937).

46 Holmes "Learning and Science" in *Collected Legal Papers* 138, 139 (1920).

goods to be bought and sold. It was argued that one of the reasons for this dichotomy was that lawyers were concerned with tests that would stand up in a court, and that it was much easier to devise tests of restrictive practices than tests indicative of a substantial degree of market control.

I still think there was substantial merit in this distinction between legal and economic notions of monopoly, but, like many distinctions, it was much too sharply drawn. There is substantial evidence in the history of antitrust cases that although the precise holdings may not have been explicitly based on indications of the degree of market control and of what is here called business performance, such indications certainly influenced the judges' decisions.

But what about the recent active development of antitrust law? Do the courts tend to find evidence of violation in particular characteristics of market structure or in various kinds of business performance or both? My impression is:

1. That the courts have moved a substantial distance in the direction of accepting the presence or absence of the market conditions associated with the notion of workable competition as appropriate tests. On all four of the important desiderata, number of firms, share of the market, collusion, and the conditions of entry, previous doctrine has been altered or extended;

2. That standards of effective business performance, though imprecisely defined, still strongly influence the manner in which tests of monopoly relating to the structure of the market are applied. This is true of determinations of whether or not the antitrust laws have been violated, but it is even more true when the courts come to the fashioning of remedies.

Not only has the legal meaning of monopoly been extended but the courts have greatly expanded the scope of action embraced within the meaning of conspiracy. The legal status of actions both of large firms and of conspiracies with respect to the conditions of entry of new firms has been reinterpreted.

In the *Aluminum* case,[47] I interpret the court to hold (1) that Alcoa's share of the domestic consumption of aluminum ingot was such as to indicate a degree of market control equivalent to monopoly, and (2) that monopoly was not "thrust upon"[48] the company by forces lying outside its control but was actively and aggressively sought in ways that had the effect of excluding potential competitors.

Although this decision probably broke new legal ground, it is, from an economist's point of view, marred by what is at best some very dubious economics. The share of the market possessed by Alcoa was incorrectly measured, the degree of market control was identified with percentage share of the market, and the evidence concerning intent to

---

[47] United States v. Aluminum Co. of Am., 148 F.2d 416 (2d Cir. 1945).
[48] *Id.* at 429.

exclude others is difficult to distinguish from ordinary, intelligent competitive action.

In measuring Alcoa's share of the market, the court excluded from the market substitute products and secondary aluminum ingot. Although the determination of what products to include in and what to exclude from a market presents a difficult problem, the existence of close substitutes in certain uses of aluminum is beyond question. With respect to secondary aluminum, the court's reasoning was ingenious but essentially incorrect. The argument was that since Alcoa's current production of primary ingot will at some future time be converted into secondary, the secondary, then coming onto the market, cannot be considered an independent source of supply. The question is whether a single producer of a product that will return to the market X years hence will, *because of that fact,* act differently with respect to current price and output than would a producer who is one of a larger number. If he does so, it can only be because he is willing to sacrifice a current profit by restricting output now in order to gain a problematical profit X years hence, which may be available because the supply of competitive scrap is not then so large as it would otherwise be. The conditions that would make such action profitable are improbable.

Lawyers sometimes describe themselves as experts in revelance. Something more than logical relevance, however, is involved in a case of this sort. There is also the magnitude of the consideration that is declared to be relevant. It was, however, on the basis of the argument stated above that Judge Learned Hand decided that "Alcoa's control over the ingot market must be reckoned at over 90 per cent." [49] If sales of secondary ingot had been considered part of the market, Alcoa's share would have fallen to the mystical sixty to sixty-four per cent, where the existence of a monopoly becomes "doubtful." [50] Even if Alcoa's share of the market had been correctly measured, it would have been wrong to infer degree of market control directly from this share. If products excluded in defining the market are close substitutes, if the entry of new firms is relatively easy, if the supply of imports is elastic with respect to price changes, even a large percentage share of the market is compatible with a small degree of market control. On the other hand, even a small share of a particular market in the hands of an industrial giant may, under certain circumstances, be conducive to a high degree of market control.[51] Market share is an important condition relevant to workable competition, but in the absence of certain tests of performance it cannot be taken as a measure of market control.

With respect to one element of business performance the court was

---

49 *Id.* at 425.
50 *Id.* at 424.
51 See Edwards, *Maintaining Competition* (1949) p. 100.

convinced that Alcoa's behavior indicated an intention to exclude potential rivals. The evidence was a tendency to build ahead of demand.

Nothing compelled it [Alcoa] to keep doubling and redoubling its capacity before others entered the field. It insists that it never excluded competitors; but we can think of no more effective exclusion than progressively to embrace each new opportunity as it opened, and to face every newcomer with new capacity already geared into a great organization, having the advantage of experience, trade connections and the elite of personnel.[52]

In this connection it is interesting to note that the leading economic authority on the aluminum industry found Alcoa's behavior to lead in exactly the opposite direction; that is, to a waiting for demand to develop before expanding capacity.[53] But, even if the court is correct, it would appear extremely difficult to distinguish between a progressive embracing "of each new opportunity" and what would ordinarily be considered desirable competitive performance.

Despite these observations, the decision in the *Aluminum* case represents a broadening of the legal meaning of monopoly in a direction favored by current views concerning workable competition.

The *Tobacco* case [54] continued in this direction. The share of the market here was, in 1939, sixty-eight per cent of the production of small cigarettes by three firms, which the Court held were joined in a conspiracy. Such a market position carried with it the power to exclude potential rivals and was therefore illegal, said the Supreme Court, even in the absence of a demonstration of actual exclusion. The Court's attitude toward the heavy advertising expenditures of the three firms was interesting but cryptic. On the one hand it was not "criticized as a business expense"; [55] on the other the Court thought that "such tremendous advertising, however, is also a widely published warning that these companies possess and know how to use a powerful offensive and defensive weapon against new competition." [56]

Both in this case and the *Aluminum* case it would seem that the decisions, based mainly on the market position of the companies, were at the same time influenced by the Court's judgment on how the market position had been used. In other words, certain standards of business performance seem to have been involved.

The *Columbia Steel* case,[57] involving the acquisition of a small west coast plant by a subsidiary of United States Steel, produced one of the most careful examinations of the market position of a company to be found in the history of antitrust cases. Though the court here re-

---

52 United States v. Aluminum Co. of Am., 148 F.2d 416, 431 (2d Cir. 1945).
53 Wallace, *Market Control of the Aluminum Industry* (1937) pp. 252, 259–60, 331.
54 American Tobacco Co. v. United States, 328 U. S. 781 (1946).
55 *Id.* at 797.
56 *Ibid.*
57 United States v. Columbia Steel Co., 334 U. S. 495 (1948).

jected a large share of the local market, with respect to certain products, as a ground for undoing the acquisition, it may well have been influenced by the spectacle of the Antitrust Division straining at the gnat of Columbia after swallowing the Geneva camel.

The *National Lead* case [58] presented a situation in which the conditions of workable competition were violated both because of the fewness of sellers—four, with two accounting for ninety per cent of the sales—and because of collusive restraints. The Court eliminated the restraints but refused to increase the number of sellers by ordering present sellers to divest themselves of part of their holdings. Apparently the majority of the judges were influenced by the finding of fact disclosing what they considered to be effective business performance in the industry:

From 1933 on there was active competition between [National Lead] and [DuPont] for customers. There has been a vast increase in sales; and repeated reductions in the price of titanium pigments have taken place and a very few increases.[59]

At another point the court says that the findings "disclose a vigorous, comparatively young, but comparatively large, world-wide industry, in which two great companies, National Lead and DuPont, now control approximately ninety-five per cent of the domestic production in approximately equal shares. . . . The findings show vigorous and apparently profitable competition on the part of each of the four producers, including an intimation that the smaller companies are gaining rather than losing ground." [60]

These and other recent cases concerning the legal meaning of monopoly appear to indicate that although the courts have moved some distance toward accepting certain of the market conditions associated with the notion of workable competition as standards of judgment—particularly share of the market and perhaps the number of firms—their application of these standards is strongly influenced by evidence relating to the character of business performance in these markets.

Collusion

When one turns to collusion, another of the elements of market structure emphasized in the literature on workable competition, interpreting the significance of recent legal actions presents a perplexing problem. The courts have certainly gone a long way in accepting various kinds of market behavior as evidence of a conspiracy among firms; so far, indeed, that it seems appropriate to inquire whether market behavior rather than conspiracy has not become the test of illegality.

---

58 United States v. National Lead Co., 332 U. S. 319 (1947).
59 *Id.* at 346–47.
60 *Id.* at 347–48.

Economists in recent years have speculated a good deal on the possible courses of behavior of firms in markets in which the number of buyers and sellers is sufficiently few to make the rival firms aware of their interdependence. Given merely the number of firms any one of a wide variety of types of behavior is possible and an explanation of a particular course of behavior becomes feasible only after an examination of a number of other elements of the market structure in which these firms operate. Among these conditions, high overhead costs, large cyclical variations in the volume of sales, and immobility of resources are combined in a substantial number of industrial markets. Given these conditions, together with a small number of firms, some economists have contended that such phenomena as price uniformity, price leadership and the relative inflexibility of prices to large variations in the national income, are frequently compatible with the independent action of firms all recognizing their interdependence.

Now independence of action is, by definition, the opposite of collusion. But it may be impossible to determine from market behavior alone whether the firms are acting independently or together. At this point we may appropriately ask, what difference does it make? With respect to the remedy to be applied it may make considerable difference. If the behavior is really the result of agreement, enjoining the agreement may, by securing independence of action, change the market behavior. But if the action of firms is already independent, this remedy is useless.

A prime example is provided by the *Tobacco* case.[61] Both the district court and the circuit court found from the record in this case evidence of a price conspiracy among the three big producers of cigarettes. Both bodies held that conspiracy does not require a formal agreement or even a meeting together of the conspirators. To the district court the essential condition was that "some character or manner of communication take place between them, sufficient to enable them to reach a definite, mutual understanding of the common, unlawful objective or purpose to be thereafter accomplished, and that they will unite or combine their efforts to that end." [62]

The conception of conspiracy in the court of appeals was, perhaps, even broader than this: "The agreement may be shown by a concert of action, all the parties working together understandingly, with a single design for the accomplishment of a common purpose." [63]

When one turns to the record in the case, there is certainly some evidence of agreement among the firms.[64] The companies admittedly

---

[61] American Tobacco Co. v. United States, 328 U. S. 781 (1946).

[62] Transcript of Record, p. 6350, American Tobacco Co. v. United States, 328 U. S. 781 (1946).

[63] American Tobacco Co. v. United States, 147 F.2d 93, 107 (6th Cir. 1944).

[64] I am indebted for an analysis of the record to the recent able Ph.D. thesis by my student, Warren Baum. See Baum, *Workable Competition in the Tobacco Industry* (unpublished in the Harvard College Library 1949).

consulted with each other on the question of opening new leaf markets.
It is probably a fact that the companies' systems of grading leaf tobacco
required explicit understandings. But to suppose that ending such
collusion or conspiracy as existed among the firms would produce a
substantially different market behavior in the sale of cigarettes than
that on which the charge of price conspiracy primarily rested is contrary both to logic and to the subsequent course of events in the industry.

There is certainly plenty of evidence that the business performance
of the big tobacco companies did not meet reasonable standards of
efficiency in the use of resources. Cigarette prices did not respond
to substantial declines in leaf prices, it required the advent of ten-cent
brands in the 1930's to bring about effective price competition; large
resources were employed in what can only be regarded from the point
of view of the community as wasteful advertising; the profits of the
three companies were inordinately high. Nevertheless, this lamentable
performance was and is quite compatible with independence of action
on the part of the firms. Under these circumstances to bring a charge
of conspiracy may have had the effect of enlarging the legal meaning
of conspiracy. But it may also have had the effect of producing in
some minds the illusion that eliminating the conspiracy will necessarily,
in some sense, make competition work better.

The charge of collusion in the *Cement* case [65] was brought under
Section 5 of the Federal Trade Commission Act [66] and the multiple
basing-point system in use in that industry was found by the Supreme
Court to be an "unfair method of competition." But there can be
little doubt, after this decision, that a similar set of facts would justify
a charge of conspiracy in violation of the Sherman Act. Whatever
ingenuity economists have displayed in demonstrating that a basing-
point system might emerge without collusion, there can be no doubt
that in the cement industry, and probably in most industries in which
this pricing system is used, collusion is involved. Furthermore, the
collusive agreements ordinarily involved in an effective basing-point
system are sufficiently central to the marketing practices of firms that
elimination of the agreements may be expected to change substantially
the character of the business performance in what were formerly
basing-point industries.

Whether the business performance will be improved in any sense
relevant to the concept of efficiency in the use of resources will depend on what alternative practices are adopted by the firms. The
abolition of a basing-point system is in itself an approach toward
workable competition as defined in terms of market conditions. By
the performance test of competition, however, the elimination of

---

65 FTC v. Cement Institute, 333 U. S. 683 (1948).

66 38 *Stat.* 719–20 (1914), as amended, 52 *Stat.* 112 (1938), 15 U. S. C. § 45 (b)
(1946).

basing-point systems is the beginning and not the end of the discussion.[67]

Considering these and other recent antitrust cases involving the charge of conspiracy or collusion,[68] it would seem that the courts have substantially enlarged the meaning of collusion or, at least, the scope of the circumstances they are willing to accept as evidence of collusion. To this extent, the enforcement agencies find their task appreciably lightened. But included among the markets in which collusion may exist are some in which the abrogation of all agreements, existing and imagined, will constitute no progress toward effective competition judged either by standards of market structure or by standards of business performance. And there are others in which, while the abrogation of agreements may improve competition in the first sense, it will not necessarily do so in the second. It is now incumbent on us to look more closely at these alternative notions of competition.

Conclusion: Objectives of Antitrust Policy

The broad public policy question underlying these various theories of competition is what objective should an anti-monopoly policy set for itself? Should it attempt to bring about a structure of industrial markets and a set of business practices such that the scope of action of individual firms is severely limited by the action of rival firms in the economy? Or should the objective be efficient use of economic resources, considering elements of market structure only when they can be shown to lead to ineffective business performance? It is the contention of this paper that neither objective can be set without regard to the other; that the tests both of workable competition and effective business performance have merits and demerits; and that these tests must be used to complement rather than to exclude each other.

In some ways the market structure tests are more precise and lend themselves more readily to administrative and judicial application. The number of buyers and sellers and the market-percentage share of each are roughly ascertainable facts, the chief difficulty being to know how much to include in a given market and what to exclude. The presence or absence of collusion, on the other hand, is sometimes

---

[67] "During the basic litigation, economic considerations are elbowed out or distorted by legalistic exigencies, both sides probably producing about equally bad or irrelevant or one-sided economics. Since serious and realistic consideration of the effects of an order cannot begin until after the order is issued, economic analysis is backward, though the heart of the legality in these cases is economic. This is unfortunate, but it seems to be the way our present system works." Clark, "The Law and Economics of Basing Points: Appraisals and Proposals," 39 *Am. Econ. Rev.* 430, 431 (1949).

[68] *See, e.g.,* United States v. Line Material Co., 333 U. S. 287 (1948); United States v. United States Gypsum Co., 333 U. S. 364 (1948); United States v. Masonite Corp., 316 U. S. 265 (1942); Interstate Circuit, Inc. v. United States, 306 U. S. 208 (1939).

difficult to discover, and the number of independent buyers or sellers considered necessary to the existence of an "adequate number of alternatives" is indeed a difficult question.

Stigler considers it necessary "that there [be] a considerable number of firms selling closely related products in each important market area. . . ." [69] A "considerable number" might mean a number large enough to eliminate recognition of interdependence. On the other hand, Edwards explicitly states that this is unnecessary.[70] The key question here is what is meant by the alternatives of which workable competition is supposed to require an "adequate number." I suggest that there is frequently no satisfactory way to assign meaning to this term without examining business performance in the market in question. The rapid expansion in the sale of titanium compounds with substantially and continually declining prices during the interwar period may have indicated that, under these circumstances, four sellers provide buyers with an adequate number of alternatives. At least the Supreme Court seemed to think so.[71] Eight or ten producers in a rapidly growing rayon industry which must meet the competition of substitute fabrics may be enough to provide buyers with adequate alternatives. Under other circumstances, this number might be too small. But whether the number is or is not sufficiently large can hardly be determined without looking at the business performance of the firms in question.

When one turns, however, to the problem of testing adequate business performance, it would have to be said that although it is probably possible to arrive at informed judgments, it is extremely difficult to devise tests that can be administered by a court of law. Among the tests mentioned in the literature are the following: [72]

1. Progressiveness: are the firms in the industry actively and effectively engaged in product and process innovation?

2. Cost-price relationships: are reductions in cost, whether due to falling wages or material prices, technical improvements, discovery of new sources of supply, passed on promptly to buyers in the form of price reductions?

---

[69] Stigler, "The Extent and Bases of Monopoly," 32 *Am. Econ. Rev.* 2–3 (Supp., June, 1942).

[70] Edwards, *Maintaining Competition* (1949), p. 9.

[71] *See* United States v. National Lead Co., 332 U. S. 319 (1947).

[72] Wallace, "Industrial Markets and Public Policy: Some Major Problems," 1 *Pub. Policy* 59, 99–100 (1940), includes among the issues involved in estimating the efficiency of business performance: (1) size of firms in relation to efficiency and economic progress and locational factors; (2) allocation of economic resources between industries, utilization of resources already invested, returns to owners; (3) the level of use of resources in the community as a whole; (4) severity of the business cycle; (5) progressiveness.

Professor Joe S. Bain in his three volume work, *The Economics of the Pacific Coast Petroleum Industry* (1944, 1945, 1947), discusses standards of performance at three levels of industry operations, crude oil production, refining, and distribution. See particularly Volume Three.

3. Capacity-output relationships: is investment excessive in relation to output?

4. The level of profits: are profits continually and substantially higher than in other industries exhibiting similar trends in sales, costs, innovations, etc.?

5. Selling expenditures: is competitive effort chiefly indicated by selling expenditures rather than by service and product improvements and price reductions?

No one familiar with the statistical and other material pertaining to the business performance of firms and industries would deny the extreme difficulty of constructing from this material a watertight case for or against the performance of particular firms in particular industries. Few, on the other hand, would deny that with respect to many industrial markets an informed judgment is possible. For example, it is possible from the record of the last two or three decades to determine that the performance of the automobile industry is relatively good, despite the existence of a small number of firms, while the performance of the construction industry is relatively bad. In any case, it is on the basis of just such industry data as we are now discussing that a decision even under the market structure test would have to be made whether the number of alternatives available to buyers or sellers in a particular industrial market is or is not "adequate."

A study of the performance of business firms in a particular industrial market may, of course, indicate the desirability of public action transcending the limits of antitrust policy. For example, one of the ways of improving the conditions of entry for new firms in the cigarette industry would be to change by legislation the present structure of excise taxes which is regressive with respect to the cheaper brands.[73] Professor Bain's study of the performance of firms in the Pacific coast petroleum industry led to a number of recommendations that lie outside the limits of antitrust action.[74] But even within these limits considerations of efficiency in the use of resources cannot be neglected in judging the acceptability of the structure of and practices in particular industrial markets.

The relative importance to be assigned to the objective of establishing appropriate market limitations on the scope of action of firms as against the objective of encouraging efficient performance in the use of economic resources no doubt presents serious difficulties. It seems probable that individual judgments will always be influenced to some extent by ideological considerations. There are those who are willing

---

[73] That is, the taxes do not increase with the base price of the cigarette as they would if the taxes were levied on an ad valorem basis.

[74] The two industry studies that have, in my opinion, gone furthest in an economic examination of the character of business performance are: Wallace, *Market Control in the Aluminum Industry* (1937), and Bain, *The Economics of the Pacific Coast Petroleum Industry* (1944, 1945, 1947).

to sacrifice a lot in the way of performance to establish market structures which severely limit the power and scope of action of individual firms.[75] There are others to whom this seems less important. How much, in fact, would have to be sacrificed in the attainment of one objective to secure a given amount of progress towards the other is the heart of the public policy problem in the area of business organization. It is only necessary to indicate here that, in my opinion, the choice of one of these objectives, to the exclusion of the other, would make a substantial amount of difference in many industrial markets.

Finally, we must ask at what level of public action this question of the appropriate objectives for an anti-monopoly policy should be considered. There are clearly three nonexclusive possibilities. The question can be raised at the level of legislation. Should the present antitrust laws be modified and, if so, how? As soon as this question is raised, it becomes obvious that a number of possible actions lying outside of traditional antitrust policy may, nevertheless, make an important contribution to an anti-monopoly policy. Taxation discriminating against size and a series of measures favorable to the development of small firms may be mentioned as examples.

Secondly, the question can be discussed at the level of adjudication of cases brought under the antitrust laws. What are and what should be the legal tests of monopoly and restraint of trade? As we have seen, these tests have, in certain respects, been substantially broadened by recent antitrust decisions and the courts can, and no doubt will, extend present trends further.

Finally, and to my mind, the most important level within the framework of traditional antitrust policy, at which the question of appropriate standards and objectives can be discussed, is at the level of the enforcement agencies. These agencies have an enormous amount of discretion with respect to the kinds of cases that may be brought and the business areas within which to bring them. This fact is by implication frequently denied by representatives of the enforcement agencies who assert that, after all, they "have a statute to enforce." The statute, however, in the words of Chief Justice Hughes, is of the same order of generality as a constitutional provision.[76] Even if the Antitrust Division and the Federal Trade Commission enjoyed appropriations five times as large as they now have, they could not conceivably bring a tenth of the cases it would be possible to bring. Under these circumstances, it is a matter of considerable importance how and where they strike.

There has, in my opinion, been too much preoccupation in the enforcement agencies with the question what cases can be won and too

---

[75] See, e.g., forthcoming article by Lewis in the *American Economic Review:* "For competition to be effective or workable, or even acceptable, in any significant lasting sense, it must not only permit, *it must compel the results we want by the necessary and continuing operation of its processes.*"

[76] Appalachian Coals, Inc. v. United States, 288 U. S. 344, 360 (1933).

little with the question what difference it makes.[77] The second question clearly involves a consideration of whether a different structure of the market and set of business practices, lying within the area subject to antitrust action, will be better, in some sense, than the existing structure and practices. At this point the alternative objectives of antitrust policy and how they should be related to each other, which has been the subject of this paper, can no longer be avoided.

VII. MEASURING THE CONCENTRATION OF ECONOMIC POWER

Meaning of Economic Power

As a result of the spectacular emergence of big business in the last half-century and the social issues that it raised, many attempts have been made to measure statistically the concentration of economic power. The term "economic power," although not always clearly defined in these studies, usually means either (1) owning, (2) controlling, or (3) managing a large share of the nation's productive capital.

Ownership

Concentration of ownership usually refers to the great family fortunes of the nation, such as those of the Mellons or the Rockefellers. Ownership itself tends to have less and less economic importance as these families move into their third and fourth generations, scatter their holdings among more varieties of investment, and become less intimately connected with actual management. Inheritance taxes, too, constantly reduce these concentrations of ownership.

Control

Concentration of control—the growth of centralized decision-making—has in the past referred primarily to the influence exerted on large areas of the economy by a few financial groups

---

[77] But see the remarks of the present chief of the Antitrust Division, Herbert A. Bergson, Assistant Attorney General: "In selecting cases we analyze the effectiveness of the relief obtainable, the competitive positions in the particular industry, and our prospects in the courts. In this respect our decision is similar to that of any businessman who proposes to invest money—he wants to know what the return will be. In anti-trust enforcement that return should not be measured in dollars and cents, but in benefits to our economy and an American system of free enterprise." Bergson, "Current Problems in the Enforcement of the Anti-trust Laws," IV *Record of the N. Y. City Bar Ass'n* 115 (April, 1949).

possessing small holdings of strategic investments.[78]   But much
of this control has been vitiated since the depression by new
government controls over banking, financial firms, and the securities markets.   Following the appearance of the classic *Modern
Corporation and Private Property* (1932), by Berle and Means,
observers have put more emphasis on the concentration of management control that comes with scattered public ownership of
corporate securities and with the abdication of stockholders from
the seat of decision-making.   When no one owns more than a
tiny fraction of a company's stock—a common case in modern industry—management has pretty much a free hand, not only in
operations, but also in determining succession.   Thus, with management in control of the proxy machinery of a scattered and un-
organized security-holding electorate, ownership of strategic blocks
of stock is relatively rare as a source of economic power.

Management

Concentration of management, the third kind of power, is the
ability of a firm to make its weight felt in the market place.   It
is the most interesting type of concentration today, because it is
probably the most important, and because it raises complex economic problems of proper social control.   However, when the
term "economic concentration" refers to the position of producing
firms in the economy, it has been used in the literature to mean at
least two different things: domination of markets for individual
products, and sheer bigness of firms.   These two meanings should
be carefully distinguished, because they are not necessarily related.   We shall review here some recent and well-known indices
of this kind of concentration in both its senses.

Giantism

The importance of big business *per se* in the economy frequently has been measured by finding the aggregate share of the
largest producing corporations in the nation's facilities, markets,
labor force, or income.   Once the data have been assembled, the
"measuring" has been simply a problem in addition, and the results have usually been sensational.

---

[78] See Means, *Structure of the American Economy,* National Resources Committee, June, 1939, Pt. I, pp. 100–101.

For example this type of analysis indicated that, as early as 1904, 40 per cent of all capital in manufacturing was invested in about 300 "trusts." [79] Berle and Means estimated in 1932 that the 200 largest non-financial corporations controlled 49 per cent of non-financial corporate wealth (total assets) and 22 per cent of the "national wealth." [80] They found further that from 1924 to 1929 these firms had a rate of growth three times that of other corporations. In Means's later and more elborate study, *Structure of the American Economy*,[81] he reported that the 49 per cent control of 1929 had risen to 57 per cent in 1933.

The most recent measure of this kind is the estimate made by the Smaller War Plants Corporation of the growth in plant facilities from 1939 to 1945. By adding war facilities to gross tangible assets stated in the 1939 tax returns, SWPC found that in 1945 the 250 largest manufacturing corporations held 66.5 per cent of all manufacturing facilities usable in peacetime, an amount equal to the entire productive plant of the economy in 1939.[82] Their share of the total (66 per cent), however, had not changed since 1939. This estimate was extremely rough, to be sure. It was almost a parenthetical part of SWPC's broad and detailed study of postwar concentration in important industries, based on sundry information available in 1945. Nevertheless, this particular finding has been prominently cited in the absence of more accurate estimates.

Implications

What do these figures show about the competitive behavior of the economy? They have been constantly publicized—and often very loosely—to support charges of monopoly, but without an explanation of what "monopoly" means. However, no responsible writer uses the figures for such simple purposes. To Berle and Means, concentration was an index of oligopoly in the economy and (in conjunction with their thesis of centralized decision-making) showed the extent to which a few executives had

---

[79] H. R. Seager and C. A. Gulick, Jr., *Trust and Corporation Problems*, New York, Harper & Brothers, 1929, p. 61.

[80] A. A. Berle and G. C. Means, *The Modern Corporation and Private Property*, New York, Commerce Clearing House, Inc., 1932, p. 32.

[81] National Resources Committee, June, 1939, p. 107.

[82] *Economic Concentration and World War II*, Senate Doc. 206, 79th Congress, 2nd Session, p. 43.

irresponsible control over a large proportion of the nation's productive plant—irresponsible in the sense of being beyond the control of market forces.[83]

In *The Structure of the American Economy* Means again emphasized this irresponsible control in his discussion of "non-market controls" (p. 154). He argued that with such concentration, allocation of resources is performed not by the price mechanism, but by the policies of a relatively few men who possess industrial power. Means stated that one important consequence of this concentration is a growing rigidity of prices in depression, when management chooses to restrict output rather than to reduce prices.

To economists, the point of this thesis was that profit maximization as a business objective had been lost along the way and that policy was being determined by influences irrelevant to economic conditions. This was hard to accept, however, for whatever the impact of concentration on the state of competition, the evidence of such studies was insufficient to jettison market forces as a basic postulate of business behavior. Analysis of price behavior in terms of a small number of profit-maximizing units (which still means control by the market, but by a particular kind of market) is more straightforward, and is at least a starting point for understanding competitive behavior.

The Market Position of Giants

To reach more specific conclusions about the competitive position of giant firms in the markets where they buy and sell, a much more intricate analysis in terms of particular products is needed. Some of the complexities of this job were brought out in the vast TNEC project, which produced 31 volumes of hearings and 43 monographs on aspects of industrial concentration. Monograph 27 (Pt. VI) contained an extensive investigation of the product structures of the nation's 50 largest manufacturing corporations in 1937. These corporations together produced 2,043 census commodities, which amounted to 20 per cent of the value added by manufacture that year.[84] They produced from 6 to 302 products apiece (with a median of 60); but for 60 per cent of the firms, ten products or less accounted for over 75 per cent of

---

[83] *Op. cit.* (Berle and Means), p. 45.
[84] TNEC, *Structure of Industry* (Monograph 27), 1941, p. 597.

total value produced by the company.[85]   As for domination of markets, these firms together produced over 50 per cent of total United States output in 478 commodities (which accounted for 74 per cent of value produced by these firms) and less than 50 per cent in the remaining 1,565 commodities.[86]

But this report does not give the whole picture; it ignores competition among these firms.   Nearly half of the 2,043 products were made by more than one of the 50 companies.   The only valid generalization that can be made from this study is that large corporations make many products, only a few of which are important dollarwise to a single firm.   The large firms' output of some of the products dominates the market; their output of other products is insignificant; and, to some extent, it is by means of the products that are important to them that they dominate the market.   But divergences from this pattern are common.

Economic Power of Giants

None of this, however, gets directly at the question of the economic power of giant firms.   After finding that the largest 50 or 100 corporations control x per cent of the nation's economy, what conclusions can we draw?   Means's analysis indicates the physical presence of bigness in the economy and in some markets, but it does not relate presence to performance.   In part, this relationship can be determined simply by measuring market domination, but we must also consider the nature of bigness *per se*.   We must determine and measure what it is in giantism that society wants to restrain.   Corwin Edwards says, "The power of the business giant consists in ability to coerce others, to close channels of opportunity, and to obtain special privileges in its dealings with those who should serve all comers impartially: for example, banks, common carriers, law courts, government executives and legislatures." [87]   Which is to say that the effectiveness of the business giant derives from its powers of discrimination.   But, although some giants do rely on such sources of power, their strategic importance must be appraised not by any of the conventional size discussions, but only by the most careful *ad hoc* analysis.

---

[85] *Ibid.*, p. 608.
[86] *Ibid.*, p. 626.
[87] Corwin Edwards, *Maintaining Competition*, New York, McGraw-Hill Book Co., Inc., 1949, p. 130.

On this point Corwin Edwards states:

> To determine when the power of the business giant has been achieved is even more difficult than to identify an industrial monopoly. Sprawling over many industries, a large concern is likely to have many sources of power and privilege and to derive its strength from a combination of all of them without necessarily enjoying a crucial advantage from any one source. In some cases the channels of opportunity are choked for small enterprises, not by the individual action of a single large rival, but by a structure of markets, credit facilities, and governmental processes which has been adapted to serve big enterprises and is therefore inappropriate to the service of small ones. Because of such conditions, the aggregate effect of bigness is likely to be more obvious than the exact points at which the effect is produced. To cope with such problems by conclusively proving that particular enterprises are excessively big may be impossible.[88]

Domination of Markets

Concentration of Facilities

Another approach to measurement of economic power is illustrated by a "concentration" study for the postwar period by the Federal Trade Commission. This study measured concentration in 26 industries by the proportion of net fixed assets held by the largest firms.[89] Data were taken from SEC files and from a sample of FTC material. These sources were used only because the complete information of a census was unavailable.

The findings of the study are shown in Table 2–2 and Chart 2–1. For at least three reasons, this report gives only a very rough picture: (1) Data were for companies rather than for products, so that all facilities of a company were classified in the industry of its most important product, and the grouping of competing firms could be only a broad-brush sketch. (2) Differences in accounting procedures and fluctuations in price levels distorted the plant accounts so that they give only a rough reflection of physical productive capacity. (3) Productive capacity, even if it were accurately reflected by net physical assets, does not measure competitive strength in terms of market shares or financial re-

---

[88] *Ibid.,* p. 131.
[89] *Concentration of Productive Facilities—1947* (published 1949).

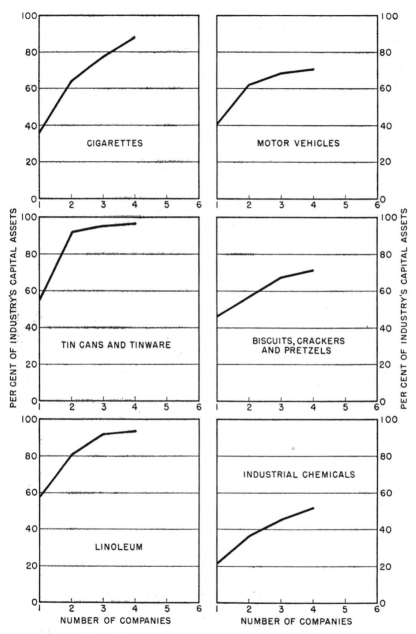

CHART 2–1. CONCENTRATION OF PRODUCTIVE FACILITIES—1947

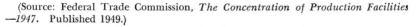

(Source: Federal Trade Commission, *The Concentration of Production Facilities —1947.* Published 1949.)

TABLE 2-2

CONCENTRATION OF PRODUCTIVE FACILITIES—1947

	Percent of net capital assets owned by—			
	1 company	2 companies	3 companies	4 companies
1. Linoleum	57.9	80.8	92.1	93.6
2. Tin cans and other tinware	55.2	92.1	95.3	96.4
3. Aluminum	55.0	85.0	100.0	...
4. Copper smelting and refining	46.8	73.5	88.5	94.6
5. Biscuits, crackers and pretzels	46.3	57.0	67.7	71.4
6. Agricultural machinery	45.3	56.8	66.6	75.4
7. Office and store machines and devices	42.0	56.3	69.5	74.3
8. Motor vehicles	40.9	62.8	68.7	70.7
9. Cigarettes	36.6	64.4	77.6	87.8
10. Plumbing equipment and supplies ..	33.2	64.9	71.3	74.3
11. Distilled liquors	29.0	53.3	72.4	84.6
12. Meat products	28.8	54.7	64.0	69.3
13. Primary steel	28.6	42.0	49.2	54.5
14. Rubber tires and tubes	27.8	49.9	70.3	88.3
15. Dairy products	27.5	48.9	55.8	59.6
16. Glass and glassware	24.9	49.1	57.4	62.2
17. Carpets and rugs	24.1	36.8	48.9	57.9
18. Footwear (except rubber)	23.6	39.6	43.4	46.8
19. Industrial chemicals	21.5	36.5	45.5	51.8
20. Woolen and worsted goods	16.7	23.5	28.1	30.3
21. Electrical machinery	15.8	28.8	41.7	47.5
22. Grain-mill products	15.6	23.5	30.2	36.3
23. Aircraft and parts	13.6	25.4	35.2	44.0
24. Bread and other products (excluding biscuits and crackers)	13.0	20.0	25.4	30.6
25. Canning and preserving	10.7	21.4	32.0	39.4
26. Drugs and medicines	8.4	16.5	23.5	30.0

Source: Federal Trade Commission, *The Concentration of Productive Facilities—1947* (Published 1949).

sources. In particular, a company that has more levels of production than other companies have—i.e., a company that starts with a rawer material and/or carries it to a higher degree of fabrication—will have a larger share of the industry's facilities than of its markets.

Obviously this FTC report is only an interim guess that can merely hint at facts If the goal of analysis is to find the limits

of managerial discretion, there is no replacement for product
data than can be combined in terms of substitute competition in
particular uses.

Concentration of Production

Economic power has also been measured by a product-by-prod-
uct analysis of oligopoly in industry.   The most famous statistical
device used for this purpose is the concentration ratio, which is
the percentage of total United States output of any commodity
(either in value or in physical terms) made by its four largest
producers.[90]   Four is the magic number because the Census
Bureau will not release data for fewer than four companies together.[91]   In a study of this kind for 1937, using a sample of 1,807
census commodities, the TNEC found that products amounting
to about half of the total value of manufacturers had concentration ratios above 50 per cent.[92]   Products amounting to nearly 20
per cent of the total value had ratios over 85 per cent.   See Table
2–3 and Chart 2–2.

What about the size of dominating firms?   Of the 3,752 different companies that appeared among the top four for one or
more products, 47 were among the 50 largest manufacturers.[93]
These 47 accounted for about 12 per cent of all appearances, and
45 of them appeared for three or more products; only 15 per cent
of all 3,752 appeared for three or more.   Thus, bigness seems to
imply a large share of a few markets, but market domination is
far more scattered than assets.

Studies based on census product data, therefore, give impressive
evidence of the extent to which a few firms dominate production in
each product.   But in appraising competitive structure from this
kind of analysis, several questions arise as to the relevance of the
data.   These doubts appear in two technical weaknesses: (1) inadequate classification of markets; and (2) irrelevance to market
structure.

Classification of Markets.   The breakdown of output into different "products" by the census classification is so erratic that sup-

---

90 See Means, *Structure of the American Economy*, pp. 110 ff.; TNEC Mono. 27,
Pt. V.
91 TNEC Mono. 27, p. 419.
92 *Ibid.*, p. 275.
93 *Ibid.*, p. 632.

TABLE 2–3

DISTRIBUTION OF VALUE OF PRODUCTS BY CONCENTRATION RATIO CLASSES, 1937

| | | Value of Products | |
Concentration Ratio Class		Per Cent	Cumulative Per Cent
0.1 to 5.0		1.2	1.2
5.1 to 10.0		1.2	2.4
10.1 to 15.0		1.6	4.0
15.1 to 20.0		2.7	6.7
20.1 to 25.0		5.0	11.7
25.1 to 30.0		4.4	16.1
30.1 to 35.0		4.8	20.9
35.1 to 40.0		9.8	30.7
40.1 to 45.0		4.9	35.6
45.1 to 50.0		7.0	42.6
50.1 to 55.0		3.0	45.6
55.1 to 60.0		6.0	51.6
60.1 to 65.0		4.4	56.0
65.1 to 70.0		4.9	60.9
70.1 to 75.0		5.7	66.6
75.1 to 80.0		7.5	74.1
80.1 to 85.0		4.9	79.0
85.1 to 90.0		2.2	81.2
90.1 to 95.0		9.5	90.7
95.1 to 100.0		1.1	91.8
[1]		6.2	98.0
[2]		2.0	100.0
Total		100.0	

Source: *Structure of Industry* (TNEC Monograph 27), 1941, p. 275.

[1] Withheld to avoid disclosing the operations of individual companies.
[2] Withheld to avoid disclosing the operations of remaining companies.

posedly non-competing items have varying degrees of substitutability. Passenger cars and chassis constitute one product, but beer cans and beer bottles are separate "products," and so are wooden and metal office furniture.

Relation to Markets. Analyses based on census classification of products determine concentration of production. This may be only loosely relevant to concentration of sellers in each market, where competitive forces come to bear. The consumer must choose between the brands of products that reach his own market, which may be more or less than the total number produced in the country. For products made only for local distribution, such as ice and bread, the national ratio understates the degree of monopoly in a single locality. For products that are partly imported,

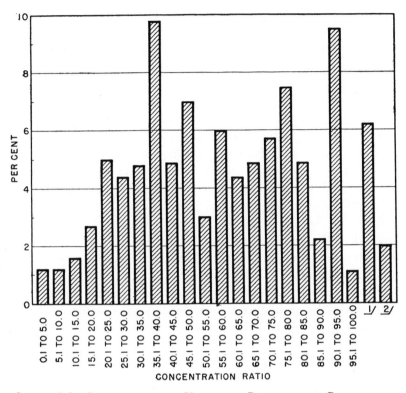

CHART 2–2. DISTRIBUTION OF VALUE OF PRODUCTS BY CONCENTRATION RATIO CLASSES—1937. (Source: *Structure of Industry,* TNEC Monograph 27, p. 276.)

1 Withheld to avoid disclosing the operations of individual companies.
2 Withheld to avoid disclosing the operations of remaining companies.

concentration in domestic production overstates market concentration. For some products such as tin, whiskey, and newsprint, concentration of domestic production is almost irrelevant.

Market Domination. Suppose, nevertheless, that the analysis had been narrowed down to a single market with relevant product groups. How close would this concentration of production of census "products" come to measuring the degree and importance of market domination? Since domination of markets presumably means the power to restrict output and to extract a monopoly profit, the degree of domination should logically be measured by either (1) the degree to which some vital factor of production, such as a raw material, pipeline, patent, or source of capital, has been subjected to monopoly control, or (2) the degree to which a monopoly rate of return has been established.

But in order to determine these two factors, we would have to know what prices, output, and distribution of incomes in the industry would have been under pure competition.[94] We simply don't have the necessary knowledge to do this, and any such index of the extent of domination would necessarily be conjecture. Intimate investigations of a few industries have in the past been able to identify the objective sources of monopoly conditions, but even these studies can make no real estimate of the intricate effects of monopoly markets. Measuring the importance of monopoly for the whole economy by industry studies of this kind, with the right data for tracing monopoly effects, would be a gargantuan chore, and is quite out of the question.

Relevance to Competition. What, then, does the concentration ratio tell about competition? How high does the ratio have to be to produce oligopoly price behavior? Sixty per cent, as in washing machines? Ninety per cent, as in typewriters? As we have seen, the structure of competition has a multitude of dimensions besides the number of sellers (see in particular Bain, *op. cit.*). The basic question is, What is the relationship of the concentration ratio to these other factors? A partial answer is given in the TNEC report itself: [95]

> This concentration . . . does not appear to result in any particular, strongly marked or unique behavior pattern. Products produced under conditions of high concentration show about the same changes in quantity and in price over periods of recovery and recession that are shown by products with low concentration. When the behavior patterns of products are analyzed in terms of their various product characteristics, changes in price are quite similar, regardless of the product characteristic, but the changes in quantity vary widely. This divergent quantity behavior, however, appears to be more closely associated with the varying economic characteristics of the products themselves than with the different conditions of competition under which they were produced.

---

[94] One of the classic suggestions in this field was Abba Lerner's index of monopoly, which compared the price of a product with its incremental cost of production, on the theory that they are equal under competition. ("The Concept of Monopoly and the Measurement of Monopoly Power," *Review of Economic Studies*, Vol. I, 1934.) Aside from its impracticality, however, this index was not a *complete* measure of the social cost of a monopoly in any market, since it did not include the size of the losses of output and distortions of income that would result, nor did it allow for the pure profits that appear with a new and growing product.

[95] TNEC Mono. 27, p. 412.

Conclusion

The technique of measuring the concentration of economic power is still an undeveloped art, and it is doubtful whether the results of the technique, even if it were perfected, would tell a more complete story than the results of present methods do.   In any statistical project, it is essential to set an objective and to study the relevance of the data to that objective.   But when the issue generates as much political heat as does the question of "monopoly," statistics are conscripted to prove much more than they can possibly show.[96]   An understanding of competitive behavior still requires close *ad hoc* study of individual markets.

---

96 A new statistical touchstone has been used recently by the Federal Trade Commission to indicate whether or not concentration is an inevitable consequence of modern technology. *Business Week* (December 23, 1950, p. 75), reports as follows:

"The new concept measures the spread between 'company concentration' (the proportion of total output produced by the few biggest companies), and 'plant concentration' (the proportion produced by the few biggest plants).   When the company share shows too large a spread over plant, the commission says, the size of the bigger firms 'must be attributed to circumstances other than technological economies of mass production.'

"FTC places all industries in one of five groups:

" (1) Low plant concentration and high company concentration.   Among these is the liquefied-gas industry.

" (2) Fairly high plant concentration but substantially higher company concentration.   These include distilled liquors, motor vehicles, steel mills, and petroleum refining.   In groups (1) and (2), the commission says, the major danger is monopoly. As a possible remedy, it suggests reducing the size of the largest companies.

"(3) Fairly low company concentration but substantially lower plant concentration. Among these are ice, bread, and fertilizer-mixing.

" (4) Both types of concentration low, as found in sawmills.   In (3) and (4), according to FTC, the biggest threat to the public interest is collusive agreement.

" (5) Both types of concentration very high.   Aircraft engines is the industry cited by the commission.   In this group, FTC concedes that there may be some valid economic reason for size."

Chapter 3

MULTIPLE PRODUCTS

Multiple Products

I. INTRODUCTION

IN MODERN AMERICAN INDUSTRY, three important facets of competition are embodied in conscious managerial action. They take the form of: (1) product policy, (2) promotional policy, and (3) pricing policy. Rapid changes in technology and demand make product-line composition an important dimension of competition. And product policy not only commands managerial attention, but is significant for the entire economy: it is the mainspring of economic progress, and hence an important test of a company's social contribution.

Although most modern firms make several products, economic theory has been developed on the premise that each firm makes only one product. The reasons for such an inadequate premise are to be found partly in the historical origins of theory, and partly in the simplicity of theoretical analysis when it is confined to single-product output. Determination of the costs of individual products in a multiple-product company is both conceptually and empirically difficult. The neglect of these problems may also be due to the notion that management views each product as a separate business activity with the characteristics of a single-product firm, but this approach has little theoretical, and no practical, support.

The purpose of this chapter is to examine, from an economic standpoint, the managerial problems of product coverage in a multiple-product firm. We are concerned with only one phase of product policy, namely, product coverage; i.e., decisions on what end products the company will make and sell. Product improvement, the other phase of product policy, is examined in various other places in this book, particularly in Chapter 10 ("Capital Budgeting").

The term "product" in this discussion will mean an end product offered for sale by the firm. Intermediate products produced as a consequence of vertical integration, and parts and components purchased for inclusion in final products are excluded from this analysis.

For the most part, we are concerned with the products that are manufactured by the firm. But product-line policy has other dimensions. Not all products sold by a company are made by it,[1] and not all products manufactured by a company carry that company's brand name.[2]

The term "product line" will be used in this chapter in a broad sense to include all the products manufactured by the firm. The term can be used in a narrower sense to refer to groups of products that are related either on the marketing side, as being complements or substitutes, or on the production side, as being made from the same materials or by similar processes.

We shall attempt to sketch a framework for a policy approach to product coverages i.e., a set of standing answers to recurring product proposals. Our analysis will have three parts: (1) opportunities for expanding a firm's product coverage; (2) criteria for deciding upon additions to the product line; (3) considerations for deciding whether or not to drop a product.

II. OPPORTUNITIES FOR MULTIPLE PRODUCTS

There are two questions to answer in considering any product addition: (1) Does it have adequate economic promise (even if technically feasible)? and (2) Can the company appropriately exploit this economic opportunity? The second question goes to the sources of multiple product advantage, which are discussed in this section.

---

[1] Major oil companies that operate filling station chains have taken essentially a merchandising view of the product line to be sold in their stations. Any product that can be efficiently sold to a motorist as an adjunct to gasoline purchase is a proper candidate, whether it is made from petroleum or not and whether or not the company itself can manufacture it.

[2] The General Electric Company will sell no final product not made by the company under its brand name, and it will not make products to be sold by others under their brand names. For this company, then, the product line is confined to its own label and manufacture. Many food packers, on the other hand, use their house-brand labels on both their own products and purchased packs, and sell to distributors for private-label sales.

Excess Capacity

Broadly speaking, the underlying reason for adding a new product to the line is to increase profits and/or competitive strength. These broad objectives may, in product-line policy, be viewed as aspects of mopping up excess capacity. "Excess capacity" has different meanings in different situations, and we shall not elaborate on them here. For this chapter, the relevant meaning is the kind of idleness that can be exploited profitably by adding new products. We may say that a new product absorbs excess capacity if it costs the going concern less to make and sell than it would cost a new company set up exclusively for that product. That is to say, this excess capacity is the source of the competitive advantage costwise of the multiple-product firm over the single-product firm.

Excess capacity can occur in any production factor that cannot be exactly and immediately adjusted for day-to-day output changes. Rigidities are thus the explanation, and since inputs that are available only in large chunks or that are bought on long-term contracts make up most of the production cost, excess capacity is quite pervasive.[3] Although classic illustrations of excess capacity are usually mechanical indivisibilities such as assembly lines and rolling mills, such cases only scratch the surface of its nature and prevalence.

The stage of development of the company determines, in part, where the major areas of excess capacity lie. For new and rapidly rising outfits that have done a distinguished job of developing and directing executives, the key asset that needs more work loaded on it may be the management team. In later stages of growth, excess capacity is also widespread in advertising, in the power of the brand name, in salesmen's time, and in distribution channels. Research can frequently be expanded by delegating laboratory chores and by keeping the key brains free for creative thinking. In the growing stages, excess capacity in administration and marketing often offers richer strategic opportunities than does the physical plant itself.

When the rate of growth is slow and expansion possibilities are remote, the indivisibilities are not so much in organization as in the durability of assets. Here excess capacity is the result

---

[3] The causes and varieties of inflexibility are discussed in Chapter 5, Section III.

of fluctuations or unexpected shifts in demand, and of technological revolutions.   This excess capacity can be seasonal, cyclical, or long-run; it can be anything from a shut-down mill that leaves a whole town unemployed, to the discovery that a wasted by-product has unsuspected profit potentials.   Whatever the reason for excess capacity, it creates opportunities for increasing profits by expanding the product line.

Classic examples of multiple-product lines developed to offset seasonal fluctuations are the coal-and-ice business, and the ski tows installed at summer resorts to create a winter clientele.   In many such cases it is difficult to decide whether alternative ways of regularizing production—e.g., manufacturing for stock or using seasonal discounts to redistribute demand over time [4] or some other valley-filler—may not be more profitable than the addition of the candidate product.   No business is more seasonal than the Christmas card industry, which is still able to equalize production over the year.   The practice of adding new products to mitigate cyclical fluctuations and thereby mop up excess capacity is common enough.   Manufacturers of building materials, banking on the past independence of building cycles and business cycles, have added industrial products.[5]

Secular Shifts

The peril of the excess-capacity criterion is, of course, that under-utilization is generally a cyclical phenomenon, whereas the product addition may be a long-term decision.   Hence the company is sometimes put in the position of using a cost criterion that includes only immediate outlays for a decision where equipment investments may be involved eventually.   The excess capacity of the depression is converted into capacity shortages, and the new product requires plant additions at prosperity peaks.[6]

---

[4] Seasonal discounts are sometimes persuasive enough to reverse the whole seasonal pattern.   This occurred in the furniture industry when bargain prices in February switched the peak sales month from late summer to mid-winter.

[5] For example, to use the excess capacity of felt mills, one firm in the early thirties added a line of products for insulating and sound-proofing automobiles. The product proved successful, even though it did not use the company's regular distribution channels and required a new sales force to sell directly to the automobile manufacturers.

[6] The Long Island Railroad created a situation somewhat like this by pricing commuter fares to cover only immediate costs.   The promotional effect of the low rate on suburban development of Long Island went far beyond expectations and put the railroad in severe financial straits.   Furthermore, efforts to raise fares to

Secular shifts that create excess capacity and call for new product-line decisions take place at every level. Familiar shifts of this sort are: the impact of substitute competition on old products, e.g., nylon driving out silk stockings, changes in the technology of production or selling, shifts in raw material supply, new competitive uses of raw materials, changes in the location of markets, and new kinds of transportation.

Product additions to offset secular declines in equipment value call for heavier planning than do short-run ventures, since they represent a change in course for the company. The range of candidate products is broadened by the increased opportunities for marginal investment in plant or markets to complement the excess capacity. Relatively minor adjustments in production and marketing were required to shift cotton looms to rayon fabrics when this fiber swept into the market. More substantial changes, particularly in distribution, were made when newsprint production shifted to Canada and domestic producers began manufacturing book, bond, and hanging paper.

Vertical Integration

An important source of excess capacity that promotes multiple-product lines is vertical integration, where the company has investments in several levels of production and distribution. The motivation for vertical integration is complex and much debated. Reduction of uncertainty, through assured quantity, quality, or costs of supply, or through assured market outlets, seems to have been more important in recent years than the hope for cost savings or greed for middlemen's profits. The motivation is seldom the desire to expand the product line. But the technical requirements for an efficient size of plant at one level are frequently out of balance with the company's own needs at other levels. Hence intermediate products need to be bought or sold. Not only scale economies, but secular shifts in technology and cyclical shifts in product-mix put the organization out of balance.[7]

---

a full-cost level were met with powerful opposition by the suburbanites, who now had a vested interest in the existing level of fares.

[7] Secular shifts are sometimes thrust upon companies by public policy. After Electric Bond and Share's holding company empire in utilities had disappeared under the 1935 Holding Company Act, Ebasco Services, Inc., the organization's service company, expanded its product line beyond the accounting, legal, and engineering services to utilities, and became a general consulting service to all

U. S. Steel's ore production in Minesota was at one time just adequate for its needs, but when it faced an increased scrap content in the furnace charge and a fall in its market share, it became a substantial ore supplier to other producers. A manufacturer of plumbing, who at one time bought a coking plant and a pig iron mill, subsequently shifted to products made from other materials and had to sell much of his coal, coke, and pig iron to outsiders. When Firestone invaded the retail tire market, it was soon selling a complete line of auto supplies—batteries, tools, and so on, partly to absorb excess retailing capacity, partly as a full-line policy. A publishing company which at one time owned a papermill to supply its own magazine paper needs eventually sold it because the range of paper grades that were inevitable parts of the output put the company deeply into the paper-marketing business.

Research

Since research creates excess capacity by making current products and their production obsolescent, it is an internal source of secular shifts in technology and demand. Research also develops new products to mop up excess capacity.

Why does a company spend money on research that may wipe out the value of its product line and plant? Theoretically, research needn't have any effect on the value of the existing product line, if new findings can be put on the shelf until present demand wanes and until sales need revitalizing with innovations.

Actually, few, if any, products have such an impregnable monopoly position. For most companies, research is part of the competitive race, and is carried on to protect demand from invasion by competitors' new substitutes. With everyone in the industry pushing research eagerly,[8] it is clear that no single firm can confidently shelve research findings and expect to find them still valuable years hence. Patents are rarely much protection against the disparate ways of doing the same thing that are characteristic of

---

industries on almost all types of problems needing experts. A recent case is Pullman, Inc., which, divested of its sleeping-car affiliate in an antitrust case, turned to general sales of stainless steel sheets as a use of the cash capital acquired in divestment.

[8] Oligopoly restraints are much weaker in research than in pricing; successful research takes more skill than price cutting; and rivals are much less able to imitate and wipe out the gains.

modern technology. The effect is to put a heavy premium on getting into the market first, establishing brand preference, and perfecting the product and technology.[9]

A broad product line is one way to exploit the unpredictable results of research. Although it is possible for a company to sell or license much of its research output, usually no outsider can use the results as profitably as can the originator. Availability of capital, technical advice in the breaking-in stages, and affiliation with the present product line, all give momentum toward exploiting a broad range of research results.[10]

Multiple-product lines enhance the value of research in another way. Rarely can one person see all the profits in research; many attitudes and backgrounds are needed. In a multiple-product firm it is easier to ferret out all the applications of research findings by distributing them throughout the firm and letting the engineers and salesmen look at them from the standpoint of their own specialties.[11]

Summary

The underlying purpose of product additions is to increase competitive effectiveness and make more money. Economic opportunities for adding products arise from various kinds of unused capacity: managerial, marketing, research, or production. The under-loaded condition may be short-lived, i.e., seasonal or cyclical, whereas the offsetting product additions are usually permanent. But often the excess capacity is chronic, being caused by secular shifts in materials, technology, or markets. Vertical integration sometimes produces unused capacity that leads to added products. But research is the most important source of new product oppor-

---

[9] Thus the risks of obsolescence of existing products fuel the drive for finding new products. And the prospect of decay of the monopoly position (and profits) of existing specialties is but a more sophisticated aspect of this drive.

[10] There is a correlation between size of company, feasible range of product line, and ability to engage in long-range basic research. This gives big business a distinctive position of strength and is a useful guide to policy for growth companies. Moreover, growth by diversification is politically far more acceptable than mere horizontal or vertical integration.

[11] An extreme illustration is I. G. Farben's discovery of a chlorination process which it applied to soap manufacture with some success. Standard Oil (New Jersey) chemists, with a petroleum industry point of view, demonstrated that the process was far more valuable in lubricants than in soaps, an application that had never occurred to the Farben men. (G. W. Stocking and M. W. Watkins, *Cartels or Competition?*, Twentieth Century Fund, New York, 1948, p. 114.)

tunities. Research speeds the turnover of the product-line, improving and obsoleting existing products.

III. POLICY ON ADDING NEW PRODUCTS

Introduction

In a dynamic economy, where product monopolies are characteristically transient and where product development is a major facet of competitive rivalry, economically sound decisions on additions to the company's product coverage are obviously of great importance. Three important problems encountered by top management in formulating policy on adding new products are, (1) scouting out potential product additions, (2) appraising these proposals and making the product selection, and (3) launching each new product venture in a way that gives it a maximum chance of success.

The first, maintaining a flow of promising proposals, is principally a question of lowering the proportion of pipe-dream schemes and raising the proportion of suggestions worth considering. The ratio of bad ideas is high and creates a danger of rejecting real opportunities by conditioned response. For many companies, product research is the main source of significant proposals. Others license new product inventions or buy them directly from independent inventors and corporate research departments, or through professional "product-finders." Product proposals also come from customers, from the company's marketing staff, from small companies that want to sell out, and from independent inventors.

The third top management problem, namely, launching the new venture, involves questions of refinement of the product design, selection of market targets, methods of distribution, pricing the new product, and making capital expenditures for production and marketing facilities. Such problems are discussed elsewhere in this book.

Top management's second problem—the appraisal of candidate product additions—is the central concern of this section. Even in large, well-managed companies, the methods used in selecting product additions leave much to be desired. A survey of the experience of 200 leading packaged-goods manufacturers in the postwar development of new products revealed that only 20 per cent of the products put on the market actually turned out to be money-makers.[12] For most of these products, expectations had been far too optimistic. This dismal experience showed that product innovation required more careful selection and more deliberate planning than these companies had anticipated. A rich mixture of market research, product testing, adequate financial resources, and persistence was needed.

Management needs a rational routine for this appraisal in the form of a set of criteria to guide its analysis. In this section we consider what questions management should ask, and what criteria it should establish. The discussion has three parts: first, standards of prospective profits from the candidate product, second, considerations of product-line strategy, and third, specific criteria of acceptability of new products.

Standards of Profitability

Usually the most important question about a new product is its prospective profitability. If the sole objective of the enterprise were to maximize profits in a strict sense, all considerations affecting additions to the product line could be subsumed under profitability; to a degree, the non-profit considerations are merely indicators of long-run profit prospects. Yet, as we saw in Chapter 1 ("Profits"), business motivations are more complex than has been assumed in economic theory. They encompass objectives such as eternal corporate life, market share, volume growth, comfortable cash reserves, assured tenure for management, and pleasant employee relations. These purposes can be forced into a concept of long-range profit maximization, but when this is done, the concept evaporates for analytical applications.

Prospective profitability, in the narrow, cash-return sense, is nevertheless the key consideration. Candidates for addition to the product line should be ranked in a priority ladder according to profitability, and should be selected from the top down, except in unusual strategic circumstances. But estimates of future earnings from new products have wide error margins. So the ladder will be nebulous at best and must be supplemented by other tests of suitability.

---

12 "The Introduction of New Products," a survey made by Ross Federal Research Corporation, for Peter Hilton, Inc.

A profitability ladder raises four questions: (1) What concept of profits is relevant?   (2) What form of profit standard should be used?   (3) How should profit prospects be measured?   (4) What rejection level should be established?

Profit Concepts

The revelant concept of profits for product-line additions is not always clear; it depends on circumstances.   The basic choice lies between some notion of incremental profits and the concept of net profits over full cost.   Incremental profits here refer to the difference in the firm's profits with and without the addition of the product in question.   It thus credits the new product with the whole increase in profitability of existing facilities that its introduction produces.   In contrast, the use of net profits means that some of the fixed overheads are loaded onto the new product, and cost burdens of existing products are correspondingly lightened.

If they are extended over a long enough period to encompass the probable life cycle of the new addition, incremental profits are the relevant concept.   Sometimes product additions are so short-lived that no capital investment is required.   Examples are sub-contracting work, war work, and production of specially designed products in a job shop.   In this special case, the usual strategic considerations (see Section III below) that enter into product-line additions are rather unimportant.   But here, as in a longer-range setting, incremental profits must be measured against the profits that could come from the best alternative use of money, time, and facilities.   If the alternative is idleness, then presumably any incremental profits will justify the addition of the product.   If, as is more common, the alternative is to use resources on some other product, the alternative return sets the standard of minimum incremental profits.

For more durable additions to the product line, a different concept of cost is needed for estimating the added profitability of the new product.   The adoption of a new product carries with it explicitly or tacitly the commitment to stay with the new venture at least until it has had a fair trial, and possibly longer.   Additions to existing costs that are often unforeseen at the time of the introduction of the new product are likely to occur, so that the businessman's rule-of-thumb of loading on the new product its full share of common overhead cost is often the most appropriate method after all.[13]

Form of Profit Standard

In order to compare the profitability of alternative uses of facilities, profit standards must be stated in a form that is relevant for ranking them. What form should a profit estimate take— unit margins, return on investment, aggregate dollar profits? The most general form is the total dollar income over the whole life of the product minus the total outlay (including investment) to produce it. But in cases where the new product is not a permanent addition, it may be easier to measure the profit return per unit of some fixed, bottleneck factor of production absorbed by the new product. Such a bottleneck factor might be executive time, machine time, or materials (e.g., steel during the postwar period of shortage and private rationing by producers). For big additions, the limiting factor is often funds for capital outlays, particularly for firms that limit investment to money available from retained earnings). In this case, return on incremental investment is the best measure. This form of profit measures the income-producing efficiency of the product relative to alternative uses.[14]

Measuring Profit Prospects

The major problem in estimating profitability is to make decent projections of revenues and costs. Ideally, these should cover the expected life-span of the product; in practice, three to five years is the limit of visibility. Forecasts of demand and costs are extremely speculative for new products; indeed, they are much more so than many firms realize. In explaining the failure of new products, the 200 companies mentioned at the beginning of this section put particular emphasis on (1) inadequate market research and (2) underestimated selling-cost requirements.[15]

---

[13] The experience of many business organizations is that new products added to mop up overhead actually produce new overheads and, in addition, incur untraceable costs, such as added drain on executive time and energy. These costs make their incremental profits quite different from those indicated by short-run marginal cost estimates. For a discussion of these cost concepts, see Chapter 5, Section II.

[14] In the extreme case, where all resources are idle and there is just one candidate product which itself cannot absorb any resource completely, the rate-of-return form is inapplicable, since efficiency is not a consideration in production.

[15] Some of the problems of exploring the market for a new product are discussed in Chapter 7 ("Basic Price") in connection with pricing a new product. Several alternative approaches are outlined in Chapter 4 ("Demand").

The hardest cost estimates to make are estimates of development and selling expenses. Pressure to get the product onto the market may cut short the research that is needed to work all the bugs out of the product. This can be an expensive shortcut, since the bad impressions made on the first venturesome customers may cause delays and perhaps foreclose market acceptance. Problems of promotional outlays are discussed in Chapter 6 ("Advertising").

Products vary widely in forecastability; for some products no refined calculations are possible at all. Consequently, any use of profit standards for appraising the candidate product is precluded. Going into some products is like making a bet on the horses. Decisions then must rest more completely on grand strategy and on criteria of acceptance like those discussed later in this section.

Level of Profit Standards

To determine how large an incremental profit is needed to justify the addition of the product to the line requires some standard of adequate return. Ideally, the market cost of new capital should always be the criterion, but it is not widely used for a number of reasons (see Chapter 10, "Capital Budgeting"). One alternative standard is supplied by the competition of rival product additions and rival internal investments of all sorts for the company's limited resources. Under such a plan, a candidate product will be rejected unless it promises a rate of return that exceeds the next best use for funds. Another standard (where resources are not limited) is in terms of some historical return on investment. (See Chapter 1, "Profits," Section IV.) Thus some companies require a minimum return equal to the company's ten-year average; others develop an arbitrary standard of adequate profits of this type that is not specifically related to anything. For example, a large automobile manufacturer, for unknown reasons, has adopted 30 per cent before taxes as a standard. Sometimes the standard is formulated in terms of unit net profit margins at some normal output rate. One company in the drug field, for example, has a minimum 50 per cent margin. Presumably, such a high standard reflects competition of highly profitable alternative products; thus it is likely to be an opportunity cost standard.[16]

---

[16] Profit standards are discussed further in Chapter 1, "Profits," Section IV, and in Chapter 10, "Capital Budgeting," Section IV.

Summary

The pivotal test for the addition of a new product is its profitability. If profit maximization were the sole goal of the enterprise, this test would encompass all others, but pluralistic motivation makes the other goals germane as well. The relevant concept of profits is incremental returns over the appropriate time period —i.e., what addition the product makes to enterprise profits over its life span. The profit prospects must be expressed in a form that allows significant comparison with alternative uses of labor, plant, and time. It is desirable to establish some standard of minimum acceptable earnings. This floor should be determined by the company's cost of capital or by the profitability of alternative opportunities.

Product Strategy

Supplementing tests of profit prospects are general considerations of strategy. These are to a degree composed of the specific acceptance criteria discussed in the next sub-section.

Multiple-product "strategy" is a shorthand name for the company's long-run purposes in product diversity. Although strategy is usually focused on profits in the long run and is confined by economic limitations, it is also affected by the technical abilities and personal preferences of management. It is a position consciously taken to simplify decision-making at crucial points. Presumably, under an enterprise system, the purpose of strategy is to make money, in the long run at least. Yet, as we have seen, this is not the whole story. (See Chapter 1, "Profits.") In a going concern, product-line strategy usually has historical roots— sometimes in the company's original purposes, but often later in a basic merger or an empire builder's dream.

Companies with no clear product-line strategy have been conspicuously profitable, and many mergers have grown in spite of the seeming lack of kinship among the products of the merging companies. Other companies say they have a product-line policy, although they are simply rationalizing a product line that grew without pattern. Yet considerable evidence indicates that many well-managed, mature, multi-product enterprises do have a logical product line that serves as a real guide to action, as is demonstrated by both product surgery and acquisitions that are consonant with announced product policies.

A few examples will show the general character of product-line strategy. A leading electrical manufacturer conceives of its broad product-line policy as a beneficent circle. Its apparatus line generates and transmits electricity; its industrial products and its lamps and home appliances build up the demand for power and help lower the public utility companies' costs; as a result, the price of current is reduced and the demand for its industrial apparatus to produce more current is expanded.

A large producer of insulating materials thinks of its product-line strategy in terms of a complete coverage of the full thermal range, with adequate alternatives throughout the range. The company wants to be considered a specialist in insulation, able to deal with any insulation problem impartially. It assumes that if it sells various alternative devices itself, customers will rely on it to select the most effective technique or material for their particular uses. The product line is an implement for selling a complete insulation service.

Product lines are sometimes conceived in terms of a framework of know-how. Thus one company views its know-how as being made up essentially of papermaking techniques. The pivotal machine converts wet pulp into dry, flat products. The company refuses to add products that depart significantly from this framework of know-how—e.g., products that involve intricate metal stamping or assembly operations. A leading automobile manufacturer looks upon its product line as essentially motive-power units, and incidentally produces the bodies and wheels that use the power. Chemical companies sometimes conceive their product-line boundaries in terms of the equipment and processes that have been peculiar to the chemical industry. But the constant stream of discoveries in by-products and methods has recently made these borders quite elastic. Chemical companies have been led toward textile and paper processes, and oil companies into chemical industry research and processes.

Sometimes product-line strategy is strictly defensive. One of the building material companies, for example, has in the last 20 years been guided in its product acquisitions by the broad line of building materials offered by the two giants in the industry, whose coverage of building materials was formerly far more comprehensive than the company's own. This policy was in part based on the belief that basic distribution economies were possible in selling a broad and related line of products all handled by the building materials dealer.

The outer limits of a product line (like the outer limits of an industry) are typically framed in terms of common raw materials, production processes, distribution channels, or final uses. These criteria—which are alternative and occasionally contradictory—are often less fundamental for determining product-line strategy than are the competitive relationships in terms of tactics for increasing profits and rivals' reactions to these tactics. Hence, considerations of product-line strategy reflect technical as well as competitive limitations on management. They thus become the groundwork for that nebulous but real aspect of the company—"grand strategy."

Acceptance Criteria for New Products

Because estimates of probable profits from new products have wide margins of error and cannot be projected far into the future, and because maximizing financial profits is not the only strategic objective of the company, supplemental standards of acceptability for new products are needed. In theory, these standards are not as fundamental as are direct estimates of profits. They rest on empirical characteristics of the firm. Nevertheless, since they are frequently easier to apply than are profitability standards, they have much value in themselves. A candidate product can be compared with the existing product line in terms of:

1. Interrelation of demand characteristics with the existing product line.
2. Use of the company's distinctive know-how.
3. Use made of common production facilities.
4. Use of common distribution channels.
5. Use of common raw materials.
6. Benefits to existing products.

These criteria can supplement estimates of the direct profits expected after adding the new product.

1. *Interrelation of Demand Characteristics*

An important factor in considering new products for the product line is the relation of their demand characteristics to the characteristics of the existing group of products. Since the right combination of products in the product line has powerful promotional value, this interrelation is a primary criterion of acceptable product additions.

What are the kinds of demand relations between the candidate product and the existing product that will improve its chances of success? Two kinds may be distinguished: the new product may be a substitute; or it may be a complement. Rigorously speaking, the distinction may be framed in terms of cross-elasticity of demand. The candidate product is a substitute if its sales fall when the price of an existing product is reduced (other things equal). If its sales gain, then it is a complement.

There are various kinds of substitute relations in demand that favor admission of the candidate product. Sometimes the new product, by extending the range of coverage, acts as a hedge against uncertainties and shifts in consumer demand. The garment industry provides many examples of product diversity to reduce risks that stem from buyers' ignorance and style change. Addition of paper, glass, and plastic containers to the product line of manufacturers of tin cans is probably partly a hedge against a revolution in container materials. Another type of substitution has to do with innovations. The acceptance of a new product which makes obsolete the company's existing product is justifiable, primarily because obsolescence is inevitable. The present product would be displaced by new ones in any event—by competitors, if not by the company itself.

Complementarity is the other general kind of demand kinship that is important in testing product additions. Typically, the question is whether the new product can fit into the pattern of demand so that the company's name established by the present products can help to sell the new one. In a sense, this condition produces excess capacity in advertising. Occasionally, another type of complementarity exists when a spectacular new product adds prestige to the existing line. Closely related to the promotional assistance of a new product, and more fundamental and common in most businesses, is the ability of a new product to make the present product line either operate or sell better. Thus the addition of fine-grain film to the product line of a camera manufacturer who sold high-speed lenses brought out the full usefulness of the lenses.[17]

---

[17] Accessories and extras, particularly in the early days of the automobile industry, served both as promotional balloons and functional improvements. For example, the roof of the 1905 Stanley Steamer was an extra, and the self-starter remained an extra for most cars for years.

A second demand characteristic is the entity of the product group as a whole. The promotional advantages of a full line often make the whole greater than the sum of its parts. The tactical advantage of a full line of sizes, grades, and supplementary products in getting good dealers and in merchandising high-margin specialties make this kind of interrelation of demand a commonly used basis for product-line policy. Some would go so far as to deny the validity of analyzing sales performance for any individual member of a product group because each member contributes to the sales and profits of the other members, and because the economic unit of merchandising activities is the whole group of products.

A "full line" may be defined as the broadest coverage of related products successfully sold by a rival manufacturer. This concept brings out the defensive nature of a full line policy. By carrying a broad product line (relative to rivals) a manufacturer has advantages in getting good dealers and in efficiently aiding in their merchandising activities by training, cooperative advertising, and "point-of-sale" materials. Consequently, whether the candidate product is needed to match a competitor's breadth of line is an important criterion.[18]

2. Distinctive Know-how

Sometimes the determining consideration in making product-line decisions is that new products must make use of the company's distinctive and almost personal source of differential advantage. An example is the M. W. Kellogg Company, which sells engineering skill in the design of giant processing equipment for chemical and petroleum industries. Fabrication and construction are carried on but are subsidiary to the principal product—technical pioneering skill. One of the company's product-line specifications is that products must fully utilize this asset and must be suitable vehicles for the sale of this service.

One of the large electrical manufacturers uses this same test in an indirect fashion. Only products that are highly engineered and that call for intricate manufacture and assembly methods are regarded as suitable, partly because the market that is developed for such products will be protected from easy invasion by these know-how requirements.

---

[18] These demand considerations are discussed further in Chapter 8 ("Product Line Pricing"), where they are applied specifically to the pricing problem.

Sometimes the distinctive asset is research power. It is a fairly conscious policy of one of the large chemical companies to choose only those new products that have been developed by its product research organization and that are distinctive enough in both chemical and manufacturing requirements to be protected for some time to come. The counterpart of this policy is to abandon products when they have degenerated to the status of commonly produced commodities. The company advances to new monopoly positions as fast as economic progress wears down the walls of the old.

For many companies, research capacity and experience is the major phase of its distinctive know-how. In such a case an admissibility standard should be framed in terms of whether the candidate product is susceptible to the kind of improvement that will put the research capacity of the company to its highest and noblest use.

Another test that may fall into this category is the volume potential test. Many large companies scorn product additions that would meet other tests, but that do not promise a sufficiently large volume of sales to use the powers of a large company fully or to overcome its disadvantages of inflexibility. They look upon small-volume new products as requiring an organization that is quicker on its feet than a large company can expect to be.[19]

3. *Common Production Facilities*

The requirement that the candidate product use existing or closely similar production facilities is a widely used test of admissibility. When applied strictly to the use of existing facilities it depends on economies of mopping up excess capacity, which are short-lived. Hence, to this extent, the test has perils of using short-run incremental cost when long-run increments are involved.

When the test is framed in terms of requiring similar production facilities, it does not run these risks, since it is not then short run in concept. In this form it bears a close resemblance to the test of distinctive know-how. Similar production facilities

---

[19] A systematic search for products developed by large research organizations whose volume prospects were too small for the developing company to commercialize was made recently by an outfit which has shown considerable success in developing fairly diverse small businesses. Professional "product finders" also prospect here.

are, in large part, a monopoly return on specialized knowledge and concentrated effort.

Most product additions fall somewhere between the extremes of idle capacity and familiar production methods. They normally make use of unused capacity of some facilities, at least common overheads, but often require additional facilities that, though different, have much in common with those for existing products.

4. Common Distribution Channels

Another popular test of the admissibility of a new product is that it must permit effective marketing through the same distribution facilities used by the company's existing products. In economic terms, this criterion is sometimes used to absorb unused capacity. More often, the economies result from savings of specialization or of large scale.[20]

The test is most applicable when the company has a single or a clearly dominant distribution mechanism. A company whose only channel is direct sales to retail stationers might require that a new product be the kind that could be handled by stationary stores and sold by the sales force that serves them. Manufacturers' postwar experience with new products traveling through unfamiliar distribution channels and requiring a different sales organization was, on the whole, quite disappointing.

Even though a product meets this distribution test, there are limits to the number and variety of products that can be efficiently sold by a salesman if he is to be more than a mere order-taker.

Sometimes the selling power rests on no more than a blanket brand name. Products that can be sold compatibly under a well-known company label are sometimes added even though they are sold through different channels and require a specialized sales force.

In addition to savings of specialization and scale, established marketing organizations of salesmen and distributors constitute a source of monopoly advantage. Frequently the dealer organization is the company's most valuable and hardest-to-duplicate asset. Development of adequate distribution is sometimes a major

---

[20] A special case of distribution mechanism economies are the savings of carload mixed-shipment rates for products that come under common freight classifications. This economy has been an important one in inducing building materials manufacturers to broaden their product lines.

barrier to entry.   Hence the selection of products that will most happily utilize this facet of competitive power is an important element in successful product line development.   The question is not whether the new product can be distributed at all through the company's marketing organization, but rather whether it can be distributed economically, both as compared with alternative candidate products, which might otherwise use these limited distribution facilities, and as compared with selling the product to other distributing organizations, while the company itself manufactures it.[21]

5. *Common Raw Materials*

Many companies look for product additions that use the same basic raw material or its by-products.   The rubber industry's product lines exemplify the application of this test.   A company with extensive asbestos mining properties has directed its product research toward developing new products that will use not only asbestos, but also the short fibers and other wastes that are left after the regular asbestos products have been manufactured.

The economic rationale for this test rests on two points: First, the basic source of raw material is controlled by the company—e.g., asbestos mines or bauxite deposits; the addition of products that use the common raw material may help develop the market for that material.   They can also put the company in a position to exploit differentials between the prices of raw materials and finished products.   Second, important savings result from intimate familiarity with intricate processing methods.   For this reason the petroleum companies rely heavily upon the common-material test.

6. *Benefits to Present Product Line*

The foregoing tests depend largely on the contributions that existing products and facilities can make to candidate new products.   This "benefits" test, in contrast, asks what the new product can offer to existing products.   Contributions through

---

21 The policy on product-line additions of one of the smaller building material producers, whose major competitors have extensive product lines illustrates the first four tests. For this company, complete competitive parity is out of the question, and its product line necessarily has some compromises and omissions. The company's criteria of selection are that a new product must (1) use the same productive facilities; (2) use the company's present technical competence; (3) sell through the same marketing channels.

interrelation to demand have already been mentioned; contributions through experience in new types of production methods which have applicability to old products has received much attention as a result of the peace-time lessons of war production. Similarly, postwar "defense" research and pilot production supported by the military organization illustrates this educational contribution of some new products.   Private ventures into new products simply for educational benefits in producing old products are long bets which few companies can take.   Old products are a generic class subject to continual evolution.   The educational benefits from an added product, either in research, production methods, or even demand interdependence, do not apply only to the present products.   Often more importantly, these benefits apply to the projected path of development of these existing products.   Remington Rand's recent acquisition of a company making a new type of "electronic brain" computing machine may illustrate the kind of contribution along the paths of projected development of existing Remington equipment.

IV. POLICY ON DROPPING OLD PRODUCTS

The problem of determining what products should be dropped is, in general, the converse of the problem of selecting products for additions.   There are, nevertheless, certain differences. These may be grouped under the following questions: (1) How does the problem arise?   (2) What are the choices?   (3) How should the problem be decided?

How Does the Problem Arise?

Candidates for deletion come partly from past mistakes in overt product-line additions, and partly from inadvertent acquisitions. These inadvertent acquisitions may result from mergers designed to acquire one group of suitable products or from backward integration that misfired and produced unforeseen by-products or unforeseen excess capacity.   Candidates for deletion also come from product obsolescence caused by basic changes in consumer taste or by striking improvements in rivals' products.

What Are the Choices?

Broadly speaking, when a product's profit or sales behavior is absolutely or relatively unsatisfactory, there are four choices: (1) improve the present operation and keep the product; (2) keep on making it but sell it in bulk for others to market; (3) keep on selling it but buy it from others who can produce it more advantageously; and (4) stop manufacturing it and stop selling it.

1. *Improvement of Present Operations*

Before ceasing to manufacture or to market a product, three avenues of improvement within the framework of existing operations should be explored: (1) improve marketing efficiency; (2) reduce production costs; (3) improve the product itself. Efforts to improve the efficiency of marketing and production usually and properly come before an effort to revolutionize the product unless it is apparent that the product is obsolete. The economist's assumption that the entrepreneur knows the least-cost combination of production factors is rarely correct for the marketing activities of even the best-run manufacturing firm. Hence the chances are good that the efficiency of merchandising the product can be improved by a research attack.

Reduction of production costs is another step often taken before product innovation. Improved efficiency often requires some redesign of the product, but this is pointed at cheapening production rather than improving salability. Improvement of existing products goes on continuously in most organizations. It is sometimes hard to distinguish improved products from new products, partly because the distinction is purposely blurred in presenting the products to the public. Product improvement is one of the most important aspects of modern-day competition in many industries. It has accounted for drastic changes in market share— for example, Goodyear's phenomenal rise as a result of pioneering the cord tire, the straight sidewall tire, and the balloon tire; or Chevrolet's rapid climb in market share in the late twenties, while Ford clung to the old-fashioned pedal gear shift. The drastic consequences for market share that can come from a single product improvement create a great compulsion to do whatever can be done to equal competitors' product standards.

Yet, surprisingly enough, this is an area of competition where oligopolists tend to forget rivals' reactions. Even the "big few" are usually heedless of the repercussions of their own product innovations; they act as though these innovations will not be imitated or at least as if the gains will more than offset any advantages of restraining competition in this area for oligopolistic reasons.

Product improvement is a major device in durable-goods industries. It expands the market by making the goods already sold out of date. In many mature industries—e.g., automobiles and machine tools—a high proportion of the market is replacement. And replacement quite largely takes place, at least among upper-crust buyers, as a consequence of obolescence rather than of physical exhaustion. Product improvement is also a major device for market segmentation. The second-hand car takes care of the high elasticity sector composed of impecunious professors and those who want mere transportation. The new car, within the limits of close rivalry, skims the more carefree spending sector of demand. This, of course, is particularly true for luxury products —e.g., Cadillacs.

Presumably, product-improvement efforts should be directed (a) at products that suffer by competitive comparisons, (b) at products that are right for the firm in the sense of meeting tests for proper product additions, and (c) where a relatively small amount of research effort will bring a relatively large amount of product improvement.

The tests of whether to commercialize a discovered improvement are essentially tests of profitability—how much improvement in sales, compared with how much increased cost to produce and sell. Of course, a rich mixture of strategy is involved, since product improvements bring future revenue in addition to present revenue. The compulsion to make defensive product improvements depends upon the market goals of the firm. A company that shoots at the top market and strives to build a reputation for the best quality at premium prices cannot choose but to make every effort to bring its product up to competitive standards.

A company, on the other hand, that starts with lower market acceptance is content to exploit the less plushy sectors, and may well hold off on product improvements until they are not only tested, but cheap to imitate.

2. Selling in Bulk

By eliminating advertising and personal selling, costs can sometimes be brought to a level that produces enough contribution margin to justify keeping the product. This alternative is particularly relevant to products that have become competitive foot-balls, or whose marketing has become too complex for the amount of executive time that can be spared for it.   Continuing to produce such a product is justified when it is a by-product.   The main question here is whether or not to devote selling energies to marketing a by-product.

3. *Buying in Bulk*

When the ailing product makes positive strategic or merchandising contributions, the possibility that it can be bought in bulk cheaper than it can be made needs investigation.

In general, buying instead of making gives the firm flexibility—it can shop around, vary its quality standards easily, and make product changes quickly, i.e., without trying to preserve capital value of obsolete plant.   Buying gives the company the advantages of the supplying firms' specialization and large-scale production—i.e., the returns from division of labor.

A few firms, nevertheless, insist on themselves making every thing and every part that carries their labels.   In part, this is a doctrine of "self-sufficiency," which supposedly makes the company independent of competitive conditions elsewhere in the economy and insures a steady and reliable supply of materials and parts.   We have seen, however (Section III), that this policy raises difficult problems of coordinating production in different size plants and carrying enough product lines to mop up excess capacity effectively.

If quality is standardized enough not to be a controlling factor, the decision to buy or to make depends on competitive conditions in supplier industries.   If competition is strong enough to push supply prices close to cost levels, and if quality and quantity are reliable, there is little point in using scarce capital in this line of activity.   If there are only a few suppliers, and if pricing follows erratic oligopolistic patterns alternating between high, rigid levels and cutthroat competition, much can be said for maintaining production within the firm, particularly if competitors in the final markets have this kind of vertical integration.

4. *Total Elimination*

The criteria for eliminating a product are substantially the opposite of those for product additions.   One approach, therefore, is to screen products that look sick enough to be candidates for deletion through the same kinds of suitability tests discussed above. Another approach is to appraise the product in terms of profits and sales results, such as whether it is slipping in market share, whether it accounts for a trifling percentage of the company's sales, and whether its net or incremental profits are satisfactory as compared with other products or with products that might be produced if it were eliminated. A product that fails the suitability tests and also shows up badly in profit results is more clearly a candidate for total elimination than one that is inherently suitable but temporarily sick.

In applying the profit tests, a distinction must be made between long-run and short-run profits. Products that show comparatively low or negative net profits may still have incremental profits—that is, they may make contributions to general overheads that would not be made if the product were dropped. This sort of short-run consideration can lead to serious errors if it is projected too far into the future. Presumably, the growth of more profitable products should soak up the excess capacity that produces these incremental profits, and the continual stream of candidate products may in the long run produce a greater contribution to overheads than the old product that is retained because of its incremental showing.

The main economic difference between dropping and adding a product is, of course, sunk costs. Deletions that are decided upon solely on the basis of net profit, with no consideration given to the fact that costs are sunk, can lead to short-run losses. But, again, it may be that this is a more valid criterion than it appears to the economist, because executive time squandered on the squeaky wheel and on passed-up opportunities to substitute new and better products overbalance the sunk cost element.

V. SUMMARY

1. Product-line composition is a major facet of modern competition; and a company's achievements in new and improved products are an important test of its social contribution.

2. An underlying reason for adding a new product to the line is that it utilizes excess capacity. Broadly conceived, excess capacity occurs when it would cost the multiple-product firm less to make and sell the new product than it would cost a new com-

pany set up to produce only that product. Vertical integration and research can be viewed as phases of excess capacity that promote multiple-product lines.

3. Prospective profitability, in the narrow, cash-return sense is a key consideration in the selection of product-line additions. The relevant concept is incremental profits over the probable life cycle of the candidate product. Some standard of adequate incremental return is needed for this profitability test. Ideally it should be market cost of new capital, with allowance for special risks. Sometimes the standard is average past return, maximum alternative return, or some arbitrary profits goal.

4. Product-line strategy is a semi-independent consideration, though presumably the purpose of strategy is to make money in the long run. Strategic considerations reflect personal, technical, and competitive limitations on the range of product diversity. These simplifying rules often center on putting the firm's distinctive strength to its highest and noblest use.

5. How the candidate product's demand dovetails with that of existing products is an important selection criterion. Complementary or substitute relationships, or the tactical advantages of a full line underlie the more conventional test of common distribution channels.

6. A candidate product that is made from common raw materials, that uses existing production facilities, and/or, that can be effectively sold through the same sales organization, is likely to mop up excess capacity and use the company's distinctive know-how.

7. The problem of deciding on what products to drop is the converse of the problem of adding products, except that long-run cost functions are not reversible and specialized capital is not perfectly mobile. Hence the possibility of salvaging product-line mistakes by partial retreat should be explored before considering total elimination.

Chapter 4

DEMAND ANALYSIS

Demand Analysis

I. INTRODUCTION

DEMAND ANALYSIS seeks to search out and measure the forces that determine sales. There are many kinds of demand analysis, which differ in purposes, methods, and degrees of refinement.[1]

In this chapter we shall be concerned with the theory and measurement of demand from a management viewpoint, i.e., in terms of the executive decisions that call for demand analysis and the kinds of estimates and forecasts that can be made practically for industrial products.

Purposes of Demand Analysis

Demand analysis has two main managerial purposes: (1) forecasting sales, and (2) manipulating demand. There are other purposes, of course, but they are ancillary to the main economic problem of planning for profit. For instance, demand analysis is an important benchmark for appraising salesmen's performance and for setting their sales quotas. It is also used to watch the trend of the company's competitive position. Occasionally a demand analysis is used in court, for damage suits and tax cases, to show what would have happened if things had been different. However, this chapter concentrates primarily on forecasting and promotion of sales.

---

[1] There is one kind that doesn't fit our initial description, because it analyzes demand, not as an effect of controlling factors, but simply as historical patterns of sales behavior that can be broken into long-run trends, cyclical fluctuations, and seasonal variations. The value of such analysis depends on stability of the patterns and on faith that they will continue into the relevant future. For the jobs that demand analysis must do, it must usually be built of sterner intellectual stuff.

Forecasting Demand

Forecasting is by far the most common use of demand studies. Since the sales forecast is the foundation for planning all phases of the company's operations, it follows that purchasing commitments, production schedules, inventory plans, cash budgets, and capital expenditure programs all hinge on the sales forecast.

To get full value from the forecasting of sales, a large company usually needs an established routine and much top-level coordination. A producer of photographic supplies uses a top-level planning committee headed by a full-time planning manager and comprised of production, selling, and finance executives. The committee is responsible for working up quarterly and annual sales forecasts that are made the basis for monthly directives to operating people. For instance, plant managers get production orders, sales branches get sales quotas, and warehousemen get estimates of shipping volume for the coming month. Working out these monthly figures from the quarterly forecast can be an intricate job of coordinating cash balances, buying, inventory levels, warehouse space, production capacity, and so forth. When operating plans cannot be set up that tie in easily with the forecasts, the committee itself tackles questions of capital outlays that are signaled to make the plan fit together.

Thus, in this company, the sales forecast plays the pivotal role in the whole scheme of things to come. In an industry, which is subject to wide seasonal swings in sales, there is an optimum production program which minimizes the total costs by balancing the costs (and risks) of inventory accummulation in slack seasons against the savings of larger lots and level production. In shooting for this operating program forecasts of sales obviously play a basic role.

Manipulating Demand

Although the scope and use of demand analysis has grown prodigiously in recent years, there are relatively few firms that take full advantage of it as a technique for formulating business-getting plans and policies. Sales forecasting is mostly passive; it estimates external economic factors and predicts the resulting sales volume the firm can expect if it continues on its present course. The forecasts are then used to program personnel, purchases, and production—the sales forecast being regarded as some-thing imposed upon the company and beyond its control.

This passive attitude toward sales forecasting stems from failure to recognize the full potentials of demand analysis as a guide for manipulating demand. When management looks upon the fore-cast of the industry's sales, now commonly prepared by many companies, as merely the starting point in manipulating as well as forecasting the company's sales, it can convert forecasting tech-niques into a powerful tool for formulating sales policy and sales strategy. Forecasts, instead of merely being indications of what general business conditions will do to the company's sales, can then become action guides by showing the probable results of the various plans and policies that management may adopt to exploit (or fight back) those externally imposed economic conditions and to select the course of action which will maximize earnings in the light of changed outside conditions.

To use demand studies in an active rather than a passive way, management must recognize the degree to which sales are a result not only of the external economic environment but also of the ac-tion of the company itself. Sales volume will differ, depending upon how much money is spent on advertising, what price policy is adopted, what product improvements are made, how accurately salesmen and sales effort are matched with potential sales in the various territories, and so forth. Estimates of what will happen with no changes in policy are important, but this is only one of many alternative programs. Passive forecasts should also be used as a benchmark for estimating the consequences of other plans for adjusting prices, promotion and/or products.

Excluded Kinds of Analysis

Our survey of demand analysis will omit several kinds of mar-ket research that do not raise major problems of economic anal-ysis. Notable among the omissions are: "consumer surveys," "product acceptance testing," and "sales analysis."

Much market research consists of so-called consumer surveys, i.e., studies of buyers' motives, attitudes, preference, and purchas-ing habits. Information is gathered from personal interviews and mailed questionnaires and is supplemented by indirect study through interviews with people in a position to observe buyers' activities. Such research, when competently and skeptically conducted, can shed much light on the character of demand and be particularly useful in the competitive struggle. It can bring about the sharpening of marketing targets, improvement of distribution methods and sales promotion techniques, and adaptation of the products to consumers' wants.

In an economy in which the consumer is king, what the public wants and will buy must govern basic decisions. A major task of demand analysis is to find out exactly what kind of product the public wants: product testing of the kind used to appraise the probable consumer-acceptability of a new product and to point to needed improvements of old products.

Sales analysis (i.e., classification and summarization of past sales by products, areas, customer types, etc.) is usually a routine operation which has little interest for economic analysts. Although the plan of classification of sales was presumably thought helpful for past managerial problems, many firms continue routine statistical breakdowns that have lost their usefulness.

Important though these kinds of demand analysis are for competitive survival and for an understanding of the operations of non-price competition, they are largely beyond the scope of this book because their interest is technical, rather than economic.

Plan of Chapter

This chapter is organized principally on the basis of the purposes of demand analysis, rather than its methods, because a purpose is the starting point for any research. It is impossible, though, to make a clean separation in the discussion between the forecasting and sales-policy purposes, which have much overlap in methods and many useful relationships. Thus, the relation of price to sales volume is usually valuable primarily for price policy on highly distinctive products; but when competition leaves no room for price jurisdiction, the relation may be useful as a forecasting device in terms of expected prices of the product and its substitutes. Such dual purposes and overlapping methods make the chapter structure a matter of emphasis and most common usage instead of a set of watertight cells.

The first step in any analysis, however, is to examine the conceptual groundwork of the problem, i.e., to find the precise question to be answered. Accordingly the next part of the analysis, Section II, surveys the theory of demand to help frame the research problem so that it will be precisely relevant for the managerial decision. Section III examines the principles underlying forecasting methods. Section IV concentrates on relationships of price to demand, and Section V deals with relations of income to demand—two aspects that are central to most sales problems. In Section VI, are presented some illustrations of more general statistical analyses that can be viewed as multiple-purpose and that have all the frailties of multiple-purpose tools. Section VII summarizes a study of automobile demand, and Section VIII, a study of demand for steel.

II. DEMAND THEORY

If demand analysis is to be helpful in solving management problems, an understanding of demand theory is needed. Theory contributes both to the design of investigations that are relevant to management problems, and to the evaluation of empirical research.

What is meant by demand? What governs its behavior? There is no single, universally useful concept of demand. Instead, there are different concepts for different problems. The demand determinants, as well as their relative importance, differ for the various concepts. The notion of demand that is appropriate depends upon the precise question to be answered. For instance, the question "How much furniture will the American people buy in the next five years?" presents one setting for analysis. It calls for a look at trends in the number and size of new families (to show expansion of the market), and consideration of recent production levels (to indicate replacement demand).

Quite a different framework is presented in the question "What will our sales to dealers in Ohio be during the next six months if we cut our price 8 per cent next week and have the cut well advertised?" This question is one of short-run regional demand sensitivity to price and promotion. These two questions are answered with two separate demand functions based on different data, assumptions, and approximations.

In order to shape an empirical analysis of demand so that it will answer the precise question that is relevant, it is desirable to be familiar with various concepts of demand and know which concept is appropriate for each sort of management problem. A convenient way to survey this domain of demand theory is to make several distinctions between different kinds of demand concepts.

Demand Schedules vs. Demand Functions

The number of television sets sold by Dumont during a particular month in 1951 was determined by many factors, among them (1) Dumont's price, (2) prices of rival sets, (3) the effectiveness of Dumont's advertising (past as well as present and absolutely as well as relative to rivals), (4) the design of Dumont's product (relative to rivals'), (5) the amount (and distribution) of purchasing power, (6) time payment terms, and (7) people's expectations as to color television, and their guesses about the effect of war on future shortages and prices.

One of these many demand determinants, Dumont's price, has been singled out for special attention in conventional economic analysis. This price–quantity relationship is portrayed as a demand schedule (or demand curve) which shows the amounts that would be sold at various prices in a given place on a given date. Classical theorists are quite aware that price is not the sole factor determining sales, and that changes in other conditions can have important sales effects on a given price. However, the effect of changes in other conditions is viewed as a "shift" of the demand schedule, meaning that the quantity sold at each price will be different because incomes are greater, or down payments lower. To sharpen traditional analysis, these other conditions are therefore frozen in some given shape, and attention is directed at the relation of price to sales.[2]

But this price relation is not usually as important to management as an understanding of the "shifts" in the demand function. For many products price has little effect on sales volume in relevant ranges of price level. Other factors, particularly the level of business activity, have a bigger impact on sales of most products.

If these shifts in the conventional price—quantity curve can be related systematically to other demand factors, such as changes in buyers' income or advertising, we can transform the *demand*

---

[2] Classical theorists had a purpose (aside from simplifying the analysis) in concentrating on the price-sales relation: their aim was to find the determinants of value, resource allocation, and income distribution in a stationary economic environment, and for this, price was the key variable.

schedule into a more general *demand function* by relating sales to several independent variables, such as those listed above for television sets.

What are the factors that should be included in a demand function? There is no general answer to this question, because the determinants of demand depend on the product and on the demand situation.

It is impossible to make a list of generic demand factors that are important for every product. Nevertheless there are a few that underlie demand behavior of so many products that they deserve a place on a check-list of possible demand determinants for all consumer goods. The most common ones are: income, sales promotion, product-improvement, and price. For consumer goods, buyers' income is the factor most nearly universal, since it determines the amount of cash in buyers' hands and strongly affects their expectations of future income. The relations of demand to prices, advertising, competition, and speculation hinge more on the nature of the product; factors that are dominant for some products may be quite irrelevant or unimportant for others. The measurable determinants of demand for producers' goods usually differ from those for consumers' goods; they also vary considerably among products. Typically, personal income is displaced by business profits (e.g., corporate profits) or by business activity (e.g., an index of industrial production). For example there is a close relation between construction activity and the demand for plaster board. Products that are durable (whether producers' goods or consumers' goods) have demand factors that are different and more intricate than are those for perishables; and products whose demand is derived often take on the determinants of demand for the parent products. We shall discuss some of these contrasts below.

Producers' Goods vs. Consumers' Goods

Generally speaking, the reasons for expecting distinctive demand behavior for producers' goods are three: (1) buyers are professionals, and hence more expert, price-wise and sensitive to substitutes; (2) their motives are more purely economic: products are bought, not for themselves alone, but for their profit prospects; and (3) demand, being derived from consumption demand, fluctuates differently and generally more violently. However, it is easy to exaggerate the differences in demand characteristics between producers' goods and consumers' goods. In the first place, the distinction itself, being based on who buys and why, is bound to be fuzzy. Is a salesman-owned Chevrolet a producer's good? In the second place there are thousands of incidental needs in any business that are simply not worth the cost of scientific purchase planning. In the third place, the human element in business purchasing is badly underrated—high-styled equipment and personal fancy create demand for milling machinery as well as for automobiles.

Durable Goods vs. Perishable Goods

Durable products present more complicated problems of demand analysis than products that give a one-shot service. Sales of non-durables are made largely to meet current demand, which depends on current conditions. Sales of durables, on the other hand, add an increment to a stock of existing goods that dole out their services slowly over several years. It is thus a common practice to segregate current demand for durables in terms of replacement of old products and expansion of the total stock.

One characteristic of demand for durables is a volatile relation to business conditions: since current output of a durable provides only a small fraction of the total current services demanded of that kind of product, sales are hypersensitive to small changes in demand for the service. If we assume, for instance, that normal annual automobile production is used (1) to replace 10 per cent of the existing stock of cars, and (2) to expand the car population by 5 per cent, then a 3 per cent increase in the demand for motor transportation will raise the new-car demand by about 20 per cent.

But demand analysis for durable goods is by no means this simple. Both replacement and expansion have manifold sets of demand determinants. Continuing the automobile illustration, replacement demand depends on the value of existing cars as transportation relative to their value as scrap iron. When expansion demand spurts up suddenly, used-car values usually go higher than scrap values; as a result the scrapping rate, and thus replacement demand falls. If the public want fewer cars (expansion rate negative) the scrappage rate must be higher than the level of new car production. This excess scrappage is possible if scrap prices are high enough, and the obsolescence price-spread between new and old cars wide enough (a) to take the old cars off the road, and (b) to cover the necessary costs of producing new cars.

The most important replacement determinant is the obsolescence rate, which sets prices in the second-hand markets. Since many cars are abandoned without regard to salvage value, scrap iron prices play a much less important role. Obsolescence is pervasive and strategic in the American economy in determining the level of business activity, and it should be appreciated for its capricious and volatile self. Physical deterioration is rarely a deciding factor in replacement of durable goods. For consumer products—and to a surprising extent for producer goods, too—style, convenience, and income play a dominant role in demand, for even such work-horse products as home furnaces.

Occasionally a technological upheaval can produce a blast of obsolescence that wipes out any distinction between expansion and replacement. Thus the demand for Diesel locomotives is not affected by fluctuations in demand for rail transport, nor cotton pickers by cotton acreage. For such major innovations, demand depends only on cultural lags, financial exigencies, and rivalry of alternative investments.

The determinants of expansion demand for durables are not different in theory from those for non-durables. In practice, however, a decision to buy a durable good is more complicated, because guesses about the future stand out more sharply in the buyer's mind. He worries about future maintenance and operating costs in relation to his future income and other demands; he takes a guess at future sales values; and he wonders whether prices will rise or fall if he postpones his purchase. Thus for durable goods [3] not only present prices and incomes, but their current trends and the state of optimism are proper variables to include in the demand function. Expectation about improved product designs are also important: leaks dry up demand and

---

[3] That is, for any purchase of a large stock of future services, such as a raw materials inventory or long-term wage contract. Price expectations play a dominant role in industrial inventory policy, but it is always called "price protection," never "speculation."

cause price concessions in current models.   This has been notable in television, where rapid obsolescence of receivers has caused a cascade of prices.

Derived Demand vs. Autonomous Demand

When demand for a product is tied to the purchase of some parent product, its demand is called "derived."   Sometimes the dependent product is a component part (e.g., demand for doors derived from demand for houses).   Sometimes dependence comes from complementary consumption (e.g., pretzels from beer).   It is hard to find a product in modern civilization whose demand is wholly independent of all others.   Demand for all producers' goods, raw materials and component parts, is derived.   So "derived demand" is quite common, and for practical analysis the distinction between it and autonomous demand is arbitrary and a matter of degree.

Demand that is derived is generally supposed to have less price elasticity than autonomous demand, assuming substitutes are equally available.   This is partly a result of dilution by other components whose prices are sticky.   A 10 per cent cut in the price of steel would cause only about a 1 per cent change in the cost of a car, assuming all other cost prices stayed the same.

Some products are so closely tied to others in their uses that they have no distinctive demand determinants of their own. When such a product has only one use and its proportion to the parent-good is fixed (e.g., television antennas), there is no point in distinguishing it as separate from the parent.   But fixed proportions are rare; more usually there is substitution leeway in the proportions as well as more than one parent use.   Crude rubber demand shows both of these characteristics when related to the population of motor vehicles.

As variability in the proportions and the number of uses increases, it is hard to tie demand down to parent products.   For instance, small electric motors have no primary uses, but to analyze their demand in terms of their thousands of parent uses is impossibly tedious.   Sulphuric acid is another such product. Capital goods (plant and equipment) have a derived demand, but variations in the actual (and expected) intensities of use are so wide that analysis in terms of finished product demand is either too broad or too approximate to be of much help.   Derived demand facilitates forecasting when proportions of the two products are fairly stable and there is a rigid time-lead in the parent product's demand.

Industry Demand vs. Company Demand

Many management problems require analyses that distinguish industry demand from company demand and explore the relationship between them. For example, a projection of industry sales is usually an intermediate step in forecasting company sales; and intelligent price leadership (and follower-ship too) is based on an understanding of the relation of the company demand to that of competing firms.

To explore this relationship in general terms we must first answer the question: What is the appropriate industry? Next we must examine the way the structure of the industry affects the relationship of company demand to industry demand. For most products the concept of an "industry" composed of a group of closely competitive firms has usefulness, despite the difficulties of neat definition. We have seen (Chapter 2) that for economic analysis an industry should ideally be defined as a group of firms serving the same group of buyers and selling products that are close substitutes for each other, but are distant substitutes for the products of other industries and thereby isolated from them by this "gap in the chain of substitutes." [4] Because the products of most modern firms are physically and/or psychologically differentiated from rivals', industries cannot, even in principle, always be defined with precision, and there are unavoidable overlaps. Conventional industrial groupings, though not delineated in terms of substitution elasticity, sometimes approximate these results.

An industry demand schedule represents the relation of the price of the product to the quantity that will be bought from all firms. It has a clear meaning when the products of the various firms are close substitutes, when they differ markedly from those of bordering industries, and when they have a well-defined price level. When, on the other hand, there is considerable product differentiation within the industry, and substitute competition with other industries, then the concept of an industry demand

---

[4] Technically this gap is sometimes defined in terms of such low substitutability that a change in the industry's price will not cause enough price retaliation to affect the industry's demand.

schedule becomes nebulous.   Adding Cadillacs and Crosleys and averaging their prices does not produce a very meaningful demand schedule.

TABLE 4–1

CLASSIFICATION OF INDUSTRIES BY NUMBER OF SELLERS AND DEGREE OF PRODUCT DIFFERENTIATION

Product Differentiation	Number of Sellers		
	One Seller (A)	Few Sellers (B)	Many Sellers (C)
Standardized Products (1)	Single-firm Monopoly	Homogeneous Oligopoly (B–1)	Pure Competition (C–1)
Differentiated Products (2)		Differentiated Oligopoly (B–2)	Monopolistic Competition (C–2)

Differences in Market Structure

The industry demand schedule is, however, a useful benchmark for studying the individual seller's demand.   The relation of the individual company's sales to its price derives from the industry's demand schedule, but the relationship differs depending upon the structure of the industry.   The two most important aspects of structure for this purpose are: (1) the number of sellers and (2) the degree of product differentiation.   Applying these two bases of classification of industries, we obtain the kinds of competitive situations shown in Table 4–1.

The competitive type of cell (A) is a single-firm monopoly—one seller of a unique product.   Here the company demand curve is the same as the industry demand curve for the entire commodity. Conceptually, the seller's price—quantity relationship is quite definite and knowable, but in practice substitute competition is so pervasive that anything resembling single-firm monopoly is hard to find in modern industry.

The competitive situation of cell (B–1) when sellers are few and their products are standardized is called homogeneous oligopoly. Aluminum, steel, and cement approximate these conditions.   In this competitive situation, business is highly transferable among

rivals.   The hallmark of this kind of oligopoly is recognized interdependence of demand, and preoccupation with rivals' reactions
to the company's pricing policy.   The company's own demand
curve is uncertain, depending upon what its rivals do.   When
products are nearly identical, sellers must usually charge the same
prices to stay in the market; so there is little uncertainty about
whether a price reduction will be met, but there is a hazard that
a price cut that is made openly may set off a chain reaction in the
form of a price war.   In general, under stabilized pure oligopoly
situation, the company's demand curve is a miniature of the
industry's demand function and has the same general characteristics.

In many manufacturing industries a few large sellers account
for a substantial portion of the industry's output.   But most
products are not uniform enough in an economic sense to make
homogeneous oligopoly a dominant competitive type.

A more common competitive situation is shown in cell (B-2),
differentiated oligopoly—few sellers and differentiated products.
Examples include automobiles, television, refrigerators and radios.
When rival sellers' products differ physically or in terms of consumer acceptance, the company's demand is less closely interdependent with the industry demand, and the individual firm has
more leeway in manipulating its price differentials, particularly
with informal concessions.   It has considerably more independence in promotional outlays and product improvement; in
fact, in this area oligopolistic restraint and uncertainties operate
less fully than in pricing policies.   Thus this competitive situation
differs from pure oligopoly.   Rivals may charge somewhat different prices and these inter-firm differentials are not rigid.
Market shares are less stable than with standardized products,
being shifted by non-price competition as well as price advantages.
Thus the firm may have an independent demand function.   It
is not a mere miniature of the industry demand, but reflects the
impact upon the company's market share of variation in its
price spreads, product superiority, and/or relative efficiency or
amount of promotional outlay.

Cell (C-1) represents industries with many sellers and a
standardized product, a competitive situation called pure competition.   The industry's demand curve is completely divorced
from that of the individual seller, who has no choice but to meet

market prices of rivals too numerous to be concerned about re-taliation. Hence the demand curve for the individual company is a horizontal straight line at the level of the market price.

Cell (C–2)—many sellers and differentiated products—is some-times labeled monopolistic competition. (The word has also been used more broadly by Edward Chamberlin and his disciples to include all competitive situations except pure competition.) The demand curve for the industry has little meaning for such industries. When the degree of product differentiation is large, the individual seller's demand function is like that of a single-firm monopolist in that he does not worry about the effect of his prices upon prices that rivals will charge. It differs from the monopolist in that the demand for a single seller may be affected by the number of rivals, their products, and prices. Generally, then, the demand curve for the firm in such a competitive situation has more price elasticity than the industry's. Gasoline stations and laundries are familiar examples in this cell.

Demand Analysis in Terms of Market-Share

The conceptual distinction between industry demand and com-pany demand is most useful when the boundaries of the industry are clearly definable in terms of a gap in the chain of substitutes (i.e., products that differ sharply in terms of substitutability from those of other industries), and when rival firms are large enough and similar enough to plan in terms of market share.

The short-run characteristics of industry demand are typically such that substitutes are not close enough to make it necessary, or even possible, to analyze demand in terms of the effect of prices relative to substitutes outside the industry. Hence, except for long-run speculations, the industry demand function can usually be expressed in terms of the absolute levels of demand determination. In contrast, the company demand schedule, in most situations that are interesting from a practical standpoint (i.e., excepting single-firm monopoly and pure competition at the other pole), often dictates a different kind of analysis. Empirical research needs to be framed in terms of price spreads or ratios over rivals, and of the effect of these price differentials upon market share. Thus the focus of the analysis is on comparative prices and the distribution of a given patronage among rival con-cerns.

For example, the sensitivity of gasoline market share to price spreads can be roughly measured. Narrowing or widening the differentials between the branded product of the price leader and the local private brand of the cut-rate distributor has a prompt effect on retail patronage. And there is considerable evidence to support the conclusion that the sensitivity of market share rises sharply when the spread widens beyond a critical point. This critical point varies among areas, and apparently also with motorists' affluence. Sensitivity also depends upon how well publicized and easily available the lower price is. In addition to open price premiums over distributors' brands, there are unpublicized differentials over the invasion brands of major oil companies that may be price leaders in other parts of the country, but do not sell their main brand in the invaded market.

Up to now we have discussed only the relation of price to sales. Price is only one of many determinants of demand. The level and distribution of incomes, the volume of business activity, the amount and quality of sales promotion—and many other factors in addition to price—determine the sales rate for the industry and for the firm. And each of these other determinants may affect company demand differently from industry demand.

In studying the effect of promotion upon sales, industry demand requires a different framework of analysis from company demand. For example, the aggregate advertising of the cigarette industry can be related to total cigarette sales (recognizing, to be sure, that cigarettes vie with other forms of tobacco and with all consumption expenditures, but so indirectly that it doesn't matter). In contrast, the company's promotional elasticity could be studied in terms of the effect upon Camel's market share caused by the absolute or relative amount of Camel advertising as compared with the other two leaders.

Market Share for Forecasting and Planning

The industry–company distinction is useful in demand forecasting, where it is common practice to predict first the total industry sales, and then the company's share of the industry market. The amount of sales of the entire industry is usually beyond the control of a single member company, unless that company happens to account for a dominant proportion of the total industry sales. Industry sales volume is largely a consequence of vast impersonal economic forces over which the individual company has little control. Here, forecasting in the sense of estimating what will happen, is the dominant activity, and company strategy plays a minor role.

The per cent of industry volume that the company obtains is, to a much greater degree, subject to control by the company, by means of its marketing (and other) activities. To be sure, the past activities (e.g., prices, amount of advertising, number of salesmen, number of outlets) affect the present and future percentage, and variation in these activities has a delayed effect upon company share. Nevertheless, this position is, over any reasonable period, subject to manipulation by the company at a cost, so that the issue is, "What promotional, pricing, and product-improvement activities would be effective and also economically justified?" Thus, doing something to change demand is dominant here, and forecasting is recessive.

When the structure of the industry makes a market share approach feasible for passive forecasting, it is usually useful for active sales policy as well. For example, in dealing with the ubiquitous problem of price-shaving, the manufacturer of a standard or premium product may make the decision to meet competitors' price concessions depend upon the effect they have on his market share. In promotion policy, similarly, this distinction is valid. For example, one oil company arrived at its advertising outlay for gasoline by observing the effect of varying its advertising upon its market share; it found that x cents a gallon tended to stabilize this share.

"Market share" concepts of demand are most usable in mature, well-defined industries whose products are relatively homogeneous —e.g., steel or cement. In this cultural setting, market share objectives often are dominantly defensive. Emphasis is put on the first step, forecasting industry sales, and the second step— planning marketing strategy to affect market share—is, for established firms, largely a matter of keeping abreast of competitive developments, e.g., overtaking product innovators, meeting price cutters, countering advertising aggressors.

Short-Run Demand vs. Long-Run Demand

A distinction between long-run and short-run demand functions is useful for many problems. Short-run demand refers to existing demand with its immediate reaction to price changes, income fluctuation, etc., whereas long-run demand is that which will ultimately exist as a result of the changes in pricing, promotion, or product improvement, after enough time is allowed to let the market adjust itself to the new situation. For example, in the short run, a cut in the price of home heating oil will increase consumption if it induces people to keep their houses hotter, but in the long run the price cut will increase consumption by inducing more people to install oil burners. Thus a temporary price cut cannot be viewed in the same light as one that is expected to stick. Consequences on competition also depend on this distinction: in the short run, the question is whether competitors will meet the cut, while in the long run, entry of potential competitors, exploration of substitutes, and other complex and unforeseeable effects may result. (See Chapter 7, "Basic Price.")

Factors that cause these differences between short-run and long-run demand fall in two categories: (1) cultural lags in information and experience; and (2) capital investments required of buyers to shift consumption patterns.

A price change today starts a chain of adjustments in customers' attitudes and competitors' prices that may not be completed for years, even if nothing further occurs. This is partly a matter of market information: there may be delay in learning about changes in relative prices among substitutes. But there is also delay in acting on these new prices, because use-patterns are sticky, and research (as in metallurgy) or alterations of the product are sometimes needed. These lags are most serious when the product whose price is changed is new. For example, reduction in long-lines telephone rates permits executive and administrative economies as compared with communication by mail or travel, but it takes time and practice to realize these benefits, particularly when the substitutes are as distant and diverse as for telephones. Although long-run growth is not wholly a price phenomenon, price-cuts can accelerate the rate of growth considerably.

Another whole set of time factors in response to price change is related to the new investment that must be made to take advantage of the new price. Thus mass consumption of frozen foods required an investment by producers and consumers in new refrigerators designed with double- or triple-sized freezer compartments. Products that require a large initial investment in consumption equipment quite commonly meet sticky and price-insensitive buying habits in established markets. In such cases, industry promotional effort expanding sales (as opposed to taking sales from rivals in the industry) may aim at selling the equipment rather than the product and must then fight in a broad arena of substitute competition on the basis of long-run price trends and performance. For example, the oil industry has promoted not fuel oil but "automatic heat" equipment in its battle with coal and gas for the home heating market.

Demand Fluctuations vs. Long-Run Trends

Many management problems call for forecasts of the way demand will shift with the passage of time. These time-patterns of demand behavior are quite different from the concepts discussed above in distinguishing between a short-run demand curve and a long-run curve.

The long-run vs. short-run distinction is based on a difference in flexibility of demand in response to a given change in prices or selling tactics, and is most useful in predicting consequences of manipulating the demand-creating factors, e.g., pricing for market penetration. The essential element of the distinction is not time but the scale of upheaval in the *status quo* necessary to make the best adjustment to new conditions.

Several kinds of time patterns can be distinguished: time-of-day, day-of-month, seasonal, cyclical, and trend. Forecasting the briefer time patterns, though important for many businesses, presents no serious analytical problems. But forecasting how sales will fluctuate from year to year and projecting long-term trends in demand encounter intriguing difficulties.

The difference between forecasting year-to-year changes and forecasting underlying trends is analogous to a distinction between business cycles and secular economic development. The external factors that are important for cyclical forecasts are different from trend projections. In year-to-year changes, much of the setting stays constant—competitive structure, market position, quality, and sometimes even prices (relative to substitutes and competitors, if not absolutely). The problem can then be narrowed down to a relation of sales pulsations to a few strategic variables, such as income, business activity, and competitive price differentials. For the long trend, in contrast everything is fluid, and the effects of year-to-year determinants are buried by basic changes in the framework, e.g., shifts in taste, technology, and way of life in a laboristic, urban, welfare state.

Forecasts of year-to-year swings in demand should be the foundation for programing the firm's operations: i.e., purchasing, production, manpower, inventory and cash plans, budgets, and schedules. Because of the importance of these annual and quarterly sales forecasts, the bulk of a company's demand analysis work is directed at exploring these capricious cyclical shifts of demand.

Projections of long-range trends of demand are useful primarily for planning investments and other long-term commitments in personnel and location. For example, in a decision to expand capacity, which usually anticipates some measure of future growth and involves a long waiting period to get a return on investment, projections of the trend and location of demand are the pivotal estimates. Though margins of uncertainty are wide and are accentuated by unknown expansion plans of rivals and by risks of obsolescence of products and methods, the decision hinges on the projection of a growth trend.[5]

In the atomic age, a long-run forecast is necessarily a speculation. The relevance of the distant past to the distant future is quite debatable. But when history is used as a basis for projections of trends, questions arise as to how far back to go, what form of curve to fit, and what kinds of corrections to make for upheavals in prices and technology. The choice of historical analysis period is arbitrary; there is no un-ambiguous past period that defines a projectible trend. And the ambiguity is intensified by the choice between linear and different kinds of curved functions that can reasonably be used for extrapolating the past into the future.

Total Market vs. Market Segments

The comprehensiveness of the demand problem sets the framework for analysis. Some problems, such as sales forecasting, call

---

[5] These uncertainties in long-range projections of sales trends make long-range "expansion programs" mostly dream stuff. In practice, definitive plant commitments are often put off until orders press on capacity; this piles capital formation on the crests of booms. Another effect of uncertainty in forecasting is the tendency to put a premium on built-in flexibility as an investment characteristic. Although a flexible plant is usually not the most efficient one, the added cost is properly viewed as insurance against forecasting errors.

for an analysis that includes the total market. Other problems, notably, some pricing, promotional, and distribution problems, call for analyses of separate market segments that have homogeneous demand characteristics.

Total market size depends partly on how broad a conception of the "product" is appropriate for the management problem. For example, is the market for Celotex insulation board confined to other brands of insulation board, or should it include the numerous close substitutes (e.g., gypsum board, rock wool, etc.)? [6] Market segments can be carved out in several dimensions, e.g., geographic areas,[7] by sub-products, by uses of the product, by distribution channels, by sensitivity to price, by size of customer, and so forth. Each of these segments may differ significantly in such things as delivered prices, net profit margins, substitutes, competition, seasonal patterns, and cyclical sensitivity. When these differences are great, analysis of demand for a single product in terms of causal relations is best confined to these individual market segments; but frequently, interflows between segments make the total market more than the sum of the parts in terms of significant controlling factors. But occasionally the similarity of behavior of different kinds of demand is stable enough to allow reliable statistical analysis of many segments combined.

Demand interrelations of market segments are more complex when the demand function includes a number of sub-products. If these articles are clearly complementary, or clearly substitutes for each other, they may be analyzed as a single product. But sub-products that are substitutes for one customer are often not substitutes for another customer. Adding the demand curves for the two customers is arithmetic that hides the relevant demand determinants. Statistically, a broad-coverage demand function that includes a whole line of products is sometimes more reliable

---

6 What is a product? Economic definitions usually run in terms of similarity from the standpoint of substitution, and involve theoretical subtleties that needn't concern us here, although the concept is reflected in some parts of this book. We have also used the businessman's typical idea that a product is homogeneous in respect to production rather than consumption: paper milk cartons are in the paper industry rather than the container industry.

7 Measuring geographical distribution of income and other basic demand determinants for setting geographical sales quotas has developed into big business. For example the magazine *Sales Management* puts out an annual "Survey of Buying Power," which estimates personal incomes in every county and in most cities of over 10,000 population.

in forecasting than analysis of a single product in a single market. When an industry demand function is made up of products that are highly similar (e.g., gasoline), forecasting accuracy is usually greater than for company sales, and probably the best demand function statistically is the total demand curve for consumer expenditures.[8]

Broadening the coverage of the concept of "product" tends to make empirical analysis easier, but also tends to make it less useful managerially. Even for forecasting, a narrow concept of "product" enhances usefulness. And for manipulating prices, promotion, product-improvement, or distribution channels in order to increase sales competitively, a segment concept of demand is often more appropriate than a product concept that has greater coverage.

Elasticity of Demand

Elasticity of demand is a common device for describing the shape of the demand function. In general it measures the sensitivity of sales to changes in a particular causal factor. More precisely, demand elasticity is the per cent increase in sales that accompanies a one per cent increase in any demand determinant. Although originally the concept referred only to price-sales relations, elasticity can be generalized to apply to each demand determinant.

Three kinds of demand elasticity are important for almost all consumers' goods: price elasticity, income elasticity, and promotional elasticity. A price elasticity of —5 means that a 10 per cent rise in prices cuts physical volume of sales by 50 per cent; an income elasticity of 1 means that sales vary in proportion to income; one concept of promotional elasticity of .5 says that $5,000 added to a $100,000 advertising budget will raise sales from $1,000,000 to $1,025,000. Per cent change, proportionality relations, and dollar changes are three different ways of stating the same basic meaning of elasticity.

The elasticity of each demand determinant has several sub-

---

8 This tendency toward increasing statistical stability is probably caused by the diminishing degrees of freedom of buyers' choice as the area of analysis broadens, and to the diminishing number of independent causal variables. Thus, in the total consumption function, prices and promotion play a negligible role compared to consumer income.

types, such as industry elasticity, market-share elasticity, and expectations elasticity, that apply the sensitivity index to the concept of demand appropriate for particular demand problems. The most important of these are industry elasticity and market-share elasticity. For price, a sharp distinction must be made between industry demand elasticity and the company's share elasticity. Industry elasticity measures the change in total industry sales as the industrywide level of price changes. Market-share elasticity relates the company's share of industry sales to the spread of its price over industry prices. Share elasticity depends primarily on the similarity of the product in the minds of buyers. For example, a Mobilgas station loses market-share promptly to a neighboring Texaco station whose price is half a cent a gallon less. The industry-share distinction in elasticity can be applied to promotion as well as price.

Although income elasticity can also be broken into industry and share elasticity, this breakdown is less significant, since income is not comparable to price and promotion as a competitive weapon. While there are shifts of market shares as a result of income changes these shifts are beyond management's control, at least in the short run. In a longer run, however, management can use product quality and promotion to aim at income sectors that are stable cyclically or that are growing in importance. Thus, to a degree, income share elasticity is manipulatable, but the actual variations in income are not controlled as are price and promotion variations.

Share elasticity is a general concept that includes the effect of various rivals' changes in price and promotion on the company's share of sales: it refers to the effects of changes by a single competitor, by several of them together, or by the entire industry, depending on the practical problem. The industry, too, has share elasticity, with respect to substitute competition—e.g., oil, gas and coal in home heating. Most commonly, however, the term refers to a company's share, paralleling the concept of company demand as opposed to industry demand.[9]

Expectations elasticity refers to the responsiveness of sales to buyers' guesses about the future values of various demand determinants, such as future price of the commodity (or of its substitutes), future incomes of buyers, or future shortages. These

[9] The term "cross elasticity" is a similar concept that has wide currency. It differs from share elasticity in that cross elasticity is measured in terms of absolute sales rather than per cent share.

various kinds of expectations have a powerful effect upon the timing of demand for many products, notably those which are durable, and hence consist of a stock of future services, and those which are storable and subject to resale. Conceivably there is an expectation elasticity for each of the major determinants of demand. Price and income expectations are normally, however, the only ones that have practical importance. Management readily recognizes that the timing of purchases is often governed by the buyers' speculations on prices and that the drying up of demand in the early stages of recession is likely to be due more to fears about future income than to the pinch of present income. Nevertheless, precise measurements of either of these concepts of elasticity of expectations is usually quite out of the question.

The concept of elasticity is easiest to use when the demand function takes the form of a hyperbola, because elasticity is then constant at all points on the curve and equal to the exponent of the variable in question.[10] For this reason, and because this form has some theoretical foundation, hyperbolic demand functions are used fairly widely in empirical work.

Demand elasticity is not by itself a measure of the importance of independent variables in causing changes in sales, since changes depend upon the volatility of variables as well as the effect of unit changes in them.

Problems of obtaining empirical estimates of the relationship of the sales to the various demand determinants will be discussed in the rest of this chapter. To do so we shall need to recognize several kinds of demand functions that are appropriate to different management problems. The purpose of the foregoing survey of demand theory has been to lay the foundation for these empirical considerations, rather than to go into the question of the measurability of each kind of theoretical concept in the present status of econometrics.

Summary

Sales are a result of many forces in addition to price. Consequently, the basic concept of empirical analysis is not usually the price-quantity schedule, but rather the mathematical relation be-

---

[10] Thus, if sales are a hyperbolic function of three variables x, y, and z, in the form $S = x^a y^b z^c$, the y-elasticity of demand is $e = \dfrac{y \delta S}{S \delta y} = \dfrac{y}{x^a y^b z^c} \cdot b \cdot x^a y^{b-1} z^c$, which reduces to: $e = b$.

tween sales and the measurable demand conditions that determine sales.

The nature of a product's demand function depends on economic characteristics, notably whether it is durable, whether it is a producers' or consumers' good, whether its demand is derived or autonomous. The relation of industry demand to company demand depends on the structure of competition. Dual classification on the basis of number of sellers and degree of product differentiation reveals competitive types that are distinctive in respect to this demand relation. Many management problems, e.g., forecasting, pricing, and promotion, call for demand analysis in terms of what causes changes in market share.

Some problems may call for study of short-run demand, while others require estimates of long-run demand, taking into account cultural lags, and capital investments required to shift consumption patterns.

Estimating year-to-year fluctuations in demand often involves finding the relation of the product's sales to a few strategic variables, such as income, industrial production, and stocks of used equipment. Projections of trends involve analysis of structural changes in terms of more basic variables.

Demand analysis must be designed for specific purposes. Conceptual distinctions help formulate both the purpose and the method of empirical analysis and educated guesses. In order to make a sophisticated and systematic demand study, the management problem should be put into a conceptual framework that draws upon demand theory.

"Elasticity of demand" is a term that is widely used to apply only to price–output relations. It can also be generalized to be a measure of the sensitivity of various demand aspects to changes in any demand determinant, e.g., income elasticity and promotional elasticity.

III. METHODS FOR FORECASTING DEMAND

Introduction

To be useful for management planning the abstract conceptions of Section II must be translated into quantitative guesses. The demand function in the previous section was conceived in a mathematical form that would be general enough for all kinds of conditions. Pragmatic analysis usually has a much more limited objective than an entire demand function, because for a single purpose, the best information comes when attention is concentrated on the few demand determinants most important for that purpose.

A theoretical demand function strives for comprehensiveness; it usually seeks to include all the forces that may influence sales. For empirical analysis, the aim should be to select from the many demand determinants only those that are variable, important, measurable, independent, and (for some problems) controllable by management. Some demand determinants are frozen, in the sense that their changes are insignificant for the particular management problem. For example, the age composition of the United States population probably affects the demand for automobiles, but it moves like a glacier, and for short-run sales forecasting it can be neglected. The analysis is therefore confined to those demand factors that have an important effect upon the particular dimension of demand behavior that is under study. To make demand analysis metrical, it is necessary to confine the determinants further to those that can be measured. Sometimes the measurement must be indirect, and usually it is only a guess. Devising measures of elusive variables is often an important part of the job. For example, in developing a formula for forecasting the sales of gasoline (and other products) at prospective service station sites, the level of income in the community must be measured indirectly from an estimate of rental values, and an index of visibility and ease of access must be devised for the site. In empirical work, demand factors are rarely independent of each other in either a causal or behavioristic sense. Theoretical demand functions normally make the assumption of independence of the various demand determinants. But in statistical analysis, covariation of determinants weakens the result for projection purposes, since one factor may be spuriously held responsible for the effects of a highly correlated factor. For some problems, the empirical analysis should be confined to those factors that management can do something about, so that controllability may enter into selection of factors.

Most sales forecasting is concerned only with short-run projections for established products. Long-range predictions for such products are not made very often, partly because the projections are precarious, but mainly because long-term decisions that require such forecasts occur infrequently. New products present an entirely different problem. The question here is whether to make the big initial investment in the first place, and for this decision the long range view is more important than the effects of next year's phase of the business cycle.

Demand forecasting for established products can usually be worked into a routine procedure, with information drawn from the existing markets and from past behavior of sales. Since most of the determinants of demand are expected to change very little through the forecast period, the analysis can often be simplified and concentrated on a few strategic short-run variables.

Forecasts for new products, on the other hand, are necessarily custom-built jobs that take more ingenuity and expense. Since the product has never been sold before, there is no empirical evidence of a base demand that can be used as a foundation for refined estimates, nor is there a structure of market prices for the product and its substitutes that can be projected into the future.

The first part of this section is concerned with methods for short-range forecasting of established products. The second part takes up the problem of forecasting demand for new products.

Forecasting Sales of Established Products

Forecasting methods for established products take a variety of forms. Some lean heavily on personal judgment and experience, while others become routinized as algebraic formulas. Different forecasting methods are not mutually exclusive; they are frequently used in teams to cross-check each other and to give estimates for different purposes. We discuss here broad categories of methods, namely customer surveys, surveys of experts, trend analysis, and correlation analysis.[11]

---

[11] In a survey of the prevalence of forecasting, the Controllership Foundation found that 36 of the 37 companies questioned made sales forecasts. Of these, 23 used estimates from the sales force, 22 used a forecast of industry sales and market share, 29 used historical trends of their own products, and 21 used correlation analysis. Although no data on buyer surveys were given, sales force estimates are frequently based on inquiries made of buyers. Twenty-three companies used at least three of these methods simultaneously, having them worked out in different parts of the organization: sales staff, market research staff, financial officer's staff, or other headquarters staff. (Controllership Foundation, *Business Forecasting*, New York, 1950.)

Survey of Buyers' Intentions

The most direct method of estimating sales in the near future is to ask customers what they are planning to buy. Since it is impractical to ask all of the customers, much may be learned by sampling or by concentrating on the few that make up the bulk of the market.

When sales are to industrial producers, this method simply puts the forecasting burden on the customer, and the seller's problem is primarily to persuade buyers to tell him their purchase (or production) plans and to know how to make discounts for unreliability. In general, an honest estimate from an industrial buyer can make the seller's guess more informed, provided the buyer has some basis for forecasting his own needs. But a user's inventory of the product often gives him much latitude in actual demand, and small changes in the price outlook can radically change his view of the proper size of stock to hold. Thus, industrial buyers' estimates should be strongly seasoned by the producer's own views of short-run price movements.

There are formidable barriers to learning the buying intentions of household consumers. In the first place it is necessary to interview and to sample, and reliable interviewing and sampling is a difficult and expensive art. The high cost often means that surveys must be few and must attempt to cover expenditure plans for several months at a clip. Consumers' inconstancy in buying intentions, as well as their inability to foresee what choice they will make when faced with the multiple alternatives of the market, restricts the usefulness of this method of forecasting and limits its use to products with big price tags and long planning periods, e.g., trips to Europe.

One inquiry into the relation between consumers' declared intentions and their actual purchases has been made in the "Survey of Consumer Finances," conducted annually since World War II for the Federal Reserve Board, by the Survey Research Center at the University of Michigan.[12] This survey estimates the total national demand for houses, automobiles, and appliances during a year on the basis of 3,000 personal interviews on buying plans.

---

[12] These surveys are published in the *Federal Reserve Bulletin* in several monthly installments starting in June of each year.

Comparisons of these plans at the beginning of the year with actual purchases during the year do not give much promise for this kind of forecasting. Chart 4–1, which contrasts planned and actual expenditures for the years 1946–1949, shows that even the direction of the year-to-year changes in plans did not correspond

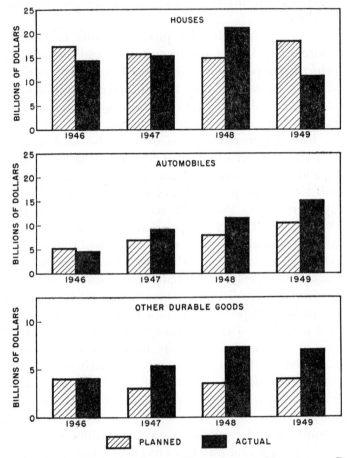

CHART 4–1. PLANNED AND ACTUAL PURCHASES OF HOUSES AND DURABLE GOODS, 1946–1949. ESTIMATED TOTAL EXPENDITURES. (Source: *Federal Reserve Bulletin,* July, 1950, p. 781.)

to actual changes for houses and durable goods. One obvious difficulty in this technique is that a year is an extremely long span in consumer's planning, first because any kind of consumer plan is pretty thin, and second because plans stand on such a low level of sophistication that changes in the economic weather may deal them a severe body blow. Depending on the product and on price expectations, a sudden change in prices may either shock consumers into a short buyers' strike or be completely ignored by them in their passion for goods.

A second difficulty, common to all interviewing techniques, is that it is never clear whether the buyer's plans are real or merely created during the interview. Most of us have trouble disentangling daydreams from plans, and few people can foresee, when confronted with a simple planning choice of buying a car or not buying one, the actual complicated buying choice they will later confront in choosing among several alternative ways of spending limited funds.

In summary, then, a direct inquiry of customers has severe shortcomings in forecasting, in that industrial customers' plans may be trigger-sensitive to short-run economic changes, while consumers' plans are fragile, capricious, and expensive to collect.

Survey of Opinions of People Who Know

A more subtle, though devious, attack can be made by asking the people who are likely to know what customers will buy. Many companies get their basic forecasts directly from their salesmen, on the theory that the grass roots contact man has the most intimate "feel" of the market. Jobbers, wholesalers, and retailers are polled for the same reason. In this kind of a forecast, the total is generally built up by adding the individual salesman's projections, then scaled down for errors of optimism by pooling the collective wisdom of top executives in second guessing and consolidating results.

The basis of forecasting by experts may be hard to identify, for it may spring largely from hunch and impulse under pressure of inquiry. For some products, however, notably industrial equipment, the salesman may be a sophisticated engineer himself who keeps close track of the capital requirements of a few customers in relation to their own sales and profit outlook. Despite its informality, this kind of forecast may be the best available for some companies.

Projection of Past Patterns

A third forecasting method, sometimes called "trend and cycle," takes an entirely different tack. By use of statistical methods for analyzing time series, the past behavior of sales is broken into several components such as a long-term exponential trend, a group of sine curves for business cycle movements, and a seasonal pattern. Using an assumption of underlying continuity, these components are projected into the future to yield forecasts for the coming month, year, or decade.

This method derives partly from the "periodogram" school of business cycle theory,[13] but the foundations of the concept were never very firm, and with the advent of modern big government as a self-conscious dominating force in the economy, there is little ground left under the method. Basic changes in institutions, motivations, and risks have disrupted the continuity of the stringent conditions necessary to use such a projection technique. But it has, for many products, a firmer economic foundation, particularly when confined to trend extrapolations and a seasonal pattern, leaving forecasting of cyclical business changes to other methods. In a growing economy, with a persistent trend of urbanization and mechanization, good long-range forecasting results have been obtained for some products (e.g., electric power) by projecting the trend alone.

Correlation Analysis

A fourth method of forecasting is correlation analysis. Like the previous method, it is statistical, but with a sharp difference. "Trend and cycle" is a demand function with time as the single independent variable.   In correlation analysis, on the other hand, the demand function states the relation between sales and other quantities in the economy (e.g., national income) that exist either at the same date or previously.   If the function has only one variable other than sales, it is called simple correlation, and if it has several, it is multiple correlation. The aim of correlation analysis is to isolate and measure the relation between fluctuations in sales and the corresponding changes in the principal demand determinants. The results are stated in mathematical form and purport to show how sales change with a unit change in each in-

---

[13] This group believes that the regularity of fluctuations in activity are self-regenerative vibrations about an equilibrium position, like the swings of a pendulum. The vibrations stem from relations between economic conditions at different dates which set up interlacing rhythmic patterns of different frequency—e.g., 40 months, 66 months and 9 years.

dependent factor, the others remaining constant and random forces averaged out.

Correlation analysis of this kind can be quite elaborate. A full description of the statistical process is beyond the scope of this book. We can only present the outlines of the methods and the results of a few analyses. However, before reviewing them, it is useful to have a general understanding of what a correlation analysis does and what the results mean.

To work a least-squares correlation, the analyst looks over historical data on market conditions to find the factors that he thinks influence sales and for which data are available over a period with wide fluctuations. His next step is usually to test the closeness of the relationship of each candidate factor to sales and to other factors and thus make a selection of independent variables. He then chooses a plausible algebraic relation between sales and these independent variables. In the simplest kind of analysis the relation is linear, such as

sales $= a$ (national income) $+ b$ (price) $+ c$ (weather) $+ d$.

But curved functions may fit better and be more logical, and indeed there is an endless choice of functions.[14] Choosing the best function ought to be done on some rational basis of causality but often the best that can be done is to pick the function that fits the data most closely.

Having defined the function, the analyst then grinds the data through a calculating machine and produces the most probable values for the constants in the equation, such as a, b, c, and d above. The coefficients a, b, and c each indicate what a given change in an independent variable (i.e., determinant of demand) will do to sales, all other conditions remaining constant.[15] This set of numerical relationships may be a valuable tool in sales forecasting. It channels estimates toward most probable values, based on the continuation of past relationships with "causal" factors that are measurable.[16] The eternal quest is for a lucky lag func-

---

14 It is possible, for instance, to bring in rates of change for some variables, or their values at previous dates or to use parabolic functions, logistic curves, or sine waves, or to put the whole thing in logarithmic form.

15 In many correlations, some of the independent variables are interrelated and a change in one is always accompanied by some change in others in the real world. In such cases sales forecasts must take account of this covariation: the coefficients mean little taken individually.

16 The independent variables in the function do not have to be causal in an inductive sense: if sunspot activity is the best index of the short position on the

tion, one with sales in close relation to something that happened, say, six months before. When, instead, sales are related to a simultaneous development, e.g., the Federal Reserve Board index of industrial production, then the forecasting problem is to map the future of this independent variable rather than sales itself. This transformation of the forecasting problem can, nevertheless, be helpful. The future level of the FRB index, for example, is the subject of so much study and conjecture that many estimates of it are readily available. Sometimes the independent factor is inherently more easily forecasted than the sales in question—e.g., population or birth-rates.

Although multiple correlation is itself an involved and expensive operation, the principle can be used on a more modest scale by graphic correlation, which gives fairly good approximations and is accessible to anyone with paper, pencil, and an eye for curves. One virtue of the graphic method is that it needs no algebraic form, and the analyst has a free hand to choose the shape of the functions. He is liberated from the simple types of formulas that must be used in the full correlation analysis, which are a travesty of the vast and intricate (if not impersonal) forces of the marketplace. But this virtue is also a peril, because there is usually a temptation to let the curve wiggle at will so long as it follows the data and thus pick up many accidental historical variations as significant relations.

Forecasting the Demand for New Products

Methods of forecasting demand for new products are quite different from those for established products. For products that are new to the economy as well as to the company, an intensive study of the economic and competitive characteristics of the product affords the key to intelligent projections of demand. Forecasting methods need to be tailored to the particular product. Possible approaches can be classified as follows:

1. *Evolutionary approach*. Project the demand for the new product as an outgrowth and evolution of an existing old product. For example, start with the assumption that color television picks up where black and white left off.

Stock Exchange, it should be used. But we must admit that a demand function in terms of factors that seem to be causal promises more durable reliability.

2. *Substitute approach.* Analyze the new product as a substitute for some existing product or service. For example, the new Foto-setter substitutes photographic composition for the established type-setting equipment (linotype).

3. *Growth-curve approach.* Estimate the rate of growth and the ultimate level of demand for the new product on the basis of the pattern of growth of established products. For example, analyze growth curves of all established household appliances, and try to establish an empirical law of market development ap· plicable to a new appliance.

4. *Opinion-polling approach.* Estimate demand by direct inquiry of the ultimate purchasers, then blow up the sample to full scale. Sending an engineer with drawings and specifications for new industrial products to a sample company is an example.

5. *Sales-experience approach.* Offer the new product for sale in a sample market—e.g., by direct mail or through one chain store—and from this try to estimate the total demand for all channels and a fully developed market.

6. *Vicarious approach.* Survey consumers' reactions to a new product indirectly through the eyes of specialized dealers who are supposedly informed about consumers' needs and alternative opportunities.

These methods are not mutually exclusive. A combination of several of them is often desirable when they can supplement and check each other. The evolutionary approach is useful only when the new product is so close to being merely an improvement of an existing product that its demand can be pretty much a projection of the potential development of the underlying product. The big problem is to estimate how the demand patterns of the new version will differ from those of the prototype.

The substitute approach has great promise when applicable. Most new products are substitutes, though not always for just one thing (e.g., air express is a substitute for inventories as well as for land transport). Sometimes the old product sets a rough upper limit to the potential market for the new. For example, packaged rail freight traffic sets an upper limit for estimates of air freight, and for a while Pullman traffic was regarded as the upper limit for airline volume. But this is a penetrable ceiling. Sales of ball-point pens, for example, have swept away old notions of fountain pen potentials. Framing the research problem in terms of finding laws of displacement rate of the occupant product also focuses attention on what needs to be done to improve, promote, or price the new product for faster encroachment.

For many practical problems it is not the upper limit of substitution, but the rate of penetration that is important—how fast the new product will displace the old, rather than its theoretical eventual potential, is important. Moreover, many new products have several uses. Each use presents a separate substitutability problem, and substitution for existing products may account for only part of the potential demand for a new product. It is said, for example, that the use of aluminum foil labels has greatly increased the sale of products using them so that the former sales of paper labels greatly understated foil sales. Much depends upon relative prices—e.g., most of the disparities in the early estimates of air travel and of air cargo were accounted for by differences in assumptions about relative prices.

The growth curve approach, even if it can be developed, has narrow applicability, and is useful primarily at the later stages of demand projection. Developing an empirical law of growth from actual rates of market development of similar products is an intriguing prospect, but small-scale investigations have so far not established reliable patterns. The method has been used, however, in projecting the probable growth path of traffic on new airline routes and new bus routes.

Opinion polling, i.e., surveys of buyers "intentions" as revealed by personal interviews, has been widely used to explore the demand for new products. This technique encounters problems of sampling, probing real intentions, and conveying the complexity of multiple alternative choice, even for established products, as we have seen. For new products these are accentuated and there are more: one has to get across a conception of what the new product is and what it will do. Engineering drawing specifications and test results will do this fairly well for skilled industrial buyers—e.g., research samples of a new chemical with a description of known properties, composition, and probable price can be sent to a sample of prospects. But for big, complex, or drastic innovations a trial run by the producer is part of a full exploration of demand.

Sales experience with a new product on a sample basis, when the experiment is properly controlled, puts estimates of demand on a more solid foundation. Trouble arises, however, in determining what allowance to make for the immaturity of the sample market and its peculiar characteristics. An inadvertent experiment of this sort occurred in the early sales of television sets as a result of the sharply localized development of video sending facilities. In blowing up the New York metropolitan sales experience, the proper allowance for program immaturity and for local peculiarities was hard to determine. Except for low-priced products that require little capital, this method comes late in the exploration process.

The vicarious approach is temptingly easy and distressingly hard to quantify. Generally, it is usable only as a cheap horseback sally. Wild enthusiasm on the part of dealers merely warrants further study, and an adamant veto sometimes shows only how uncomprehending human beings are. Such opinions are worthless unless confined to the area of the dealer's experience, and are then only as good as his insight. Vicarious surveys are no better than the ability of the dealer to guess what buyers will do and to report it disinterestedly.

Criteria of a Good Forecasting Method

There are thus a good many ways to make a guess about future sales. They show contrasts in cost, flexibility, and the necessary skills and sophistication. How do we pick the best one for a particular demand situation? In addition to technical tests of appropriateness and efficiency, there are certain economic criteria of broader applicability.

Accuracy

It is well to have an accurate forecast, but the problem is, how accurate? This question can be answered only in terms of the value of marginal precision compared to its cost. What are the returns to precision? Higher sales because the inventory was there when demand swung up; bigger advertising impacts because customers were hit when they were ready to buy; more bulk buying with better discounts; and so forth. Can these marginal gains from accuracy be matched against the cost of using a $40,000 economics staff instead of a salesman's guess? Not by precise meas-

urement, but by judgment. In principle, such marginal estimates set the relevant rule.

Plausibility

The executives who use the forecasting results must be willing
to believe in the method. This usually means they have to understand how the estimate was made. Plausibility is thus a tight
checkrein on econometricians who want to use matrix algebra and
differential equations, and seriously limits the market for higher
mathematics.

Plausibility requirements can often improve the accuracy of
results as well as their chances of being accepted. Experienced
executives have a "market feel" and an appreciation of the whole
compass of the problem that can contribute to research only if
they understand what their specialists are doing.

Durability

Unfortunately, a demand function fitted to past experience may
back-cast exquisitely, and still fall apart in a short time as a forecaster. The durability of the forecasting power of a demand
function depends partly on the reasonableness and simplicity of
functions fitted, but primarily on the stability of the underlying
relationships measured in the past. Of course, the importance of
durability determines the allowable cost of the forecast.

Flexibility

The need for flexibility stems directly from the need for durability. Flexibility can be viewed as alternative to generality.
That is, a long lasting function could be set up in terms of basic
natural forces and human motives, which, albeit fundamental,
would nevertheless be hard to measure and thus not very useful.
A set of variables whose coefficients could be adjusted from time
to time to meet changing conditions is a more practical way to
maintain intact the routine procedure of forecasting.

Availability

A demand function in terms of statistical time series that are
published weekly or monthly (e.g., the Federal Reserve Board
Production Index, the Bureau of Labor Statistics Wholesale Price
Index) may not be as relevant as one in terms of the biennial

Census of Manufactures, but it is obviously more useful. Immediate availability of data is a vital requirement, and the search for reasonable approximations to relevance in late data is a constant strain on the forecaster's patience.

Summary

There are two broad varieties of demand forecasting: (1) the short-run, routine estimates of sales fluctuations for an established product, and (2) special-purpose estimates of long-run promise needed for investment decisions, particularly in new products.

Short-run forecasts on the basis of past trends and cycles rest on faith in the continuity of history and must be used cautiously. Correlation analysis also uses past performance as a guide, but tries to find significant causal relations between sales and controlling factors that can be predicted more easily than sales can directly.

Demand forecasts for new products call for more ingenuity, and produce rough guesses. The methods suggested either tie the new product to demand for substitutes that it will compete with, or use controlled experiments in marketing the product on a pilot-distribution scale. The various methods are supplemental and the ones to use depend on the nature of the product and the money and time available for research.

The ideal forecasting method is one that yields returns over cost in accuracy, seems reasonable (consistent with existing knowledge), can be formalized for reasonably long periods, can meet new circumstances adeptly, and can give up-to-date results.

IV. PRICE RELATIONS

Introduction

In this section we discuss problems of measuring price–quantity relations, the conventional demand schedule of economic theory, and examine some methods, and illustrations of ways to go about it. Demand analysis designed to highlight the role of price as a controlling factor is useful for forecasting, but its major role is in market management: pricing, advertising, distribution, product design. Companies that have no control over prices nevertheless need to know whether expected changes in market prices will affect industry sales. A closer analysis of price relations, moreover, may reveal to such companies unseen areas for positive pricing policy that had been lying dormant.   For industry price leaders and for companies without any close rivals, information on price elasticity is basic to a marketing policy.

When a clear-cut group of similar products defines a recognized and recorded industry, there are two kinds of price–quantity relations that can be usefully distinguished.   The first is the schedule of industry demand, i.e., the relation between sales of the entire industry and an average or benchmark price.   The second is company demand, i.e., the relation of a single company's sales to its own prices.   If competitors' prices are assumed fixed while the company's price varies, the company's demand curve has a higher price elasticity than the industry demand curve, because product similarity makes comparison of price easier and more significant for buyers.   Greater company elasticity is a necessary condition in one economic definition of an "industry" that contains more than one company.

In reality the company's price change either instigates or follows changes by other companies, so that the actual sensitivity of a single firm's sales to a change in price is less than would prevail if rivals' prices remained constant.   When products are homogeneous and there is close followership, uniformity of industry prices produces a company's demand schedule that is for practical purposes a miniature of the industry schedule.

The difference between the shape of the demand schedules for the industry and company depends partly on how long-run the question at hand is.   There are lags in rivals' price reaction as well as in demand reaction to a new price.   Competitive prices may follow a change within a day or not for months or years.   Rivals' reaction time varies approximately with buyers' price sensitivity and is thus a function of such things as product differentiation and the rate of long-run adjustment of demand to new prices.

Measurement of the pure relation between price and sales volume, for either an industry or a company, has been a hard nut to crack statistically.   The heart of the difficulty is that the setting for analysis, i.e., other determinants of demand, changes too rapidly to produce an adequately homogeneous set of data.   To get a demand schedule for a single product of one firm (the practical problem of importance), it is necessary to hold constant the product itself, buyers' incomes, expectations, and preferences, and the relation of competitors' prices to the company's price.   With all of these things frozen, we need data on actual sales at several different prices, which can then be correlated to get a demand schedule. The whole study can be put into either a short-run or long-run setting.

For most companies selling highly fabricated products, there are three major blocks to such analysis: (1) Prices are almost never shuttled back and forth enough in a uniform market to produce the requisite data.[17] (2) Rivals' reactions to price changes are hard to study systematically and to predict; individual reactions to price cut can range from a price war to upgrading of products and better advertising. Since a company's sales are intimately related to what its competitors do, there can be no demand schedule without some kind of regular relationship with competitors' prices and promotion at each price level. These difficulties are closely related to the degree of product differentiation. When homogeneous materials are sold in an oligopoly market with a price leader calling the signals, prices may be uniform, but they also tend to be too rigid for statistical analysis. (These matters are more fully discussed in Chapter 7, "Basic Price.") (3) The product itself changes physically, as well as psychologically; and its margin of superiority over competing and substitute goods may also change with improvements in these goods.

In estimating a price–quantity relationship for a moderately differentiated product, some of these problems can be solved by analyzing prices in terms of spreads or ratios of rival products. For example, the price of top-grade frozen orange juice might be expressed as a premium over (a) unadvertised brands of frozen juice or (b) over fresh oranges, depending on the pricing problem. Sales would be measured in terms of share of the frozen juice market or the share of the total consumption of oranges. What we have in this kind of relationship is a measure of share-elasticity of demand with respect to other frozen juice or all other ways of consuming oranges. Share-elasticity with a near substitute is an incomplete price picture, but it gives the most important informa-

---

[17] For such products, price swings do not need to be very wide to cover the probable range of optimum prices. But for many reasons—inertia, timidity, and Fair Trade laws—industrial prices are sticky and fluctuations are restricted to a small part of even this range. Prices of agricultural staples, in contrast, fluctuate frequently and widely.

tion for short-run pricing problems. This method can also be put to good use in measuring geographical share elasticity, that is, the relation of price differentials between localities to share of total market. For instance, how much gasoline and cigarette demand flow from New York to New Jersey when New York has a one- or two-cent tax differential over New Jersey? Or what price advantage does a super market on the outskirts of town need in order to attract x per cent of the patronage from stores located in residential areas?

This approach washes out some dynamic variations, such as supply-caused changes in price levels of oranges and shifts of demand caused by income, baby-booms, and the like. But not all dynamic shifts go: changes in incomes, differences in advertising, and the price of orange squeezers affect the distribution of demand among rival products as well as its total size.

In using a demand schedule there is always a problem of deciding what conditions it is relevant for. Does it hold for a single income level on both upswings and declines of business activity? Does it shift horizontally with income changes? Vertically? Clearly, if the demand function is to be put to use in sales management, some guesses as to the nature of shifts are necessary.

We have arrayed a formidable list of problems raised in trying to find price—sales relations; problems of accuracy, usefulness, and relevance. When these are fortified by the belief common in many industries that demand is quite inelastic with respect to price, it is easy to see why very little work has been done in this branch of demand analysis outside of farm products.

Methods for Estimating Price Relations

Price relations, like forecasts, can be sketched out empirically by several different means. However, an important difference is that price studies offer opportunities for deliberate experimentation that are obviously not possible in making forecasts. Aside from this, the basic approaches are similar. In the paragraphs that follow we shall discuss controlled experiments, questionnaires, engineering estimates, and correlation analysis.

Controlled Experiments

The most promising method of estimating short-run price elasticity for the product of an individual firm is usually by controlled experiments. The essence of this method is to vary separately certain determinants of demand which can be manipulated, e.g., prices, advertising, packaging, and try to conduct the experiment so that other market conditions either remain fairly constant or can be allowed for. Geographic differentiation is one way to manipulate prices or marketing strategy, comparing sales in separate localities, and usually reversing the arrangement as a check to eliminate the effects of other factors. Or prices and promotion can be manipulated through time in the same market, although this is usually less informative.

The Parker Pen Co. conducted a price experiment recently to determine whether they should raise the price of Quink, which was then selling at a loss to the company and at little profit to the dealer. The increase in price from 15¢ to 25¢ was tested in four cities. Results indicated such low elasticity of demand that the sales loss was more than offset by the added profit margin. After the price was advanced, experimentation was continued in cooperation with 50 dealers. In some stores the old package priced at 15¢ was placed next to a package marked "New Quink, 25¢." Two out of five customers bought the 25¢ package. In other stores Quink was placed on display beside competitive inks priced at 15¢ and at 10¢. In order to test specifically cross-elasticity of demand Quink was sold at 15¢ for two weeks, then at 25¢ for another 2 weeks. At the higher price there was a slight decline of Quink sales in relation to sales of two competitive inks. Consumer panel reports indicated that volume declined at first and then began to rise both absolutely and relative to competitors. Several competitors followed the price advance of Parker, which is the largest ink manufacturer.

Another example of field tests of competitive cross-elasticity is the Simmons Mattress experiment. Identical mattresses, some bearing the Simmons brand and others an unknown brand, were offered for sale, first at the same prices and then at various price-spreads, to determine the effect on sales. With parity prices the Simmons brand outsold the other fifteen to one; with a five dollar premium, sales were eight to one; and with a 25 per cent premium, sales were equal. A parallel experiment with Cannon towels produced similar results.

Field testing of prices is sometimes used in connection with the introduction of new products. Thus, a manufacturer of duplicating supplies introduced a new product in two supposedly comparable geographic areas at different prices. The indicated demand elasticity was less than unity so the product was priced at the higher level. A similar case is that of a large food manufacturer who was faced with the problem of setting the price for frozen orange juice when it was first introduced. He experimented with three different prices in different cities. All three prices were below the then parity level of fresh oranges. Sales did not appear to differ significantly among the three price levels.

To cite another example, a new type of roll-around shopping cart which collapses into an eminently portable form was developed recently. Experimental probing for the right price, included an effort to sell it house-to-house for $4.98. But it wouldn't go. Simultaneously, a large Chicago department store was supplied with a lot to be offered at $3.98. At this price and through this channel the shopping carts sold well. Efforts to pare the costs enough to make it profitable to sell at this price through department stores were unsuccessful, however, so the product had to be withdrawn from the market.

For products that are normally sold by mail order, opportunities for experimental analysis of demand are rich. Price, promotion, and even product design, can be varied among keyed mailings, chosen as successive samples of the same prospect population. Several years ago a mail-order house sent out a batch of catalogs in which the price of one item varied from $1.88 to $1.99 and then observed the relation of sales to the range of prices to find the price elasticity.

A new product that is not to be permanently sold by mail can be experimentally offered by direct mail at different prices to carefully controlled and geographically separated sectors of a mailing list. By analyzing the actual order response to each of the series of prices, some conception of demand elasticity can be obtained. This approach may be viewed as a variant of the prospect questionnaire method, but it avoids the difficulty of bridging the gap between declaration of intention and actual purchasing action. It has limitations both in the difficulty of getting satisfactory comparability of the market sectors and in the failure to duplicate the actual purchasing environment.

There are serious problems in determining demand schedules by controlled experiments. Such experiments are expensive, hazardous and time-consuming. In planning the study it is not always clear just what conditions should be held constant. Moreover, it is difficult, costly, and dangerous to set up a pricing experiment that will include all the effects of a price change that you want to measure, and exclude all the effects of other factors that you don't want. It is hard to reflect realistically the reaction of rivals to the price change. And dealers' responses are often atypical since they are privy to the experiment. The temporary impact of a local price raid may be all that is measured, whereas the problem concerns the effect of full-scale and more permanent price reductions. For example, the great responsiveness of sales to price-cuts in the Macy experiment conducted by Whitman (discussed below) probably measures stocking-up to take advantage of a short-lived opportunity and also reflects lags by competitors in meeting Macy's prices. Sufficient reaction time to feel the full effect of price is seldom possible before other conditions change significantly. Thus, the results often have limited generality, since they are tied to the particular conditions of the experiment.

Pricing experiments are costly and hazardous. They run risks of unfavorable side-reactions of dealers, consumers, and competitors. Nonetheless, this method deserves wider use than it has had, and constitutes one of the most promising implements for demand analysis in current markets.

Consumer Questionnaires

Personal interviews and written questionnaires are widely used to probe the buying motives, intentions and habits of customers and prospects. They are sometimes helpful (in the absence of better measurements) in guessing at the sensitivity of demand to price. Little confidence can be placed in answers to questions that ask consumers what they think they would pay, or how much they would buy if prices were lower, or if price-spreads over competitors and substitutes were different. This kind of frontal attack on the intricate psychological problem of buyers' intentions and actions is still a highly dubious method of analysis, even when the market consists of a few large industrial customers. Not until the psychometric techniques of depth interviewing have advanced far beyond their present status can much be expected from such direct probing.

But collateral information obtained from such interviews can brace up a guess at price sensitivity. For example, interviews revealed that most buyers of a branded baby food chose it on their doctor's recommendation, and that most were quite ignorant about substitutes and about prices. This knowledge, together with other information, led the manufacturer to guess that demand for his product was quite inelastic.

Occasionally questionnaire research can indicate the outer limits of price. For example, an automatic timer developed for photographers was never commercialized because questionnaires indicated that the lowest profitable price was far above what most photographers *said* they would pay. But in general such research is a frail foundation for pricing decisions.

Engineering Estimates

For producers' goods, it is sometimes possible to guess at the effect of price upon the sales of a capital good by making engineering estimates of the cost savings and other benefits that can be produced by the product for a sample of prospects. By applying some standard of capital earnings, e.g., a three-year crude pay-out, it is possible to translate estimates of savings into demand for equipment.

The cost savings of customers will vary because prospects differ in size, wage rate, efficiency of displaced equipment, and other such conditions. To estimate the way these divergent conditions affect the quantity of equipment that will be purchased, a sample of prospects that is representative of various strata of customer size, wage rates, equipment efficiency, etc., is selected. From estimates of the cost savings and the number of prospects in each category, the sample results can be blown up to yield a projected schedule of equipment sales at various prices. Estimates of the cost savings of new equipment types can be supplemented and verified by test installations in major prospect categories.

The most difficult practical problems usually arise not in estimating the cost savings in a particular situation, but in translating these savings into a demand schedule that reflects a composite of all situations. Comprehensive knowledge of the operations of a buying industry are required for the equipment, both to determine the appropriate conversion factors for capitalizing cost savings and to select the sample and blow it up.[18]

Correlation Analysis

Often, information on price elasticity can be found by applying the correlation technique described in Section III to historical records of prices and sales. The important problem in this method is to design a function that can sift out the price relations from data that show the composite effect of all sales determinants.

Correlation analysis of price elasticity has been applied most extensively to demand for agricultural products, notably by Henry Schultz. Using very simple relationships [19] Schultz found fairly high correlations of price and consumption for most farm products [20] over periods of about fifteen years. Table 4–2 shows some of the estimates of price elasticity for the most recent period he studied.

Farm products have economic characteristics that make them particularly susceptible to this kind of analysis: they are homogeneous and staple, so that their demand curves change very slowly over the years; they are sold in highly competitive markets, where prices are flexibly adjusted to demand and supply; supply varies widely from year to year, but annual production, once under way, is hard to control by producers. Wide swings in supply plus highly stable demand can in these conditions be assumed to pro-

---

[18] This approach concentrates on obsolescence replacement, since it is here that pricing affects engineering feasibility. Cultural lags of ignorance, uncertainty, and speculation contaminate this relationship. Buying equipment on the basis of its prospective earnings on capital is unfortunately not yet sufficiently common to be the sole basis for analysis of demand. The age, distribution, and the status of depreciation reserves of existing equipment, though they should be irrelevant, may properly enter into forecasts of the rate of displacement of obsolete machinery. (See Chapter 10.)

[19] For instance, he used functions in the forms

$$x = a + by + ct$$
$$x = Ay^m e^{nt}$$

where x is per capita consumption, y is the deflated price, and t is time, while $a,b,c,A,m,n,$ and e are constants. In another form of analysis, price and consumption were used not in absolute terms but as deviations from a long-term trend; time was omitted as an explicit variable. Another variant of the analysis was a correlation of year-to-year changes in price with corresponding changes in consumption, a method first used by Henry Moore (*Economic Cycles: Their Law and Cause*, New York, 1914).

[20] An important exception was wheat, for which price behavior was largely governed by a world market rather than a national one.

TABLE 4–2

PRICE ELASTICITY OF DEMAND FOR AGRICULTURAL
PRODUCTS 1915–1929

(Estimated by Henry Schultz)

Sugar	.31
Corn	.49
Cotton	.12
Hay	.43
Wheat	.08
Potatoes	.31
Oats	.56
Barley	.39
Rye	2.44
Buckwheat	.99

Source: H. Schultz, *Theory and Measurement of Demand*, University of Chicago Press, Chicago, 1938. Table 49.

duce a series of prices that, when plotted against consumption, trace out the shape of the demand curve.

These are far different pricing conditions from those prevailing in manufacturing industry, where prices are a combination of rigid, official quotations and undercover concessions, where products are rarely comparable, and where current demand is more closely matched by current production. Nevertheless, in some industries, price data for this kind of analysis is produced inadvertently. Price wars, regional differences in competitive and substitute price spreads, and the distortion of relative prices caused by inflation create research opportunities that are too often neglected. Statistical analysis of such price experience can sometimes provide usable knowledge about how prices and price spreads affect both the company's market share and the industry's battle with substitutes. A state sales tax on soft drinks recently created data inadvertently that demonstrated a high price elasticity for one bottling company. This company found that a one cent per bottle tax could not be added to the wholesale price without cutting volume enough to lower total revenue. Differences in state taxes on gasoline, together with geographical differences in laid-down cost, have furnished oil companies with data for making correlation analyses of the relationships between price and volume.

When a product's price is rigid, changes in substitutes' prices shift the relative price of the product and give data on price elasticity. For example, in studying the price elasticity of policy-loans made by an insurance company, it was found that the policy-loan rate stayed constant while competing lenders reduced their rates. Thus the relative price of policy-loans was rising in a way that was measurable and could be related to changes in loan volume, both absolutely and relative to competitors' volume.

Price Elasticity—An Illustrative Study

One of the best studies of the short-run relation of price to sales was done for Macy's department store by R. H. Whitman.[21] In several respects this is an ideal field for such research: (1) prices are an important sales factor—they are featured in advertising, and customers shop between stores; (2) prices are unusually flexible—seasonal patterns and style cycles make careful price administration a must for managing large inventories profitably; (3) there is substantial and regular competition among stores, but with some leeway for price policy; (4) there is keen competition between substitute products on the same counter, which presents the raw material for well controlled experiments.

Whitman was thus able to sidestep some of the obstacles discussed earlier in the chapter. For instance, he used a very short time period (two and one-half months), which stabilized consumer income, but which nevertheless saw many price changes. He analyzed only staple products in order to obviate the style cycles problem. He assumed that when Macy's changes its price the pattern of reactions of other stores during the analysis period would be repeated under similar conditions in the future. These simplifying circumstances neutralized the effect of several independent variables that must be used in most demand situations, and permitted him to use simple correlation of price and quantity sold to find price elasticity.

Whitman created his data by systematically manipulating price over a wide range during a short period. Parallel experiments were performed for a number of staples.

When correlation analysis is worked out in its mathematical (least-squares) form, the first step is to set up an algebraic function to express the relation. There is usually room for

21 "Demand Functions for Merchandise at Retail," *Studies in Mathematical Economics and Econometrics,* University of Chicago Press, Chicago, 1942, pp. 208–221.

judgment in deciding on the best form to use. In choosing his demand equation, Whitman rejected the common form, $q = a + bp$ and used instead $q = Ap^a$. ($q =$ quantity sold; $p =$ price; $A, a,$ and b are constants.) [22]   In geometric language, he used the hyperbola in Chart 4–2B, rather than the straight line in 4–2A.

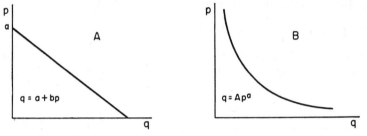

CHART 4–2. ALTERNATIVE FORMS OF DEMAND FUNCTION

As mentioned in Section II, an important feature of the hyperbolic demand curve is its constant elasticity: regardless of the level of price, the ratio of a small fixed per cent change in price to the resulting per cent change in quantity sold is constant. This ratio is equal to the constant a, which is the price elasticity of demand, and which is negative. For example, if a is -5, a drop in price of 1% will increase sales by 5% and revenue by 4%. In the simplest case, where $a = -1$, sales vary inversely with price just enough to keep total revenue constant for all values of p.

In the straight-line demand curve, on the other hand, a $1 change in price will produce a constant absolute change in quantity sold regardless of the level of price. In this case there is a price which gives a maximum revenue, namely $a/2$.

Whether the hyperbola is more realistic is not clear *a priori:* there is certainly a price where none at all can be sold, and the amount that can be given away is also finite. But for the relevant range of actual prices, Whitman found it a better fit to the facts than a straight line.

The price elasticities that resulted from this analysis told a significant story and were surprisingly reliable in a statistical sense. Chart 4–4 presents the demand schedule for one product, showing a price elasticity of about -6 (with a standard error of .78) and a correlation coefficient of $-.89$, which indicates a

---

[22] Exponential functions of this type are used in logarithmic form for correlation analysis:

$$\log q = \log A + a \log p.$$

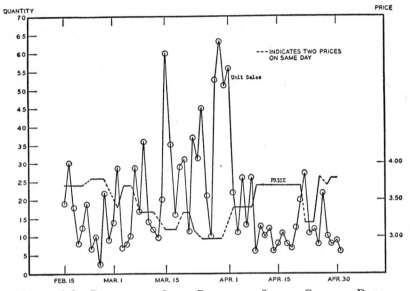

CHART 4–3. DEPARTMENT STORE PRICES AND SALES. ORIGINAL DATA. (Source: R. H. Whitman, "Demand Functions for Merchandise at Retail," *Studies in Mathematical Economics and Econometrics,* Chicago, University of Chicago Press, 1942, pp. 210, 214.)

close relation between sales and prices. Other commodities showed comparable price elasticities and correlations. Moreover, by comparing results for the same calendar months in two successive years, Whitman found that the change during the year was relatively slight compared to the margin of probable error.

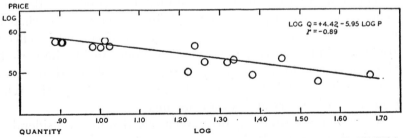

CHART 4–4. DEPARTMENT STORE DEMAND FUNCTION. (Source: R. H. Whitman, "Demand Functions for Merchandise at Retail," *Studies in Mathematical Economics and Econometrics,* Chicago, University of Chicago Press, 1942, pp. 210, 214.)

These price elasticities are relatively high, and mean that sales are sensitive to prices for these products. For these products. price is a powerful weapon in competition—probably too powerful to be used freely.   Low elasticity, in contrast, shows products where price competition is too ineffective to be important, compared to the returns from advertising.

Whitman also ran a multiple correlation analysis to find the relation of sales to prices of other products, using as independent variables both the product's price and an index of competing products.[23]   The closeness of fit for this equation was not impressively high, but the analysis did contribute some information on cross elasticity of demand, which for different products ranged from 1.4 to 16.2.

As we indicated above, this analysis had a rather ideal short-run setting, which is unattainable for most products.   It is much more common for prices to change from year to year than from day to day, and for reaction patterns to be much slower.   Nevertheless, it is highly probable that there are other areas where it can be useful.

Summary

Price–sales relations have long occupied a central position in economic theory.   And knowledge of this part of the product's demand function could take much of the guess-work out of pricing.   Nevertheless, empirical investigations of the effect of price on a manufacturer's sales remain a relatively untouched field of demand analysis.   This is one reason why many companies do not have independent price policies but, rather, follow the industry leader or use cost criteria of pricing.   Price relations are extremely difficult to analyze for manufactured products: the frequency and range of price variation is inadequate; a price change is generally felt only after a long gestation period; and its effects are buried in the shifts of the over-all economy during the period.   Since price relations depend on the closeness of substitutes and the behavior of their prices as well, there are different price relations for an industry and for a company.

A method for studying price relations that has considerable promise is the controlled experiment.   There are various forms of experimentation with prices in the market that can reveal an approximate price–sales schedule over the range of possible prices.   Other methods, including consumer questionnaires, en-

---

[23] The equation took the form: $Q = Ap^a P^b$.

gineering estimates, and correlation analysis, can, under appropriate conditions, produce usable estimates. For agricultural commodities, correlation analysis of the relation of short-run behavior of sales to short-run changes in prices has been widely used.

V. INCOME RELATIONS

Introduction

Buyers' income is a basic demand determinant, and an understanding of income–sales relations is necessary to all kinds of sales planning problems. There are two facets to income relations: the effect of income changes on sales, and the distribution of sales among buyers of different income levels. Income changes have been widely studied in demand analysis, and they are a primary tool for forecasting. Sales distribution among income levels, although vital for decisions on product design, pricing, advertising, and distribution channels, has been relatively neglected, because the necessary data are much too scarce and expensive to provide working information.

Income–sales relations, in contrast to the relation of sales to price, are strong enough to be revealed by simple statistical investigations. This probably explains why analysts have been content with relatively crude measures. In many studies no attempt is made to remove the effect of price changes in measuring income relations, yet removing the income effect is a universal undertaking in measuring price–quantity relations from comparable data. In this section we discuss these relatively simple studies of income and the kind of information that they produce.

Kinds of Income Functions

The relationships between buyers' income and quantity of commodity bought can be divided into six broad groups by distinguishing between (1) dynamic changes in income of the same group of buyers, and (2) static differences in income among different groups of buyers and by subdividing each of these two classes by distinguishing among (a) buyers' aggregate income, (b) aggregate income per bracket, and (c) individual or average income per person in each bracket. A diagram of the resulting six-cell classification pattern of income function is illustrated in Chart 4–5.

TOTAL SALES   SALES PER BRACKET   SALES PER CUSTOMER

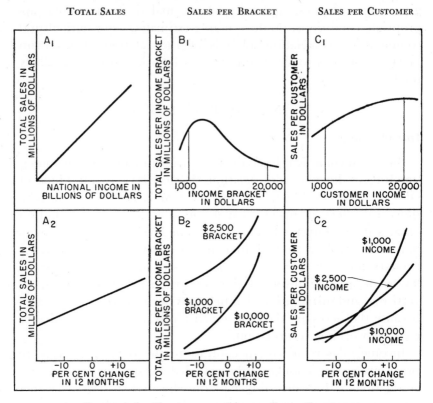

CHART 4–5. VARIETIES OF INCOME–SALES FUNCTION

Cell A_1 shows the relationship between aggregate income and aggregate sales under conditions of total adaptation when spending habits have had a chance to settle down for each level of aggregate income. Cell A_2 in contrast, shows the relationship between aggregate sales and changes in aggregate income under a dynamic condition of partial adaptation, that is, when the income of the measured group fluctuates from year to year, possibly with progressive expansion over a long period of time. Cell B_1 shows the total sales of the commodity per income bracket in a stable situation after total adaptation to the income level of each group. On the horizontal axis is average income per income bracket; on the vertical axis, purchases per person in each bracket multiplied by the number of persons in each income bracket. Cell B_2 shows what happens to sales in a single bracket when the average income of that bracket changes. For example, it might show how total sales of Cadillacs to cattle farmers of Elko County, Nevada, vary as their income goes from $2,000 to $10,000 to $50,000. The third tier of charts shows the relationship between the per capita expenditures for the commodity in question and the per capita income bracket under a stable situation of total adaptation. It differs from the second tier, B_1, only in showing expenditures in per capita rather than in total form. Both show the basic relationship between consumption and income bracket, when people are accustomed to the income. Cell C_2, in contrast, shows the relationship between per capita sales and income changes for one income bracket under a dynamic situation where adjustment to the new income level is not yet complete. Corresponding to Cell B_2, it would show Cadillacs per 5,000-acre ranch in Elko County.

The sales in this group of charts, which portrays different aspects of income in relation to demand, can refer to sales of any group of commodities, either for the industry as a whole or for an individual company. Thus industry demand functions in respect to income do not differ from those of the firm in the underlying nature of the relationship, though they may differ in sensitivity to any of the various aspects of income discussed above.

In this section we discuss the kind of function shown in Cell B_1 and A_2. As we have mentioned in previous sections, Cell B_1 shows a relation that is important for long-run sales policy while A_2 reflects the basic relation needed for short-run sales forecasting.

Sales Distribution by Income Brackets

The income relation in Chart 4–5, Cell B_1 is an aspect of the standard of living of the people who buy the product. It thus says something about their tastes and the things that are important to them in buying, whether brand name, quality, price, styling, or size. The curve also shows the importance of the product in their budgets, which itself suggests something about price elasticity.

The shape of the curve is useful for answering questions about actual and proposed penetration of markets at different income levels. For instance, if the curve climbs steeply to a peak at $6,000, what are the costs in price cuts of shifting that peak to $4,000? They are probably higher than the cost of making a peak at $4,000 in a curve that is flat from $4,000 to $9,000. But even though shifts are too expensive by outright price cuts, they may be feasible by some kind of discrimination, e.g., a line of standard and delux models (see Chapter 8).

The location and sharpness of peaks is significant in setting up cushions against demand fluctuations. Some kinds of income are much more volatile than others, and have different demand elasticities. A choice can thus be made between selling high specialty items on a feast-and-famine basis or establishing roots in solid mass markets with low margins and medium quality. Knowledge of income-sales relations is one factor in an intelligent choice between these two marketing strategies.

A formidable obstacle in this kind of analysis is the scarcity of good data on consumption patterns at different income levels. Some estimates are made by the Federal Reserve Board on personal income distribution, and studies of family budgets for different incomes are occasionally made by the Bureau of Labor Statistics to keep the Consumers' Price Index up to date. But this information is expensive to collect and cannot be gathered in much detail. Chart 4–6 shows some results from one of the most detailed income budget studies. There are other ways for a company itself to make some guesses about income distribution, for instance, by analyzing the residential areas where buyers live. These may be good enough for practical purposes, but in general, income distribution has not yet received the detailed study that income fluctuations have.

Income Fluctuations

The relation of changes in demand to changes in buyers' income is basic for short-run forecasting and has been the subject of much statistical study, particularly in terms of total national income or disposable personal income. There have also been similar analyses of corporate income (profits) in relation to business investment that have found significant correlations.[24]

A major problem in analyzing income changes is to decide how minutely to sort out distinctive fluctuation patterns of different

---

[24] However, the high correlations that are found from this kind of analysis can be quite misleading as causal explanations, because the relation is usually between a total (e.g., gross national product) and one of its parts. To say that demand for machinery will increase next year if GNP increases probably means no more than to state the casual relation in the other direction. Indeed private capital formation and its components have been used with some success for forecasting GNP.

customers.   Both the demand elasticities and the income volatili-
ties of different users may be so different from each other or from
national totals that a breakdown is needed.   For instance, residential and industrial consumers of electricity bear little resemblance to each other in either the income-sensitivity of
demand or in the width of swings in their income over time.

The net relation of sales to, say, national income is therefore
not simple, since it depends upon the underlying relations of the
incomes of the particular group of buyers to the national aggregate.   For example, if a function is fitted statistically to historical
data for hay-baler sales and national income, this curve is valid
for the future only if hay farmers' income fluctuations either conform rigidly to the national pattern or maintain the same relationship to national income as in the past.   This problem is quite
general in using broad aggregates statistically, since they usually
include much more than is relevant to the analysis of a single
product's demand.

Changes in income through time raise a problem in long-run–
short-run differences in demand, i.e., the difference between the
first and second tiers of Chart 4–5.   It has been fairly well established that consumption patterns show a cultural lag with
respect to income changes.   That is, it is common to find that
when a family's income increases from $4,000 to $5,000 during
a year, expenditures on food and housing in the second year are
still below the level normal for $5,000 families, and the converse
is true when income falls.   This lag probably applies as well to
changes in real national income, although not for changes in
aggregate money income, which may be offset by proportional
price changes.   The lag has two complementary consequences:
(1) demand for staple goods is less sensitive to income changes in
the short run than it is eventually; (2) for a period, consumers
accumulate excess cash balances which they are apt to spend
freely on such things as extra suits and trips to Mexico.

Total Consumption Functions

The consumption function has had wide currency among
economists and business analysts since the middle thirties.   A
basic element of J. M. Keynes' *General Theory* was the idea that
total consumption expenditures had a fairly fixed relation to the
level of national income, and that as income rose, the proportion

of it spent on consumption decreased. When this theory was tested statistically for the 1920's and 1930's, some sensationally high correlations were found in a number of different analyses.[25] Straight-line functions in the form (consumption) $= a + b$ (income) fitted the data as closely as more complicated curves, and yielded correlation coefficients well above .95. The slope of the line b is usually about .8 or .9, which indicates that when personal income increases $1 billion, consumption increases about $850 million. The constant term a is always positive, indicating that if a depression gets deep enough, consumption will be larger than income, i.e., there will be negative savings, provided the whole function does not then shift.

At one time the consumption function was thought to have great predictive powers, and it may yet develop them, but in recent years its has proven a treacherous projection, largely because cash balances have been extremely high relative to incomes. In any event, it is important to note that total consumption is more stably related to income than is any sub-class of consumption (e.g., durable or non-durable goods). Although consumers may make the choice between spending and saving largely on the basis of income, their choice on how to spend seems to depend on relative prices, availabilities, and existing stocks, as well as on income. For instance, when appliances and cars are expensive or hard to get, money is channeled into other product lines such as clothes or entertainment where supply is more expansible. The net effect is to maintain total demand at about what it would be with more ample hard-goods production. That is, the choice between spending and saving is largely independent of the decision on what to buy. The close relation between national income and total consumption is by no means necessarily carried over to demand for individual products.

Product Consumption Functions

Nevertheless, when some fairly wide error margins are tolerable in demand estimates, it is possible to find a consumption function for individual broad product groups. An illustration of a simple method is given in Chart 4–7, which shows such a function for

---

[25] The best-known study of the consumption function is by Paul Samuelson. The results have been published as an Appendix to Chapter XI of Alvin Hansen's *Fiscal Policy and Business Cycles*, New York, W. W. Norton & Co., Inc., 1941.

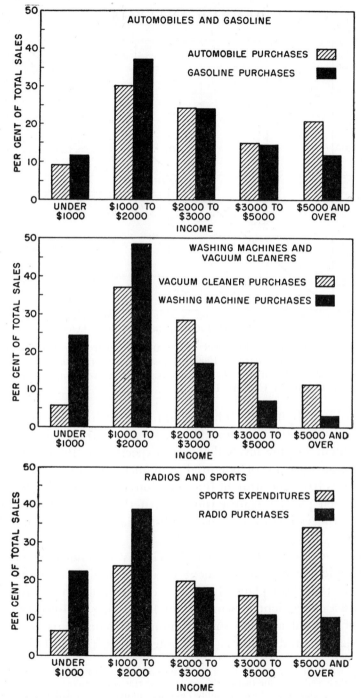

CHART 4–6. SALES DISTRIBUTION BY INCOME BRACKETS—1935–1936. (Source: National Resources Planning Board, *Family Expenditures in the United States*, Washington, D. C., 1941, Statistical Tables, p. 26.)

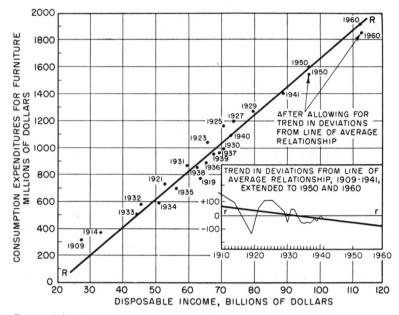

CHART 4–7. RELATION BETWEEN DISPOSABLE INCOME AND CONSUMPTION EXPENDITURES FOR FURNITURE—1909–1941, EXTENDED TO 1950 AND 1960. (Source: Frederic Dewhurst and Associates, *America's Needs and Resources*, New York, Twentieth Century Fund, 1947, p. 728.)

household appliances.[26]   The straight line in this chart is drawn free-hand using the data for 1909–1940, and extrapolated to full employment income levels that were expected for 1950 and 1960 to make an estimate of potential appliance sales for those years. Deviations from the straight-line function show a distinct upward trend when plotted against time, and if the trend is taken into account the estimates are raised substantially, as shown on the chart.[27]

Such free-hand methods have the virtues of being inexpensive and simple for top management to understand.   If the trends found in them can plausibly be expected to hold in the future, they are a convenient benchmark for forecasting.   However, this kind of method also has some limitations: when it is tried on more specific product lines (e.g., toasters), it is frequently hard to

---

[26] This was a method used by the Twentieth Century Fund to predict consumption levels in their elaborate forecast of the structure of the postwar economy.

[27] Although this procedure resembles graphic multiple correlation, it is not exactly equivalent.   In graphic correlation the straight line would be redrawn to fit the points adjusted to eliminate the trend element.

fit a line-function at all accurately, and for a single company's product, the correlation may become still worse. The flywheel effects in the relation of total consumption to national income tend to disappear as analysis narrows down to single products.

Measurement of Income Elasticity of Demand

Estimates of the sensitivity of sales to changes in national income have been carried out by the Department of Commerce for a large number of products by multiple correlation analysis.[28] Excerpts from the report of this work are reprinted here to show the method and the broad picture of consumption habits in the results themselves.

INCOME SENSITIVITY OF CONSUMPTION EXPENDITURES

By Clement Winston and Mabel A. Smith

The measure of sensitivity

Sensitivity to income changes of the expenditure for a commodity or service is measured by a coefficient which is derived by correlating dollar expenditures during the years 1929–40 with disposable personal income and a trend factor. The coefficient expresses the average percent by which expenditure varied, in the base period, corresponding to a one percent change in disposable income—holding constant the effect of trend.

If the coefficient for a specified commodity or service is less than 1, this indicates that changes in expenditure for the item were proportionately smaller on the average than the changes in aggregate disposable personal income. A coefficient greater than 1 implies that fluctuations in income were associated with relatively larger fluctuations in outlays for the corresponding good or service. For example, the consumption of luxuries increased and fell off more sharply than income, and hence these goods have sensitivity coefficients greater than 1. In contrast, expenditures on certain basic necessities were much more stable than income, and these items accordingly have coefficients much less than 1.

It should be borne in mind, however, that such a coefficient may be altered when relevant factors other than income are introduced explicitly. Although this analysis considers only the effects of income and a trend factor, clearly other influences can be important in explaining fluctuations in specific expenditure items. This is particularly true where the rate of secular growth in the base period was not

---

[28] The principal differences of the Commerce method from the method just discussed are that Commerce used least-squares multiple correlation instead of a simple graphic analysis; and they used an exponential function instead of a linear one. (See Appendix at end of the reprint.) Reprinted from *Survey of Current Business*, Jan., 1950, pp. 17–20.

constant. In such cases a markedly different value of the sensitivity coefficient might result from a more extensive analysis than could be undertaken for the complete break-down of consumption expenditures. It has been necessary to exclude a number of categories for this reason. An example of an expenditure item which is not covered in the tables because the rate of growth was not constant during the years 1929–40 is personal outlays for airline transportation.

Categories have also been omitted where income is largely irrelevant to the size of expenditure, in which case the sensitivity coefficient is subject to a considerable margin of error. Standard clothing issued to military personnel is an example of a category for which no cyclical association with aggregate disposable income would be expected. Also, several items have been excluded because the data do not permit the derivation of a sufficiently dependable measure of the income sensitivity.[29]

The distinction between the income-sensitivity of expenditures discussed in this article and the income-elasticity of demand which is frequently employed should not be overlooked. The difference arises primarily through the use of dollars expended rather than quantities purchased. The relation between the movement of prices of a specific commodity or service and the changes in over-all prices reflected in disposable personal income will influence the degree of response of dollar outlays to changes in income, whereas income-elasticity measures the effect of income on the demand for a commodity when its price is held constant.

Moreover, technical problems exist in estimating demand relationships from aggregate expenditure data over time. For example, there may be situations where supply considerations are the governing factor in determining the amount purchased. In spite of these reservations, a classification of consumer expenditures by sensitivity is useful in summarizing how the demand for these goods and services may be expected to vary with cyclical changes in income.

By methods discussed in the appendix to this article a sensitivity coefficient was obtained for each of the expenditure items. For total consumption expenditures on goods and services, the sensitivity measure is 0.86. That is to say, other things being equal, a change of 10 percent in disposable personal income during the base period was associated on the average with a change of about 8½ percent in total consumption expenditures.

For presentation purposes all expenditure items have been grouped about this over-all or average sensitivity figure. All items with coefficients that fall in the interval 0.7 to 1.0 are considered as having average sensitivity to income, those under 0.7 as below average, and those

---

29 In the great majority of excluded cases, the coefficient of partial determination of expenditure by income was found to be less than 0.7. A few of the categories included also have coefficients less than 0.7, and such cases are indicated in the table.

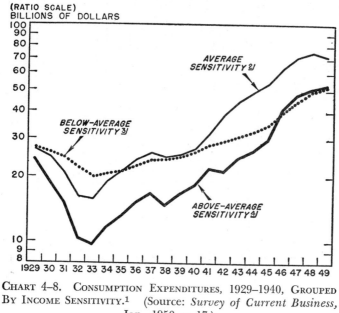

CHART 4–8. CONSUMPTION EXPENDITURES, 1929–1940, GROUPED
BY INCOME SENSITIVITY.[1]   (Source: *Survey of Current Business,*
Jan., 1950, p. 17.)

[1] Income sensitivity is measured by the percentage change in spending associated
with a 1 percent change in disposable personal income.
[2] Income sensitivity coefficients between 0.7 and 1.0.
[3] Income sensitivity coefficients less than 0.7.
[4] Income sensitivity coefficients of 1.0 and over.

with coefficients equal to or greater than unity as above average.

The groupings are, of course, arbitrary, but they serve the purpose
of separating the expenditure items in a simple manner for analytical
purposes. For specific applications, however, more detail than these
broad classifications provide may be desirable. Consequently, the
value of the sensitivity coefficient for each of the items has been listed
in Table 4–3, where the durable and nondurable goods and service
items have been arrayed according to the responsiveness of expenditures to changes in disposable personal income.

Durable goods highly sensitive

It is immediately evident from the table that the durable-goods
groups tend to have a high income sensitivity. For example, a change
of 10 percent in consumer income is associated, on the average, with
a change of 20 percent in expenditures for automobiles, and with 25
percent for radios, phonographs, and other musical instruments. Of
the 22 durable-goods groups only 2 show coefficients which are less
than 1, and for the majority of them the sensitivity measure is 1.4 or
higher.

Table 4–3

Personal Consumption Expenditure Items Classified According to Sensitivity to Changes in Disposable Personal Income [1]

Above-average sensitivity	S	*Average sensitivity*	S	*Below-average sensitivity*	S
Durable goods		**Durable goods**		**Durable goods**	
Boats and pleasure aircraft	3.1	Ophthalmic products and orthopedic appliances	0.8	China, glassware, tableware, and utensils	[3] 0.7
Radios, phonographs, parts, and records	2.5	**Nondurable goods**		**Nondurable goods**	
Pianos and other musical instruments	2.3	Food purchased for off-premises consumption	[a] 1.0	Miscellaneous household paper products	[3] .7
New cars and net purchases of used cars	2.0	Purchased meals and beverages—tips	[a] 1.0	Drug preparations and sundries	.6
Luggage	1.9	Purchased meals and beverages—retail, service, and amusement establishments	[a] 1.0	Purchased fuel (except gas) and ice	.6
Jewelry and watches	1.8	Nondurable toys and sport supplies	[a] 1.0	Tobacco products and smoking supplies	.5
Cooking and portable heating equipment	1.7	Cleaning and polishing preparations	.9	Gasoline and oil	.5
Tools	1.7	Shoes and other footwear	.8	Magazines, newspapers, and sheet music	.5
Furniture	1.6	Food produced and consumed on farms	.8	Purchased meals and beverages—schools and school fraternities	.5
Writing equipment	1.6	Toilet articles and preparations	.8	**Services**	
Miscellaneous electrical appliances	1.4	Food furnished government and commercial employees; and withdrawn by non-farm proprietors	.8	Intercity bus—fares	[3] .7
Floor coverings	1.4			Chiropodists and podiatrists—services	[3] .7
Wheel goods, durable toys, and sport equipment	1.4			Admissions—professional hockey	.6
Durable house furnishings, n. e. c.	1.3			Funeral and burial services	.6
Products of custom establishments, n. e. c.	1.3			Interest on personal debt	.6
Monuments and tombstones	1.3				
Tires and tubes	1.2				
Books and maps	1.2				
Automobile parts and accessories	1.2				

Durable goods (Cont.)	
Refrigerators, and washing and sewing machines	1.0
Nondurable goods	
Purchased meals and beverages— dining and buffet cars	1.6
Flowers, seeds, and potted plants	1.6
Stationery and writing supplies ..	1.4
Semidurable house furnishings ..	1.1
Clothing and accessories except footwear	1.1
Purchased meals and beverages— hotels	1.0
Services	
Ticket brokers' mark-up on admissions	2.1
Admissions — legitimate theaters and opera	[4] 1.9
Fur storage and repair	1.6
Watch, clock, and jewelry repairs	1.5
Steam railway (excluding commutation) fares	1.4
Sleeping and parlor car—fares and tips	1.3
Baggage transfer, carriage, storage, and excess charges	1.3
Private flying operations	1.3
Domestic service	1.3
Taxicab—fares and tips	1.2
Dressmakers and seamstresses (not in shops)—charges	1.2

Services	
Care of electrical equipment (except radios) and of stoves	[2] 1.0
Personal business services, n. e. c.	[2] 1.0
Accident and health insurance— net payments	[2] 1.0
Dancing, riding, shooting, skating, and swimming places	.9
Chiropractors—services	[2] 1.0
Amusement devices and parks ..	.9
Boat and bicycle rental, storage, and repair	.9
Baths and masseurs	.9
Admissions—professional baseball	.9
Miscellaneous curative and healing professions—services	.9
Osteopathic physicians—services	.9
Commercial, business, and trade schools—fees	.9
Dentists—services	.9
Telegraph, cable, and wireless ..	.9
Laundering in establishments ...	.9
Fire and theft insurance on personal property—net payments ..	.8
Veterinary service and purchase of pets	.8
Classified advertisements	.8
Correspondence schools—fees	.8
Commercial amusements, n. e. c.	.8
Athletic and social clubs—dues and fees	.8
Beauty parlor services	.8
Costume and dress suit rental	.8

Services (Cont.)	
Foundation expenditures for education and research	.6
Foundation expenditures for religious and welfare activities ..	.6
Automobile insurance—net payments	.6
Upholstery and furniture repair .	.6
Services furnished without payment by financial intermediaries except insurance companies	.6
Net purchases from second-hand furniture and antique dealers ..	.5
Housing—clubs, schools, and institutions	.5
Owner-occupied nonfarm dwellings—space rental value	[4] .5
Moving expenses and warehousing	[4] .5
Trust services of banks	.5
Street and electric railway and local bus-fares	.5
Tenant-occupied nonfarm dwellings—space rent	[4] .5
Cemeteries and crematories	.5
Steam railway—commutation fares	.5
Rental value of farm houses	.4
Telephone	[4] .4
Religious bodies	.3
Legal services	[4] .3
Privately controlled hospitals and sanitariums—services	.3
Postage	[4] .3
Museums and libraries	.3

TABLE 4-3 (Continued)

Above-average sensitivity Services (Cont.)	S	Average sensitivity Services (Cont.)	S	Below-average sensitivity Services (Cont.)	S
Net payments—mutual accidents and sick benefit associations ..	1.2	Entertainments of nonprofit organizations, except athletics ..	.8	Miscellaneous household operation services	.2
Practical nurses and midwives—services	1.2	Golf instruction, club rental, and caddy fees	.8	Water	[4].2
Rug, drapery, and mattress cleaning and repair	1.2	Other instruction (except athletics)—fees	.8	Expense of handling life insurance —life insurance companies	.2
Miscellaneous personal services ..	1.2	Physicians—services	.8	Gas	[4].2
Cleaning, dyeing, pressing, alteration, storage, and repair of garments, n. e. c. (in shops)	1.2	Shoe cleaning and repair	.7	Electricity	[4].2
Billiard parlors and bowling alleys	1.2	Admissions—motion-picture theaters	.7		
Express charges	1.1	Social welfare and foreign relief agencies	.7		
Photographic studios	1.1	Barber shop services	.7		
Housing—transient hotels and tourist cabins	1.1	Admissions—other amateur spectator sports	.7		
Radio repair	1.0	Private duty trained nurses— services	.7		
Automobile repair; greasing, washing, parking, storage, and rental	1.0				

---

[1] The classification is based on the relationship of personal consumption expenditures for each item with disposable personal income and a time factor for the period 1929–40. The figures in the S column indicate the percent change which is associated with a 1 percent change in disposable personal income; for example, an increase of 1 percent in disposable personal income is associated with an increase of 1.8 percent in the expenditures on jewelry and watches, all other factors being equal.

[2] Value between 0.95 and 1.00.

[3] Value between 0.65 and .70.

[4] Coefficient of partial determination less than 0.7.

Source: U. S. Department of Commerce, Office of Business Economics.

n. e. c.: not elsewhere classified.

TABLE 4–4

PERSONAL CONSUMPTION EXPENDITURES IN 1948 CLASSIFIED
BY INCOME SENSITIVITY [1] (Millions of Dollars)

Type of good	Above-average sensitivity [2]	Average sensitivity [3]	Below-average sensitivity [4]
Durable	21,599	416	1,504
Non-durable	20,860	65,142	14,498
Services	7,485	9,416	32,582
Total	49,944	74,974	48,584

[1] The sensitivity groups shown omit certain items which account for only about 3 percent of total expenditures.
[2] Includes all items with income-sensitivity coefficients of 1.0 and over.
[3] Includes all items with income-sensitivity coefficients between 0.7 and 1.0.
[4] Includes all items with income-sensitivity coefficient less than 0.7.
Source: U. S. Department of Commerce, Office of Business Economics.

Expenditures for the durables are, in general, more readily post-ponable than most items in the consumer budget. As a result, purchases of hard goods tend to fall more rapidly than income during the downswing in the business cycle and rise at a more rapid rate on the upswing. Nevertheless, even in this category there are two groups with relatively low sensitivity to income, namely, ophthalmic products and orthopedic appliances, and china, glassware, tableware, and utensils. These groups are generally less readily deferred than is the case with the other durable commodities. As a result, such expenditures fluctuate less over the course of the business cycle.

At first glance it appears from the table that among the nondurable goods and services there is not the same tendency toward concentration into one sensitivity group as shown by the durables. However, this is primarily the effect of the kind of detail shown. When the relative importance of the groups, based on dollar expenditures, is considered, it is found that the nondurable outlays fall predominantly in the middle sensitivity group, while the major service expenditures are of low sensitivity.

For example, nondurable goods with sensitivities between 0.7 and 1.0 represented two-thirds of dollar expenditures on nondurables in 1948. For the services about 60 percent of the expenditures are for items listed in the below-average sensitivity class, most of the remainder falling in the middle group. In contrast, more than 90 percent of all durable goods in terms of dollar outlays are represented in the upper sensitivity class.

These results are reflected in the behavior of the totals for durables, nondurables and services. The over-all coefficients for durable and nondurable goods and for services are 1.6, 0.9, and 0.6, respectively. In general, therefore, the durable goods are above average in sensitivity, the nondurables are average, and the services are below average. Nevertheless, it is important to note that substantial amounts spent in the nondurable and service categories are found outside of the representative sensitivity class.

Wide range in services

Among the services a considerable number of groups possess income sensitivities far in excess of the low average for the category as a whole. As seen in Table 4–3, there are 23 items in the first sensitivity class with indexes ranging from about 1 for automobile and radio repair to more than 2 for ticket brokers' mark-up on admissions.

The most important service groups with above average sensitivity from the standpoint of dollar volume are domestic service; services connected with clothing, such as cleaning and pressing of garments, fur storage and repair, and dressmaker and seamstress charges; and various transportation items including steam railway, sleeping and parlor car fares, baggage transfer charges, and taxicab fares. Auto repair is listed in this group, but as noted above, it is a borderline case.

A large number of services are also found in the average sensitivity class. Outstanding among these are medical services, accident and health insurance, and a large part of the recreation group. These health and recreation expenditures account for 60 percent of the total service expenditures in the average sensitivity class.

In Chart 4–8, there are presented the annual values of personal consumption expenditures for the three sensitivity groups for the years 1929–49. The difference in the cyclical behavior for these three groups is immediately apparent.

From 1929 to 1933 expenditures for goods and services in the upper sensitivity class declined by 57 percent, compared to 41 percent for the average and 26 percent for the low-sensitivity items. Similarly, on the upswing from 1933 to 1940, the increases for the three groups were 92, 71, and 29 percent, respectively.

Changes in the war and postwar years

The expenditure behavior in the three sensitivity classes diverged during and after the war from the patterns traced in the prewar years. The war period was marked by high income and shortages, and the factors that had previously operated to influence expenditures were temporarily superseded by conditions in which prices and distribution were controlled and spending tended to be a function of supply. In the postwar years of sustained capacity operations, the increases in income and expenditures likewise were not the normal cyclical changes characteristic of the base period, but reflected unusually large price movements following the wartime distortions in the economy. As a result, after 1940 the sensitivity measures did not have their earlier significance, although in the current period the peacetime cyclical movements are beginning to merge.

In interpreting the results presented, it should also be remembered that the postwar period differs markedly from the period on which the coefficients are based. Disposable personal income in the early years varied from $45 to $82 billion. The present level of income, however, is over $190 billion. Inferences drawn from the observed relationships at points so far beyond the range of income and after so long an intervening time are subject to a considerable margin of error.

Consequently, in attempting to apply the procedures outlined in this study for the purpose of appraising consumption possibilities for the future, it is particularly important to employ the measure described in conjunction with a careful analysis of changed market conditions. The results of the study of income sensitivities can best be applied to a particular field of production or distribution when supported by a full knowledge of that field, its relation to other industrial segments, and the special conditions existing in the economy.

APPENDIX

To derive a measure of the sensitivity of expenditures to income it is necessary to evaluate the net effects on expenditure of changes in income over these years. This is accomplished by adjusting for the effect of other forces which, in addition to income, may influence the relationship.

The method employed for this purpose was that of multiple correlation, relating consumption expenditures in the base period 1929–40 for each of the groups to disposable personal income and a time factor allowing for a constant rate of growth. The general form of the equation used in determining the income sensitivity coefficients is: $C = AY^sB^t$ where $C =$ consumption expenditures, $Y =$ disposable personal income, $t =$ time, and A, s, and B are constants derived from the data by least squares procedures. From this form of regression the exponent s is taken as the approximate measure of the income sensitivity for each expenditure item.

The time factor has been introduced as an aid in accounting for the variation in expenditures not explained by income alone. This procedure is based on the assumption that the resultant of all forces other than income on expenditure tends to be exhibited as a relatively smooth time trend. The assumption does not always hold; moreover, the sensitivity coefficient may change as additional factors are explicitly introduced. In most cases, however, it is felt that the coefficients would be little altered by a more extended analysis, since in the great majority of the categories, income and time factors alone yield high coefficients of partial determination. Where the trend is important in accounting for variations in expenditure, it is desirable where possible to replace it by the specific factors which it represents, e.g., population. However, such an analysis is beyond the scope of this article.

In presenting the expenditure categories by sensitivity to income in table 1, it was decided to include only those groups for which the analysis in terms of income and time appeared adequate. For this reason, a number of expenditure items were eliminated. The criteria of exclusion have been indicated earlier. Generally, these groups account for a very small portion of total expenditure, and all omitted items together represent about 3 percent of consumer spending.

In a small number of categories, the income sensitivities shown in the table have standard errors in excess of 20 percent, corresponding to a coefficient of partial determination less than 0.7. Such cases are indicated in the table.

Regional Differences in Income Behavior

Every sales manager knows that standards of living and consumption patterns differ in different parts of the country. Regional sales quotas are determined so as to reflect these disparities. The *Sales Management* "Buying Power Index" is one tool that is widely used to gauge the relative sales potential of states, counties, and even towns throughout the country. If the total income of, say, New Hampshire last year was .3 per cent of the national income, the New Hampshire sales manager may get a quota of .3 per cent of the total sales forecast.

But this kind of allocation method neglects an important cause of regional demand differences, namely the relative volatility of incomes. The Commerce Department has made a study of the cyclical behavior of state incomes, showing that when national income rises 10 per cent, income in New Hampshire rises only 7 per cent, whereas Iowa income rises 15 per cent. Table 4–5 and Chart 4–9 present the results of this analysis for all of the states. An important refinement is to plot the deviations from the average relation against time to find a trend for forecasting purposes. Chart 4–9 shows this for New York.

TABLE 4–5.

SENSITIVITY OF INCOME PAYMENTS OF EACH OF THE STATES TO
UNITED STATES INCOME PAYMENTS—BASED ON PERIOD 1929–1940

State	Per Cent Change in Income for State Associated with a 10 Per-Cent Change in National Income Payments [1]	State	Per Cent Change in Income for State Associated with a 10 Per-Cent Change in National Income Payments [1]
Iowa	14.8	Minnesota	11.0
Nebraska	14.6	Oregon	10.8
South Dakota ...	14.3	Wyoming	10.7
Nevada	14.2	Colorado	10.7
Arizona	13.5	Florida	10.4
North Dakota ...	13.4	Oklahoma	10.4
Michigan	13.0	Louisiana	10.3
Idaho	13.0	Kentucky	10.3
Kansas	12.3	Delaware	10.2
Utah	12.2	Pennsylvania	9.9
Montana	12.2	Missouri	9.6
Illinois	12.2	Connecticut	9.0
New Mexico	12.0	West Virginia ..	8.9
Indiana	11.8	New York	8.5
California	11.7	Vermont	8.5
Mississippi	11.6	New Jersey	8.4
Wisconsin	11.5	Georgia	8.4
Texas	11.4	South Carolina ..	8.2
Washington	11.4	Maryland	8.2
Arkansas	11.2	Virginia	7.9
Alabama	11.2	North Carolina ..	7.8
District of		Maine	7.6
Columbia	11.2	Massachusetts ...	7.3
Tennessee	11.1	Rhode Island ...	7.1
Ohio	11.0	New Hampshire .	6.8

[1] Derived from regressions.

Source: See Chart 4–9.

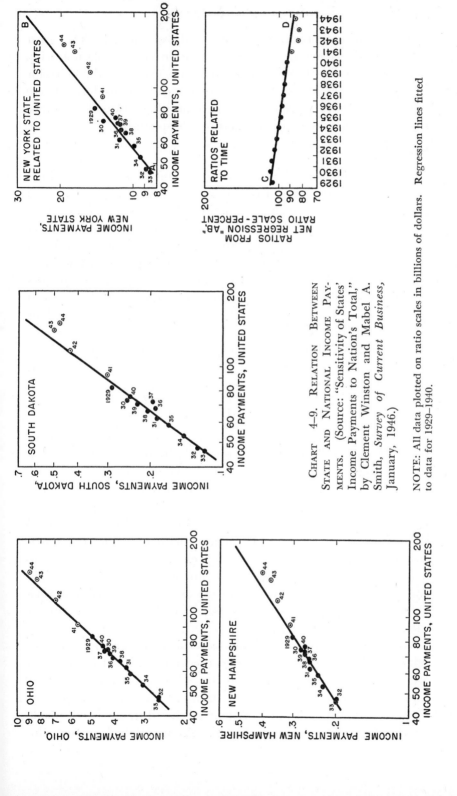

CHART 4-9. RELATION BETWEEN STATE AND NATIONAL INCOME PAYMENTS. (Source: "Sensitivity of States' Income Payments to Nation's Total," by Clement Winston and Mabel A. Smith, *Survey of Current Business*, January, 1946.)

NOTE: All data plotted on ratio scales in billions of dollars. Regression lines fitted to data for 1929–1940.

These estimates were probably made obsolete by the great changes in the economic structure that occurred during the forties. New industries in the South and Far West, changes in the behavior of farm income, and so forth are new facts to consider. These figures are therefore presented more as an illustration of a promising method than as a basis for future sales planning.

Summary

The functional relation of sales to income is for most products the sharpest and easiest to determine. There are, however, a number of types of income function with different uses. One function is the relation of sales per customer to the income bracket of the customer. This function has implications for cyclical behavior of demand and for selection of appropriate promotional effort. Another kind of income function is the relation of sales fluctuations to fluctuations in income of either a single buyer, a group of buyers, all buyers, or the whole potential market. This kind of function probably has less stability than it was once thought to have, but it is still a good benchmark for refined demand analysis. The income aggregate that is used must, however, be closely tailored to the particular product.

VI. MULTIPLE RELATIONS

We have seen in Sections IV and V that analysis of demand in terms of a single controlling factor has a limited field of application: consumer income is closely correlated with demand only for broad product lines and, since there may be no direct causal relation at all, the reliability of income–demand functions depends on the stability of some intervening relations. Empirical analysis shows price as the dominant factor only for very short-run situations where all other influences are relatively fixed. The natural route to a general demand function is therefore multiple correlation analysis where we can use as many independent variables as we wish and get some idea of the relative influence of each on demand.

We have already discussed the basic principles of multiple correlation in Section III, and the detailed mechanics of the method are laid out in any statistics text. This section, therefore, is limited to a few illustrations of its use. We shall first present three fairly simple studies of demand for durable goods made by the Department of Commerce. As mentioned earlier, durable products inherently have more complicated and volatile demand functions than non-durables. The big problem in analyzing them is to decide how many of the obviously important factors can be incorporated economically into the demand function. Added precision falls rapidly as variables are added, while added costs of computation skyrocket.

The fourth illustration is an analysis of life insurance sales, which is a straightforward multiple correlation, but uses what is almost a plethora of variables.

Commerce Department Studies of Durable Goods

Household Furniture [30]

The yearly values of furniture sales, 1923–1940, were correlated with disposable income, residential construction, and the price of furniture relative to other prices. Of several functional forms that were tried, the best turned out to be a hyperbola:

$$F = .0036 \, Y^{1.08} \, R^{0.16} \, P^{-0.48}$$

where F = furniture expenditures per household, Y = disposable personal income per household, R = value of private residential construction per household, and P = ratio of the furniture price index to the Consumer Price Index.

As explained in Section II, the exponents in this equation show the per cent change in sales that accompanies a 1 per cent change in each independent variable—Y, R, or P—when the other two stay constant. Price elasticity was about –0.5, quite low; income elasticity, $+1$, shows furniture sales should increase about 10 per cent when national income rises 10 per cent.

The multiple correlation coefficient for this function was .996, which means that for the 18 years used in the computation, there was virtually no deviation between actual and calculated furniture sales. But the real test of the value of the equation is its ability to estimate sales outside the base period used for computing the function, and after five years of war and shortages. The degree of fit to postwar years, shown in Chart 4–10, is surprisingly close, considering the changes that occurred between 1940 and 1950. Indeed, the fit is closer than we can reasonably expect and may be the accidental net effect of some opposing tendencies that individually would have distorted the estimate. For example, the high cost of construction relative to other prices tends to raise the estimate, while a trend to smaller dwellings tends to lower it.

---

[30] *Survey of Current Business*, May, 1950, page 8.

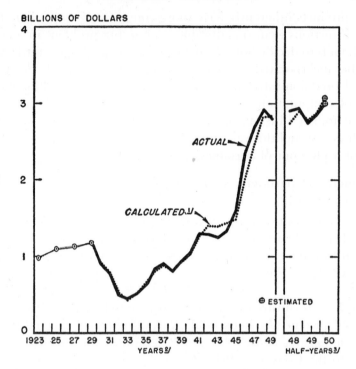

BILLIONS OF DOLLARS

ACTUAL→

CALCULATED⊔

⊕ ESTIMATED

1923 25 27 29 31 33 35 37 39 41 43 45 47 49   48 49 50
              YEARS²/   HALF-YEARS³/

CHART 4–10. PERSONAL CONSUMPTION EXPENDITURES FOR FURNITURE: ACTUAL
AND CALCULATED.   (Source: *Survey of Current Business,* May 1950, p. 8.)

[1] Calculated from a linear least squares regression for the years 1923–1940, based
on disposable personal income and the value of residential construction, both
adjusted for changes in the number of households, and on the ratio of furniture
prices to the prices of all consumers' goods and services.

[2] Data for 1924, 1926, and 1928, are not available.

[3] Half-yearly totals, seasonally adjusted, at annual rates. Data for the first half
of 1950 were estimated on the basis of first quarter data.

Several other such factors could be suggested.

Because furniture is highly durable, we might expect that the
amount and age of furniture already in use would have some
influence on demand and should be included in the demand
function to get a correlation this high.   Actually, the stock of
consumers' furniture probably has been incorporated into the
function as well as can be expected by its relation to the value
of residential construction.   To the extent that replacement demand for furniture is correlated with replacement demand for
housing (which is one determinant of construction activity), it
plays a part in relating furniture sales to the construction variable.

To be sure, this relation puts an extra forecasting burden on the construction estimate which it may not be able to carry.

When the analysis is done in physical rather than dollar units (furniture sales and residential construction measured in constant dollars), the price elasticity is −1.2 rather than −.5. Analysis in real terms is closer to theoretical concepts of demand than the money analysis, and is more relevant for some purposes: certainly physical volume of housing and physical sales of furniture are more closely related than the corresponding dollar volumes are.

Electric Refrigerators [31]

A rather different method was used in fitting a demand function to refrigerator sales, because in this case there was a distinctive problem of time trend. Throughout the analysis period, 1927–1941, the strong upsurge of sales tended to override the influence of the other variables and to obscure the numerical relation of sales to income and price. But in the postwar years, refrigerators had become a mature product and had displaced most iceboxes in wired homes. Thus the trend was leveling off, and price and income were emerging from their secondary position to become dominant factors. The shift in trend made a new scene for forecasting that had little to do with earlier relations.

The variables used in this analysis were time (to catch the trend), disposable income, and the change in disposable income from the preceding year. This last variable, change in income, was used in correlation analysis as a rough indicator of buyers' optimism about the future, and thus their willingness to spend cash balances and to go into debt.

The equation that resulted from this analysis is:

$$Y = 2812.8 + 34.4X_1 + 35.6X_2 + 2024.3X_3,$$

where Y = thousands of refrigerators sold, X_1 = disposable income in billions of 1939 dollars, X_2 = change in disposable income from preceding year, and X_3 = logarithm of time (1925 = 1), i.e., trend with a declining rate of growth.

The multiple correlation coefficient in this case was .96, considerably lower than that for furniture. The estimating ability of the equation can be seen in Chart 4–11, where it is compared

---

[31] *Survey of Current Business,* June, 1950, p. 8.

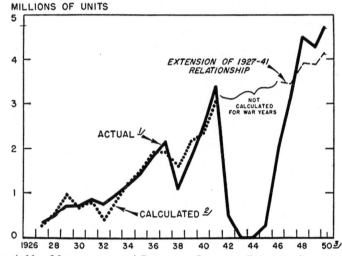

CHART 4–11. MANUFACTURERS' DOMESTIC SALES OF ELECTRIC REFRIGERATORS.
(Source: *Survey of Current Business,* June, 1950, p. 8.)

[1] Data represent sales from *Electrical Merchandising,* less exports from U. S. Bureau of the Census.

[2] Calculated from a linear least squares regression for the years 1927–1941. Equation: $Y = -2812.7546 + 34.3788X_1 + 35.6204X_2 + 2024.2754X_3$, where $X_1 = $ real disposable income in billions of 1939 dollars, $X_2 = $ change in real disposable income from preceding year in billions of 1939 dollars, $X_3 = $ time in logarithms $(1925 = 1)$, $Y = $ manufacturers' domestic sales of electric refrigerators in thousands of units. Coefficient of correlation $R = 0.96$.

[3] Data are for first half of 1950, seasonally adjusted, at annual rates.

Sources of data: Actual—McGraw-Hill Publishing Co., Inc., *Electrical Merchandising* and National Electrical Manufacturers Association; calculated—income, U. S. Department of Commerce, Office of Business Economics.

with the actual volume of sales for both the computation period and the early postwar years. The postwar estimates are clearly too low, largely because there was no opportunity in the base period to bring into the function the relation of refrigerator sales to residential construction after the product had become fairly mature. Construction was undoubtedly a dominant factor in postwar demand.

The lesson of this analysis is that for new and rapidly growing products, statistical correlation of past performance is a shaky foundation for forecasting. Until the market matures to a state where much of production is for replacement rather than new equipment, the data for one period are not very relevant for following years unless a complicated form of demand function is used.

Automobiles [32]

The demand function for automobiles was estimated by using a modified hyperbolic function with the following independent variables: disposable income, change in income from the preceding year, prices of automobiles, and time. The correlation was made for the period 1925–1940, and produced the function:

$$Y = 2.8 \times 10^{-4} X_1^{2.5} X_2^{2.1} X_3^{-1.3} (0.985)^t$$

where Y = new car registrations per 1,000 households, X_1 = disposable income per household in 1939 dollars, X_2 = current income per household as a per cent of preceding year's income, X_3 = ratio of automobile price index to Consumer Price Index, and t = year minus 1933.

The multiple correlation coefficient is .98, and the closeness of the function's fit to actual data is shown in Chart 4–11.

For the computation period this function is quite clearly a better estimate of demand than the refrigerator function in Chart 4–10, partly because there are more variables used, and partly because the time trend is much weaker. Nevertheless, when the automobile function is extrapolated to postwar years, its estimating error is substantially larger than that of the refrigerator function. The weakness of the automobile function for forecasting lies in a heavy reliance on the time variable to catch the effects of some slowly moving factors of great importance to automobile demand. When World War II disrupted the regularity of these implicit demand factors, it made the time variable quite obsolete for forecasting. Specifically, in the base period, the time trend reflects fairly well the slowly increasing age at which cars were scrapped, i.e., it shows the decreasing replacement demand per car in use. In the postwar years this trend was no longer relevant because the war had produced a tremendous demand for replacement which had not been satiated by even 1950. If the demand function had been formulated to include replacement demand explicitly, in terms of normal scrappage age and number of cars at or beyond scrappage age, the postwar estimates would have been substantially closer to reality.

[32] *Survey of Current Business,* June, 1950, p. 6.

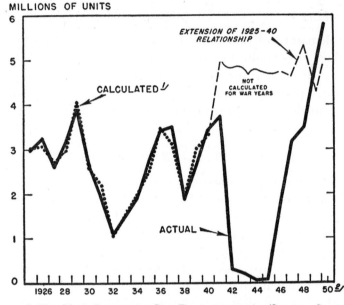

MILLIONS OF UNITS

CHART 4–12. NEW PASSENGER CAR REGISTRATIONS. (Source: *Survey of Current Business,* June, 1950, p. 6.)

[1] Calculated from a least squares regression for the years 1925–1940. Equation: $Y = 0.0002797 X_1^{2.455} X_2^{2.12} X_3^{-1.314} (0.985)^t$, where $X_1 =$ real disposable income per household in 1939 dollars; $X_2 =$ percentage of current to preceding year in real disposable income per household in 1939 dollars; $X_3 =$ percentage of average retail price of cars to consumers' prices; $t =$ year minus 1933; $Y =$ new private passenger car registrations per 1,000 households. Coefficient of correlation $R = 0.98$.

[2] Data are for first half of 1950, seasonally adjusted, at annual rates.

Sources of data: Actual—R. L. Polk & Company; calculated—income and households, U. S. Department of Commerce, Office of Business Economics; prices, U. S. Department of Labor, Bureau of Labor Statistics, and Automobile Manufacturers Association.

A time factor is a convenient gadget for fitting estimates to actual demand in the base period, but for mature products, such as automobiles, as well as for innovations, the time function rapidly gets out of date. A demand function that uses controlling factors explicitly is usually more durable than one that lumps them together in a time trend. The question for the analyst is whether the added durability of forecasting power justifies the added investment necessary in constructing and maintaining a more elaborate function.

"Normal" Demand Functions

Before leaving these three demand functions for durable goods we should point out that although they do not forecast postwar demand accurately, this very failure may reveal their usefulness for another purpose.

An empirical demand function like these can be construed as showing some "normal" level of sales which would have prevailed if there had been no postwar backlog of demand stored up from earlier years.   The difference between actual and estimated sales is then the result of a special circumstance—i.e., the war—and can be expected to disappear eventually.   For example, in the automobile case, 1950 production was from this point of view about 20 per cent above what could be expected in the long run at the 1950 level of income, prices, and so forth.   If correct, this is valuable information for long-run planning: by comparing actual demand with "normal" demand, management may be better able to decide how much of the demand is "pent up" and hence whether or not current demand should be met with short-run expansion, such as a third production shift, as opposed to long-run expansion.   Permanent expansion would allow lower costs, but of course only if the demand is sustained.

Thus the demand function would be used, not for explicit forecasting, but for keeping present conditions in focus relative to underlying normality.   The assumption of underlying normality is a big one, though, and must be carefully checked.   It requires that the demand function be derived from a period of "normality"—which is impossible to define satisfactorily—and also that present normality be the same as base period normality.

"Normality," like the time factor, is a confession of ignorance or excessive computation costs: a more adequate demand function —one that estimates current "abnormal" demand more closely— can be used for *both* short-run forecasting and estimating normal demand by using for independent variables either the expected values for the coming months or the average values that seem reasonable for the long-run future.

Regional Demand for Life Insurance

Multiple correlation analysis has been widely used to find and assign weights to the factors that make Maine's sales differ from Alabama's. This kind of demand analysis is primarily used to estimate the territorial distribution of potential sales, in order to plan retail distribution, set sales quotas, and apportion local advertising.

Analysis of regional differences in demand is usually more complicated and more uncertain than analysis of time series, because factors that are unknown and unmeasurable cover a wider range of variation. Topography, local traditions, important industries, and the like, all change more from place to place than from year to year. Yet, for sales management purposes, regional analysis is important, since it is the basis for matching one salesman's performance against another's and for planning sales effort in each region. An example of this kind of demand analysis is found in a study of regional variations in life insurance sales made by D. R. G. Cowan.[33]

Cowan used seven independent variables in his analysis and yet did not produce a correlation as high as those in the Commerce Department's three-variable studies. (Cowan's multiple correlation coefficient was .95.) [34] The results of his analysis are shown in Chart 4–13. Each line represents the functional relation of sales to a separate independent variable when all others are held constant.[35] The upper left-hand panel shows how closely the estimate from the total function fits the actual sales data.

The seven independent variables in this function were chosen *a priori* to reflect different dimensions of the market that Cowan expected to have the most significant effects on sales. As the chart shows, it turned out that two variables—the proportion of Negroes and the proportion of foreign-born in the population had no measurable influence.

[33] *Sales Analysis from the Management's Standpoint*, Chicago, University of Chicago Press, 1939.

[34] It should be kept in mind that a correlation of .95 with seven variables is by no means as good a fit as a correlation of .95 with three variables. This is because increasing the number of variables, like reducing the size of the sample, has the effect of increasing the probable sampling error.

[35] Each state was a separate region in this analysis. Variations in independent factors are among states, not through time, and the income relation should by no means be considered equivalent to the income—demand functions discussed above.

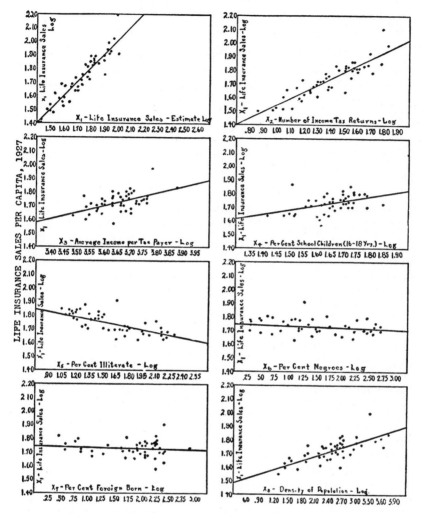

CHART 4–13. INSURANCE SALES AND SEVEN REGIONAL FACTORS. (Source: D. R. G. Cowan, *Sales Analysis from the Management Viewpoint,* Chicago, University of Chicago Press, 1938, p. 36.)

Summary

This section illustrates some applications of multiple correlation to demand analysis. In using this statistical approach, the important problem is to find a few efficient causal factors, rather than to compile a catalog of influences on sales. Efficient indicators are found not only by insight into demand determinants, but by adaptation of statistical analysis to the problem and by experimentation with different functional relations. For instance, the durability of a demand function is often enhanced by converting dollar values into physical units and occasionally by using a time lag between variables. When such refinements are not feasible, flexibility is a more economical substitute for durability than is elaborateness.

VII. DEMAND FOR AUTOMOBILES

In Section VI we discussed an analysis of automobile demand made by the Department of Commerce. In this section we present another study,[36] made by Roos and von Szeliski, that is quite different from the Commerce study. The reason for summarizing it here is that it reveals the structure of demand by analyzing explicitly certain determinants that were reflected only indirectly in the Commerce study. Whereas Commerce made time a fourth factor to reflect all of the trends in the use of automobiles, this study probed deeper into the demand for both replacement and expansion to find relevant market data. The Commerce study was simpler, less expensive, and had quite as good a fit to the base period data. But it probably does not have the durability of the General Motors study.

Major Factors Affecting the Year-to-Year Changes in Sales of New Automobiles

As with all durable goods, the demand for new automobiles is derived from the demand for services which they yield. Since the automobile yields transportation services for a period from five to fifteen years, the demand for these services may be satisfied by running the old cars another year or by buying used cars instead of new cars. Thus the consumption of automobile services is disassociated from the purchases of new cars, and, as is to be expected, the former is far more stable than the latter. The number of cars in use held up relatively well even in the trough of the depression, while the sale of new cars suffered a great decline.

(1) *Consumer Income*

The level of consumer income is, of course, a major factor in determining the number of new car sales. When the level of income is high, sales will be high; conversely, when national income is low, car sales will be low. This is illustrated in Table 4–6

---

[36] *Dynamics of Automobile Demand*, General Motors Corp., 1938, pp. 21 ff. The summary is from U. S. Steel Corporation, *TNEC Papers*, Vol. I, pp. 73–103.

and in Chart 4–14, which relate new car sales to consumer disposable income.

TABLE 4–6

RETAIL PASSENGER CAR SALES, DISPOSABLE INCOME, MINIMUM COST
OF LIVING AND SUPERNUMERARY INCOME, 1919–1938

Year	Retail Passenger Car Sales(a) (thousand units)	Disposable Income(b) (billion dollars)	Necessitous Living Costs(c) (billion dollars)	Supernumerary Income(d) (billion dollars)
(1)	(2)	(3)	(4)	(5)
1919	1,591	$61.38	$21.92	$39.46
1920	1,657	66.29	25.44	40.85
1921	1,471	53.60	22.22	31.38
1922	2,088	56.45	21.38	35.07
1923	3,351	64.98	22.30	42.68
1924	3,172	66.02	22.98	43.04
1925	3,252	69.46	23.86	45.60
1926	3,495	72.94	24.18	48.76
1927	2,705	72.53	24.02	48.51
1928	3,396	74.92	24.08	50.84
1929	4,036	78.50	24.30	54.20
1930	2,652	71.21	23.68	47.53
1931	1,903	60.29	21.52	38.77
1932	1,096	46.67	19.42	27.25
1933	1,526	45.23	18.82	26.41
1934	1,928	52.38	20.10	32.28
1935	2,531(e)	55.55	20.90	34.65
1936	3,639(e)	63.06	21.66	41.40
1937	3,749(e)	68.97	22.76	46.21
1938	1,850(e)	64.20	22.66	41.54

Source: Data used by Roos and von Szeliski in *The Dynamics of Automobile Demand.*

(a) For 1919–1925 the data represent factory production, less exports and foreign assemblies, less assumed changes in dealers' stocks; for 1926–1929 the data are estimated by General Motors from retail sales of General Motors passenger cars and new car registrations of other passenger cars; for 1930–1938 the data are estimates of the Automobile Manufacturers Association.

(b) Figures for 1929–1938 are Department of Commerce income payments series, plus entrepreneurial savings, less Federal income, gift, estate and inheritance taxes; figures for 1919–1928 are a backward extension of 1929–1938 figures, on basis of data provided in Kuznets' *National Income and Capital Formation, 1919–1935,* less Federal and direct taxes.

(c) Estimated at $200 per capita for 1923 and varying with the National Industrial Conference Board Index of the Cost of Living for other years.

(d) Equals column (3) minus column (4).

(e) Model year (12 months) ending in October.

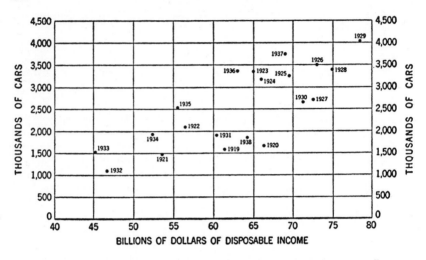

CHART 4–14.   RELATION OF PASSENGER CAR SALES TO DISPOSABLE INCOME.
(Source: Table 4–6.)

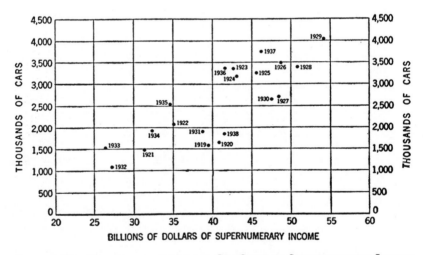

CHART 4–15.   RELATION OF PASSENGER CAR SALES TO SUPERNUMERARY INCOME.
(Source: Table 4–6.)

A somewhat more refined analysis is possible if consumer income is adjusted by deducting necessitous expenditure.   Before distributing his income among different commodities or between savings and spending, the individual consumer must first allocate a portion to meet his necessary living costs.   Messrs. Roos and von Szeliski estimate the subsistence or necessitous living cost to have been $200 per capita for 1923 and to have varied in other years with the National Industrial Conference Board index of the cost of living.

Deducting these costs from disposable consumer income, they obtain estimates of "supernumerary income" which is available for expenditures on automobiles and other goods (Table 4–6, Column 5).

Charts 4–14 and 4–15 demonstrate that for a given amount of disposable or supernumerary income the sales of automobiles are characteristically much higher when income is rising than when it is falling. The reason for this has long been known. The demand for automobiles, as for most durable goods, depends not only on the level of income but on psychological factors such as the state of confidence. Declining business activity and decreasing income give rise to uncertainty and to fears that income will decline still further. As a result, even relatively high levels of income may be associated with a low volume of sales. Conversely, increasing business activity and income lead to increased confidence, and to the allocation of an increasing proportion of present and future income to automobile purchases.

The rate of change of the national income may be taken as an approximate index of this psychological factor. If the rate of change, as well as the level of national income, is taken into account, the relationship to sales is seen to be much closer than appears from the use of national income alone.[37] Although the introduction of the rate of change of the national income as a factor in the analysis does help to explain variations in the demand for automobiles, it is not an entirely satisfactory measure of consumer confidence, since other phenomena have appreciable influence on the psychological reactions of automobile buyers. A given rate of change may have little effect on sales at one time and a great effect at another. The rate of change in income is, therefore, at best only an approximate index of these psychological factors.

(2) *Potential New Owners and the Maximum Ownership Level*

The concept of Messrs. Roos and von Szeliski of potential new ownership and of the maximum ownership level is an important contribution to the analysis of the demand for automobiles, since it not only explains the relationship between income and automobile sales but also presents a logical analysis of the major forces determining the sales of automobiles.

Briefly summarized, their explanation is as follows:
(a) At any given time under given economic conditions there is a maximum number of cars that will be kept in operation. In the long run, changes in this maximum ownership

---

[37] S. L. Horner, "Statement of the Problem," *The Dynamics of Automobile Demand.*

level depend, of course, on the growth of population, on the development of highways, and on technical progress. From year to year, however, the level changes in response to the economic status of consumers, and to other factors such as price and durability of the car.

(b) The number of potential new owners is equal to the difference between the maximum ownership level and the existing consumers' stock of cars.

(c) The number of new owner sales is proportional to the number of potential new owners, and to factors dependent on income, price, trade-in allowance, volume of installment credit, and similar factors.

(d) Thus the demand factors are made to enter twice in the analysis of automobile sales, first in determining the maximum ownership level under any given set of economic conditions, and second in determining the nature of the reaction of sales to changes in the number of potential new owners.

(e) By means of these concepts, the relationship between income and automobile sales is explained. Assuming other factors to remain constant, the maximum ownership level at any given time depends on the level of income at that time, but the stock of cars in operation depends on previous income. The number of potential new owners is the difference between the maximum ownership level and the stock of cars in operation and depends therefore on the difference between this year's and previous years' income. Thus, while it is the change in income from past levels which determines the number of potential owners, it is the current level of income which determines the relation between the volume of sales and the number of potential new owners.

(f) The maximum ownership level is a potent force in determining the volume of new car sales. A sudden increase in income may increase the maximum ownership level to a figure far above the number of cars in operation and thus lead to a very large increase in car sales. This is undoubtedly what happened in 1937. On the other hand a sudden decline in income may decrease the maximum ownership level to a figure below the number of cars in operation. In that case there will be an actual liquidation of part of the stock of cars in operation. This is what happened during the depression years 1930–32.

(3) *Replacement Demand*

Messrs. Roos and von Szeliski's theory with respect to replacement demand is as follows:

(a) Not only do consumers adjust the *number* of cars in operation towards the maximum ownership level, but they also
adjust the *quality* of the cars in operation towards some
optimum level by means of replacement.

(b) Replacement demand depends on the pressure for replacement, and on such economic factors as price, income and
trade-in allowances.

(c) The age distribution of the cars in operation combined
with experience tables for scrapping furnishes a measure
of the pressure for replacement. The studies of car survival which have been made since 1926 show that car life
during the last fifteen to twenty years has slowly increased.
Griffin's study of 1926 shows 50% of the cars surviving
about seven years, whereas the most recent study based
on 1933–37 registrations shows 50% surviving about nine
years. From these studies may be computed the percentage of an original group of cars that is scrapped after the
first, second, third, etc., year of service. By application of
these percentages to the figures giving the age distribution
of the cars in operation in any year a measure of the
replacement pressure during that year is obtained. This
index represents the theoretical scrapping rate.[38]

(d) Theoretical scrapping, however, merely indicates normal
replacement pressure. It is not equal to actual replacement since this varies with economic circumstances. In
times of prosperity people scrap more cars than is indicated
by theoretical scrapping. The converse is true in periods
of depression. Thus in 1929 actual scrapping was about
one-third higher than theoretical scrapping, whereas in
1933 it was about 60% lower than the theoretical rate.[39]
Replacement sales therefore depend not only on theoretical
scrapping but on income and price and other economic
factors.

(4) *The Price of Automobiles*

The almost continuous reduction (until 1933) of car prices
undoubtedly contributed significantly to the great development
of the automobile industry. The effect which price changes have
on year to year changes in sales is, however, a more difficult question.

One of the major difficulties encountered is the fact that manufacturing specifications change so frequently. Since price changes
do not occur separately but in conjunction with changes in car

---

[38] See Roos and von Szeliski, *op. cit. supra,* pages 47–53.
[39] *Ibid.,* page 52, chart 15.

models, it is impossible to segregate satisfactorily the influence of price changes on car sales.

A second difficulty in analyzing the effect of price changes is the fact that there have not been sufficiently wide fluctuations in car prices to warrant very reliable conclusions. A long-run decline in car prices has been associated with a long-run increase in sales. But since year to year changes in price have not been large, it is difficult to discover what effect they have had on year to year changes in sales.

Another major problem in any statistical analysis of the effects of changes in car prices upon volume of sales is the construction of a price index. Automobiles have improved so rapidly in quality, and the changes in design and construction have been so frequent, that it is next to impossible to construct a satisfactory price index. The Bureau of Labor Statistics index of wholesale prices, which is an average of prices of different makes, has been shown to be seriously in error.[40] The index used by Roos and von Szeliski is the average delivered price of the lowest priced cars freely available in volume (Ford, Chevrolet, and Plymouth). Their assumption underlying the use of this index is that this average price determines the number of cars sold, and that the prices of other cars merely determine the distribution of sales among the various makes.[41]

Roos and von Szeliski conclude that price has not been a very important factor in determining automobile sales. The usual measure of the responsiveness of quantity sold to price is the elasticity of demand, or the ratio of the percentage change in the quantity sold to the percentage change in price. It was found that this elasticity was not constant but varied from year to year with changes in economic conditions, particularly with changes in income and in the maximum ownership level.

The figures in Table 4–7 give the statistical estimates on the elasticity of demand for the years 1919–1938:

These are presented as the *best* estimates of the elasticity of demand. The authors point out that the elasticity may be anywhere between .65 and 2.5, and that 1.5 is probably a good representative figure. It will be noted that there has been a long-run tendency for the elasticity to increase except in periods of depression.

For comparison, there are given in Table 4–8 their findings on the income elasticity or the responsiveness of demand to changes in supernumerary income.

---

[40] A. T. Court, "Hedonic Price Indexes," *The Dynamics of Automobile Demand*, pages 99–103.

[41] This index is available only since 1926. For the years 1919–1925 the Bureau of Labor Statistics index was used.

TABLE 4–7

ELASTICITY OF DEMAND FOR AUTOMOBILES WITH RESPECT
TO PRICE, 1919–1938

1919	1.03	1929	1.41
1920	1.04	1930	1.51
1921	1.04	1931	1.46
1922	1.05	1932	1.44
1923	1.05	1933	1.30
1924	1.15	1934	1.34
1925	1.22	1935	1.34
1926	1.26	1936	1.33
1927	1.33	1937	1.38
1928	1.37	1938	1.53

Source: Roos and von Szeliski, *The Dynamics of Automobile Demand*, p. 94.

TABLE 4–8

ELASTICITY OF DEMAND FOR AUTOMOBILES WITH RESPECT
TO INCOME, 1919–1938

1919	1.55	1929	2.39
1920	1.55	1930	2.62
1921	1.56	1931	2.57
1922	1.61	1932	2.44
1923	1.69	1933	2.19
1924	1.80	1934	2.19
1925	1.94	1935	2.20
1926	2.08	1936	2.25
1927	2.20	1937	2.40
1928	2.25	1938	2.58

Source: Roos and von Szeliski, *The Dynamics of Automobile Demand*, p. 89.

Since the income elasticity is considerably higher than the price elasticity it is evident that the influence of price on sales is not sufficiently powerful to overcome the effect of the wide swings in income during the business cycle. Even if the price elasticity were equal to the income elasticity, it would require a 50% reduction in price to offset a 50% decline in income. Since cash costs for raw materials, tools, wages, salaries, taxes, and other out of pocket expenses constitute about 90% of the wholesale price of a car it is obvious that such reduction in price unaccompanied by a reduction in costs would be disastrous.[42]

---

[42] See S. M. Dubrul, "Significance of the Findings," *Dynamics of Automobile Demand*, pages 123–39.

Secondary Factors Affecting Retail Sales

The factors listed above account for all but a small part of the annual variation in retail sales of automobiles. There are, however, some secondary factors which are highly correlated with those we have considered and whose influence it is therefore difficult to segregate from the rest. In certain years these forces may be of particular importance in stimulating or discouraging sales.

(1) *Used Car Allowances*

The used car allowance is one such factor. Since the net cash cost to the buyer of a new car is the difference between the new car price and the used car allowance, it is obvious that the size of the allowance must affect new car sales. In the statistical study made by Roos and von Szeliski it was, however, impossible to measure this effect.

(2) *Financing Terms*

Financing terms have become progressively easier. The percentage of installment contracts running more than 12 months rose from 14.5% in 1928 to 68% in 1937. The percentage of down payments that were under standard terms ($33\frac{1}{3}$% on new cars, 40% on used cars) rose from 6.1% to 23.3% during the same period. Beginning in 1935 the easing of financing terms was particularly marked.[43] This undoubtedly has had an important effect on the increased volume of purchases of new cars since 1935.

(3) *Operating Costs*

Operating costs are particularly important as a long-run trend factor determining the maximum level of ownership. The better the quality of the car and the lower the annual operating and maintenance costs, the greater is the number of cars that will be kept in operation.

Operating costs were not included as a separate variable in the statistical study. The variation in operating costs has, however, closely paralleled the variation in automobile prices, and it is difficult therefore to separate their respective effects on the volume of automobile sales. Roos and von Szeliski have made estimates of the elasticity of demand for automobiles when the effects of operating costs are included and also when they are excluded. It is the latter series which has been used in the section on prices (Table 4–7).

(4) *Dealers' Used Car Stocks*

Dealers' used car stocks undoubtedly have important effects on sales of new cars in some years. When used car stocks are large,

---

[43] Roos and von Szeliski, *op. cit. supra,* page 68.

dealers tend to push the sales of used cars with greater vigor, and they lower their trade-in allowances. Both of these have a depressing effect on sales of new cars. Unfortunately no data are available on the number and value of used cars in dealer hands, and it is difficult to get any statistical evidence on this point. However, even a superficial examination of the automotive journals indicates that this is at times a major problem.

NOTE:

The demand function in this study took the form

$$S = j^{1.2} p^{-.6} [.0254C \, (M - C) + .65X]$$

where $S =$ sales

$j =$ supernumerary income

$p =$ index of automobile prices

$C =$ number of cars in use during the year

$M =$ maximum ownership, a function of real supernumerary income, durability, and the number of families

$X =$ replacement pressure, a function of income, price and the theoretical scrapping rate

This function is somewhat similar to the Commerce Department function, in that it uses a hyperbolic function of income and price, but the variables used are quite different. Since it is not in a form susceptible to least-squares computations, the regression line was fitted by a method of successive approximations. Price and income elasticity in this function are not, as is normal in hyperbolic functions, equal to the exponents of j and p, since income and price also enter into the values of M and X. This is why their elasticities were found to vary from year to year, as shown in Tables 4–7 and 4–8.

VIII. DEMAND FOR STEEL

The analysis of the demand for steel, which is presented below,[44] parallels the automobile study in its scope but raises problems of a different kind and describes the procedure in more detail. The most glaring difficulty in analyzing the demand for steel is the vast variety of its uses. Automobiles provide a fairly homogeneous service to all buyers, but "steel" is a generic name for materials

---

44 "A Statistical Analysis of the Demand for Steel, 1919–1938," U. S. Steel Corporation, *T.N.E.C. Papers*, Vol. I, pp. 169–196.

This study was done by Jacob Mosak and Gregg Lewis under the direction of Theodore Yntema, for the U. S. Steel Company's testimony before the TNEC.

which have demand patterns as diverse as machinery and tin cans.

The discussion of the problems raised by this analysis is to a considerable degree a summary and application of principles discussed in the previous sections of this chapter.

Statement of the Problem

This analysis undertakes to measure the importance of the level of steel prices in determining the quantity of steel [45] sold. More specifically the question to be considered in this study is:

> If the average level of steel prices in any year had been higher or lower than it actually was by a certain percentage, but everything else had been the same,[46] by what percentage and in what direction would the quantity of steel sold in that year have changed? In other words, what is the *price elasticity of demand for steel?*

Some General Considerations on the Demand for Steel

It may seem that the economic and statistical problems involved in an econometric analysis of the demand for steel are simple. The demand for no other product, however, is more complex, or presents greater analytical problems.

A. Steel Is Not a Homogeneous Commodity

The steel industry is generally pictured as a mass-production industry, selling only a few types of steel products, a pound of which is like every other pound of the same type in physico-chemical composition, degree of processing or fabrication, general shape and dimensions.

Actually, the steel industry produces thousands of steel products, most of which are practically made-to-order to the chemical, physical, shape, and dimension specifications of each buyer.[47] And each of the many steel products has its own price.

It is obvious that a demand analysis cannot reasonably be made for each of these innumerable steel products. Thus, one is confronted at the outset with the problem of combining all steel products into a composite whose quantity and price can be measured.

---

[45] Throughout this paper the term *steel* should be understood to include only those products sold by the steel production industry—i. e., what is generally understood as the steel-works and rolling mills industry—to consumers outside that industry. The term *products-made-from-steel* includes all products into which steel so defined enters as a raw material of production.

[46] Except to the extent that changes in other factors affecting the demand for steel are caused by the change in the level of steel prices.

[47] See, for example, the list of steel products in the *Census of Manufacturers,* 1929 (United States Department of Commerce, Bureau of the Census, 1933), pp. 953–958. Each type listed is composed of many different steel products sharing only the common characteristics of the type. See also the list of steel products for which prices are published weekly in the steel trade journal, *The Iron Age.*

B. Steel Is a Raw Material, a Producers', Not a Consumers', Good

Steel as it is sold by the steel producers usually is *not* a finished product ready for use (consumption) by the ultimate consuming public. It is a raw material used by its buyers, along with labor, machines, and other raw materials in the production of products-made-from-steel.

Thus the demand for steel does not depend solely and directly upon the conditions determining consumers' purchases—but is indirectly derived from the conditions affecting the output of products-made-from-steel.

This complicates the analysis because the amount of steel sold to a producer of products-made-from-steel depends largely on:

(1) His current and expected output of products-made-from-steel. This is in turn dependent upon an interrelation of numerous factors such as:
   (a) The current and expected conditions of demand for his output, which will tend to be complex.[48]
   (b) His current and expected costs of production, including not only the cost of the steel he uses, but many other costs as well.
   (c) The institutional arrangements of the market in which he sells his products-made-from-steel.
(2) The amount of steel he uses per unit of product-made-from-steel, which will depend upon
   (a) The technological characteristics of his product-made-from-steel; of steel and substitute raw materials; and of his production methods.
   (b) The price of steel.
   (c) The cost of using substitutes for steel.[49]

C. Steel Is Used in the Production of Many Widely Differing Kinds of Products-Made-From-Steel

That products-made-from-steel are almost innumerable and widely diverse in kind is a point that need not be labored. One has only to observe the number of products-made-from-steel which enter into everyday activity.

---

[48] If the product-made-from-steel is a *producers'* good, such as a machine, the conditions of demand will tend to be especially complex, since they must in turn be derived from the output of a further product.

[49] The cost of using substitutes will depend not only upon the price of the substitute itself, but also upon:

(i) The cost of the machinery, labor, etc., that the use of the substitute requires.

(ii) The gain or loss in sales volume that the use of the substitute might entail. It should be emphasized that machines and labor, as well as raw materials, may be, at least in part, substituted for steel. Thus, a reduction in the costs of labor may lead to the use of more labor per unit of output and reduce the quantity of steel used, through reduction of fabrication losses by more careful processing.

If the factors, and the relations among the factors, determining the outputs of all types of products-made-from-steel were more or less identical, the diversity of products-made-from-steel would present no great analytical difficulties in determining the demand for steel. It is obvious, however, that since products-made-from-steel enter into so many differing aspects of economic activity, the determinations of their outputs must also differ greatly. The way in which the output of refrigerators is determined is certainly much different from that for automobiles, and that for automobiles different from that for battleships.

It is clearly an impossible task to make an analysis of the output of every type of product-made-from-steel.[50] Thus again we have the index number problem of combining the many products-made-from-steel, the factors which determine their outputs and the quantity of steel used per unit of output into a reasonable number of economic composites.[51]

D. Steel Is Largely Used in the Production of Durable Goods [52]

The most important consideration involved in the analysis of the way economic factors act in relation to each other in determining the demand for steel is that the major part of the quantity of steel sold is used in the production of *highly durable* products-made-from-steel.[53]

It is elementary economics to observe that goods are valuable—that is, can command a price on the market—only for the services they provide.[54] Thus the demand for goods essentially is derived from the demand for the services of the goods.

The peculiar characteristic of *durable* goods is that they can provide services over a long period of time. Once a stock of durable goods has been built up—as is true in advanced economic societies—it is possible to obtain an almost undiminishing flow of services from them for a long period of time *without the production of any new durable goods. Consumption,* that is, may go on without a corresponding *production* of new durable goods. New durable goods will be produced only when it is economically desirable to replace "worn out" durable goods and to enlarge the stock of durable goods. Thus it is

---

50 Inasmuch as the production of a few types of products-made-from-steel takes the major part of the quantity of steel sold, the problem is not as difficult as it might appear. Thus the main types could be analyzed and combined together as representing the demand for steel, without serious loss of accuracy from the omission of the many less important products.

51 Whether this can be accomplished by the usual index number techniques without serious loss of information or without producing spurious results is a question that has not yet been satisfactorily answered.

52 See C. F. Roos and V. von Szeliski, "Factors Governing Changes in Domestic Automobile Demand" in *The Dynamics of Automobile Demand* (General Motors Corporation, New York City, 1939).

53 Tin plate, which is used mainly in the production of tin cans, is the most important exception.

54 The service which apparently non-useful goods provide is the satisfaction of ownership.

obvious that the production of new durable goods tends to be largely dissociated from the consumption of the services of the stock of durable goods. For the same reason, the amplitude of cyclical fluctuations in the production of new durable goods will tend to be greater than the variations in the consumption of durable goods and in the production and consumption of perishable goods. Since the demand for steel is derived largely from the production of new durable goods, it follows that there will be great cyclical fluctuations in the quantity of steel sold.

Upon what factors does the demand for new durable goods depend? Inasmuch as the conditions of demand for *producers'* durable goods differ in some respects from those for *consumers'* durable goods, each of these types will be discussed separately.

(1) *Factors Affecting the Demand for New Producers' Durable Goods.* Broadly speaking, a producer will not purchase a new durable producers' good unless he can reasonably expect that the return attributable to the new good over its "life span" will be sufficient to cover all the costs (including a reasonable profit) attributable to the purchase and use of the good. That is, the purchase must be expected to be a profitable one.

Among the most important factors determining the profitability of such purchases are:

(a) The current demand and the future demand expected by the producer for his output of goods and services.
(b) His present stock (number of units, age and efficiency of the units, and expected life span of the stock) of durable goods.
(c) The purchase price of the new durable good, including financing charges.
(d) The expected life span and efficiency of the new durable good. That is, the expected life "capacity" of the new durable good.
(e) The "costs of using" the good—i.e., the labor, material, managerial costs, etc., involved in the use of the good.
(f) The expected sale price per unit of the output of the good.
(g) The current and anticipated costs of (including the "costs of using") substitutes, such as labor, for the new durable goods.

(2) *Factors Affecting the Demand for Consumers' Durable Goods.* The most important factors affecting the demand for consumers' durable goods are: [55]

(a) The current and anticipated amount of consumers' disposable cash income.
(b) The distribution of such income among economic classes.
(c) The size (number of units, age distribution, efficiency, and expected life span) of the stock of consumers' durable goods.
(d) The present and anticipated price of the new durable good.
(e) The costs of operating (including maintenance) the new durable good.

(f) The cost of obtaining competing consumer services, including the "costs of living."

(g) Consumers' tastes.

It is apparent that the *demand* for new durable goods is determined by a complex composite of factors. Moreover, not all of the factors are directly measurable. Since the complete "fund of services stored" in durable goods can be used up (consumed) only over a more or less long period of time, *anticipations* are of paramount importance in determining the output of new durable goods. Thus there arises the problem of "measuring" changes in producers' and consumers' states of mind.[56]

There is a further and very important analytical problem. Since the amount of any commodity bought and sold depends not only on its price but also on a complex set of other factors, an analysis which attempts to isolate the influence of price is more difficult when the other factors are numerous, important, and subject to great or rapid changes. If, for example, as is the case for certain staple agricultural commodities, only a few factors other than price tend to be important in determining the quantity sold, and tend also to follow a slow and regular routine of change, the problem of isolating the effect of price is simplified. In the case of durable products-made-from-steel, however, factors other than price are numerous, exert very important effects, and tend to have large and irregular variations. Thus the problem of isolating the effect of the price of steel on the quantity of steel sold is exceedingly difficult.[57]

E. Steel Is Durable and Can Be Stored

Since steel itself is durable, it may be kept in stock for fairly long periods without serious physical deterioration.[58] Thus, purchasers of steel may currently buy more steel than they require for current (or anticipated near future) consumption, building up a stock of steel for future production requirements. Conversely, the building up of such a stock in the past enables a steel purchaser currently to *buy* less steel than he *consumes,* the balance of such consumption coming from depletion of his steel inventories. If *changes* in the size of steel inventories in the hands of consumers (buyers) tend to be large, then it is obvious that the size of such inventories is an important factor influencing the sales of steel producers.

---

[56] Inasmuch as current anticipations depend for the most part on the recent and current behavior of factors which in many cases can be measured, an approximate measure of anticipations can often be obtained from study of the measurable factors.

[57] An excellent discussion of the problem of isolating the effect of price in the derivation of quantity-price demand relations is contained in Henry Schultz, *Theory and Measurement of Demand* (Chicago, 1938), pp. 61–104.

[58] There are, of course, exceptions to this statement; for example, cold reduced auto sheets should be used promptly.

The size of steel inventories in the hands of consumers [59] will depend for the most part on:

(1) Buyers' anticipations as to future prices of steel.

(2) Their expected production requirements, which will depend largely on their expected sales of products-made-from-steel.

(3) The expected length of time it will take to get delivery from steel producers on future orders of steel.

(4) The cost of carrying such inventories.

If the steel buyer expects that prices of steel shortly will be higher, or that near-capacity operations of steel producers may delay delivery on his orders at a time when his steel requirements will be high, he may currently buy more than he needs for current consumption, stocking steel as protection against future higher prices or delivery delay. On the other hand, if his steel requirements turn out to be smaller than expected, he may find himself with unnecessarily large inventories of steel on hand. Thus he may consume from stock, curtailing his buying below his current production requirements.

However, such changes in inventories, which are largely speculative, for the most part exert only a short run effect on steel buying. The effect usually is a short run shift in the time of the actual purchases, without changing the total amount of steel bought over a one or two year period from what it otherwise would have been.

The reasons for this are:

(a) Inventories of steel cannot be reduced below a certain minimum (which depends largely on the level of the producers' operations) without serious inconvenience. This is especially true when there is danger of delay in delivery of orders of steel.

(b) On the other hand, the cost of carrying inventories and the risks involved tend to set an upper limit to their size. The larger the inventories, the higher is the carrying expense, and the further into the future must the user anticipate prices of steel and his own production requirements. Such anticipations become more risky as they extend longer into the future. The situation seldom arises when the costs of carrying are low enough, and the future certain enough, to justify changing inventories by more than a few months' production requirements.

---

[59] This section deals only with changes in inventories of steel in the hands of *consumers*. However, steel producers themselves may keep stocks of steel. Inasmuch as the largest part of the steel produced is made to order to the buyer's specification, changes in inventories of finished steel in the hands of producers are ordinarily small. There is some evidence, however, that changes in inventories of steel ingots, semi-finished steel, and *standard* types of finished steel in the hands of producers may at times be quite large. Such changes of inventories in the hands of *producers* are relevant to the discussion of this paper only if it is necessary to derive estimates of steel sales from figures on steel production.

This is not to say, however, that *year-to-year* fluctuations in steel inventories are unimportant in explaining *year-to-year* changes in steel buying. In periods of rapid change in business activity and business outlook—such as the period from the middle of 1936 to the middle of 1938—changes in the size of inventories may be very important.

Thus in analyzing the demand for steel it is necessary to include as a factor net changes in steel inventories in the hands of steel buyers, or in the absence of such data, the factors upon which the size of steel inventories depends.

F. Steel Is Not Sold in a Single One-Price Market [60]

Largely because steel producers and steel buyers are located over a wide area, and also because it is impossible at all times for all buyers and sellers of steel to have "perfect knowledge of the market," there tend to exist at any time certain differentials between the prices paid for the same type of steel by different buyers.[61] These differentials are of two main types:

(1) First there are the more or less permanent price differentials between buyers in different geographic areas. These differentials have arisen partly from varying costs of assembling raw materials and converting them into finished products at different locations, partly from varying costs of transportation of the finished product into different areas, partly from the forces of competition, and partly from certain long established institutional arrangements in the pricing of steel.[62] These same forces, however, tend to keep the differentials more or less constant, so that year to year changes in the price of steel are about the same in all areas.[63]

(2) The second type of price differential is the concession from the prevailing price. Because of competition among steel producers, it is obviously advantageous at certain times for certain steel producers to offer steel at lower prices than their competitors.[64] By so doing they can often take a substantial

---

[60] This section is not to be interpreted either as an attempt to describe fully or to appraise the pricing and selling arrangements in the market for steel.

[61] Obviously this problem is not confined to the marketing of steel. Such price differentials will almost always arise when there is more than one seller and one buyer.

[62] Discussions of the basing-point method of pricing are especially relevant here. See the description in Daugherty, de Chazeau and Stratton, *Economics of the Iron and Steel Industry* (McGraw-Hill Book Company, New York, 1937), Vol. I, pp. 533–544.

[63] Mill net indexes for different basing point areas support this conclusion.

[64] Price concessions are especially advantageous (from the short-run point of view of the individual seller) for producers (1) having relatively small steel producing capacity (2) operating at a low percentage of capacity. By making concessions such producers may gain enough business to raise their operation to a rate at which they can make substantial profit gains (or loss reductions).

share of the steel market away from competing steel companies.[65] However, the same forces of competition require that such price concessions be kept from the knowledge of competitors; otherwise the concessions will be met and become general.[66] When concessions do become general, data on the price cuts ordinarily become market knowledge available to the steel trade journals who report "going" market prices.[67]

The combination of these two types of prices differentials means that at any time there tends to be more than one price for the same type of steel. Thus there arises the problem of combining these prices into single composite prices for the various types of steel.[68]

Factors Which Might Be Expected to Influence the Quantity of Steel Sold

From the discussion of the previous pages it is clear that the following factors might reasonably be expected to influence the quantity of steel sold:

(1) The price of steel—including both the level and the direction of change.
(2) Consumers' disposable cash income.
(3) The distribution of the income among income classes.
(4) The stock (number of units and efficiency) of durable goods—both consumers' and producers'.
(5) The cost of living.
(6) The prices of goods and services which compete with products-made-from-steel for the outlays of producers and consumers.
(7) The costs of maintaining and operating products-made-from-steel.
(8) Industrial profits.
(9) The psychological atmosphere—i.e., producers' and consumers' anticipation as to future economic conditions.
(10) Industrial production.

Since some of these variables are very highly related to others, however, and since others tend to change slowly and smoothly from year to year, certain of them were omitted in the actual analysis. The factors which were used in the final statistical analysis were:

(1) The price of steel—both its level and direction of change.

---

[65] See the recent discussion in Paul M. Sweezy, "Demand under Conditions of Oligopoly," *Journal of Political Economy*, XLVII, No. 4 (Aug., 1939), pp. 568 *et seq.*

[66] See Sweezy, *op. cit.*

[67] Undoubtedly there are times when price concessions are important, and when it is difficult for the trade journals to verify or measure the extent of the concessions. Ordinarily the trade journals can measure the extent of the concessions only when the market for some type of steel "breaks wide open."

[68] This, too, is a difficult index number problem that has never been satisfactorily solved. Ideally the solution requires separate demand analyses for each group of buyers subject to the same price differentials.

(2) Industrial production—both its level and direction of change.
(3) Consumers' income—both its level and direction of change.
(4) Industrial profits—both its level and direction of change.
(5) The cost of living.
(6) A time-trend variable.

As will be pointed out below [69] these six factors can be taken as approximately representing all of the preceding ten.

The Period Studied

The period 1919 to 1938 was chosen for analysis for the following reasons:

(1) It was a long enough period to provide observations on the nature of the demand for steel under practically all types of conditions so that somewhat general inferences could be drawn from the data. The period covered includes both years of boom and years of decline.[70]

(2) This period is of more current interest than earlier periods, because the inferences drawn are of more accurate current application.

(3) Data for years prior to 1919 are very often not available.[71]

However, after the analysis was begun it was found desirable to exclude the years 1919–1921 from some of the demand relations. The analysis indicated that the situation in these three years was abnormal because of the World War. The magnitude and the direction of the fluctuations in economic activity were not typical of the rest of the period, and the inclusion of these years, it was thought, obscured the ordinary steel demand relations. The statistical analysis, however, was in most cases carried through for both the complete and the abbreviated periods.

Annual data, rather than monthly data or data for periods longer than a year, were selected for analysis for three reasons:

(1) Monthly data were not available for some of the series.

(2) The use of monthly data unnecessarily complicates the analysis for the purposes of this paper because it introduces short-term factors—such as seasonal variations and short-run speculative activity—which are practically excluded by using annual data.[72]

(3) The use of longer-period data was considered undesirable because

---

[69] See section A, under "The Demand Relation Hypotheses."

[70] When annual data are used, the statistical technique here employed requires a period as long as fifteen or twenty years in order to get a sufficient number of observations. The reasons for this are technical and will not be discussed here.

[71] For example, reliable data on consumers' income, industrial profits, the cost of living, and industrial production are not available in good form before 1919.

[72] Ideally, of course, it would be desirable to use monthly, or even shorter-period data, since intra-year variations tend to affect annual measures. However, the extra analysis was considered to be too great to compensate for the small loss of information involved in using annual data.

(a) A much longer period of years would have to be studied in order to get a sufficient number of observations.

(b) The effect of year to year changes in demand conditions on steel sales was desired.

(c) It is extremely difficult to isolate the causative effect of price when longer-period data are used. The use of longer-period data introduces many new factors into the analysis which can be considered as unimportant in studying year to year changes.

The Demand Relation Hypotheses [73]

The final problem remaining prior to the actual statistical determination of the demand for steel is that of setting up an economically logical hypothesis as to the way the factors considered earlier act together in determining the quantity of steel sold. This is by far the most important part of the whole analysis of the demand for steel. It is obvious that the final inferences drawn—concerning the influence of the price of steel on the quantity of steel sold—will depend on the demand relation hypothesis set up.

The problem of setting up a demand relation hypothesis for steel is a perplexing one. Products-made-from-steel are so numerous and so diverse that it is almost impossible to analyze the way economic factors act together in determining the output of even the most important. Moreover, data which would be helpful are lacking at critical points. Then, too, information as to the economic-technical problem of the amount of steel used per unit of products-made-from-steel is almost completely unavailable. A similar situation exists for the problem of setting up an hypothesis as to the determination of steel inventories.

The lack of information at critical points, and the absence of a completely suitable body of economic theory have forced recourse to what is largely an empirical determination of the demand hypothesis.

A. Actual Variables Included in the Demand Relation Hypothesis

Five general hypotheses as to the actual variables to be included in the demand relation hypothesis were set up. The basic variables included in these various hypotheses are shown in Chart 4–8. The five general hypotheses were:

The quantity of steel sold [74] depends upon:

(h–1) The price of steel,[75] and the volume of industrial production.[76]

(h–2) A time-trend variable in addition to those of (h–1).

---

[73] See Roos and von Szeliski, *op. cit.*, section III.

[74] Measured by steel ingot production, and estimated shipments and bookings.

[75] *The Iron Age* composite price of finished steel.

[76] The Federal Reserve Board index of manufacturing production excluding iron and steel.

(h–3) The same variables as (h–2) and in addition two variables measuring respectively the rate of change in the price of steel and the rate of change in the volume of industrial production.[77]

(h–4) The price of steel, a time-trend, consumers' supernumerary income, and industrial profits.

(h–5) The same variables as (h–4), and in addition three variables measuring respectively the rates of change in the price of steel, supernumerary income, and industrial profits.[78]

In (h–1) it was assumed that industrial production measured accurately the composite influence of all factors affecting the demand for steel except the price of steel. It was assumed that industrial production reflected the composite effect of the most important demand factors, viz., industrial profits, consumers' income, the replacement pressure on the stock of durable goods, and, also indirectly the psychological outlook. Since all of these factors have actually been more or less highly correlated with industrial production, such an assumption is not unreasonable.

In (h–2) an additional time-trend factor was included. The time-trend was included explicitly as a variable to act as a proxy measure for all factors influencing the demand for steel which tend to change slowly and smoothly over a long period of time. Thus it serves as a composite measure for such factors as population, the size of the stock of durable goods, and long-time changes in various price and cost levels (including the level of the prices of steel), industrial technology, and people's tastes. The inclusion of such a variable makes it possible partly to isolate the effects of these long-run factors.

It is commonly recognized that a very important factor determining the current level of activity in durable goods production— and thus in steel sales—is the business outlook of producers and consumers, their anticipations as to future prices, profits, income, etc. Such anticipations are very largely determined by the rapidity and direction of change in recent and current business activity. If present levels of activity are higher than they have been in the recent past, it is easier to believe that conditions will continue to improve than if activity is currently on the decline. For this reason the rate of change of industrial production was included in (h–3) as a factor measuring changes in anticipations. Similarly the rate of change in the price of steel has been included in (h–3) as a

---

[77] The rates of change are for any year in each case measured by the link relative for that year. (The link relative is equal to that year's figure divided by the figure for the previous year.)

[78] The measure of the rates of change is the link relative, except for profits where the rate of change is measured by first differences. (The first difference for any year is equal to the figure for that year less the figure for the previous year.)

measure of steel buyers' anticipations as to the near future price of steel.

In (h–4) and (h–5) industrial profits and consumers' supernumerary income and their respective rates of change have been substituted for industrial production and its rate of change to measure the composite of factors other than the price of steel influencing the demand for steel.

Of the five general hypotheses it would seem that (h–5) is probably the most complete and the most reasonable. The final answer, of course, cannot be given until the form of the five general hypotheses is set up and tested.

B. The Form of the Demand Relation Hypothesis

The next step in the analysis is the formulation of an hypothesis as to the way the economic variables act together in determining the demand for steel.

Each of the five general hypotheses outlined above was studied by familiar graphical multi-factor correlation techniques,[79] in order to find out

(i) What mathematical relation seems to be the most reasonable expression of the relation between the factors.

(ii) Whether any of the five general hypotheses should be discarded or modified.

The graphical analysis indicated that for all of the hypotheses a simple additive relation would probably give as satisfactory results as any other (such as the multiplicative or combinations of the additive and multiplicative).[80]

It was also decided from the graphical analysis to use only (h–2), (h–4), and a modification of (h–3) which excluded the rate of change in the price of steel [81] and the time-trend.

Thus four mathematical relations were formulated for further examination by mathematical statistical techniques. Translated verbally these relations were:

---

[79] See Henry Schultz, op. cit., pp. 184–186, including the sources cited in footnote 7 on p. 185.

[80] The additive relation has in its favor the simplicity with which the statistical analysis may be carried out. More complicated forms of mathematical relations have, of course, certain logical advantages arising from their greater generality. It is well known, however, that if it is desired to study a demand relation near the average values of its variables, the linear arithmetic form gives practically the same results as more complex forms. Since it was considered feasible to study the relation only near its average values, and since there was no clear indication from the graphical analysis that a more complicated form was a more likely one, the additive relation was selected. However, the statistical analysis was also carried through for (h–2) using a simple multiplicative (linear logarithmic) relation.

[81] The graphical analysis indicated that no significant information would be added by the rate of change terms in (h-5), and the rate of change of the price of steel in (h-3), and that the inclusion of these terms might break down the statistical analysis.

Relation I

Production of steel ingots and castings is equal to:

Price of steel multiplied by a constant value

plus Industrial production multiplied by (another) constant value

plus Time (in years) multiplied by (another) constant value

plus a constant balancing value.

Relation II

The same as Relation I plus

The rate of change of industrial production multiplied by a constant value and excluding the time-trend.

Relation III

Estimated steel shipments are equal to:

Price of steel multiplied by some constant value

plus Industrial profits multiplied by some constant value

plus Supernumerary income multiplied by some constant value

plus Time (in years) multiplied by some constant value

plus a constant balancing factor.

Relation IV

The same as Relation III except that estimated steel bookings were substituted for estimated steel shipments.

The only problem remaining was to find the numerical values of the various constant multiplying and balancing factors in the relations. Once this was done it was easy to find out how much of a change in the quantity of steel sold (as represented by bookings, shipments, or ingot production) has been associated with a given change in the price of steel, industrial production or any other of the independent variables.

The Statistical Findings

The constants were determined by the least squares multiple correlation technique.[82]

The same statistical procedure also gives the percentage of the total variation in the quantity of steel sold over the period studied that is accounted for by the economic factors included in the relations, and the amount that can be directly attributed to the separate variations of each of the factors.[83] These percentages are shown in Table 4–8.[84]

---

[82] For an excellent description of the techniques followed see Schultz, *op. cit.,* Appendix C.

[83] For a rigorous definition of the term "variation" as used here, and the details of the procedure used in attributing variation in steel sales to the various "causative" economic factors, see Schultz, *op. cit.,* pp. 741–743. Simply stated, the percentage of variation directly attributable to any factor is the ratio of the variation in the quantity of steel sold which would have taken place if only that factor had varied in the way it did, to the variation in the quantity of steel sold that actually took place.

[84] Except for Relation II the period studied was 1922 to 1938; for Relation II, it

TABLE 4–9

VARIATION IN STEEL SALES RELATED TO VARIATION IN DEMAND FACTORS

| Relation Number | Quantity of Steel Sold Measured by | Relation Accounted for by All Factors in Demand | Percent of Variation in Quantity of Steel Sold | | | | | |
| | | | Directly attributable to variation in | | | | | |
			Price of steel	Industrial production	Industrial profits	Super-numerary income	Rate of change of industrial production	Time trend
I	Production of Steel Ingots and Castings	96	0	88				0
II	Production of Steel Ingots and Castings	96	9	81			1	
III	Estimated Steel Shipments	91	1		41	19		0
IV	Estimated Steel Bookings	90	9		90	6		1

Two conclusions are indicated by Table 4–9:

(1) In each of the demand relations, the included factors accounted for 90 percent or more of the observed variation in the respective measure of steel sales.

(2) Over the period studied only a small fraction (10 percent or less) of the variation in steel sales was directly attributable to variation in steel prices, while the major part of the variation was accounted for by included factors other than the price of steel.

It should be emphasized again, however, that these conclusions depend upon the accuracy of three assumptions:

(a) That the demand relations set up are good approximations to the true demand relations both as to factors included and the form of the relation.

(b) That the variables used more or less accurately measure what they are supposed to.

(c) That the statistical technique yields approximately correct constant values for the demand relation.

In appraising the second conclusion drawn from Table 4–9 it should be kept in mind that the relative proportion of the total variation of steel sales attributable to variation in the price of steel over any period will depend in part on the amount of variation in steel prices relative

---

was 1920 to 1938. It will be noted that in all cases the sum of the percentages of variation directly attributable to the separate factors is not equal to the total variation accounted for by all the factors in the relation. The reason for this is as follows: In obtaining the percentages attributable to any factor we assume that none of the other factors varied. Actually, of course, this is not true; all of the factors varied, the changes in some factors tending to *increase* the quantity of steel sold *while* other changes were tending to *decrease* sales. The net result of all the simultaneous changes is the amount of variation accounted for by all the factors.

to variation in the other factors. Over the period 1922 to 1938 relative variation in steel prices was considerably less than the relative variation in the other factors.

A more useful measure of the importance of the price of steel is the elasticity of demand coefficient. This coefficient is the ratio of the percentage change in the quantity of steel sold to the corresponding percentage change in the price of steel, other factors being fixed at some level.

Table 4–10 shows the values of the elasticity of demand found in the four demand relations when the values of the demand factors are at their average levels for the periods studied.[85]

TABLE 4–10

ELASTICITY OF DEMAND FOR STEEL

Relation Number	Elasticity
I	+ 0.12
II	+ 0.52
III	− 0.21
IV	− 0.88

The values are consistent in this very important respect: they indicate that at most *a one percent decrease in the price of steel would cause (other factors remaining the same) less than a one percent increase in steel sales (and conversely).* If this is true, and if fluctuations in the other factors continue to be as great and as important as they have been in the past, the volume of steel consumption cannot be stabilized by compensatory changes in the price of steel.

Which of the above values of the elasticity of demand is the most likely? The values obtained from Relations III and IV are probably better than those from I and II for the following reasons:

(a) On *a priori* grounds it seems reasonable that a change in the price of steel would lead to a change in the opposite direction in steel sales. Relations I and II both indicate positive relations between steel prices and sales.

(b) Steel ingot production is probably not as accurate a measure of steel sales as the estimates used in Relations III and IV.

(c) Industrial production (and its rate of change) is probably not as good a measure of the composite of factors other than price of steel as the combination of the two factors, industrial profits and supernumerary income.

The difference in the values obtained from Relations III and IV can be due only to the difference between the estimates of steel sales used in each case, for the relations are identical in other respects. From Chart 4–16 it is apparent that fluctuations in the steel bookings

---

85 These values of the elasticity have been computed at the arithmetic mean point of the factors influencing the demand for steel.

BASIC SERIES USED IN STATISTICAL ANALYSIS

Year	Steel Ingot Production (thousands of gross tons)	Steel Bookings (thousands of gross and net tons)	Steel Shipments (thousands of gross and net tons)	Industrial Production (1923-25=100)	Industrial Profits (billions of dollars)	Supernumerary Income (billions of dollars)	Composite Price of Steel (cents per pound)
1919	34,671	25,233	20,783	85	6.419	28.2	3.115
1920	42,133	30,212	27,217	83	4.468	32.8	3.737
1921	19,784	7,609	12,375	73	−0.055	25.0	2.437
1922	35,603	30,391	23,705	87	4.380	28.9	2.124
1923	44,944	25,439	29,173	100	5.867	35.5	2.697
1924	37,932	26,214	24,154	95	4.998	35.6	2.505
1925	45,394	30,557	29,639	105	6.971	37.5	2.334
1926	48,294	29,138	30,847	107	6.774	39.8	2.315
1927	44,935	28,488	28,827	107	5.880	40.6	2.202
1928	51,544	33,761	32,560	110	7.566	43.0	2.165
1929	56,433	39,167	36,197	116	8.083	46.8	2.209
1930	40,699	26,977	26,280	95	1.366	41.7	2.048
1931	25,946	17,133	18,431	86	−3.145	34.1	1.957
1932	13,681	9,129	10,385	73	−5.375	23.1	1.901
1933	23,232	15,027	15,607	82	−2.379	20.2	1.879
1934	26,055	18,777	16,222	83	0.157	25.1	2.033
1935	34,093	22,751	21,050	93	1.674	27.8	2.058
1936	47,768	33,888	28,766	104	3.903	36.0	2.077
1937	50,569	30,212	31,620	106	3.872	38.8	2.464
1938	28,350	19,413	18,176	89	2.165	34.0	2.394

figures used in Relation IV tend to lead industrial profits, while steel shipments (used in Relation III) do so to much less degree.

In the graphical analyses that were made of the various demand relations, there were clear indications that if the lags of shipments and industrial profits behind bookings were removed, Relations III and IV would both give about the same results for the elasticity of demand, yielding a figure of 0.3 to 0.4. The evidence and argument adduced in the preceding pages of this paper support the conclusion that such a value—or one even lower—for the elasticity of demand for steel is not a statistical happenstance, but a reality.

Although these findings are not absolutely conclusive in establishing this very low elasticity of demand for steel, they certainly afford no basis for the view that the price of steel is a practical medium for stabilizing production.

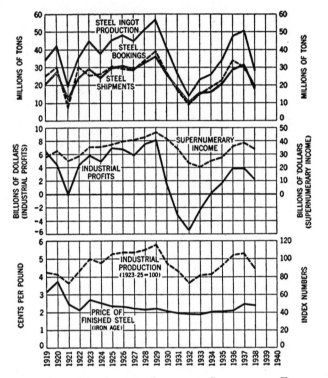

CHART 4–16. DEMAND FOR STEEL AND INFLUENCING FACTORS.
(Source: Table 4–11.)

Chapter 5

COST

I. INTRODUCTION
DECISION-MAKING COSTS
DETERMINANTS OF COST BEHAVIOR
Prices of Input Factors
Technology
Lot Size
Other Factors
Efficiency

II. COST CONCEPTS
INTRODUCTION
OPPORTUNITY VS. OUTLAY COSTS
PAST VS. FUTURE COSTS
SHORT-RUN VS. LONG-RUN COSTS
VARIABLE VS. CONSTANT COSTS
TRACEABLE VS. COMMON COSTS
OUT-OF-POCKET VS. BOOK COSTS
INCREMENTAL COSTS VS. SUNK COSTS
ESCAPABLE VS. UNAVOIDABLE COSTS
CONTROLLABLE VS. NON-CONTROLLABLE COSTS
REPLACEMENT VS. HISTORICAL COSTS
ILLUSTRATION OF COST CONCEPTS
CONCLUSION

III. COST AND OUTPUT RATE
INTRODUCTION
NATURE OF SHORT-RUN COST OUTPUT FUNCTIONS
DIFFERENT APPROACHES TO DETERMINATION OF COST FUNC-
TIONS
HOW TO DECIDE WHICH APPROACH IS BEST
Statistical Approach
Accounting Approach
Engineering Approach
STATISTICAL DETERMINATION OF COST OUTPUT FUNCTIONS
Suitability of Plant for Statistical Analysis
Measurement of Output
Selection of Time Unit of Observation
Selection of Period for Analysis
Selection of Cost Elements
Selection of Form of Cost Observations
Deflation of Cost Data

Cost

I. INTRODUCTION

THE PURPOSE of this chapter is to show how economic analysis can produce, from orthodox accounting records, cost estimates that are relevant for management decisions. In the preceding chapter we examined various concepts of demand in their managerial context and surveyed methods of measuring them. In this chapter we shall look at costs in much the same way to find out what concepts of cost are useful for various kinds of managerial problems, and how these concepts can be reduced to numbers.

Most of the raw material for these special cost estimates comes from traditional double entry record systems that are the basis for balance-sheets and income statements to serve the legal, financial, and tax needs of the enterprise. The interesting cost problems of managerial economics arise in adjusting and supplementing this basic historical record of costs in order to produce the kind of special-purpose costs that management needs in various problems. To do this we draw upon economic analysis for ideas about what costs are appropriate for different decisions, and upon statistical and engineering analysis for techniques to convert conventional financial accounts into estimates of cost concepts that are tailored to a managerial decision problem.

Estimates of these decision-making costs are used only by management. They do not tie into the routine financial accounts. In fact, rigid validation of any kind would be the kiss of death for such special costs. They do not and should not conform to the accounting rules, which are designed primarily to assure formal comparability among periods and among enterprises, and to facilitate verification by disinterested auditors.

Decision-making Costs

Business decisions involve plans for the future and require choices among rival plans. In making these choices, estimates of the effect of each alternative plan upon future expenses and revenues are needed, and cost estimates must be tailored to the economic characteristics of the choices. It should be recognized at the outset that the only costs that matter for business decisions are future costs; "actual" costs, i.e., current or historical costs, are useful solely as a benchmark for estimating the costs that lie ahead if one course of action is chosen as opposed to another.

Many policy decisions can be framed in terms of profitability calculations that are estimates of what changes in the amount (and time distribution) of future expenses and future revenues can be expected from a proposed plan as compared with some other plan. The only expenses and revenues that need be included in such calculations are those that will differ; the unchanged quantities cancel out in the comparison.

Methods of estimating the costs of alternative programs are necessarily conjectural. They involve guessing what would happen to each item of expense under Plan A and under Plan B. What does it take to get good estimates of these decision-making costs? The first requisite is a precise picture of the alternative programs involved in the choice. An explicit definition of the differences among alternatives usually requires economic analysis of the situation. A second requirement is an understanding of different cost concepts, in order to select the one that is most relevant. In operating a modern multiple-product enterprise, the situations requiring decisions are so varied not only among themselves, but in the character of the alternatives available that many different concepts of cost are needed for significant comparison of the alternative plans. The third requisite is flexible classification of the accounting records on several alternative bases. Since decision-making costs require classifications according to rival operating plans, multiple classifications are a desirable informational foundation for such cost estimates. A fourth requisite is ingenuity and skill in quantitative analysis, since typically the desired cost conjectures can be improved by statistical analysis of accounting data.

Decision-making costs can be found from traditional accounting records only by reclassifications, deletions, additions, recombinations of elements, and repricing of input factors in the process of shaping the cost conjectures to fit the concept of cost relevant for the management planning choice. Traditional accounting, because of the need for verifiable data to fulfill its financial reporting function, uses "original cost," i.e., historical prices of input factors, so that costs do not (with a few exceptions, such as inventory valuation during deflation) reflect changes in price levels or managerial mistakes in investment. Traditional accounts are classified primarily on the basis of the object of expenditure, which is handy for verification. When a classification by function (process or department) is superimposed, it also is generally a formalized, unvarying classification, and the assumption is usually made that the original outlay can be spread among functions proportionately to one or several allocation bases, such as direct labor hours, square feet of space, and the like.

Records of historical outlays, based upon these rigid classifications and formal proportionalities need to be drastically reworked for decisions about the future. Classification should depend upon the nature of the rival programs being considered, and therefore change from problem to problem.[1]

Valuation as well as classification depends on the purpose of analysis and differs with the economic characteristics of alternative programs. A single piece of equipment will have different values in terms of its disposal price, replacement cost, value in its present job, and value in alternative jobs. The only values that are irrelevant for all decisions on what to do with a specific asset are its original cost and its book value.

Control and appraisal of executive performance requires an approach to cost analysis that is essentially different from studies to aid decision making. For managerial control, costs must be classified according to areas of executive responsibility, and according to the degree of authority over expense delegated to the executive. Thus once one of the alternative plans is chosen, responsibility for carrying it out in an acceptable manner is assigned, and expenses must be reclassified in a manner that will measure

---

[1] The required flexibility in the classification of costs can be obtained in many ways. One method is to make multiple copies of the original record of the transaction, which can be classified in several different ways. Punch-cards and mechanical tabulation are widely used for cost analysis.

how the performance of each executive compares with some standard or budget (see Chapter 1, Section V). Thus the basic classification by objects of expenditure required for pecuniary history and financial reports must be so set up to enable easy re-classification on a basis that parallels the structure of managerial organization.

To get a clear picture of the kinds of cost notions that are appropriate for different kinds of management decisions, we shall examine in Section II a panorama of concepts of cost and indicate some of the managerial problems for which each type of conceptual distinction is useful. In succeeding sections we shall discuss the problems of empirical analysis for three major cost problems: cost—output relations, cost—size relations, and product costs in multiple product operations. Before taking these up, however, we shall consider briefly, and in general terms, the cost determinants that are the root of cost analysis problems.

Determinants of Cost Behavior

Cost behavior is the result of many forces. Determination of the functional relationship of cost to each major force helps to provide the informational foundation for various cost forecasts, and estimates of the alternative costs of rival programs which characterize cost analysis in managerial economics. The multiple conjectures of conditions that are needed for these decisions can be sharpened by a knowledge of cost functions, as well as by a clear understanding of cost concepts that are relevant for each.

The patterns of cost behavior can be conceived as a single comprehensive cost function, which states the complex relationship of cost to the many determinants which operate for a particular establishment. Alternatively, cost behavior may be analyzed pluralistically in terms of a number of separate cost functions, each showing the relationship of cost to a single determining factor (e.g., the cost—output function). Though this piecemeal approach is abhorrent to mathematical economists, it is useful in applied economics for focusing attention on one relationship which is of significance for the problem at hand.[2] Such a partial analysis is often the most practical approach to statistically significant answers in empirical studies.

---

[2] To isolate one aspect of cost behavior, however, involves some analysis of the other forces that are also operative in order to remove or allow for their influences.

What forces determine the behavior of costs—e.g., account for differences in cost per ton-mile among railroads, and from month to month on the same road? The determinants of cost differ so much from firm to firm and from problem to problem that no general set is applicable to all. Nevertheless, there are a few determinants that have enough importance in modern manufacturing enterprises to deserve special attention: (1) rate of output (i.e., utilization of fixed plant), (2) size of plant, (3) prices of input factors (materials and labor), (4) technology, (5) size of lot, (6) stability of output, and (7) efficiency (of management as well as labor).[3]

The relation of cost to rate of output is examined in Section III, and the relation of cost to size of plant in Section IV, so they need not be discussed further here.

Prices of Input Factors

The effect of changes in wage rates and material prices upon costs must usually be anticipated for the future in choosing among alternative programs. Such relations can usually be developed quite simply for the past by special-purpose index numbers of prices applied to the physical quantities of input factors. In projecting for the future, however, all the problems of price forecasting are encountered, plus the special political uncertainties of forecasting wage rates and labor perquisites. But changes in wages and prices affect not only the cost per unit of inputs but also the minimum-cost mixture of labor, materials, and capital. High wages and low materials prices warrant a larger amount of wastage and rejects than the reverse relation does, since the cost of conserving materials is the labor time spent in careful planning and precise operations. High wages also promote substitution of capital equipment for labor inputs and stimulate technical research

---

[3] Some of these determinants of cost behavior are examined in accounting analysis of short-run cost fluctuations by a process called "variance analysis." The disparity between standard cost and the reported ("actual") cost, called variance, is partitioned among the various determinants of cost behavior—e.g., output rate, material prices, wage rates, labor efficiency. Standard costs usually presuppose norms for all of these cost determinants. Departures of actual conditions from standard operating conditions for each determinant are studied to find out how much of the cost variation can be assigned to each cause. The usual procedure is to work from known factors (such as material price variance) toward unknown causes by successive substraction. Another approach is by multiple correlation analysis. (See Joel Dean, "Correlation Analysis of Cost Variation," *Accounting Review*, March 1937, pp. 55–60.)

in automatic machinery and the use of mechanical energy. For short-run problems the impact of wage rates and material prices on production methods and on improved technology can be largely ignored. But for the more distant future, cost forecasts should take account of the possibility that cheaper materials will be found, that technical advances stimulated by high wage rates will develop methods for displacing man hours.

It is theoretically possible to distinguish between labor-saving equipment adoptions that are caused by technical advances and those that represent a speed-up in the rate of adoption of existent techniques as a result of changes in relative prices (e.g., wage increases). A further distinction can be made between exogenous technical improvements and those that are induced by past or prospective changes in wage rates. Little is really known about the extent to which high wages spur on technology or change the character of technological process, although much is known about the way in which they alter the pattern of adoption of existing technology and hence the depth of capital.

In general, however, the equipment that embodies the existing level of technology usually limits the range of substitution between materials and labor that can be induced by changes in relative prices. Since equipment design prescribes the labor-material mix within fairly rigid limits, the design itself must be changed before high labor prices relative to material or to equipment can have the effect upon the proportional factors of production envisaged in theory.[4] An example of time lag is seen in the problem faced by a manufacturer of highly automatic printing presses immediately after the war. In designing a new line of presses that would have a gestation period of about five years from drawing board to introduction, the management tried to guess what kind of wage level of pressroom labor might be expected by 1951. Thus it was engaged in trying to foresee the factor price substitutions associated with technology.

---

[4] Occasionally, price-induced substitution of labor-saving equipment for labor may be quite important in the short run. This occurs when a high proportion of potential uses of an existing machine lie below the margin of adequate return on the investment so that changes in relative prices can lift them above the margin and make the equipment practical. For example, applications of punch-card accounting which were not economical at prewar wage levels suddenly became highly desirable at postwar wage levels.

Technology

Knowledge of the relation of cost to technological progress *per se* is needed for management problems of cost forecasting as well as for planning the capital expenditures associated with technical advances. The relationship of technology to cost behavior is more subtle than can be encompassed by continuous functions and trend analysis. Often a single change in equipment alters not only the technology but also the scale of the plant and its flexibility for changes in output. Conceptually we distinguish between changes in scale and technological changes by saying that an increase in size may employ a different and better technique, provided it was already a part of the "state of the arts." This change is not a technological improvement: the increased size was necessary to make use of more elaborate technology economical.

An important management problem that involves forecasts of technology is replacement of equipment. Here, the immediate problem is to determine the degree of obsolescence of an old machine which is a candidate for replacement. But to do this requires forecasting the rate of obsolescence of the new machine as well. (See Chapter 10.) Thus projection of technical progress is basic to replacement decisions.

When cost forecasting must go beyond the horizon of foreseeable technical advances, some economists have simply extrapolated past trends in cost into the future.[5] For the economy as a whole, the figure of 3 per cent per year increase in output per man hour has become a popular guess at the future rate of productivity increase and has even been written into labor contracts as a basis for annual increases in wages. It originates in estimates of the average rate of productivity increase in industry for the first part of this century. But much too little is known of the nature of

---

[5] This kind of trend analysis was used in a cost study made for the U. S. Steel Corporation under the direction of Theodore Yntema. In order to adjust earlier cost data to the level of 1938 technology, a trend was fitted to the average annual rate of technological cost reductions. Such a trend might be projected into the future as one means of forecasting technical change. The same general approach is used for the economy as a whole in the Twentieth Century Fund study, *America's Needs and Resources* (1947), and in other forecasts which assume that a long-term trend of improvement in output per man hour can be projected forward.

industrial development or the prospects for peace for anyone to say whether such extrapolation is justified.

Lot Size

The relation of cost to lot size (i.e., size of a single production job) is easy to understand; yet methods of estimating savings and determining optimum lot size differ greatly and cannot all be best. If costs of setting up machinery (or other constant costs per lot) are large, so that the economy of large lots is marked, then knowledge of the lot-size cost curve is indispensable for production planning. It may also be helpful for quantity discounts, and for price differentials among products when there are big differences in their average lot size. But production savings from bigger lots are not the only cost effects. As production cost per unit goes down with lot size, storage and risk cost per unit goes up, so that the optimum size of lot depends also on the volume, stability and predictability of sales of individual products.

Other Factors

In addition to lot size there are other dimensions of production that affect cost behavior importantly in some firms. One is the volatility of output rate: stability and planability of output bring savings in various kinds of hidden costs of interruption and learning.[6] Another is variability of the product-mix, where costs of adaptation are sometimes greater than the cost impact of lot size or change in output rate.

Efficiency

Knowledge of the relation of cost behavior to these determinants is a benchmark for making the kinds of cost projections needed for decisions. Nevertheless, cost functions must be treated with a certain degree of skepticism when human characteristics are brought into the picture. Contrary to the suppositions of orthodox economic theory, the least-cost way of making a given output

---

[6] Size and direction of changes in output rate from the preceding period were tested statistically as determinants of cost behavior in empirical studies of a furniture factory, a hosiery mill, and a belt shop worked out by the author. (See Section III.) Departures of actual sales from planned sales were also tested as a factor in the behavior of costs in three departments of the Lord and Taylor department store. See Joel Dean, "Department Store Cost Functions," in *Studies in Mathematical Economics and Econometrics,* Chicago, University of Chicago Press, 1941.

is not always known, not always politic, and sometimes not even sought.

There is usually some uncertainty as to the least-cost way of producing a given output under specified operating conditions, factor prices, and technology.   To find the lowest-cost operating pattern for a given output rate often involves a choice among several dimensions of operation.   For example, output could be increased by increasing: (1) speed of machines; (2) number of machine hours per day; (3) number of days of operation per month; and/or (4) number of machines operated.   Whether or not a cost study indicates the best method to use, the firm rarely has full flexibility in respect to each of these dimensions.   Repair requirements, union rules, and shift differentials affect the choice.[7]

There are, moreover, great differences through time and among firms in the intensity of the compulsion to attain the least-cost combination, as we have seen in Chapter 1.   Profit maximization in the short run is seldom the dominant objective and the pressure for efficiency is not, as assumed in theory, constant and always sufficient.   Instead, it varies dramatically over the cycle and with the fortunes of the firm.   Thus the complexity of cost behavior and the high tensions that are necessarily created in a drive for cost minimization are dominant reasons for the wide zones of uncertainty that surround most cost projections of whatever sophistication.

II. COST CONCEPTS

Introduction

The word "cost" has many meanings in many different settings. The kind of cost concept to be used in a particular situation depends upon the business decision to be made.   There is a widespread and unfortunate notion that financial accounting costs are universally practical for all kinds of business decisions because they are "actual" in the sense of being routinely recorded somewhere.   Cost considerations enter into almost every business de-

---

[7] Coal mine operators claim that the shift from the eight-hour day to the seven-hour day raised all operating costs because equipment had been synchronized to meet an eight-hour cycle of operation.   The seven-hour day required more supplies and a new combination of men and equipment. (*Economic Consequences of the Seven-Hour Day*, W. E. Fisher, Philadelphia, University of Pennsylvania Press, 1939, p. 39.)

cision, and it is important, though sometimes difficult, to use the right kind of cost.

The costs reported by orthodox financial accounts provide an impeccable pecuniary history that is admirably suited to the legal and financial purposes for which it was designed. But for business decision-making, the relevant cost concept will usually be quite different from "actual full costs" reported by conventional accounting. Hence an understanding of the meaning of various concepts is essential for clear business thinking. One way of getting clear-cut distinctions among different notions of cost is to set up several alternative bases of classifying costs and show the relevance of each for different kinds of problems. Such a classification provides the framework for the discussion that follows in this chapter.

What is the use of defining and distinguishing concepts of cost that have no counterpart in the costs reported by the firm's conventional accounting system? One useful purpose is to scout the fallacy that the cost estimates produced by conventional financial accounting are appropriate for all managerial uses. Actually they serve only the special purposes of financial accounting. The second purpose is to demonstrate the notion that different business problems call for different kinds of costs by flashing a panorama of cost concepts. These distinctions aid the development of special estimates of relevant cost concepts by defining the concepts that would be ideally appropriate for various purposes.

Although there are difficulties, workable approximations of these concepts of cost can be developed, given, first, a clear understanding of the management problem and of the concept of cost that is relevant for it; second, familiarity with the business and its records; and, third, ingenuity and boldness. The raw materials for making these special cost estimates are largely found in the accounting and statistical records of the company, though sometimes they need to be supplemented by special collections of data.

Cost concepts differ because of differences in viewpoint. Financial records aim at describing what was, whereas the useful decision-making concepts of cost aim at projecting what will happen under alternative courses of action. These special-purpose costs differ from "actual costs" in content as well as viewpoint. Different combinations of cost ingredients are appropriate for various kinds of management problems. Disparities occur from deletions, from additions, from recombination of elements, from price-level adjustments, and from the introduction of measurements which do not appear anywhere in the accounting records.

Opportunity vs. Outlay Costs

A distinction can be drawn between outlay costs and opportunity costs on the basis of the nature of the sacrifice. Outlay costs are those that involve financial expenditure at some time and hence are recorded in the books of account. Opportunity costs take the form of profits from alternative ventures that are foregone by using limited facilities for a particular purpose. Since they represent only sacrificed alternatives, they are never recorded as such in the financial accounts.

Whenever the problem allows an opportunity to buy all input factors for cash, outlay cost is the correct concept to use. In this situation, cash is the scarce factor and the standard of value of input factors relative to all other conceivable uses of cash.

Such complete market access is almost never within the bounds of practicability, and thus some concept of opportunity cost is usually relevant. Indeed, for many problems, opportunity cost is the more important cost. In a cloth mill that spins its own yarn, for example, the cost of yarn is really the price at which the yarn could be sold if it were not woven into cloth. For the problem of measuring the profitability of the weaving operations in order to decide whether to expand them or abandon them, it is this opportunity cost—the foregone revenue from not selling the yarn—that is relevant. In periods of boom demand, the use of a versatile bottleneck factor, such as scarce steel or scarce loom capacity, for making one product, involves the opportunity cost of not using it to make some other product that can also produce profits. The opportunity cost of producing heating oil in a modern, flexible refinery, for example, is the value of the gasoline that might otherwise have been made. For this reason, "gasoline equivalent" costing has considerable acceptance in this industry.

For short-run decisions like those illustrated above, the alternatives are clear, and the opportunity cost of foregoing them is calculable. But opportunity cost has a broader meaning and a wider usefulness than is implied in these straightforward applications. It is useful for long-run decisions involving problems of major strategy. For example, the cost of getting a college education is not confined to the outlays on tuition and books, but also includes the earnings that are foregone by not working full time.

In military affairs, to cite another example, the cost of sending bombers on a particular mission is not the price of the gasoline and ammunition but, rather, the damage that they would have done the enemy had they been sent on a substitute mission. Opportunity costs also play a role in sales strategy. For example, in determining whether a gasoline station should do major automotive repair work, the owner should consider the cost of such work in terms of the amount of gasoline and oil that will not be sold because the attendant is flat on his back under a truck. Managerial skill is scarce in most companies. Ventures that demand executive time must have high productivity to cover the opportunity cost of foregone management activities.

Opportunity cost plays an important role in capital expenditure budgeting, as we shall see in Chapter 10. Under conditions of capital rationing, the cost of acquiring a $100,000 gasoline station in New York City is not usually the interest that would have to be paid on the borrowed money but, rather, the profits or cost savings that could have been achieved if the $100,000 had been invested in four suburban gasoline stations, or in pipelines or refinery facilities. Investing equity money in the venture involves opportunity costs measurable in terms of sacrificed income from alternative investments. Estimates of cost of capital are essentially founded on an opportunity concept of investment return.

Opportunity cost is the cost concept to use when the supply of input factors is strictly limited. Such rigid supply may occur for technical reasons, e.g., the limited number of television channels available in a single locality; for social reasons, e.g., wartime rationing; for private reasons, such as lack of ready cash, or because the problem is too short-run to adapt facilities to their most profitable long-run relation to the job. In business problems the message of opportunity costs is that it is dangerous to confine cost knowledge to what the firm is doing. What the firm is not doing but could do is frequently the critical cost consideration which it is perilous but easy to ignore.

Past vs. Future Costs

Most of the important managerial uses to which cost information is put actually require forecasts of future cost, rather than "actual costs," i.e., unadjusted records of past cost. Management decisions are always forward-looking and therefore require comparative conjectures concerning future situations. Cost forecasting is required, whether or not this is recognized. When historical costs are used instead of explicit projections, the assumption is made that unvarnished cost history is the best available estimate of probable future costs under the situations involved in the decision.

The universality of this principle, that future costs are the only costs that matter for most executive decisions, will be readily recognized after an examination of some of the major managerial uses to which cost information is put. Among them are: expense control, projection of future income statements, appraisal of capital expenditures, decisions on new products and on expansion programs, and pricing.

For expense control, cost forecasting is necessary for setting scientific standards that will realistically reflect the operating conditions that will govern the level of costs during the future accounting period for which the budget is set. The essence of expense control is to have a plan or standard by which performance can be judged. The budget expense must therefore be a forecasted expense to fit the future conditions.

Projections of income statements require cost forecasts. Modern management calls increasingly for estimates of income expectations. These profit-and-loss projections require estimates of cost behavior under assumed future conditions. Choices between various kinds of major courses of action can usually be made more intelligently if explicit forecasts of the revenue and cost to be expected from each of the alternative strategies are calculated. This calls for multiple cost forecasting under different sets of assumed conditions.

For price policy also, it is future cost rather than past cost that is needed. To the extent that costs are relevant at all, it is expectations that govern policy decisions and that also should guide the determination of specific prices.

The fact that the future is always uncertain does not detract from the necessity for making explicit forecasts of future costs. With crude implements and unsubstantiated guesses, it is often possible to make a more accurate projection than that which is obtained when historical cost is used, for with historical costs, the implied though usually unrecognized assumption is that the future will be exactly like the particular period in the past when the costs were incurred Rarely does this represent the best guess that can be made concerning the future.

Short-Run vs. Long-Run Costs

Another kind of cost distinction which differs from the preceding ones can be drawn between the pattern of behavior of costs in the short run and in the long run.

The distinction between short-run and long-run cost behavior is a basic one in economic theory. Roughly, the short-run costs are those associated with variation in the utilization of fixed plant or other facilities, whereas long-run cost behavior encompasses changes in the size and kind of plant. Strictly, then, the distinction is based upon the degree of adaptation of all input factors to rate and type of output. When there is perfect flexibility in the size of plant, labor force, executive talent, and so forth, long-run cost behavior is involved. Anything short of perfect flexibility produces cost behavior that can be changed with leeway, improved, given time and investment resources. Such alterable costs are short run. The conventional dichotomy of long-run versus short-run cost curves needs to be expanded in economic theory to envision a whole family of cost curves that differ in degree of adaptation, so that the conventional long-run cost curve is the limiting case of perfect adaptation. In the real world, adjustments to higher output, new materials, or new product designs typically take a variety of forms that fall short of the perfect adaptation of the long-run cost curves. They progress gradually by widening a succession of bottlenecks rather than by adding an entire balanced unit.

Most business decisions involve some degree of short-run imbalance in the sense that for the range of most problems in going concerns some factors are fixed. There are occasions, however, when an approximation to complete long-run costs is germane—notably when deciding upon the initial size of plant or an enterprise and, to a lesser degree, when deciding upon expansion. The reduction of unit cost that comes from higher utilization of existing plant by spreading overhead over more output is often confused with savings of bigger size of plant. This confusion contributes to the delusion that more sales volume is a panacea for all company ills.

Variable vs. Constant Costs

Variable costs are distinguished from constant costs on the basis of the degree to which they vary in total with changes in rate of output. Strictly, variable costs might be confined to those that vary as a continuous function of output, and fixed costs to those that vary not at all. Since fixed costs are constant in total, they vary per unit with output rate. Costs that are proportionately variable in total are constant per unit. Many costs fall between these extremes, varying less than proportionately or changing by jumps, e.g., the number of foremen in a given plant. Fixed costs are, of course, not less susceptible to reduction than variable costs. They depend partly on management's zest for taut supervision and on the kinds of amenities, such as window washing, that are deemed desirable. One of the hazards of this concept is that "fixed" costs are erroneously viewed as not cuttable.

Which cost items are fixed and which variable depends on the degree of adaptation of costs to output rate, i.e., the degree to which the adjustment is short-run as opposed to long-run. The distinction also depends on the size and the suddenness of the change in output, and on the amount of pressure put on management to increase efficiency and to defer postponable expenditures.

The distinction between variable and constant costs is important in forecasting the effect of short-run changes in volume upon costs and profits. The break-even chart illustrates this application in predicting profits; and the flexible budget illustrates an application to control of costs by setting standards that are adjusted for volume changes.

Traceable vs. Common Costs

A traceable cost is one which can be identified easily and indisputably with a unit of operation, e.g., a product, a department, or a process. In accounting terminology, direct costs are distinguished from indirect costs on the basis of traceability to different products. In economic theory, traceability is the source of distinction between common costs and separable costs. Common costs are used broadly to cover costs that are not traceable to plant, department, and operation, as well as those that are not traceable to individual final products. The distinction is useful because in some situations important costs which cannot be traced to individual units of a product are nevertheless variable with output and are affected in complex ways by specific output decisions. Electric power for running machines is frequently an example of a non-traceable cost which is nevertheless variable with output. Many costs that are by nature traceable get lost and become overheads because in practice record systems are designed for other purposes and fail to exploit the full traceability potential of the operation.

Common costs that are not traceable to individual products are, in economic analysis, further classified into joint-product costs and alternative-product costs. Two products are joint when increasing the output of one product (e.g., hams) necessarily increases the output of the other product (e.g., pork shoulders). If increasing the output of hams should bring a decrease in the output of shoulders, then the products would be alternative.[8]

When does traceability of costs matter for management? It becomes important when multiple products that incur common cost differ considerably in production or marketing processes, and when cost has significance in decisions on adding or subtracting from a product line, product pricing, or product merchandising. (See Chapters 3, 7, 8.) It is not necessary that costs be traceable all the way to the product for this distinction to be useful for management. The degree of traceability varies from cost to cost, some costs being traceable as far down as divisions, others down to departments, and others down to cost centers.

Out-of-Pocket vs. Book Costs

Out-of-pocket costs refer to costs that involve current payments to outsiders as opposed to book costs, such as depreciation, that do not require current cash expenditures. In concept, this distinction is quite different from traceability and also from vari-

---

8 See Section V of this chapter for a discussion of the relation of jointness of products and controllability of product-mix to costing of individual products.

ability with output.   Not all out-of-pocket costs are variable; e.g., the night watchman's salary.   Not all out-of-pocket costs are traceable, e.g., the electric power bill.   Conversely, book costs are in some instances variable, e.g., depletion of ore or oil and, in some instances, are readily traceable and hence a part of direct costs. The distinction primarily affects the firm's cash position, but it is also significant for other than liquidity decisions.

Book costs can be converted into out-of-pocket costs by selling assets and leasing them back from the buyer.   The rental payment then replaces the depreciation charge and interest cost of owned capital.   Basically, then, the distinction depends on the durability of the asset and on whether or not the company owns it.[9]

Incremental Costs vs. Sunk Costs

Incremental costs are the added costs of a change in the level or nature of activity.   They can refer to any kind of change: adding a new product, changing distribution channels, adding new machinery.   Although they are sometimes interpreted to be the same as marginal cost, the latter has a much more limited meaning, referring to the cost of an added unit of output.

Sunk costs are the costs that are not altered by the change in question.   Most business decisions require cost estimates that are essentially incremental and costs that are not altered by the contemplated change are sunk and irrelevant.   Incremental costs, though familiarly short-run, are not necessarily so.   Indeed, the principal peril in using incremental costs is failure to recognize when the commitment involved in a decision will outlast the period of idleness and even the period of useful life of fixed equipment, so that the long-run incremental costs of full adaptation are part of the problem.

Incremental costs are not necessarily variable, traceable, or cash costs.   In many short-run problems, the most important incremental cost is the foregone opportunity of using strictly limited facilities in their present work, rather than shifting them

---

[9] Sometimes book costs are called "imputed" costs.   But "imputed" should refer strictly to costs that never show up in conventional accounts, e.g., interest on equity capital.   By "book" costs, we refer to costs that are met by cash outside the current accounting period, but they are conventionally recorded in determining what may legally be paid in dividends during this period.

to a new activity. Similarly, sunk costs can be cash costs (e.g., the president's salary); they can be variable (e.g., when the change in question is of customers rather than products); and they can be traceable. The clearest kind of sunk cost is amortization of past expenses, e.g., depreciation (here, indeed, the big problem is to keep from overstating sunk costs by recognizing incremental capital costs), lost opportunities, use depreciation, and obsolescence, for instance, of a branded product line by private label sales.

Escapable vs. Unavoidable Costs

The distinction between escapable costs and unavoidable costs is basically similar to that between incremental costs and sunk costs. The only difference is that escapable costs refer to decrements in cost associated with various kinds of contractions in the enterprise activity, whereas incremental costs refer to new projects which take on added costs. It is the net effect on cost that is important, not just the costs directly avoidable by the contraction. Added costs elsewhere may be partially offset, since retrenchment often results in increases in activity in other parts of the organization. These additions to cost must be offset against the direct reductions in escapable costs in order to estimate the net impact of the change. And the difficult problem usually lies in estimating these indirect effects, rather than the direct savable costs. For example, the escapable cost of closing an apparently unprofitable branch warehouse shifts storage loads onto other units and increases transportation charges. Similarly the costs that can be eliminated by dropping a credit sales system may be less than the costs of maintaining it.

Escapable costs are those eliminated by a contemplated retrenchment, and the kind of retrenchment determines their magnitude. Costs that appear to be avoided are often really only postponed—e.g., the deferral of maintenance of basic assets, such as a railroad's right-of-way. Hence escapable costs are highly correlated with controllable or discretionary costs, but they are not the same. For example, during the 1949 recession, one executive eliminated all window washing and desk wiping, thereby saving thousands of dollars. Chopping out fat is not, in this sense, an avoidable cost, since such savings are not associated with a specific curtailment decision.

Controllable vs. Non-Controllable Costs

The distinction between controllable and non-controllable costs is clear from the terms, but the controllability of a particular expenditure depends upon the level of management. Some costs are not controllable at the shop level since they depend on decisions upstairs, but at some level all such costs come into the discretionary area of an executive. The controllability distinction is primarily useful for expense and efficiency control by setting up budgets that correspond to areas of managerial responsibility, as discussed in Chapter 1 ("Profits").

All costs are controllable in the sense that they are assignable to some executive for control responsibility. But costs are not equally cuttable. And a controllability distinction might be made in terms of susceptibility to economy. Whether a particular cost can be cut does not, as is sometimes supposed, depend on whether the cost is variable or is traceable. Quite often, in fact, direct and variable costs are the hardest to cut and many constant costs (e.g., research, institutional advertising, and the salaries of top executives) are eminently compressible.

Replacement vs. Historical Costs

Replacement costs and historical costs are two methods for carrying assets on the balance sheet and establishing the amounts of costs that are used to determine income. Historical cost valuation states cost of plant and materials, for example, at the price originally paid for them, whereas replacement cost valuation states the costs at the prices that would have to be paid currently. Costs reported by conventional financial accounts are based on historical (original outlay) valuation. During periods of substantial change in the price level, historical valuation is a poor projection of the future cost that is relevant for many management decisions. The relevant quantity is the loss in value of assets incurred by the decision, measured by the cost of replacing those assets, either today or when replacement is expected. This problem is discussed more fully in Chapter 1, Section III, in connection with measurement of profits.

Illustration of Cost Concepts

This array of distinctions in cost concepts can be tied together by showing how they may appear in a single business decision. Consider the market expansion problem of a company that bottles soft drinks and distributes them in several adjoining states. The company is faced with a shrinking demand and has a limited cash fund to use in reversing the sales trend. The question is whether or not to expand distribution into two more states for this purpose, and more immediately, how much the expansion would cost.

Opportunity vs. Outlay Costs

A basic choice must be made between expansion and some alternative use of the firm's limited resources, e.g., another layer of advertising in the established markets or some basic changes in the product line. The profit that could otherwise be earned in these alternatives is the opportunity cost of using the cash fund for expansion. And if the prospective earnings from expansion are less than the alternative earnings of the fund, there is a real loss incurred in making the expansion investment. But the alternative earnings (i.e., opportunity costs) can only be determined by comparing projected cash outlay costs and revenues, which are thus the basic data for the decision.

Long-Run vs. Short-Run Costs

There are several degrees of intensity of cultivation of the market for soft drinks, ranging from mere grocery chain distribution to an elaborate system of automatic dispensers in public places. Stepping up selling intensity involves increasing the amount of capital invested in distribution channels, advertising displays, machinery, and trucks. In going into the venture the company can choose a cost structure with either a high labor content, which it could use to probe the new markets experimentally, or with a high capital content, which would presumably have a more potent selling pressure, but which would involve the company deeply in a long-term commitment. The question of whether any conclusive success can be had without a full-blown investment involves a distinction between long-run cost and short-run cost.

Incremental vs. Sunk Costs

The only costs that matter for this decision are the added costs. Each alternative marketing program has its own set of incremental costs for equipment, bottles, deliverymen and executive time, and so forth. These are the outlays that are relevant to the decision on the kind of selling job to undertake, as well as to the prior decision whether market expansion is preferable to increased advertising or new products. To the extent that existing operations are unaffected, the different programs have the same kinds of sunk costs. But it is important to determine in each case which costs are really sunk in respect to the particular decision.

Variable vs. Constant Costs

This familiar distinction, on the basis of the relation of costs to output, is used in finding the level of sales needed to make the project worth trying.

Escapable vs. Unavoidable Costs

Although this distinction is applicable principally to retrenchment problems, it has some usefulness here in considering the choice between a full-scale selling operation and various short cuts. Thus, much of the cost of dispensing and delivery equipment is avoidable by using relatively idle units and trucks from other areas or by limiting the operation to the wholesale level. The bottle inventory, on the other hand, is probably largely unavoidable.

Traceable vs. Non-Traceable Costs

The separable costs of this project are, aside from material, almost entirely in the distribution operation within the new areas. Most of the production costs in the bottling plant are common to the entire sales volume, since the products are homogeneous and the plant highly mechanized with, as we assumed at the outset, substantial excess capacity. There is much conjecture involved in any attempt to allocate production labor, power, and so forth, to any particular segment of output. Advertising in area-wide media, e.g., radio network, is also common to the total output, although local promotion is of course separable.

Joint vs. Alternative Costs

The costs that market expansion incurs jointly with existing output are the common costs that are more productive when applied to the whole output than to any part of it. The clearest cases are produced by economies of large scale in purchasing, uniform advertising copy for local media, and stabilized production levels. In an excess capacity situation, alternative costs are less usual than joint costs, but taking partly idle trucks from old markets to the new ones, and using management time to sell the new markets rather than to concentrate on the ailments of the existing markets, are cases of alternative costs.

Out-of-Pocket vs. Book Costs

In an expansion problem, book costs, such as depreciation, are not yet existent, since the new equipment hasn't been bought. The question is still, What will be the gross earnings of the investment over its probable life, and do they justify the outlay? Transfer of old dispensers, bottles, and trucks to the new areas brings separable book costs into the picture. These costs are important to the long-run but not the short-run problem of cash budgeting.

Replacement vs. Historical Costs

This distinction comes into the problem when past experience is used as a guide to cost levels in the proposed operation, as well as in considering costs of maintaining fixed equipment. It is clear that to be relevant, historical costs must be adjusted throughout to reflect current or future price levels.

Conclusion

The distinctions made in this section are of different kinds. One kind of distinction cuts aggregate accounting costs into two pieces that add up to total accounting costs, i.e., variable vs. constant costs, traceable vs. non-traceable costs, cash vs. book costs, incremental vs. sunk costs, controllable vs. non-controllable costs, escapable vs. unavoidable costs.

The remaining distinctions are based upon viewing the cost problem from an economic as opposed to an accounting standpoint—namely, opportunity vs. outlay cost, future vs. past cost, short-run vs. long-run cost, and replacement vs. historical cost. The set of distinctions is summarized in Table 5–1.

From the foregoing classification, it is clear that cost is a relative matter. What is cost depends upon what sacrifices are really produced by a particular business decision. These different cost concepts do not necessarily correspond to any accounting category. Financial accounting has a specific task—namely, to determine the over-all asset status (balance sheet) and the origin and disposition of funds (operating statement) during a specific and arbitrary time period. To do this well, accountants need unchanging and conventional definitions of costs. This approach wars with the notion that a particular item is a cost under some circumstances and not under others.

It is better to use a rough approximation of the concept of cost that is correct for a particular decision than to have an accurate estimate of an irrelevant concept. The unsophisticated executive is in danger of taking the easier course of using conventional accounting costs as though they were appropriate for all purposes. Instead, it is better to modify reported costs as necessary to make the best possible guess at the concept theoretically relevant for each decision.

TABLE 5–1

CLASSIFICATION OF COST DISTINCTIONS

Dichotomy		Basis of Distinction
Opportunity Costs	Outlay Costs	Nature of the Sacrifice
Past Costs	Future Costs	Degree of Anticipation
Short-Run Costs	Long-Run Costs	Degree of Adaptation to Present Output
Variable Costs	Constant Costs	Degree of Variation with Output Rate
Traceable Costs	Common Costs	Traceability to Unit of Operations
Out-of-Pocket Costs	Book Costs	Immediacy of Expenditure
Incremental Costs	Sunk Costs	Relation to Added Activity
Escapable Costs	Unavoidable Costs	Relation to Retrenchment
Controllable Costs	Non-Controllable Costs	Controllability
Replacement Costs	Historical Costs	Timing of Valuation

Since it is usually impractical to keep cost records in sufficiently flexible and detailed form to give off estimates of various concepts of cost by established routine, back-of-the-envelope guesses are typically needed to give management the right cost tools for its decisions.

III. COST AND RATE OF OUTPUT

Introduction

This section deals with problems of measuring short-run cost behavior empirically and examines some estimates that have been made in this field.   In surveying empirical studies, we shall first sketch in theoretical terms the nature of short-run cost functions, then describe the main problems that must be solved in empirical cost studies, and finally, summarize the findings and the essential methods of some of the investigations.[10]

Economists have long speculated about the shape of the relationship of cost to output, since it plays a key role in determining the theoretically optimum level of production.   The accepted economic doctrine has been that marginal costs rise continuously as output rate increases above some given level, and that the resulting average-cost curve has a U-shaped relation to output. In contrast with this doctrine, businessmen have quite generally supposed that marginal cost is constant, at least over the output range of normal experience.

A very few statistical cost studies have been made, some of them by the author.   These studies are not conclusive as to the shape of the cost function, since they covered only a few firms, and since they did not include years of over-full employment, when production capacity is crowded to the limits imposed by cost behavior or physical size.

More such empirical studies should be made.   Not only are they needed to make enterprise economics more realistic; they are also needed to put executive decisions on a sounder economic foundation.   Knowledge of cost-output relations is, as we have

---

10 I am indebted to the publishers of the following of my studies for permission to draw upon them in preparing this section: *Statistical Determination of Costs, with Special Reference to Marginal Costs,* University of Chicago Press, 1936; *The Relation of Cost to Output for a Leather Belt Shop,* National Bureau of Economic Research, 1941; *Statistical Cost Functions of a Hosiery Mill,* University of Chicago Press, 1941.

seen, important for various kinds of managerial problems: expense control, profit prediction, pricing, and promotion, to mention a few.

For both phases of managerial economics, it is important that the cost research be done thoroughly, drawing upon economic and statistical analysis, as well as accounting and engineering disciplines. Thorough studies which face explicitly the research problems discussed below have great practical value as measurement benchmarks and as pilots for shortcuts in connection with the rough approximation studies that must be used for particular decisions.

Although forecasts based upon cost functions are subject to estimating error, this does not destroy their usefulness, since management cannot escape guessing about future costs in reaching decisions. No careful forecast of costs could be as inaccurate as the tacit assumption that current costs and the current structure of controlling factors will continue indefinitely. Yet, this is exactly the assumption that is made when decisions are reached on the basis of "actual costs," which means current or past costs.

Nature of Short-Run Cost–Output Functions

In dealing with cost as a function of output, economic theorists distinguish between short-run and long-run cost functions. In the long run all input factors (i.e., buildings, machinery, supervisory personnel, labor, and materials) are assumed to be completely adapted for minimum total cost at the plant's rate of output. In the short run, some of the input factors, e.g., plant, machinery, or management, are assumed to be physically fixed and not capable of immediate adaptation to changes in the rate of output within the short-run limits of flexibility. Thus, only some of the input factors are variable in response to changes in output rate. This situation is sometimes called partial adaptation, in contrast to the long-run adjustment called total adaptation. Clearly, there exist a great many short runs, depending upon the number and importance of the factors that are fixed, and upon how complete the adjustment of the variable factors is. In this section we are concerned with one of these short-run cost functions.

The basic proposition is that there exists in the short run a functional relation between cost and a set of independent variables, which may include, for example, volume of production, size of production lot, prices of input services, and variety of output. The independent variables will be different for each type of manufacturing operation, although in general the most important variable is rate of output. The independent variables are considered to determine cost behavior.

The output relation is the most important to study because it is subject to faster and more frequent changes. (Indeed, in economic analysis the cost function usually refers to the relationship alone between cost and rate of output, and thus assumes that all of the other independent variables are kept constant.) Moreover, once the cost–output function is determined, estimates of future costs of production at various levels can usually be obtained by adjusting the cost function to reflect the effect of other forces, such as wage rates, material prices, and lot size.

The cost function of economic theory is strictly static, i.e., it shows costs for alternative levels of stable output rate. Such a static function is inadequate as a picture of short-run cost behavior, however, because the short-run relation of cost to output rate may itself be higher when output is increasing than when it is decreasing, or it may simply be higher when output rate is changing than when it is stable. This static function is thus but a first approximation, although usually a fairly good one, to the dynamic cost function. Moreover, a statistically derived cost function taken from observations at different points of time at best represents the average relationship, including effects of output fluctuation, for the period as a whole, and is not even the timeless one of economic doctrine.

The characteristics of the fixed equipment play a dominant role in the determination of a plant's pattern of short-run cost behavior —i.e., the shape of the relation between total cost and rate of output. The critical characteristic for this purpose is the degree of segmentation possible in the plant, that is, its potentiality of varying the rate of flow of output without changing the proportions of variable inputs to fixed equipment in use (e.g., the ratio of man hours to rotary printing press hours). Segmentation in this sense refers to the technical nature of the fixed equipment which permits a wide range of choice in the machine hours used per week.

The degree of segmentation varies widely for different plants, ranging from none to complete and continuous segmentation. An example of no segmentation is a single blast furnace, which must be operated continuously. An approximation of complete segmentation may occur in hydro-electric generation at Grand Coulee Dam, where there is provision for 18 generators, each of which might theoretically deliver power at any rate from almost nothing up to its full capacity. Common examples of discontinuous segmentation are found in plants that are inhibited by labor contracts or managerial prejudice from operating at other than full shifts (no overtime or part shifts).

The point where a plant falls on this segmentation scale depends on the technical nature of the equipment, the success of managerial efforts to segmentize, and the nature of the labor contract. Three sources of segmentation can be distinguished. The first is physical divisibility, where fixed equipment consists of a large number of homogeneous units. An example of this is a hosiery mill where the knitting of stocking legs is done on 81 nearly identical knitting machines.[11] This may be called "unit segmentation." Under such circumstances the successive introduction or withdrawal of the machine units permits wide variability in the services of the machinery despite its over-all fixity. It is further possible to introduce segmentation by varying the number and hours of the shifts per period that the fixed equipment is employed. It is convenient to designate this device as "time" segmentation. If the technical nature of the fixed plant is such that it can be used at varying speeds, "speed" segmentation can be obtained by more or less intensive use of the service of the equipment, i.e., by operating machines at faster or slower rates.

The means of attaining segmentation, as well as the technical structure of production, will determine the degree of segmentation that can be achieved in any instance. Unit segmentation is characterized by discreteness in the flow of services, as each successive unit of plant is brought into operation. The units may be so small in certain cases, however, that for practical purposes the discontinuities can be neglected. Time segmentation may also be

---

[11] In the theoretical analysis the assumption is that the machine units are of uniform efficiency. In practice, however, the machines and their labor complements may differ in efficiency. If so and if the machines are brought into operation in order of decreasing efficiency when output is increased, a progressive cost curve would result. This source of variation may be unimportant in a particular plant where union rules prevent management from taking advantage of the hierarchy of machine efficiency.

characterized by marked discontinuities, for example, when the choice is between one or two shifts of eight hours rather than between an eight- and nine-hour shift. On the other hand, speed segmentation permits continuous variability in plant use, although the range within which machine speed-up, etc., is a practical method of achieving segmentation is narrow.

Cost behavior depends not only on the possibilities for segmenting fixed plant but on the rigidity of the proportions of fixed and variable inputs at different levels of production. The output of some equipment can be increased by putting more men to work on it, but there are many machines that have a fixed requirement of one or two men and can make no use of more labor input. Such variable and fixed relations are also present in the rate of materials throughout. In general, the more specialized the machine design, the more rigid are its labor and materials requirements or capacity.

When other factors such as price levels and technology are stable, these two conditions—degree of segmentation and varia-

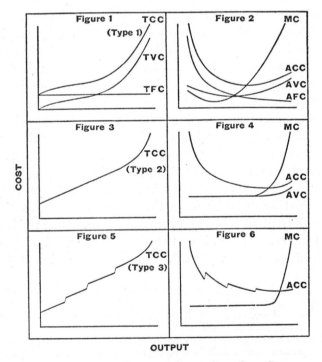

CHART 5-1. THREE TYPES OF SHORT-RUN COST BEHAVIOR

bility of factor mix—are sufficient to determine the short-run cost behavior of a plant.

Three types of behavior are important: (I) absence of segmentation with factor proportions variable; (II) perfect segmentation; and (III) discontinuous segmentation. The Type I behavior pattern results in the short-run cost function portrayed in Figure 1 of Chart 5–1, where output is measured on the horizontal, and cost on the vertical, axis. The course of total variable cost, i.e., that part of cost which fluctuates in response to output variation, is indicated by the cubical parabola TVC. Total fixed cost which arises from the firm's inability to adapt certain input factors to prevailing output rates is designated by the horizontal line TFC in Figure 1. The vertical addition of the total fixed and total variable cost gives the curve of total combined cost TCC.[12] Since the total variable cost function rises first at a decreasing, then at a constant, and finally at an increasing, rate, the total combined cost function obviously has the same shape, but an intercept higher by the amount of the fixed cost.

The corresponding behavior of unit costs is shown in Figure 2 of Chart 5–1. The fixed cost per unit will be represented by a rectangular hyperbola indicated by the curve AFC. Variable costs per unit (AVC) will be falling, constant, or rising, depending upon the phase of operations. Average combined cost, shown by the curve ACC, is obtained by vertical summation of the average variable and average fixed cost. The marginal cost function denoted by MC in Figure 2 represents the increment in total cost associated with a small change in the rate of output, or, alternatively, it shows the additional cost that must be incurred if output is increased by one unit. The marginal cost function, which is given by the slope of the total combined cost curve will, under the conditions postulated, decline at first and then bend upward, continuing to increase over the remainder of the output range.

In Type II behavior, where for any output level, fixed and variable inputs can be mixed in minimum-cost proportions at all levels of output, up to some maximum, the total cost curve is linear over the output range. This characteristic of the cost function, which

---

12 "Combined" cost here means the sum of fixed and variable cost or aggregate cost and is the sum of the component costs: e.g., overhead, productive labor costs, and non-productive labor cost.

results from perfect segmentation and fixed factor proportions, produces a total cost curve which is proportional to output below the
level of the physical capacity of the equipment, and sharply rising
at greater than capacity production. That is to say, marginal cost
is constant as the level of operations increases up to the capacity
point, at which it increases rapidly. This is illustrated by the
total cost curve Type II drawn in Figure 3 of Chart 5–1. The
derivative unit cost functions—average variable, average combined, and marginal cost—are shown in the corresponding Figure
4. Marginal cost and average variable cost coincide over the
operating range up to the point at which no more fixed equipment
can be brought into operation.

The Type III case applies when there is discontinuous segmentation of the given plant. The only difference between this
and Type II behavior is that there are breaks in the cost function,
a sharp change in the level of the total cost curve. Even though
there may exist discontinuities in the total cost of operations when,
for example, successive machines are brought into operation, this
need not influence the level of marginal cost. Discontinuities
introduced into a cost function with an initial linear phase are
pictured in Figure 5 of Chart 5–1. In Figure 6 the behavior of
the average and marginal cost curves for this discontinuous case
are illustrated. It may be that cost functions of Type III are
prevalent in mechanized industry. However, opportunities for
segmentation are greater than economists have generally recognized. In many industries the development of versatile and
adaptable plants, in order to produce a variety of products in a
wide range of proportions, and in order to operate efficiently at
many rates of output, have brought about much time, speed, and
unit segmentation, which have reduced the practical importance
of discontinuities.

Different Approaches to Determination of Cost Functions

We have seen that for several kinds of management problems
it is desirable to find an empirical approximation of the theoretical
short-run cost functions discussed above. Empirical functions are
necessarily approximate because (1) they cannot include every
kind of short-run cost factor, nor find the exact relation of cost to
the factors used, and (2) a theoretical cost function applies to one
point in time, whereas empirical functions, to be useful, must

apply to a future period which will have many minor changes in production circumstances.

There are several approaches to an estimate of cost function:

1. Classification of accounts into fixed, variable, semi-variable, on the basis of judgment and inspection.

2. Estimation of the relationships of cost-output on the basis of engineering conjectures.

3. Determination of the cost function and the degree of output variation by statistical analysis.

The method of statistical analysis of past behavior of costs is the most thorough and "scientific," since it deals with each major problem of determining empirical cost relationships explicitly. The other two methods must cope with each of these problems, but they do so less consciously and usually less successfully.

How To Decide Which Approach Is Best

These three approaches, statistical, accounting, and engineering, are not always mutually exclusive. Often it is desirable to use two or more to supplement each other. Nevertheless, it is usually desirable to try to determine at the outset which of the three should receive greatest emphasis.

Statistical Approach

The statistical approach, when conditions are appropriate for its use, is likely to produce more reliable results than the other methods. However, it is more time-consuming and expensive if applied in a thorough manner. In essence, it uses multiple correlation analysis (discussed in Chapter 4) to find a functional relation between changes in costs and the important cost determinants, such as output rate, lot size, output fluctuations, and so forth. Although ideally it should have an algebraic form fitted by least-squares analysis, much can be learned by graphic analysis.

The power of statistical analysis lies in its ability to pick out the fixed cost elements in each cost component, such as direct labor or fuel consumption, and to show whether marginal cost is constant or variable with changes in cost determinants. These relations are derived from the shape of the cost function found statistically.

The conditions necessary for reliable statistical analysis are discussed later in the section.

Accounting Approach

The accounting approach involves classification of expenses as
(1) fixed, (2) variable, and (3) semi-variable, on the basis of
inspection and experience. This approach is the simplest and
least expensive of the three. Hence, it should normally be used
whenever feasible as a supplement to the other methods if it is not
used as the principal method. To be most successful the requisite
conditions are:

1. Experience with a wide range of fluctuation in output rate.

2. A detailed breakdown of accounts kept on the same basis
over a period of years.

3. Relative constancy in wage rates, material prices, plant size,
technology, and so forth.

Since the accounting approach provides no way to correct data
explicitly for changes in cost prices or for changes in other conditions that affect cost behavior, a constancy of these cost conditions is essential if accurate results are to be obtained. The
statistical method can tolerate more variation in underlying conditions because it possesses a means of dealing with these variations. Uniform coverage of the output range is not essential for
success of the accounting method. A group of observations at
each extreme of the range is sufficient. The accounting method
isolates constant cost easily by inspection. It identifies variable
cost easily, but determines less accurately the pattern of variation
of these and of semi-variable costs. This approach needs to be
supplemented by graphic statistical analysis to separate the
variable and fixed components of semi-variable cost and to determine the linearity of output relationship for semi-variable and
for variable costs.

Engineering Approach

In essence, the engineering method consists of systematic conjectures about what cost behavior ought to be in the future on
the basis of what is known about the rated capacity of equipment,
modified by experience with man-power requisites and efficiency
factors, and with past cost behavior. Hence, it depends upon
knowledge of physical relationships supplemented by pooled
judgments of practical operators. It should, and usually does,
make use of whatever analyses of historical cost behavior are ap-

propriate and are available, as a means of making the judgment better. Typically, the engineering estimate is built up in terms of physical units, i.e., man hours, pounds of material, and so forth, and converted into dollars at current or prospective cost prices. The cost estimates are usually developed at a series of peg points that cover the contemplated or potential output range.

The engineering approach is the only feasible method when the inadequacy of experience and records provides little systematic historical basis for estimating cost behavior. The approach is also a desirable supplement to statistical or accounting analysis when it is desired to project cost behavior beyond the range of past output experience, or when it is necessary to estimate the effect of major changes of technology or plant size upon cost behavior over a familiar or unfamiliar output range.[13]

Although statistical studies of cost are rare in industry, they are by far the most interesting kind of cost analysis from an economic standpoint. The rest of this section is therefore devoted to statistical methods for determining cost functions.

Statistical Determination of Cost–Output Functions

Our main interest here lies in determining the net effect of rate of output on cost when the influence of the remaining variables has been allowed for. If the statistical cost function can be determined in such a way as to eliminate the influence of all other cost determinants apart from output rate, the resultant cost function is the empirical counterpart of the theoretical cost function described above.

In general, three steps are needed to eliminate the influence of these irrelevant cost forces. The first is to select a period of observation in which dynamic elements, such as changes in the size of plant, technical production methods, managerial efficiency, and so forth, were at a minimum. The second is to rectify the cost and output data recorded in the firm's accounts in order to remove the effect of remaining irrelevant factors, such as changes in wage rates, prices of materials, tax rates, special accounting allocations, lags caused by the production cycle, and so forth.

---

[13] It is also an efficient method when the operation in question is susceptible to complete theoretical analysis. An engineering cost function with a high degree of accuracy was developed for an airline on the basis of aerodynamic theory. (A. R. Ferguson, "Empirical Determination of a Multidimensional Marginal Cost Function," *Econometrica*, XVIII, No. 3 (July, 1950), pp. 217–235).

The third step in removing other cost influences is to hold their effect constant by means of multiple correlation analysis. Cost may be affected by other operating variables beside the rate of output, e.g., size of production lot, change in output from the previous period, style variety, and so forth. Hence it is necessary to take account of these additional independent variables which reflect operating conditions suspected to exercise an important influence on short-period fluctuations in cost.

All three of these general methods of purification must usually be employed. Operationally they break down into smaller steps. These may be conveniently discussed in terms of the following problems:

1. Determination of the suitability of the particular plant for statistical analysis.
2. Measurement of output.
3. Determination of time unit of observation.
4. Choice of period of analysis.
5. Selection of cost elements.
6. Determination of form of cost observations.
7. Deflation of cost data.
8. Matching of costs with output.
9. Allowance for other determinants of cost behavior.
10. Selection of form of function.

Each of these problems will be discussed in general terms in the light of experience in making statistical determinations of short-run cost behavior for a hosiery mill,[14] a leather belt shop,[15] and a furniture factory.[16]

Suitability of Plant for Statistical Analysis

Firms typically operate a number of technical units. Some are appropriate for statistical determination of cost–output functions; some are not.[17] Five criteria are useful for judging the suitability of a plant for statistical analysis:

---

[14] Joel Dean, *Statistical Cost Functions of a Hosiery Mill,* Chicago, University of Chicago Press, 1941.

[15] Joel Dean, *The Relation of Cost to Output for a Leather Belt Shop,* New York, National Bureau of Economic Research, 1941.

[16] Joel Dean, *Statistical Determination of Costs, with Special Reference to Marginal Cost,* Chicago, University of Chicago Press, 1936.

[17] The following analysis is from the standpoint of top management of a

a) *Age of plant.* The first requisite is a large amount of accumulated data to analyze. Usually, four or five years' operation is necessary before statistical analysis can be done with precision.

b) *Homogeneity of product.* The smaller the number of different products the easier it is to measure output and to put cost estimates to practical use. Also the less the products themselves have changed (in ways that affect cost) the easier and more durable is the study. For example, in this respect a ball-bearing plant is better than an automobile body plant.

c) *Homogeneity of equipment.* Similarity of machine units is desirable in order to eliminate cost variations due to use of more efficient machines for some levels of production than for others. In the hosiery industry, for example, selection of better equipment during times of slack production is relatively unimportant, because union restrictions prohibit allotment of work which discriminates against operators of inefficient equipment during periods of low or part-time employment.

d) *Technical changes.* If the production technology is altered through new developments during the analysis period, there is a change of cost function, and statistical results do not reflect a single type of cost behavior. However, if only minor changes have occurred, they can be allowed for in the analysis and a practical approximation to a single cost function can be made.

e) *Length of production cycle.* The production cycle, which is the average length of time it takes the initial inputs in a process to emerge as finished products, should be short. This will minimize the reallocation of recorded costs and output necessary to place them in the accounting period which is appropriate, i.e., so that costs attributable to a certain output are actually matched with that output.

f) *Volume variation.* The nature of the operations should be such that the production volume varies from month to month in such a fashion as to include a wide range of volume and a fairly uniform coverage of this range.

---

multiple-plant firm faced with the problem of selecting which plants can best be studied by statistical analysis (as opposed to other methods of determining the cost function). From the standpoint of the manager of a single plant, the problem is whether his plant qualifies for a statistical approach. The substance is the same from either viewpoint.

Measurement of Output

Measurement of output is usually the hardest problem in statistical determination of cost. The theoretical cost functions discussed above assume that output consists of homogeneous units of a single product. Actually, however, almost all modern plants produce a number of varied products. This is true even when output appears at first blush to be homogeneous, as in the hosiery mill and the leather shop.

There are two kinds of solution for the problem of output heterogeneity, not necessarily exclusive. The first is to construct a single index of output from a weighted combination of the various kinds of product. An index is easy to compute, but it is accurate only when there is little variation in the product-mix or when products are not very different; that is, an index is useful when the problem is not serious. The second solution is to introduce each significant aspect or dimension of output as a separate independent variable in a multiple correlation analysis. This kind of solution is particularly useful when different dimensions of output have distinctive cost influences. For instance, a common measure of railroad traffic is ton-miles carried, but it is reasonable to assume that hauling costs vary in linear relation to miles and in some higher degree parabolic relation to tons carried.

In the studies reviewed here, output was in most cases homogeneous enough to permit the index-number solution for measuring output. An index of output was computed for the furniture factory by weighting each article of furniture in proportion to its deflated standard cost. The weights in the output index for the hosiery study were determined on the basis of relative direct labor costs. In the belt shop, square feet of single-ply equivalent belting was chosen as the measure of output, primarily because the cost of operation was more closely related to area than to weight, dollar value, or the standard costs of output, all of which were studied as alternative measures. The second kind of solution was also used in the belt shop, where weight per square foot of belting was introduced as an independent variable in the analysis. Two dimensions of output were examined as separate independent variables in a study of department store costs: number of transactions and value of transaction.

In an analysis of cost behavior for the entire U. S. Steel Corporation, which sells a tremendous variety of products, an index of output was constructed by correcting the actual tons of each of the many steel and non-steel products shipped in each year by the ratio of the product's average mill cost in the period 1933–1937 to the over-all average mill cost of all rolled and finished steel products. Thus the crude number of tons of all products was converted into equivalent tonnage, weighted for average cost.[18]

Selection of Time Unit of Observation

Should the unit of observation be a week, a month, or a year? The smaller the unit, the less chance that the effect of fluctuations in output rate during the observation unit will be missed. This can be serious when the year is the unit, for example. On the other hand, the smaller the observation unit, the greater the problem of matching recorded output with the cost that caused it, and the greater the problem caused by arbitrary assignment of cost to time periods. The best unit of observation is the briefest period that will not cause serious gestation lags, arbitrary time allocations, or incompleteness of data. A month is the observation unit most satisfactory for these studies, but for the hosiery mill, test studies were made in terms of weeks and quarters as well. The U. S. Steel Corporation analysis used a year as the unit.[19]

Selection of Period for Analysis

The observation period for collecting data shoud have the following characteristics: (1) wide range of output variability and uniform data coverage for the range; (2) constant size of plant; (3) little change in technology; (4) stable managerial methods; (5) uniform cost records covering changes in volume, cost, and other operating conditions; (6) number of observations large enough to permit generalization and yet small enough to be manageable in correlation analysis. The observation period, moreover, should be recent and relevant to future operations.

---

[18] *TNEC Papers*, Vol. I, U. S. Steel Corporation, New York, 1940, pp. 223–324. This analysis was done under the direction of Theodore Yntema for the period 1927–1938.

[19] *TNEC Papers, op. cit.* Using a period as long as a year made it possible to measure output in terms of tons shipped rather than tons produced, since fluctuations in inventory (the cushion between production and shipments) were small relative to a year's output.

In the furniture factory, for example, the study covered the years 1932–1934, and 47 two-week accounting periods were used in the analysis.

Selection of Cost Elements

When, as is usual, one plant of a multiple-plant firm is being studied, a decision must be made on what elements of cost should be included in the study. Those that are arbitrarily allocated to the plant and that bear no apparent relationship to its operating conditions should be excluded. To find out whether the omission of overhead common to several plants causes understatement of the marginal cost of one plant, the omitted overhead should be correlated with the output of the plant (as was done in the hosiery and leather belt studies).

Another problem is to decide whether the separate components of combined cost should be studied statistically. Cost analysis in terms of individual elements and components of expense has several advantages. In the first place, individual accounts may require different corrective devices, corresponding to the varying influences which give rise to the need for rectification. Irrelevant influences may differ in kind for different expenses and may also operate with varying intensity on the various categories of cost. The same considerations apply to the influence of independent variables as well as to the influences that are removed by rectification. An independent variable may affect only certain components of cost. A flexible budget can be more detailed and more accurately adjusted to variations in operating conditions, and the estimates more precisely modified to accord with changed input prices, if the analysis is so made that separate correction and reflation of the components is possible. Again, if underlying conditions affecting only a few cost elements change, it is possible to readjust the costs affected so that it is not necessary to scrap the entire findings concerning the cost–output relations.

Selection of Form of Cost Observations

It is convenient to analyze combined cost in the form of totals for the accounting period rather than in the form of cost per unit of product. Experimentation with these alternative approaches in various cost studies has shown that analysis in the form of total rather than average cost yields more convenient and reliable findings.[20]   The conversion of cost in total form to average and marginal form, which may be desired for interpretative purposes, is a simple matter.   Marginal cost, for example, is the rate of increase in the total function or the slope of the net regression line of total combined cost on output.   When the total cost function is linear, marginal cost is simply the coefficient of net regression of total combined cost on output.

Deflation of Cost Data

To obtain empirical cost functions of lasting generality (analogous to the static theoretical functions described above) it is necessary to hold the prices of input factors constant at some base level.   Two assumptions are implied in this formulation: (1) that substitution among the input factors does not take place as a result of changes in their relative prices; (2) that changes in the output rate of the enterprise exert no influence on the prices paid for its factors.   The short-run cost function which is sought here will not be descriptive of actual cost behavior.   It will in general be true that near-capacity rates of output of any one firm will occur in the rising phase of the business cycle when other firms will also be expanding operations.   While an individual firm may be in itself sufficiently small to have no influence on factor prices, increases in its output will be highly correlated with a rise in the output of the industry, which will generally exert a significant influence on prices of factors.   Consequently, as a firm increases its rate of output to a marked extent, the increase will be accompanied by a rise in factor prices with consequently rising marginal cost.   The analysis of cost behavior under these conditions is, of course, a significant problem; but the treatment here is an attempt to approximate a static model for which prices are assumed to remain unchanged no matter what the rate of output of the individual firm.[21]

---

[20] Several problems are encountered in the statistical analysis of average cost. First, selection of the most suitable specification for the average cost function is more difficult.   Second, slight errors in the choice of the function produce magnified errors in the derived marginal cost function.   Third, since average cost is a quotient of two variables, each of which is subject to error, the statistical distribution of the quotient may be less likely to conform to the assumptions upon which multiple regression analysis is based.

[21] Whether or not it is correct to assume that the firm's rate of output does not affect input prices, such an assumption is the only practical approach to the determination of the firm's cost–output functions.   Although influences attributable to

Since the influences on cost (apart from output) affect the various elements of combined cost differently, composite correction is not likely to be accurate. Specialized rectification devices were therefore used for the various elements of cost.[22]

Matching Cost with Output

Rectification of the time lag between the recording of cost and of the output causing it ordinarily involves two steps: (1) the determination of the proportion of cost recorded in a period other than that in which the corresponding output is recorded; (2) the determination of the length of the recording time lag. Sometimes these magnitudes are readily found, but it is usually necessary to resort to estimates based on technical considerations and engineering opinions. These estimates can be supplemented by statistical analysis designed to test objectively the correctness of the engineering calculations.[23]

The recording of the cost of machinery repairs and depreciation involves timing problems that warrant special attention.

Capricious fluctuations in repair expenditures tend to obscure the cost–output relation. Special studies of individual machines over a long period of time can sometimes determine what part of repairs are a function of operations and what part a function of the ravages of time. When there is wide discretion in the timing of maintenance, e.g., a railroad's right-of-way, a spurious relationship to output is sometimes produced to give the illusion of close "control" of expenses. Repair outlays are cumulative, as well as fortuitous, so that some kind of lag correction is usually required. In the belt shop, for example, machinery repairs are adjusted to be one-fifth of the current figure, and four-fifths of the outlay three months later. Fortunately repair cost in these studies was

changes in the output of the industry may have been represented in the observations, these could hardly be disentangled and purged by multiple correlation procedures.

22 This procedure is substantiated by the experience of Ehrke and Schneider in their statistical analysis of cost in a cement mill. Their correction for price changes in the factors was first undertaken by using the *Groszhandels Preisindex*. Finding this unsatisfactory they constructed a special index for the prices of labor, limestone, clay, coal and coke. See Kurt Ehrke, *Die Ubererzeugung in der Zementindustrie*, Gustav Fischer, Jena, 1933.

23 In the hosiery study, recorded production was adjusted for a recording lead based upon the length of the production cycle. This was necessary because of the practice of recording output before its actual completion.

small enough so that its adjustment could not affect the form of the marginal cost function.

Depreciation presents a similar problem. Ideally, use-depreciation should be separated from time-depreciation, since only that part of depreciation which arises from the actual operations of a plant is relevant in determining the cost occasioned by different levels of operation. The shape of the marginal cost function depends upon whether use-depreciation is a linear, increasing, or decreasing function of intensity of utilization. This relation as well as the magnitude of use-depreciation depends upon maintenance standards and upon the effects of uninterrupted high speed utilization upon the deterioration of equipment. Depreciation caused by physical deterioration due to the passage of time, and by losses in value as a result of technological progress or changes in product specification (obsolescence) affects merely the height of the intercept of the total cost function on the cost axis, not the shape of the function itself.

Unfortunately, depreciation is usually charged on a "straight-line" basis, i.e., as a linear function of time, so that time- and use-depreciation cannot be differentiated in these studies. Marginal cost was understated only to the extent that significant losses of value, in excess of time-depreciation, arose from use after maintenance expenditures have been incurred.[24]

Allowance for Other Determinants

There are usually other determinants of cost whose influence has not been removed by selection of the sample, by rectification of the data, or by the devices for getting a comprehensive measure of output. The effect of some of these factors is averaged out in the course of the statistical analysis. When feasible, multiple correlation analysis can be used to determine explicitly the relation

[24] Use-depreciation may be defined as the loss in value of productive assets not offset by maintenance that is in excess of time-depreciation. Use-depreciation will be zero if the loss in value occasioned by physical deterioration due to the passage of time is not increased by more intense use. For example, an automobile body die, which will be obsolete in one year by a planned change in design, may have zero use-depreciation if no conceivable rate of production could diminish its efficiency or hasten its scrapping. Since the loss in value attributable to use may be reduced or completely balanced by maintenance, use-depreciation represents only the loss in value not restored or avoided by maintenance. To the extent that productive assets are fully maintained in the sense that no residual loss in value results from use, use-depreciation, as we have defined it, may be neglected in estimating marginal cost.

of these factors to cost. Variables selected for testing are those that management thinks have an important effect on cost. One statistical test that can be used requires the candidate variable to have a significant net regression with cost.

Each influence selected as relevant is accordingly separately examined in order to ascertain: (1) the reasons for its influence on cost; (2) the best statistical series available for its measurement; (3) its net correlation with cost. The list of candidate variables differs for each establishment. Those tested for the belt shop, for example, included: change in output; variability in rate of output within accounting period; size of manufacturing lot; proportion of special orders; and rate of labor turnover. In the hosiery study time was used as a catch-all to reflect several changes in efficiency, among other influences.

In the study of U. S. Steel costs,[25] the effects of technological change over the 17-year analysis period were eliminated in four steps: (1) total cost was plotted against output; (2) a least-squares straight line was fitted to the cost—output observations; (3) deviations of actual observations from the line were plotted against time, each observation being for a particular year; (4) a straight line was fitted between the deviations and time, and this line was used to adjust cost observations to a 1938 level of technology.

Selection of Form of Function

Before the correlation analysis can be made, it is necessary to select the form of functional relationship between cost and the independent variables. Most interest attaches to output relationship, but others present similar problems and receive similar treatment.

The choice of the form of the cost—output function to be specified in an empirical study is in practice usually limited to those illustrated by Types I and II in Chart 5–1, namely, a cubic function of the form

$$X_1 = b_1 + b_2 X_2 + b_3 X_2^2 + b_4 X_2^3 \text{ [26]}$$

or a linear function of the form

$$X_1 = b_1 + b_2 X_2$$

---

25 *TNEC Papers*, Vol. I, U. S. Steel Corporation, New York, 1940, p. 253.

26 The choice of a cubic function to represent the pattern of cost behavior in this instance is based on its convenience and simplicity. While it is the simplest functional form descriptive of the behavior postulated, it is, of course, not the only admissible form.

where X_1 is total cost, X_2 is output, and the b's are constants.

The Type III function is virtually impossible to determine by statistical analysis, since the random scatter of observations is usually of about the same magnitude as the separate jumps in the total cost curve. The resulting empirical function thus has no statistical significance with respect to the size or location of the discontinuities, and will appear in a form such as Figure 4 of Chart 5–1.

To reach a choice concerning the shape of the total cost function, three investigations were made: First, the process of manufacturing was examined in the light of the theoretical analysis of segmen-

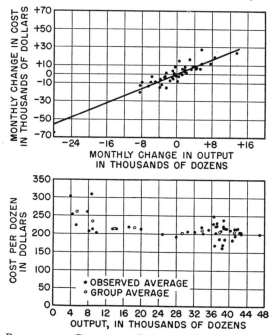

CHART 5–2. RELATION OF CHANGES IN COMBINED COST TO CHANGES IN OUTPUT: HOSIERY MILL. (Source: Joel Dean, *Statistical Cost Functions of a Hosiery Mill*, p. 43.)

tation and variable proportions presented earlier. Second, the statistical distribution of cost observations was examined by graphic multiple regression analysis. This usually included a study of the scatter of first differences of cost on output, as illustrated by Chart 5–2 from the hosiery mill study. Here the linear relationship of first differences in the top panel, combined with the lack of any evidence of rising per unit cost at extreme output in the bottom panel, substantiated the hypothesis that the relationship of total cost was linear.   A third step was to fit not only a straight line but also curves, usually parabolic and cubic regressions, for total cost and output.   Then various statistical tests were applied to find which functional form fitted best.

In none of the plants studied did the first-difference tests or the tests of significance for the higher-degree functions indicate that a curvilinear total-cost curve fitted the data better than a straight line.   The Type II function above was therefore concluded to be the best form to use.   This is equivalent to saying that marginal costs were constant over the range of output observed, since an increase in output (X_2) of one unit raises total cost by b_2X_2, regardless of the level of output.

However, output is not indefinitely expansible.   Such flat curves indicate that there is probably some critical output level where marginal cost rises very steeply and that for a number of reasons these producers never pushed production to that critical level during the analysis period.   (These studies were made during the thirties, when low demand played an important part in determining cost behavior.)   This is not the place, however, to discuss or evaluate the various theoretical reasons why output was kept below the critical level, even though marginal cost was lower than price.   It is enough to note that for practical purposes straight-line cost functions apparently have more usefulness than theory would lead us to believe.

Findings of Empirical Studies

Chart 5–3 shows for the leather belt shop the total, average, and marginal combined cost curves in relation to output that were derived from multiple correlation analysis using output and average weight per foot of belting as independent variables.   The total cost relation to output is linear within the range of observation and yields a hyperbolic average cost curve, i.e., a curve that falls continuously, and a constant marginal cost curve that lies below the average cost curve.

For the hosiery mill, a multiple correlation function was computed with total cost the dependent variable, and both output and time as independent variables.   The partial relation with output was then transformed into average and marginal cost form.   Chart 5–4 shows in its upper sections the partial regression of total cost on output and in its lower section the average and the

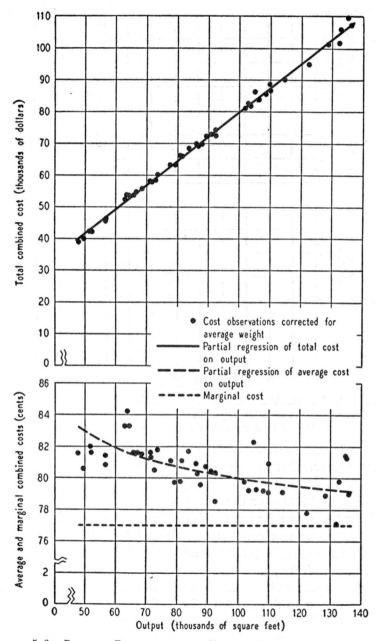

CHART 5–3. PARTIAL REGRESSIONS OF TOTAL, AVERAGE, AND MARGINAL COMBINED COST ON OUTPUT: LEATHER BELT SHOP. (Source: Dean, *Relation of Cost to Output for a Leather Belt Shop*, p. 27.)

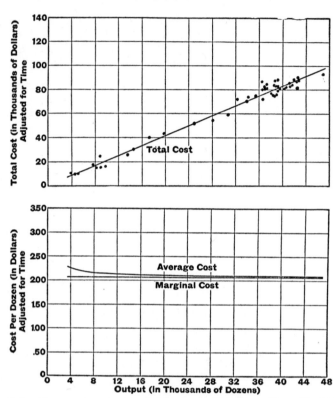

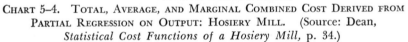

CHART 5–4. TOTAL, AVERAGE, AND MARGINAL COMBINED COST DERIVED FROM
PARTIAL REGRESSION ON OUTPUT: HOSIERY MILL.   (Source: Dean,
Statistical Cost Functions of a Hosiery Mill, p. 34.)

marginal cost curves derived from this relation.   From these results, it is seen that the operating cost of producing an additional
dozen pairs of hose (not including the cost of materials) was approximately $2.00 over the range of output observed.

Chart 5–5 shows for the furniture factory another kind of analysis, where one cost component—direct labor—is related to several of its determinants by graphic multiple correlation.   The
top section of the chart shows the basic relation of direct labor
cost to output, and the lower sections show how other factors
cause this cost to deviate from its basic output relation.   Thus,
larger lot sizes and increases in production tend to lower unit
costs, while introduction of new styles, decreases in output rate,
and higher labor turnover raise costs to different extents.   When
significant relations in this form can be found for important cost
components, such as indirect labor, inspection cost, and main-

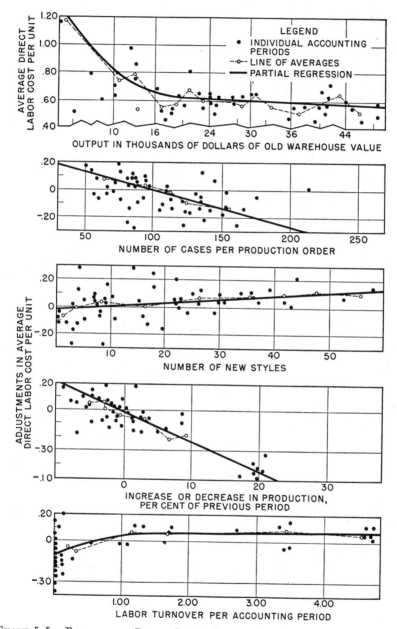

CHART 5–5. RELATION OF DIRECT LABOR COST TO FIVE INDEPENDENT FACTORS: FURNITURE FACTORY. (Source: Dean, *Statistical Determination of Costs with Special Reference to Marginal Costs*, p. 111.)

tenance, the analysis provides a basis for a more accurate and so-phisticated type of flexible budget then is commonly used. Not only cost forecasting but expense control can be built upon this kind of chart.

IV. COST AND SIZE OF PLANT

Introduction

In the studies of short-run cost behavior discussed in Section III, plant size was approximately constant. We now turn to the long-run problem of finding empirically the effect of varying the size of plants upon cost.

Knowledge of how plant size affects cost can be useful to man-agement in several ways: Though the size of a unit such as a retail store is not the only or necessarily the most important influence governing its profitability, plant size is subject to man-agerial control. Consequently, a knowledge of the relation of cost to size is needed to formulate a rational policy of plant size and plant location, and to set standards of operation that are ad-justed for uncontrollable differences in cost due to size.

In many industries the choice of plant size is closely tied in with problems of location. When transport costs and other barriers are high, location may govern the size of plant, despite impor-tant savings of size—e.g., the size of petroleum refineries located in foreign countries.[27]

Theoretical Framework of Measurement Problem

Before we can intelligently survey the methods and sample the findings of empirical studies of cost–size relationships, we need to examine the underlying concepts in theoretical terms. The theoretical framework of this problem can best be constructed un-

---

[27] Just now the optimum size of catalytic cracking refineries appears to be 60,000-barrel units, and although it is possible to make a 70,000 or 50,000 unit, costs are higher for each of these sizes than for the 60,000 unit. Two 60,000 units are as efficient as one, but not much more so. Despite higher refining costs, small units are installed. For example, a 20,000 unit was recently built in Billings, Montana, and units down to 1,000-barrel capacity have been built in foreign countries by American firms. This is because savings in transportation costs of crude oil and refined products more than offset the diseconomies of scale at these locations, or because tariff and import and export restrictions in foreign countries overbalance the cost savings and larger refinery operations.

The perishability of these barriers and of the spread between crude prices and product prices enter continuously into decisions on whether to locate the refinery and how big it should be and where it should be.

der the usual static assumptions of atomistic competition, homo-geneous products, constancy of input factors and their prices, and stability of the state of the arts. The relationship we seek is the statistical counterpart of the long-run cost curve showing the effect of plant size upon cost. This hypothetical relationship between cost and size of plant is shown in Chart 5–6. The short-run cost

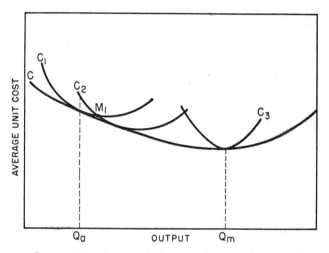

CHART 5–6. THEORETICAL LONG-RUN COST CURVE.

curves C_1, C_2, and C_3, represent cost variation with output rate of a few alternative sizes of fixed plant and reflect the notion that for each product there is a minimum-cost plant size (C_3) which makes the best compromise between indivisibilities of big ma-chinery and the high cost of coordinating big plants. When all of these short-run curves are drawn on the chart, an envelope curve (C) can be traced showing for each output rate the mini-mum-cost level and the size of plant that produces it. Such an envelope is the long-run cost curve. It does not pass through the minimum points of the short-run curves (except C_3), since there is in general some slightly different size plant that can produce that output at even lower cost.[28]

The long-run cost curve in this pristine form is quite remote

[28] When the range of possible plant sizes is not continuous—e.g., when only the three plants shown are possible—the long-run curve is scalloped, being merely the chain of short-run curves. It is difficult to say how common such discontinuities are in practice. Although cement kilns, turbines, and assembly lines suggest this situation, there is more output variation possible in their design than is apparent to the layman.

from management problems of plant size. No plant is built with the expectation of an absolutely fixed output rate, such as Q_m. It is important to know not only minimum-cost points, but cost behavior with fluctuating output rates, changes in product-mix, and the like, discussed in Section III. Furthermore, flexibility for adaptation of plants to new types of product as they develop is an important part of long-run decisions. Since there is no way to draw all of these aspects on a two-dimensional graph, Chart 5–6 can only be considered a conceptual benchmark, and it is so presented here.

To clarify the measurement problem, it is desirable to distinguish plant size from two other phases of size that sometimes confuse the issue: size of firm, and depth of plant. Size of plant is different from size of firm, even when there is only one plant. The firm encompasses several economic functions in addition to production. Each of these operations usually has a different cost–size relationship and a different optimum size. Big companies find a practical solution for this disparity in having units that differ in size for each economic function—e.g., two-man retail shoe stores and 200-man shoe factories. Despite oceans of speculation, little is really known about the relation of size of firm either to cost or to more subtle and relevant measures of over-all economic efficiency, such as profitability. Our problem here is the narrowed one of finding how cost varies with the size of plant for a particular function, such as retailing shoes or generating electricity.

The problem of size of plant must also be distinguished from depth of plant. Plant depth is a different dimension of "size" which is analogous to the degree of vertical integration for the firm. It is roughly measured by the ratio of value added to sales. A pure assembly plant is not comparable to a plant that manufactures its own parts and subassemblies. Such differences in plant depth confuse the conception of the relation of plant size to cost or obscure its measurement.

In this section, "size" refers to the volume of final output rather than the amount of work done in the plant, and plants of different sizes are assumed to make the same transformation of materials and labor into product.

Methods of Empirical Analysis

Four methods of approach to the study of the problem of cost and size of plant merit consideration.

(1) Analysis of changes in actual cost which accompanied the growth of a single plant over a period of time.

(2) Analysis of differences in actual cost of plants of different sizes operated by separate firms and observed at the same time.

(3) Engineering estimates of the alternative cost where the same technology of manufacturing is used in plants of different sizes.

(4) Analysis of differences in the actual costs of different-sized plants operated by one corporation.

The first approach encounters insuperable difficulties in the way of correcting the data for changes in products, technology and management, unless the firm displays very little technical advance during its growth. Successive observations of the firm as it adapts itself are likely to represent an expansion path which traces only growth in number of plants operated and seldom large-scale increases in plant size. Problems of rectifying cost data for changes in prices, and for differences in valuation and in accounting procedures also arise. Such a project requires complete information about one establishment over a period of continuous and substantial growth, and this is obtainable only by the closest cooperation with the enterprise. An example of this kind of study was made for a cement mill by Kurt Ehrke and Erich Schneider. The team had full access to records, and the product remained much the same over a long period of time, but technological advances could not be isolated from pure size influences.[29]

The second approach—simultaneous observations of plants that differ in size and in ownership—encounters other difficulties. Differences in products, techniques, accounting methods, valuation base, price levels and managerial effectiveness, are likely to obscure the relationship of cost to size except in unusually homogeneous industries.

Although output is almost perfectly homogeneous and measurable in electric generating plants, measurement of the effects of size present many difficulties. Power plant costs are closely tied

---

[29] *Die Ubererzeugung in der Zementindustrie,* 1858–1913, Jena, G. Fischer, 1933. Also see Theodor Beste, *Die Optimale Betriebsgrosze als betriebswirtschaftliches Problem,* Leipzig, G. A. Gloeckner, 1933.

to the age and location of the plant, and technology shows wide variations. The Federal Power Commission makes regular studies of long-run cost functions for power plants which demonstrate the heterogeneity of costs in the wide scatter of individual plants of the same capacity around the line of average relation. A study of 196 steam-electric plants that used bituminous coal was made by the U. S. Geological Survey.[30] These plants were selected from 400 plants in northeastern United States because full and consistent data were available. To remove variations in input prices, the cost of coal was taken at the average cost of $5.35 per ton for all plants. Costs of distribution and fixed costs were omitted. The relation between size and variable costs per kilowatt hour for 8 size groupings of plants is shown in Chart 5–7.

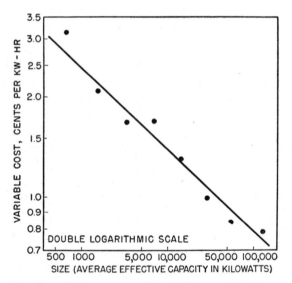

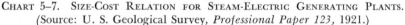

CHART 5–7. SIZE-COST RELATION FOR STEAM-ELECTRIC GENERATING PLANTS. (Source: U. S. Geological Survey, *Professional Paper 123*, 1921.)

Another industry in which output and input are fairly homogeneous and size of plant varies greatly is creamery. Table 5–2 gives the results of a study of 78 Canadian Prairie Province creameries.

The third method, engineering conjectures of costs of plants of different size, is the only one that has wide usage in the business community. In making these estimates of future costs, some

---

[30] U. S. Geological Survey, *Professional Paper 123*, 1921.

TABLE 5–2

THE RELATION OF VOLUME OF OUTPUT TO COST OF MANUFACTURING
A POUND OF BUTTER IN 78 CREAMERIES—PRAIRIE PROVINCES, 1933

(Production per Factory in Thousands of Pounds)

	Less than 100	100– 199	200– 299	300– 399	400– 499	500 and More	Average
Number of factories	4	14	22	19	5	14	78
Items of cost in cents							
Plant wages	1.36	1.32	1.05	0.90	0.79	0.76	0.91
Materials and miscellaneous	1.47	1.28	1.28	1.31	1.30	1.18	1.25
Overhead	1.26	0.73	0.66	0.70	0.52	0.48	0.60
Administration	0.73	0.56	0.53	0.71	0.76	0.76	0.69
TOTAL COST	4.82	3.89	3.52	3.62	3.37	3.18	3.45

Source: Department of Agriculture of the Dominion of Canada, *Technical Bulletin 13,* "An Economic Analysis of Creamery Operations in Manitoba, Saskatchewan and Alberta" (Ottawa, March 1938).

rough analyses of past costs are used. For example, in chain stores, technology has been stable enough to make experience with stores of different size projectable into the future. But technical advances can destroy past cost–size relationships, and they do not always work in the direction of stepping up the savings of scale. There is always a question as to how adequately such estimates take account of all operating circumstances.[31]

An example of the use of engineering estimates of cost and size of plant is provided by the following data on petroleum refineries.[32] The estimates refer to the "approximate costs under present conditions of three modern refineries which might be built in three different typical locations"; they were presented to "show how present day refining costs compare with other elements in the cost of finished products at different locations. Of

[31] Recent experiments with pulverizing big plants and operating in several smaller units have indicated that imponderables missed by engineering estimates are significant. Gains from the standpoint of employee morale and management efficiency have offset economies of specialization.

[32] Testimony of Robert E. Wilson, president of the Pan American Petroleum and Transport Company, *Hearings before the Temporary National Economic Committee,* Part 15, Petroleum Industry, Section II, pp. 8636–37.

course estimates of this sort can only be made by making numerous assumptions, but the effort has been to approximate the actual possibilities as of June 1, 1939 in various localities."

As presented (see Table 5–3), the estimates show increasing cost with increasing size. A cursory examination of the breakdown of costs reveals, however, that this is mostly due to the item "pipe line rate to refinery." This charge is hardly relevant to the cost of production, since either the raw material or the product must be transported for sale in any given market. The apparently higher cost of the Gulf Coast refinery is explained also by a higher price of input factors. In the case of all other cost elements, the cost either remains constant or declines as size increases.

TABLE 5–3

ESTIMATED COSTS AND SIZE OF REFINERY

Location of Refinery	Mid-Continent	Gulf Coast	Chicago District
Size of refinery (bbl. crude capacity per calendar day)	5,000	15,000	60,000
Estimated capital investment	$2,000,000	$5,000,000	$16,000,000
Kind of crude run	Mid-Continent	East Texas	Mid-Continent
Gravity of crude (API)	36.0–36.9	38.0–38.9	36.0–36.9
Field price of crude	$1.02	$1.10	$1.02
Gathering charge	.05	.05	.05
Pipe line rate to refinery	..	.125	.345
Direct refinery operating expense (not including fuel)	.16	.11	.08
Taxes, overhead, insurance, etc.	.04	.035	.03
Depreciation (not including obsolescence) at average rate of 7 per cent	.077	.064	.051
Miscellaneous charges	.06	.05	.04
Total cost per barrel of crude processed	$1.407	$1.534	$1.616
Total cost per barrel of products	1.529	1.667	1.757

Source: Testimony of Robert E. Wilson, president of the Pan American Petroleum and Transport Company, *Hearings before the Temporary National Economic Committee*, Part 15, Petroleum Industry, Section II, pp. 8636–37.

The fourth method is most promising. Because of the difficulty of finding comparable plants of different ownership, the relationship between cost and plant size may be most easily studied by analysis of individual units of multiple-plant firms. When several units are operated under a single ownership, they are apt to be more alike in operating techniques, accounting methods, and management.

This approach is not entirely satisfactory, however, since the units of a multiple-plant organization are not only somewhat dissimilar under the best conditions (e.g., in age) but also not completely autonomous. The costs of administrative functions, to the extent that they are performed centrally, must be omitted from analysis, unless they can be satisfactorily allocated to the operating units. Furthermore, differences in managerial effectiveness, although likely to be lessened, are not entirely eliminated.

Some of the irrelevant variations due to differences in operating conditions can be removed by careful selection of the sample, rectification of data, cross-classification, and introduction of the source of variation as an independent variable in correlation analysis. For example, one could select stores of a chain that are similar with respect to locality, maturity, and product proportions and classify stores according to non-quantitative characteristics such as the supervisors.

Problems of Measurement [33]

To determine empirically the relationship between cost and scale of plant requires careful consideration of alternative concepts of scale and cost in order that those used are at once theoretically relevant and empirically measurable.

Measuring Size

To find an appropriate concept of size of plant that will permit practical measurement is not an easy matter. It involves choice among several alternatives:

(1) Amount of fixed equipment
    in physical terms, e.g., number of spindles
    in value terms, e.g., total assets, physical assets, capital assets, tangible net worth

---

[33] The analysis of measurement problems is based on materials the author prepared for the Committee on Price Determination, which were published in its study, *Cost Behavior and Price Policy*, National Bureau of Economic Research, New York, 1943, pp. 231–263. It is used here with the permission of the publisher.

(2) Output capacity

   maximum physical capacity, e.g., rated capacity of a blast
      furnace

   economic capacity, e.g., "efficient" capacity throughput of
      a refinery.

(3) Input capacity

   physical capacity, e.g., size of "charge" of furnace, number
      of employees or man hours

   economic capacity, e.g., "efficient" capacity, "normal"
      capacity.

If the problem is stated as one of physical size of plant, this
implies measurement in terms of fixed factors not readily modified in the short run.   The amount of fixed equipment is difficult
to measure in physical terms that permit comparison unless the
equipment is highly standardized and made up of a large number
of homogeneous units.   Railroads, for example, might be ranked
in size on the basis of trackage or rolling stock, both of which
measures are homogeneous and important.   However, they give
very different results.   Value measures of fixed plant make it possible to summarize and compare heterogeneous physical units,
but they involve complex problems of what to include as fixed
plant, and of determining the current cost of plants of varying
ages, constructed at different price levels.   Hence, measurement
of scale of fixed plant by the amount alone is much less significant than the prevalence of the practice would indicate.

Another major alternative is to frame the problem in terms
of output capacity of the equipment.   Satisfactory measures of
output capacity are difficult to find, partly because output units
are not homogeneous, and partly because "capacity" is so hard
to determine.   Concepts of physical capacity appear to be inappropriate for this purpose, because the theoretical framework of
the problem has been constructed in economic terms.   There is
no definitive concept of capacity in economics, since in theory output is determined by the relation of costs to prices rather than by
some characteristic of the plant alone, such as "designed" capacity.   There are indications, however, that in some industries
engineers' ideas of "physical capacity" coincide approximately
with minimum average cost; for the marginal cost function is
nearly flat over most of the range of output, and curves upward
only as physical capacity is approached.   This means that average

cost per unit declines over most of the range and reaches a minimum at or near the physical limit of the fixed equipment. (See Chart 5–4 in Section III.) Under these conditions minimum average cost is a reasonable and useful concept of economic capacity which come close to physical capacity—probably well within the error range for an estimate of either concept.

But not even this economic capacity is the theoretically correct concept for determining the long-run cost function, which, as Chart 5–6 shows, does not pass through the low point of the series of short-run cost curves, but is rather the envelope of these curves. Hence what is required is the point of tangency of each curve with the envelope of the entire series. That is to say, to find the long-run cost curve empirically, we want to observe a series of plants each operating at that output rate (and at maximum efficiency) for which it has the lowest cost possible with full adaptation of plant.

It is hard to see how actual observations of cost and output could meet these requirements, however. If competition were perfect we would expect to find observations only at Q_m on Chart 5–6. Under conditions of fluctuating demand and uncertainty, there will be many observations of higher cost plants that are operating, at lower profits, perhaps, as long as prices cover their marginal costs. With imperfect competition, moreover, there will be a variety of price levels in the industry and some sales for each company at its own price, but by no means necessarily at the output rate corresponding to tangency to the envelope curve. A multi-plant company will operate as many of its plants as it needs at minimum cost and keep the rest shut down, rather than operate all of them at the level we want to observe. Moreover, if the observation represents an annual average of several positions on the short-run curve, it will necessarily be higher than the minimum point of the short-run curve, reflecting as it does a variety of output levels. An important kind of deviation from the data we are looking for is produced by ambitious and growing firms that buy plants early in anticipation of market expansion. Such a firm with sales at Q_a on Chart 5–6 would have a plant such as C_2 rather than the minimum-cost C_1 plant, and thus give a misleading indication of the envelope curve.

It is clear, then, that actual observations of output will not produce the long-run cost curve we seek. Nevertheless, it may be

hoped that in industries with a continuous range in possible size
of plant, i.e., without the scalloped curve mentioned early in this
section, a statistical averaging of observations will give a curve
of about the same shape as the theoretical function.[34]   For management purposes of making choices between plant sizes, the
shape rather than the level is after all the important result to find.

Size can be measured by input capacity as well as by the amount
of fixed equipment and output capacity, i.e., by the capacity of
the plant to use workers or consume raw material.   Although
theoretical analysis is not commonly made in these terms, the same
basic discrepancies between theoretical and empirical relationships
are involved.   There are instances, however, when an input
measure of capacity may prove desirable (notably when output is
so varied that no satisfactory index can be constructed).   Here
again it is difficult to find the capacity point along the input scale.
If size is measured simply by average input of a major raw material
over a period of time, it is assumed that all plants have operated
at full, or at a uniform proportion of, capacity, and this is not
likely to be true.   Each study will require consideration of different alternative measures of size.   In general, a measure which
corresponds most closely to economic capacity is the best.

Measuring Cost

Recorded cost is affected by many factors other than size of
plant.   Removing these variables in order to compare the effect
of size on cost for several plants is the central and most difficult
problem of methodology.   The most important of these irrelevant
influences—some of which have been explicitly treated in Section
III—are changes in:

(1) rate of output
(2) "state of the arts"
(3) accounting valuations and procedures
(4) prices paid for input factors
(5) managerial skill

---

[34] Whether or not this is so depends upon whether the positions of the observations on the short-run curves differ systematically with the scale of output.   If, for
example, small plants were operated at a higher percentage of capacity than large
plants, the long-run curve may be tilted to the left.   If the responsibility for
maintaining price when demand is low is borne by the firms with larger plants
in the industry, firms with smaller plants can shade price, keep some plants operating at high rates, and thus produce this kind of empirical curve.

(6) locational advantages

(7) character of products

Differences in rate of utilization of capacity have an important effect upon cost per unit through the spreading of fixed factors and through the operation of the law of diminishing returns upon increased application of variable factors. Thus, as indicated earlier, the position of a cost observation on the short-run cost curve for a particular scale of plant obscures the relationship between scale and cost. Two methods of removing this irrelevant variation are promising. The first is to try to average out differences in utilization rate by including many plants, by using a long observation period (e.g. a year, so as to smooth out monthly variation in output rate), and by excluding plants known to have extreme under-utilization. The second method is to introduce percentage of utilization as an independent variable in a multiple correlation analysis.

Technical advance is likely to becloud the effects of size of plant. Plant size of multiple-unit firms may be systematically associated with age and hence with technology. For example, recent suburbanization of department stores makes small units more modern than big ones. For single-plant firms, growth is likely to be associated with efficiency and as the firm grows it may obtain more competent technical advice. Hence the expanded plant is likely to embody more advanced technology, and size and technical progress may be inextricably intertwined.

A fairly clear theoretical distinction between these two factors may be made. At a given level of technology or state of the arts, differences will exist between the various sizes of plant in respect to the type of machinery, the size of machines, and the organization of production; but these differences will be associated only with the scale of plant and will involve no technical improvements that were unknown when any of the plants were designed.

This theoretical distinction is difficult to make in practice, because even when plants of various sizes are built at the same time, cultural lag and ignorance of the best current technical processes will result in variations in technology that are not solely attributable to differences in size. Furthermore, the science of plant design and of production organization and management is not exact. Hence a wide range of differences in technology may exist because of differences in opinion. Despite these difficulties, these two forces must be disentangled if the relationship between cost and size of plant is to be determined.[35]

Differences in accounting valuation and in accounting procedures are likely to affect average cost as reported in the records of the several firms, and thus to obscure the true relationship between cost and size of plant. Two plants of identical size and technology may have been constructed at the same time under different types of corporate promotion, which may lead to the overvaluation of one plant on the books, and thus result in higher recorded average cost. Furthermore, the way in which overhead is allocated to production may have considerable effect upon reported average cost. Differences in prices paid for plant and equipment may be considerable if they have been purchased at different times, under different solvency conditions, or in different regions. Removal of these distorting influences constitutes one of the more important research problems.

Differences in the prices paid for input factors, i.e., labor and materials, may tend to conceal the cost–price relationship. Geographic and chronological differences in wage rates and material prices, to the extent that these differences are not a function of the size of the firm (i.e., are not economies of large scale buying), should be removed from the data.

Adjustment for differences among plants in factor prices presents the same kind of problems of rectification discussed for short-run cost research in Section III. But since the likelihood of price-motivated substitution is greater for long-run adjustments, a cost function in terms of fixed prices may omit an important economic fact. Moreover, measurement is sometimes more elusive for regional disparities.

Differences in managerial skill may cause some distortion of the observed relationship between cost and size of the plant, for a superior management may, to a degree, equalize the differential advantages of size.

Differential locational advantages not fully compensated by rent differences further complicate cost comparisons. Depart-

---

[35] Since new plants are usually built in bunches at cyclical peaks, it may be possible to find the relation between cost and scale by analysis of a group of new plants constructed at about the same time. For example, many petroleum refineries of different size were built during the war, presumably with similar technology.

ment store operating costs, for example, appear to be lower in small cities than in large. For this reason crude comparisons which fail to take account of differences in location are misleading.

Differences in products constitute one of the most serious obstacles to collection of suitable data on this point. The number of industries in which plants of varying size make the same product or comparable products in the same proportions is limited.

Shoe-Chain Study

To illustrate the method of interplant comparison within a company, we shall survey a study of a shoe chain.[36]

The purpose of this study was to determine by statistical analysis the relationship between the size and the operating cost of the retail stores of a large shoe chain. Out of the several hundred stores operated by the corporation, a sample of 55, all located in a single large city and under the control of one supervisor, was studied. The sample of stores was selected to provide a fairly uniform coverage of various operating conditions, such as the ratio of the sales of various types of shoes to total sales and, at the same time, to be representative of sales volumes of the stores in the chain as a whole. Stores recently opened were excluded because immaturity might mean systematic under-utilization of capacity. Annual data on retail operations and costs for each store were made available for the years 1937 and 1938.

Measurement of Size

The first problem was to decide on the appropriate concept of size. Size, however measured, cannot in theory be dissociated from some concept of capacity. As we have seen, there are several available concepts of size that can be measured, and that are relevant to cost. Three are of particular importance: (1) physical size of plant and equipment, (2) input capacity, and (3) output capacity. For plant and equipment of shoe stores, number of seats in a store, area of floor space, or number of standard lighting units are possibilities for physical-unit measures, but they were found to vary too much for irrelevant reasons to provide a trust-

---

[36] For a more complete analysis of this study, see *The Long-Run Behavior of Costs in a Chain of Shoe Stores,* by Joel Dean and R. Warren James, Chicago, University of Chicago Press, 1942. Permission to summarize this study and present some of its findings was granted by the University of Chicago Press.

worthy indication of size for inter-store comparison. Input indexes were also inadequate, because the major input is labor service, which can be measured only in big chunks—i.e., the number of salesmen per store. There is too much variation in the scale of operations of, say, a two-man store, to measure size continuously and accurately. Moreover, the skill of the sales force varies widely among stores.

Actual output in the form of total annual sales was therefore found to be most representative of size. Although actual observations could not be confined to output at economic capacity, the use of an annual aggregate averaged out short-run fluctuations to a large extent. As discussed previously, this measure of size probably shows the shape of the long-run curve, but not its absolute level.

The next problem was to select for the shoe stores the most satisfactory index of output. Output of a retail store is best viewed as the production of sales service—i.e., the contribution of the shoe salesmen to the prospective purchaser in the form of fitting and selection, help, and advice. Although the quality and quantity of sales service per transaction differed among transactions, there were several influences making for uniformity of service standards, notably the fact that the sample stores were confined to one chain and one city and were under a single supervisor. Theoretically, the best measure of output would weight the components of physical sales on the basis of the quantity (and quality) of selling time and effort they require.

Several alternative indexes were considered: (1) Total store sales in dollars, (2) shoe sales in dollars (excluding rubbers, hosiery, etc.), and (3) shoe sales in number of pairs. Although the dollar volume of store sales represented the most comprehensive index, it weighted shoes according to their price, which does not accurately reflect the amount of service associated with the sale. Low-priced children's shoes typically require greater sales service than more expensive men's shoes. Shoe sales in pairs had the advantage of giving all types of shoes equal performance and hence afforded the least objectionable weighting of any of the measures considered. This was the index of output used.

Measurement of Cost

Cost components as well as combined cost were studied statistically. Separate analysis of cost components is valuable for the following reasons: First, for purposes of control, it is important to trace the sources of total cost variability. Knowledge of the cost-size pattern for individual components affords clearer insight into the causes of abnormal cost behavior in individual stores and gives a basis for designing new stores. Second, a partial check of total cost estimates was provided by separate analysis of components, since components can be combined in order to arrive at total cost. All costs were included except two elements of central administrative expense that were allocated to individual stores arbitrarily.

Findings

The relation of total cost to physical volume of shoe sales for 1937 and for 1938 is shown in Chart 5–8. The use of logarithms of the cost and of the output variables not only produces a better fit, but shows up clearly the effect of relative changes of output

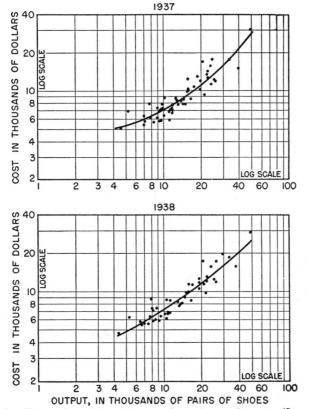

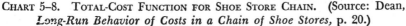

CHART 5–8. TOTAL-COST FUNCTION FOR SHOE STORE CHAIN. (Source: Dean, *Long-Run Behavior of Costs in a Chain of Shoe Stores*, p. 20.)

on cost.   The parabolic shape of the fitted regression shows that
the relative change in cost is increasing, i.e., the elasticity of total
cost is increasing over the whole range of output.   Hence total
cost elasticity moves from values of less than unity to values greater
than unity.   The average cost curve correspondingly displays the
familiar U-shape with a minimum point at an output of approximately 32,000 pairs for 1937, and about 38,000 pairs for 1938.   A
direct analysis of average cost behavior was made to supplement
this relationship derived from total cost logarithms.   Chart 5–9
shows the results of this correlation analysis for the years 1937
and 1938 in terms of average cost per hundred pairs of shoes
sold.

Applications

Cost–size studies of this type have three uses.   The first, quite
obviously, is to establish an optimum size of store as a criterion
for planning on the number of stores in an area in relation to the
density of the market.   That is, if sales potential appears to be
600,000 pairs, it would be nice to have 20 stores scattered through
the area, each selling 30,000 pairs.   One grocery chain has indeed
established a rather rigid size and layout of store which prevails
in most of its units and is the goal to be reached in the few deviate
units.

However, there are locational and other complications to consider in planning a chain, and it is frequently necessary to have
a single store in, say, Times Square, selling 50,000 pairs, even
though the unit cost is higher than optimum.   When this is the
case, cost–size studies have a second application in balancing
the benefits of better market orientation against the losses of de-
parting from the minimum-cost size.   Economies of size for
gasoline stations, though substantial, must be balanced against
accessibility in choosing a location which typically governs size.
A third use of cost–size studies is in setting up expense standards for control purposes.   Here, the analysis in terms of cost
components (not presented under *Findings,* above) is most useful.
By knowing an over-all statistical relation of lighting expense or
labor cost to the size of individual units, much speculation and
argument can be wrung out of cost control, and managers will
cease to be blamed for variances from cost standards that are
quite beyond their control.   A cost–size study such as this one has

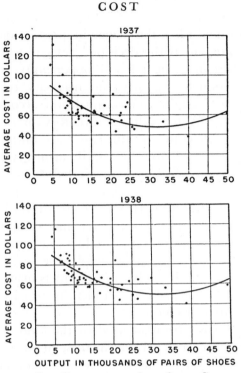

CHART 5–9. AVERAGE-COST FUNCTION FOR SHOE STORE CHAIN. (Source: Dean, *Long-Run Behavior of Costs in a Chain of Shoe Stores*, p. 25.)

actually been used as the basis for expense control in a consumer-finance company with a large number of branch offices.

V. COSTS OF MULTIPLE PRODUCTS

Introduction

Monistic production is exceptional in modern American industry; multiple-product production is the overwhelming rule. Determination of the costs of individual articles produced and sold in multiple-product operations is therefore of great practical importance for some kinds of problems. For example, it can be used: to guide birth and death decisions that affect product line; to influence product modification and redesigning; to select the most appropriate system of price differentials among members of an existing product line; and to indicate opportunities and limits for non-price competition by revealing the incremental profits of different products.

The individual product costs that are needed are the increments that will occur if and when the change in question occurs, i.e., the costs that are different if the decision goes one way rather than the other. These incremental and opportunity costs that are needed for decision-making have no necessary relation to the product costs obtained by conventional cost accounting, which are useful principally for valuing inventory in computing net income. These conventional "full costs" are built from records of historical outlays and from necessarily arbitrary allocations of overheads, many of which are unaffected by (and therefore irrelevant to) the particular decision.

As pointed out in Section II, some costs are traceable to individual products, e.g., purchased parts and components, while other costs are common to several products, i.e., not easily identified with a single product. For example, the cost of the factory building is common to all the types of products made there. The problem of product costing arises in identifying parts of common costs with particular products.[37]

Some common costs are unaffected by the kind of change that is up for decision, e.g., a 10 per cent increase in output. Common costs that are fixed do not need to be allocated, since they are irrelevant for any decision for which they are constant.[38]   It is the common costs that vary with the decision that need to be allocated to individual products.

Some decisions involve such a major overhaul of the cost structure that special cost studies are needed to determine the incremental costs. But the occasions for such decisions are quite rare. More frequent are problems that are closely related to variations in rate of output. For these decisions short-run variable costs are most important, and warrant special attention to the allocation of variable common costs.

---

[37] The distinction between traceable and non-traceable costs, as we have seen, is a function of the record system as well as of characteristics of production methods and cost behavior, and many costs that are traceable in nature become lumped when accounts are classified for other than costing purposes.

[38] For any problem that has a large enough scope to meet these fixed costs, their present allocations may forecast future costs poorly. Some problems do require estimates of long-run costs of individual products, e.g., the decision to add a light truck to a passenger car line. Costs that are fixed and not traceable in the short run are relevant for such decisions, because they do vary in the long run. These long-run costs are likely to be quite different from the arbitrary allocation of short-run fixed overheads.

Accounting Allocations of Product Cost

When an executive asks the cost of a product, the answer he gets is a historical, fully-allocated, average unit cost. There are comparatively few executive decisions for which this kind of cost is relevant, although it occasionally approximates the relevant concept. There are problems of public relations for which full unit costs obtained by orthodox accountancy are precisely relevant because of their authoritarian ring. Hence, allocations of full cost should not be abandoned altogether, but they need less emphasis than they get in cost analysis and in management decisions. Serious economic errors may result if these full unit costs are used for decisions for which they are inappropriate. For many management problems, a better decision will be made if cost allocations are confined to overheads that vary with the decision. To get this kind of cost, apportionment of overheads should conform as closely as knowledge permits to cost behavior rather than be dominated by consideration of equity ("each product bearing its fair share of the overhead load").

Accounting practice in determining the cost of individual products generally treats all non-traceable costs alike, in that no distinction is made between alternative products and joint products, and no distinction between joint costs with fixed proportions of products and those with variable proportions. In effect, common costs are viewed as all joint costs with the proportion of products fixed.[39] These costs are allocated to individual products by one or more bases of allocation, such as traceable cost or sales value. These bases or formulae are essentially arbitrary in the sense that equally defensible formulae can give quite different cost estimates, and also in the sense that the allocation is not modified to fit the situation—i.e., does not distinguish between variable and fixed overheads or between manipulatable and fixed product-mix. For instance, the cost of heating a kiln might be allocated to different qualities of chinaware that pass through it on the basis of relative direct labor costs or relative prices. A shift in product-mix toward a greater proportion of low priced

---

[39] In fact, the *Cost Accountant's Handbook* (Theodore Lang, Ed., New York, The Ronald Press, 1944, p. 501) defines joint products simply as products processed together in approximately equal proportions. Behavior of common costs as the product-mix varies plays no part in the definition.

utility ware will lower the total allocated heating cost, but it won't affect the actual cost of keeping the kiln hot.

When a large proportion of the costs are traceable, and these costs are also variable in the short run, overheads are light and errors in allocation do not matter much. But when overheads are large and partly fixed in relation to output, then economic errors of accounting allocations can be serious. Routine allocations should be confined to variable overheads since, as was mentioned above, only the variable costs are useful in decision-making. When variable overheads are highly correlated with direct labor in the aggregate, then the use of direct labor to prorate variable overheads among individual products can produce estimates of variable costs which may be a good enough benchmark for projecting the costs of the article into the future. It is when traceable costs are small in relation to common costs and when common costs are largely fixed that the product costs that are obtained by conventional cost accounting are of least managerial usefulness. Under these circumstances, a cost figure is produced for each product which may prove in with the financial accounts. But it is hard to think of an executive decision for which this "actual cost" figure is truly relevant.

The most widely used method of allocation of common costs is some measure of direct labor costs. Common bases for allocation of overhead costs according to a research study of the NACA are shown in Table 5–4. Other methods not mentioned are focused on equalizing reported profits from each product—e.g., allocating common costs on the basis of sales value.[40] Sales value methods are, of course, circular and have no usefulness in product-line problems, since they provide no basis for comparing costs with revenues.

To use product cost data for decision making, we must understand the cost characteristics of the product line that determine the relevance of various costs to a particular problem. The distinctive aspects of product-line costs that must be considered here are (1) jointness of products, and (2) controllability of product-mix.

---

40 An example of the sales value method of allocation is found in W. Albert Bush, "Pickle Costs," *NACA Bulletin,* November 1, 1938.

TABLE 5–4

BASES USED IN APPLICATION OF OVERHEAD *

Bases Used	Number of Companies Using as Major or Only Base	Using as Secondary Base	Total
Actual direct labor cost	96	13	109
Actual direct labor hours	27	21	48
Actual machine hours	30	13	43
Weight basis	7	39	36
Standard machine hours	13	22	35
Standard direct labor hours	29	4	33
Unit of product	11	18	19
Material cost	..	11	11
Prime cost	5	5	10
Standard direct labor cost	5	..	5
Miscellaneous	1	2	3

* "Practice in Applying Overhead and Calculating Normal Capacity," *N.A.C.A. Bulletin,* XIX (April 1, 1938), Section III, p. 922.

Quoted in *Cost Behavior and Price Policy,* National Bureau of Economic Research, New York, 1943, p. 183.

Jointness of Products

For product-costing it is desirable to distinguish two broad categories of common products: joint products and alternative products. When an increase in the production of one product causes an increase in the output of another product, then the products and their costs are traditionally defined as joint. In contrast, when an increase in the output of a product is accompanied by a reduction in the output of other products, it is a case of what may be called alternative products. Slag and steel are joint products, but steel rails and steel sheets are alternative products.[41]

[41] A common case of alternative products arises with flexible equipment that can be applied to several kinds of product—e.g., a petroleum products pipeline. If it is used for one product, it is unavailable for all others. Many bottlenecks in industry have this characteristic, so that it is a ubiquitous short-run problem in costing multiple products.

The case of products whose proportions cannot be varied in production (a rigid joint relation) is probably rare in manufacturing industry. When it exists, the problem of allocation of costs of individual product members is insoluble; in fact, there is no point in seeking a solution for most managerial problems.

In principle, two joint cost situations can be distinguished. First, when the proportions of the end products can be varied; second, when these proportions are fixed. The case of fixed proportions presumably cannot exist in the long run, since changes in technology and the development of new breeds of animals can alter the proportion—e.g., make the pig's hip bone vestigial in, say, 10,000 generations. Even in the short run, to be meticulous, it may be maintained, as Professor Viner does, that in all cases of joint products, it is possible to vary the proportions in some degree, so that there is no instance of absolutely invariable proportions of end products. (See Jacob Viner, article on "Costs," in *Encyclopedia of the Social Sciences,* Vol. IV, page 473.)

Nevertheless, there are enough situations where the costs of manipulating the product-mix in the short run are prohibitive, so that fixed proportions are an important practical case. Under these circumstances, separate product costs are indeterminate. There is not even much point in contemplating the separate costs of bringing hams and shoulders to the slaughter-house, since each unavoidably accompanies the other. When one product is much less important than the other, it may be called a by-product, a gratuitous use of a waste material, but there is no real distinction between joint products and by-products. Where the march of technology is rapid, as in chemistry, by-products soon become joint products and may even take on senior status.

In the case of common costs that are not joint between two products, increasing the output of one product is either unassociated with an increase in the output of the other, or requires a sacrifice or reduction of the output of the other. In the first instance, the separate incremental costs are, at least in principle, determinant; in the second case, where sacrificed production of other products is involved, the concept of opportunity costs is frequently the most important. For example, the principal cost of canning tomatoes is the foregone opportunity to pack tomato juice.

The existence of alternative products is generally the result of incomplete adaptation. Given the facilities to adapt production exactly to the level and nature of demand, there would be no need to choose between products and to forego opportunities. In a war economy, shortages of particular materials and labor make choices between alternative products a major type of problem. Joint products, on the other hand, are generally considered to result from the technical nature of the production process, rather than solely from the scale of existing plant.[42]

Assigning common costs to individual products is more difficult and less useful when the products are joint than when the products are alternative. The cost of an alternative product can always be computed in terms of the foregone profits from the other product, whereas the cost of a joint product (as distinguished from the cost of the product package) is essentially indeterminate. When the proportion of joint products is fixed, cost allocation is impossible as well as footless, since there is no alternative but to produce the package. When proportions are variable, marginal costs with respect to changes in product-mix would be useful in deciding between alternative product-mixes. But opportunities for altering proportions are far scarcer with joint than with alternative products, and this kind of marginal cost is therefore rarely needed. Even when their proportions are manipulatable, separate costs of the individual products are for practical purposes indeterminate, although in theory marginal cost might be estimated by vast and horribly expensive experiments (as discussed later).

For joint products of both fixed and variable proportions, cost problems relate more commonly to the incremental effect of an increase in output rate to meet new demand for one of the joint products. Such an increase involves higher output for all of the products and may therefore cause a reduction in prices of joint products in order to get rid of them—e.g., more slag from increased output of steel. Thus the added revenue from one joint product must cover not only the marginal cost of the whole product package, but also any loss of revenue from lowered prices of the other joint products as well.

Controllability of Product-Mix

We can distinguish between a production situation in which the proportions of different products (product-mix) follow a necessary functional relation and one in which there is some management discretion in determining the proportions. These

---

42 Ultimately, whether two products are joint products or alternative products depends on whether increasing their output as a team gives a greater or a smaller profit than increasing either one of them singly. This is a question of relative prices as well as of technology.

two situations are applicable to joint products. Thus, for joint products, an increase of one unit in product A may necessarily raise output of B by 6.5 units, or it may require an increase in B of from 4.5 to 9.5 units, with a minimum cost point at 6.5. A rigid relation—i.e., where product-mix is not controllable—however, does not mean the same proportion at all outputs: the necessary ratio may be 6.5 at 100,000 unit output, and 10.5 at 300,000.

For alternative products, output proportions are ordinarily fully controllable. Despite flexibility of production, there can also be a pragmatic approximation to an invariant product-mix with alternative products caused by inflexibility of demand. Market restrictions on the sales mix can nullify freedom to manipulate the production mix. For example, the ratio of long-distance calls to local calls is frozen by demand rather than by production inflexibility. This is likely to happen only when demand is highly insensitive to changes in relative prices or promotional activity and when there is no escape through competitive jockeying or modification of the product. The effect on the desirability and the possibility of determining separate product costs is the same as if it were physically impossible to vary the proportions if the market restrictions are really iron-clad. For many purposes it is thus convenient to consider rigid joint demand as demand for a single product, which raises no problem of sorting out the parts of common cost.

Allocation of Variable Overheads

The problem area has been narrowed to the allocation of short-run, non-traceable, variable cost under conditions where the proportions of common products can be varied.

In terms of abstract theory, this cost can be allocated correctly among the products by systematically varying both the total volume of output and the proportions of the various multiple products and observing the effect upon total variable common costs.[43]

---

[43] Theoretically this could result in the determination of pure functional relationship between costs and volume and between costs and various dimensions of product-mix. Given these functional relationships, it would then be possible to estimate the costs of any specified proportion of products and rate of output. It would also be possible to estimate the independent effect upon cost of varying the output of one product while holding all others constant, thus arriving at the cost allocation for that product.

Empirical exploration of this suggested solution has been limited. Under favorable circumstances some progress can be made by multiple correlation analysis. These circumstances include: (a) the ability to remove by data rectification most of the extraneous influences that affect costs, (b) variation in both the rate of output and the proportion of products with fairly complete coverage of the range, (c) a small enough number of products so that the product-mix could be measured by a small number of independent variables, and (d) ability to confine the situation by sampling to a pure short-run static one with no change in product line.

From this imposing array of requisites, it is clear that this approach cannot be widely used, at least in this full-blown form. It may be useful, however, as a check on the answers given by the allocation methods of cost accounting. This can sometimes be done with rough scatter diagrams in a relatively simple situation.

A simpler empirical approach is to isolate by statistical analysis the common variable costs as a function of aggregate output and then to allocate these costs among multiple products on some basis that seems reasonable, though it is bound to be somewhat arbitrary. Several alternative allocation methods are available.

When there is a traceable element of cost which in the aggregate is highly correlated with output, and/or with the variable common costs to be allocated, then proration of variable overheads on the basis of this single input—e.g., direct labor hours—gives a pretty good approximation to normal marginal costs for individual products. A second method is to allocate all variable overheads to individual products on the basis of the relative size of the product's total of traceable costs—e.g., the sum of direct labor and direct materials. This solution assumes not only that the direct costs are variable, but also that the amount of direct cost will pull along, or at least indicate a corresponding amount or proportion of indirect labor and other variable overheads caused by the production of one more unit of a particular product. A third approach, patterned on cost accounting practices, would be to allocate each variable overhead separately, selecting from a battery of traceable inputs the one that appeared to be most closely related. For example, electric power might be allocated on the basis of machine hours, inventory expenses on the basis of direct materials, and indirect labor on the basis of direct labor. A fourth approach is to find by statistical analysis how each element of overhead cost varies with each of several dimensions of output, and use these relationships as the basis for allocating the variable portions of each element of overhead cost separately to individual products on the basis of their dimension characteristics. This would involve finding, for each element of overhead that varies significantly with output, a different criterion for allocating its variable portions to individual products. For example, in a furniture factory, certain clerical and stockroom costs vary with the number of production orders, and spoilage may depend on the number of new styles.

Petroleum Refining—An Illustration

An illustration from the petroleum industry may help to point up the foregoing analysis. An estimate of the refinery-door cost of home heating oil is needed for pricing and marketing problems arising from the fierce fight between natural gas and home heating oil in many markets. Management must find out the lowest price at which it can afford to accept business in an effort to retain existing home heating markets. The problem is for simplicity conceived as a short-run one, in the sense that adjustments of output and of product-mix must be achieved with existing refinery facilities and techniques.

Separable costs of refining are negligible.[44] Hence, the allocation of common costs is the central problem in determining the cost of individual petroleum products.

Crude oil yields a mixture of joint and alternative products. Residual fuel oil is a joint product with invariant proportions in respect to the group of upper and middle distillate products as a whole. Increasing the output of the distillate group necessarily increases the output of residual, and the ratio of residual fuel oil to the group cannot be readily manipulated. But within this distillate group, products are alternative to each other rather than joint. As a result of modern refinery processes—catalytic cracking and polymerization—the range of practical variation in proportions of these products has been greatly increased. Heating oil can now be largely converted into gasoline, and the product proportions can be varied over a wide range.

---

44 In the latter stages of preparing and blending a product such as gasoline, there are some added operations and materials (e.g., lead) that are traceable to individual products, but these are an unimportant part of total cost.

Some of the common costs to be allocated in the short run are constant costs—e.g., depreciation, interest, and repairs on refinery facilities used in common. But the important costs vary as a function of output, notably crude oil, and some of the labor. For the problem of heating oil prices, common fixed costs are irrelevant; it is the common variable costs that are significant for the pricing problem.

The most satisfactory way to estimate the cost of heating oil for this management decision is its gasoline opportunity cost. The cost of heating oil is the foregone gains that could have been realized by converting the oil into gasoline, which is usually the most important product.[45] Gasoline is the important product, because it is the one that justifies the refinery investment. It is the big-volume, high-margin product, the demand for which is inelastic, largely because there is little substitute competition. Hence there is also less risk of losing the market than there is for heating oil. Thus costing heating oil on the basis of gasoline conversion value employs a concept that is relevant for deciding the minimum price at which it would be better to convert into gasoline rather than to sell as heating oil to retain the market threatened by natural gas (abstracting here from longer-run considerations).

None of the alternative methods of allocation are very satisfactory. One which has been traditional in the industry is to look upon all products other than gasoline as undesirable by-products and implicitly as joint products of invariant proportions, and deduct the amount realized from their sales from the variable costs as a whole, thereby obtaining a variable cost for gasoline. The same approach could be used for heating oil, looking upon gasoline as a by-product. This approach has the disadvantage of making the cost of gasoline so estimated depend upon the prices obtainable from the other products, in an illogical way, since the higher the price of heating oil, the less the cost of gasoline. But the main objection is, of course, that it is economically unrealistic to view as by-products of fixed proportions distillates that are really alternative products of plannable proportions.

---

[45] For large companies an important limitation of this gasoline opportunity cost is that the prevailing price of gasoline overstates the equivalent gasoline value to the company, since producing more gasoline would probably depress its price.

Another solution is to allocate common costs on the basis of relative sales value of the various products. This solution is obviously circular and irrelevant to the problem. Moreover relative prices change mercurially, and not always in close relationship to the price of crude oil, the raw material.

Summary

Determination of the costs of individual products is needed for various management problems. These decision-making costs need to be tailored to fit the problem. The product costs supplied by conventional cost accounting are not multiple-purpose costs, but primarily useful for costing inventory for computing enterprise profits. As decision-making costs, they are defective in several respects: first, overheads that are not variable with the decision and, hence, are not costs for that problem, are nevertheless allocated to individual products; second, the method of allocation is necessarily arbitrary; third, no distinction is made between joint products and alternative products in determining their costs; and fourth, there is no recognition of the significance of controllability of the product-mix in estimating the incremental and opportunity costs that are relevant for specific decisions.

Analysis of the economic characteristics of the managerial problem and of the production process can help correct these defects. Allocations can be confined to those overheads that are variable with the decision and are appropriately valued. And the accuracy of these allocations can sometimes be increased.

VI. COST AND PROFIT FORECASTING

Forecasting profits is an essential part of operations planning. It is the basis for planning cash and capital expenditures, pricing policy, and income tax reserves. Typically, book profits (i.e., what the company's accountants will report), rather than "economic" profits are predicted.

Forecasting book profits involves projection of the entire income statement, which requires prediction of most aspects of the company's operations. Since profits are residuals that result from the forces that shape demand for the company's products and govern the behavior of its costs, their prediction is subject to wide margins of error, from cumulation of errors in forecasting revenue and costs, and from the interrelation of the various components of the income statement.

Three approaches to profit forecasting may be distinguished. (1) Spot projections: prediction of the entire income statement for a specified future period by forecasting each important element separately. (2) Break-even analysis: determination of the functional relation of both revenue and costs to output rate, and derivation of the functional relation of profits to output as a residual. This profit function may also be determined directly by statistical analysis of past profit behavior in relation to output. (3) Environmental analysis: determination of the relation of the company's profits to key variables in its economic environment (such as general business activity and general price level.)

In practice, these three approaches need not be mutually exclusive, but can be used jointly for maximum information. In making spot projections of the income statement, use can be made of the functional relations of cost to output and to its other determinants. Similarly, direct measurements of the impact of outside economic forces upon the company's profits can facilitate good spot guesses, and can also enhance the accuracy of break-even analyses.

Spot Projections

Predicting a company's profits by building up a conjectural income statement for a specific future period is a sort of by-product of the forecasts and plans of operating activities that characterize modern management. Forecasting of sales, prices, product-mix and channel-mix come to focus in the prediction of revenue. Forecasting of costs involves the same kind of analysis required to set expense control standards in budgetary control. It calls for empirical knowledge of functional relation of costs to their major determinants: output rate, technology, product-mix, factor prices, and the like.[46] It also requires prediction of the probable level of these underlying operating conditions.

Revenues and costs are interrelated in complex ways. Profit forecasting must, therefore, take account of management's latitude in "controlling" costs in adversity through intensifying the drive for efficiency and through manipulation of discretionary expenditures (e.g., research and advertising).

---

[46] The care and precision with which these relations should be estimated depends upon the value of reducing forecasting error. As in any business problem, cost puts a damper on perfectionism, and it is usually necessary to settle for rough-and-ready methods.

Spot projections of profits are made periodically as a by-product of complete budgeting. Variants of conventional profits are also predicted on a spot basis, for example income tax profits, or net cash generated internally.

Break-Even Analysis [47]

The break-even chart is an important practical application of empirically determined cost functions. In recent years, break-even charts have come into wide use by company executives, investment analysts, labor unions, and government agencies. Our purpose here is to appraise this alarmingly popular gadget as an instrument for forecasting profits.

We shall consider, first, the nature of break-even analysis; second, its limitations; third, its principal contributions; and, fourth, ways to make this kind of analysis more useful.

Nature of Break-Even Analysis

A break-even chart is a diagram of the short-run relation of total cost and of total revenue to rate of output. These relations should be conceived of as static, i.e., as alternative cost and revenue schedules possible at a single point in time. The total cost function, like its parallel in theory, is drawn on the assumption of constant factor prices, plant scale and depth, technology, and efficiency. The total revenue function assumes selling prices and product-mix unchanged. Chart 5–10 is a typical break-even chart.

The spread between the revenue line and cost line defines the profit function, which is the empirical counterpart of the short-run relation between profits and output rate, with traditional constancies. This family of conjectural income statements is more important than is indicated by the name "break-even chart," which places unfortunate emphasis on the zero-profit member of the family.

Break-even analysis (which will refer not only to the presentation device, but also to the basic relations themselves and the methods generally used to determine them) produces flexible projections of the impact of output rate upon expenses, receipts, and profits, assuming other things equal. It thus provides an

---

[47] This discussion is based on the author's paper on "Cost Structures of Enterprises and Break-even Analysis," *American Economic Review*, Vol. 38, No. 2 (May, 1948), pp. 153–164.

important bridge between business behavior and the theory of the firm. If determination of this profit-output relation will produce reasonably accurate predictions, then break-even analysis has considerable significance for economic research and public policy, as well for investment analysis and company management.

Most break-even analyses are based on the concept of static cost and revenue functions, but they differ in attainment of this ideal. At one extreme are charts that involve an all-out attempt to remove dynamic influences. In statistical studies this is done by rigorous sampling, deflation, lag corrections, multiple correlation, and other statistical refinements discussed in Section III.

At the other extreme stands the "migration-path" break-even chart which is developed from annual data that cover a long period of years, with no correction for the substantial changes that have occurred in dynamic factors such as prices, efficiency, technology, and plant. Output is measured by sales volume in current dollars rather than by an index of physical production. A sort of dynamic total cost function, which appears to be linear and which often shows only moderate scatter, has been obtained for many enterprises. Sometimes subgroups of consecutive years show different lines of fit. The result is not a static total cost function but a movement-path on a series of shifted static functions.[48] A possible explanation for the linearity of this path is cost-plus formula pricing by the enterprises studied. A sort of dynamic profit function can also be determined directly by correlation of historical profits and output, with constancies abandoned. Scatter diagrams of this sort are used in investment analysis.

Break-even analysis should be distinguished from two other managerial tools: flexible budgets and standard costs. The variable expense budget is built on the same basic cost–output relationships, but it is confined to costs and is primarily concerned with the components of combined cost, since the purpose is to control cost by developing expense standards that are flexibly adjusted to activity rate. This purpose often leads to measures of activity that differ among costs and operations, so that they cannot be readily added or translated into an index of output for the enterprise as a whole. Standard costs, on the other hand, are

---

[48] The pioneering work of Walter Rautenstrauch is an example of this sort of analysis. See his *Economics of Enterprise* (John Wiley & Sons, Inc., 1939), Chs. VI and VII.

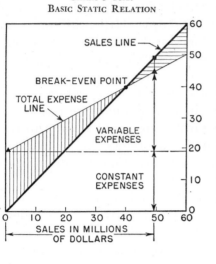

CHART 5–10A.
BASIC STATIC RELATION

SALES LINE

BREAK-EVEN POINT

TOTAL EXPENSE
LINE

VARIABLE
EXPENSES

CONSTANT
EXPENSES

SALES IN MILLIONS
OF DOLLARS

CODE:

○ BREAK-EVEN POINT
△ TOTAL EXPENSE LINE
□ ANNUAL SALES

A shows the generic structure of the break-even chart. The horizontal axis represents some measure of output, such as physical volume of production, per cent of full-capacity output, or sales volume. The sales line relates total revenue on the vertical axis to total output on the horizontal axis and is always drawn as a straight line. There are usually two kinds of cost shown: variable costs (assumed to vary with output), and constant costs (assumed independent of output). The total-cost line adds these two components, and is also drawn as a straight line. The vertical distance between total sales and total cost is total profit at outputs greater than where the two lines intersect. Short of this break-even point it represents losses.

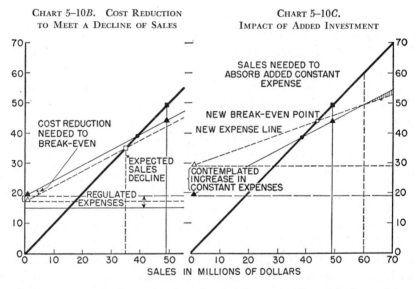

CHART 5–10B. COST REDUCTION
TO MEET A DECLINE OF SALES

COST REDUCTION
NEEDED TO
BREAK-EVEN

EXPECTED
SALES
DECLINE

REGULATED
EXPENSES

CHART 5–10C.
IMPACT OF ADDED INVESTMENT

SALES NEEDED TO
ABSORB ADDED CONSTANT
EXPENSE

NEW BREAK-EVEN POINT
NEW EXPENSE LINE

CONTEMPLATED
INCREASE IN
CONSTANT EXPENSES

SALES IN MILLIONS OF DOLLARS

B illustrates how a break-even chart is used to find the amount of cost reduction needed to meet a given amount of sales decline. In the form shown here the chart assumes that selling prices, material prices, and wage rates and labor efficiency will all remain unchanged in the face of a sales decline.

C illustrates how a break-even chart can be used to determine the effect of a contemplated new investment on cost behavior. The new investment is assumed to increase fixed costs and reduce unit variable costs. Therefore the new total-cost line is above the old one for low outputs and below it for high outputs. The intersection of the two cost lines shows the level of output that must be exceeded to make the new investment profitable.

CHART 5–10. BREAK-EVEN CHART.

328

CHART 5–10*D*. TEN YEARS OF BREAK-EVEN POINTS

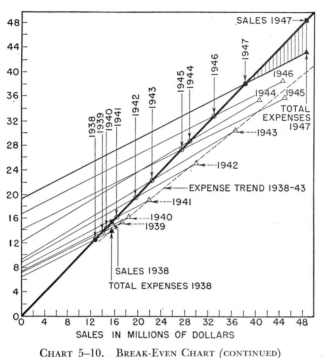

CHART 5–10. BREAK-EVEN CHART (CONTINUED)

D shows how the total-cost line and the break-even point shift from year to year with changes in selling prices, materials prices, wages, and the nature of production. However, if the horizontal axis had been calibrated in physical units, or if a price index had been used to deflate the cost and revenue data, the shift in the break-even point would have been reduced substantially.

Charts adapted from *Fortune*, Vol. 39, No. 2 (February, 1949), p. 82.

___

quite foreign to break-even analysis. Typically, they are unchanging unit costs, which are used as expense goals or as a substitute for current unit costs. The analysis of departures of current costs from standard cost usually attempts to segregate the variance attributed to rate of activity (as well as that due to other causes). This analysis of variances involves some knowledge or assumptions concerning the basic relationship of expenses to rate of utilization.

Limitations on Profit Projections

For profit forecasting the static break-even chart has serious limitations which its users have frequently ignored. These limitations arise from four general sources: errors of estimating the true static cost function, oversimplification of the static revenue function, dynamic forces that shift and modify these static functions, and managerial adaptations to the altered environment. Awareness of these sources of error can improve the analysis and sharpen interpretation and application of the resulting projections.

The principal problem area of break-even analysis is empirical determination of the enterprise's cost curve.[49] Typically the static cost function has not been established with much sophistication or precision. Since profits are residuals, the profit function gets the full impact of these inaccuracies. To understand the nature and importance of this source of forecasting error let us see how successfully break-even analysis has solved the problems of measuring cost, measuring output, matching cost with output, and holding other things constant.

Measuring Cost. We have seen earlier that enterprise cost data are largely the by-product of the requirements of financial accounting. They are collected, classified, and apportioned under fairly rigid conventions that impose serious qualifications on the meaning of the resulting cost and profit functions. Errors from this source are of three types: exclusion of imputed cost, wide discretion in the timing of semi-investment expenditures, and valuations and allocations that are necessarily arbitrary.[50] We have discussed these errors in Sections II and III of Chapter 1 in connection with the nature and measurement of profits.

The inclusion of selling costs also impairs the accuracy of the estimate of total cost, and this makes profit prediction more unreliable.[51] There is no necessary functional relation between output and costs incurred to modify the firm's demand curve. Selling activity may remain substantially constant yet the demand

---

[49] Section III deals with precise determination of such cost functions. The discussion here relates to the short-hand methods of determination used for practical break-even analysis.

[50] Allocation errors arise from the necessarily arbitrary proration of common costs among operating units, and the allocation of capital wastage over time periods. Depreciation is a good example of the problems of time-allocation. When, as is common, depreciation is recorded as a straight-line function of time, it is treated as a constant cost and is thereby excluded from the estimate of marginal cost. The amount of error from this omission depends on the extent to which obsolescence exceeds the loss of value due to use deterioration that was not made up by properly recorded maintenance.

[51] See Chapter 6, "Advertising."

curve may shift with fluctuations in national income and tastes. Moreover, there is much latitude for manipulating the amount and timing of many kinds of selling expenditures.

A high correlation between output and selling outlays does not necessarily mean a stable or meaningful relationship. To be sure, some selling costs, such as salesmen's commissions, may be a function of sales. But sales may depart from current production for short periods, so that even these expenses may not be related to output. When the advertising appropriation is determined by mechanistic standards (e.g., x per cent of expected or past sales), this expense is often projected as proportionate to output. This is not, however, evidence of a true functional relationship. Output may depart from history and from forecasts without causing changes in the advertising plan or commitments. Moreover, the effect of advertising will be spread indeterminately over future output as well as present.[52]

Even the empirical production cost function is likely to be somewhat nebulous in a large enterprise because of disparity among constituent plants. Typically, plants differ considerably in size, technology, factor prices (because of geographical variation), and other locational advantages. For example, a large gypsum company has geographically scattered board mills that embody the history of various stages of technical advances and that also differ in scale, in depth, and in wage rates and material prices. These plants form a hierarchy in respect to marginal cost and average unit cost. The costs associated with a specified company-wide output rate are thus a composite of the costs of those mills which are operated at that time. Since it is not possible to move up the cost hierarchy as output rate expands, because of the uncontrollable geographical distribution of demand, cost will not be the same for any given composite output rate.

Measuring Output. Perhaps the most difficult problem for break-even analysis is to get a good index of output for a multiple-product plant with variable product-mix. A specially constructed

---

[52] Even when budgeted as a fixed percentage of expected sales, much advertising should be treated as a fixed cost, since once the advertising plan is established its total is unaffected by the actual output rate of the period. Better still might be to view some advertising as a capital investment, since benefits stretch into the future, and there is wide discretionary latitude in its timing.

index of physical output with weights based on inputs at constant prices is usually the best solution.

Output indexes used in most break-even analyses are not very satisfactory. Sales volume in current dollars is generally used. This kind of index, which weights diverse products in ratio to selling price rather than to inputs, is unreliable if articles differ in contribution margin [53] and if the product-mix varies. It is also erroneous if selling prices change during the analysis period.

The use of sales (in properly weighted physical units) rather than production to measure output is satisfactory only if selling is the dominant activity of the firm, or if the production and sales rate are closely synchronized. Otherwise serious error is introduced, particularly if the analysis period is short. Normally, it is better to measure activity by production, and to reconstruct any expenses that are a function of sales or orders, on the assumption the output is sold in the period produced.

Matching Cost with Output. To find the relation between cost and output the costs must be synchronized with the output to which they contributed. This problem has not been recognized or solved in most break-even analyses. The importance of the resulting error differs among establishments and depends on the length of the record period in relation to the production cycle. A production gestation period of any length results in a recording of costs to some degree in a period earlier than the recording of the output for which they were incurred. Removal of this error is tedious and never entirely satisfactory for short analysis periods. The use of annual data largely obviates the problem but hides important variations of cost and output within the year.

The wide latitude in timing many expenditures also causes errors of matching. Outlays for maintenance and for many administrative and selling activities are properly attributable to past and future outputs as well as that of the current period. Hence true costs associated with any output have a penumbra of indeterminacy. Outlays, however, may be made to have a fairly definite relationship to output by company policy that controls the timing of expenditure. Thus railroad management has often "controlled" maintenance outlays to conform much more closely

---

[53] Contribution margin is the difference between price and marginal cost. It can be approximated often by price minus traceable (direct) cost.

to fluctuations in traffic than the timing of their true incurrence would justify.[54]

Holding Other Things Constant. The problem of actually obtaining the assumed constancy of plant, technology, methods, product, and prices cannot be satisfactorily solved in workaday break-even chart analysis. Analysis of past cost behavior underlies, in some degree, all empirical cost functions (unless the whole projection is based on engineering conjecture). Yet no past period can be found with the assumed constancy of dynamic factors.

In the empirical work of the economists, illustrated in Section III, chief reliance has been placed on careful selection of the enterprise and the sample period. In normal break-even chart analysis, this kind of sample selection is out of the question. Much use must be made of conjectures that imagine away these difficulties. Multiple correlation analysis has been used with some success in removing the influence of "other factors." But its widespread use in break-even analysis is limited by its expense and unfamiliarity.

In most break-even analyses adjustments for changes in factor prices have not been made carefully or at all. The use of current dollar sales as an output index does not solve the problem. The direct impact of changes in factor prices can be easily removed by tailored index numbers; but indirect influences through substitution among input factors cannot. Rigid limits upon such price-motivated substitutions are, however, imposed by modern technology.

There are severe limitations on the research refinements that are practical for break-even analysis. It is costly to get precise estimates of cost functions by careful research. The error range from cheaper methods is often tolerable practically, particularly when shifts of the cost functions cause estimating errors that are much wider. These shifts often have more practical interest than the function's precise shape, at least over the range of normal

---

[54] The cost function derived from such expenditures may do a good job of forecasting future expenditures and short-term recorded profits. But even so, profits will differ materially from a concept of "real" profits over the long term. Hence it may be argued that the source of distortion should not be removed since it is the timing of expenditures, not of cost incurrence, that is relevant for expense control and possibly for profit forecasting. But this assumed that the change in output (and other sources of distortion) will always follow the same pattern in arriving at a specified output rate.

operations, for changes in factor prices are dramatic in their impact today and changes in technology and product design often take place continuously.

Validity of Revenue Functions. The revenue function of break-even analysis holds selling price constant over the range of output, an assumption that is practical for many enterprises because of the inflexibility of selling prices and the existence of an area of price discretion. This departure from the assumptions of economic theory is made because break-even analysis is not concerned with the effect of price on quantity sold, but is confined to projections of the effects on costs and profits of various outputs that result from shifts in the firm's demand function. Analysis of demand is viewed as a separate problem.

The accuracy of a profit projection based on this constant-price revenue line will be impaired by changes in list price, concessions, product-mix, and distribution-channel ratio. Changes in list price call for a new sales line that alters the profit function and the break-even point. Changes in price concessions, which in some industries are great and are likely to be correlated with output, will also vitiate the profit forecast, and are harder to allow for.

Changes in the composition of demand impair the accuracy of the static sales line and may vitiate the profit projection. Whenever products differ in contribution margin and there is variation in product-mix from period to period, profits will vary at a given output rate, if output is measured by an index that is appropriate for getting a production cost function. Under these circumstances, the constant-price sales line is inaccurate, even as a static function. Two different combinations of products that are equal in amount as measured by the output index will not yield equal revenue. Only by measuring output in current sales dollars can total revenue be a single valued function of output. But if this is done, cost will not be the same for output of different product composition.

Changes in the proportion of output that goes through the various distribution channels have serious effects in some firms, where the contribution margin differs greatly among channels (for example, between original equipment and retail dealer sales of automobile accessories). The channel-proportion is often neither stable nor precisely correlated with output.

One way out of these difficulties that has been found helpful is to set up a family of revenue lines, each one applicable to a specified product-mix and distribution-channel ratio.

Dynamic Forces. Dynamic forces impose added limitations on profit projections from static and partial cost and revenue functions, however accurately determined. Concentration on short-run cost functions has led to neglect of other elements of the cost structure of the enterprise. Changes in factor prices, technology, and scale and depth of plant, shift and modify the static cost function. These changes take place continuously and their impact is intertwined so that it is normally not possible to separate them empirically from short-run adjustments.

It was pointed out earlier that the distinction between short-run and long-run cost is continuously blurred. Conceptually, the basis of the distinction is the degree of adaptation of cost to output rate. This conventional dichotomy of long run versus short run should be expanded in theory to envision a whole family of cost curves that differ in the degree of adaptation, with the conventional long-run cost curve as the limit of perfect adaptation. Adjustments to higher output take a variety of forms short of adding an entire balance plant unit. They represent jumps from one short-run curve to another, not just movement along one curve.

In Section IV we also discussed the subtle relation of technology to cost behavior. Changes in scale, in flexibility, and in management methods are often all represented in a single technical improvement.

These dynamic changes in costs and selling prices are likely to be highly correlated with the firm's output. This relationship will reduce the reliability of forecasts of profits that are based upon assumed independence. A single company's volume decline is not likely to be independent of a downturn of general business activity. And it is improbable that management's adaptation to this changed situation would produce an output-expenditure pattern just like that produced by the operating plans of today's volume expectations.

Break-even analysis is virtually useless for some firms. This is particularly likely when materials that fluctuate widely in price are a predominant cost, when the product-mix varies greatly and profit margins differ among products, when advertising or sales promotion are important and highly shiftable, or when the product design or technology changes continuously over short periods.

Profits Controllable. Profits in modern enterprise are not so purely passive as economic doctrine implies. Profits are controllable by management to an important degree. Costs are more reducible and manipulatable than economists have recognized. Profit maximization in the short-run sense is seldom the dominant objective, and the pressure for efficiency is not, as assumed in theory, constant and always sufficient. It varies dramatically over the cycle and with the fortunes of the firm. There are, therefore, significant fluctuations in the intensity of the compulsion to attain the least cost combination. Top management of a major railroad estimated in 1947 that two years of systematic indoctrination at all management levels would be required to get the efficiency drive back to the prewar level.

This range of management discretion can affect costs because there is much room for improving efficiency in even the best-managed concerns, and because a wide area of uncertainty exists as to the least-cost combination for specified conditions of output, factor prices, and technology. For example, the methods for determining economic lot size differ greatly and cannot all be best.

Another condition that makes reported profits significantly controllable has been mentioned; namely, the wide time latitude that exists in the incidence of real cost upon expenditures. Important parts of production, selling, and administrative expense relate to past or future output and can be postponed over long periods.

Price jurisdiction provides another means of controlling profits. In the first postwar years, prices that would have been high enough to retain the prewar break-even point would for many companies have put profits so high at postwar peak output rates that they would have had serious consequences for public and labor relations.

This controllability of short-term profits means that the empirical profit function is less reliably determined and forecasted and has less economic meaning than has been supposed.

Summary of Limitations. The projection of the short-run, static profit-output function of break-even charts is not a reliable forecast of future profits. The break-even point indicated by charts presupposes continuation of today's relative prices and expenditures patterns. Hence it does not accurately forecast the probable future shifts in price structure when business conditions change. A break-even chart is an oversimplified analysis of expected profits at various levels of output. The basic premise that profit is a single-valued function of output is wrong. Profit will, of course, vary with changes in output; but it also will vary with changes in production plans and in the intensity and kinds of selling efforts. The profit function will also be buffeted about by the vast impersonal forces of the market. Hence, at best, any single break-even chart can show profit expectations only under a single set of assumptions regarding external market conditions and internal management strategy.

In typical break-even analysis, the static cost function has not been determined with much precision. Concentration on short-run cost functions has led, moreover, to neglect of other elements of the enterprise cost structure, which impairs the accuracy of projections of the short-run cost function. Changes in the composition of demand and in costs and in prices are, moreover, likely to be highly correlated with the firm's output. Despite rigidities of prices and of wage rates, a decline in general business activity will shift the functional relationships that were presumed to be independent.

Usefulness of Break-Even Analysis

The empirical short-run profit function has more stability than the foregoing discussion of its limitations might imply. One reason is that shifts in the cost function tend to be accompanied (with some lag) by similar changes in selling prices in many imperfectly competitive enterprises. This relationship is partly the result of the use of cost plus formulas to set and adjust prices. Another reason is that the pressure for efficiency is intensified in periods of adversity. The controllability and postponability of expenditures can in some degree compensate for uncontrollable shifts in selling prices and stickiness in factor prices.

Under modern competitive conditions, selling price and the intensity of selling efforts are not normally adjusted frequently to short-term shifts of the firm's demand. Hence the assumptions of constant selling price and essentially passive selling cost adjustments are more realistic and useful for short-run adjustments under normal conditions than economic logicians might think.

Managerial Usefulness. Ambitious claims have been made for the managerial usefulness of break-even charts. They include not only profit projections but also expense control and price determination. For these added purposes, as for profit projection, the limitations discussed above impair but do not destroy its usefulness.

Empirical cost functions can be highly useful for expense control. But for this purpose they must deal with components of cost, and should be confined to those costs that are controllable at each area of responsibility. Although this kind of flexible budget may be built up to a break-even chart, it is not a by-product.

Thus conceived, the break-even analysis no longer concentrates on the break-even point or on a single static profit function. Instead, it provides a flexible set of projections of costs and revenue under expected future conditions and under alternative management programs. Profit prediction under these multiple conditions becomes then a tool for profit-making.

Building Flexibility into Break-even Analysis

A statistical illustration of some of the refinements that can be added to "break-even" profit forecasting is provided by an analysis of the United States Steel Corporation made by H. H. Wein,[55] in connection with the first postwar round of wage controversy. Since the analysis rested largely on published financial data, it could make no allowance for shifts in product-mix. Moreover, it was for the short and unusual period 1929–1939. The purpose of this work was to give the fact-finding board in these cases some idea of the effect upon profits of the various wage and price demands. Although its results were crude, the study illustrates the kind of approach that can expand the conventional break-even chart into a more flexible forecasting tool.

A set of relations between the various elements of cost and the rate of output were developed by simple correlation analysis. The cost data for these correlations were deflated by suitable price indices in an effort to remove the effect of changes in prices during the analysis period. The resulting simple relation, together with

---

[55] The results of this analysis are presented in H. H. Wein, "Wages and Prices— A Case Study, *Review of Economic Statistics,* May, 1947.

the price factors, were then aggregated into a generalized equation which related profits to rate of output, prices, cost of materials and services, wage rates, labor productivity, depreciation, interest, and taxes on other than income. The equation took the following form:

$$Q = ax - \left[\frac{xr}{b + cx} + (d + ex)f + (g + hx) + i \right]$$

where

Q = profits	$d + ex$ = physical volume of
a = average sales-	purchases
price per ton	f = price of materials
x = tons of steel pro-	and services
duction	$g + hx$ = depreciation and de-
$b + cx$ = productivity	pletion
r = wage rate	i = taxes and interest.

In this equation some of the quantities were taken as fixed (taxes, interest); some varied in a linear relation with production (material costs, depreciation, productivity); and the total wage bill increased at a decreasing rate as output was raised.[56] It can be seen that the correlation analysis indicated elements of fixed cost in purchases of materials and in depreciation and depletion, as well as in taxes and interest.

With this kind of equation it is possible to calculate profits under any assumed conditions of wage rates, prices, and rate of output.

By algebraic manipulation it is possible to use such functions to answer a variety of questions. For instance:

(1) What will be the effects on profits of contemplated wage and price increases?

(2) What sales volume will be necessary to maintain a given profit level when costs or prices change in a specified way?

(3) What productivity gain will be needed to maintain profits with rising wages and constant prices?

(4) What will be the effect on profits of a change in prices of purchased materials, sales volume remaining constant?

Chart 5–11 shows such an analysis for U. S. Steel. By setting profits equal to zero and solving the equation for output with wage

---

[56] Although average revenue per ton was found to be a U-shaped function of output (when expressed relative to the general price level in the economy), this further complication was not brought into the analysis.

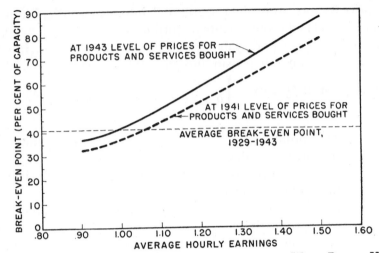

CHART 5–11. BREAK-EVEN POINT AS A FUNCTION OF WAGE RATES: U. S.
STEEL CORP. (Source: *Review of Economic Statistics,* Vol. 29, No. 2, May,
1947, p. 118.)

rates variable and the other terms constant, a functional relation
was found between wage rates and the break-even point. Chart
5–12, also from Wein's analysis, shows for the automobile industry

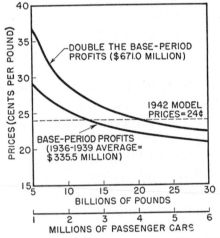

CHART 5–12. RELATION OF PRICES TO PRODUCTION THAT IS NECESSARY TO
YIELD A GIVEN PROFIT, AND DOUBLE THAT PROFIT: AUTOMOBILES. (Source:
Review of Economic Statistics, Vol. 29, No. 2, May, 1947, p. 120.)

a form of the equation where price is the dependent variable, output fluctuates, and the other terms are fixed. For each assumed
level of profits there is a separate line of this sort.

This kind of empirical investigation is essentially a refinement of traditional break-even analysis. Cost relations are determined more rigorously, since factor prices are held constant. The expression of the results in a comprehensive equation, which reflects prices as well as cost functions, facilitates flexible application in estimating profit under any given combination of prices and output.

Nevertheless, the analysis has the basic deficiencies of break-even analysis. It assumes that profits have a single-valued functional relation to output, and it assumes that the revenue function is linear and is independent of the cost function. It does not take into account dimensions other than output rate, such as variations in product mix, changes in the structure of formal or informal price discounts, and in promotional outlays. In many companies these vary substantially and affect profits importantly.

Of course, all such studies suffer from the limitations of statistical analysis in general. They require extensive data for homogeneous periods which will continue into the future. That is, they are short-run studies that require data over long periods. A drastic change in cost structure may be brought about by installing new labor-displacing machines, renovating the product-line, chopping back institutional advertising, or throwing out the research department.

Environmental Analyses

Factors that control profits have a tendency to move in regular and related patterns; rate of output, prices, wages, material costs, and efficiency are all interrelated by their connections with the national markets and their interactions in the aggregate business economy. Theories of business cycles have as an underlying hypothesis the idea that the national values of production, employment, wages, and prices show systematic patterns of behavior as business activity fluctuates, and although it is not always clear what the pattern is in detailed analyses, the hypothesis has some justification for broad averages.

These patterns of confluence raise the possibility that profits of a company can be forecast directly by finding a relation to key variables in the economy that either control or combine the movements of the myriad of direct forces that are felt in the income statement. The problem is to find a direct functional relation between company profits and national activity that shows statistical significance.

These aggregate statistics are most useful to industries in which fluctuations of prices and output lag a few months behind the national averages. For these industries the forecasting problem is much simplified when the current state of the nation preludes the company's activity, prices, and output. For example, a multiple correlation analysis of the profits of a manufacturer of building materials revealed that profits were highly correlated with fluctuations in general building activity and a time trend of company growth. Building permits led construction activity and the purchase of building materials sufficiently to permit fairly accurate projection of construction activity put in place, which was the measure of building activity used in this analysis.

Projecting profits on the basis of empirical relation to general economic activity encounters additional difficulties when the economic series must itself be forecast. Then the accuracy of the forecast of profits depends upon the precision of the projection of the economic indicator, as well as upon the closeness of its relation to the company's earnings.

This approach to profit forecasting is in sharp contrast to the particularistic break-even analysis. The relations are approximate and empirical; their value rests not so much on plausibility (although this helps) as on stability of the relation and ability to forecast the independent variable.

A study of this kind has been made by William M. Bennett,[57] to find the elasticity of manufacturing profits with respect to changes in industrial production for thirteen industries. This was done in two steps, by finding, first, the functional relation of production rates in each industry to the Federal Reserve Board index of industrial production; and, second, the relation of profit margins to the rate of operations.

In the first step, multiple correlations were run between production indices for the thirteen industry groups and the total FRB index. To allow for secular trends, "time" was used as a second independent variable. The results are presented in Table 5-5. These equations show by the X-coefficients that manufac-

---

[57] Of Cyrus Lawrence and Sons, Inc., New York. Mr. Bennett presented this unpublished material in a lecture to the author's class at Columbia in the winter of 1948, and has kindly permitted me to summarize it here.

TABLE 5–5

RELATION OF PRODUCTION INDEXES IN MANUFACTURING TO TOTAL FRB INDEX

Sub-group	Formula for sub-group index
Manufacturing: 1919–1940	$-1 + 1.015x$
1941–1948	$-18 + 1.15x$
Durable	$-40 + 1.52x - 1.5t$
Automotive	$-63.2 + 1.7x - 1.6t$
Furniture	$1.5 + 1.1x - 2.5t$
Iron and steel	$-39.5 + 1.5x - 1.5t$
Lumber	$-2.5 + 1.5x - 5.1t$
Non-ferrous metals	$-35.8 + 1.6x - 2.9t$
Non-durable	$41.3 + .51x - 1.3t$
Chemicals	$6.2 + .77x + 2.6t$
Food	$40.8 + .54x + .72t$
Paper	$21.7 + .59x + 2.4t$
Textiles	$30.8 + .64x + .73t$

x = total FRB index (1935–1939 = 100)
t = year minus 1929
Period used in correlation is total period for which index has been published through 1948.

turing is slightly more volatile than the FRB index as a whole, and that durable goods fluctuate more widely in output than do non-durables.[58] They show, further (by the sign of the t-term), that non-durables have been rising faster than the FRB index during the analysis period, and that durable output has been rising more slowly.

In the second step, profit margins (i.e., profits as a per cent of sales) were correlated with production as a per cent of full-capacity production for each of the thirteen industries. Full capacity is a dubious concept for an industry, but in this analysis it was assumed to be shown by the highest previous peak in the industry's production index—a method of measuring capacity that is consonant with the findings of empirical cost studies. The functional relation that was used in the correlation took the form:

$$\text{Profit margin} = a + \frac{b}{OR}$$

where OR is operating rate, i.e., production as a per cent of capacity.

---

[58] That is, an increase of 10 points in the FRB index is usually accompanied by a 15-point rise in steel production and a 5-point rise in food.

This form of profit output function, being based on historical data of profit margins over the business cycle takes account of the shifts in the break-even point caused by changing conditions of cost and efficiency.[59] Considering the horse-back estimate of capacity that was used, the stability of the relation is surprisingly good for the broader industry groups. (See Chart 5–13.) Results were less stable but still usable for the smaller industry segments. The correlation equations from this second analysis are given in Table 5–6.

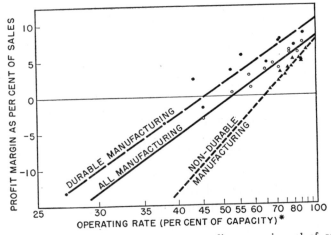

* Calibration of horizontal scale is spaced according to reciprocal of operating rate, to show the regression lines in the straight-line form that was used in the least-squares analysis.

CHART 5–13. PROFIT MARGIN AS A FUNCTION OF OPERATING RATE.

Combining the analyses of sales and profit margins produces estimates of the elasticity of profits with respect to total industrial production for each industry. Table 5–7 shows what effect to expect in profits when the FRB index drops 10 per cent from its postwar full-employment levels.

The principal shortcoming of correlation analysis for this kind of profit forecasting is again the dearth of clearly relevant data. In such studies, history more than one business cycle old rarely can give reliable clues to the future. Since a single cycle seldom

---

[59] Profit margins in historical data are affected to an important extent by changes in the price level and the resulting profits and losses in inventory valuation. Since this element of profit margins is unrelated to rate of operations, it was eliminated before the correlation was run.

Table 5–6

PROFIT MARGINS IN MANUFACTURING RELATED TO RATE OF OPERATION

	Profit Margin before Income Tax as % of Sales	Indicated Break-even Point
Manufacturing	$17.3 - \dfrac{9.1}{OR}$	52.5
Durable	$19.2 - \dfrac{8.8}{OR}$	45.5
Automotive	$13.6 - \dfrac{3.7}{OR}$	27.4
Furniture	$17.4 - \dfrac{10.5}{OR}$	60.1
Iron and steel	$15.6 - \dfrac{6.8}{OR}$	43.2
Lumber	$23.5 - \dfrac{15.4}{OR}$	65.3
Non-ferrous metals	$15.0 - \dfrac{6.1}{OR}$	40.6
Non-durable	$21.9 - \dfrac{14.2}{OR}$	64.2
Apparel	$14.4 - \dfrac{11.3}{OR}$	77.8
Chemicals	$26.6 - \dfrac{15.1}{OR}$	57.0
Food	$9.5 - \dfrac{4.4}{OR}$	47.5
Paper	$32.0 - \dfrac{24.4}{OR}$	76.0
Textiles	$29.2 - \dfrac{22.2}{OR}$	76.0

OR = operating rate as per cent of capacity.
Break-even point equals value of OR when profit margin = 0.
Correlation period = 1929–1939.

encompasses more than a decade, a plausible correlation usually requires quarterly or monthly data, with necessary and sometimes dubious adjustment for seasonal fluctuations.

Summary

Profit forecasting can be done on many different levels of refinement, depending on the range of visibility into the future, the kind of information sought, and the funds available for analysis. Three major forecasting methods are spot projections, break-even analysis, and environmental analysis.

A spot projection is a conjectural income statement for a spe-

TABLE 5–7

RELATION OF INDUSTRY PROFITS TO FRB INDEX

	(a) Decline in Sub-group Production with 10% Decline in FRB Index [1]	(b) Decline in Profit Margin with 10% Decline in FRB Index [2]	(c) Decline in Aggregate Profits with 10% Decline in FRB Index [3]
Manufacturing	11%	12%	22%
Durable	13%	12%	23%
Automotive	17%	8%	24%
Furniture	13%	32%	41%
Iron and steel	14%	9%	22%
Lumber	20%	27%	42%
Non-ferrous metals	16%	12%	26%
Non-durable	5.4%	11%	16%
Apparel	7.6%	16%	22%
Chemicals	5.8%	8.5%	14%
Food	6.1%	7%	13%
Paper	7.0%	12%	18%
Textiles	7.6%	12%	19%

Decline measured from levels in the closing months of 1948.

[1] From Table 5–5.

[2] From Tables 5–5 and 5–6.

[3] Column $c = 1 - [(1 - \text{col. a}) \times (1 - c\ \text{col. b})]$

cific future period.   Forecasts are made of sales volume and prices and costs of producing the anticipated sales.   The profit forecast is no more than the residual of these projections.   The completeness and accuracy of the information in this kind of forecast depends on the quality of the parent forecasts, that is, on the sophistication and care with which all future conditions in the company can be projected.

Break-even analysis is a more general type of forecasting method, since it uses only a functional relation between profits and the level of output and leaves the problem of output forecasting unsolved.   For even forecasting of the profit–output relation, however, break-even analysis is subject to many limitations.   Its basic difficulty is that profits are the net result of far too many factors to be presented in any two-dimensional diagram.   Prices, product-mix, efficiency, and technology are only some of the influences that are important in year-to-year changes.   The break-even chart is an attempt to measure static, short-run relations on the basis of dynamic data reflecting long-run developments. It can be found only by careful analysis of qualifying factors, and can be used only in a multiple form that shows alternative profit forecasts on the basis of different conjectural conditions. More expense is necessary to use break-even analysis accurately than most companies are willing to undergo.

Environmental analysis is a broad-gauge approach to forecasting through empirical relations of profits to variables external to the company. It is a speculation with wide error margins, but a saving virtue is that it is *obviously* so; it hasn't the illusion of precision of many break-even charts.

Chapter 6

ADVERTISING

I. INTRODUCTION
NATURE OF ADVERTISING COSTS
Promotional Elasticity of Demand
Advertising Activities of Rivals
Long-Run Aspects
PLAN OF CHAPTER

II. CONTRIBUTION OF ECONOMIC THEORY
SIMPLIFIED THEORETICAL ANALYSIS
SHAPE OF ADVERTISING COST FUNCTION
REFINED THEORETICAL ANALYSES
LIMITATIONS
CONTRIBUTIONS
PRACTICAL APPLICATION OF MARGINAL APPROACH
SUMMARY

III. METHODS FOR DETERMINING TOTAL ADVERTISING BUDGET
ALTERNATIVE METHODS
PERCENTAGE-OF-SALES APPROACH
ALL-YOU-CAN-AFFORD APPROACH
RETURN-ON-INVESTMENT APPROACH
OBJECTIVE-AND-TASK APPROACH
COMPETITIVE-PARITY APPROACH
SUMMARY

IV. CYCLICAL FLUCTUATIONS OF ADVERTISING
STABILIZING EFFECTS OF ADVERTISING
ALTERNATIVE POLICIES
TESTS OF CYCLICAL POLICIES
CRITERIA FOR CYCLICAL ADVERTISING
Changes in Advertising Effectiveness
Income Elasticity
Changes in Profit Margins
Improvement of Products
Perishability of Advertising Impact
Promotional Elasticity of Market
Proportion of Investment-Type Advertising
SUMMARY

V. MEASUREMENT OF THE ECONOMIC EFFECTS OF AD-
VERTISING

The Objective

Difficulties

Methods of Measurement

Comparative Analysis of Historical Data

Analysis of Historical Data for Individual Companies

Summary

Chapter 6

Advertising

I. INTRODUCTION

A VAST AMOUNT OF MONEY is spent every year on advertising; in 1949 for example, over five billion dollars was spent.[1] Almost every important enterprise in the country wrestles with the problem of planning its advertising budget over a period of years; deciding how this outlay should fluctuate from year to year with changes in business conditions; and how each yearly total should be apportioned among products, territories and classes of prospects. Yet in making these critical decisions, most executives have to play by ear. Few firms have a valid theoretical or research basis for deciding upon the level of advertising expenditures; e.g., whether they should spend $100,000 or $200,000 a year.

The purpose of this chapter is to provide a background of concepts and methods for attacking the practical problems of planning and controlling advertising expenditures. Advertising, as a pure form of selling cost, encounters the same economic problems as other kinds of selling cost. Hence, this chapter can illustrate the general approach of managerial economics to other kinds of marketing outlays. The discussion starts from theoretical foundations, but operates in the no man's land between the rigorous and abstract analysis of the economic theorist and the largely intuitive performance of the practitioner.

Our discussion is confined not merely to advertising, but to the problems of control and allocation of advertising expenditures; it does not deal with problems of advertising techniques, such

---

[1] Annual advertising expenditures during the inter-war period averaged roughly 3 per cent of national income. The postwar average is around 2 per cent. (H. Zeisel, "U. S. Advertising Volume Passes 5 Billion, Hits New High", *Printers' Ink*, June 16, 1950, pp. 28–30.)

as creating copy, choosing media, or fitting advertising into the company's merchandising program to achieve a proper balance between mass selling and personal selling.

Nature of Advertising Costs

Advertising costs, being one kind of selling costs, are designed to increase the demand for the firm's products; i.e., to shift the demand curve to the right of where it would otherwise be.

Advertising costs, along with other elements of pure selling expenditures, call for quite a different kind of economic treatment from production costs. The dividing line between production costs and selling costs is sometimes drawn at the factory door. Costs incurred through final factory inspection are classified as production costs; all costs incurred beyond that point are classified as selling costs. This classification is not appropriate for economic analysis, however. Here selling costs are those that adapt the demand to the product, and production costs are those that form the product and take it to market. In other words, selling costs are incurred to get the business; production costs are incurred to take care of the business. Pure selling costs are designed to shift the demand schedule, i.e., to obtain sales that would not otherwise have been obtained at the same price. They include only those elements of distribution costs that are designed to affect demand. They do not include physical distribution expenses, such as transportation and handling costs. These costs are viewed as production costs, since they are functionally related to output in the same general way as manufacturing costs. Like them, they are a result of sales. Selling costs, in contrast, have no necessary functional relationship to output; they are a cause, not a result of sales.

Like pricing and product innovation, advertising is a device for manipulating the firm's sales volume. Like product improvement, it shifts the whole schedule of demand for the product. Price affects the volume obtainable from any given demand schedule. Thus short-run profit depends on the combinations of price, product improvement, advertising outlay, and other selling activities. These four influences are, of course, interactive. The price charged may affect the responsiveness of volume to additional advertising expenditures; changes in the product are almost certain to do so. And the price that will maximize profits may be different when advertising is stepped up or when the product is improved.[2]

Advertising not only shifts the firm's demand curve to the right of where it would otherwise be, but it may also make demand less elastic.[3]

Promotional Elasticity of Demand

Sales of various products differ greatly in their responsiveness to advertising. Some articles, such as perfumes, are highly responsive; others, such as heavy machinery, are relatively inert. In analyzing this responsiveness, a useful concept is promotional elasticity of demand, which is analogous to the familiar price elasticity of demand.[4] Promotional elasticity measures the responsiveness of sales to changes in the amount of advertising with constant price. In one form, it is the ratio of proportionate change in sales to the proportionate change in the advertising that causes the change.

In analyzing response to promotion, a distinction may be made between (1) industry elasticity, i.e., the responsiveness of the entire industry's sales to advertising; and (2) share elasticity, i.e., the responsiveness of a firm's market share to changes in its share of the industry's advertising.

The promotional elasticity of a product will probably change over the product's life cycle of public acceptance, and its market

---

[2] Since the practical problem is often to get the right combination of advertising and other merchandising activities, the advertising budget problem is not only, "How much should the total selling effort be?" as the economists have usually phrased it, but also, "What part of the selling job should be done by mass selling as opposed to personal selling and other devices?" The answer to this question requires a basic decision on marketing strategy that governs the general scale of advertising outlay relative to other costs. It can have a wide variety of answers, even for a single product. Often industry giants are able to employ mass advertising media that are hopelessly inefficient for small competitors; little firms must usually concentrate on advertising of narrow geographical coverage or on promotional supplements to advertising, such as rich dealer discounts, service extras and personal persuasion. But every firm faces problems of substitution at the margin among the various types of selling cost to balance their marginal returns.

[3] Some economists call the shift "informational" advertising, and the reduced elasticity "puffing" or product-differentiating advertising.

[4] If any general relationship could be established between a product's promotional elasticity of demand and its price elasticity and/or income elasticity, it would have important practical uses. I can see no theoretical basis for such a relationship, however.

elasticity and share elasticity may also vary with the stage of market development.[5]

Advertising Activities of Rivals

The effectiveness of a company's advertising will depend on how rivals react to it. Retaliation against competitors' successful advertising may take the form of an attempt to match or better the advertising or an effort to improve other merchandising activities, or the product itself. Some assumption should be made about the probable reaction of rivals, since each possible reaction is likely to cause the seller to have a somewhat different marginal advertising cost curve. Though much advertising is defensive it is quite common for companies to assume blandly that rivals will make no response to a particular outlay.

The advertising activities of rivals are important in two ways: (1) The amount and quality of competitors' present and past advertising influence the responsiveness of sales to the firm's own advertising. The position and shape of its marginal selling-cost curve are likely to vary in accordance with the activities of rivals. (2) Rivals may react defensively to a firm's advertising plan by adjusting their own advertising (or other) outlays. Rivals' reactions to advertising are less certain, less immediate, and less precisely imitative than are their price reactions, but they raise essentially the same problems.

The sinister effects of advertising in strengthening a firm's monopoly power have been overemphasized. In many industries the efforts of rivals to differentiate their products have tended to offset each other.[6] Even though the individual firm's selling

---

[5] For example, when the electric blanket was first introduced, industry sales were apparently highly responsive to educational advertising. As the new product gained acceptance as a safe and customary feature of bedroom comfort, and as the number of reliable suppliers increased, the power of advertising to expand the total market (market elasticity) appears to have declined, while share elasticity increased. In the early stages of public acceptance, rival advertisers of electric blankets encroached little upon one another's sales and had the primary effect of educating the public, but at a later stage advertising may primarily ration the established market among rival sellers.

[6] For example, despite large and continuous advertising outlays, leading producers of branded gasoline are unable to obtain any significant price premiums over other advertised brands. Neil H. Borden (in *The Economic Effect of Advertising*, Chicago, Richard D. Irwin, 1944, Part II) made an interesting attempt to measure the effect of advertising upon elasticity of demand in nine industries. His findings, though rather inconclusive, do not support the thesis that advertising generally has the effect of reducing price elasticity of demand.

activity may be designed to enhance market imperfection, the over-all effect of rival selling activity has been to reduce, to some extent, elements of imperfection by overcoming those due to consumer ignorance and inconvenience. For example, the advertising of rival consumer-credit institutions has tended to melt down the walls of ignorance and bashfulness that give the neighborhood pawn-broker monopoly power.

Long-Run Aspects

Advertising has long-run impacts as well as the short-run effects we have discussed so far. All advertising has in some degree a delayed and cumulative result that gives it the characteristics of an investment outlay. Moreover, the goal of advertising in many firms is not to maximize short-run profits but, rather, to attain broad strategic advantages in market position and security that contribute to long-run profit maximization.

Plan of Chapter

This chapter discusses three parts of the practical problem of controlling advertising expenditures:

(1) the level of the total expenditure over a period of years;

(2) fluctuations in annual outlays over the course of a business cycle;

(3) measuring the effects of advertising for control purposes.

The next section will summarize the contributions of economic theory to the analysis of these three problems. Section III contains an appraisal of some methods actually used to solve the first of these problems, i.e., determining the total advertising appropriation. Section IV considers the second problem, i.e., cyclical policy of advertising, and Section V wrestles with the third problem, i.e., measurement.

II. CONTRIBUTION OF ECONOMIC THEORY

The theory of monopolistic competition has made advertising a legitimate problem of economic analysis.[7] Analysis of the role of selling costs in the firm's competitive adjustment developed concepts that can be useful in planning and controlling adver-

---

[7] For a simple discussion of selling costs in the setting of monopolistic competition, see Neil Borden, *The Economic Effects of Advertising, op. cit.,* Chapter 6.

tising.   This section attempts to appraise the contributions made
by such analysis.

Simplified Theoretical Analysis

The marginal approach to advertising outlays is illustrated in
its simplest form in Chart 6–1. In this simplified short-run

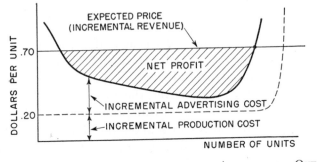

CHART 6–1. SHORT-RUN DETERMINATION OF ADVERTISING OUTLAY BY
MARGINAL ANALYSIS.

analysis, advertising cost is assumed to include all pure selling
costs.   Physical distribution costs are included in production cost.
Incremental production costs (i.e., the added costs of producing
an additional unit of the product) are assumed in the short run
to be constant at 20 cents a unit over the practical range of sales.
Unit price is also assumed to be constant over this range, so that
average revenue and marginal revenue and price are equal and
constant.   Incremental advertising costs (i.e., the additional advertising outlay that will be required to produce an additional
unit of sales) are drawn as a curve which first declines, then is
constant, and then rises at an accelerating rate.   The rationale for
the shape of this curve will be discussed later.

In terms of this diagram, it is obviously profitable to push
advertising outlays up to the point of intersection of the incremental cost of advertising and production with the price line.
If incremental production cost is 20 cents a unit, and, if price is
70 cents, the added profit per unit is 50 cents.   When the added
advertising cost of getting business exceeds 50 cents a unit, the
business is not worth getting, so the intersection marks the cut-off
point.   Thus, in general, advertising outlays should be increased
in every market and medium up to the point where the additional

cost of getting more business just equals the incremental profits from that business.

The assumptions underlying this simplified exposition are fairly realistic. A passive price policy is common enough, at least for short-run adjustments like those under study here (see Chapter 7, Section I). Hence a constant price (i.e., a price that is not changed as a result of changes in advertising outlays) is a moderately good approximation of reality. Empirical findings for industries whose production is mechanized indicate that incremental production costs are constant over the range that is significant for determining advertising policy in the short run; and, as will be discussed later, there is much theory and some empirical evidence to support the shape of the selling cost function drawn here. Abstracting from fluctuations in business conditions and consumer incomes is a necessary simplification that emphasizes the incremental character of the measurement problem, i.e., to find the added sales with, as opposed to without, an added advertising outlay.

Shape of Advertising Cost Function

The incremental advertising cost curve in Chart 6–1 shows the general form of the relationship between advertising outlays and the demand they cause. Under usual conditions of static analysis, it is reasonable to assume that as advertising outlay is increased its unit cost first declines then levels to a minimum, and thereafter rises.

The declining phase of the curve is partly explained by economies of specialization. Larger appropriations may make feasible the use of expert services and more economical media.[8]

More important than specialization, usually, are economies of repetition. Each advertising attack starts from ground that was taken in previous forays, and where no single onslaught can overcome the inertia of existing spending patterns; the hammering of repetition (e.g., the radio jingle) often overcomes skepticism by attrition.

The rising phase of the advertising cost curve is caused pri-

---

[8] Reduction of unit costs sometimes stems from scale economies, e.g., from the use of mass media with national coverage. Such media are usually accessible after long-term growth of the firm but not in the range of discretion on its advertising outlay for any one year.

marily by tapping successively poorer prospects as the advertising effort is intensified.[9] Presumably the most susceptible prospects are picked off first, and progressively stiffer resistance is encountered from layers of prospects who are more skeptical, more stodgy about their present spending patterns, or more attached to rival sellers. The rise may also be caused by progressive exhaustion of the most vulnerable geographic areas or the most efficient advertising media. Promotional channels that are ideally adapted to the scale and market of the firm are used first.[10]

For firms with expansible markets, the selling cost curve is likely to be stepped rather than continuous; and a double bottom may occur if an enlarged appropriation gives access to new and more efficient advertising media.

The short-run marginal advertising cost curve will probably have the same form for all commodities regardless of their elasticity of promotion. The shape of the curve is determined by variations among prospects in accessibility and in susceptibility to advertising, and by the diminishing utility of additional units of the product to any one user. Great differences among commodities may be expected, however, in the relative length and depth of the declining and rising phases, as well as in the level or position of the curve. Moreover, discontinuities in the array of appropriate media (e.g., the gap between local newspapers and national magazines) may cause steps and irregularities in the curve, such as double bottoms.

The relationship of advertising to sales is more intricate than short-run marginal analysis indicates. The selling cost function will differ with the nature of the business strategy involved. If the firm uses advertising to achieve a major expansion, both the production and the advertising cost functions are dynamic and irreversible. If the firm subsequently abandons its attempt to grow, it will not be able to return exactly to its original position. After expansion has been achieved, expenditures may fall below the level of the first attack with no resulting loss of revenue; and

---

9 For statistical evidence of diminishing returns, see D. R. G. Cowan, "Differential Selling Cost in Relation to Wholesale Prices," *Advertising and Selling*, Jan. 1938, pp. 50–52. Also W. L. Mitchell, "How Retail Advertising Expenditures Vary with Sales Volume and Size of City," *Dun's Review*, Jan. 1941, pp. 13–20.

10 For example, W. L. Mitchell (*op. cit.*) found that stores in medium-sized towns are more liberal advertisers than are similar stores in large cities or in small towns. This he attributed to differences in the character of advertising media available.

they may continue at that level, since the firm will then be reaping the return on its initial outlay. This cumulative action of the advertising outlay gives it its investment aspects.

Refined Theoretical Analyses

The foregoing sketch is an extreme simplification of the conventional analyses of modern economic theory. Refined analyses add two important complications: (1) Unit production cost is drawn as a curve shaped like the selling cost curve, rather than as a line of constant cost. A curved production cost makes the drawings, but not the reasoning, more intricate in short-run analyses. (2) Average revenue is drawn as a sloping line or curve on the demand chart instead of as a horizontal line that assumes price is not affected by advertising outlays. A sloping average-revenue function introduces complications, since both price and advertising are then variable.

Chamberlin first varies price with advertising constant then varies advertising with price constant.[11] Buchanan varies price and advertising simultaneously.[12] He starts his analysis with the firm's original demand schedule and the corresponding marginal revenue curve, which, with the production cost curve, makes it possible to determine optimum price. He then assumes various amounts of advertising. A specified advertising outlay will move the demand curve to the right, and may change its shape. The horizontal distance between the two curves measures the effect of advertising in the form of the increase in quantity that can be sold at each price. A new optimum price and output for the changed situation are then determined. The average unit selling cost required to make the change is also found.

By this method, a whole series of demand curves resulting from various amounts of increased advertising is plotted and the optimum price-output point for each amount is determined. The unit advertising costs required to attain each demand shift are determined, and are plotted as a curve. When the various optimum price-output points are connected in a curve, the most profitable short-run advertising outlay and price can be found by these

---

[11] E. H. Chamberlin, *Theory of Monopolistic Competition*, Cambridge, Harvard University Press, 1942, Chapters 4–8.

[12] N. S. Buchanan, "Advertising Expenditures, A Suggested Treatment," *Journal of Political Economy*, August, 1942, pp. 537–557.

two curves where the corresponding incremental curves intersect.

Boulding[13] worked out an ingenious analytical solution by means of two series of contour lines which portray the surfaces produced by varying price and selling costs simultaneously. This he converted into a selling cost table, which gives estimates of the sales that will result from specified combinations of price and selling costs.[14] Shone uses a three-dimensional surface to find an optimum combination of the three variables: price, output, and advertising.[15]

All these theoretical analyses assume that each amount of advertising cost is spent in the best possible way. Barford,[16] however, tackles the problem of finding the best way to spend the money. He deals mathematically, under many simplifying assumptions, with the determination of an optimum combination of various media and campaigns. Like other theoretical analysts, he assumes that the advertiser knows what effect his outlay will have on sales.

Despite their eloquent logic, the refinements of these theoretical analyses do not take us much beyond our first simplified version. Their added complexity is caused, as we have seen, by assuming two conditions that are in the short run not relevant to many advertisers: rising marginal production costs and a policy of making price variable in respect to advertising outlay. The analyses share other limitations, which we shall examine next.

Limitations

A major defect of this kind of analysis is the assumption that the firm has knowledge or dependable estimates of the effect of advertising on sales volume.[17] These estimates raise some of the toughest statistical problems in managerial economics, and in contrast, using the knowledge is a simple matter.

This problem leads us to another deficiency, namely, that the

---

13 K. E. Boulding, *Economic Analysis*, New York, Harper & Bros., 1941, pp. 578–593.

14 Sales, total gross revenues, and total production revenue are shown in the table for each price-selling cost combination. The table shows the various combinations of selling costs and prices that will dispose of a given output as well as the combination that will be most profitable.

15 R. M. Shone, "Selling Costs," *Review of Economic Studies*, 1935, p. 225.

16 B. Barford, "The Theory of Advertising," *Econometrics*, 1940, pp. 279–280.

17 The more refined models require that the price-sales relation and the cost output function, as well, be known.

analyses do not satisfactorily recognize the cumulative effects of past advertising on future sales. A dollar of advertising spent today may be thought of as having two impacts: (1) its immediate and independent effect on demand and (2) a delayed and more durable impact which, in an economic sense, is an investment. This neglect of long-range problems goes to the root of the problem of objectives. The objectives of advertising are dominantly long-range to assure the firm eternal life and a place in the sun. For example, advertising tries to create enough volume to permit economies of large-scale production and research, which will make life hard for a new entrant. Advertising tries to bring closer the distant day when product acceptance will permit some price premium over less familiar brands. Such long-range goals can be brought into the static theoretical analysis only when management has occult powers of divination. When uncertainty is part of the picture, they may be excluded even in theory.

These analyses make the conventional but dubious assumption that the businessman tries to maximize profits by keeping his marginal costs and revenues equal. Surveys of business behavior, supported by some modern theory, indicate that competitive conditions and ignorance of relevant quantities rule out this procedure. The theorist's profit maximization can be viewed as including many intangible and non-pecuniary gains, but it then becomes pretty indefinite. Another shortcoming is that even the more intricate theoretical analyses take no specific account of the important and difficult problem of rivals' reactions. (See Chapters 2 and 7.)

Contributions

Despite these limitations of static economic analysis, theory makes some conceptual contributions of practical importance. Except for long-run investment advertising, the marginal approach to determination of outlay provides in concept a simple and definitive test of how much to spend and when to stop. As such it is useful as a guide in thinking about advertising appropriations and in determining what to shoot for in estimates. It may have great usefulness in guiding empirical measurement. The fact that it manipulates esoteric functional relationships and assumes that the businessman has knowledge where he hasn't restricts its immediate usefulness. But these very restrictions may broaden its future usefulness as a guide to the kind of questions that empirical selling-cost research should try to answer.

Practical Application of Marginal Approach

Perhaps the most promising area for applying the marginal approach quantitatively is direct mail advertising. Here the distorting conditions that make it hard to find the marginal cost of advertising are at a minimum. Keyed responses make it possible to trace a large part of the results directly to a specific advertisement. Quality of copy can be held constant (or manipulated independently) by sending identical copy to large numbers of prospects. The cumulative effects of advertising are usually less troublesome, and response lag is short enough so that cyclical changes do not cause important distortions. Finally, and perhaps most important, sectors or strata of prospects can be walled off and separately tapped.

An example of the way a publisher might determine the amount to spend on direct mail advertising in promoting a specific book will illustrate how the incremental approach can be applied quantitatively in this sort of advertising. The procedure can be sketched by the following steps:

1. Marshal the candidates for direct mailing in the form of mailing lists. These lists will vary in "quality," i.e., appropriateness for the particular book.

2. Array the lists in a guessed ladder of susceptibility to direct mail advertising.

3. Starting at the top of the ladder and working down, test each list by sending the promotional literature to an efficient sample of the list.

4. Estimate the probable marginal advertising cost of each list by computing the ratio of (a) the sales obtained from the sample mailings and (b) the added advertising cost of the mailings; e.g., for List A, 50 cents a copy.

5. Estimate the incremental profit per copy. Roughly, it is the spread between price and incremental printing costs (e.g., $1.00 a copy).

6. Rearrange the sample lists in a new ladder in respect to the estimated marginal cost of advertising. Starting at the top, make full mailings to each list down to the rung where incremental profit just fails to cover estimated marginal advertising cost (e.g.,

stop at List M where a marginal advertising cost of $1.00 a copy was indicated by the sample).

Summary

In theory, optimum advertising outlays can be precisely determined under specified conditions of production cost behavior and advertising effectiveness, but the most exhaustive solutions to the problem are too complex to present here. When the situation is severely restricted to short-run advertising with fixed price and constant marginal costs of production, the solution is greatly simplified and yet is still useful for many problems.

The basic feature of theoretical solutions is the use of marginal analysis—the ubiquitous equating of marginal cost to marginal revenue—to maximize net profits. The difficult problem in applying this conceptual model is to find an empirical estimate of the effect of advertising cost on sales. For some kinds of advertising, e.g., direct mail, a fairly good guess may be made.

Another difficulty in using this concept (as well as the more intricate theories) is the non-reversible effects of most advertising: the impact of advertising cumulates and dissipates slowly, and it is not easy to return to the starting point, once an advertising venture is under way.

The contribution of the theory to management is that it brings out the relevant (even if unmeasurable) quantities in advertising, as opposed to irrelevant (but measurable) ones.

III. METHODS FOR DETERMINING TOTAL ADVERTISING BUDGET

Having reviewed the theoretical foundations of selling cost analysis, we turn now to the methods that are actually used to determine advertising outlays. Our central concern is with the philosophy underlying the methods; we shall not trouble with the mechanics of administrative controls.[18]

Analytically, it might be desirable to separate the determination of the average level of advertising outlay over a period of

---

18 We shall use "budget" and "appropriation" interchangeably, though a distinction might be made between the long-range expenditure plan (budget) and the outlay authorized for a given year (appropriation). The words "expenditure" and "outlay" will, unless otherwise qualified, apply to future plans, and will refer to the budget.

years from decisions about its cyclical fluctuations. In this appraisal, however, a clear distinction is not feasible, since the typical firm does not plan advertising expenditures for more than one year at a time.[19] If a policy of stable or contra-cyclical expenditures is contemplated, some conception of the long-run average level of outlay is needed. But if expenditures are to move up and down with business conditions, such a distinction is less necessary. However, the whole institution, and even the concept, of periodic business cycles may now be obsolete.[20] Accordingly, we shall deal with some fluctuation problems as we meet them in yearly budgeting methods and then deal more generally with the problem of cycles later. In any event, the foresight required for any kind of accurate long-range planning is rarely possible.

Alternative Methods

The marginal approach was reviewed in the preceding section; its impeccable logic provides a framework for appraising the methods described in this section, even though its problems of application are at times insurmountable. Several alternative approaches to the problem of planning total advertising expenditures will be examined: (1) a fixed percentage of sales; (2) all you can afford; (3) whatever amount promises a better than specified return on investment; (4) objective and task; (5) competitive parity.

Percentage-of-Sales Approach

Determination of the advertising budget as a percentage of past or expected sales is a method that was dominant in the past and is still widely used.[21] The method has several variants: a fixed percentage or a percentage that varies with conditions is

---

19 A survey by the editors of *Printers' Ink* showed that out of 126 advertisers, 107 made their advertising appropriation by the year, and 19 set their advertising budget from one to six months. "Flexible Advertising Budget Essential to Sound Selling," Part I, *Printers' Ink*, January 18, 1946, page 84.

20 Discussed in Section IV.

21 A survey of budgeting practices of industrial users in 1939 made by the National Industrial Advertisers Association and reported in *Sales Management Handbook*, J. C. Aspley, Editor, 1947, showed that 48 per cent of the 383 respondent companies used some variant of the percentage-of-sales method. Of 215 companies advertising consumer goods in 1935, 54 per cent stated that their appropriations were a predetermined percentage of sales, either of the past year, or of the year of the budget. N. H. Borden, *Economic Effects of Advertising, op. cit.,* Chapter 25.

taken of historical or projected sales either in dollars or in physical volume.

This general approach to the problem is hard to support analytically. The purpose of advertising is to increase demand for the company's products above what it would otherwise be—advertising should be viewed as the cause, not the result of sales.[22] The amount that should be spent in shifting the demand schedule should depend on how much the shift is worth. The volume of sales the company already has tells nothing about the cost or worth of getting more.

It would appear even less rational to base the budget on the volume of sales the company expects to get. Sales will be the result of the level of national income, the accumulated effects of past advertising, and the advertising that is currently being decided upon. To the extent that sales are determined by forces other than current advertising, the criterion of expected sales is irrelevant. To the extent that they are determined by future advertising, the criterion is based on circular reasoning.

How, then, can the widespread use of this method be explained? To some extent it may be due to top management's desire for the certainty and the illusion of control that comes from relating this essentially discretionary element of expense in a systematic way to revenue. There is an element of safety in limiting advertising outlays in this manner, since expenditures are timed to come when the company has the gross revenue to afford them and when their tax effect may be favorable. But this element of safety could be intensified by making advertising a function of expected profit, which normally fluctuates cyclically more violently than expected sales. If this method rests upon the belief that the added sales per dollar of advertising is higher when national income is high, it would be more logical to make advertising outlay vary directly with national income.[23]

Another possible explanation for the popularity of this method stems from competitive relationships. If all, or most, members of an industry used this method and employed the same percent-

---

22 A stable or declining demand is not evidence that advertising is ineffective, for without it sales might have been lower.

23 Except insofar as the amount expendable on the firm's products departs from the fluctuations of total national income, which might be expected for products with unusually high or low income elasticity of demand.

age of sales, competitors' advertising outlays would be roughly proportional to their market shares. This condition would have a
restraining effect on competitive warfare in advertising, and would
ease ulcers in peace-loving firms. Much advertising is essentially
defensive anyhow.

Thus, although the percentage-of-sales approach appears on its
surface to have no logical justification, it has features that make
it attractive: it provides a formula answer with an illusion of
control; it permits the cyclical timing of outlay to fluctuate
roughly with ability to pay; and it may tend toward competitive
stabilization. But inertia and the lack of a more logical and
equally definitive standard are probably the most important explanations for the popularity of this essentially mechanistic
method.

All-You-Can-Afford Approach

An approach to the determination of the advertising budget
that is probably more widely used than is admitted is for a company to spend on advertising all that it can afford. In practice,
this amount is sometimes a predetermined share of the profits,
though sometimes it is gauged by the amount of liquid resources
and borrowable funds.

At first blush this method seems to make no sense at all, yet
on further analysis it appears that the effects of advertising outlays upon profits and liquidity are important considerations in
setting outer limits for advertising. These limits may prove to
be beyond the range of profitable advertising outlays, but they are
often well within it. In any event, they ought to be staked out.

Normally, a time lag occurs between advertising outlay and
sales results. Even if the advertising outlays bring highly profitable results ultimately, financial embarrassment may develop if
short-term cash and credit limits are ignored—especially if the
time lag of response is long. The limit of what a company can
afford ought to involve ultimately the availability of outside funds.
In this sense the firm's resources set a real limit on advertising
outlay. However, this limit may be above the limit set by a
marginal-return criterion.

The effect of advertising outlay upon the company's earnings
statement is also a valid factor in timing. Even though an added
thousand dollars of advertising brings a smaller increment of sales

and profits at a profits peak, it may be justified because the government pays 45 per cent of the outlay, and because a lower earnings figure is often more respectable at such times.

Corporate income taxes favor concentration of advertising at cyclical peaks and penalize attempts to accumulate advertising reserves to be spent in depressions. One reason is that future tax rates are quite likely to be higher in prosperities than in depressions and the carry-back and carry-forward provisions of the law are probably inadequate to remove this tax incentive for bunching of expenditures. Moreover, Section 102 discourages retention of earnings for future depression advertising. The vast amount of money spent during the war in advertising unavailable civilian products showed the widespread acceptance of the philosophy of relating advertising outlays to profits, with a weather eye on their tax effects.[24] Union negotiations and public opinion also frequently make it embarrassing to show high profits in prosperity; hence timing advertising outlays to manipulate reported earnings makes sense as a modification of a purely marginal approach. Considered purely as a capital investment in distant-future benefits it may be desirable from the viewpoint of capital budgeting to limit advertising outlay of an earnings plow-back nature to some fixed proportion of current earnings. Over the cycle this method would lead to advertising outlays that fluctuate violently, for a company's profit cycle normally has much greater magnitude than its sales cycle. It might lead to unprofitable curtailment in hard times.

Used uncritically, the all-you-can-afford method is unsatisfactory, largely because there is no relation between liquidity and the richness of advertising opportunities. If another $1,000 of advertising will bring in $2,000 of added profits, it is hard to say that it cannot be afforded. A management that limits advertising to liquid funds or to percentages of profits may forego money-making opportunities.

But spending money on advertising up to the limit of all-you-can-afford spending may at times go far beyond the point at which the added earnings from advertising equal their cost. Spending money because you have it and without regard to benefits is hardly an economical way of determining the advertising budget.

---

24 (See J. D. Scott, "Advertising When Buying Is Restricted," *Harvard Business Review*, July, 1943, pp. 443–454.)

The all-you-can-afford method, however, is helpful in some ways in determining the advertising appropriation: (1) it produces a fairly defensible cyclical timing of that part of advertising outlay that has cumulative, long-run effects; (2) when marginal effectiveness of advertising can be guessed, it budgets well for firms operating short of the point at which incremental advertising costs and profits are equal; (3) when nothing can be known about the effects of advertising, it sets a reasonable limit on the gamble. Actually, everything above a respectable return on capital could be spent on advertising, since excess earnings have low utility to management as such, compared with the possible contribution of continuous advertising to eternal life for the firm.

Return-on-Investment Approach

Advertising has two effects: (1) It increases sales today. (2) It builds good will to increase sales tomorrow. The first primarily involves problems of selecting the optimum output rate for maximizing short-run profits. The second involves selection of the pattern investment of capital funds that will produce the best scale of production and maximum long-run profits. Thus, another approach is to treat advertising primarily as a capital investment rather than as a current expense. Determination of the amount of advertising then becomes a problem of capital expenditure budgeting. Advertising investment must compete for funds with other kinds of internal investment on the basis of prospective rate of return.

Each piece of advertising affects immediate sales and, at the same time, adds another brick to the good-will structure, but the relative importance of the two effects can vary widely. At one end of the spectrum is institutional advertising, with a long time-lag and untraceable effects, e.g., the sponsoring of symphony concerts. This is almost pure capital investment. At the other end is advertising of special sales events by retail establishments. Such advertising usually has only a small element of capital investment. Metrical separation of these two components is probably impossible. Interaction makes the problem even more complex, since the level of the reservoir of cumulative good will modifies the efficiency of advertising directed at immediate sales.[25]

---

[25] The possibility of using multiple correlation analysis has been discussed and explored for some time. The main findings of a published study of this type by

The timing of advertising over the years that is produced by a return-on-investment approach will differ unpredictably among companies.[26] This may be unimportant in some cases, where the lag in response is long and diffuse. But dimming memories and the incursions of rivals usually dissipate the good will built by advertising through evaporation or run-off. This is particularly dangerous when costs of re-entering lost markets are high. Hence a part of the advertising investment problem is to find what rate of current expenditure is required to offset this deterioration and to maintain the level of this good-will reservoir. Thus a concept analogous to plant replacement operates in estimating return on advertising investment.

The chief deficiency of the return-on-investment approach is the difficulty of even guessing at the rate of return on advertising investments. Problems of distinguishing investment advertising from outlays for immediate effect; problems of estimating the evaporation of the cumulative effects of advertising; and, most important, problems of measuring the effect of advertising accumulation upon long-run sales volume and upon the possibility of eventual price premiums conspire to make the return on advertising investments highly conjectural.

These measurement difficulties rule out this approach as a sole criterion for budgeting investment-type advertising, but they do not invalidate the investment approach itself. For other kinds of investment, e.g., research laboratories and department-store escalators, it is equally impossible to estimate the return precisely. Yet few would, for this reason, kick out such items from the capital expenditure budget. Institutional and cumulative advertising should be analyzed in the intellectual setting of the capital budget, viz., long-range strategic and profit objectives, competition of alternative investments for limited company funds, and balancing of risks against prospective return on investment in rationing capital. This kind of investment perspective should be an integral part of an intelligent approach to the advertising budget.

Sydney Hollander, "A Rationale for Advertising Expenditure," *Harvard Business Review*, January, 1949, are summarized later.

26 The pattern will depend upon the philosophy of budgeting and upon the prospective profitability of capital expenditures that vie with advertising for funds. Only if the marginal efficiency of institutional advertising has sharp cyclical fluctuations will anything but an accidental cyclical pattern evolve from this criterion alone.

Objective-and-Task Approach

The war brought to prominence the objective-and-task method of determining the advertising appropriation.[27]   The popularity of this approach during the war apparently came partly from the need to justify advertising expenditures as business expenses (for purposes of taxes and contracts) during a period when x per cent of civilian goods sales would support only trivial outlays.

Under this approach the advertising budget is the amount estimated to be required to attain predetermined objectives.   The orthodox procedure involves an impeccable and highly salable sequence of steps: (1) define the objectives; (2) outline the tasks, i.e., the specific means of attaining the objectives; (3) determine the cost of accomplishing these tasks.   This cost is the advertising appropriation.[28]

An objective is properly stated as a change, the difference between results with the advertising and without it.   The objective usually applies to the coming year's sales, although it may refer to invasion of a specific market or the establishment of distribution outlets.   In this respect, the actual advance that this method represents over the percentage-of-sales criterion may easily be overestimated.   In general practice, the sales volume objective is based on the preceding year's volume.   Expected changes in business conditions, competitors' actions, and so forth, are then considered as a basis for deriving the current year's outlay from the preceding year's outlay.

Some companies fall back on intermediate objectives such as establishing brand familiarity or preferences, promoting applications of the product, or simply broadcasting the sales message. Many such objectives simply list the roles of advertising in the broader merchandising scheme without referring to specific sales effects.   For example, a recent study for the Association of National Advertisers reports the advertising goals of the Armstrong Cork Company as keeping the company's name before customers and attracting the attention of those who are not buying now by providing salesmen an access to prospects, making prospects easier

---

[27] On the basis of a postwar survey, *Printers' Ink* concluded that this was the method most widely used by advertisers (December 28, 1946, p. 26).

[28] For a complete and thoughtful treatment of this approach, see A. H. Haase, *The Advertising Appropriation*, New York, Harper & Bros., 1931.

to sell to, publicizing the Armstrong name, and carrying the sales message beyond the range of personal coverage.[29] Nobody can quarrel with thinking through goals of advertising as completely as possible, since it contributes to better copy and media policy. But this kind of "objectives" contribute nothing to determining the size of the advertising appropriation. For this purpose objectives must be expressed so that they are measurable and costable, e.g., a 10 per cent increase in sales next year, over what they would have been without this advertising.

In its bald form, the objective-and-task approach begs the question. The important problem is to measure the value of objectives and to determine whether they are worth the probable cost of attaining them. In other words, what intensity of demand (i.e., what position and shape of demand schedule) is an economically sound objective? Objective-and-task assumes that the candle is always worth the cost. In many cases, the high marginal productivity of advertising (up to the limit of the money available) bails out the advertiser, but this good fortune does not make his basic thinking any clearer.

After valuing and costing legitimate objectives, the next and vital step is either to cut back or to expand plans in the light of these prospective costs. In this way, the objectives can be reshaped and really determined by the cost of attaining them, rather than vice versa. In this form the approach has the virtue of sharpening issues and directing research and planning into relevant channels.

When the objective has been stated so that the task can be defined in terms of costs, the problem has been stated in a form that is appropriate for either the marginal analysis attack outlined in Section II or the investment approach. Objectives in terms of near-future sales volume can be expressed as the short-run marginal advertising cost function in Chart 6–1, while specific long-run objectives can be viewed as investments to be built into the capital budget on a rate-of-return basis. For instance, if the objective is to get mass volume for a new product at a premium price, the task of advertising is to establish and maintain the corresponding brand preference; the budgeting problem is to determine the relation between the necessary initial and continuing outlays and

---

[29] *Marketing Handbook*, Nystrom (Ed.), Ronald, New York, 1948, p. 1235.

the resulting level of price premium, and to compare the premium profits with the required investment in advertising.

To sum up, the objective-and-task approach uses a straightforward sequence of attack that is good for all business problems. In its simple form, however, the approach begs the question. The economic problem is to determine what objectives are worth the cost of attaining. This cost can sometimes be measured, but can only rarely be compared with the ultimate value to be derived from attaining objectives. However, this method can be extended into highly promising experimental and marginal approaches. Through such approaches, objectives can be reformed in the light of costs. Economic tasks can thus be adapted to the peculiar goals and situations of individual companies and nicely integrated with other elements in the company's merchandising plan.

Competitive-Parity Approach

The essence of the competitive-parity approach is to base in some systematic way the company's advertising outlay on the outlays of other members of the industry. Specifically, the company's percentage of total competitive advertising might be made equal to its share of the market.[30]

This method of budgeting is widely used, and it finds some support in the writings of practitioners. The defensive nature of a large proportion of advertising outlay, designed to check the inroads of trouble-makers, may account for the method's popularity.[31]

This approach appears at first to have slim warrant in principle. What competitors spend on advertising does not tell a firm how much it can spend to make added benefits just equal the added costs. The size of this optimum outlay is affected by rivals' advertising, since competitors' advertising influences the productivity (incremental cost) of the firm's advertising. But it cannot be determined by merely matching competitors' appropriations. Hence what rivals choose to spend does not in itself provide any

---

[30] A variant, which is quite different conceptually, is to spend as much as necessary to retain desired market share.

[31] For example, in the antitrust case against the big three tobacco companies the explanation advanced by American and by Liggett & Myers for following the lead of Reynolds in a 1931 price advance was that the revenue was needed to match Reynolds' increased advertising. (328 U.S. 805)

valid measure of what the firm's advertising budget should be.

The parity approach is sometimes defended on the grounds that the advertising percentages of competitors represent the combined wisdom of the industry. This argument assumes that rivals know what they are doing and that their goals are the same as the firm's. Actually, since great differences normally exist among competitors in the ratio of advertising to sales, the industry average is often relatively meaningless. As an example, a breakdown of an industry average that appeared in *Printers' Ink* (Feb. 8, 1947) follows:

No. of Companies	Per Cent of Sales Devoted to Advertising
1	9
1	3
3	2
2	1

No correlation appeared between outlay and size of firm. Further analysis revealed that the smallest firm (one of the heaviest advertisers) was bent on a program of aggressive expansion; one of the concerns that spend 2 per cent manufactured only a restricted line and had no ambition to grow; the largest concern was well established and was making a very satisfactory showing with an expenditure of only 3 per cent. This case illustrates the limitations of an industry average as a tool for determining outlay, in that companies differ in objectives, brand maturity and marketing methods. It also suggests the advantages of knowing rivals' objectives and competitive situations as well as their advertising outlays.

Another difficulty is that, to the extent that this rationale is valid, the future and not the past advertising outlays of rivals should constitute the standard. Usually these outlays cannot be determined soon enough or with enough accuracy to be useful in planning appropriations.

Advocates of parity advertising claim that it safeguards against advertising wars that can be started when other methods are used to determine outlay. Parity advertising may thus play a role analogous to that of price leadership in preventing price wars. But degenerative retaliation in advertising is much less likely than in price competition. This is because precise retaliation in advertising is more difficult, less often necessary, and less compulsive in the eyes of defenders than price retaliation. Quality of copy and appropriateness of media vary, and time is required to plan campaigns.　Advertising is a more diffuse basis for buyers' comparisons of competitors than price, and differentials in advertising cause smaller shifts than do price differentials in price wars. Moreover, uncertainty about the results of the aggressor's advertising slows reaction of other firms, who rather hope for industry-wide benefits from the outlay through expansion of the total market.　(Particularly in the early stages of product acceptance—e.g., frozen orange juice—the market-widening effect may be vastly more important than the market-sharing aspect.)

Behind the desire to offset competitors' effectiveness, presumably lies the desire to retain market share (or to expand that share by a planned amount).　To do this does not necessarily call for parity in advertising outlay.　Advertising is only one of many forms of selling effort.　The amount competitors spend on it simply reflects their apportioning of the sales dollars among all the various possible forms.　One firm's proportion may be wrong for another firm.　If a firm is to match its competitors in some way, it should match their total sales effort in effectiveness, rather than their apportionments among various devices.　For example, an oil company might counter a rival's gasoline advertising by reducing prices (informally, usually), stepping up its octane rating, improving its service stations, or invading new market areas.　One frozen-food company meets a rival's heavy advertising by slightly wider dealer margins and (they say) more uniform quality of pack. Better quality of copy and media, greater cumulative prestige, and superior product attributes may make it possible for a firm to do 10 per cent of the advertising done by its competitors and still keep 20 per cent of the sales.

The parity approach is a dangerous guide to use literally. Since competitors' advertising affects the productivity of a firm's advertising, it also affects the firm's optimum outlay for both short-run and long-run profit maximization.　But the firm's optimum outlay is not actually determined by parity with competitors' expenditures.　Firms differ so much in objectives, competitive maturity, marketing methods, and the quality and cumulative prestige of advertising that competitors' advertising ratios are a pretty useless criterion.　In the face of these differences in competitive situations, the possibility that parity will stabilize competitive warfare is not usually great enough to justify its use.

Summary

Viewed against the logical background of marginal analysis, most methods actually used for determining advertising budgets seem to have no economic foundation. Fixed percentage-of-sales makes the budget an effect of what it should cause; all-you-can-afford reflects a blind, ignorant faith in advertising; objective-and-task shows nothing about the value of the objective; and competitive parity is a narrow goal not tailored to the company's needs. While the investment approach is sound conceptually, in recognizing the time dimension of advertising, it is hard to nail down with empirical data.

The difficult problem in applying economic analysis to advertising is to find the empirical equivalents of the theoretical curves. The deep uncertainty surrounding the productivity of advertising is perhaps the origin of such methods as percentage of sales and objective and task. But whatever rationale these methods may once have had, their basic weakness is that they hide rather than highlight the economic issues in the advertising problem. Despite its limitations, economic analysis can be helpful in reaching a better decision on the amount of advertising by focusing attention on the relevant (even though unmeasurable) relationships as opposed to the irrelevant (but measurable) ones. Though the complete theoretical solution to the advertising problem is too complex for practical use, manageable approximations may sometimes be feasible. New statistical methods and sources of data are continuously expanding the range of measurable quantities in executive problems.

IV. CYCLICAL FLUCTUATIONS OF ADVERTISING

How should a company's advertising appropriation fluctuate with general business conditions? When national income changes 10 per cent, should promotional outlays also change by 10 per cent, or should they change 15 per cent, 5 per cent, or not at all? This is a difficult question for management to answer, but it is important from both the private and social viewpoints, since there is at least some possibility that contra-cyclical advertising outlays can have a stabilizing effect on business activity. This section discusses the problem from the company's viewpoint and describes the kind of economic analysis that is needed to find the most profitable promotion policy to cope with fluctuations in business conditions.

Stabilizing Effects of Advertising

Recently the notion that we can advertise our way out of future depressions has gained wide acceptance. Can advertising help to stabilize cyclical fluctuations?[32] Orthodox economists have to some extent taken the view that advertising in net effect does not alter propensity to consume; it merely channels consumption among rival goods.[33]

But if advertising can really alter the consumption function, it has a double multiplier effect. First, advertising, like any business spending, creates employment, which in turn produces more spending. Second, by increasing the propensity to consume, it raises the whole multiplier.

To the extent that advertising does affect the consumption function, aggregate advertising has in the past probably accentuated business fluctuations rather than offset them, since advertising cycles have corresponded closely to general business cycles. Cyclical fluctuations of advertising expenditure are even more mechanically tuned to business cycles than changes in other types of investment when they result from budgeting practices that relate appropriations to sales or to profits. Various studies of cyclical variation in the advertising expenditures for specific products indicate that the violence of fluctuations varies roughly with the income elasticity of the product. Thus advertising for consumer durables is more volatile than it is for foods.

The effectiveness of advertising as a stabilizing influence depends upon several conditions: (1) how well it can overcome spending timidity in recession periods; (2) how far it can offset contraction in other kinds of business spending, notably inventory

---

32 This discussion is based upon the assumption that we will continue to have swings in business activity. The government's full employment commitment, the new tools of economic policy, the immense role of the government in the economy, and the jumpy preparedness on all sides to avoid depression may have made the conventional idea of business cycles obsolete, but it is too early to say that inadvertent fluctuations are gone forever.

33 For a summary of the economists' case against advertising, see F. P. Bishop, *The Economics of Advertising*, Robert Hale Ltd., 1946, especially Chapters I, VI, and VIII. See also K. W. Rothschild, "A Note on Advertising," *Economic Journal*, 1942, p. 112.

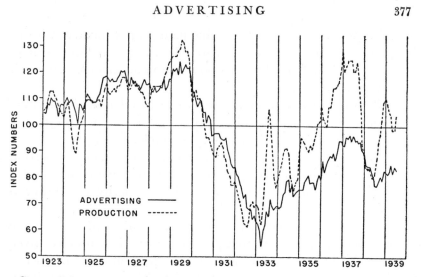

CHART 6-2. ADVERTISING INDEX AND FEDERAL RESERVE INDEX OF INDUSTRIAL PRODUCTION—1923–1939. (Source: L. C. Wagner, "Advertising and the Business Cycle," *Journal of Marketing,* October, 1941.

and plant and equipment outlays; and (3) how rapidly it can produce results—long and uneven response lags and a high proportion of institutional promotion dilute the effect of advertising on the immediate consumption function. Since these conditions are quite difficult to specify, it is still very much a moot question what the influence of advertising might be. Advertising at 2 per cent of the national income is probably one-fifth to one-half the size of other capital expenditures made by business. Thus it might be a fairly significant lever if drastic anti-cyclical expenditures could be induced. But to implement an over-all plan would require some incentive and financing scheme to persuade businessmen to lay out cash at a time when common sense tells them it is both risky and unproductive to invest in advertising. This section is concerned with the conditions that determine whether or not their fears are justified.

Alternative Policies

Although the aggregate advertising expenditure moves up and down with business conditions, individual firms can have divergent cyclical patterns. The range of policy as to the cyclical pattern of advertising is wide:

1. Advertising outlay may fluctuate proportionately with ex-pected (or last year's) sales, so that the percentage spent on advertising will tend to be about the same in prosperity as in depression.

2. Advertising outlay may fluctuate in relation to forecasted profits, so that a uniform percentage of profits will be poured into advertising at all phases of the cycle.

3. Advertising outlay may fluctuate more than proportion-ately with sales or with profits, so that the advertising percent-age will be higher than average in prosperity and lower in depression.

4. Advertising outlay may fluctuate less than proportionately with sales or profits, so that percentage-wise it will be relatively great in depression, and less than proportionate in prosperity. This pattern might be roughly achieved by setting a minimum total outlay for a depression period, regardless of how low sales and profits fall.

5. Advertising outlay may be held constant in total dollar outlay regardless of cyclical fluctuations in sales or profits.[34]

6. Advertising outlay may fluctuate inversely with sales or profits in order to mitigate these fluctuations.

Each of these possible courses of action has its advocates and practitioners.

Tests of Cyclical Policies

Only two important attempts have been made to test statis-tically the effects of various cyclical advertising policies. In his pioneer investigation, Roland Vaile studied the sales behavior of more than 200 companies during the period from 1920 to 1924.[35] Firms that decreased their advertising between 1920 and 1921 suffered a somewhat greater decline in sales than did non-advertis-ing firms, and companies that increased their advertising had pronounced gains in sales. These gains were not, however, pro-

---

[34] For example, O. A. Keyser recommends, on the basis of the experience of one company, that advertising expenditures be held constant over the cycle by using funds accumulated in boom times. His recommendation is based on a theory of cycles that attributes fluctuations to cumulative psychological movements of fear and optimism. O. A. Keyser, "A Counter-Cyclical Fund for Advertising," *Adver-tising and Selling*, April 1947, p. 34.

[35] R. S. Vaile, "Use of Advertising During Depression," *Harvard Business Review*, Vol. 5, p. 323.

portional to the increase in advertising linage. During the up-swing after 1924, this latter group showed the most pronounced gains, and sales of non-advertisers lagged farthest behind. Depression advertising was apparently more effective for products that were habit-forming or were bought largely by men. A divergence between sales of advertisers and non-advertisers was noticeable for convenience goods and producers' goods. No attempt was made to trace the effect of these various advertising policies upon profits.

A later investigation by L. C. Wagner [36] dealt with the cyclical advertising policies of a group of twenty-two companies from 1933 to 1939. During the upswing of 1935 and 1936, the fifteen firms that increased their advertising showed relatively greater sales and profits than did the firms that did not. During the down-swing of 1937–1938, the eight firms that increased their advertising found that their sales decreased less, but the difference in profits between this group and the group that decreased appropriations was negligible. Wagner concludes that during the '30s, companies were wise to follow the business cycle in their advertising appropriations.

These two studies make important contributions; more studies of this sort are needed. Unfortunately, however, these two are not conclusive, partly because differences among companies in size, efficiency, product acceptance, and marketing methods also affected results. To be conclusive, comparisons must be made among companies that are similar in every important respect except in advertising policy.

Criteria for Cyclical Advertising

Consideration of a contra-cyclical or even a level advertising budget is, for most companies, strictly academic. Some cyclical fluctuation is inevitable; the practical problem is, "How much?" —e.g., whether the advertising outlay should be a greater proportion of sales in depression than in prosperity. The optimum degree of fluctuation is certainly different for different products. Since empirical research has not gone far enough in this area to provide dependable guides, cyclical policy is largely a matter of judgment. Some factors that should be known to make the judg-

---

[36] L. C. Wagner, "Advertising and the Business Cycle," *Journal of Marketing*, October, 1941, pp. 124–135.

ment more rational are: (1) cyclical changes in advertising effectiveness; (2) income elasticity of demand; (3) changes in profit margins; (4) improvement of products; (5) perishability of advertising impact; (6) promotional elasticity of market; and (7) proportion of investment-type advertising.

Changes in Advertising Effectiveness

In a sense, the whole cyclical problem is to find how the advertising cost curve shifts with business fluctuations. Taken in this sense, each of the other considerations listed above is encompassed in this one. They are all either determinants or indicators of cyclical changes in the efficiency of advertising. Broadly conceived, the advertising cost function must include all the long-run aspects of advertising which, in Section II, we saw were usually intractable in quantitative marginal analysis. If we limit the cost function, therefore, to the immediate response in sales and to current-expense advertising, then the cyclical shift of the advertising cost curve becomes one of several factors, including production costs and prices in the short run which management must consider in designing a cyclical advertising policy.

There is reason to believe that responsiveness to advertising does change cyclically and that it is directly correlated with changes in income, since demand, to be effective, must be backed by purchasing power. In times of depression when buyers are over-cautious, more advertising dollars must be laid out to bring in a dollar of sales. Moreover, anticipation of bad times to come dries up buying, even when incomes are still holding up. To some extent, these declines in propensity to buy may be offset by reduced competition for attention as fringe advertisers fold up. But it is more important that in many industries the price spread between advertised and unadvertised products widens in depression and puts a heavy selling job on the advertising dollar.

A valuable indicator of the extent of these cyclical shifts may be the income elasticity of demand.

Income Elasticity

Income elasticity of demand for a product measures the extent to which its demand curve shifts in response to buyers' incomes. This aspect of demand is discussed in Chapter 4 where a table of such elasticities is shown for consumer products. The promotion problem is to find a relation between income elasticity and changes in the effectiveness of advertising.

When depression strikes, many just get out of the market altogether for big purchases—cars, furniture, trips—and the occasional luxuries. For the "convenience goods" and necessities consumers apparently shift patronage more responsively to price differentials, but at least they stay in the market. When incomes rise and expectations of unemployment and of better bargains recede, however, consumers re-enter the durable goods market and tend to make consumption more conspicuous.

This leads to the hypothesis that for products that have low income-elasticity, i.e., necessities and convenience goods, the marginal effectiveness of advertising changes much less than for the durables and luxuries. If this is true, it provides an important guide to cyclical advertising policy, since income elasticity can be measured fairly acurately for many products. However, much remains to be learned about this relation before it can be advanced as an established criterion for advertising policy.

Changes in Profit Margins

Ideally, advertising outlay should be expanded to the level where the last advertising dollar spent brings in a dollar of incremental profit; i.e., sales revenue minus marginal production costs. Cyclical swings in competitive intensity usually lower the incremental profit spread in depression and raise it in prosperity, e.g., through varying amounts of price discrimination, and thus leave less room for advertising in bad times than in good.[37]

To illustrate, let us go back to our book example (Section II of this chapter), summarized in the following table:

	In Prosperity	In Depression
Publisher's net price	$4.00 per copy	$3.50 per copy
Marginal production cost	3.00 " "	2.75 " "
Incremental profit	1.00 " "	0.75 " "
Cut-off point (barely profitable list)	16th list	8th list
Advertising outlay to circulated profitable lists	$30,000	$15,000

[37] There are, of course, numerous exceptions. Extreme rigidity of actual (as opposed to nominal) prices, accompanied by the usual cyclical fluctuations in cost prices and labor efficiency, would make incremental profits higher in depression than in prosperity. Here, as in the other cases, we presume that incremental production costs are approximately constant over the actual range of output.

In prosperity the net selling price was $4.00 and the marginal production cost was $3.00. His incremental profit per copy was $1.00. This set a limit on the amount of money that could advantageously be spent on direct mail advertising, since the $1.00 profit cut-off of mailing lists whose "quality" was so low it did not pay to solicit them. If in depression the net price dropped to $3.50 and marginal costs to $2.75, then incremental profit would be $0.75 a copy. This 75 cents would cut off more lists than would the $1.00 profit, if the will to spend and susceptibility to advertising did not wither cyclically. But they will, since profit shrinkage comes at a time when the selling cost function is usually rising so that advertising is cut back still more. In general, these conditions call for sharp restrictions of advertising. However, in depression, the effectiveness of advertising may sometimes be maintained to some extent by dramatic price cuts and product improvements which make good advertising copy, or by drops in advertising costs and by new developments in production techniques.

Improvement of Products

The introduction of new products or dramatic improvement of old ones during a period of low demand can increase the effectiveness of depression advertising. After examining several hundred Harvard Business School cases, Borden concluded that "as a general rule mere increase in advertising expenditure does not by itself produce profitable results. . . . In order to be effective and profitable [it] must be accompanied by merchandising efforts which bring about the offering of particularly desirable products at attractive prices." [38] The experience of Philco bears out this generalization. [39]

Perishability of Advertising Impact

The factors so far considered concern the short-run shifts of the "static" advertising cost curve. Turning to the time aspects of advertising, we have three types of problems: timing of adver-

---

[38] N. H. Borden, *The Economic Effects of Advertising*, Chicago, Richard E. Irwin, 1944, p. 728.

[39] See S. M. Ramdell, "How Philco Doubled Sales During the Depression," *Printers' Ink*, October 22, 1931, p. 17.

tising relative to sales, long-term irreversible trends in the market, and longest-run advertising objectives.

Cyclical timing of advertising must be related to the durability of advertising impressions in buyers' minds and to the time lag between exposure and purchase. For example, a product with a high turnover of customers, i.e., teen-agers, graduating classes or brides, justifies considerable cyclical stability of advertising because the impact is not very storable. A product bought frequently and in small purchase-units, like cigarettes or candy— "impulse items"—also leaves little latitude in cyclical timing, but here it is because of the brief time-lag in advertising response. But when returns from advertising are spread over several months —which is typical for large and dramatic purchase items such as automobiles or trips to Europe—the seller has greater flexibility in timing than he would for small convenience items. The long gestation period can be used to time attacks at strategic turning points in the cycle, where they face less competition or are most feasible financially. Thus advertising at the beginning of recovery upturns will plant seeds which can be harvested in prosperity without the heavy costs of matching the heavy noise level of competitive advertising in the later stage. But this tactic requires knowledge of the durability of impacts, length of cycles and cost of re-entry into the market if sales efforts are dropped during slump periods. Such a scheme calls for more foresight or faith than most people have.

Promotional Elasticity of Market

The second time factor is the rate of long-term growth of the total market and the extent to which advertising can increase the rate. This is the promotional elasticity of the market. Refrigerators, vacuum cleaners, gasoline, and electricity all had vigorous underlying growth trends during the early thirties, which gave strong boosts to the effectiveness of advertising in spite of general depression. This secular boost to promotional elasticity justifies more stable or even contra-cyclical advertising outlays.

Proportion of Investment-Type Advertising

Some advertising is directed at creating long-term good will rather than at producing immediate sales. The proportion of the total outlay allotted to this investment-type advertising differs among products and companies and affects the appropriate cyclical policy.   Normally, the firm has wide time latitude—in terms of months and even years—in this type of advertising.   Investment-type advertising can be made to vary with gross profits in order to dampen fluctuations in reported earnings.

It has been argued that corporate income taxes, as a practical matter, force this kind of pattern of variation.   This argument is correct only: (1) if the advertising outlays would not otherwise be deductible—e.g., if carryback provisions are inadequate; (2) if corporate income taxes are progressive—e.g., wartime excess profits taxes; or (3) if changes in corporate income tax rates can be forecasted (as they could with reasonable certainty toward the close of the war).   These conditions have existed in the past and will probably be met again in the future.   Timing advertising to reduce taxes leads to extreme cyclical fluctuations of advertising.

On the other hand, there is much that can be said for maintaining a minimum level below which the firm will not go in depression.   Such a level can be justified, first, by the notion that good will evaporates and is eroded by competitors' activities and, second, by the possibility that it would cost more to regain a favorable sales or brand-preference position lost as a result of low advertising in depression than it would to retain it by continuing at a minimum level in depression.[40]   Another justification for a minimum outlay in depression is that costs per unit of impact, e.g., to get one reader to recall seeing a particular advertisement, are lower because of lower space rates and less competition for attention.

Thus how the time latitude of investment-type advertising should be used cyclically involves a balancing of these benefits of a minimum maintenance level against the easier availability of funds and the stabilization of reported profits that favor extreme cyclical fluctuations.

Summary

The practical problem of most firms is to determine the degree of cyclical fluctuation that should be permitted in advertising. The degree should differ among products.   Characteristics that

---

[40] See "Why Advertising Should Be Continuous," *Printers' Ink*, April 28, 1938, p. 12.   Executives of eleven large corporations that advertised heavily and successfully during depression give their reasons for such a policy.

favor extreme cyclical fluctuations are: large shifts in the marginal efficiency of advertising; high income elasticity of demand; sharp constriction of margin over production cost and intensified price competition in depression; the absence of dramatic product improvement in depression; a low proportion of investment-type advertising and a short response lag; and the lack of strong growth in the potential market. Converse conditions favor cyclical stability.

V. MEASUREMENT OF THE ECONOMIC EFFECTS OF ADVERTISING

The principal hope for developing a sound method for planning and controlling advertising lies in improved measurement. All approaches to the problem that have any merit require for their successful application good estimates of the relationship of advertising outlay to sales results.

The marginal approach requires estimates of the effect of added advertising on sales and on potential prices. Similar estimates are also needed for a sophisticated application of the objective-and-task approach. And the investment approach requires estimates of the return on advertising investments. Thus, research to improve estimates of the effects of advertising is the key to scientific budgeting.

Despite the vast amount of research on advertising, surprisingly little has been directed to this problem. Primary attention has been given to the problem of how to get the most out of a given advertising expenditure. Determining the size of that expenditure from its effectiveness has been relatively neglected. The amount of money spent on advertising and the lack of defensible objective criteria for determining how much to spend argue cogently for more research on the problem of budgeting.

Conditions are now more favorable for such research. Research techniques have been refined in recent years, and the theoretical analysis that must underlie sound planning and interpretation of empirical studies has developed quite completely. Moreover, the advertising industry has matured enough to be able to study this kind of attack seriously.

The Objective

The measurement problem is to find how much the firm's demand schedule shifts as a result of specified amounts of advertising outlay.[41] In other words, the problem is to determine how much of current demand has been produced directly by advertising, and to determine how much this man-made demand increases as more money is poured into advertising.

Although this concept is clear enough, the presence of growth and cyclical swings in demand makes measurement exceedingly difficult. The effect of advertising is not on the surface, but must be sorted out from the impact of the other forces in the market. The thing to find is the difference between what the volume was with the advertising and what it would have been without advertising. This becomes complicated when advertising accelerates growth, piles up boom demand, or enables a firm to hold its own in the face of competitive inroads, cyclical downturns, or secular declines.

Difficulties

The mere statement of the measurement problem reveals some of the manifold difficulties.[42]

The difficulty of allowing for the effects of non-advertising determinants of demand is a major problem. Growth trends and changes in income, in relative prices, in competition, and in the firm's own product and its other marketing activities obscure the effects of advertising. The firm's demand function moves as a result of all these forces. Hence, it is necessary to eliminate, or to allow for the influence of, these other factors in order to isolate both revenue and selling cost functions.

---

41 Theoretically, the effects of advertising should be measured in terms of the shift of the whole revenue function of the firm, not just the alteration of sales at the current price. Many firms, however, do not vary price with advertising. Normally, little is known about the demand function at other than the current price. Furthermore, the range of actual price discretion may be quite narrow, so that much of the revenue function is really horizontal except in so far as advertising eventually gives it a slope (i.e., differentiates the product from competitors' products).

42 For discussions of difficulties, see Committee on Price Determination, *Cost Behavior and Price Policy*, National Bureau of Economic Research, 1943, Chapter 9; also H. E. Smith, "Imputation of Advertising Costs," *Economic Journal*, 1935, pp. 682–699.

Another difficulty is caused by differences in the effectiveness of copy and the suitability of media. Variations in *quality* of the advertising obtained for a given outlay make measurement of the effects of different *quantities* of expenditure difficult, because the observed results may be due to variations in skill. To some extent, these fluctuations can be averaged out.

The uncertain time lag between advertising outlay and sales response is another source of trouble. Reaction to advertising is delayed and is sometimes spread over a long period. Hence, it is difficult to trace its impact. The time-distribution of response differs considerably among products as well as among types of advertisement.[43]

Another measurement complexity is caused by the limited objectives of much advertising. Although the ultimate purpose is to produce sales, advertising may not do so directly. Its role may be merely to produce a favorable climate of opinion for other sales-getting activities. Consequently, measurement is often made in terms of readership, brand familiarity, or brand preferences. Results that are measured in these intermediate terms are, of course, useful for testing media and copy. But they are not sufficient as a guide in budgeting unless the sales-producing worth of a unit of readership or familiarity can be measured.

Multiplicity of products and the economies of blanket brands and omnibus advertisements often make separation of the effects upon individual products difficult, although, of course, it is easy enough to judge the over-all effects on the joint products. But determining the optimum advertising, pricing and output for individual products is virtually impossible.

Methods of Measurement

Measurement methods may be classified in various ways. On the basis of source of data, they fall in two categories: historical data created by accident, and controlled data created by experiments. Historical accident data may be studied in two ways: (1) by comparative analyses of differences among firms, and (2) by analysis of the behavior patterns of a single firm. Controlled

---

43 Kinds of advertising, therefore, differ in susceptibility to measurement, forming a sort of spectrum of intractability, with institutional advertising at one end and specific commodity sales offers (e.g., department-store special sales) at the other.

experiments are usually confined to a single firm, though they involve comparisons among its territories or selling units.

Comparative Analysis of Historical Data

When the problem is attacked by comparisons among firms, it is desirable to have the greatest possible uniformity in all respects except advertising outlay. Differences in products, price policies, merchandising methods, or markets may invalidate comparisons.

An example of this kind of analysis is found in a statistical study by Brown and Mancina,[44] using the expense data for department and specialty stores compiled by the Harvard Bureau of Business Research. They tested the hypothesis that the relationship between selling cost and sales is a straight-line function. They found that this hypothesis was not supported by the data. Two cross-section analyses of the same general sort by Vaile and by Wagner have already been mentioned (Section IV).[45]

Analysis of Historical Data for Individual Companies

Another approach is to determine patterns for a single firm from its historical data. This approach has been attempted in various ways. Under some circumstances, multiple correlation analysis has some promise as a means of removing the effects of extraneous factors and isolating the impact of advertising on sales. It is not easy, however, to obtain data that will include adequate variation in the amount of advertising and that will also show either constancy or significant variation in the other measurable factors that govern sales. Such data are sometimes created inadvertently, but they usually have to be produced by controllable experiments. In addition to the general measurement difficulties discussed above, correlation usually has special difficulties, e.g., important factors that cannot be measured, and interdependence of the seemingly independent variables.

An example of the use of this method to determine the behavior

---

44 G. H. Brown and F. A. Mancina, "A Note on the Relationship Between Sales and Advertising of Department Stores," *Journal of Business of the University of Chicago,* January, 1940, pp. 1–16. (A correction appeared in the April issue of this publication, p. 205.)

45 R. S. Vaile, "Use of Advertising During Depressions," *Harvard Business Review,* Volume V, pp. 323–330, and L. C. Wagner, "Advertising and the Business Cycle," *Journal of Marketing,* October, 1941, pp. 124–135.

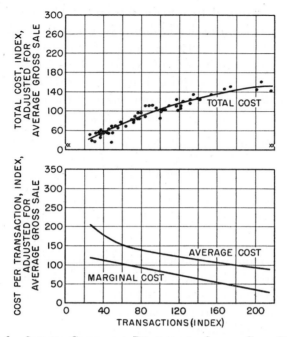

CHART 6–3. SELLING COSTS IN A DEPARTMENT STORE: COAT DEPARTMENT. TOTAL, AVERAGE, AND MARGINAL COMBINED COST DERIVED FROM PARTIAL REGRESSION ON TRANSACTIONS. (Source: see footnote 46.)

of selling costs for the coat department of Lord and Taylor is shown in Chart 6–3.[46]

A published example of the application of this method to advertising costs is found in a study by Sidney Hollander.[47] He used graphic multiple correlation analysis to isolate the pure relationship of advertising outlay to the sales of a nationally advertised proprietary drug product. The dependent variable was sales. The independent variables were (1) applicable disease rates; (2) consumer purchasing power; (3) current advertising expenditures on the product; (4) current advertising expenditures on a closely related product of the same company (5) cumulative advertising; and (6) time.

Price was not included and the effects of competition were,

46 For a summary of the method and the statistical results, see Joel Dean, "Department Store Cost Functions," in *Studies in Mathematical Economics and Econometrics,* Chicago, University of Chicago Press, 1941.

47 Sidney Hollander, "A Rationale for Advertising Expenditures," *Harvard Business Review,* January, 1949, pp. 79–87.

after study, presumed to remain constant.   The relationship of
current advertising to sales is shown in Chart 6–4.   An attempt
to deal quantitatively with the cumulative effects of advertising
is perhaps the most important contribution of this study.   Although Hollander's description is not sufficiently explicit to show
just how he did it, his general conception of the problem and the
practical results he claims for his findings are significant:

> By means of the cumulative advertising formula developed in
> this case, it proved feasible to determine in a rather general
> fashion the value of cumulative advertising effect in terms of
> current expenditure.   It is also possible to say how rapidly
> the advertising effect will diminish if not replenished and what
> rate of current expenditure is required to maintain that rate of
> equilibrium.[48]

Another version of this method is a simple comparison of sales
in different areas where advertising has differed significantly, but
where other dynamic factors that affect sales have been about the
same.   Accidentally created data occasionally make such comparisons possible.   Another simple approach that is occasionally
possible is to isolate a burst of sales growth that is associated
historically with intensified advertising and not attributable to
other dynamic variables.

Unfortunately, however, historical data that are produced accidentally are not often adequate for estimating the firm's incremental advertising costs.   Instead, data must usually be created
by controlled experiments.   Indeed, this is the most promising
approach to the measurement problem.   It is likely to be a costly
one but the stakes are high.   The experiment must be designed to
overcome the difficulties discussed above and any other difficulties
peculiar to the product or the company.[49]   Correlation or variance analysis is often needed to get valid findings, even from
controlled data.

Short of a completely controlled experiment, there are a number
of intermediate approaches that have promise.

Advertising that permits keyed responses (e.g., direct mail or
coupon clippers) usually makes measurement of results com-

---

[48] *Ibid.,* page 8.

[49] See William Applebaum and Richard F. Spears, "Controlled Experimentation
in Marketing Research," *Journal of Marketing,* January, 1950, pp. 505–517, for an
examination of methods and limitations of controlled experiments.

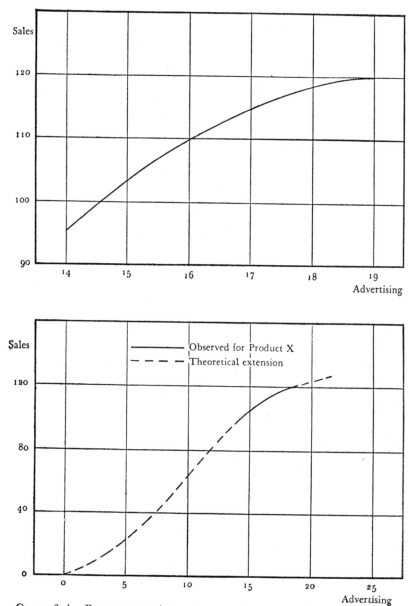

CHART 6–4. RELATION OF ADVERTISING TO SALES FOR A PROPRIETARY DRUG, OBSERVED AND GENERALIZED. (Source: Sidney Hollander, "A Rationale for Advertising Expenditures," *Harvard Business Review*, January, 1949.)

paratively easy, for reasons discussed in Section II. Though results are distorted by outside influences, and "inquiries" have to be converted into sales, a fairly satisfactory estimate of marginal advertising costs can often be obtained here.

Another method is to vary advertising outlay systematically among areas and to compare the first differences in sales (i.e., the percentage increases and decreases). This method was tried with some success by a chain finance company. Local advertising was manipulated systematically in selected areas; and quarterly first differences in advertising were correlated with quarterly first differences in business, lagged one quarter. Although the scatter was great, an increment selling cost relationship was discernible.[50]

A different attack is to study the behavior of the firm's market share as related to its share of outlay. By systematically varying the firm's proportion of the total outlay by major rivals, and by studying its impact upon the firm's market share (with lag corrections if possible), it may be possible to eliminate the effect of "other factors" and also to allow for the dilution of reader attention and for rivals' gains that come with more advertising by the whole industry. The hazard of willfully letting market share drop might be mitigated if this kind of research were conducted on the basis of numerous small territorial samples.

A kindred approach is to manipulate the advertising outlay over a fairly narrow range and see how much is needed to hold market share. For example, an oil company has inadvertently done some experimenting of this type and has come to the conclusion that when advertising falls below x cents a gallon, it loses market share; when it rises above that amount, its gains in market share are dubious and costly.

Another kind of analysis is to study rates of growth that result from a manipulation of advertising. This approach has normally worked best on an area basis. Sometimes small areas can be found whose past pattern of sales is highly similar to the national pattern or to the pattern of other small areas. By systematically varying the amount of advertising in these areas, the effects upon the patterns of sales growth can be studied. It is not uncommon to test alternative copy and media in this way. But this general

---

[50] For other applications of this approach, see H. R. Tosdal, *Problems in Sales Management*, New York, McGraw-Hill Book Co., 1939: "Colwell Co.," pp. 369–375; "Dressler Co.," pp. 382–386; "Beckett Co.," pp. 386–391.

approach can also be used to measure the effects of different total outlays.

Direct surveys of advertising effect by questionnaire are expensive and by no means infallible. But if carefully done they may yield a rich fund of data for economic analysis. An example of the kind of information that can be found is a statistical study by Banks, applied, in this case, to a comparison of media.[51] The study illustrates the marginal approach to determining optimum advertising media. Using data provided by *Life* magazine studies for 1938–1941, Banks calculated the incremental cost of enlarging the circle of readers (translated into "rememberers") by means of additional magazines and by means of additional issues of the same magazine. A rising incremental selling cost was found.

Summary

Measuring the effects of advertising is a question of estimating sales with and without the outlay, everything else remaining constant. The empirical problem is, then, one of comparing alternative situations, and this can be done by observing either several companies at the same time or one company at several times. Since empirical data show the net effect of changes in all demand determinants, the big problem is to isolate the effects of advertising. Although analysis of advertising effects is not essentially different from analysis of the effects of other demand determinants, there are greater ranges of uncertainty because of the uneven quality of advertising. Dollar outlay is thus quite inaccurate as a measure of advertising effort. There is, moreover, a diffuse time lag in both the intended and actual fruition of advertising that is usually harder to judge for advertising than for changes in prices and styling.

Research on the economic effects of advertising is a principal hope for more scientific determination of the advertising appropriation, for better cyclical timing of outlays, and for better apportionment of a given outlay among products, areas, and media.

---

[51] Seymour Banks, "The Use of Incremental Analysis in the Selection of Advertising Media," *Journal of Business of the University of Chicago,* Oct. 1946, pp. 232–243.

Chapter 7

BASIC PRICE

I. INTRODUCTION
PURPOSE AND SCOPE
KINDS OF PRICING PROBLEMS
SYSTEMATIC ATTACK ON PRICING
Pricing Objectives
Pricing Theory
Pricing Research
Pricing Policies
KINDS OF COMPETITIVE SITUATIONS

II. PRICING PRODUCTS OF LASTING DISTINCTIVENESS
ECONOMIC THEORY FOR MONOPOLY PRICING
Econometric Problems
POTENTIAL COMPETITION
SUBSTITUTE COMPETITION
SUMMARY

III. PRICING PRODUCTS OF PERISHABLE DISTINCTIVE-NESS
DETERIORATION OF A PRODUCT'S DISTINCTIVENESS
Elements of a Cycle
Speed of Degeneration
STEPS IN PIONEER PRICING
Estimate of Demand
Decision on Market Targets
Design of Promotional Strategy
Choice of Channels of Distribution
POLICIES FOR PIONEER PRICING
Skimming Price
Penetration Price
PRICING IN MATURITY
SUMMARY

IV. PRICING STANDARD PRODUCTS WHEN COMPETITORS ARE FEW
INTRODUCTION
Importance of Oligopoly Pricing
THE PRICING PROBLEM OF OLIGOPOLY
NON-PRICE COMPETITION
PRICE LEADERSHIP
Requirements for Leadership Pricing
Qualifications of Price Leader
Problems of the Price Leader

Basic Price

I. INTRODUCTION

FROM THE FIRM'S-EYE VIEW, modern competitive activities are of three sorts: (1) product improvement (and innovation); (2) sales promotion; and (3) pricing.   The interdependence, as well as the existence of this trilogy, needs to be recognized in approaching pricing problems.   Product strategy is discussed in Chapter 3 and promotional strategy in Chapter 6.

In this and the next two chapters we shall outline a systematic attack upon some important pricing problems from the standpoint of the seller.   In doing so we develop a philosophy of price-making and implement it by indicating how economic analysis and marketing research can be used to improve practical pricing.

Purpose and Scope

The scope of this analysis is restricted in several respects: (1) It is confined to the pricing policies of manufacturers.   Price problems of wholesalers and retailers are considered only in so far as they affect the policies and decisions of manufacturers. (2) It deals only with those manufacturers who are sufficiently independent in their competitive position to have a significant degree of discretion in setting prices.   Usually this means that products are substantially differentiated or that sellers of a standardized product are few.   (3) It places chief emphasis upon the problems of the multiple-product firm.   Most modern firms make several products, yet formal economic theory has usually dealt only with single-product manufacturers.

In this introduction we shall sketch a general approach to price-making by outlining a breakdown of pricing problems, suggesting a systematic attack on pricing, and examining briefly the kinds of competitive situations that are important for practical pricing.

Kinds of Pricing Problems

To systematize our analysis, we have classified the principal pricing problems of a manufacturer as follows:

1. Basic price: determination of the company's price level or basic price, including its adaptation to cyclical fluctuations.

2. Product-line pricing: determination of the relation among prices of members of a product line.

3. Price discount structures: determination of the structure of price discounts and allowances, including differentials for distribution channel quantity, geographical location, terms of payment, and the like.

The first problem will be discussed in this chapter; the second and third problems will be discussed in the next two chapters.

What is meant by "price level" of a company that makes many products? It may be thought of as an average of the net prices of its individual products. It thus corresponds in concept to a price index: it reflects some weighted average of (frequently) divergent price movements. Thus, in December, 1949, the 4 per cent price increase in steel was the net effect of a complete readjustment, with a rise in sheet prices, no change in stainless steel prices, and a drop in the price of exported steels.

When one product dominates the line, or when all products are related to the price of a single basic product by constant price differentials, then the notion of a "basic price" can supplant the more nebulous concept of price level. A basic price of this kind corresponds in benchmark properties to the price of wheat on the Chicago grain exchange, where a single quotation can be translated into actual prices of specific grades of wheat by a fixed formula.

The firm's price level may also be measured in terms of the level of aggregate profits produced by the prices. In a sense, this is a price index weighted with profits. In public utility regulation, for example, pricing problems are put in two groups: (1) rate level, where the concern is that aggregate earnings shall not be "unreasonable"; and (2) rate structure, where regulatory attention is concentrated on prevention of "undue discrimination."

Since practical pricing problems generally arise in a cyclical setting, adaptation to the business cycle must be considered in solving them. Although cyclical changes can be made through impromptu adjustments and informal concessions on individual sales, this chapter discusses a group of alternative explicit policies that can be formulated to meet the cyclical problem.

But sales revenue depends not only on list prices, but also on the use that is made of discount structures in the terms of individual sales, and on the proportion of sales of various products. A company's price level is the net effect of these dimensions of price structure. Discount structures and product lines are often designed for promotional or cost-saving effects, or for price discrimination, as contrasted with the basic revenue-generating role of the price level itself. They are therefore discussed in separate chapters because they involve distinct strategic and analytical problems. Patterns of prices for related articles are studied in Chapter 8, "Product-Line Pricing," and the structure of discounts associated with circumstances of sale in Chapter 9, "Price Differentials."

Systematic Attack on Pricing

A systematic approach to pricing requires not only a logical classification of pricing problems, but also an explicit conception of pricing objectives, pricing theory, pricing research, and formulation of price policy.

Pricing Objectives

Since pricing is not an end in itself, but a means to an end, an explicit formulation of the company's pricing objectives is essential. The fundamental guides to pricing are the company's over-all goals. Normally, the broadest of these is survival. Most companies will tolerate all kinds of upheaval in product lines, organization, and even personnel, if necessary, to assure continued existence. But on a more specific level, company objectives relate to rate of growth, market shares, maintenance of control or of ownership, and independence of operations, as well as making money. Since these goals may not always be compatible, a major problem is to sketch out long-range plans that will reconcile them. Such plans call for decisions on the types of products and market areas to attack, in terms of income brackets, geography, distribution channels, and cyclical volatility.

Price policy starts at this point by deciding how prices, as one of the company's weapons, are to be used in the over-all strategy. For example, a policy choice as to general level of price in relation to competitors ("premium pricing" vs. "chiseling") must be coordinated with company goals in respect to quality and services built into the product, and with consideration of long-run demand elasticities, cross-elasticities, and the nature of potential competition.

Pricing Theory

The main applications of economic theory to practical pricing are, first, to pick concepts of demand, competition and cost that are relevant to each kind of pricing problem, and second, to design research projects for getting quantitative estimates of these concepts. Economic theory also throws some light on the social and economic desirability of various pricing policies, a consideration that is frequently important in private pricing decisions and a primary concern of public policy.

Pricing Research

Pricing research yields information on the structure of competition, the behavior of the firm's costs, and the characteristics of demand. Modern techniques of economic and statistical analysis can improve the accuracy of estimates and predictions of critical pricing factors. Still, research attacks on pricing are not yet very common. There are understandable reasons for this. First, professional economists have only recently given much attention to the executives' problems of private pricing policy. They have been preoccupied with the measurement and explanation of the behavior of the entire economic system of prices; they have studied prices primarily from the viewpoint of public policy. Second, since the factors that should govern pricing decisions are highly complex and dynamic, a purely scientific analysis may be too complicated to carry out. Moreover, many of them are not susceptible to accurate measurement and prediction.

Pricing Policies

A pricing policy is a standing answer to recurring questions. A systematic approach to pricing requires that decisions on individual pricing situations be generalized and codified into a policy coverage of all the principal pricing problems. Policies can and should be tailored to various competitive situations. Du Pont, for example, has different pricing policies to meet the different structures of its various markets. Nylon and other innovations over which du Pont has great price jurisdiction, have been priced as specialties while they were sheltered competitively. Cellophane, however, has been aggressively priced for market expansion, with drastic reductions in price. And sulphuric acid, which is sold under conditions of undifferentiated oligopoly (see Section IV), is priced to meet all comers.

A policy approach, which is becoming normal for other sales activities, is comparatively rare in pricing. Most well-managed manufacturing enterprises have a clear-cut advertising policy, product policy, customer policy, and distribution-channel policy. But pricing decisions remain a patchwork of *ad hoc* decisions. In many otherwise well-managed firms, price policy has been dealt with on a crisis basis. This kind of price management by catastrophe discourages the kind of systematic analysis needed for clearcut pricing policies.

The following proposals, considered by a large manufacturer of machinery, illustrate what is meant by pricing policy:

1. Prices should aim at maximizing profits for the entire product line, i.e., they should stimulate profitable combination sales.

2. Prices should be set to promote the long-range welfare of the firm, e.g., to discourage competition from entering the field.

3. Prices should be adapted and individualized to fit the diverse competitive situations encountered by different products.

4. Pricing policies should be flexible enough to meet changes in economic conditions of the various customer industries.

5. A predetermined and systematic method of pricing new products should be provided.

6. Replacement parts prices should be determined from an organized classification of parts by type and manufacture.

Kinds of Competitive Situations

Since different competitive situations require quite different pricing, good solutions for pricing problems require an understanding of the competitive environment in which the company sells its various products.

In pure competition, sellers have no pricing problems because they have no price discretion; they sell at the market price or not at all. Price policy has practical significance only when there is a considerable degree of imperfection in competition, so that sellers can make some sales in spite of disparities with competitors' prices.

In our analysis of pricing, we shall be concerned with only those kinds of competitive structures that are thus marked by a zone of price discretion.[1] How much price discretion a seller has depends on a number of conditions:

(1) The number, relative sizes, and product lines of competitors who sell products to do the same job.

(2) The likelihood of potential competition.

(3) The stage of consumer acceptance of the product.

(4) The degree of potential market segmentation and price discrimination (see Chapter 8, "Product-Line Pricing").

(5) The degree of physical difference between the seller's product and those of other companies.

(6) The opportunities for variation in the product-service bundle.

(7) The richness of the mixture of service and reputation in the product bundle.

Competitive situations that raise policy problems of pricing can be classified on the basis of the kind of product. The important situations are those where the product has: (1) lasting distinctiveness; (2) perishable distinctiveness; (3) little distinctiveness and a few competitive sellers. The first two situations occur where the individual seller's product is differentiated enough to have some of the characteristics of pure monopoly demand.

The dividing line between differentiated products and homogeneous products is drawn on the basis of the buyer's attitude, that is, in terms of cross-elasticity of demand (discussed in Chapter 4, Section II). If one product can be sold at a premium (or a discount) without disrupting competitors' prices or sales, the product is distinctive from an economic viewpoint, regardless of its physical nature. To be sure, all sellers have some degree of monopoly power, stemming from geographical or personal advantages, but one can arbitrarily set some level of cross-elasticity, above which products are similar and below which they are distinctive.

The distinction between lasting and perishable price discretion is made in terms of the probability that the seller's monopoly

---

1 For an analysis of these and other types of competitive situations, see Chapter 2, "Competition."

power will in the future deteriorate because of competitive encroachments (see Section III).

In the third competitive situation in which price policy has practical importance, the product does not differ dramatically from products of rival sellers, but the number of rivals is small and each watches the others closely. Where a few competitors dominate the supply of a fairly uniform product, changes in relative price produce big shifts in market share. This competitive situation is referred to in economic writings as oligopoly (or homogeneous oligopoly). In this situation, there is no such thing as a demand function for an individual firm. The quantity that it will sell at various prices depends upon the competitors' reactions to those prices, which may be hard to forecast.

The dividing line between oligopoly competition and the competitive situations where each seller has a distinctive product (sometimes called monopolistic competition) is also hazy, since there are varying degrees of product differentiation. Cement, steel, aluminum, and gasoline, for example, call for oligopoly pricing policies, whereas machine tools and locomotives raise problems of monopoloid pricing.

Most multiple-product firms typically sell different products under different competitive conditions. Moreover, one firm often sells the same product at the same time in several markets that differ in competitive characteristics, and these characteristics themselves change with the turnover in sellers and product types.

II. PRICING PRODUCTS OF LASTING DISTINCTIVENESS

Products of lasting distinctiveness are extremely rare in the economy, if "lasting" means more than ten years, and "distinctiveness" means no acceptable substitutes. Although it is frequently possible to build up a fairly long-run monopoly position in a single product, an unrestrained mining of the profits inevitably stirs outsiders into an intense search for substitutes and imitations. Control of scarce mineral deposits is one of the strongest bastions of monopoly, but in copper and tin, for instance, monopoly power that was established with strenuous political effort was constantly harassed by new discoveries of ore that could be profitably mined at the ruling price. Metallurgical and chemical progress, furthermore, have found entire arrays of substitute materials that displace monopolized metals at various price levels. Patents have also proven a shaky barrier to competitive entry. Many industries have found that inadequacies of patent protection make it more profitable to pool technical advances among firms than to try to exploit individual discoveries. It is often best to assume, therefore, that new products that are distinctive at the outset will inevitably degenerate over the years into common commodities with the entry of competition. The pricing of such short-lived specialties is the subject of Section III.

Before dealing with other problems on a practical level, it is worth while to examine pricing theory for the pure long-run monopoly, since it illuminates a few factors relevant in the short-run case as well. It may be taken as a first approximation to reality where long-run consequences are ignored.

By "pure" monopoly, we do not refer to the arid ideal of absence of all substitutes; instead, we refer to a company whose products' substitutes are so distant and scattered that its sales depend on its own price level and on economic conditions, but are not affected by prices of any other particular group of sellers. Although the company's price level may affect the actions of substitute competition, these are only fringe effects that chip away at the marginal buyers. "Pure" monopoly thus contrasts not only with pure competition, where no sales are possible above the selling price and where no individual company's actions are especially important, but it contrasts also with oligopoly where each seller is vitally interested in the policies of each other seller.

Economic Theory for Monopoly Pricing

Chart 7–1 shows in simple form the traditional economic approach to monopoly pricing. The demand schedule for the distinctive product of the monopolist is shown in revenue functions of three forms: total revenue, average unit revenue, and marginal revenue. The behavior of cost in respect to output is also diagrammed in comparable forms. The problem as conceived by the theorist is to find the price and the rate of output (determined by the price) that will maximize profits.

In section (A) of Chart 7–1, TR shows the seller's total revenue per month (or other time-unit) for various output rates, and TC shows the total cost of producing the indicated outputs. The point of maximum total profit is an output of 300,000 units per

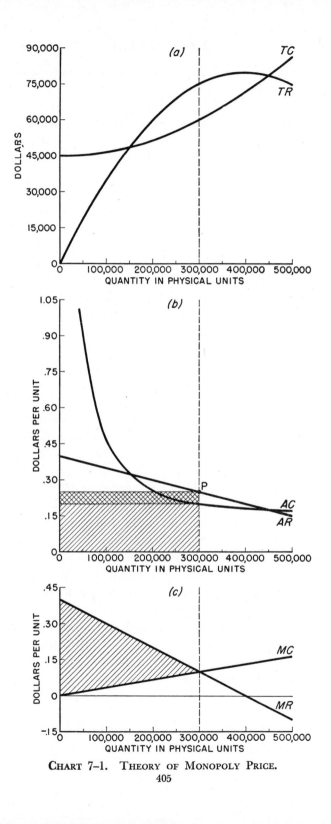

CHART 7–1. THEORY OF MONOPOLY PRICE.

month, where the spread between the total revenue and the total cost curve is greatest ($15,000).

In section (B), AR shows the same demand curve in the form of average revenue per unit (price) associated with a series of output rates. AC is the corresponding average unit cost curve. The price that will maximize profits (25¢) can be determined from this diagram by finding the unit profit which, when multiplied by output, gives the largest total profit, as indicated by the crosshatched area of the rectangle in the diagram ($15,000).

Section (C) shows the same demand and cost behavior in marginal form. MR depicts the additional revenue produced by the sale of an additional unit at each output rate. Similarly, MC shows, for the relevant range of output, the additional cost of making an additional unit. The point of maximum profit is the output rate at which marginal cost and marginal revenue are equal (10¢). The triangular area between the two marginal curves equals contribution profits, the excess of total revenue over incremental costs (in this case, $60,000). Deducting the fixed cost ($45,000) gives net profits ($15,000).

The main contributions to practical pricing of this kind of theoretical analysis are to point out the kinds of demand and cost relations that need to be guessed, and to show how these functional relations should be used to indicate the most profitable price.

This solution is logical enough so far as it goes, but it doesn't go very far. It shouldn't be taken very literally in practice as a description or a prescription. A major qualification of its usefulness is the restraints on profit maximization as a pricing objective. These restraints, which are partly political, are discussed in Chapter 1 ("Profits"). On even purely economic grounds, however, the solution is oversimplified and difficult to apply. For the pure monopoly situation assumed here, there are formidable econometric problems of estimating the demand and cost curves. For more provisional monopolies, the analysis cannot take account of potential competition and the reactions of substitute competitors, or of the effects on future prices or patronage, all of which are vital factors in most monopoly pricing problems.

Econometric Problems

This approach obviously requires usable estimates of demand and cost. Since demand analysis is discussed in general terms in

Chapter 4, it is necessary here only to point out that monopoly pricing raises particularly tough problems in this field. In demand analysis for competitive selling, the range of relevant prices is usually very narrow, since the general level of prices is set by cost conditions in the industry. The monopolist has a far wider discretion in setting prices, and finding the best one calls for estimates of the effect of price volume over a wide and dubious price range. Such estimates require elaborate research of the kinds suggested in Chapter 4 (in correlation analysis, survey questionnaires, and controlled experiments).

In general, the elasticity of demand is much lower for short-run estimates than for any relevant long period (aside from speculative reactions). The short-run decline in demand as price increases reflects principally the consumer's decision to do without, but with some time allowance for adjustments, it reflects also the switch to substitutes that become practical as prices increase. Similarly, price cuts produce responses in demand that increase with time. They depend on cultural lags, on the amount of capital investment needed to take full advantage of the new price, and on the rate at which substitute competition is excluded from the market as prices fall.

But no demand curve, for whatever time span, can take account of the full range of reaction to price changes in terms of speculative buying, emotional and political ire, and substitute improvements that may appear. A price change of any kind has a tendency to stir up inquiries and new ideas about the monopoly, and for this reason, many monopolists have preferred to maintain rigid prices for years at a time rather than to maximize short-run profits; that is, they consciously ignore changes in conditions for any period short enough to put into this kind of demand—supply diagram.[2]

To get the cost side of the price picture requires estimates of future cost behavior. Such forecasts require knowledge of the functional relation of cost to operating conditions, such as output rate, scale of plant, prices of labor and materials, and technology. They also require projections of these operating conditions themselves. Estimates of these functional relations can, in many situ-

---

[2] George J. Stigler, "The Kinky Oligopoly Demand Curve and Rigid Prices," *Journal of Political Economy*, Vol. LV (October, 1947), No. 5.

ations, be obtained by statistical and engineering studies of cost behavior, such as those described in Chapter 5 ("Costs"). It should be recognized, however, that such cost curves are expensive and relatively transitory, and that they do not touch the problem of projecting into the future the operating conditions themselves.

As we have seen, the practical pricing problem of a monopolist is usually to find a price that he can keep for long periods under varying conditions of demand. This calls for cost forecasts that cover a range of factor prices, and even encompass some technical progress and product improvement.

Thus, the theorist's solution to the monopoly pricing problem is apparently quite inadequate for any real case of long-run monopoly, first, because the curves as conceived are difficult to approximate in practice and, second, because even in the pure monopoly case, there are far more dimensions to the problem than can be comprehended in the two-dimensional conception.

Potential Competition

But the theoretical solution misses much more of the pricing problem when long-run monopoly is provisional rather than permanent. A provisional monopoly often springs from striking innovations (e.g., nylon or punched-card accounting). It may, however, grow from an accumulation of technical or selling superiorities, where, once having gained the bulk of the market, the company can make the most of large-scale economies in production, distribution, and research, to hold off potential competition (e.g., G.M.'s Diesel locomotives). Regardless of origin, the demand curve for provisional monopoly must reflect not only the entry of high-cost marginal producers when prices rise, but also the possibility that once having entered the market, such competitors can beat the large-scale economies presently enjoyed only by the dominant firm.

Cost estimates are essential for applying this long-run pricing criterion quantitatively. The cost that is relevant for this purpose is not the seller's own cost, but rather, the cost to a potential new entrant working at the current price level and using the available technology. The profit that is relevant is not unit markup percentage, or the earnings rate of existing firms, but rather the entrants' prospective rate of return on investment. And the investment that is relevant is not confined to production facilities, but should also encompass investment in cumulative advertising and in distribution arrangements required to compete effectively. For example, before World War II, a large manufacturer of branded breakfast food was asked what it would cost to enter his business. He pointed out that the cost of making plants that could produce as cheaply as his would be $2,000,000, whereas the cost of developing a market for selling the output of the plants would be $20,000,000.

The classical economic doctrine is that entry is governed by profit margins over average unit costs. When profits rise above normal entrepreneurial profits new firms are supposed to enter; their entry increases supply, which in turn depresses price and shuts off the entry stimulant. This thermostat approach to potential competition has its limitations under modern conditions. In many industries the important potential competitor is a large, multiple-product firm operating in neighboring industries. For such a firm, the most important consideration for entry is the prospect of large and growing volume of sales. Existing margins over costs are not the dominant consideration. Such firms are normally confident that they can get their costs down as low as competitors if the volume of production is large. Thus, it is the relationship between price and their estimate of their own potential cost that is significant, rather than the margins now being realized in the industry.

Substitute Competition

The theoretical pricing solution is also inadequate when substitute competitors react directly to price changes by changing their own prices. The demand curve in Chart 7–1 can be drawn only on the assumption of a given set of substitute prices. This is a valid approach, so long as the distinctive product is only a minor competitor to each of its substitutes. When this is the case, the product's price changes effect the demand for its substitutes too little to warrant price changes.

In practice, there are usually a few substitutes that are vitally affected, and others that are only remotely so. For instance, aluminum competes very directly with copper on a price basis for use in electrical cable, where the important consideration is cost per unit of capacity. But price is only one of many factors in aluminum's competition with steel and glass for structural and cooking purposes.

When there are close competitors on price for some uses of the product, the demand curve is to this extent indeterminate unless reactions of substitute rivals can be forecast.   This is the oligopoly problem discussed in Section IV, but there are few products, however distinctive, that can ignore rivals' reactions entirely.   Chemical companies, for instance, in pricing a new product, must consider the possibility that old products thereby made obsolete will resist displacement by reducing prices down to their incremental cost.

Summary

In pricing a sharply differentiated product whose distinctiveness promises to be fairly permanent, it is desirable to start with the economist's theoretical solution for the monopoly pricing problem.   Despite its omission of important pricing considerations, this model shows what kinds of estimates of demand and cost behavior are needed, and how the price that will maximize immediate profits can be selected.   The next step is to make the econometric estimates needed to project this maximum-profit price.   As a first approximation, projections of the future short-run behavior of costs can be used in conjunction with estimates of the firm's demand schedule to indicate the price that promises greatest immediate profit.   But this provisional solution must be modified: (1) by estimates of the effect of today's prices on future sales;   (2) by estimates of the effect of prices upon the entry of potential competitors; and   (3) by estimates of the long-run effects of the prices of substitutes.

III. PRICING PRODUCTS OF PERISHABLE DISTINCTIVENESS

In the pricing situation just examined, the possibility that competitive inroads would curtail monopoly jurisdiction over price was relatively remote.   Usually, however, the probability of progressive competitive degeneration of a monopoly's position enters importantly into pricing strategy.   New products have a protected distinctiveness which is doomed to progressive degeneration from competitive inroads.   Before discussing this pricing problem itself, we shall examine the character of this degeneration.

Deterioration of a Product's Distinctiveness

The tendency toward a cycle of competitive degeneration is quite general. The invention of a new marketable specialty is usually followed by a period of patent protection when markets are still hesitant and unexplored and when product design is fluid. Then comes a period of rapid expansion of sales as market acceptance is gained. Next the product becomes a target for competitive encroachment. New competitors enter the field, and innovations narrow the gap of distinctiveness between the product and its substitutes. The seller's zone of pricing discretion narrows as his distinctive "specialty" fades into a pedestrian "commodity" that is so little differentiated from other products that the seller has limited independence in pricing, even if rivals are few.

Throughout the cycle, continual changes occur in promotional and price elasticity and in costs of production and distribution. These changes call for adjustments in price policy.

Elements of Cycle

Appropriate pricing over the cycle depends on the development of three different aspects of maturity, which usually move in approximately parallel time paths: (1) technical maturity, indicated by declining rate of product development, increasing standardization among brands, and increasing stability of manufacturing processes and knowledge about them; (2) market maturity, indicated by consumer acceptance of the basic service-idea, by widespread belief that the products of most manufacturers will perform satisfactorily, and by enough familiarity and sophistication to permit consumers to compare brands competently; and (3) competitive maturity, indicated by increasing stability of market shares and price structures.

Of course, interaction among these components tends to make them move together. That is, intrusion by new competitors helps to develop the market, but entrance is most tempting when the new product appears to be establishing market acceptance.

Speed of Degeneration

The rate at which the cycle of degeneration progresses varies widely among products. What are the factors that set its pace?

An overriding determinant is technical—the extent to which the economic environment must be reorganized to use the innovation effectively. The scale of plant investment and technical research called forth by the telephone, electric power, the automobile, or air transport makes for a long gestation period, as compared with even such major innovations as cellophane or frozen foods. Development comes fastest when the new gadget fills a new vacuum made to order for it. Electric stoves, another example, have risen to 50 per cent market saturation in the fast-growing Pacific Northwest, where electric power has become the lowest-cost energy. Products still in early developmental stages also provide rich opportunities for product differentiation, which with heavy research costs, hold off competitive degeneration.

But aside from technical factors, the rate of degeneration is controlled by economic forces that can be subsumed under (1) rate of market acceptance, and (2) ease of entry.

By "market acceptance" is meant the extent to which buyers consider the product a serious alternative to other ways of performing the same service. Market acceptance is a frictional factor caused by cultural lags, and may endure for some time after quality and costs make products technically useful. The slow catch-on of the electric garbage-disposal unit is an example. On the other hand, the attitude of acceptance may exist long before any workable model can be developed; then the final appearance of the product will produce an explosive growth curve in sales. The anti-histamine cold tablet, a spectacular example, reflected the national faith in chemistry's ability to vanquish the common cold. And, of course, low unit cost may speed market acceptance of an innovation. Ball-point pens and all-steel houses started at about the same time.

Ease of competitive entry is a major determinant of the speed of degeneration of a specialty. An illustration is found in the washing machine business before the war, where with little basic patent protection the Maytag position was quickly eroded by small manufacturers who performed essentially an assembly operation. The ball-point pen cascaded from a twelve-dollar novelty to a 49-cent football, partly because entry barriers of patents and techniques were ineffective. Frozen orange juice, which started as a protected specialty of Minute-Maid is speeding through its competitive cycle.

At the outset, the innovator can control the rate of competitive deterioration to an important degree by non-price as well as by price strategies. Through successful research in product improvement he can protect his specialty position both by extending the life of his basic patent and by keeping ahead of competitors in product development.[3] Ease of entry is also affected by a policy of stay-out pricing, which may, under some circumstances, slow down the process of competitive encroachment.

Steps in Pioneer Pricing

Pricing problems start when a company finds a product that is a radical departure from existing ways of performing a service and that is temporarily protected from competition by patents, secrets of production, control of a scarce resource, or by other barriers. The seller here has a wide range of pricing discretion resulting from extreme product differentiation.[4] To get a picture of how he should go about setting his price, we shall describe the main steps of the process (of course the classification is arbitrary and the steps are interrelated):

1. Estimate of demand.
2. Decision on market targets.
3. Design of promotional strategy.
4. Choice of channels of distribution.

Estimate of Demand

Pioneer products present more difficult estimating problems than a relatively stable monopoly because the product is beyond the experience of buyers and because its distinctiveness is perishable. How can demand for new products be explored? How can we find out how much people will pay for a product that has never before been seen or used?

---

[3] The record of the International Business Machines punch-card equipment illustrates this potentiality.

[4] A good example of pricing latitude conferred by protected superiority of product is provided by the McGraw Electric Company's "Toastmaster," which, both initially and over a period of years, was able to command a very substantial price premium over competitive toasters. Apparently this advantage resulted from (1) a good product that was distinctive and superior, and (2) substantial and skillful sales promotion. Similarly, Sunbeam priced its electric iron two dollars above comparable models of major firms with considerable success. And Sunbeam courageously priced its new metal coffee-maker at $32.00, much above competitive makes of glass coffee-makers, but it was highly successful.

The problem of estimating demand for a new product can be broken into a series of sub-problems: (1) whether the product will go at all (if price is in a competitive range); (2) what range of price will make the product economically attractive to buyers; (3) what sales volumes can be expected at various points in this price range; and (4) what reaction price will evoke from producers of displaced substitutes.

The first step is an exploration of the *preferences and educability of consumers,* and of the technical feasibility of the new product. How many potential buyers are there? Is the product a practical device for meeting their needs? How can we improve it to meet their needs better? What proportion of the potential buyers would prefer this product to already existing products (prices equal)? For example, is the basic idea of an aluminum pipe wrench, that will weigh a fraction of the conventional wrench, compatible with plumbers' folkways?

Sometimes it is feasible to start with the assumption that all vulnerable substitutes will be fully displaced. For example, to get some idea of the maximum limits of demand for a new type of reflecting-sign material, the company started with estimates of the aggregate number and area of auto license plates, highway markers, railroad operational signs, and street name signs. Next, the proportion of each category needing night-light reflection was guessed. For example, only rural and suburban homes could benefit by this kind of name-sign.

It is not uncommon and possibly not unrealistic for a manufacturer to make the blithe assumption at this stage that the product price will be "within a competitive range," without having much idea of what that range is.[5]

The second step is marking out this *competitive range of price.* Vicarious pricing experience can be secured by interviewing selected distributors who have enough comparative knowledge of customers' alternatives and preferences to judge what price range would make the new product "a good value." Direct discussions with samples of experienced industrial users have produced re-

---

[5] For example, in developing a new type of camera equipment, one of the electrical companies judged its acceptability to professional photographers by technical performance without making any inquiry into its economic value. When the equipment was later placed in an economic setting, the indications were that sales would be negligible at any price that would be worth while to the company.

liable estimates of the "practical" range of prices. Manufacturers of electrical equipment often explore the economic as well as the technical feasibility of a new product by sending engineers with blueprints and models to see customers, such as technical and operating executives.

In guessing the price range of a radically new consumers' product of small unit value, the concept of barter equivalent can be a useful research guide.[6] But asking prospective consumers how much they think they would be willing to pay for a new product is unlikely to give a reliable indication of the demand schedule. People don't know what they would pay. It depends partly on their incomes and on future alternatives. Early in the postwar period a manufacturer of television sets tried this method and got highly erratic and apparently unreliable results, because the distortion of war shortages kept prospective buyers from fully visualizing the multiple alternative ways of spending their money. Another deficiency, which, however, may be less serious than it appears, is that responses are biased by the consumer's confused notion that he is bargaining for a good price. Not until techniques of depth interviewing are more refined can this crude and direct method of exploring a new product's demand schedule hold much promise of being accurate.

While inquiries of this sort are often much too short-run to give any real indication of consumer tastes, the relevant point here is that even such rough probing often yields broad impressions of price elasticity, particularly in relation to product variations such as styling, placing of controls, and use of automatic features. It may show, for example, that $5.00 of cost put into streamlining or chromium stripping can add $50 to the price.

The third step, a more definite inquiry into the *probable sales from several possible prices,* starts with an investigation of the prices of substitutes. Usually the buyer has a choice of existing ways of having the same service performed; an analysis of the costs

---

[6] For example, a manufacturer of paper specialties tested a dramatic new product in the following fashion: A wide variety of consumer products totally unlike the new product were purchased and spread out on a big table. Consumers selected the products they would swap for the new product. By finding out whether the product would trade even for a dish pan, a towel, or a hairpin, the executives got a rough idea of what range of prices might strike the typical consumer as reasonable in the light of the values she could get for her money in totally different kinds of expenditures.

of these alternatives serves as a guide in setting the price for a new way. Comparisons are easy and significant for industrial customers who have a costing system to tell them the exact value, for example, of a fork-lift truck in terms of warehouse labor saved. Indeed, chemical companies setting up a research project to displace an existing material often know from the start the top price that can be charged for the new substitute in terms of cost of the present material. But the comparison is usually obfuscated by the presence of quality differences that may be important bases for price premiums. This is most true for household appliances, where the alternative is an unknown amount of labor of a mysterious value. In pricing a cargo parachute, the alternatives are: (1) free fall (padded box from a plane flown close to the ground, (2) landing the plane, (3) back shipment by land from a distant air terminal, or (4) land shipment all the way. These alternatives differ widely in their service value and are not very useful pricing guides. It is hard to know how much good will be done by making the new product cheaper than the old by various amounts, or how much the market will be restricted by making the new product more expensive. The answers usually come from experiment or research.

One appliance manufacturer tried out new products on a sample of employees by selling to them at deep discounts, with the stipulation that they could if they wished return the products at the end of the experiment period and get a refund of their low purchase price. Demand for frozen orange juice was tested by placing it in several markets at a range of three different prices all lower than the equivalent price of fresh fruit, but the result showed rather low price elasticity.

The fourth step in estimating demand is to consider the *possibility of retaliation* by the manufacturers of displaced substitutes, by price cutting. This development may not occur at all if the new product displaces only a small market segment, but if old industries do fight it out, their incremental costs provide a floor to the resulting price competition and should be brought into price plans.[7]

---

[7] For example, a manufacturer of black-and-white sensitized paper studied the possibility that lowering his price would displace blueprint paper substantially. Not only did he study the prices of blueprint paper, but he also estimated the out-of-pocket cost of making it, because of the probability that blueprint paper manufacturers would fight back by reducing prices toward the level of their incremental costs.

Decision on Market Targets

When the company has developed some idea of the range
of demand and prices that are feasible for the new product, it
is in a position to make some basic strategic decisions on market targets and promotional plans. To decide on market objectives requires answers to several questions: What ultimate
market share is wanted in the new product? How does it fit
into the present product line? Production methods? Distribution channels? These are questions of joint costs in production
and distribution, of plant expansion outlays, and of potential
competition. If entry is easy the company may not be eager to
disrupt its present production and selling operations to capture
and hold a large slice of the new market. But if the prospective
profits shape up to a substantial new income source, it will be
worth while to make the capital expenditures on plant needed to
reap the full harvest.

A basic factor in answering all these questions is the expected
behavior of production and distribution costs. The relevant
data here are all the production outlays that will be made after
the decision day—the capital expenditures as well as the variable
costs. A go-ahead decision won't be made without some assurance that these costs can be recovered before the product becomes
a football in the market. Many different projections of costs will
be made, depending on the alternative scales of output, rate of
market expansion, threats of potential competition, and measures
to meet that competition that are under consideration. But these
factors and the decision that is made on promotional strategy are
interdependent. The fact is that this is a circular problem that
in theory can only be solved by simultaneous equations.

Fortunately, it is possible to make some approximations that
can break the circle: Scale economies become significantly different only with broad changes in the size of plant and the type
of production methods. This narrows the range of cost projections to workable proportions. The effects of using different
distribution channels can be guessed fairly well without meshing
the alternatives in with all the production and selling possibilities. The most vulnerable point of the circle is probably the
decision on promotional strategy. The alternatives here are
broad and produce a variety of results. The next step in the
pricing process is therefore a plan for promotion.

Design of Promotional Strategy

Initial promotion outlays are an investment in the product that cannot be recovered until some kind of market has been established. The innovator shoulders the burden of creating a market —educating consumers to the existence and uses of the product. Later imitators will never have to do this job. So if the innovator doesn't want to be a benefactor to his future competitors, he must make pricing plans to recover his initial outlays before his pricing discretion evaporates.

His basic strategic problem is to find the right mixture of price and promotion to maximize his long-run profits. He can choose a relatively high price in pioneering stages, together with extravagant advertising and dealer discounts, and plan to get his promotion costs back early; or he can use low prices and lean margins from the very outset, in order to discourage potential competition when the barriers of patents, distribution channels, or production techniques become inadequate. This question is discussed further below.

Choice of Channels of Distribution

Estimation of the costs of moving the new product through the channels of distribution to the final consumer must enter into the pricing procedure, since these costs govern the factory price that will result in a specified consumer price, and since it is the consumer price that matters for volume. Distributive margins are partly pure promotional costs and partly physical distribution costs. Margins must at least cover distributors' costs of warehousing, handling, and order-taking. These costs are similar to factory production costs in being related to physical capacity and its utilization, i.e., fluctuations in production or sales volume. Hence these set a floor to trade-channel discounts. But distributors usually also contribute promotional effort—in point-of-sale pushing, local advertising, and display—when it is made worth their while.

These pure promotional costs are more optional. Unlike physical handling costs they have no necessary functional relation to sales volume. An added layer of margin in trade discounts to produce this localized sales effort (with a retail price fixed) is an optional way for the manufacturer to spend his prospecting money in putting over a new product.

In establishing promotional costs, the manufacturer must decide on the extent to which the selling effort will be delegated to members of the distribution chain. Indeed, some distribution channels, such as house-to-house selling and retail store selling supplemented by home demonstrators, represent a substantial delegation of the manufacturer's promotional job, and usually involve higher distribution-channel costs than do conventional methods. Rich distributor margins are an appropriate use of promotion funds only when the producer thinks a high price plus promotion is a better expansion policy on the specialty than low price by itself. Thus there is an intimate interaction between the pricing of a new product and the costs and problems of floating it down the distribution channels to the final consumer.

Policies for Pioneer Pricing

The strategic decision in pricing a new product is the choice between: (1) a policy of high initial prices that skim the cream of demand; and (2) a policy of low prices from the outset serving as an active agent for market penetration. Although the actual range of choice is much wider than this, a sharp dichotomy clarifies the issues for consideration.

Skimming Price

For products that represent a drastic departure from accepted ways of performing a service, a policy of relatively high prices coupled with heavy promotional expenditures in the early stages of market development (and lower prices at later stages) has proved successful for many products.[8] There are several reasons for the success of this policy:

(1) Demand is likely to be more inelastic with respect to price in the early stages than it is when the product is full-grown. This is particularly true for consumers' goods. A novel product, such as the electric blanket or the electric garbage-disposal unit, is not yet accepted as a part of the expenditure pattern. Consumers are still ignorant about its value as compared with the value of conventional alternatives. Moreover, at least in the early stages,

---

[8] A rule-of-thumb in the relationship between factory door cost and consumers' price is that the final price to the consumer should be at least three or four times the factory door cost. Such a markup is frequently used to provide adequate margins for the promotional outlays needed for new-product flotation and for anticipated reductions in the retail price as distributor competition intensifies.

the product has so few close rivals that cross-elasticity of demand is low. Promotional elasticity is on the other hand quite high, particularly for products with high unit prices, such as television sets. When customers are pretty much in the dark about what the unfamiliar product can do for them, then education and puffing can be particularly effective in increasing demand.

(2) Launching a new product with a high price is an efficient device for breaking the market up into segments that differ in price elasticity of demand. The initial high price serves to skim the cream of the market that is relatively insensitive to price. Subsequent reductions in the price tap successively more elastic sectors of the market. This pricing strategy is exemplified by the systematic succession of editions of a book, which sometimes start with a fifty-dollar limited personal edition and end up with a twenty-five-cent pocket edition.

(3) The skimming-price policy is safer, or at least appears so. When demand elasticity is unknown, high introductory prices serve as a refusal price (Chapter 8, Section III) during the stage of exploration. That is, the company will not market the product at all unless initial prices cover the early high costs of production and selling—costs that, if success were certain, would be considered part of the investment outlay in the new product.

(4) Many companies are not in a position to finance the product flotation out of distant future revenues. High cash outlays in the early stages result from heavy costs of production and distributor organizing, in addition to the promotional investment in the pioneer product. Even when the effects on market expansion make a low initial price clearly more profitable than a high price, the company may be unwilling or unable to mortgage its future earnings to pay for these early investments. High initial prices thus finance the costs of raising a product family when uncertainties block the usual sources of capital.

Chart 7–2 shows the history of prices of six new drugs from the time that they were introduced up to the end of 1949.

Penetration Price

The alternative policy is to use low prices as the principal instrument for penetrating mass markets early. This policy is the reverse of the skimming-price policy in which price is lowered only as short-run competition forces it. The orthodox skimming

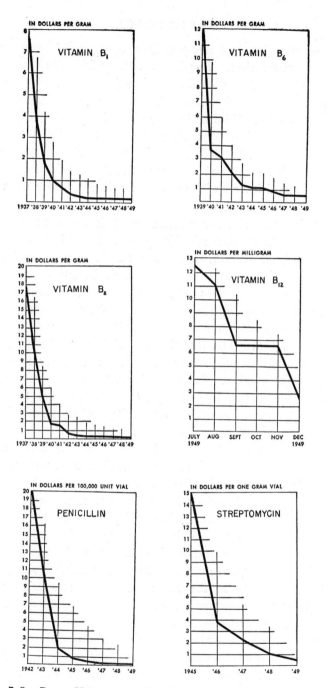

CHART 7–2. PRICE HISTORY OF SIX NEW DRUGS FROM THE TIME THEY WERE INTRODUCED UP TO THE END OF 1949. (Source: Merck & Co., Inc., *A Progress Report on Cortisone*, Rahway, N. J., 1950.)

421

policy has the virtue of safeguarding some profits at every stage of market penetration. But it prevents quick sales to the many buyers at the lower end of the income (or preference) scale who are unwilling to pay any substantial premium for novelty or reputation superiority. The active approach in probing possibilities for market expansion by early penetration pricing requires research, forecasting, and courage. The low-price pattern should be adopted with a view to long-run rather than to short-run profits, with the recognition that it usually takes time to attain the volume potentialities of the market.

A decision to price for market expansion can be reached at various stages in a product's life cycle: before birth, at birth, or in childhood, adulthood, or senescence. The chances for large-volume sales should at least be explored in the early stages of product development research, even before the pilot stage. A more definitive exploration is often called for when the product goes into production and when the price and distribution plans are decided upon. The question of pricing to expand the market will probably arise once again after the product has established an elite market. Some products have been rescued from premature senescence by pricing them low enough to tap new markets. A familiar example is the reissue of important books in twenty-five-cent pocket-sized versions. These have produced not only commercial but intellectual renascence for many authors. The pattern of sales growth of a product that had reached stability in a high priced market has been known to undergo sharp changes when it was suddenly priced low enough to tap new markets. A contrasting illustration of passive policy is the recent pricing experience of the airlines. Although safety considerations and differences in equipment and service cloud the picture, it is pretty clear that the bargain-rate coach fares of scheduled airlines were adopted in reaction to the cut rates of non-scheduled airlines. This competitive response has apparently established a new pattern of traffic growth for the scheduled airlines.

What conditions warrant aggressive pricing for market penetration? This question cannot be answered categorically, but the generalizations that follow may be helpful. First, there should be a high price-elasticity of demand in the short run, i.e., responsiveness of sales to reductions in price should be great. Second, savings in production costs as the result of greater volume should be substantial. This is not a necessary condition, since if elasticity of demand is high enough, pricing for market expansion may be profitable without scale economies. Third, the product must be of such a nature that it will not seem bizarre when it is first fitted into the consumers' expenditure pattern. Fluorescent lighting, which exemplifies these three traits, showed a dramatic growth of sales in response to early penetration pricing. Its 1942 price was about one-third its 1939 price and volume had grown eighteenfold.

A fourth condition that is highly persuasive for penetration pricing is the threat of potential competition. One of the major objectives of most low-pricing policies in the pioneering stages of market development is to raise entry barriers to prospective competitors. But stay-out pricing is not always appropriate; its success depends on the costs of entry for competitors and on the expected size of market. When total demand is expected to be small, the most efficient size of plant may be big enough to supply over half the market. In this case, a low-price policy can capture the bulk of the market and successfully hold back low-cost competition, whereas high prices are an invitation for later comers to invade established markets by selling at discounts. In many industries, however, the important potential competitor is a large, multiple-product firm for whom the product in question is probably marginal. For such a firm, the most important consideration for entry is not existing mark-ons but the prospects of large and growing volume of sales. Present margins over costs are not the dominant consideration because such firms are normally confident that they can get their costs down as low as competitors' costs if the volume of production is large. Thus, when the total market is expected to stay small, potential competitors may not consider the product worth trying, and a high-margin policy can be followed with impunity.

On the other hand, when potential sales appear to be great, there is much to be said for setting prices at their expected long-run level. A big market promises no monopoly in cost savings, and the prime objective of the first entrant is to entrench himself in a market share. Brand preference costs less at the outset than after the competitive promotional clamor has reached full pitch.[9]

---

[9] When a leading soap manufacturer developed an additive that whitened clothes and enhanced the brilliance of colors, the company chose to take its gains

An off-setting consideration is that, if the new product calls for capital recovery over a long period, there is a risk that later entrants will be able to exploit new production techniques which undercut the pioneer's original cost structure.

Profit calculation should recognize all the contributions that market-development pricing can make to the sale of other products and to the long-run future of the company. Often a decision to use development pricing will turn on these considerations of long-term impacts on the firm's total operation strategy rather than on the profits directly attributable to the individual product.

An example of market-expansion pricing is found in the experience of a producer of asbestos shingles. Asbestos shingles have a limited sale in the high-price house market. The company wanted to broaden the market in order to compete effectively with other roofing products for the inexpensive home. It tried to find the price of asphalt shingles that would make the annual cost per unit of roof over a period of years as low as the cheaper roofing that currently commanded the mass market. Indications were that the price would have to be at least this low before volume sales would come. Next, the company explored the relation between production costs and volume, far beyond the range of its own volume experience. Variable costs and overhead costs were estimated separately and the possibilities of a different organization of production were explored. Calculating in terms of anticipated dollars of profit rather than in terms of percentage margin, the company reduced the price of asbestos shingles and brought the annual cost down close to the cost of the cheapest asphalt roof. This reduction produced a greatly expanded volume and secured a substantial share of the mass market.

Pricing in Maturity

To determine what pricing policies are appropriate for later stages in the cycle of market and competitive maturity, we must be able to tell when a product is approaching maturity.

What are the symptoms of degeneration of competitive status toward the commodity level?

---

in market share rather than in a temporary price premium. Such a decision was sound, since the company's competitors could be expected to match or better the product improvement fairly promptly. Under these circumstances, the price premium would have been short-lived, whereas the gains in market share were more likely to be retained.

(1) Weakening in brand preference, which may be evidenced by a higher cross-elasticity of demand among leading products: the leading brand will not stand as much price premium as it started with, without losing position.

(2) Narrowing physical variation among products as the best designs are developed and standardized. This development was dramatically demonstrated in automobiles and is still in process in television receivers.

(3) The entry in force of private-label competitors, such as the mail-order houses' own-label refrigerators and paint sprayers.

(4) Market saturation (assuming that the market can be defined). The ratio of replacement sales to new equipment sales serves as a symptom of the competitive degeneration of durable goods. Saturation in the radio market was once thought to be one per home, but was later expanded to one per house room.

(5) The stabilization of production methods. A dramatic innovation that slashes costs (e.g., prefabricated houses) may disrupt what appears to be a well stabilized oligopoly market.

The first step for the manufacturer whose specialty is about to slip into the commodity category is to reduce real (*de facto*) prices as soon as symptoms of deterioration appear. This step is essential if he is to forestall the entry of private-label competitors. Examples of failure to make such a reduction are abundant.[10] Refrigerators and tires are examples. This does not mean that the manufacturer should declare open price-war in the industry. When he moves into mature competitive stages, he enters oligopoly relationships where price slashing is peculiarly dangerous and unpopular. (See Section IV of this chapter.) With active competition in prices precluded, competitive efforts move in other directions, particularly toward product improvement and market segmentation.[11] As the product matures and as its distinctiveness narrows a choice must sometimes be made as to the rung of the

---

[10] By and large, private-label competition has speeded up the inevitable evolution of high specialities into "commodities" and has tended to force margins down by making price reductions more open and more universal than they would otherwise be. From one standpoint, the rapid growth of private-label share in the market is a symptom of unwise pricing on the part of the house-brand sector of the industry.

[11] Product improvement at this stage, where most of the important developments have been put into all brands, amounts practically to market segmentation: it means adding refinements and quality extras that put the brand in the elite category, with an appeal only to the top income brackets. This is a common tactic in food marketing, and was the response of the General Tire Company to the competitive conditions of the thirties.

competitive price ladder it should occupy—roughly, a choice between a low relative price and a high one. What does it mean to say that a company has a "low price policy" for a mature product? First, the product, which is physically similar to competing products, is sold at the lower end of the array of the industry's real prices. Second, the company's product bundle usually shows a lean mixture of services and reputation. Third, the company usually has a lower gross margin than do other industry members, although not necessarily a lower net margin. The choice of a low price policy may be dictated by technical or market inferiorities of the product, or it may be because the company has faith in the long-run price elasticity of demand and the ability of low prices to penetrate an important segment of the market not tapped by higher prices.

Summary

In pricing products of perishable distinctiveness, a company should study the cycle of competitive degeneration in order to determine its major causes, its probable speed, and the chances of slowing it down. Pricing in the pioneering stage of the cycle involves difficult problems of projecting potential demand and of guessing the relation of price to sales. The first step in this process is to explore consumer preferences and to establish the feasibility of the product, in order to get a rough idea of whether demand will warrant further exploration. The second step is to mark out a range of prices that will make the product economically attractive to buyers. The third step is to estimate the probable sales that will result from alternative prices.

If these initial explorations are encouraging, the next move is to make decisions on promotional strategy and distribution channels. The policy of relatively high prices in the pioneering stage has much to commend it, particularly when sales seem to be comparatively unresponsive to price but quite responsive to educational promotion. On the other hand, the policy of relatively low prices in the pioneering stage, in anticipation of the cost savings resulting from an expanding market, has been strikingly successful under the right conditions. Low prices look to long-run rather than to short-run profits and discourage potential competitors.

Pricing in the mature stages of a product's life cycle requires a technique for recognizing when a product is approaching maturity. Pricing problems in this stage border closely on those of oligopoly, which will be considered in the next section.

IV. PRICING STANDARD PRODUCTS WHEN COMPETITORS ARE FEW

Introduction

Up to this point we have discussed two competitive situations: (1) pricing a sharply differentiated product that is relatively impregnable to competitive encroachment; and (2) pricing a new, distinctive product in the expectation that the seller's pricing discretion will be eaten away by competitive inroads as the product passes from the pioneering stage into maturity.

We turn in this section to a third situation: competition among a few sellers of a relatively homogeneous product that has enough cross-elasticity of demand so that each seller must, in his pricing decisions, take account of rivals' reactions. This competitive situation is called, in economic writings, "oligopoly." Two kinds are distinguished: "pure oligopoly," when rivals sell quite similar products, and "differentiated oligopoly," when rivals' products are sufficiently different in the buyers' minds to make brands an important feature of marketing and to allow differences in price to prevail, yet sufficiently similar to make a seller watch rivals' prices closely.[12]

The power of every monopolist is qualified by substitutes, and his pricing is never completely independent in the sense of being untouched by competition. But a monopolist competes with a broad range of alternative ways to spend money, while an oligopolist competes directly with two or three or fifteen particular firms whose products are not only close substitutes but also similar in respect to cost behavior. The costs as well as the demand of rival producers of tin cans will be similarly affected by a major change in business conditions that will affect producers of glass and paper containers differently.

---

[12] In economic writings, the word "rival" is distinctively associated with oligopoly competition. The word gives nicely the right sense of personalized competition, as compared with pure competition, where prices are set by "the vast, impersonal forces of the market place."

Importance of Oligopoly Pricing

We saw in Chapter 2 ("Competition") that oligopoly (pure and differentiated) looms large in American manufacturing in so far as statistics of industrial concentration validly indicate its importance. These statistics may understate its importance in the economy, since they are national aggregates and don't take account of local market oligopolies of producers with less than national distribution. Individual markets that have more than ten competitive sellers are fairly rare, except in metropolitan areas.

There is furthermore a strong tendency in modern industry for both competitive and monopoly sellers to gravitate toward oligopoly situations. In industries that approach pure competition (i.e., where firms are numerous, products similar, and competition intense) each firm has a strong drive to develop a product that differs from competitors' products either physically, psychologically (by enhanced reputation), or by a richer mixture of service. Successful development of such products reduces the number of sellers who are closely competitive.

Conversely, as we have seen, a seller who has a successful innovation is vulnerable to the encroachment of substitutes that become progressively closer approximations to his product, so that the innovator's distinctive specialty of today tends to degenerate toward a commonplace commodity of tomorrow. This process creates an oligopoly where monopoly was before. The history of competition in electric refrigerators, automatic washing machines, radios, television receivers, and frozen foods shows how rapidly an ephemeral monopoly can be eroded down to an oligopoly plateau by entry of big competitors.[13]

Thus the setting of the problem is a dynamic economy in which the seller is constantly threatened with improvements in rivals' products and merchandising, in which sharp swerves occur in consumer desires, and in which market invasion by undreamed-of substitutes is a constant threat.

---

[13] The erosion of trust monopolies in the steel, oil, paper, and can industries has a similar pattern. In these cases, the innovator produced not a new product, but a new organization—the combine—to control the industry's output. The competitive response to such mergers is frequently not different from the response to product innovation: imitative mergers of independent rivals to maintain parity with the new industry leader.

The Pricing Problem of Oligopoly

In industries where a few competitors dominate the supply of relatively uniform products, periods of low demand and excess capacity create serious competitive problems. This is particularly so in industries with heavy plant investments, and high barriers to entry. Each manufacturer is acutely aware of the disastrous effects that an announced reduction of his own price would have on the prices charged by competitors. As a result, these companies have by painful experience developed a pronounced aversion for attempting to gain market share by open and announced price cutting. The main conditions that cause this aversion may be summarized thus:

> 1. The seller knows that price cuts will be met promptly (either precisely or with differentials that are likely to preserve competitors' market shares). This reaction virtually destroys the effectiveness of overt price cuts as a means of extending a firm's market share.
> 2. Price reductions are not easily reversible. Once industry prices are cut, it is usually difficult to get them back up again until the cost and demand situation again commands higher prices.
> 3. Open price competition often degenerates into an uncontrolled price war, [14] particularly where marginal cost is considerably below average cost over the relevant range of output.
> 4. Sellers doubt that a lower price throughout the industry will expand total sales enough to offset the reduction in unit revenue. They usually believe that industry demand is highly inelastic.

Under these circumstances, substantial uniformity of published price is to be expected and market share is largely determined by secret price concessions and by non-price competition.

Under conditions of "pure" oligopoly, there is no such thing as a demand function for the individual firm. What the firm can sell at a given price and with a given amount of selling ac-

---

[14] The distinction between price war and price competition is frequently impossible to make on objective grounds, particularly in "sick" industries where demand is falling secularly. The only indisputable evidence of war is prices below marginal costs. The existence of warfare depends ultimately on the attitudes and plans of competitors about the situation, and in fact there are as many degrees of price warfare as there are of military war, where aggression ranges from diplomacy, through guerrilla tactics and fifth columns, to open battle.

tivity depends upon rivals reaction to the firm's market policy. To draw a demand curve, some stable pattern of market shares acceptable to all sellers must be established automatically for each price the firm might set.

To analyze this problem of interdependence, economic theorists have set up various assumptions about the chain of reactions to rivals' prices. These assumptions suggest the adventures of Dick Tracy, and give about equally convincing results. But the fact that the "equilibrium" price is by logical analysis indeterminate does not mean that it is so in practice. Actually, the seller in many industries has, from his knowledge of rivals' cost and demand situations and personal traits, and from industry experience, a very good idea of the probable reaction of major rivals to his price or other market actions.[15] When, as is quite common, price makes little difference in the industry's total sales (even though small price disparities shift business quickly), then the pattern of rivals' reactions to a price cut can be quite clearly foreseen.

What determines the likelihood that rivals will meet an announced price change? It depends on whether the change is compatible with the dynamic setting, i.e., with changes in demand, costs, and substitute prices. During a business decline, when demand is drying up, rivals' excess capacity and low marginal costs typically cause informal price concessions that undermine the official prices. Under the circumstances an announced rise in price is unlikely to be followed but an announced cut in price will be followed immediately. On the other hand, when demand is booming and when costs and substitutes' prices are rising, price reductions are less likely to be followed than price advances.

When the dynamic changes in demand and cost conditions that prompted a given price change are viewed in much the same way by all rivals, they do not cause serious uncertainties concerning rivals' reactions. But these uncertainties do become serious: (a) when rivals are quite differently affected by the same general changes in conditions, (b) when rivals differ in their estimates concerning the future conditions for which they are pricing, and

---

15 For example, any major oil company selling a well accepted house brand of gasoline knows that an open reduction in its price in a market in which the brand's share is substantial will be met promptly and precisely by house brands of major companies, by other brands, and by lesser rivals, with a fairly predictable pattern of differentials.

(c) when rivals have drastically different notions about the industry elasticity of demand with respect to price.[16]

Since these disruptive influences are continually at work to some degree in many industries, a critical problem of oligopoly is to devise industry practices that can reconcile the need for adjustments to changing industry demand with the need to maintain the precarious price structure that has been established.

Two important releases from this dilemma are (1) non-price competition, and (2) price leadership. When these are inadequate or slow to relax conflicting pressures in a new demand situation, there are still several varieties of underground price competition that can be used to maintain a façade of industrial peace in the industry without resorting to war. We shall discuss these in turn below.

Non-Price Competition

The hallmark of oligopoly is domination of the market by a few sellers whose products are highly similar. But competitors' products do not need to be absolutely alike to make rivals' reactions an important factor in pricing and merchandising strategy. Indeed, absolute uniformity of the entire product-package of rival sellers, including illusions and services, is rare. The degree of difference of "products" varies in a continuous range of competitive situations between pure monopoly and pure oligopoly, and the economic distinction that has been mentioned above between homogeneous (pure) oligopoly and differentiated oligopoly on the basis of the uniformity of products and the resulting cross-elasticity of demand with respect to price is therefore hazy.

It is not actual physical uniformity of products, but instead, believed uniformity that is relevant for pricing decisions and that is reflected by cross-elasticity of demand. Nevertheless, cross-elasticity is so difficult to measure that in practice the distinction between homogeneous oligopoly and differentiated oligopoly must be based upon the physical similarity of rivals' products.

Illusory differentiation of products is apparently most effective in consumers' goods where purchases are small and the buyer is consequently relatively uninformed. Spectacular success has been

---

[16] Many industries have had, at one time or another, a discordant personality, such as Firestone or Carnegie, whose heterodox views disrupt the whole pattern of reasonable oligopoly behavior.

achieved in creating brand preferences for products not significantly different physically from rivals' products (e.g., aspirin tablets). And the product need not always be a small purchase item. The physical homogeneity of beer is illustrated by the following *New York Times* dispatch:

> MILWAUKEE, Nov. 17 (1950)—Wisconsin beer distributors lined up at a booth at their convention here and tasted beer from three different taps.
> Jack Whitnall, booth manager, asked them to identify the brands.
> After twenty-seven tests, he counted twenty-six misses.

For producers' goods, on the other hand, because purchases are made in quantity by informed specialists, illusory differentiation is more difficult. Here, physical homogeneity is countered by differences in the package of services and by reciprocity, friendship, and assurance of supply.

Non-price competition is viewed with far more equanimity than price cutting, and is frequently quite unrestrained. The basic reason may be that retaliation is much more difficult against advertising or product improvements than against price cutting. Indeed, differences in the probability of retaliation is a major determinant of the channels of competition in an oligopoly situation. Direct and open price competition is, as we have seen, so quickly and easily met that fear of retaliation rules it out as an effective device for expanding market share when the product is homogeneous. The next most hazardous form of competition from the standpoint of retaliation is covert price concessions. They cannot actually be kept secret for long, and price discrimination based upon buyer alertness is not apparently a very stable nor acceptable basis of market segmentation.

The likelihood of immediate retaliation when competition takes the form of product improvements is remote. Patent and know-how barriers, plus the long and usually secretive gestation period, delay imitation, and the transient gains of innovation are also important. Moreover, the belief is quite general that product-improvement will broaden the market more than corresponding price reductions.

In promotional outlays, advertising, and personal selling, direct and immediate retaliation is difficult. The great variation in efficiency of marketing activities demonstrates the importance of "know-how" barriers to retaliation. The best way of doing things is too peculiar to each firm's situation to permit speedy imitation. Cultural lags are ever present. Moreover, retaliation often takes a different route. A sampling campaign by one soap manufacturer is met by a contest rather than a duplication of the sampling campaign. The sales effects of a particular promotional strata· gem are far less clear than the effects of price cutting, and there is usually a less compelling necessity to retaliate. Furthermore, it is commonly felt that non-price competition such as advertising, improvement of products, and styling is more likely to expand demand for the whole industry than lower prices would.

Price Leadership

The institution of price leadership is another way for oligopoly competitors to achieve the delicate adjustment to changing cost and demand conditions without precipitating a price war. One firm takes the initiating role in all price changes, and the other firms follow along, matching the leader's price exactly, or with established differentials. Price leadership in action may be seen most clearly in a mature and stable industry with a highly standardized product, such as steel, oil, cement, or building materials. But it plays an important part in many industries that have considerable product differentiations.

Requirements for Leadership Pricing

Price leadership is, in essence, a tacit concurrence by major firms in the industry with the wisdom of the leader's pricing decision.[17] It greatly reduces the number of possible reactions of a price change, and thus gives a modicum of certainty to the pricing aspects of market forecasting. It does not, of course, involve agreements that would explicitly violate the Sherman Act. The origins of leadership in any one industry are often too intricate and obscure to be analyzed. Round-table conferences are not

---

[17] A distinction should be made between "followers," in a positive sense, and merely the "rest of the industry." Some firms are price leaders because they control most of the industry's output, and set their prices with little regard to the marginal producers. There is little leader–follower relation in such industries. Much more important are the industries in which the leader's market share is not dominating and where successful leadership requires reasonably loyal followers. There are always marginal firms who follow no one, but these can be neglected if prices are stabilized on the bulk of production.

needed to set it up. All that is needed is one firm whose price policy is consistently acceptable to most of the industry. The leader may take responsibility for setting prices that followers will accept independently without starting a price war, but in more sophisticated industries, where members have better *rapport*, followers, too, accept responsibility for behaving in the best interests of the group. Indeed, "leadership" can function with all degrees of group action, up to a cartelized market-quota system. The form it actually takes depends on the size structure of the industry's firms, on disparities in their cost function, product differentiation, and geographical distribution, and on the pattern and stability of demand.

Qualifications of Price Leader

What are the requisites for being a price leader? (1) A substantial share of the market. Typically, although not necessarily, the largest firm becomes the leader, because this firm is presumed to have the greatest stake in "industry welfare"; to be able to "enforce" followership (although it rarely can or does); and to be best informed about industry demand and supply conditions, and hence best equipped to determine industry price policy. (2) A reputation for sound pricing decisions, based on better information and more experienced judgment than the other firms have. (3) Initiative. Often the company that first develops a product or area retains the price leadership, whether or not it retains the largest market. Often a company may take leadership by default by developing aggressive pricing. Thus the company that believes that lower prices will penetrate large and profitable markets wrests leadership from more conservative rivals whether or not its decision appeals to followers.

In some industries the price leadership shifts among major firms. But more commonly, one firm remains the leader for long periods.

Leadership structure is sometimes segmented. Geographical and product segmentation are common. Thus, in gasoline pricing, different companies are market leaders in different areas. Broad-line chemical manufacturers are typically price leaders for some chemicals and followers for others.

Problems of the Price Leader

Broadly conceived, the problem of the price leader is a problem of industrial statesmanship; the leader makes (within the willingness of his followers) decisions for the entire industry. Narrowly conceived, the leader's problem is a compromise between the price solution that is best for the leader and the price solution that is best for certain other members of the industry.

The price leader's problems of industrial statesmanship are serious, particularly when industry conditions are changing rapidly. If he fails to reconcile his own and the industry's interests with those of the followers, he may easily impair his own position in leadership and market share.[18]

In many industries, price leadership has been fairly responsive to changes in cost and in demand, but generally it has managed to dampen the amplitude of cyclical fluctuations. Under leadership, prices have not gone as high in boom periods or as low in depressions. Since a price change for the industry may have a wide range of unpredictable effects on individual firms, the leader is usually reluctant to stir up the market with frequent price adjustments to meet changed demand and costs perfectly. Continuous change would undermine the loyalty of hard-hit firms and give an appearance of vacillation by the leader. Price leadership usually produces few, but large and dramatic, price changes in the industry over the cycle. After World War II, a few leaders, notably International Harvester and General Electric, tried lowering prices in an attempt to curb inflation, but they were too far out of line with market conditions to be followed. They subsequently raised their prices again.

Even in normal conditions, however, the leader usually leads only in price rises. On downslides the leader actually becomes a follower. Any competitor can lead real prices down, and the typical situation in most industries is for nominal followers to take the initiative here. The reaction of the leader is typically, first, to adjust his real prices down to the market, and later to bring his quoted price into line.

---

[18] The stable price policy of U. S. Steel in the deflation of 1920–1922 caused unhappiness among some of the independents. They reacted by disrupting the market to such an extent that Bethlehem Steel, acting in a quasi-leadership role, acquired them and thus stabilized the industry again. As a result, Bethlehem's market share was substantially increased. (TNEC Monograph 13, p. 106.)

It is important for the leader to know how long the lower price level will last. A temporary drop should be met only by informal concessions from the official price, since frequent changes in announced prices disrupt followers' adjustments and weaken the leader's prestige. Only when market weakness indicates a fairly long-run shift in conditions should the major move of changing official prices be made.

The leader thus has a further problem of making sure that temporary price concessions do not undermine the official price so much that it must be shifted. The impact of the leader's concessions on the stability of the official price level depends on (1) the manner in which concessions are made; (2) the leader's share in the market segment that is weak; and (3) the industry's pattern of adjustment to distress sales that disturb the price peace.[19]

A statement to the T.N.E.C., made by Mr. S. A. Swensrud, now President of the Gulf Oil Company, illustrates the leader's scrutiny of symptoms of market weakness:

> In any territory all suppliers are watching the same things. They watch the statistical position of the industry as a whole, that is, production of crude oil and gasoline, sales of petroleum products and stocks of crude oil and gasoline. . . . They watch the ambitions of competitors to increase their share of the business in the territory. They gage these ambitions by reports of salesmen on price concessions to commercial customers, by observations of the amount of business done by trackside operators and sellers of unbranded and locally branded gasoline, by the reports of salesmen as to competitive offers being made to dealers, and by reports of salesmen as to the extent of secret price cuts, discounts, and the like being offered by retailers. All these facts are constantly before local managers and central organizations.
>
> Now suppose that secret price cutting by dealers in some particular area breaks out into the open in the form of a cut in the posted price because some dealer becomes disgusted with the uncertainty as to how much business he is losing to com-

---

19 In the sulphuric acid industry, for example, sales of acid at prices substantially below the general price level by steel companies who make it as a joint product, apparently do not pull down the price level, since this segment of supply is comparatively small and since the industry has adjusted price-wise to the steel companies' practice of dumping their acid regardless of the effect on price. Two sizable food manufacturers, for example, have for many years made it a practice to dump some of their output at any price they can get in order to regularize their output.

petitors granting secret discounts. As the openly admitted price reduction operates, the local officers of all suppliers are assailed with demands from dealers, relayed and in some instances emphasized by salesmen, for a reduction in the tank-wagon price. . . . The local manager of the leader marketer of course faces more demands than any other manager. He attempts to gage the permanence of the retail cut. Frequently local managers elect to make no change in the tank-wagon price. Ordinarily this decision springs from the conclusion that the local price war will soon run its course because it is not supported by weakness in basic markets. On other occasions the local manager concludes that the causes of the retail price cutting rest primarily on the availability of sufficient low-price gasoline so that the condition may be considered deep-seated, and he therefore authorizes or recommends a local reduction in the tank-wagon price. . . . Thus the particular local territory becomes a subnormal territory, that is, one in which prices are out of line with those generally prevailing in the marketing area.

The major sales executives of all companies watch carefully the number and size of subnormal markets. . . . If the number of local price cuts increases, if the number and amount of secret concessions to commercial consumers increase, if the secret unpublicized concessions to dealers increase, it becomes more and more difficult to maintain the higher prices. . . . Finally, some company, usually the largest marketer in the territory, recognizes that the subnormal price has become the normal price and announces a general price reduction throughout the territory.

In summary, therefore, the so-called price leadership in the petroleum industry boils down to the fact that some company in each territory most of the time bears the onus of formally recognizing current conditions. . . . In short, unless the so-called price leader accurately interprets basic conditions and local conditions, it soon will not be the leading marketer. Price leadership does not mean that the price leader can set prices to get the maximum profit and force other marketers to conform.[20]

The price leader often merely formalizes what is generally recognized as inevitable in the trade, or merely forecasts sooner, and more accurately what later becomes recognized. Forecasting is thus a critical part of leadership. It determines what attitude to take toward a deteriorating market and it signals the time for an

---

[20] Quoted by George J. Stigler, in *The Journal of Political Economy*, Vol. LV, October, 1947, Number 5, page 445.

advance. If forecasts of developing cost and demand conditions are accurate and trusted by the industry, there are substantial gains, but when the leader has a history of blunders, followership is weak and the leader can only formalize changes that are generally recognized as inevitable in the trade. In the long run, however, being a leader is not the same as being merely an initiator of price changes. Leadership attaches to a firm, not an act, and is established only by a career of coordinating the economic and political welfare of the industry as a whole with the interests of the individual members.

Another problem of the leader is to find what pattern of price differentials among firms is acceptable. Products are never identical. Differences in quality, in brand acceptance, promptness of delivery, and reliability, are reflected in both formal and real prices.

When there are significant differences in quality, service, or reputation, it becomes more difficult to find a formal or informal price that will be generally acceptable. Typically, the price leader himself operates in the upper-quality strata, with a rich mixture of services, and attempts to get some price premium for his superiority.

The problem then is to learn by observation and experience the critical price differential that permits a competitor to make serious inroads in market share. This price differential usually differs among firms. For large competitors whose product and services are equal to his, the leader cannot permit any open underpricing without suffering significant losses in his market share; whereas, for sub-standard competitors with poorer product acceptance, a 5 or 10 per cent open price differential may be tolerated without significant loss of market share to large firms. The permissible differential may vary from one sub-standard competitor to another.

Shifts in this pattern of differentials may reflect quality changes, but again they may show dissension in the ranks in the face of new market conditions. The leader must decide what these shifts mean and whether they can be tolerated. The stabilizing pattern of price differentials varies among phases of the business cycle. When demand is slack, cross-elasticity is apt to be high and the critical differential correspondingly low.

Occasionally a large company finds that by reducing its prices it will hurt small competitors enough to create serious political repercussions. Although this reason for not reducing prices is always suspect as sheer rationalization, there are instances where it is valid.[21]

Problems of a Container Manufacturer

To illustrate oligopoly pricing problems, we shall look at a leading integrated manufacturer of light containers. The pricing problem that troubles him most is the instability of the price level that results from concessions by small non-integrated manufacturers, whom we shall call "converters." He feels the need for objective criteria for determining the level of price that will keep these price wars at manageable levels of frequency and intensity.

Characteristically, the announced price level is set so high that weeds, in the form of converters, grow like mad, and continuous cultivation is required to keep the weed population and the growth of individual plants at a tolerable level. In a sense, the problem is to find the level of price that will keep down the cultivation work enough to warrant the sacrifice in revenue from lower prices.

This critical price level will, of course, fluctuate in response to several factors. The main one is the price that converter-manufacturers pay for raw material under secret concessions. This price will depend on how hungry the non-integrated producers of raw materials are for business now, and how fearful they are about future business.

Looked at in a long-range setting, the big producer has a problem of stay-out pricing. The basic econometric relationship is between price (in the form of a spread over raw-material cost) and the volume of containers produced by converters. Over a longer period, this is a function of the converter population and the number of machines they have. This relationship between converter output and price spread is sensitive, because entry is

---

[21] For example, a leading electric lamp manufacturer found itself in the embarrassing position of producing almost the entire output of one type of incandescent lamp. It had one small competitor, whom it had helped to bring into existence. This competitor had such high costs that if the big company reduced the price of these lamps in line with its general company policy and in line with its falling costs, it would almost certainly drive the small company out and find itself in the embarrassing position of having an unchallenged monopoly in this product.

cheap and easy. Capital of $25,000 or less will put a converter into business. Moreover, shutdown costs are small and overhead costs low, so that converters can and do close up for several months, when price conditions are unfavorable. Thus, price squeezes initially bring only temporary withdrawal in the form of shutdowns. Not even mortality in the form of bankruptcy has, in the past, proved permanent; it has served merely to permit new entrants to come in with the low costs of the bankrupt investment levels. Second-hand machines operate adequately, since there has been no important technical advance in converting machinery for many years.

A high posted price level from which concessions are made, both on an individual basis and in periodic forays of different markets, produces some price discrimination (discussed in Chapter 9). There appears to be a geographic pattern of price weakness, with the soft spots where there are important converters. Moving the official level down to a lower price would, therefore, sacrifice some profits from discriminatory pricing.

Costs of Converters

Converters are not at a serious cost disadvantage from economies of scale: four machines can be run about as cheaply as forty. Technical progress has been slow: the basic machine was developed fifty years ago. Second-hand equipment produces poorer quality stuff, but not at much higher cost.

The major item of cost of the converter is raw material. The price he pays for it varies considerably over time and probably among converters. It depends basically upon demand for the material and on the opportunity costs of forgoing its sale for other uses. The basic process is flexible, so that the stock could be converted into raw material for various other end-products. This opportunity-cost sill is, however, frequently pierced. Market mills in 1950 were selling material to converters at prices that produced a lower netback than alternative uses of ingredients and equipment in that year's tight market. They did this because they feared for the future. Giving the converter prices below opportunity cost kept him alive and protected a market that was likely to be needed in the future. The converter squeezed by a narrow price differential goes to his supplier with the plea that the price be reduced to avoid bankruptcy. Thus, in such periods, the converters, because of their adversity, tend to beat down the price of material.

The converter's selling costs are low and fairly easily computed. Typically, he hires either a true agent at 5 per cent, or pays salesmen strictly on a commission basis, or does his own selling. Physical handling costs are in some respects advantageous as compared with integrated producers. In general, the converter caters to a local market and can truck his stuff, saving handling costs at freight yards.

Marketing Advantages

The converter has important service advantages—three-hour delivery instead of three-week. The customer deals directly with the owner of the converting operation instead of with a salesman. One disadvantage is a shorter line. Few converters carry a full line of sizes and kinds. Big mills also often have somewhat higher quality and a secret ingredient called "integrity," not always sold by small converters.

During World War II, shortages forced many buyers to adopt a policy of having at least two suppliers to assure adequacy. The harvest of this practice was reaped after the war. Many buyers have decided they want an integrated bag manufacturer and a converter as their two suppliers: the converter for fill-in business and fast delivery; the integrated manufacturer for the bulk of the line.

Effect of Price on Entry

The central pricing problem of the big, integrated firm is to find for containers the price level that will hold down to some goal level the market occupancy of converters. Today, converters do about 30 per cent of the volume. During the great depression, converters' volume grew rapidly from negligible proportions to more than half of the business. The presence of converters as a substantial part of the supply brings periodic instability to the price. Customers of integrated mills who are offered a 5 or 6 per cent concession by a converter insist that the integrated mill meet the concession. Big producers are loath to let the business go at the concession, for several reasons. One is that they remember the effects of doing this during the depression. Another reason is uncertainty as to which big mill will lose the business to converters. Converters now have a third of the market, and if their prices are not met they will get more. But from whom will they take it? If it were known that the loss would be spread evenly among the big companies, it might be tolerated, but every manager worries that the loss will be all his. Once the first scared producer meets the price-cut of a converter, others must follow.

Another deterrent is the uncertainty about how much larger converters might grow if allowed to get as much business as they want; at a 5 per cent differential they may prosper so that they themselves can produce the raw material, as has been done, and thus become major, instead of minor, contenders. A fourth reason is a quasi-political one. Moving the price spread down to a level that would kill off converters might lay the big producers open to antitrust suits and would certainly stir up political trouble.

Underground Price Competition

The discussion of price leadership has indicated that the most important device for short-run sales expansion is the secret price concession. The form of the concession is not important, as long as the buyer understands the real offer. It may take the form of high turn-in values, down-grading of high quality lines, better payment terms, and so forth. There are many ways to lower real prices without taking open responsibility for the action.

Oligopolists are not exactly alike. They may put emphasis on different products and aim at different market segments. For example, in the rubber industry, the big four differ in the relative importance they ascribe to tires in the product line, and to the private-label market, and in the structure of market segmentation and price discrimination through second- and third-line tires and "fighting" brands. Underground price competition in the tire industry takes such forms as concessions to mail-order houses and filling station chains, special prices for "test tires" (allegedly slightly used), and so forth. This hidden price competition is nonetheless real, and is just as beneficial to consumers as is open competition—at least to some consumers. But it does not have the explosive consequences that open reductions in the manufacturer's first-line branded tires have.

Many price erosions start on the periphery of the industry,

where minor producers are continually chipping away at the official price structure. When the market becomes intolerable for some manufacturer at the posted price levels, the trade journals start talking about a "soft" market, which is the sign that secret price concessions are becoming more open and general and will soon shape up to the real and acknowledged price in the market. Characteristically, the first-line competitors adhere quite strictly to their published price. But when the undercover concessions of the second-line competitors eat into the market share of the big producers, breaches in the price peace result.

The industry leader has the problem of determining whether and how to reduce the level of official prices to meet undercover concessions. Much depends upon whether or not the conditions that produce concessions are viewed as temporary. As we saw above, a decline in demand may be regarded as short-lived. Because of the difficulty of reinstating official prices once demand has returned to normal, the big producers may decide to meet price competition on an informal plane, as, for example, in the steel industry in 1937 and early 1938. If, on the other hand, changes in demand, cost, or supply are regarded as structural and more or less enduring, some big producers may decide on a change in official prices. For example, in the winter of 1948 a price war occurred in asphalt tile. First-line manufacturers departed from public schedules quite generally, quoting special prices in the hope that the situation would soon right itself. A leading manufacturer, whose general policy is to lower quoted prices fairly promptly when such conditions develop, played along on an informal basis considerably longer than usual, because he felt that a permanent move to the going market level would be very damaging to his profits. But as the situation continued to deteriorate, he eventually lost hope and moved his published prices down to the bottom market levels.

When are undercover concessions significant enough to warrant open reduction of prices? Here are a few strategic indicators:

1. When they spread over a wide geographic area.

2. When they continue for several months.

3. When first-line competitors indulge quite generally in undercover cutting.

4. When earnings at the higher price level are really more than adequate and invite the entry of new competitors.

5. When the price-cutter is out to broaden the market. If his motive seems to be to capture a bigger market share by secret concessions, the leader may merely meet these informal concessions.

6. When substitute prices are low enough to encroach the leader's market. For example, in the summer of 1949 insulation-board sheathing was forced down publicly by informal concessions on lumber sheathing and gypsum sheathing. The experience of many industries indicates that official prices must be cut down close to the lowest level of known shaving if the price-shaving is to be dried up. When informal price concessions amount to 15 per cent, a 5 per cent reduction in official prices will not do the job.

The main economic function of underground price competition is to give resilience and stability to an otherwise brittle oligopoly situation. Undercover price concessions make it possible to develop an informal hierarchy of prices which allows products of sub-standard acceptance a share of the market without setting off a price war. Such concessions for standard products take the shock of short-lived slumps in demand, and serve as a device for exploratory raids. They may also be the means of relating prices in different markets for the same product, e.g., in copper: a producer's market, an export market, an outside market, and a re-sale-copper market. Analogously, within a market informal concessions are a basis for price discrimination according to the elasticity of demand and the bargaining ability of the buyer.

V. COST-PLUS PRICING

Surveys of actual business practice in setting prices have indicated that the most pervasive pricing method used is to make a cost estimate and to add a margin of some kind for profit—what is known as cost-plus pricing. This approach is basically different from the economists' solution to the pricing problem discussed in the preceding sections of this chapter. Cost-plus pricing is so extensively used that it deserves the special attention given to it in this section.

Use of Cost-Plus Pricing

Two investigations of pricing behavior have been made in England, one by a group at Oxford University, who interviewed business tycoons,[22] and another by Clive Saxton, who depended on a mail questionnaire.[23] A similar study of business behavior, based on comprehensive personal interviews, has been under way in this country for several years.[24] According to these studies, a majority of businessmen set prices on the basis of cost plus a "fair" profit percentage. By "cost" they usually mean full allocated cost at current output and wage levels (although there are important modifications). By "fair profit" is meant a fixed percentage mark-on, which differs greatly among industries and among firms.

The standard of profit mark-on is usually set quite arbitrarily. There are many rationales given for its level, but in general no one seems to want more than a "fair" profit. The results of the Oxford study, summarized in Tables 7–1 and 7–2, give an idea of the importance of cost-plus pricing and the reasons executives give for using it.

Several different concepts of the cost component may be used in formula pricing. In general, "cost" means either actual, expected, or standard cost. Actual cost usually means historical cost for the latest available period. It reflects recent wages and material prices, and overhead loading at the then current output rate. Expected cost is a forecast of actual cost for the pricing period on the basis of expected prices, output rates, and efficiency. Standard cost is a conjecture as to what cost would be at some "normal" rate of output, e.g., 75 per cent of capacity, with efficiency at some standard level, which may be an optimum or simply a normal level.

Occasionally (particularly for pricing specially designed products) the cost base is purely conjectural. It is built up from engineering estimates plus cost experience and may even be projected into future operating conditions.

Formulas for cost-plus pricing differ widely among industries and even among firms within an industry. This variation is probably in part a reflection of differences in accounting methods and differences in the relative importance of overhead cost and

---

22 R. L. Hall and C. J. Hitch, "Price Theory and Business Behavior," *Oxford Economic Papers* #2, 1939.

23 *Economics of Price Determination,* London, Oxford University Press, 1941.

24 Begun in 1941 by a Committee of the Conference on Price Research under the co-chairmanship of Theodore Yntema and Joel Dean, the study has not yet been completed.

selling expenses.   It may also indicate that the basic formula is in part a reflection of the general level of price that competition in that industry permits.

A few examples of pricing formulas will clarify this approach. An equipment manufacturer starts with the cost of materials and direct labor, and adds 100 per cent for overhead, 25 per cent for selling expense, and 10 per cent for profit.   A rubber company adds 10 per cent of material cost for purchasing overhead, then adds 155 per cent of direct labor for general overhead.   He then

TABLE 7-1

DEGREE OF ADHERENCE TO FULL COST PRINCIPLE *
(Per cent of companies classified according to types of markets)

	Not Adhering	Adhering Rigidly	Adhering Normally	Adhering in Principle	Total
Monopoly	25%	50%	25%		100%
Oligopoly	25		75		100
Monopolistic Competition	28	45	18	9%	100
Monopolistic Competition with Oligopoly	16	26	47	11	100
Total	21	32	39	8	100

* Source: R. L. Hall and C. J. Hitch, "Price Theory and Business Behavior," *Oxford Economic Papers,* #2 (May, 1939), Table 6, page 26.

TABLE 7-2

REASONS FOR ADHERING TO FULL COST PRINCIPLE *

Number of Companies

General

Belief that this is the "right" price   5
Loyalty to Association   2
Experience proved its advisability   2

Reasons for not charging more than full cost
Fear of competitors or potential competitors (including
  belief that others would not follow increase) ....   11 plus 6 of the 7 textile firms

Buyers technically informed regarding costs   3
They do not go in for a high profit   2
They prefer a large turnover   2

Reasons for not charging less than full cost
Competitors will follow cuts   11
Demand unresponsive to price   9
Quasi-moral objections to selling below cost   8
Trade Association minimum prices   3

	Number of Companies
General	
Difficult to raise prices once lowered	2
Convention with competitors	1
Price cuts not passed on by retailers..................	1
Reasons for not changing prices (however fixed) once settled	
Conventional price in minds of buyers	5
Price changes disliked by buyers	4
Disinclination to disturb stability of market prices	3

* Source: R. L. Hall and C. J. Hitch, "Price Theory and Business Behavior," *Oxford Economic Papers*, #2 (May, 1939), Table 2, page 21.

adds 20 per cent of this sum for profit. The following table shows examples of pricing formulas for various kinds of manufactures. For comparability, the components are stated as percentages of the list price.

	Appliance Mfgr.	Boiler Mfgr.	Truck Mfgr.
Material	29%	25%	39%
Labor	7	10	6
Overhead	8	15	20
Sales Expense	3	19	7
Discounts	40	22	25
Profits	13	9	3

The formula mark-ons for overhead and selling expense sometimes are tied to current output rates, but probably more often based on standard costs or reflect some form of "normal" output rate. As a result many formula plans may amount to out-of-pocket-costs-plus pricing.

Determination of Profit Mark-Up

The percentage that is added for profit in cost-plus formulas differs strikingly among industries, among member firms, and even among products of the same firm, although it has been suggested that 10 per cent is a typical figure. Some of this variation may be due to differences in competitive intensity, some to differences in cost base (e.g., the degree to which profit has already been included by padding of overhead), and some to differences in turnover rate and risk. The size of this profit factor, however, often reflects habits or custom and some vague notion of a "just" profit.

Rate-of-Return Pricing

In contrast to this arbitrary way of setting the percentage of unit cost to be added for profit, some large companies determine the average mark-up on costs necessary to produce a desired rate of return on the company's investment. For example, Western Electric tries to set its prices to produce, on the average, an 8 per cent return on net investment.

A notable statement of the methods of applying this kind of pricing policy was made in 1924 by Donaldson Brown, then vice president of General Motors, in an article that reflected the company's pricing practice.[25]

Under this policy, pricing starts with a planned rate of return on investment. To translate this rate of return into a per cent mark-up on cost, i.e., to find the profit margin, it is necessary to estimate a "normal" rate of production, averaged over the business cycle. Total cost of a year's "normal" production can then be estimated, and this is taken as standard cost in the computation. The ratio of invested capital to a year's standard cost is then computed. This is called capital turnover. Multiplying capital turnover by the goal rate of return gives the mark-up percentage to be applied to standard cost.[26] This mark-up is an average, both among products and through time. The long-run base price that is obtained by applying this mark-up to standard cost will be altered with changes in wage rates and prices of material, but not for fluctuations in output away from the "normal" rate of production. During periods of high production, earnings will give a higher-than-normal rate of return on investment, because actual unit costs will be lower than the standard unit cost used as a mark-up base, [27] and in low-production years, actual earnings will be correspondingly lower.

---

25 Donaldson Brown, "Pricing Policy in Relation to Financial Control," *Management and Administration*, Vol. 7, pp. 195–198, 283–286, 417–422.

26 In algebraic terms:

$$\frac{\text{invested capital}}{\text{standard cost}} \times \frac{\text{earnings}}{\text{invested capital}} = \frac{\text{earnings}}{\text{standard cost}}$$

For instance, if capital turnover is 0.6 and the goal rate of return is 20 per cent on invested capital, the mark-up on standard cost is 12 per cent.

27 Since some costs are fixed, a 10 per cent increase in output will produce a less-than-10-per cent increase in total costs, and thus a fall in average unit costs. But the standard unit cost used in pricing is fixed, i.e., does not change with short-run fluctuations in output.

Actual prices of specific products will vary from the base price, derived from the long-run mark-up on standard cost, to meet varying conditions of demand and competition for each product. But if the goal rate of return is to be attained over, say, a ten-year period these deviations must be made to balance so that the weighted average of mark-ups keeps close to the planned over-all mark-up. The planned margin is thus a benchmark for controlling short-run pricing actions and appraising the extent to which they drive earnings away from the goal rate of return.

This method of cost-plus pricing is in two respects more refined than most: (1) it builds price on cost that is "normalized" for fluctuations in rate of output, and (2) it develops a profit mark-up that is related to a rate of return. But this relation does not necessarily remove the arbitrary element in setting the unit profit mark-up percentage. It may merely transfer arbitrariness to the rate-of-return goal. The method does, however, have the advantage of pointing pricing at some planned rate of earnings on investment, although there is no assurance that this planned rate will be earned, except when demand and competitive conditions are favorable enough to permit it.

Rate-of-Return Goals

How should the rate-of-return goal be set? The concept and determinants of a profit standard depend on its purpose. Profit standards are discussed in Chapter 1 as a substitute for profit maximization as a company's earnings goal, in Chapter 3 as a tool of product-line policy, and in Chapter 10 as a guide for determining the total capital budget. For a general goal of reasonable profits, the relevant concept is an average return that cuts across cycles and conforms to the standards of reasonableness that are embraced by the crucial outsiders, e.g., union leaders, potential competitors, antitrusters, or "the public." For product-line policy and for capital budgeting, the relevant concept is a marginal return on an added product or added investment, to be compared with alternative uses of funds and with the cost of outside capital. Although none of these concepts is exactly relevant for setting a pricing profit standard, the problem is akin to the over-all earnings goal, since pricing is one way to manipulate earnings.

The standard of earnings that has been taken for granted in

economic analysis, though to a lesser extent apparently in business practice, is "all you can get." Enchanting and defensible
though this standard is, it is not a very helpful criterion for cost-
plus pricing. Indeed, it is fundamentally a denial of this whole
approach. But within the cost-plus framework, perhaps the most
sensible standard is a recent average return of companies that are
comparable in products, processes, and risks. Such a standard
provides some measure of the competitive return that is allowable
in the industry without loss of market shares or invasion of
markets. But industry averages are hard to compute: they raise
questions of the most relevant companies to include and the appropriate averaging period, and are no protection against the
competitor who pays no heed to averages.

Objective profit standards must be used cautiously for pricing.
Actually attaining the average return deemed reasonable by any
of these standards requires prices that produce above-average earnings in boom years, in order to offset the low earnings or losses of
poor years. Moreover, mark-ons must be adequate to offset
mark-downs and competitive price concessions, if the standard of
reasonable earnings is to be attained.

Different pricing formulas are sometimes used for different
members of the company's product line. For example, a manufacturer of control mechanisms varies the profit mark-up among
products according to the characteristics of the buying industry
and the intensity of substitute competition. High specialties
have a longer mark-up. Also, the amount added for dealer discount in the formula commonly differs among products. Thus
formulas frequently overstate the rigidity of actual pricing practice. Prices that are presumably set by cost-plus formulas are
sometimes substantially modified by competitive consideration,
either by differentiating the formula for different items, or by setting prices below or above the formula. Often, however, a pricing formula, by applying a uniform mark-up, operates to cut off
potential profit at the top of the line and potential sales at the
bottom of the line, where products are intensely competitive.

Inadequacies of Cost-Plus Pricing

The popularity of the cost-plus method does not necessarily
mean that it is the best available method. In most situations it
is not, for several reasons:

1. It ignores demand. It fails to take account of the buyer's needs and willingness to pay, which govern the sales volume obtainable at each of a series of prices. What people will pay for a product bears no necessary relation to what it costs any particular manufacturer to make it.

2. It fails to reflect competition adequately. The effect of a price upon rivals' reactions and the effect upon the birth of potential competition are omitted from this simple formula.

3. It overplays the precision of allocated costs. The costs of individual products cannot be determined exactly in multiple-product firms where common costs are important and are arbitrarily allocated to products. Equally defensible bases for apportionment yield significantly different product costs. Hence the figures on full costs used in the formula are generally less factual than their role in pricing warrants.

4. It is based upon a concept of cost that is frequently not relevant for the pricing decision. For many decisions, incremental costs rather than full costs should be controlling. Moreover, it is not current costs, and certainly not past costs, that are needed to price future output, but rather forecasts of future costs. Opportunity costs, i.e., alternative uses of facilities, are important, but they are not usually reflected in accounting systems.

5. It involves circular reasoning in some degree if current full cost is used as the base. To the extent that unit costs vary with output, and thus with sales volume, this cost depends partly on the price charged, provided that demand has significant elasticity and fixed overhead is important.

Justification of Cost-Plus Pricing

In the light of these economic short-comings in cost-plus pricing, what is the explanation for its widespread use? Several reasons have been suggested by economists and businessmen and are presented here. Although they conflict with each other, there is little basis for choosing among them, and different reasons may apply in different situations.

Suggested Explanations

1. Cost-plus pricing is an illusion; executives don't really do it that way (they deceive investigators because "cost-plus" sounds like a logical and respectable pricing formula). It may be true

that businessmen tend to overstate their adherence to this pricing rule. In personal interviews many of them speak of "adjustment to take account of competitive conditions" as an afterthought. Hence the cost formula may be a pricing ideal that is actually attained less frequently than surveys indicate. Moreover, the formula is sometimes really used as a means of expressing the result of a price decision and as a means of comparing prices of different products rather than as a means of making such a decision. But in spite of the possibility that survey tabulations may overstate the frequency and slavishness of cost-plus formula pricing, there is ample evidence of its widespread use in American industry today.

2. Since maximizing profits, at least in the short run, is not actually the company's objective, cost-plus pricing isn't really illogical after all. There is considerable evidence that maximization of profits in the short run and probably also in the long run is not the single or even the principal objective of most business enterprises. The notion of a "just price" is still strong in business mores. Compunction against charging more than a "fair profit margin" is a significant pricing factor. Some businessmen say they aim at maximizing volume rather than profits.

3. It is the logical way to maximize profits in the long run. In part, this contention is based on the view of classical economists that in the long run prices tend to equal costs of production (including a return on capital). But this theory states a survival tendency under idealized conditions of perfect competition rarely approximated in America today. In part, this justification is based on an untested (but sometimes plausible) theory that pricing up to levels justified by demand will pull in potential competition. The pull of high prices and high unit profits differs among industries according to barriers to entry, prospects of great growth in demand, prospective economies of scale and technology, and so forth.

4. It is the safest though not the most profitable method of pricing. In pricing a new, made-to-order article, a cost-plus formula may set what amounts to a refusal price. The seller automatically saves himself from tying up facilities with work that would yield subnormal profits. But even here the protection is negative and incomplete. Formula pricing keeps a firm from losing money by getting orders. but not from losing money

by failing to get orders. It sets ceilings on profits, but not floors. When a buyer can produce the product himself (e.g., automobile components) prices benched on costs may be safer. But logically, the buyer's probable costs, not the seller's, should govern (although, frequently, they are not too different).

A major uncertainty in setting a price is the unknown reaction of rivals to that price. When the products and production processes of rivals are highly similar, cost-plus pricing may offer a source of competitive stability by setting a price that is more likely to yield acceptable profits to most other members of the industry. Cost-plus pricing may reduce the hazards of price warfare. If these results are to be obtained legally, costs and standards of acceptable profits need to be fairly similar (or compensatingly different) among firms.

Under certain circumstances, cost-plus pricing may be viewed as the safest way to cope with unforeseeable cyclical shifts in demand. If demand has a negligible price-elasticity and is subject to violent cyclical shifts, setting a price on the basis of normal full costs for the cycle average of output rate may assure a predetermined total profit over the cycle. For example, a company may set its pricing sights to earn, over the cycle, an average of 10 per cent on its investment. Such a decision implies the existence of a "normal business cycle" that will hold for the future.

For the same assumed conditions, another kind of cost-plus safety pricing is based on some sort of Jeremiah criterion. By envisioning the worst probable cyclical demand shift, a price is built up that will produce a predetermined profit level under these circumstances. An example is pricing to break even at 30 per cent capacity. Pricing to cover bond interest at x per cent capacity is another version.

Cost-plus pricing also has features of political safety as a guide to inflation pricing, particularly for large firms whose prices are pivotal and whose profits are conspicuous. But here the firm's practical problem is to justify and limit profits, not to maximize them.

5. It is a resort of desperation, in the absence of the knowledge required for more reasonable methods. It is difficult to estimate at all precisely the impact of price upon sales volume. Ignorance of the firm's demand curve obviously makes it impossible to take its influence on price into account. The reaction of rivals to a

given price policy that has a pronounced effect upon volume is also hard to forecast. The effect of today's price on tomorrow's demand and upon potential competition may also be hard to estimate. Faced with the necessity of guessing at almost every factor that ought to enter into scientific pricing, executives often take refuge in the pseudo-certainty of a price built up by rather arbitrary mark-ons from a cost bench that is "known" but not always relevant.[28]

Role of Cost in Pricing

If mechanistic formula pricing is not the best way to use costs in pricing, how should they be used? In Section II, we discussed the all-important use of costs in conjunction with demand estimates, namely, to probe for the price that will be most profitable (or to hit upon a sales goal that will yield some acceptable amount of earnings). The basic use of costs in pricing is thus to forecast the profit consequences of various alternative prices.

Nevertheless, there are some situations in which cost appropriately plays a more direct role in determining prices. Among these are: (1) product tailoring; (2) refusal pricing; (3) monopsony pricing; and (4) public utility pricing.

Product Tailoring

Most new products are moulded to meet a zone of competitive price, and much selling effort goes into giving the maximum quality in that price range. In an extreme form, however, a selling price is predetermined exactly, and by working back from this, product design is arrived at. An example of this inverted cost-price relation is a manufacturer of model airplane building kits who starts with a target retail price and works backward by first deducting estimated retail and wholesale margins, then deducting manufacturer's selling cost and desired profit, and finally

---

28 Professor William Fellner, in an article in the *Journal of Political Economy* (June, 1948), supported the view that full-cost pricing is a logical approach for businessmen faced with uncertainty in forecasting demand and cost conditions. He maintains that entrepreneurs, seeking to protect themselves against possible detrimental shifts in their demand and cost curves, will operate at that price and output rate at which the margin between average unit cost and price is a maximum. However, Professor Fellner does not contend that businessmen consciously follow his line of reasoning, but rather that businessmen's use of full cost pricing can be reconciled with economists' opposition to it once the typical uncertainty of forecasting future events is brought into the picture.

selecting the components of the kit whose costs will not exceed what money is left over.   One chemical company uses this process to guide development of new materials to displace existing chemicals in specific uses.   The predetermined displacement price controls the entire process of research, production, and distribution.

This inverted relation, where price appears to determine cost, is directly applicable only when product design is fluid and when the target price is sharply defined by the economic situation in respect to substitutes and demand.   But this approach has the virtue of starting with market-price realities; it looks at the problem from the viewpoint of the buyer in terms of what he wants and what he will pay.   It views the product as a vehicle to be modified by economic determinants in order to satisfy specified consumer wants.   In spirit, this approach has a general applicability, since the consumer is king and product design is quite generally subject to modification.

Refusal Pricing

Pricing products that are designed to the specifications of a single buyer are another area in which cost plays a direct role. Such products might logically be priced on the basis of estimated incremental cost, plus a gross margin equivalent to that which the seller could get if he used the facilities in the next best way then open to him.[29]   This system at least could set a price floor.   Here, the seller is really engaged in refusal pricing, for he is deciding whether or not to make the product at all; he is not deciding what to charge for a product that he is already committed to manufacture.   But even here cost sets only a floor for prices; otherwise, the seller might miss potential immediate profits and ignore the effects of price upon future business.

Monopsony Pricing

Another situation in which cost is an unusual limiter of price is in selling to powerful and knowledgeable buyers, the limiting case being monopsony, i.e., where there is only one buyer.   An example is found in the automobile parts industry.   Here buyers

---

[29] For instance, if a textile mill interrupts its regular production of shirting to fill a special government order for an experimental arctic fabric, the loss in shirting sales is the real cost of the special job and determines the margin.

are few and powerful, and know a great deal about suppliers' costs. They are in a position to make the product themselves if they don't like the seller's prices. But even here it is not the seller's own costs, but the costs that the buying automobile company would incur if it made the product itself that are relevant. Thus the seller's cost in this kind of pricing is only an indicator of the relevant basis for setting the price that will keep competition out.

Public Utility Pricing

Another place where cost can determine price directly is in public utility pricing, which is beyond the scope of this analysis. Since the test of the average price level of a utility is usually the reasonableness of its earnings, which are often measured by its cost of capital, the standard of price regulation is cost-plus pricing in its purest form.

Summary

This analysis may be bluntly summarized as follows:

1. Although cost estimates should play a vital part in pricing, analyses of demand, of competitive environment, and of political impacts are also major considerations.

2. Effective use of costs for setting prices requires a clear understanding of cost concepts and of the principle of different costs for different purposes.

3. The widespread use of cost-plus formula pricing is explained and justified in various ways: (a) that it is an ideal rather than a method of pricing, (b) that it is sensible when a company's goal is adequate profits rather than maximum profits, (c) that it is the safest course in the long run, and (d) that it is a resort of desperation in the face of ignorance about demand elasticity and competitive structure.

4. Despite its popularity, cost-plus pricing has serious deficiencies: (a) it ignores demand, (b) it fails to reflect competition adequately, (c) it overplays the precision of historical costs, and (d) it is based on a cost concept that is frequently irrelevant.

5. One valid role of cost estimates in practical pricing is to project the effects of proposed prices upon accounting profits and upon real economic profits. In many situations, the relation of

cost to price is inverted and cost analysis should be used to tailor the product and its cost to fit a predetermined selling price.

VI. CYCLICAL PRICING

Many of the decisions on the company's general price level relate not to new products or to changing competitive conditions, but to the company's response to alterations in the entire economic environment—what we usually call business cycles.

Whether future fluctuations will actually be cycles in a periodic sense, as some economists believe, or merely a succession of independent fluctuations, we needn't try to decide here. It may be, moreover, that the cycles we knew before World War II have disappeared or been seriously altered in their nature by the postwar climate of armament races, guaranteed full employment, and income supports. But fluctuations in inventory, in capital outlays, and in national income, are likely to continue in some form, and they raise certain generic problems of pricing, which will be discussed in this section.

Since 1932, there has been a good deal of controversy on the public policy level concerning the cyclical effects of existing pricing practices in business. The central question is whether prices have been too rigid for stable employment. Again, we cannot go into this intricate question in this book, [30] but price rigidity itself is an important question in private price policy, and its existence should be recognized.

It is now generally agreed that the prices of agricultural products and certain raw materials and manufactured goods have been predominantly flexible over the cycle. The prices of certain other raw materials and most manufactured products generally have been inflexible. Many of the firms that this book is primarily concerned with, i.e., price leaders and firms with a certain amount of independence in price determination, fall into the second category. It has been common practice in a large number of industries to change prices infrequently and to attempt to limit price cuts in periods of declining demand, as well as to refrain from major price increases in periods of rising demand. In the great depression, agricultural prices declined significantly

---

[30] For a survey of the controversy, see A. C. Neal, *Industrial Concentration and Price Rigidity*, Washington, American Council on Public Affairs, 1942.

more than the prices of most manufactured goods, while in the inflationary period following World War II farm prices rose much faster than finished-goods prices.

The rigidity of many industrial prices is more apparent than real. In periods of declining business activity, concealed price concessions and changes in the various extras, guaranties, discounts, and so forth, associated with the price quotation tend to impart some flexibility to even the most inflexible nominal prices. In periods of boom and inflation, gray market operations achieve the same result. Nevertheless, the conclusion that major portions of the economy are characterized by significant price inflexibility seems to have been satisfactorily established.

Reasons for Price Inflexibility

The main reasons for price inflexibility may be put into four groups on the basis of cyclical changes in conditions of: (1) demand, (2) competition, (3) costs, and (4) profits.

1. *Demand.* It is a common belief among industrialists that demand for their products is highly inelastic; i.e., that responses of the buying public to changes in price are relatively small. In many cases, this belief is well grounded in fact. An increasing portion of the nation's output consists of durable goods; the purchase of such goods is deferable, often for long periods, since the community already has a large stock of them in use. As a result, sales are generally much more responsive to changes in consumer income or to changes in producers' prospects of profit than to changes in the prices of the goods in question. This would appear to be true for durable consumers' goods as well as for durable producers' goods. In addition, major price cuts often result in consumer anticipation of further reductions, and thus in smaller increases in sales than would be the case if consumers felt that the price cuts were to be final.

Whether or not it is true that sales are only negligibly expanded by cyclical reductions of price, many manufacturers formulate their pricing policies on this assumption that demand is inelastic. Sumner Slichter quoted a prominent machine-tool manufacturer on this subject, as follows:

> Since the experiences of 1920 and 1921, in which an attempt was made by several machine tool builders to increase sales by lowering prices, it has been the general

belief in our industry that this is a hopeless process, and it has not since been tried. . . .

Of course, there is some relation between the price of machine tools and sales. Any given proposal is ordinarily based on the length of time required to pay for the new investment with all the factors taken into account. . . . This time has to be so short to be attractive that it has to be an absurdly good proposition anyway, and 15 per cent on the investment one way or the other doesn't seriously handicap or seriously improve the proposal.[31]

Alfred Neal has pointed out that demand for consumers' durable goods also shifts widely with business conditions:

With customers well stocked with durable goods from the buying splurge of the previous prosperity, the physical limitations to the market alone are likely to make price cuts on established lines ineffective. Moreover [credit buying makes consumers sensitive to income anticipations, so] many consumers are unlikely to want to commit themselves to making a series of payments for a durable good in a period when their own incomes are uncertain. Even more than this, however, the consumer's credit is likely to be weaker in depression than in good times.[32]

Dr. Neal suggested that a better line of attack for consumers' durable goods industries in depression would be to concentrate on differentiation and innovation. For example, electric refrigerators, a new product, suffered no depression during 1929–1932.

2. *Competition.* We have seen throughout this chapter that much industrial pricing is done under oligopoly conditions, where price competition always contains the seeds of a cutthroat battle. The instability of price equilibrium is so dangerous that even the leadership mechanism must be used cautiously. Major price changes cause follower adjustments that are always unpredictable to some extent, and to minimize these uncertainties, official prices are kept fixed as long as there is hope of maintaining them. The

---

[31] Sumner Slichter, "Corporate Price Policies as a Factor in the Recent Business Recession," 1937, *Proceedings of the Academy of Political Science,* vol. 18, 1938–40, No. 2, pp. 24–25, note.

[32] Neal, *op. cit.,* pp. 159–160.

effect is to freeze prices and to delay changes, usually until other prices have started moving.

3. *Costs.* Much of American industry seems to be characterized by relatively stable incremental and variable costs per unit over wide ranges of output. Thus great changes in demand and in production may be experienced with only minor changes in marginal or average variable costs, aside from those causes by changes in prices of materials and labor. Prices of some materials, particularly those of concentrated supply (e.g., nickel) and semi-finished components, are increasingly rigid. Wage rates, although recently more prompt in upward adjustments, are likely to be quite rigid downward. Thus variable cost per unit tends to remain relatively constant over long periods and widely differing outputs. Fixed cost per unit, as reported in conventional accounts, varies inversely with volume and with cyclically sensitive material prices. Current full costs, consequently, appear cyclically rigid and the prevalence of cost-plus pricing imparts some of this cost rigidity to prices.

4. *Profits.* The role of custom and tradition in setting prices in many areas must not be underestimated. The concept of the "just price" is surprisingly common and in many industries restrains price rises as well as price declines. This factor has been of some importance in limiting price increases in manufacturing industry during the recent inflationary period. For price leaders and producers who have considerable latitude in price-making, obtaining a "reasonable" profit is often a more common goal than profit maximization.

The question of why prices are inflexible in many areas of the economy is generally answered in terms of the above set of factors. Not all of them are effective in every industry and at all times. Prices that are rigid in one period are not necessarily rigid indefinitely. The most rigid price has some flexibility and conditions making for inflexibility often break down under the impact of major shifts in economic conditions. Even the most sheltered industrial enterprise finds itself thinking in a new light about its problems when it is hit by catastrophic changes in the rest of the economy. Nevertheless, price rigidity is so pervasive a phenomenon that we must conclude that the above-listed factors are of major importance in determining the behavior of many industrial prices.

Policies on Cyclical Price Flexibility

The preceding analysis of price inflexibility is concerned with reasons for rigidity in broad areas of the economy. But each industry and each firm has particular problems of cyclical pricing. Since very few have completely rigid prices, they must make some decisions on responses to changing economic conditions.

The practical problems of cyclical pricing are a good deal more complex than a clear-cut choice between rigid prices and flexible prices. Problems arise as to the degree, the timing, and the pattern of cyclical price changes. Moreover, since changes in actual unit prices may be accomplished in various ways, a choice of the form of cyclical adjustment enters. Finally, the strategic overtones of market stratification cannot be neglected.

A cyclical change in the level of net prices may take a variety of forms that run the gamut of the chief dimension of prices: (1) changes in list prices, (2) changes in product-mix and product-line differentials, and (3) changes in the structure of discount and merchandising allowances. The decision as to the form of a given change in price level has an important strategic impact. The basic decision, however, is whether and how much to alter the net price level of the firm in adapting to cyclical fluctuations. It is this underlying problem that is the principal concern of this section of the chapter.

In formulating policy on cyclical pricing, several possible policies might be considered:
1. Price rigidity.
2. Price fluctuations that conform to cost changes.
   a. Current full cost.
   b. Standard full cost.
   c. Incremental cost.
3. Price fluctuations that conform to prices of substitutes.
4. Price fluctuations that conform to changes in the general price level.
5. Price fluctuations that stabilize market share.
6. Price fluctuations that conform to changes in industry demand determinants.

These policies might be characterized more accurately as objectives, since some of them cannot be fully attained. Furthermore, a choice among these alternatives is open only to firms that have some real freedom of choice as to cyclical policy—actual or potential price leaders or members of an industry where products differ enough to permit wide independence of price action.

Price Rigidity

Absolute or approximate stability of the company's price level over the course of the business cycle is a policy followed by some producers of industrial materials and equipment. It is largely based upon two beliefs: (1) that the wide cyclical fluctuations in demand are caused by basic economic changes (e.g., in incomes, profits, and expectations which are largely beyond the control of the seller, and (2) that changes in the firm's prices within the range of feasibility will be ineffective in altering these conditions or in tempering these cyclical fluctuations in demand. In fact, there is evidence that reductions in some prices during a depression might be more likely to accentuate than to check the decline in demand.

Price Fluctuations that Conform to Cost Changes

Confining cyclical changes in price to changes in company costs is another popular cyclical price policy. This policy has several variants, depending upon which concept of cost is employed: current full cost, incremental cost, or some variant of standard cost. In essence, it amounts to stabilizing some sort of unit profit margin. This policy has been defended in terms of a "just price." That is, price reductions in depressions are limited to the company's savings in unit cost (in some form), and price hikes in boom periods are voluntarily restricted to the sellers' increases in cost.

This policy has little to commend it. It shares the shortcomings of all cost-plus formula plans. It ignores all demand and competitive considerations. If prices are tied to current full cost and if overhead is important, then this policy may signal price advances when demand falls off and when substitutes' prices are declining. Conversely, in prosperity it would produce declining or sluggishly rising prices. Admirable though such pricing restraint may be in inflation, a successful anti-inflation policy needs a broader economic foundation than this pricing formula offers.

In oligopoly industries where the leader has substantial jurisdiction over price levels, most changes in basic prices are timed so that they may be explained and justified by cost changes. Such an occasion is used to make a whole series of price changes, both upward and downward, to remedy maladjustments brought on by rigid prices. Thus the increase in the price of steel to meet the wage increases of 1949 also includes decreases in export prices and no change in stainless steel. In contrast, the more "perfectly" competitive industries show prompt and continual adjustments of prices to demand and cost changes.

Normally an increase in factor prices does change the price at which maximum profit can be obtained and, other things being equal, it will call for a higher price. Presumably, the price increase will result in some reduction of quantity of goods demanded. The amount of the reduction will depend on the elasticity of demand. Shifts in the revenue function that result from the changed situation associated with the higher factor costs and from anticipation of price advances often counterbalance and hide the curtailment of sales that is caused by higher prices.

When purchased materials or components make up the important part of production costs, changes in their prices become an overwhelming consideration in setting selling prices. Typically, industries differ in the immediacy of this cost pressure from prices. In the rubber industry, for example, the big four, with long inventories in rubber, will not feel a cost squeeze as soon as the smaller companies, but later on the smaller ones will benefit more from a cost reduction. It may be argued that, since prices should logically be based upon replacement costs, inventory position is irrelevant. However, it is necessary to take realistic account of how competitors think about these costs rather than of how they *should* think.

There is a lively controversy among practical men on how cost-plus pricing should operate when the price of materials is rising substantially. Three levels of sophistication may be distinguished. At one level the doctrine is that price should be based on original cost of materials, since that is what was paid and is therefore the "actual cost." A more sophisticated view, possibly reflecting the benefits of courses in economics, is that prices should be based on replacement costs, since historical costs produce illusory, jumbled-dollar profits, and replacement costs come nearer to indicating real economic income. The third, and for some situations the highest, is to realize that your competitors, having eschewed economics courses, will price on original cost and will force you to do likewise.

Price Fluctuations that Conform to Prices of Substitutes

The use of substitute products as a cyclical pricing guide is an appropriate price policy in many situations. By keeping the spread between the firm's product and substitute products stable, or by manipulating it to obtain specified volume objectives, this cyclical pricing policy can protect or improve the company's market position. It may also stabilize the industry's share of the vast substitute market. In industries that have strong price leadership, the cyclical price policy employed by many price followers is of this type. Such firms follow the leader, either precisely or with some manipulation of price spread, when quality or reputation differences permit it. This kind of a competitively sensitive cyclical price policy has much to commend it.

Conformity to Changes in Purchasing Power

Keeping your price in line with the falling purchasing power of money is a depression pricing standard that has strong appeal. But this kind of blanket index of purchasing power is an inferior pricing guide. Purchasing power is an average that covers up great disparities in the behavior of the prices it summarizes. These component prices are more relevant for the company than their average. A single product should be priced in line with its own direct and indirect substitutes.

Price Fluctuations that Stabilize Market Share

Although market share is determined by many factors (product characteristics, marketing skill, and so forth), price is an important background determinant, particularly when products and services are dissimilar. Moreover, price policy has a profound effect upon the larger share of the substitute market. Market share can be a useful pricing guide for cyclical pricing. This policy is not at all the same as meeting all comers on price; nor is it even the same as maintaining the present price differentials among competitors. The price spread at the peak of the boom may have quite a different effect upon market share when recession sets in. Obviously, the adoption of such a policy presupposes moderately accurate and current information about what is happening to market positions. It also requires alertness and flexibility in pricing.

Price Fluctuations that Conform to Changes in
Demand Determinants

The demand schedules, both of the industry and of the firm, shift continuously as a result of changes in general business conditions and changes in special outside conditions that affect the product. If these shifts in demand are pronounced, they should be taken into account in setting prices. In fact, they are often more important than the elasticity of demand.

One recession pricing policy is to change prices in relationship to some appropriate index of shifts in demand for the product. Sometimes it is possible to find a direct relationship between some index like disposable national income and the past fluctuations of the price of the product. This functional relationship can then provide a rough criterion of the appropriate price at any given or forecasted level of demand.

The use of any such historical relationship as an absolute recession pricing criterion has severe limitations that destroy its usefulness in most industries. Implicitly, this pricing method assumes (1) that flexible rather than rigid prices are appropriate; (2) that changes in the price in the past have adjusted for changes in demand correctly (in the sense of attaining past pricing objectives); (3) that these past pricing objectives are today's objectives; and (4) that cost behavior and competitive reactions will be the same as in similar periods in the past.

Preserving Caste

One of the strategic problems in adjusting prices to changes in business conditions is to keep the product in the quality and service stratum that has been selected as a long-run merchandising policy objective. The quality and service sector in which the firm elects to operate partly determines the appropriate cycle pricing. Price policy must be synchronized with other aspects of marketing policy that are required for the chosen quality level.

It is often possible and desirable for a manufacturer to cater to several different quality layers of the market by differentiating products, brands, and services. But his cyclical pricing must be separately tuned to each such market segment. Quality stratification of competition does not mean that any given manufacturer is forever frozen in one layer. He may gradually move up or down the quality ladder. But if he does, it should be by long-term plan rather than inadvertently by an inappropriate cycle pricing policy.

Competition is not confined to firms in the same quality category, although direct rivalry is keenest for such firms. There is much overlapping, since caste lines are not clean. Customers shop and shift.

During a depression, many companies are tempted to "trade-down," i.e., apply to a product of lower quality a brand that has gained acceptance as a symbol of high quality—for example, the Packard 120, brought out in the thirties. Trading-down may be a sound, long-term policy. Moreover, it may be appropriate to time the downward move with a cyclical decline in demand. But trading-down should be recognized as a long-term shift in quality and service caste which can be reversed only at great expense over a long period of time. It should not be confused with cyclical price adjustment. And cyclical adjustments should be of a magnitude and form that will not inadvertently plunge a product from its chosen quality level.

Summary

1. Fluctuations in general business activity constantly shift the demand and cost conditions of the firm. To simplify decision-making in meeting new conditions, it is desirable to have some kind of company policy on cyclical price behavior.

2. Much publicity has been given to the thought that flexible prices would help to cut short the descent into depressions and reduce fluctuations in business activity. Nevertheless, there is little support for this idea either in accepted economic theory or in history. Whatever social merits flexible prices may have, they are difficult to achieve in most manufacturing industries, where inelastic demand, oligopoly tensions, cost rigidity, and "fair profit" concepts are common forces making for "price stability" over the cycle.

3. For companies that have some independent discretion as to the behavior of their prices, there are many different policies possible for simplifying the relation of price to cycles. However, pricing rules that are mechanistically based on cost behavior, or on movements of broad aggregates such as the FRB index, make little sense and may be dangerous if closely adhered to. Cyclical

changes in the company's demand function and the company's strategic goals should be the overriding considerations in cyclical price policy. Cyclical demand behavior varies not only for different products but for different qualities of the same product, and the company must make basic strategy decisions on whether to go into a depression with fighting prices and down-grading, or to sit it out in order to maintain a quality-and-price reputation untarnished.

Chapter 8

PRODUCT-LINE PRICING

Product-Line Pricing

I. INTRODUCTION

PRODUCT-LINE PRICING is an important practical problem for most modern industrial enterprises. Since almost every firm makes several related products, product-line pricing is an important phase of price policy. Yet the theory applicable to this pricing problem has never progressed beyond broad generalities that have almost no applicability outside the simplest discrimination situations.

The problem of product-line pricing is to find the proper relationship among the prices of members of a product group. This problem is here broadly conceived to include not only the pricing of products that are physically distinct, but also the pricing of those that, though physically the same, are sold under demand conditions that give the seller an opportunity to charge different prices. Thus use-differentials (e.g., fluid milk versus cheese milk), seasonal differentials (e.g., morning movie specials), and style-cycle differentials are all phases of product-line pricing.

The justification for this heterodox approach is that the essential economic feature of the product line is the cross-elasticity of demand that exists among parts of the seller's output—a product line should, from a pricing standpoint, be defined by demand relationships.

The dividing line between the kinds of price differentiation that are here included in product-line pricing and those that are viewed as price differentials associated with distribution is of course arbitrary. A convenient and administratively useful distinction can be made between: (1) distribution differentials, i.e., price differentials based on the nature of particular buyers, e.g., quantity discounts, trade-status discounts, cash discounts, and geographical differentials (discussed in Chapter 9, "Price Differentials"); and (2) product differentials, i.e., price differentials that are tied solely to the characteristics of the product and its use (e.g., quality spreads, size differentials, and other dimensions of product-line pricing).

Our analysis of product-line pricing is divided into two parts: the first sets forth a general approach to the problem; the second applies this approach to some specific cases.

II. GENERAL CONSIDERATIONS IN PRODUCT-LINE PRICING

The underlying approach to product-line pricing that is set forth in this chapter is relatively simple and has been developed elsewhere. Cost should not be a direct determinant of price; instead its role is to set lower limits for price and to help select the price-output combination that is most profitable. The important determinants of the pattern of relative prices of a company's products are differences in their competitive situations and demand elasticities.

Surprisingly enough this principle is not widely employed in product-line pricing. This may be because the principle is not recognized or accepted. Consequently it is desirable to determine exactly what principle (if any) underlies the firm's structure of product prices. To this end we consider alternative policies of cost relationship. But even if the suggested principle of pricing is accepted, difficulties of applying it may block its adoption. Therefore we discuss in this section problems of exploring demand relationships and competitive differences and of making and using cost estimates for pricing related products.

Alternative Policies of Price Relationship

A logical approach to product-line pricing is to start with a picture of the alternative kinds of policy regarding the relationships among prices of members of a product line. This approach assumes that it is desirable to have some kind of underlying system of relationship of product prices, which is debatable. But before adopting a philosophy of chaos it is well to examine systematic patterns, several of which are sketched below.

1. *Prices that are proportional to full cost, i.e., that produce the same percentage net profit margin for all products.*

Under this scheme, each product assumes its full allocated share of all common and overhead expenses, and each produces a uniform percentage profit over this full cost. This is the pattern of product-line prices that is produced by a strict adherence to cost-plus pricing in its conventional full-cost form. In the illustration in Table 8–2, this rule gives equal prices for the three products, since full costs are assumed equal.

Relative prices are thus determined by the accounting conventions that govern the allocations of common costs among products. In practice these allocations are necessarily arbitrary from an economic viewpoint. Moreover, this plan gives no considerations to market factors.

2. *Prices that are proportional to incremental costs, i.e., that produce the same percentage contribution-margin over incremental costs for all products.*[1]

The price pattern resulting from this policy can be quite different from that resulting from the full cost policy, as can be seen from the contrast in the illustrative prices in Table 8–2. When product A is priced at $1300 under the principle of incremental cost plus a uniform contribution mark-up, product B is priced at $325 for our arbitrary equated unit, and product C is $1950.

This pricing approach is largely, but not entirely, free from the defect of arbitrary allocation of common costs found in the first plan, since incremental costs usually require little arbitrary allocation of variable overheads. A pattern of product prices that produces contribution margins that are the same for all products is the result of cost-plus pricing when the base is incremental cost. But this price pattern also take no account of differences in demand and competitive conditions. If members of a product line differ in superiority over competing products or are able to tap market sectors that can stand differential prices or different degrees of non-price competition, then a pattern of product-line prices that is proportional to incremental costs misses significant profit opportunities. Incremental cost is a handy tool

---

[1] Incremental cost is the additional cost of added units. It is often moderately well approximated by those out-of-pocket costs that are directly traceable to the product. Contribution-margin is the spread between price and incremental cost.

TABLE 8–1

PRODUCT-LINE COST STRUCTURE

	A Tabulating machine	B Rental service	C Tabulating service
Incremental costs:			
1. Materials	200	30	750
2. Labor	400	120	150
3. Total	600	150	900
Overhead costs:			
4. Depreciation	100	400	50
5. Labor	200	440	20
6. Rent, power, etc.	100	10	30
7. Total	400	850	100
Full Cost (3) + (7)	1000	1000	1000

TABLE 8–2

ALTERNATIVE PRODUCT-LINE PRICE STRUCTURES

Pricing principle:	Mark-up	Prices A	B	C
1. Prices proportional to full cost	30%	1300	1300	1300
2. Prices proportional to incremental cost	117%	1300	325	1950
3. Prices proportional to conversion cost	62.5%	1300	1575	406
4. Prices related to demand elasticity		1300	1500	500

Tables 8–1 and 8–2 illustrate the kinds of product-line price structure that result from the alternative price policies discussed in the text. The product line is three alternative forms of a single service—statistical tabulation. The illustrative firm manufactures tabulating machines and offers (1) to sell the machines directly, (2) to rent them to customers on annual lease, and (3) to perform special tabulations for customers who need the service only rarely. Table 8–1 shows hypothetical cost data for these three products, set up somewhat as in cost accounting form. These are average unit costs, where for comparative purposes, the units chosen are such as to give equal unit "full costs." Some assumed rates of output are of course implicit in the data. Table 8–2 shows the varieties of price structure that are produced by following three different cost-plus rules, and by taking demand elasticity into account as in the text.

for product-line pricing; but its usefulness is destroyed if it becomes the basis for a mechanical cost-plus pricing formula.

3. *Prices with profit margins that are proportional to conversion cost, i.e., that take no account of purchased materials cost.*

The pattern of relative prices produced by this policy may diverge considerably from either of the other mechanistic policies just discussed. Table 8–2 illustrates possible divergences. Under conversion cost-plus pricing, product A would be $1300, B is $1575 and C, $406. Conversion costs, i.e., the labor and overhead required to convert raw materials into finished products, may be approximated by deducting purchased materials costs from allocated full cost.

This pattern of relationship of product prices to costs was staunchly advocated by W. L. Churchill [2] on the grounds that conversion costs (roughly the cost elements of "value added") reflect the firm's social contribution, whereas purchased costs do not. Hence the amount of profit earned on individual products, he reasoned, ought to be proportional to the expenditures that reflected the firm's additions to the social welfare as opposed to the activities of the firm as a mere distributor of materials and components that entered into its products. Recently, F. Heath has publicized the notion under his brand name of "Scientific Pricing." [3] Few economists would support this monistic view of the economic contribution of the firm.[4]

The notion that some elements of cost are more worthy of bearing a profit markup than others is hard to justify, particularly since this mechanistic approach to pricing ignores the differences in price elasticity among products, and in present and potential competition.

4. *Prices that produce contribution margins that depend upon the elasticity of demand of different market segments.*

Buyers with high incomes are usually less sensitive to price than those that make up the mass market, and it is often profitable to put higher profit margins on products for the plushy "class" markets than for the rough-and-tumble "mass" markets. Product-

---

[2] W. L. Churchill, *Pricing for Profit*, New York, The Macmillan Co., 1932.

[3] See "Philosophy of Conversion Cost Pricing," *National Association of Cost Accountants Bulletin*, Vol. 31, No. 2 (October, 1949), p. 137.

[4] Differences among one firm's products in the degree of vertical integration should be no more relevant for pricing than differences in integration among firms.

line prices that exploit differences in demand elasticity among
sectors of the market can be quite different from the patterns of
product prices produced by the three variants of cost-plus pricing
just discussed. In Table 8–2, for instance, we may suppose that
demand elasticity for sales is higher than for rentals, since buyers
are reluctant to take on the obsolescence risk of owning a machine;
whereas the tabulating service has high promotional value for
introducing the machine to new customers and thus warrants a
low, come-on price. Variations in style and features among
models of a single product can create a partial barrier to flow of
demand between such market segments. Ignorance, snobbishness,
and inertia are mainstays of the segmentation that makes such
price discrimination effective. Its most useful applications, therefore, are to new and exotic products; rational product comparison
is impossible and the buyer resorts to blind faith in the seller's
reputation. Royalty licensing of patents and "unit-charge" leases
of equipment, where the rental depends upon the output of the
machine, are examples of highly individualized segmentation.
Film rentals based on a percentage of the gate or of gross profits
also represent an attempt to charge each buyer a personal price
depending on the service-value of the product to him.

5. *Prices that are systematically related to the stage of market
and competitive development of individual members of the product line.*

Many products pass through life cycles. They start as novelties,
develop into distinctive and protected "specialties," and then
degenerate into undifferentiated commodities. This pattern of
economic evolution and the strategy of pricing for pioneering and
maturity stages were discussed in Chapter 7 ("Basic Price").

A product-line pricing policy that specifically recognizes that
a company's various products are at different stages in their life
cycles, and hence face different market acceptance and competitive
intensity, has much to commend it. When these differences
among products are great, the resulting pattern of product prices
can be quite divergent from that produced by cost-plus plans, as
is illustrated in Table 8–2.

A company's products change in their relative customer-ac-
ceptance. The by-products of one period become the main
products of a later period. For example, heating oil has grown
up from a dumped by-product to a major earning product. This

situation has been likened to that of the members of a human family: big brothers who contribute more than their pro-rata share of joint costs; self-supporting members whose price covers their pro-rata share; weak sisters who contribute more than incremental cost but are not self-supporting; and problem children who fail to cover costs savable by their elimination.[5]

This approach to the product-pricing problem is free from the restrictions of cost theology and margin uniformity. Moreover, it recognizes the dominant role of demand considerations in pricing. Its main contribution to product-line pricing is advance recognition of the probability of independent life cycles of monopoly power for the several products. Objective indicators of the stage in the cycle and suggestions for pricing strategy were discussed in Chapter 7. For finding the pattern of product prices that will achieve these strategic goals, it is necessary to use criteria of competitive intensity and price elasticity of demand.

The foregoing classification of policy alternatives is not exhaustive. But a background of analysis in terms of pure types will serve to sharpen the issues and highlight the basic choices. As in other policies, exceptions to the selected underlying scheme of relationship are expected. Moreover, different policies are likely to be appropriate for different product lines, and a combination of patterns is often desirable.

The important factors to consider in designing any product-line price structure are the demand relationships among products, differences in their competitive settings, and their costs.

Demand Relationships in the Product Line

Two demand characteristics peculiar to multiple-product lines are significant for pricing purposes. The first is the interdependence of the demand for various members of the product line. Interdependence takes many forms. Products may be substitutes for each other, e.g., different models of radios or grades of tires. They may be complementary, e.g., tabulators and punched cards. They may be complementary in the more remote and subtle sense of augmenting one another's acceptability, e.g., in enhancing the reputation of the firm.

Interdependence also has a time dimension. The sales of one

---

[5] E. S. Freeman, "Pricing the Product." *National Association of Cost Accountants Yearbook, 1939.*

product today may affect the sales of another product tomorrow. Striking examples are introductory models, such as trial subscriptions and children's editions of magazines, midget pencil sharpeners, and diminutive sporting equipment. But this time aspect extends into any product group in which the sale of one product tends to tie the customer to future purchases of other products, as exemplified by the slow-speed phonographs and their records.

A second demand characteristic in multiple-product lines is their importance as instruments for market segmentation and price discrimination.[6] They provide opportunities for breaking the market into smaller sectors that differ in price elasticity and hence can profitably be charged different prices. Product design and pricing are major methods for achieving segmentation. Not only can market segmentation increase profits by setting prices that take advantage of the different elasticity of demand in each sector; it can also increase total sales by penetrating mass markets at prices that cover incremental costs and contribute a little to overhead.

Big differences in demand elasticity among a company's products can be caused by differences in their competitive environment. A product's cross-elasticity of demand is determined by the similarity of competing products. Close competition causes high share-elasticity of demand, and makes competitor's prices controlling. Distance from these substitutes (i.e., marked superiority over competitors' products) reduces share-elasticity and usually permits higher profit margins.

The selection of market segments and of separation devices is intimately tied up with the buyers' sophistication as well as with the character of the product. For many products, ignorance and snobbishness create a demand for quality that can easily be exploited. Slight additions to cost in decorating, packaging, or servicing can add rich margins to the price. Chromium plate on cars, "streamlining" of washing machines, the lighting and decor of restaurants, and the media used for advertising are examples of devices used for this purpose.

The amount of leakage between market segments, i.e., transfer

---

6 The general nature of market segmentation and price discrimination is discussed in Chapter 9, ("Price Differentials").

of high-margin buyers to low-margin market is related, if other things are equal, to the price differentials that are used. Consequently, the practical pricing problem is to find the right price structure to maximize the margins without breaking down the walls of the segments. For example, some people are skeptical about the quality of the private branded products of mail-order houses compared to nationally advertised manufacturers' brands. This skepticism is the basis for segmenting the market and charging different prices. But as the price disparity widens, the barrier of skepticism and ignorance is broken down by more consumers who take the trouble to investigate the real product differences. The drastic invasion of the replacement tire and battery business by mail-order chains illustrates the way that leakage between sectors tends to increase as the price disparity increases.

Incremental concepts—comparing added revenue with the expected added cost—can alone provide a clear criterion of whether or not an additional division of a market is worth while. Incremental cost sets a lower limit for price in the most elastic sector of the market. For example, in deciding whether or not to sell a typewriter to a mail-order house for private branding a manufacturer should compare the added revenue (adjusted to allow for the potential loss of sales of the manufacturer's own brand) with the incremental cost of producing the additional machines. The costs of carving up a market into segments (e.g., brand-name advertising) and of policing the separating walls cannot be neglected.

Competitive Differences

An analysis of competition is frequently a vital phase of product-line pricing because differences of competitive setting among products call for differences in profit margins or distribution margins. Even though it is not possible to measure the relevant aspect of competition in a way that will indicate definitively how prices and margins should differ among products, an analysis of the structure of competition can be used to indicate a range of prices for particular products, and to rank products by various objective indications of competitive intensity.

The practical problem is to measure these competitive differences among products. Although there is a general underlying approach, its application depends on the nature of the product and the industry; hence it will be clearer to pin it down in terms of a concrete example, namely, a manufacturer of a diverse line of processing equipment designed to serve one particular manufacturing industry. This producer has the problem of measuring differences among nearly 100 distinct machines in its product line. The problem breaks down into two parts: (1) measuring the present intensity of competition; and (2) predicting the probability of entry of potential competition.

Existing competition can be measured indirectly by several of its symptoms: (a) the number of competitors; (b) the extent of the company's market occupancy (market share); and (c) the degree of similarity of the competitive product.

The number of existing competitors and their comparative size as measured by some such index as a concentration ratio (see Chapter 2, Section VII) differs widely among particular machines or closely related groups of machines. For example, group A products may have one competitor, group B three, and group C several hundred. In general, the fewer the competing sellers, the higher the margins, aside from other dimensions of competition.

Market share is a closely related indicator of competitive intensity, since products of this company varied from 90 per cent share down to about 20 per cent. Supposedly a product with a dominent market share can stand a higher mark-up, since the presumption is that it has competitive superiority.

The degree of similarity of competitive products, including customer services such as installation, application, engineering, and field services, is often hard to measure, though it can sometimes be approximated by rough indicators. For machinery, the relevant measure is usually the operating savings of this machine over those obtainable by the best competitive machine, and when these savings for typical or marginal users can be estimated, they are a fairly definitive guide to a price premium related to rate of return or payout on the customer's investment. Typically, some machines are so close to competitive equipment that little pricing discretion exists, and the only problem is a strategic one of setting a small premium or discount to compensate for differences in the bundle of services.

This equipment manufacturer must also price with a weather eye on potential competition. Here one necessarily operates in the realm of conjecture. There are, however, a few objective indexes that can be used to rank individual products in a ladder of probability of the entry of competitors. Some of these indexes are: (a) incentives for competitive entry; (b) patent barriers, (c) financial barriers, and (d) technological barriers.

According to the classical view, competitors' incentives to bring out equipment that will match or better this company's machines are related to profits. Although this is reasonable theory, there are some indications, mentioned in Chapter 7, Section III, that invasion, particularly by large firms, is related less to current profits in the industry than to the potential volume of business, and possibly also to the average unit price. This company's machines range in sales volume per year from under 100 machines to many thousands, and in unit price from under $50 to many thousands of dollars. Hence it would be possible to get a rough indication of outsiders' interest by a dual classification, first on the basis of sales volume in units (for the whole industry) and second, on the basis of unit price of the machine. High sales volume tempts entry, while high prices discourage entry, since most big companies would hesitate to develop and manufacture a large complicated piece of equipment that sells at a high price when the unit sales volume expectation is small. A simpler and adequate way to measure this aspect of entry incentives may be merely to rank products in terms of estimated industry dollar sales.

Patent barriers differ greatly for this company's machines. Although this factor cannot be quantified, the machines can nevertheless be grouped roughly on the basis of the value of their patents.

Financial barriers can be quantified by guessing how much money it would take to develop a competitive product and set up, manufacture, and sell it, although if the threat is from large, multiple-product firms, the costs of entry are hard to guess.

Technical barriers to entry, beyond patent roadblocks and financial requisites, are sometimes important in this field. The importance of nontransferrable know-how as a barrier can sometimes be measured by the intricacy of the equipment and the closeness of tolerances. A rough ranking of integral machines on this basis was possible for this company and, as is pointed out later, this factor is of considerable importance in assaying potential competition on replacement parts.

Cost Estimates

The first three of the policies of product-line pricing that were sketched at the beginning of this chapter imply that cost should be the dominant if not the sole consideration in determining the relationship of prices within a product line. Is this philosophy sound? Correctly used, cost estimates are indispensable for accurate analysis of almost every kind of pricing problem. The valid practical questions concern the kind of cost concept to be used in deriving estimates and the role of cost estimates in pricing.

Cost estimates are needed in product-line pricing to project roughly the effects upon profits of different price structures. Each set of prices will produce a particular product-mix (i.e., proportions of sales of various members of the product line) and a corresponding total revenue and total cost. Although different price structures can be designed to yield equal total revenues, they will nevertheless involve different total costs, since cost varies with the product-mix. The pricing problem, then, is to find the price structure with the biggest expected difference between total revenue and total cost.

A common approach to such profit estimates is to compare for each product its unit full cost (current or normal) with its price, and thus get unit net profit. But this method brings into the pricing problem the conventional overhead allocations of cost accounting and ignores the non-cash opportunity costs that are measured by alternative uses of plant. A more promising approach is to compare the incremental costs of each product with its price. Such a comparison, together with sales estimates, indicates the contribution to overhead and profit for each alternative price for each product. Experimentation with prices in this way shows the pattern that produces the greatest total contribution of all products combined to overheads and profits. This method is free from the arbitrary cost allocations of overheads in the net margin method which may complicate and obscure the maximizing process. This approach does not imply that prices of articles in a product line should be equal to incremental costs—far from it. Nor does it mean that prices of related products should be proportionate to their marginal cost. (See Chapter 9, "Price Differentials.") The margin between price and incremental cost should normally differ greatly, depending on the demand factors discussed above. These differences should *not* be determined by the allocation of overheads (which is necessarily quite arbitrary) or by the moral principle that each item in the line should "pull its own weight." So long as each product makes some contribution, the aggregate profit on the line is likely to be greater if the seller gets whatever marginal contribution he can from each product than if he attempts to price products so that each makes a uniform net profit.

One function of cost in product-line pricing is to set a floor below which price should not ordinarily go without raising the question of whether that product should remain in the line. For this purpose, the product's incremental cost (which is about the same in practice as the avoidable cost that could be saved if the product were eliminated) is the relevant cost concept. As has been pointed out, it is the product's marginal contribution to common overhead and profit that is strategic.

When using incremental costs in setting prices, a manufacturer must have a clear picture of the volume increment that is contemplated. Incremental cost sometimes will differ in amount depending upon the nature, the size, and the duration of the increase in volume. Output increments in slack months, or for products that improve the balance of utilization of equipment, will cause relatively low incremental cost, but a sudden big increase may raise it before complete adjustments in production flow are made. And the incremental cost of the kind of business that can be quickly cut off (e.g., subcontracting, and private-brand sales) is lower than the incremental cost of business that carries commitments to continue to supply. Thus the nature of the sale commitment determines the kind of incremental cost estimate that is appropriate.

The kind of cost estimates that are appropriate also depends upon the pricing objective. It is usually assumed that businessmen want to make as much money as possible, but, as we have seen in Chapter 1 ("Profits"), maximizing profits is not always the company's pricing goal. If the objective is to make a specified, limited profit, cost estimates play a quite different role in pricing than when maximum earnings are the objective. Cost may determine prices directly and mechanistically, rather than indirectly through selection of optimum prices. Relevant cost concepts and estimates, then, are those that will measure the particular concept of profits (e.g., accounting profits vs. economic profits) that is employed in the profit objective. For example a telephone company which was allowed a 6% net return by its regulatory commission should base its rates on full accounting costs, including corporation income taxes, to achieve the kind of profits allowed.

When additional business is taken at prices that are close to incremental cost, consideration must be given to the risks of spoiling the market by pulling down the whole price structure or of diverting high-price business into low-price business. Properly, these risks are a part of the incremental cost of this kind of price decision.

Thus strategic considerations may overreach economic considerations and restrict the importance of the effect upon short-run profits of a particular pattern of product prices. The strategic factors in product-line policy can be highlighted by classifying products in terms of the size of contribution margin and the reasons for low contributions.

Products that make a substantial, though below-average, contribution margin are candidates for elimination only when and if something better is found to take their place. Of course, a continuous effort must be made to improve or displace these below-average products, but most product lines contain some products of this type. They are of several kinds: (1) *Loss-limiters*, i.e., products whose purpose is to limit the loss from otherwise idle facilities. The existence of such products is justified when there is unused marketing or manufacturing capacity. Loss-limiters should normally be squeezed out or cut to a minimum volume when demand surges above capacity. (2) *Line-fillers*, i.e., strategic products that complete a product line by offering a full range of colors, sizes, designs, or types of product. Here the direct contribution may understate the true marginal contribution of the product, because of demand interdependence (see above). Nevertheless, unless strategy is absolutely determining, it is desirable to know and consider the cost of strategy in terms of the apparent contribution margin of such products. (3) *Price-meeters*, i.e., products whose role is to carry out company policy of meeting every competitive price with some member of the product line. Again, the strategic value of such products may exceed their apparent marginal contribution.

Products that make above-average contributions are usually

sheltered from the full blast of competition by the ability of the seller to manufacture or market more cheaply or to design more attractively or to keep ahead of the technological profession. It is desirable and proper that such competitive superiorities be reflected in higher margins.

Subject to these policy restrictions, a major job of cost estimates is to help select the most profitable pattern of prices in order to implement policies that take advantage of differences among members of the product line in competitive conditions and in demand elasticity among members of an existing product line. For this job incremental costs of individual products rather than fully allocated costs are normally appropriate. Cost estimates have another important job with respect to new-product pricing. These long-run pricing problems, which often amount to decisions on whether or not to add the products to the line, call for estimates of the long-run added costs of having, as opposed to not having, the product. Such long-run incremental costs are usually moderately well approximated by average full cost (including fixed overheads). These estimates should be projected into the future and should take account of economies of scale and technology. A third job of costs is to determine what should be the rock-bottom for short-run price concessions. For this decision short-run incremental costs provide a guide.

III. SPECIFIC PROBLEMS OF PRODUCT-LINE PRICING

The philosophy of product-line pricing that has been sketched can be illustrated by applying it to a few sample problems.

Pricing Products that Differ in Size

How should we determine price differentials for members of a product line that differ only in size? The first question is whether price should differ at all with size. If buyers' benefits do not vary and if costs differ little (e.g., in shoe sizes), a uniform price is sensible. Moreover, custom may force uniformity even when costs differ materially.

But if it is decided that price should vary with size, the next question is whether any kind of systematic pattern in respect to size is desirable. Having a pattern has its advantages. Price determination is made easier when new sizes are subsequently fitted into the line. The appearance of equity is given to the buyer. Management's time is saved by a blanket decision that can be systematically extended to individual pricing decisions.

Assuming that some systematic pattern is desired, which one should be chosen? In general, the possible choices are included in the five categories listed in Section I. The most common types are prices proportional to full costs and prices proportional to product size. Except when cost savings are possible on volume output for popular sizes, these two philosophies often produce price ladders with rungs in the same order, but different distances apart. They both have advantages of being easy to compute and to justify, but neither of them is necessarily the most profitable or strategic method of size-pricing. If the different sizes of products vary in competitive intensity and in opportunities for profitable market segmentation, proportioning price to any dimension of cost probably sacrifices potential profits, at least in the short run. Other strategic considerations should modify the pattern of prices. The demand for the various sizes is usually interrelated, particularly in its future dimensions. Low prices on small sizes may induce buyers to get acquainted with the product, and future sales of larger sizes may result.

The logical role for size as a pricing criterion is as a measure of value to the buyer. But size can be measured by a variety of dimensions, and it is important to find the most relevant. For some products the choice is not difficult, e.g., weight for different-size bags of sugar or flour. For other products, such as intricate durable equipment, it is hard to find an objective measure of size that is closely correlated to economic worth to the buyer (partly because buyers differ in the dimension that is relevant). What is the value of a 10-column calculator compared with an 8-column model? A 20-ton elevator compared with a 10-ton elevator? Is the usefulness of a radial power saw measured by the size of its blade or by its horsepower? Since the weight capacity of a parachute is roughly proportional to its volume, which increases more steeply than either diameter or cost, should the price-size gradient be determined by capacity or by costs?

In selecting the pattern of relationship of price to size, much depends on whether the typical buyer has freedom to substitute one size of product for another, so that two sizes are in competition. If substitution is possible, then much can be said for lower prices per service unit for larger sizes, so that the buyer will be induced to shift to the larger sizes. This situation is especially desirable if the manufacture of larger sizes permits important savings, and if the purchaser of the bigger package will be more likely to form the habit of using the brand. Habitual use shelters the seller from competition during a longer consumption period.

The intensity of competition often varies with size. Since different sizes sometimes go into quite different uses, the service value, as compared with alternatives, bears little relation to size or to the seller's costs. For example, potential use of parachutes differs in different sectors of the size range, from lowering whole airplanes to dropping caged carrier pigeons. Competition from other parachutes, as well as from substitutes, is more intense in some sectors of this size-use range than in others.

An example of the size-differential pricing problem is found in the fractional-page advertising rate of magazines. Often, eighth-page, quarter-page, half-page, and full-page space is offered at prices that are not proportional to space. A decision on this pattern of prices should involve: (1) an estimate of the incremental costs of each type of fractional-page advertisement in order to estimate the marginal contribution to profits and general overhead that each size makes under present prices and also under other possible price schedules; (2) some kind of estimate of the pulling power of advertisements of various sizes in order to estimate the service value of different-size ads to the typical buyer of space; (3) an investigation of the hypothesis that advertisers who buy eighth-page ads later grow up to buy full-page ads. One magazine recently found that the number of eighth-page advertisers who eventually became full-page advertisers was extremely small. The proportion of advertisers who would have to grow up to full-page ads in order to justify the sacrifice in contribution margin with the present eighth-page rate was several times the proportion of advertisers who had actually become full-page advertisers.

Pricing Products that Differ in Quality

How should we determine the relationship among prices of members of a product line that differ in quality? This decision depends primarily upon the strategic objectives of having products that differ in quality. Sometimes the purpose of high-quality items is to bring prestige to the entire line (e.g., 50-dollar cuff links to glamorize a line of medium-priced men's jewelry). Then the price of the prestige items should not be set with any view to its effect on sales of the product itself, but rather with a view to its effect upon attitudes of customers toward the lower-priced, high-volume members of the line.

There is considerable support for the belief that demand is less responsive to price at the high end of the quality scale. Table 8–3 shows that for washing machines the gross and net margins over factory billing price, over factory cost and over full cost widened systematically from the stripped model to the super deluxe.

TABLE 8–3

UNWEIGHTED AVERAGES OF GROSS AND NET MARGINS FOR DIFFERENT
PRICE LINES OF WASHING MACHINES, 1941 [a]

Retail List Price	$49	$59	$69	$79	$89
	Sample I [b]				
Unit factory cost	$26.39	$28.16	$31.12	$35.10	$36.69
Total unit cost	30.61	32.89	36.22	40.45	42.40
Factory billing price .	30.94	33.55	37.92	43.61	47.48
Percentages			(per cent)		
Factory billing of retail list	63.1	56.8	55.0	55.2	53.3
Factory cost of factory billing price	85.3	84.0	82.1	80.5	77.3
Total cost of factory billing price	98.9	98.1	95.5	92.8	89.3

[a] Records of the Office of Price Administration. These costs were applicable to the closing months of the year and show in general much lower operating profit margins than the industry enjoyed for the year as a whole (10.4 per cent of sales reported for 1941) and higher ratios of factory cost to total cost and to selling price than was experienced for the year as a whole. (OPA *Economic Data Series No. 8,* Table 5.) This indicates either that costs reported had not been adjusted downward for "variances" or the difference between anticipated costs as shown by the company's standard cost systems, or that costs had been adjusted in anticipation of curtailed operations under wartime restrictions. These facts do not invalidate the use of the data here for these factors should have had an equivalent effect on the costs of the respective models and we are interested in inter-model comparisons, not the absolute level of costs for particular models.

[b] Five companies.

(The author is grateful to Richard Hefflebower for permission to use this table. It was developed by Mr. Hefflebower for a study of the washing machine industry not yet published.)

When the purpose of low-end articles in the firm's quality scale is primarily to counter price competition by keeping some items in the line competitive with the lowest-priced product in the market, then an entirely different pattern of quality-price differentials is needed. The main purpose of the "fighting brand" may be to maintain the "never undersold" claim for the entire product line. Another purpose of the low-quality item in the line may be to take up the shock of cyclical flexibility in pricing. Thus third-grade gasoline is normally introduced and pushed in depression phases of the cycle and disappears in prosperity phases. Similarly, third-grade tires appear and are emphasized when competition is severe. Under such circumstances, the price of the "fighting brand" is determined not at all by costs, but solely by the competitive prices it is designed to meet by competition within a narrow range.

In many industries the typical firm operates in two distinct markets: a brand market and a dumped market.[7] The methods of determining output rates are distinctly different for these two types of market. In the branded-product market, the method is "all you can sell," which means that price concessions are not used in the short run to expand sales, the seller being acutely aware of the overtones of spoiling the market. "All you can sell," then, for any one month, is determined pretty much by hustling during that month in the setting of product-acceptance developed by past advertising and merchandising, and by the dynamic changes in business conditions.

Unbranded output is dumped into the other markets in the amount needed to use up the remainder of the plant's capacity.[8] In this dumped market the manufacturer, regardless of his size, acts pretty much as he would under conditions of pure competition. He "follows the market"—i.e., sells at the best price he can get. In so doing he does not allow for the possibility that low prices in the unbranded, cut-rate trade may reduce the sales

---

[7] This kind of double-standard output determination is apparently found in industries that have the following characteristics: (1) low (and fairly constant) marginal production costs relative to total costs (often associated with heavy mechanization and continuous-process production); (2) brand names that command price premiums; and (3) oligopoly.

[8] In many industries, capacity is fairly definite at one-, two-, or three-shift operation, depending upon the nature of the process. Capacity is defined partly by engineering convention, but behind this definition may lie a rising average unit cost beyond the rated capacity.

of his price-maintained branded output. The branded product gets priority on production capacity; its output is determined by market reaction to a fixed price. Selling costs are the long-run method of market expansion, and prices of branded products are not adjusted to stabilize seasonal and cyclical shifts of demand. The unbranded segment of output takes up the slack to keep production at economical rates. It is dumped at whatever price it can bring, down to (and sometimes below) short-run marginal production costs.

Price lining—i.e., a predetermined pattern of relationship in the price to the ultimate buyer—is a common example of quality differentials. The widespread use of price lining in retail establishments and its growing acceptance as a philosophy of product-line planning on the part of manufacturers raises important problems of pricing the product line. But they are not solely pricing problems. Quite largely, from the manufacturer's viewpoint, they constitute a problem of product design and selection. Inverted pricing may be involved, which starts with the retail price goal and works back through distributor margins and selling costs to necessary manufacturing costs, and hence to the design and selection of a product that will fit into the product line strategically.

However, part of the impact of price lining is absorbed by differences in margins, both in the distribution channels and at the level of manufacturing. The tailoring of the design of the product to fit the retailer's price line must sometimes be supplemented by variation of manufacturer's (and dealer's) profit margins.

Charm Prices

The belief has long been held that prices ending in odd figures, e.g., $4.95 and $9.95, have greater effect than even prices such as $5 and $10. Although this point has been debated for years, empirical research does not yet permit a conclusive answer, but the evidence does throw serious doubt on the validity of this "charm price" theory. Several years ago, a mail-order house systematically experimented by pricing the same article in different catalogues at odd prices and at even prices, e.g., $2.98 and $3.00. The results were shockingly variable. Sometimes moving a price from $2.98 to $3.00 greatly increased sales, and sometimes it lowered them. But the experiment did cast considerable doubt on the charm price doctrine. More recently, a mail-order house priced the same item at $1.99 in one million catalogues, $1.98 in the second million, and so forth, down to $1.88. There was no clear evidence of concentration of sales response at any figure such as $1.95. Inflation has done much to dissolve the rigidity of conventional price brackets. Tabulation of prices quoted in New York daily newspapers showed a clear concentration at "bargain" figures such as $4.95 and $9.95, but it also showed an almost continuous coverage of the intervening price range.

Nevertheless, rightly or wrongly, the conviction that certain pricing points are peculiarly effective at the retail level may, and perhaps should, lead manufacturers to select their prices and possibly modify their products in order to reach the consumer market at these prices.

Pricing Special Designs

In pricing special designs, it is common practice to estimate "normal" full cost, then add to cost a fixed percentage to represent a "fair" or desirable profit. Let us examine the usefulness and adequacy of this cost-plus procedure.

To an important degree, the price decision on special orders is really a decision as to whether or not to produce the product at all. Hence cost plays a peculiar role in special-order pricing. An essential foundation for special-order pricing is good judgement in estimating accurately the future cost of unfamiliar products. Analysis of previous cost experience in the kind of detail that can be focused on the estimating problem is called for here.

The problem of pricing special designs can be usefully analyzed by seeking answers to these questions:

1. What price is required to secure the order?
2. What is the lowest price that will make the business acceptable to the producer in the short run, in the light of available alternatives?
3. What adjustments in the short-run figure are made possible (or necessary) by long-run future benefits (or drawbacks)?

Business-getting Price

To estimate what is the highest price that can be charged without losing the business is often a sheer guess. Partly for this reason, many quotations on special orders are really a form of refusal pricing. Bidding in the dark on what the product is worth to the buyer, the seller tries to accept no business that will not produce the desired unit net profits over "normal" cost. He may carry this concept further, and have a policy of "discouragement pricing" on special orders in order to channel demand into purchase of his standard models.

At the other extreme, there are cases where the maximum price is pretty definitely known, so that the real problem is whether or not this price is acceptable to the seller. Between these extremes lies a dim area where estimates of buyers' benefits and alternatives and guesses at rivals' bids may give some indication of the upper limit.

Where buyers are few and powerful and are also potential producers (e.g., automobile companies buying from parts producers), pricing on the basis of full current cost may be logical. Buyers' intimate knowledge of the seller's production processes and costs makes them sensitive to high unit margins, and their ability to produce the product themselves may make stay-out pricing on the part of the sellers a wise strategy. But even under these circumstances it is not the seller's costs that are relevant but those that the buyer would incur if he made the part himself, or the costs of some other potential supplier. The seller's costs are useful primarily as a guide in estimating these pertinent costs.

Acceptable Price

A second problem is to determine the lowest price that the seller can afford to accept, considering his alternatives. A useful concept for this purpose is "parity price." A parity price, as the term is used here, is one that yields the same total contribution-profit as would have been obtained from the available alternative uses of the plant facilities (or of the bottleneck factor, e.g., skilled labor). The pricing action of the firm should depend upon what these alternatives are. If the alternative is idleness, the parity price is incremental cost. Revenue from a special order must exceed the incremental cost if this business is acceptable. But this incremental cost does not give price answers automatically and must, in fact, be used with care.

If, however, the alternative is the production of regular lines, the parity price is quite different. Then it is incremental cost plus the dollars of contribution (to profit and overhead) obtainable from the displaced regular production, i.e., alternative uses of the production facilities (or in general the limiting scarce factor, e.g., steel). If the alternative is the production of some other special order, that should determine the "parity price." Long-run considerations, such as the possibility that the special business will become permanent, the danger of spoiling the market, and so on, should modify this first approximation.

"Load Factor" Price Differentials

Charging different prices at different times for the same product or service in order to improve the seller's load factor has important profit potentialities for many producers. Increasing interest in employment stability and in the annual wage may well accentuate interest in this pricing problem. The impact of cost considerations on this aspect of product-line pricing is greater than on most other aspects.

Examples of load factor price differentials are: off-peak rates for electric energy, morning movie prices, August fur sales, summer coal discounts, advance dating of merchandise, and so on. Off-peak pricing is not necessarily confined to the same product sold at different times. It may take the form of a slightly or totally different product used to fill in valleys and priced with this objective in view. Much private-brand merchandise is made in off-seasons and sold at favorable prices because of this scheduling latitude. Similarly, the price differential between stable products and more highly styled products of the same type may in part be justified by the greater ability to make the stable merchandise off-season because its inventory obsolescence risk is smaller.

If a seller uses price as an instrument for improving the load factor and stabilizing operations, how should he determine how much of a price differential is desirable? Analysis of demand, cost and competition should enter into this determination. Shiftability of demand and elasticity of demand should be dominant considerations. The probable effect of a price differential in changing the timing of demand is hard to predict exactly. Experience with other products, plus experimentation, is one way to find out about the price sensitivity of such demand shifts. Examination of the circumstances of consumption, purchase, and resale provide indications of the barriers, costs, and risks of shifting demand of consumers and merchants. In general, a smaller price differential may be required to induce wholesalers and retailers to incur added inventory costs and risks than would be needed to induce consumers to shift their consumption patterns.

A second demand consideration is the degree to which lower prices will tap new sectors of the market and thus increase total demand rather than merely alter its timing. Demand elasticity differs greatly among products. August fur sales and morning movies, for example, are supposed to bring in customers excluded from the market by normal price levels. Summer discounts on coal probably do not.

Cost considerations are important, but price differentials should not necessarily be proportional to cost differentials. Instead, cost analysis should be used to set limits to price differentials and to guide the selection of the most profitable pattern of time and product discount. The economies of stable operations and larger lots are the sources of cost differentials. The difference between the total annual cost with the present load factor, and the total costs with the improved load factor gives the savings estimate. If the discount results primarily in net additions to total business, incremental cost at the valley sets a rock bottom for such discounts. If the effect is merely to transfer demand from peak to valley, then logically the difference between marginal cost at the peak and the marginal cost of producing in an off-peak period sets the outside limit for the price differential. Often it is more practical to estimate the cost effects in terms of total costs before and after the contemplated change in the time-distribution of demand. This method brings out incremental cost as the foundation for estimates of the total dollar contribution before and after the contemplated change.

Pricing Repair Parts

All manufacturers of durable goods face the problem of pricing spare parts. It is an important problem. For some firms the sales receipts from repair parts exceed those from new equipment. For even more firms the gross profits from parts do, or will at some stage, exceed gross profits from new equipment.

But typically, the number of repair parts is very large for a big, full-line machinery manufacturer, and the sales frequency for individual parts is low and erratic, presenting the manufacturer with a choice between ridiculously small production lot sizes and large costs and risks of carrying the parts in inventory. This problem is accentuated as the machines get older, and it seems to be hard to make customers appreciate the costs, risks, and nuisance of standing perpetually ready to supply such parts on short notice.

One solution for the repair parts problem of ancient machines is to set a policy that no repair parts will be supplied for any machines that are, say, over fifteen years old. Unfortunately, however, customers put much stock in the prospect (usually valueless) of having easy access to parts forevermore, and the parts problem therefore needs a less frontal attack.

Competition and Repair Parts Pricing

Essentially the problem has many aspects of monopoly pricing. The amount of monopoly power normally is greater for repair parts than for the integral equipment, because, once the buyer has bought the original equipment, he is usually committed to a single source of replacement parts.

This monopoly power is, however, always restricted by competition of various forms. These differences in competitive intensity are an important guide to pricing. For example, they justify a different mark-up for jobbed parts than for made parts.

Competition takes several forms, which may act independently or together:

1. Manufacturers are frequently requested to quote spare parts prices as a part of the price quotation for the original equipment; buyers have been known to reject such equipment because parts prices were too high. Some buyers also keep records of the cost of repair parts per unit produced by the equipment, e.g., per ton of coal mined. Since this cost reflects not only the durability of the equipment but also the price policy on parts, this practice has a restraining influence on parts pricing. Thus parts pricing is sometimes a significant dimension of original equipment competition. Consequently, considerations of broad competitive strategy enter into determining the general level of repair parts prices.

2. Another source of competition that affects repair parts pricing is the buyer's alternative of making his own repair parts. Estimates of buyer's shop costs, plus opportunity profits, can translate this factor into a rough price limit.

3. A major source of parts competition in some industries comes from companies who specialize in making parts but who make no original equipment. In the mining machinery industry, for example, there are specialized competitors who produce high-quality parts and who sell at standard prices. There are also competitors, regarded as bootleggers, who price systematically below the parts price of the manufacturer of the original equipment.

Influences of Convention

In the machinery industries, buyers' rough, rule-of-thumb standards influence sellers' price policies. One rough check, for example, is that the sum of the prices of all spare parts should not be more than double the price of the integral machine. For some kinds of machinery, buyers have a dollars-and-cents price per pound that they consider "reasonable."

In examining the prices of repair parts, some buyers have developed the notion that "eye appeal should be right." This means that the price should be consistent with the prices of other repair parts, considering the size and complexity of the item. Some manufacturers price spare parts by a criterion of weight adjusted roughly for complexity. Cost is widely used as a standard of price consistency among the repair parts made by a given manufacturer. This method usually makes parts prices proportional to their "normal" full cost.

Suggested Approach

Logically, spreads among the prices of machine parts should *not* be related to relative average costs or to relative weight. Instead, their comparative prices should be governed primarily by buyers' alternatives. Parts that are readily available either because specialized parts manufacturers supply them, or because they are jobbed rather than made by the producer of the machine, should be sold at relatively low prices. In other words, they should have a relatively low mark-up over incremental cost. Parts that the buyer can himself rebuild or can make fairly easily in his own shops ought to be priced low, in recognition of this potential competition. Parts that are sheltered from competition, on the other hand, should be priced to reflect this profit opportunity. Differences in usefulness among the parts themselves have no role in pricing, however, since parts seem to be about equally indispensable.

One large manufacturer of equipment found an inverse relationship between complexity of manufacture and intensity of competition. Different classes of replacement parts were distinguished on the basis of complexity of the company's own fabricating operations: (1) parts purchasable in finished form from mill supply houses; (2) parts purchasable in blank, or semi-finished form from mechanical-products houses that will complete the blank part for a standard finishing fee; (3) parts that could be reproduced by simple hand tool methods, usually by the customer's mechanic; (4) parts that could be reproduced by rough machining, often in the customer's tool rooms; (5) parts that would require precision machining, usually by an outside machine shop.

Production engineers can quite speedily classify parts in groups such as these. Ideally, if worth the cost, it might be possible to guess at the customer's alternative for each part, or, on the average, for each category in the form of a margin over the manufacturer's standard or out-of-pocket cost. But even if the classification is only used to indicate a rough ladder of profit mark-up, it can be a useful device for improving repair parts pricing.

Orderliness of pricing patterns may have some value as a guiding principle but its value is probably overrated. It is doubtful whether buyers who want a car gear of a particular size study the prices of all other sizes and worry about size-price consistency.

There are limitations to this general attack on the problem of pricing repair parts. The cost of making the estimates that would be required to set a price usually makes it impractical to have "scientific" pricing of every individual repair part. Moreover, the difficulty as well as the cost of estimating at all accurately what the buyers' future competitive alternatives will be limits the usefulness of this approach for trivial parts. Finally, the threat of potential competition should restrain the seller from taking extreme price advantage of his monopoly situation in repair parts.

Pricing Leases and Licenses

Royalty licensing and leasing of capital goods and patents are applications of market segmentation pricing. These practices represent one of the nearest practical approaches to perfect price discrimination because they charge each user a price that closely conforms to the benefits he receives. Thus this pricing practice reaps for the seller a share of the gains of the most advantageous users, and at the same time sets up the minimum price barrier for those whose uses of the equipment would be less advantageous. There are vast differences in benefits from a piece of equipment among its potential buyers. Benefits are determined by the purpose for which the equipment is obtained, the rate of utilization, the efficiency of alternatives, and so forth. Hence charging a uniform, lump sum to all potential buyers for the life-time stream of services of the machine gives to the most advantageous users an unearned surplus and cuts off the patronage of users whose benefits fall below this price line.

In determining the royalty price, the development costs that were incurred in creating the equipment are irrelevant. Since they are, at the time, sunk costs, they have no bearing in pricing the equipment. For example, in determining rentals on movies, the entire production costs of the film should be ignored. Only the incremental costs of distributing it and the amount that the public is willing to pay to see it are relevant considerations in setting royalty prices.

The costs that will be incurred in *producing* a machine, however, are not sunk, and hence are relevant. The expected cost of selling the rental service should be included as well as the servicing cost. These production, selling, and servicing costs may well set a sill of a minimum annual rental that rejects the potential customers who have no promise of profitability. This element of the price is a device for rejection and selection. It selects the customers who will benefit enough to justify the unit royalty.

How to price the royalty charge for the use of patents is a problem of importance. The objectives of price policy here may be: (1) to stimulate wide use of the patent among both competitors and others so that competitors will help carry the burden of promotion of the new product; (2) to discourage competitors from developing alternative processes or infringing the patent; (3) to ward off governmental disapproval; and (4) to obtain maximum profits consistent with the other three objectives.

To attain these objectives, certain pricing principles discussed above should be applied. First, the cost of developing the patented process is wholly irrelevant. It is a *sunk* cost, which will be the same whether the seller licenses or does not license the patent, and whether he charges little or much for it. The buyer does not know or care whether the invention cost millions of dollars or came as a costless stroke of genius. Those costs that will be incurred in the future in connection with administering the license are the only relevant costs for pricing. They should be used to select among alternative royalties the one that will yield the greatest net profit contribution over and above these incremental costs. Second, the probable cost that potential competitors would incur if they developed a similar process themselves is a relevant pricing factor, if they can be estimated with any degree of accuracy. They would have a bearing on the royalty price that would discourage competitors from developing a similar process. Normally, it is not practical to do much with this factor because of the wide error of estimating such a cost. Third, the principal consideration in pricing should be buyer's benefits, i.e., the worth of the process to the licensee. To estimate this service value at all accurately is usually difficult. Yet it is better to guess at the right concept, even if error margins are wide, than to use the wrong concept (e.g., the cost of development).

Sometimes it is practical to gauge the buyer's value by comparing the licensed process with the cost that would be incurred by the buyer if he obtained the same results by his next-best method. A prominent petroleum additive is said to be priced to the petroleum industry so that the product properties that it gives to petroleum products will be cheaper by this method than by any other available method. When the results of the licensed process cannot be obtained by other means, then its value can sometimes be gauged roughly in terms of the price premium for the finished product or in terms of lessened sales resistance obtainable if the patent is used. For example, the value of the "Sanforizing" process for shirt manufacturers takes the form of premium prices and/or greater sales volume for shrink-proof shirts.

Chapter 9

PRICE DIFFERENTIALS

I. INTRODUCTION
  KINDS OF DISCOUNTS
  EFFECT OF DISCOUNTS ON AVERAGE REALIZED PRICE
  PRICE DISCRIMINATION
    What Is Price Discrimination?
    Is Price Discrimination Bad?
  THE VARIETIES OF NON-DISCRIMINATORY PRICES
  MARKET SEGMENTATION
  GOALS OF DIFFERENTIAL PRICES

II. DISTRIBUTOR DISCOUNTS
  NATURE OF DISTRIBUTOR DISCOUNTS
    Discounts vs. Profits
    Form of Distributor Discounts
    Examples of Distributor Discounts
  HOW TO DETERMINE DISTRIBUTOR DISCOUNTS
    Objectives
    Distributors' Operating Costs
    Competitors' Discount Structures
    Effect on Distributor Population
    Costs of Selling to Different Channels
    Opportunities for Market Segmentation

III. QUANTITY DISCOUNTS
  WHAT KIND OF QUANTITY DISCOUNTS?
    Product-Quantity vs. Mixed Order
    Physical vs. Dollar Measures of Order Size
    Incremental vs. Total-Order Size
    Order Size vs. Cumulative
    Combination of Quantity and Channel Discounts
  WHAT SIZE OF DISCOUNT?
    Objectives
    Legality

IV. CASH DISCOUNTS

V. GEOGRAPHICAL PRICE DIFFERENTIALS
  GEOGRAPHICAL PRICING METHODS
    Postage-Stamp Pricing
    Zone Pricing
    Single Basing-Point Pricing
    Multiple Basing-Point Pricing

501

Price Differentials

I. INTRODUCTION

In the preceding chapters we examined problems of establishing the company's basic price level and the prices of individual products. Our discussion included pricing a new product over its cycle of competitive degeneration, pricing under conditions of oligopoly, adapting the company's prices to cyclical fluctuations in business conditions, and pricing members of product lines. In this chapter we shall discuss problems of establishing a structure of price differentials designed to accommodate various circumstances of purchase.

By modifying the list price, these discounts and differentials tailor the net price to the peculiarities of particular purchase situations. Although this individual adaptation of the price is usually accomplished by several general schedules of price discounts, their combined impact gives the buyer a personal net price.

Kinds of Discounts

The principal bases for price differentials are: (1) the trade status of the buyer; (2) the amount of his purchase; (3) the location of the purchaser; (4) the promptness of payment; (5) the time of purchase; and (6) the personal situation.

Only the first four types are discussed in detail in this chapter. Time-of-purchase discounts and informal price concessions will be examined only briefly.

Prices that vary over time, e.g., the seasonal discounts of the anthracite coal industry, are quite common. These variations range from time-of-day differentials, as found in movie tickets, restaurant prices, and utility rates, through day-of-week and end-of-month discounts, and on up to seasonal and (conceivably) cyclical differentials. The purpose of discounts based on time of purchase is usually a combination of (1) an effort to establish discriminatory market segmentation, and (2) an effort to modify the time pattern of demand in order to produce more favorable behavior of costs.

Informal price concessions are also a common practice, but they do not find their way into official discount structures. Devices for this kind of personal discrimination are legion. They include trade-in allowances, special prices to promote combination sales, additional services without compensating charges, leniency in accepting returned goods and in extending credit, and free goods and combination offers. These concessions often serve as the mechanism for changing the basic price level in the firm and in the industry. (Chapter 7, "Basic Price.")

Effect of Discounts on Average Realized Price

The average net realized price per unit obtained by the manufacturer depends not only upon the formal structure of price differentials for various classes of purchasers, but also upon the proportion of sales made in each class, and the departures from formal price structures. Consequently, competitors usually differ in net realization per unit, even when their formal price structures are quite similar. For these reasons, and because of differences in formal discount structures, there is often little relation between the average recovery to the manufacturer per unit and the list prices of competitive products.[1]

Price Discrimination

The elaborate structure of discounts related to trade channels, quantities, geographical location, terms of payment, time of purchase, and the extra charges for special services that are an integral part of every price quotation[2] create price differentials that usually involve some price discrimination.

---

[1] In the tire industry, for example, the big four brands had, in 1943, the lowest average retail list price, but also made the highest recovery at wholesale; and small tire companies that had high list prices had substantially lower average recovery. In the tire industry there is, moreover, a clear relationship between average recovery and relative expenditure on selling and advertising. Small firms with large selling expenses recovered almost as much per tire as the big four that advertised heavily. But the recovery of small firms that did little advertising was much lower.

[2] For a detailed account of the intricate texture of a modern price quotation, see Reavis Cox, "Non-Price Competition and the Measurement of Prices," *Journal of Marketing*, April, 1946, pp. 370–383.

Although price discrimination has been an important legal concept since the passage of the Interstate Commerce Act of 1887, it did not plague manufacturers seriously until the Robinson-Patman Act was passed in 1936. This concept now plays a central role in the legal appraisal and reform of manufacturers' discount structures. But discrimination started out as an ethical, rather than economic, concept, and it thus has many meanings. The legal definition, while obviously important, is by no means the most useful one for management's pricing policy and profit-making purposes.

Intelligent determination of prices from the seller's standpoint requires an understanding of what is involved in price discrimination, specifically, the answers to two basic questions: (1) exactly what is it; and (2) is it bad?

What Is Price Discrimination?

Price discrimination is said to exist when differences in prices charged by a seller do not exactly match differences in costs. In a world of multiple-product firms and large common overhead costs, this definition is not sufficient for detecting discrimination, since it does not specify either the concept of cost or the base for an "equal" spread between cost and price.

As to cost concepts, the choice lies essentially between (1) average full costs, and (2) marginal costs. To define discrimination as price differentials not equal to average full costs, which is the accepted practice in FTC regulation, is in several respects inadequate. First, the allocation of common costs and overhead to different products makes determination of the average unit cost of individual products largely a matter of "judgement" in choosing among several defensible bases of apportioning non-traceable common costs. Untraceable costs are particularly prominent in marketing operations. Unit costs are most indeterminate for the various conditions of sale—quantity, location, channel—which are the basis for a firm's structure of price discounts.

An especially ticklish problem is the allocation of promotional costs. Some apparently discriminatory price concessions are really promotional costs that need to be allocated over a broader base than the transactions in question. Even explicit promotional outlays are hard to assign properly. For example, if a cigarette manufacturer hands out free samples at a baseball game, this is discrimination against the people who pay money for his brand;

and yet the handout is a form of promotional expense, not economically different from billboard advertising.

The meaning of "equal" spread between cost and price is also hard to define precisely.   It may mean equal markups on cost, or equal ratios of price to cost, or equal returns on investment.   For long-run equality of advantage to the seller, it ought to mean equal returns on investment, but the job of computing returns on different kinds and conditions of sale is much too expensive and conjectural for practical trade regulation.   Equal markup on cost is the concept most commonly used in legal questions of discrimination, although this concept also provides formidable problems of cost analysis.   (It should be noted, however, that equal prices are never discriminatory in law, regardless of cost disparities.)   Thus, a test of price discrimination in terms of price disparities that do not conform to cost disparities has serious defects of concept and measurability.

A concept theoretically preferable to average unit cost for testing the existence of price discrimination is marginal cost.   The most rigorous and, indeed, the only fully satisfactory cost disparity type of definition of discrimination is that all prices are discriminatory unless they precisely equal marginal cost.   Marginal costs can (in principle) be definitively identified with a particular customer's purchase, and they measure the added social burden of a unit of output.   This definition of discrimination, however, has little practical usefulness, since marginal-cost pricing cannot earn a "normal" return on capital except at peak output rates that crowd the plant's capacity.   At such levels of over-full production, marginal costs are rising rapidly, and are highly sensitive to the rate of output.   Prices set equal to marginal cost would at these levels fluctuate wildly with small changes in output.

In an effort to make the marginal cost definition more useful in practice, economists have tried defining discrimination as prices that are not proportional to marginal costs.   By this test, prices are discriminatory unless they produce contributions to overhead and profits from each sale that are in the same ratio to incremental costs.   A variant of this concept is that a seller discriminates whenever *differences* in his prices for different channels, quantities, locations, seasons, products, and so forth, are not equal to differences in the marginal costs in these various situations. Charging the same price when marginal costs differ (e.g., the same price for different sizes of orders) is also by this test discriminatory. It is apparent that, by any of these three marginal-cost tests, price discrimination is quite common.

Any marginal-cost test has shortcomings: (1) Measurement difficulties impair its practical usefulness. Although there are some simple situations where marginal costs can be identified and estimated fairly accurately, it is quite common to have a high degree of product jointness in production, where marginal cost depends on the product-mix of the increment. For joint products, marginal costs are difficult to find and unstable as a price base. (2) Since interest and time-depreciation on durable equipment are not usually marginal costs, disparities in capital turnover (ratio of sales to investment) among products or sales situations cause wide differences in the return on specialized investment when unit contribution margins are proportional to marginal cost. Thus profits as measured by gross return on investment will differ under even a non-discriminatory pattern of prices, and some sales will advantage the seller more than others. Both society and the seller will gain by adjusting prices in order to increase output on the high-return investments and reduce the use of low-return facilities. Hence a test of discrimination in terms of prices that are proportional to marginal cost is not meaningful in theory as a guide for public or private policy.

The deficiencies of concept, but not of measurement, of this proportionality definition might be removed by a definition of discrimination in terms of the rate of return on specialized capital that is produced by the spread between marginal cost and price. Prices would be non-discriminatory when this rate of return is uniform. This definition involves the usual measurement difficulties, since common investment is even more difficult to divide indisputably than common marginal costs. Splitting off the specialized investment used exclusively for one product or one sales channel is one of the most formidable of statistical problems in cost accounting. Moreover, this rate-of-return formulation neglects capital wastage, since depreciation, except in so far as it is a function of output, is excluded from marginal costs. For private policy, this omission is not damaging for short-run pricing decisions, but differences in perishability of the value of equipment are an important source of discrimination (by this definition) in a longer-run framework.

However, definitions of price discrimination that are framed in terms of marginal costs are, no matter how valid or interesting to economists, quite irrelevant to the legality of a price structure, since the law is framed according to some cost accounting idea of average full costs. As we shall see, neither marginal nor average cost concepts contain a fully adequate criterion for detecting discrimination that damages the public welfare. Thus cost disparity produces no definition of discrimination that is universally satisfactory.

Is Price Discrimination Bad?

The second question, whether price discrimination is bad for the economy, cannot be answered in the framework of the particular pressures that produced anti-discrimination legislation. Instead, it must be approached more generally in terms of welfare economics. Modern welfare economics theory does not support the contention that a disparity in cost-price relations is bad for the economy, except under certain assumed conditions that are highly unrealistic.

The underlying principle here is that national welfare is maximized if every consumer buys every product up to the amount where its marginal utility to him just equals three other things: the marginal utility of his money in other uses, the marginal utility of the product to other consumers, and the marginal cost of making and selling the product. This magnificent balance is always far from fulfillment in the real world. Even if prices precisely equaled marginal costs (a condition prevailing under pure competition and rarely found), the marginal utility of money is not the same for all individuals. It varies widely among people and depends on income, wealth, and expectations. The heart of the welfare problem is to compare what different people in different circumstances get out of a given product. Only if we could measure and compare "products" in different situations on the basis of utility could an absolute definition of price discrimination be formulated. If it were possible to make such measurements, discrimination would have to be defined as selling "utility" at different rates per util (i.e., unit of utility), but it is clearly quite out of the question to apply in practical life a test of price discrimination that makes prices that are proportional to "values" to individual buyers the only ones that are not discriminatory.[3]

With the usual inequalities of income distribution present, price discrimination conceived in economic welfare terms can be avoided only by charging different persons drastically different prices for the same "product" without regard to marginal costs of the seller. Surgeons' fees are the chronic example of this kind of pricing. From the standpoint of welfare, none of the definitions of discrimination in terms of disparity of prices and the seller's costs is an adequate test of price discrimination. None tells us anything about what is really important for economic welfare, namely, prices that produce disparities in "real value" among buyers. Indeed, a good case can be made for the social desirability of many forms of price discrimination (i.e., by cost disparity criteria). Such discrimination is widely practiced by governments and is frequently motivated by welfare considerations. Notable examples are subsidized low-cost housing, food-stamp plans, veterans' benefits, farm price supports, and even the progressive income tax (under suitable assumptions as to the distribution of benefits from government). These are all forms of price discrimination that work in the direction of equalizing real income.

Thus, no blanket condemnation of price discrimination is possible in the real world of widely disparate incomes. Some forms are good and some forms bad in terms of the social criterion of the general welfare.

The connotations of injustice in price discrimination which produced the Robinson-Patman Act were not born of concern about economic welfare or justice, but were rather the reaction of independent retailers to an unpalatable competitive situation, namely, the invasion of their markets by giant food and drug retailing chains. The chains were getting big discounts from their suppliers and were passing them on to consumers in low prices that small independent retailers had difficulty meeting. The independents, in their fight for legislative protection made much of the disreputable position of price discrimination, but

---

[3] A 35-cent shoe shine really costs an advertising executive less, psychically, than the same shine at 10 cents costs a clerk. From a cost disparity standpoint, the price discrimination runs in the clerk's favor. Yet, from the standpoint of welfare economics, it favors the executive.

were not concerned with its effects upon economic welfare. Hence a definition of price discrimination in terms of average full cost was adequate for their political purposes.

The Varieties of Non-Discriminatory Prices

Table 9–1 illustrates the variety of price structures that a company might set up in an attempt to escape a charge of discrimination. The product, e.g., shoes, is sold by a manufacturer to retailers who have a preference for buying in small amounts for immediate delivery to avoid making long bets on future style changes. Production must be scheduled to follow the erratic behavior of sales, and entails considerable costs of setting up and adjusting machines for small lot sizes and for warehousing an inventory to meet unexpected spurts in demand.

If buyers place a single order for a whole year's purchases, it facilitates the manufacturer's production planning and enables him to lower costs substantially. Moreover, buyers that take over the warehousing operation help lower the manufacturer's overhead costs of warehousing such as depreciation and interest on the capital tied up in inventory. A single order also reduces selling costs such as salesmen's visits and clerical work.

It is assumed in Table 9–1 that each buyer takes 1,000 pairs during the year in any event, and will choose either of two purchase patterns. This means that either kind of order must be burdened with a full share of overhead costs for productive plant. However, the small-order business must carry the whole load of warehousing and inventory costs.

How is the manufacturer to fix prices that do not discriminate between these two purchasing patterns? This depends on the definition of discrimination, which is discussed above. Some of the alternative pricing methods are shown in Part B of Table 9–1, together with the prices that result and their relative profitability. It should be noted that the most legal of these is probably No. 4, where price differences equal differences in full cost, although it would also be legal to charge a uniform price regardless of cost differences.

No. 1 is included only for completeness, and indicates that there is usually excess production capacity, probably intentionally so. When rate of production has risen to a pitch which strains the seams of the equipment, marginal cost increases to

TABLE 9–1

VARIETIES OF NON-DISCRIMINATORY PRICES

PART A: Unit Costs for Two Sizes of Purchase.

Kind of Cost	Size of Purchase		Col. (2) as % of Col. (1)
	10-unit orders	1000-unit orders	
	(1)	(2)	(3)
Unit Marginal Costs:			
Material	$0.50	$0.50	100
Labor	.60	.50	83
Selling Costs	.40	.20	50
Total marginal cost	1.50	1.20	80
Unit Overhead Costs:			
Depreciation	.18	.15	83
Interest on capital	.30	.15	50
Other	.52	.30	58
Total overhead cost	1.00	.60	60
Unit Full Cost	$2.50	$1.80	72
Investment per pair	$3.00	$1.50	

PART B: Non-Discriminatory Prices for Two Sizes of Purchase.

Pricing Method	Unit Price		Markup on Full Cost		Profit on Investment	
	Unit Orders		Unit Orders		Unit Orders	
	10	1000	10	1000	10	1000
1. Prices equal to marginal cost.	1.50	1.20	−40%	−33%	−33%	−40%
2. Prices with equal contribution margins over marginal cost ($1.30).	2.80	2.50	12%	39%	10%	46⅔%
3. Prices proportional to marginal cost (86⅔% markup).	2.80	2.24	12%	24%	10%	29⅓%
4. Prices with equal markups on average cost (30¢).	2.80	2.10	12%	16⅔%	10%	20%
5. Prices proportional to average cost (12% markup).	2.80	2.02	12%	12%	10%	15%
6. Prices giving equal profit on investment.	2.80	1.95	12%	8⅓%	10%	10%
7. Prices that equalize buyers' costs of selling.	2.80	2.30	12%	28%	10%	33%
8. Prices that are uniform.	2.80	2.80	12%	56%	10%	67%

a level that permits profitable pricing by this rule, but this rarely happens.

No. 7 is an attempt to price according to value to the buyer, and necessarily includes the assumption that all buyers operate at about the same scale with the same cost functions and retail price levels, but that buying in large lots increases costs of storage and obsolescence by 50 cents.

Market Segmentation

The practical problem of putting price discrimination to work involves breaking the market into sectors that differ in price elasticity of demand.   To the extent that it is feasible to seal off such segments of the market, charging different prices for different sectors can increase total profits and, in many instances, can also increase the total volume of sales.   Occasionally it raises revenue enough to warrant production that would otherwise not be turned out at all.   This occurs when a single price could not cover average costs at any volume of output.

The notion that there is but one price at which a product will move, and that knowledge and competitive leveling will make it impossible to charge different prices at different places, is a pervasive one.   It may stem from the idealized concept of a perfect market.   Yet, examples of simultaneously charging a variety of prices, even in the same store, are numerous.   A large New York department store, for example, at one time sold the same mop on different floors at 94¢, 98¢, and $1.07, with much higher sales at the latter price than at the two lower prices.   The classic experiment with two scales side by side at the door of the store, one free, the other with a charge, showed that many more people would pay money to be weighed than would take advantage of a free service.

This kind of price-partitioning of the market is called market segmentation.   Requirements for profitable market segmentation are: (1) the existence of differences in demand elasticity among buyers because of disparities in income, tastes, ignorance, and competitive alternatives; (2) the means for segregating groups of buyers who differ in elasticity of demand; (3) no legal or cultural deterrents to charging discriminatory prices (i.e., prices that are not equal or proportional to marginal costs); and (4) no substantial leaks between market segments where different prices are charged (i.e., little selling by low-price buyers to high-price markets).

Price discounts of various sorts are a major means of achieving market segmentation. Product-line design and pricing, discussed in Chapter 8, is another way.

The practical problem of accomplishing profitable market segmentation has three parts:

1. Determining which parts of the market differ enough in elasticity of demand to warrant segmentation.

2. Selecting and developing devices for separating and sealing off these segments.

3. Determining the appropriate pattern of price differentials.

Economic theory provides the conceptual rules for maximizing profits in the short run through price discrimination, after markets have been segmented; it furnishes little guidance for practical application. The selection of market segments and of separation devices is intimately bound up with the nature of the market and of the product, and cannot be treated by theory. Precise knowledge of the demand elasticity of each segment can rarely be obtained. Hence the tools of practical policy must usually be forged through experimentation.

Incremental concepts alone, i.e., comparison of the expected added revenue with the expected added cost, can provide a criterion of whether or not an additional divison of a market is worth while. Incremental cost sets a clear lower limit for price in the most elastic sector of the market. For example, the decision to sell a typewriter to a mail-order house for private branding can best be made by considering the added revenue (including the potential loss of sales of the manufacturer's own brand) as compared with the incremental cost of producing the additional machines. Good guesses on demand elasticity can come from experimentation and from study of differences among sectors in intensity of competition (since it is cross-elasticity, not market elasticity, that is usually important for this decision).

Price discrimination can also affect long-run demand. Introductory offers and children's offers that are designed to build future revenue in a higher profit sector of the market can be a double-edged weapon for profitable pricing. They can bring both immediate profits from market segmentation and future profits from later sales promoted by today's lower prices. Thus the real revenue obtainable from such introductory offers is greater than the apparent revenue of the initial sale. For example, the *Reader's Digest* sells a slightly expurgated school children's edition for 15 cents. The cash marginal contribution obtained from such sales understates their true contribution. Some allowance should be made for the value of establishing the *"Reader's Digest* habit" in millions of school children.

The orthodox theoretical solution of the price discrimination problem is based solely on differences in demand elasticity and on incremental cost. It assumes perfectly sealed sectors of the market. In practice, however, boundary-sealing is usually imperfect. Since the amount of leakage is largely determined by buyers' inertia and ignorance of prices in other sectors, the greater the differences between prices from one sector to another, the more leakage there will be. Consequently, the practical pricing problem often hinges on this relationship between price differentials and the amount of flow of demand between segments, e.g., shifts from deluxe to standard models. Experimentation with different price spreads can furnish indications of this leakage factor. Leakage can sometimes be reduced by modifying and adapting products to each market segment, so that their characteristics create a barrier to cross-elasticity.

An extreme form of market segmentation is to charge different prices to individual buyers—each buyer being a market segment. This practice calls for leak-proof walls between segments and is most practical in its full form in selling a monopolized service. Monopoly pricing power is created when the buyer is abysmally ignorant of the market, as in morticians' services. The classic example of such segmentation is the pricing methods of surgeons and obstetricians. Here the charge is often based on "ability to pay," under the implied condition that demand is highly inelastic, and that sectors of the market are sealed by the non-transferability of the service. The pattern of charges also reflects custom and ethical overtones, but the general level of charges is influenced by the supply of doctors relative to the demand for medical services.

In general, individualized discrimination sets prices according to a "benefits received" criterion. (When the marginal utility of money is taken into consideration, the medical example can be fitted into this general scheme: from this viewpoint, an appendectomy is worth more dollars to a rich man because the dollars have lower marginal utility.)

Goals of Differential Prices

From the seller's standpoint, the differential prices that result from the application of various discount structures and from product-line pricing may serve several purposes. It is, therefore, desirable to look first at the company's whole structure of price differentials in terms of these purposes, which may be grouped as follows:

(1) *Implementation of marketing strategy.* The patterns of price differentials (product-price differentials and the various discount structures) should implement the company's over-all marketing strategy. These price differentials should be efficiently geared with other elements in the marketing program (e.g., advertising and distribution channels) to reach the sectors of the market selected by strategy. In doing so, the job of a particular structure of discounts may be quite specific. For example, an oil company whose strategy was directed at large and few service stations served by giant transport trucks would grant large quantity discounts for big purchases.

(2) *Market segmentation.* A major objective of differential prices is to achieve profitable market segmentation when legal and competitive considerations permit discrimination.

(3) *Market expansion.* Differential pricing that is designed to encourage new uses or to woo new customers is a common goal of product-line pricing, but it also extends over various phases of the discount structure, depending upon the circumstances of a purchase by a new user.

(4) *Competitive adaptation.* Differential prices are a major device for selective adjustment to the competitive environment. Discounts are often designed to match what competitors charge under comparable conditions of purchase, in terms of net price to each customer class. When products are homogeneous, competitive parity is a compelling consideration.

(5) *Reduction of production costs.* Differential prices can sometimes help solve problems of production. Seasonal or other forms of time-period discounts may be partly for

the purpose of regularizing output by changing the timing of sales. For example, since electricity cannot be stored, classifications of electric rates are designed to encourage off-season uses and to penalize uses that contribute to peaks.[4]

In designing patterns of differential prices that will achieve these five purposes, their legality must be investigated. Living within the law must, of course, be an overriding consideration in discount policy. Determination of the structure of discounts for differences in quantity, trade channel, and location is more circumscribed by legal restrictions than is any other major phase of private price policy. A thorough analysis of the legality of price differentials, however, is inappropriate in this book. Hence we shall not venture far into this complex and changing domain.

Price differentials are considered in this chapter primarily from a policy viewpoint (i.e., how they should be used) rather than from a descriptive viewpoint (i.e., how they are actually used). The origins of discount systems are obscure in many industries, and existing systems are maintained through inertia and custom. Indeed, stability in discount practices has much appeal in itself for members of an established industry, since it eliminates an area of uncertainty in competitors' behavior. A firm bent on reforming its price structure faces a multiplicity of markets and product-service packages, where the reactions to a new discount system are hard to predict. Competition for the favor of distributors may undermine the best laid schemes for rational discounts.

The discount structure is, however, the main area for adaptation of prices to changed economic conditions and competitive status. A drop in demand hits the discount structure first, and its first impact there is in secret shading of quantities and classifications. Similarly, a competitor who is at a disadvantage in the quality, reputation, or distribution of his products uses the informal or formal structure of discounts to even up these weaknesses. The important effect of this mechanism is on the net price, and is properly a subject of Chapter 7. In this chapter, we take up the design of a rationally functional discount structure, rather than

---

4 Sometimes these off-peak differentials are so successful that they convert a former valley into a new peak. Commuting rates on railroads, designed to encourage off-peak use of facilities, have sometimes created a new peak load requiring greater facilities.

the pathology of price competition. Our investigation will be confined to four major elements of the structure of discounts: (1) trade-channel discounts; (2) quantity discounts; (3) cash discounts; (4) geographical differentials.

II. DISTRIBUTOR DISCOUNTS

Nature of Distributor Discounts

Distributor discounts [5] are price deductions that systematically make the net price vary according to the buyers' position in the chain of distribution. Since discounts relate to the channels through which the product flows to market, they are sometimes called trade-channel discounts. These differential prices distinguish among customers on the basis of their marketing functions (e.g., wholesaler vs. retailer), and are thus also called "functional discounts." Pricing distinctions among categories of users are not always associated with marketing functions. Special prices given to manufacturers who incorporate the product in their own original equipment (e.g., tires and spark plugs sold to automobile manufacturers), special prices to other members of the same industry (e.g., gasoline "exchanges" among petroleum companies), and special prices to the Federal Government, to state governments, and to universities, are examples of common forms of discounts that are close enough to trade-channel discounts to be grouped with them.

Discounts vs. Profits

At the outset we should distinguish among four concepts that are often viewed as synonymous: (1) distributor's discount; (2) distributor's realized gross margin; (3) distributor's net profit margin; and (4) rate of return on distributors' investment.

A *distributor's discount* is a deduction from the list price (or a differential in net price) granted to a particular kind of marketer. Differences in these functional discounts govern the differentials in net price paid at the various levels of the distribution chain.

The *realized gross margin* is the difference between the price the distributor pays for merchandise and the price at which he sells it. Only if suggested resale prices are adhered to is the dis-

---

[5] Throughout this discussion of distributor discounts, we shall use the term "distributor" in the generic sense of including wholesalers, jobbers, and dealers.

tributor's realized gross margin the same as his discount. Competition and the pricing policies of the distributors themselves usually make average gross margins quite different from discounts.[6]

The distributor's *net profit margin* is the difference between his realized gross margin and his costs of doing business (usually expressed as a percentage of his sales). Its size depends on how much of this allowed margin he passes by concessions from suggested selling prices, and what it costs him to perform his distributive functions. This net profit margin, however, is not in itself particularly significant. It is aggregate net profit or rate of return on investment that is relevant for most pricing purposes. These depend on the distributor's volume of sales as well as upon his net profit margin.

Form of Distributor Discounts

Distributor discounts assume various forms, determined largely by industry custom. Nevertheless, there are times when a decision must be made as to the form of discount to be offered. Such a decision involves (1) a choice between *net prices* at each distributive level and *list prices* that are modified by a structure of discounts; (2) a choice between *single* discounts and a string of *successively* applied discounts (e.g., 30 per cent and 20 per cent, the first going to retailers, the combination going to wholesalers selling to retailers).

Net prices are rarely used as the device for quoting differential prices to distributors. Typically, manufacturers who use them sell directly to franchised dealers and thus have a fairly simple distribution-channel pricing problem. Net prices are also used when sales are made solely to wholesalers and when sales are made to other manufacturers. The simplicity of net prices produces some savings in billing and bookkeeping. List prices with discounts, however, are more flexible: they make for ease in dealing with diverse trade channels, and they permit prices to be adjusted cyclically or even seasonally by merely varying the discount. It

---

[6] The disparity between allowed margins and the margins actually realized by dealers is pronounced in some industries. For example, the average retail list price of the big-four leading brands of tires was 7 per cent above the average retail price in 1941. For small companies with high list prices, list prices were 23 per cent above realized prices on the average, and for small companies with low list prices, list prices were 16 per cent above realized prices. For these estimates the author is indebted to Richard Hefflebower.

is supposed that discounts from list prices give manufacturers greater control over the realized margin of various types of distributors. But real control is achieved only when such discounts are coupled with resale price maintenance. Serial discounts (e.g., 40 per cent and 10 per cent, rather than 46 per cent) give the wholesalers a picture of the whole trade-channel structure of suggested resale prices. But it is doubtful whether they make adherence to them more likely. Serial discounts are often very elaborate. In the plumbing industry, for example, discounts of 35, 5, 5, 5, 10, 5, and 2 per cent are found. Although such discount structures may be intended to reflect distributors' costs at different stages of the flow to market, the competition between kinds of distributors and the wide variability of distributor costs make the discounts only remotely relevant to costs. The principal effect of successive discounts is to increase bookkeeping expense. The main reason for keeping them, rather than using a single-discount equivalent, is the thick crust of industry tradition.

Examples of Distributor Discounts

Distributor discounts differ widely among industries. They also differ somewhat among firms within an industry. Examples of discounts granted to various kinds of distributors in selected industries are shown in Table 9–2. The range of net prices that may result is illustrated in Table 9–3.

How to Determine Distributor Discounts

The economic function of distributor discounts is to induce independent distributors to perform marketing services. To build a discount structure on a sound economic basis, it is necessary to know: (1) the objectives of the discount structure; (2) distributors' operating costs; (3) discount structures of competitors; (4) effects of discounts on distributor population; (5) costs of selling to different channels; (6) opportunities for market segmentation.

Objectives

To find out exactly what services the manufacturer wants from each type of distributor requires a broad, carefully thought-out distribution plan that fits the product, the competitive position of the seller, and the folkways of the industry. The primary con-

Table 9-2

Trade-Channel Discounts in Various Industries

Channel Discounts
(from list price)

Type of Business	Manufacturer's Agent	Distributors	Wholesalers	Dealers
Air Conditioning	50 & 10%		50%	40%
Automotive Accessories	50 & 10%		50%	40%
Electrical Appliances				35 or 40%
Farm Equipment		40 & 20%	25%	30%
Heating Controls	40 & 10 & 10% indiv. units; 50 & 10% package units		40 & 10% indiv. units; 50% package units	25 & 5% indiv. units; 33⅓% package units
Machinery	5%			30% stocking 10% non-stocking
Motorcycles		30% motorcycles; 50% parts		25% motorcycles 45% parts
Musical Instruments—				
Percussive	10% commission		50 & 10%	50%
Office Supplies	2 & 10% commission		50 & 20%	50%
Radios			60%, 60 & 5%, 60 & 10%, 50 & 10% (varies with line & quality)	40%; on certain line 33⅓%
Scales	50 & 10%		50%	40%
Industrial Division	50%			
Stoves and Heaters			33⅓ & 25% or 40 & 25% if bought in car-load lots	33⅓% deluxe models 40%
Toys	5%		50 & 5%	40%
Water Coolers			40 & 5% max.	30 & 5% max.

520

Source: Trade Discount Practices, Report No. 558, The Dartnell Corp.,Chicago.

TABLE 9–3

NET PRICES RESULTING FROM SPARK-PLUG MANUFACTURER'S
SCHEDULE OF DISTRIBUTOR DISCOUNTS

	Price In cents per plug
1. Automobile manufacturers	
a. For original equipment (not individually packaged)	6
b. For replacement parts	24
c. Average prices to one automobile manufacturer	13 to 15
2. National distributors (branded and packaged in individual cartons)	
a. Largest service-station group buyer	23
b. Large oil company	23
3. Distributors who sell branded products to dealers and garages	27.1
4. Mail-order houses and other large private-brand sellers	18
5. Secondary jobbers and fleet owners in purchases of 1,000 or more (branded and packaged)	29
6. Retailers and garages (who buy from secondary jobber or distributor); "fair-traded" price structure:	
Quantity 1– 99	39
" 100–299	36
" 300–over	32
(The "300-over" price is supposed to require a minimum annual sales of $5,000)	
7. Car-owner "fair-traded" prices:	
Quantity 1 plug	65
" set of 6 or 8 plugs	59

sideration in working out such a plan is the allocation of marketing functions between the manufacturer and the distributing chain and among the links in that chain. The problem is to find which functionary can do each specific job most economically and effectively. For example, a large electrical manufacturer selling refrigerators through distributors and dealers decided that in one of its major markets the function of the retail dealer should be confined to displaying six basic models, taking orders for them, and arranging the terms of the individual transactions. In the plan that this manufacturer worked out, the wholesaler, in addition to his traditional function of selecting the dealers and helping them do a better selling job, performs for his retailers many of the service functions normally conducted at retail. He receives the merchandise, inspects it, delivers it to the customer's premises, installs it, and takes complete charge of all subsequent mechanical service.

Distributors' Operating Costs

The most important function of trade channel discounts is to cover the operating costs and normal profits of distributors. Discounts should be closely aligned to these costs if distributors are to play the part planned for them. Margins that are too rich produce excess selling effort or too many distributors, while margins that don't cover costs will not move the goods.[7]

Distributors who are in the same nominal trade status category sometimes differ widely in functions. And their operating costs depend in part upon what functions they perform. The manufacturer must decide whether or not to vary the trade-channel discounts according to the functions performed by the distributor. For example, one building-materials manufacturer gives a 5 per cent margin on certain products to wholesalers who resell in carload lots shipped directly from the manufacturer to the retail dealer. But a margin of 12 per cent is given on shipments that are warehoused by the wholesaler and sold by him in less-than-carload lots. The differential in margins is estimated to cover the costs of performing the warehousing and reshipping functions.

In some industries distributive functions are jumbled, and it is hard to set discounts that will take account of the functions actually performed. What is a wholesaler? The question is not easy to answer. Some wholesalers perform retail functions and nominal wholesale functions in varying degrees, so that the difficulty of classifying individual customers into clean functional groups impairs the practical effectiveness of functional discounts.[8]

Even with identical functions, costs differ among individual distributors with variations in operating efficiency. Size economies are apparently quite pronounced in some distributive trades, though they are often obscured by correlated differences in functions (services). Big service stations, for example, enjoy definite

---

[7] Although it might be expected that competition would determine the proper discounts, this relation is clouded by wide variations in selling-effort and service of different distributors, i.e., the possibilities of product differentiation. But adequate knowledge of these costs is hard to acquire. Cost records are inadequate and not readily available to the seller. Moreover, distributors' costs vary, depending upon the functions, efficiency, size, product-mix, and location of each distributor.

[8] In the famous Standard Oil (Indiana) case (173 F. 2nd 210) an important root of the FTC's complaint was that one of the company's jobber customers was also selling at retail.

economies, which are particularly dramatic when combined with self-service features.

Should trade discounts be determined by the costs of the inefficient or by the costs of the efficient? One solution to this problem is to set trade discounts to cover the estimated operating costs (plus normal profits) of the most efficient two-thirds of the dealers. When cost estimates are uncertain, a practical test of excessive margins is the extent to which rehandlers pass margins on by knocking down realized prices.

Another check on distributors' costs is an estimate of the manufacturer's cost of performing the distributive function himself. Many companies periodically consider doing more of the marketing job themselves (e.g., bypassing the wholesaler), and such estimates are frequently available as by-products of these trade-channel policy studies. Moreover, some companies operate through different channels in different sections of the country, and thus have some cost experience in performing distributive functions.

When a distributor handles a variety of products, his costs vary among products. Consequently, his average cost for all products is a poor indication of the specific costs for a single product. The manufacturer must decide the extent to which distributor discounts should vary among products to conform to these cost differences. For example, the lumber dealer's cost of handling a carload of roofing is about half that of handling a carload of insulation board, which makes a higher margin on insulation board appropriate.

If these cost differences are great, and if the distributor can determine them with some degree of accuracy, the distributor discount that will be sufficient to secure adequate distribution and induce the desired amount of sales assistance should differ among products.[9] But since the benefits of individualized discounts are paid for by increased complexity, they may incur ill will if industry traditions run against them.

To an important and generally unrecognized degree, distributors' operating costs depend upon their price policy. For example, the low selling costs of mail-order chain stores, although partly due to stripped-down services, are quite largely due to their

---

[9] Particularly when the amount of assistance that the manufacturer wants differs among products and varies with the stage of popular acceptance of a given product.

price policy. If everyone, including the house-brand manufacturers, were to follow the same policy of low prices, the sales costs
of these chains would rise.[10]

Competitors' Discount Structures

We have now discussed the ways the distributor's costs should
enter into the determination of his discounts. Now we turn to
a second practical guide, namely, the discounts granted by rival
sellers. In a sense, dealer discounts are a means of purchasing
the dealer's sales assistance in a competitive market. In trades
where custom has sanctified a uniform margin, discounts granted
by competitors are a particularly compelling benchmark.

In many industries the actual (as opposed to the nominal) discounts granted by rival sellers vary. The manufacturer must decide whether he is to be guided by the higher or by the lower discounts. Specifically, a manufacturer whose product is at some
disadvantage in consumer acceptance may consider an attempt to
buy distribution by granting larger margins than do competitors.
The success of such an effort usually depends upon the following
conditions: (1) whether the high margin merely compensates for
low turnover and thus gives the distributor no real economic incentive; (2) whether the margin incentive will actually induce
the distributor to push the product; (3) how much influence the
distributor has in the buyer's brand decision; (4) whether the
dealer has opportunities for profitable market segmentation in
the form of personal price discrimination; and (5) whether competitors are likely to meet the wider margins. Thus, in general,
the success of such a plan requires that consumers have considerable indifference to brands and great confidence in the distributor,
and that the manufacturer have a small enough market share so
that large competitors will not feel compelled to meet the wider
margin.

A related question is: Should a lower price be offered to dealers
who handle only your brand? In the oil industry, for example,
the retail gasoline dealer who handles a house brand exclusively
gets an "undivided dealer" discount, which is more favorable
than the discount granted a non-exclusive dealer. An exclusive

---

10 The total distribution margin of the mail-order chain is usually higher than
the dealer's margin. The savings come from buying at the factory price and performing the wholesale functions themselves.

dealer usually gets price advantages from quantity discounts in any case, particularly in relation to the small dealer who must handle a wide line of products for several manufacturers.

The competition from substitute distribution channels should also be studied. Costs of alternative routes may place the selected channel at a disadvantage in terms of the ultimate price to the consumer for a comparable product-service combination. This factor may set ceilings on channel discounts for a chosen distribution route. Cheap substitute channels have been a salutory stimulant for the seller to seek more effective channels.

Effect on Distributor Population

The effect of varying margins upon the entry of new distributors and upon mortality is a third factor in determining distributor discounts that deserves more study than it has had. A new and expanding industry such as television, which needs many well-trained distributors, might adopt a discount policy calculated to expand the distributor population rapidly. On the other hand, oil companies may use a narrow margin to reduce the service-station population down to large service stations, which have important economies of scale. States with wider service-station margins have more stations per car and also have smaller stations on the average.

Costs of Selling to Different Channels

The cost of selling to various kinds of distributors varies. For example, it usually costs less to sell to mail-order houses or chain stores for private branding than to sell through jobbers, wholesalers, and retailers. These varying selling costs have an important bearing on legal requirements for channel discounts.

The Robinson-Patman Act forbids pricing practices that constitute "discrimination" where their effect may be to "injure, destroy, or prevent" competition among sellers, buyers, or their customers. Ordinarily, since the various trade levels do not compete with one another, price differences among them would not adversely affect competition and hence would not raise the question of illegal discrimination.

The Federal Trade Commission has, in several cases, however, applied the anti-discrimination provision of the Act to trade-status discounts. Court decisions in these cases indicate that, to be legally safe, differences in trade discounts among distributors of the same trade level should be confined to probable cost savings. The wide differences in the character of distributors in the same trade categories make this limitation important. Mail-order houses, chain stores, and small independent retailers are all retailers, since they sell to ultimate consumers. As such, they should receive the same price, except in so far as discounts are supported by savings in the cost of selling to them. Thus different discounts to subdivisions of distributor categories should be based on the manufacturer's selling costs.

But the law applying to trade-status pricing is still in flux. Consequently, when a manufacturer sets up or revises a structure of functional prices, he should make a careful study of the current legal picture before he applies other considerations.

Opportunities for Market Segmentation

Trade-channel discounts can be one means of achieving profitable market segmentation.[11]

In some industries the market is broken down into several fairly distinct sub-markets, each of which has its own peculiar competitive and demand characteristics. These sub-markets provide a ready-made opportunity for market segmentation. In the tire market, for example, the following sub-markets may be distinguished:

1. The original-equipment market, characterized by skill and bargaining strength of buyers and by big cyclical fluctuations in demand.

2. The individual-consumer replacement market, characterized by unskilled buying, brand preferences, and cyclical stability.

    a. The manufacturer's brand segment.

    b. The distributors' brand segment.

3. The commercial-operator replacement market, characterized by large buyers who are price-wise and quality-wise (e.g., bus companies).

4. The government-sales market, characterized by large orders, formal bids, and publication of successful bidder's price.

---

[11] Product-line pricing can also be used for this purpose, as was mentioned in Section I.

5. The export market, characterized by international competition.[12]

Both the elasticity of aggregate demand and the cross-elasticity of demand among sellers vary in the various sub-markets. For example, for original equipment, price probably has little influence on the total number of tires purchased, since the price of the tire paid by automobile manufacturers is considerably less than 5 per cent of the wholesale price of the car, and no feasible reduction in tire prices would affect car prices enough to increase perceptibly the demand for cars. On the other hand, small price differentials among the big four in the original-equipment market could create explosive shifts in market shares—that is, cross-elasticity is probably quite high.

Pricing a product that is a component of the finished product of another manufacturer and that also has a resale market presents intricate trade-channel pricing problems. In the pricing of spark plugs or tires for automobiles, for example, the practical question for many suppliers is not so much how to price for the original-equipment business, but *whether* to price for it. Original-equipment business has been presumed to carry with it, directly or indirectly, replacement business, as well as to contribute to the prestige of the product's manufacturer. But this assumption should be regarded as an open question subject to research, rather than as a foregone conclusion, and the alternative costs of getting replacement business by other ways should be investigated. Small manufacturers of tires have been able to sell exclusively in the replacement market without any original-equipment business. It is estimated that the big four account for more than 90 per cent of the tires placed on new vehicles.

In the individual-consumer replacement market, there is some evidence that the level of price affects the timing of demand within fairly rigorous limits set by the age of the tire. But the buyers' responsiveness to price differences (as indicated by switching from one seller to another) is probably lower than in other markets where buyer knowledge is greater. Market segmentation is further increased in this market by the differential between manu-

---

[12] Richard Hefflebower, *Price-Making and Competition in the Rubber Tire Industry,* an unpublished manuscript.

facturers' brands and distributors' brands and by the multiplicity of prices and claimed quality represented by the several brands of each manufacturer.   By offering a variety of price lines, manufacturers are able to separate sectors that differ in price responsiveness.   They can meet price competition of distributors' brands and the brands of second-line manufacturers without pricing their first-grade tires at lower levels, and can shelter the price structure to some degree from decline in buyers' income.

Price discrimination among individual consumers in the replacement market is a common form of market segmentation. The manufacturer's pricing problem here is whether to keep the initial margins high enough to permit dealers to make individual concessions to customers.   Realized margins that are substantially lower than official margins do not necessarily mean that the official margins should be reduced.   This disparity may be justified in industries where competition at the dealer level is strong and where opportunities for personal differentiation are important. A dealer can then get the full price from some customers who are averse to shopping and bargaining and can give substantially lower prices, with the flavor of a bargain, to more careful shoppers. This kind of individual pricing can yield a higher dealer profit than can uniform pricing.   A conspicuous example of such pricing is found in the operation of automobile dealers under normal competitive conditions.   It is normally appropriate to permit the dealer considerable latitude when the unit cost of the article is high, when trade-ins and service concessions provide a convenient mechanism for veiled price reductions, and when the customer is not tied tightly to the dealer by strings of continuity of service or by customer relations.

A related pricing problem of the manufacturer is whether to establish different distributor margins for high-quality, high-priced lines and for lower-level products.   In some industries different distributor margins for different qualities have been worked out quite systematically.   Differences in dollar margins per unit result from the application of a uniform percentage margin to products that differ in retail list price.   But sometimes there are systematic quality differences in percentage margins. In the tire industry, for example, dealer margins have varied from 22.9 per cent for lower quality lines to 29.3 per cent for top-grade tires.[13] High unit dollar-margins for high-quality products, whether achieved by uniform percentage margin or by differential percentage margins, are a device for market segmentation. They result in discriminatory prices, in so far as the official margins are the realized margins and in so far as differences in distributor costs are less than the differences in dollar margins.[14] The manufacturer must decide whether his profits or his long-run strategic goal are sufficiently more favorable on high-quality products to justify such a pattern of margin incentive.

Market segmentation and price discrimination produce long-run as well as short-run gains. Market segmentation sometimes makes it possible to build plants big enough to get economies of size otherwise unobtainable. Manufacturers have built bigger plants specifically to take on private-label business (a common form of segmentation) in order to get scale economies quickly, with the plan of later paring away the private-label business as acceptance of the manufacturer's own brands grows.

III. QUANTITY DISCOUNTS

Quantity discounts are reductions in the net price that are systematically related to the amount purchased. Our analysis is confined to commercial discounts. It does not include package-size differentials at the consumer level. (See Chapter 8, "Product-Line Pricing.")

Illustrations of commercial quantity discount structures are found in Table 9–4 and Chart 9–1. Chart 9–1 summarizes some findings on the size of discounts and the quantities needed to get them, while Table 9–4 shows some maximum discounts available. The information is taken from OPA data on ceiling prices. For each commodity, the maximum discount was computed as the ratio of (1) the spread between the highest and lowest price to (2) the highest price. The quantity required to obtain this maximum discount was expressed as a multiple of the quantity for the highest price.

Quantity discounts have loomed large in managerial pricing in

[13] Margins for Group I independent dealers, November, 1941. Richard Hefflebower, *Price-Making and Competition in the Rubber Tire Industry, op. cit.*

[14] It is clear that inventory investment is higher for premium goods, that is, stock turn is usually lower and it may take more sales effort to persuade a customer to pay the premium price.

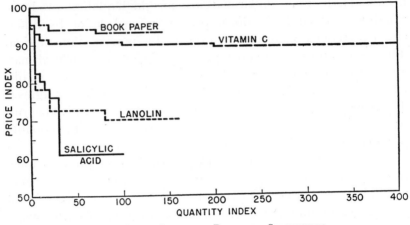

CHART 9–1.   QUANTITY DISCOUNT STRUCTURES.

recent years. A revolution in price and wage levels, together with changes in distribution technology, made many quantity discount structures obsolete in the postwar period. Moreover, court

TABLE 9–4

MAXIMUM QUANTITY DISCOUNTS AND QUANTITY REQUIRED
TO OBTAIN THEM—SELECTED PRODUCTS

Commodity	Maximum Discount [1] (Ratio of high–low to high)	Quantity to Get Max. Discount [2] (as multiple of quantity for highest price)
Cocoa Beans & Cocoa Products	.0217	22
Titanium Pigments	.049	80
Broom Corn	.0625	9.32
Kapok	.068	20
Book Paper	.0695	144
Antimony Metals	.103	89.2
Vitamin C	.108	400
Oil of Wormseed	.113	400
Tungsten	.116	200
Oil of Lemon	.165	200
Acetic Acid	.185	10
Lanolin	.300	160
Salicylic Acid	.391	40

[1] Spread between highest prices (for smallest quantity) and price for maximum discount quantity expressed as ratio of highest price.

[2] As multiple of quantity for highest price bracket.

Source: OPA Price Ceilings.

decisions and intensified Federal Trade Commission activity under the Robinson-Patman Act, prompted a re-examination of the basis for quantity pricing.

Recently, many companies have given serious consideration to the abandonment of quantity discounts. Their reasons are various. One reason is the difficulty of establishing a legally acceptable cost justification. Allocations of common costs are necessarily arbitrary, and the burden of proving their validity is put upon the manufacturer. Another reason, from the experience of some companies, is that quantity discounts tend to force the basic price down to the level of the net price of the largest buyers and tend to get passed on to dealers' customers. Naturally, dealers who are unable to merit big discounts are unhappy.

Quantity discount systems play a part in raising the efficiency of the economy. Quantity discounts by a food manufacturer, for example, pass on to a chain store some of the economies of buying in larger lots. If the resulting savings give the chain competitive advantages, through lower prices to its customers, then the discounts tend to foster the survival of the fittest throughout the distribution channels. This situation tends to reduce the cost of distribution and the price to the ultimate consumer. Thus quantity discounts up to the limit of cost savings appear to serve the public interest, at least in so far as economic efficiency and standard of living are concerned. Efficiency is of course not an unmixed social good. Many believe that encouragement of small entrepreneurs is a social benefit worth considerable sacrifices in efficiency. Just how to balance these opposing benefits is a serious social question beyond the scope of pure economics.

But quantity discounts are important pricing tools for most firms and must be integrated into the general marketing strategy to gain company objectives. The problem of quantity discount structures may be broken into the following parts:

1. What type of discount system should be chosen?
2. How big should the discount be for various sizes of purchase?

What Kind of Quantity Discounts?

Assuming that a manufacturer has decided to offer quantity discounts, the next question is, "What kind?" Possible types of discount structure may be classified on three independent bases, as follows:

1. With respect to the way "size" is measured.
   a. Aggregate of all products bought from seller.
      i. Dollar-value measures.
      ii. Physical-unit measures (e.g., carload discounts).
   b. Separately based on the quantity of individual products.
      i. Dollar measures.
      ii. Physical measures (e.g., integral case discounts).
2. With respect to the form of calculation.
   a. Incremental, i.e., discounts figured on the increased volume over a specified amount.
   b. Absolute, i.e., discounts figured in terms of total quantities.
3. With respect to number of transactions.
   a. Cumulative, i.e., based on aggregate purchases over a period, such as a year.
   b. Non-cumulative, i.e., based on the size of a single order.

Product-Quantity vs. Mixed Order

The choice between (1) discounts that are based on the aggregate size of mixed orders, and (2) discounts for each product, based on the individual amounts ordered depends largely upon the product line and upon buying practices. If quantity discounts are based solely on quantities of individual products, some of the clerical savings of large order size are missed. On the other hand, if discounts depend only on the aggregate size of a mixed order, important savings in handling costs that can be obtained from integral-case lots of a single product are missed. From the seller's standpoint, the individual-product form of discount is, in general, preferable to the composite-order form, when the purpose of the discount is to reduce handling costs.

A combination of the two types that preserves the advantages of both is sometimes feasible. For instance, some sellers levy an "order service charge," which covers the constant cost—mostly clerical—of filling an order regardless of its size. This charge can then be combined with individual-product discounts based on broken or integral cases of various sizes.[15]

---

[15] A minimum-order requirement combined with individual-product quantity pricing approximates this scheme. For example, one building material company renders no bill for less than $10.00.

Physical vs. Dollar Measures of Order Size

The choice between a discount based on dollar values and one based on physical quantities depends on the variety of products in an order. Since cost savings are easier to analyze in terms of physical quantities, they are preferable legally. But in some industries—the classic case being drugs—orders are likely to be long and intricate, with quantities that are hard to add in physical units. Quantity discounts in such industries are therefore usually related to dollar values of orders.

Physical measures of order size are preferable to dollar measures for other than merely legal reasons. They make possible a discount structure that encourages integral-case purchasing. Savings in packaging integral cases are often important. Passing on part of these savings may induce buyers to order case units, but this gesture is usually not enough: price incentives must be supplemented by persuasion and case size must be tailored to meet stock-turn needs of typical buyers. Moreover, physical discounts are less likely to be distorted by changes in the price level. And they make order computations easier under changing price conditions.

Incremental vs. Total-Order Size

The choice between the incremental and absolute forms of figuring the discounts is purely a matter of convenience and custom. Both are widely used. The incremental form simply shows the buyer more dramatically the marginal cost of expanding his order; it is therefore often persuasive in inducing large orders and, indeed, overbuying. A given discount scale can be translated into either incremental or absolute form.

Order Size vs. Cumulative

A basic choice must be made between a discount based on total purchases over a period and a discount based on single order size. Cumulative discounts are thought to be effective, in part, in discouraging divided accounts, i.e., buying from several competitors simultaneously. More important, they provide a means for making broad concessions to large buyers.

Cease and desist orders of the Federal Trade Commission have indicated that cumulative discounts of the following kinds are of dubious legality:

1. Discounts based on a single buyer's total annual purchases of one or several products from a single seller.

2. Discounts based on the buyer's total purchases of a particular article from *all* manufacturers (as opposed to a single seller).

3. Discounts based on the combined annual purchases of a group of buyers from a single seller.

Discounts of the first type usually cannot be justified by the direct evidence of cost savings because the cumulative effect of the size of a year's purchases on operating costs is practically impossible to sift out of the accounting records, assuming that there is such a cost effect. The fact that larger annual orders may provide opportunity for stabilizing production (through off-peak scheduling, production for stock, and so forth, has not often proven an adequate defense. Cost savings from stabilized production are difficult to determine and to trace to annual orders.[16]

Discounts of the second type certainly cannot be justified before the FTC by cost savings, which would have to be related to the rate of output for the total industry.[17] This kind of discount structure is actually designed to meet competitors' cumulative discount structures. For one seller to capture customers from another seller, it is necessary to meet not only his list prices, but the discounts that have accrued from previous purchases.

Discounts of the third type can be set up by classifying buyers according to industry and by basing discounts for each buyer on his industry's purchases. This procedure might have promotional effects where sales to a single buyer occur infrequently or sporadically, but any such saving in selling costs could not offset, in the FTC's view, the impairment of competition.

In summary, cumulative discount structures have a highly dubious legal standing, and, from this viewpoint, are inferior to order-size discounts. Moreover, they do not directly attack the problem of high-cost small orders, since the buyer is given no incentive to make infrequent large purchases in circumstances

---

16 But in a recent FTC order (Minneapolis-Honeywell Regulator Co., January 14, 1948), cost data were accepted as justification for at least some of the discount brackets in an annual discount structure. It thus appears that cumulative discount systems are not *per se* illegal if supported by cost accounting.

17 Savings from high output by the whole industry would be Marshallian "external economies" that the Commission would view with deep skepticism.

(such as impending deflation) when he prefers hand-to-mouth living by frequent short orders.

This brief examination of the various kinds of quantity discounts leads to certain general conclusions: (1) order size is a better basis than are annual purchases; (2) discounts based on the quantity of individual products ordered have advantages over those based on aggregate size of order (but it is desirable, when feasible, to use both these bases; (3) physical quantities are preferable to dollar values as a measure of order size; and (4) there is no clear preference of form for calculation of discounts.

Combination of Quantity and Channel Discounts

An important practical problem is the integration of quantity discounts with trade-channel discounts. One manufacturer of grinding wheels has set up a combined discount structure that takes account of differences in (1) quantities, (2) distribution channels, and (3) product categories.

His quantity-discount plan is based on the size of orders of each product, measured in physical quantities and conditioned on the purchase of integral cases. This quantity-discount schedule, which is the same for all products and for all types of buyers, is shown in Table 9–5. Column 3 shows the net unit price for various quantities of a particular product sold through a particular kind of distributor.

TABLE 9–5

QUANTITY DISCOUNT STRUCTURE FOR GRINDING WHEELS

1	2	3
Number of Wheels	*Quantity Discount*	*Net Unit Price*
1 to 9	None	$2.65
10	25%	1.98
20	30%	1.85
50	35%	1.72
100	40%	1.59
250	45%	1.46

Functional discounts for different categories of distributors are superimposed upon this quantity-discount structure, but the same quantity discounts apply, regardless of the trade category and the size of the annual purchases.

TABLE 9–6

RELATIVE PRICES FOR GRINDING WHEELS TO ONE CLASS OF DISTRIBUTORS,
COMBINING QUANTITY AND MATERIAL DISCOUNTS

Product	Product Discount	Quantity Bracket					
		None	25%	30%	35%	40%	45%
A	46%	.54	.405	.378	.351	.324	.297
B	25%	.75	.5625	.525	.4875	.45	.4125
C	0	1.00	.75	.70	.65	.60	.55

The list price is the same for each size of wheel, regardless of
the material from which it is made. Net prices for wheels made
of different materials are varied by means of product discounts.
This method of price differentiation has flexibility, since the
pattern of relative product discounts can be varied without altering base list prices.

This three-way discount structure appears quite complex, but
in practice it operates simply. Precalculated multipliers are used
to reflect the combined effect of quantity discounts, product
discounts, and trade-channel discounts. A sample of the multipliers obtained by the combined effect of product discounts and
quantity discounts is shown in Table 9–6.

What Size of Discount

Having arrayed the various forms of quantity discount we now
turn to the question of the amount of discount to be granted for
orders of different size.

In dealing with this problem, the first step is to think through
the specific market objectives of quantity discounts. The second
is to consider whether the discounts needed to attain these objectives are legal (i.e., whether the chances are good that they
will be legally defensible).

Objectives

What merchandising job do we want quantity discounts to do?
One important job of quantity discounts is to reduce both the
number of and the losses from small orders. For example, it is
common for a firm to find that 80 per cent of its orders account
for only 20 per cent of its sales. The cost of making these sales

frequently causes an actual out-of-pocket drain of cash. Quantity discounts can help correct the size-distribution of orders in three ways: (1) they may stimulate a given set of customers to order the same amount of business in bigger lots; (2) they may induce the same customers to give the seller a larger share of their total business in order to get savings of quantity buying; and (3) they may turn away small accounts and attract bigger accounts, thus altering the size-distribution of the customers themselves.

To manipulate the size distribution of orders, the discount system must be framed in reference to competition. The seller must decide, by over-all market strategy, which competitors he wants to better in what sectors of the market. The important factor competitively is the impact of net prices charged to strategic customer classes, not the formal quantity-price structure *per se*. In some situations there is no room for such pin-pointing of market targets, since discount structures of the industry are uniform, and deviations will be met by retaliation in some form. But frequently there are differences in the net quantity prices offered by various competitors to a given category of trade. The quantity discount structure can then be integrated with the company's selling strategy and assigned a designated part of the total distribution job.

Legality

The legality of a quantity discount structure hinges on cost savings that can be proved. That injury to competition results from such structures is now virtually taken for granted. In the Morton Salt Company case (68 S.Ct. 822, May 3, 1948), the Supreme Court held that the Federal Trade Commission need only show a reasonable possibility that the discount may have had the effect of injuring or suppressing competition. The Commission does not need to prove that the discount has actually done so. The unusual degree of reliance upon the experience of the Federal Trade Commission in this case led Justice Jackson to state in his dissenting opinion, "The law in this case in a nutshell is that no quantity discount is valid if the Commission chooses to say that it is not." Other recent cases (e.g., Rigid Conduit decision, 168 F. 2nd 175) confirm this trend and indicate a basic shift in authority as courts rely more and more on the FTC's interpretation of the factual situation.

Thus all quantity discounts are discriminatory and, therefore, illegal, unless they can be justified by: (a) the seller's good-faith effort to meet a competitor's lower price; or (b) lower costs resulting from savings in manufacturing, delivery, and selling. But the possibility of defense based on meeting competition was whittled down considerably by the Standard Oil Company (Indiana) case.[18] It now appears likely that meeting competition must be confined to an individual case basis that precludes systematic structures of discounts, even when discounts can be supported by provable cost savings.

The immediate practical problem, then, is to determine the cost savings that are related to order size. To establish these cost savings by tracing them to orders that differ in size is the job of distribution cost accounting. Unfortunately, however, it cannot furnish unassailable determination of cost savings. Since cost estimates are a function of the basis selected for allocating common costs, the results are inevitably somewhat arbitrary.

Although the precedents of individual cases are conflicting and shifting, certain practical guides can be formulated tentatively.

In the sale of standard products, savings in production costs seldom provide safe grounds for quantity discounts. When the planning and scheduling of production is substantially divorced from the size of orders (as is common in products that are standard and made for stock), it is not possible to establish that the reduction in unit overhead production costs from obtaining a given output rate is due to a particularly large or small order.

In the sale of special-order products, production economies offer some possibility of justifying quantity discounts. Nevertheless, these economies are restricted in various respects. Cost savings that are incapable of objective measurement cannot be safely used to support quantity discounts.

The contention that large orders reduce style risk and facilitate planning is seldom tenable. The shifting of these risks depends upon the timing of the order rather than upon its size. Advance-season orders that do shift part of the style risk to the buyer might justify lower prices, but not necessarily because they are large or small.

---

[18] Standard Oil Company (Indiana) vs. FTC (173 F. 2nd 210), March 11, 1949.

A large order that enables a producer to increase his output cannot be costed on a marginal basis. A cost formula that does not allocate both direct and indirect costs uniformly to all purchasers must itself be minutely justified before it can be used to support discounts. Each buyer must assume his percentage share of the maintenance of every department needed for the conduct of the business, regardless of the immediate use or non-use of that department by the buyer in question. In the significant Goodyear Tire case, the Federal Trade Commission refused to take differences in manufacturing overhead into consideration, despite the fact that large buyers' requirements could be made in off periods, thus permitting fuller average utilization of facilities.

Cost savings, as a practical matter, are thus largely confined to selling and distribution expenses. Savings in selling expenses are usually important. Business-getting costs per unit tend to decline as order size increases. Since these costs are almost the same per order, regardless of its size, they can be substantially lower per unit of sale for large orders than for small. Clerical and bookkeeping expenses decrease in the same way.

Economies in physical distribution, e.g., office, packing, and delivery costs, are also often substantial. Credit collection, recording, billing, and accounting costs per unit all tend to be about the same in aggregate for a large order as for a small one. Hence these costs also are smaller per unit for big orders. Economies in transportation rates, packing labor, and containers, may also be significant for large orders.

It is important to note that a legal limit on the range of discounts may be imposed, even if cost savings can be established. The Robinson-Patman Act authorizes the Federal Trade Commission to fix maximum limits on the quantity that is subject to further discounts, when the Commission finds that purchasers of the large quantities are so few that such discounts would be "unjustly discriminatory or promotive of monopoly." In 1950, the Commission was seeking to limit quantity discounts allowed by tire manufacturers to dealers in the replacement market by establishing the carload as the maximum discount unit. Such a restriction would bring the large chain distributors up to the price level of many individual tire dealers, regardless of the cost savings that might be achieved by manufacturers dealing with mass distributors.[19]

IV. CASH DISCOUNTS

Cash discounts are reductions in the price which depend upon promptness of payment. Probably the most typical cash discount terms are 2% off if paid in 10 days, full invoice price due in 30 days. The size of discount ranges widely, however, from ½% 10 days to as much as 4% 70 days. Terms of 2% 10 days, full invoice price 30 days, amount to an interest rate of about 36% a year. It is only a matter of viewpoint and industry practice as to who pays this interest cost. If normal practice is to pay promptly, the seller plans revenue at 2% off list price, and a buyer who waits the full 30 days pays a heavy interest charge relative to his competitors. If most buyers wait out the 30 days, it is the seller who pays, and the prompt payer who earns, the 2% interest for the 20-day loan. The real answer depends on competitive effects in the buyer and seller industries.

The cash discount is a convenient way to identify bad credit risks. In some of the garment trades, where mortality is notoriously high, the cash discount is as high as 8%, which makes the full wait extremely expensive competitively. The higher price to the credit buyer thus reflects his weak bargaining position. In the fertilizer industry there was a two-way cash discount to farmers: the quoted price applied at a designated settlement date; earlier payment conferred discounts; but payment imposed a substantial interest charge.[20]

Since the purpose of the cash discount is to promote prompt settlement of bills, it is really an indirect collection cost. The manufacturer's problem in essence is not to pay too much for quick payment, as compared with (a) carrying the account, and (b) alternative ways of attaining prompt settlement. By discouraging customers from credit buying, the manufacturer gets a reduction in working capital, which may mean a saving in interest on bank loans. But he may be paying 36% in order to save 3% interest. Hence the reduction in collection expenses and in risks

---

19 *Business Week,* Oct. 8, 1949, p. 21.
20 See Corwin Edwards, "Types of Differential Pricing," *Journal of Marketing,* April, 1942, pp. 156–167.

rather than savings in interest must be the principal justification for cash discounts.

Unfortunately, there is no real information on the effects of cash discounts on bad-debt losses and on speed of collection. Immediately following the war, many companies drastically reduced or eliminated cash discounts. Possibly because of the unusually liquid position of buyers, this experiment did not indicate that significantly slower collection resulted from a 1% cash discount than from a 2% discount.[21]

V. GEOGRAPHICAL PRICE DIFFERENTIALS

The preceding sections of this chapter concerned trade discounts, quantity discounts, and cash discounts. We now turn to a fourth aspect of the firm's system of price differentials, namely, the geographical structure of prices. The practical problem of deciding how a company's delivered price should be related to the geographical location of the buyer involves (1) an examination of the various methods of geographical pricing; (2) a survey of the factors that are important in working out a policy on geographical pricing.

Geographical Pricing Methods

Geographical pricing methods may be classified as follows:
A. Uniform Delivered Pricing Methods.
    1. Postage-stamp pricing.
    2. Zone pricing.
B. Basing-point Pricing Methods.
    1. Single-basing-point.
    2. Multiple-basing-point.
    3. Full-freight-equalization.
C. F.O.B. Pricing Methods.
    1. Uniform F.O.B. price with no freight absorption.

---

[21] These reductions produced a prodigious outcry from distributors that was hard to explain. The typical cash discount is in reality a price reduction. Its elimination amounted to a price increase. But this indirect price increase was trivial compared with direct advances that were taken calmly in that period. Apparently the violence of the reaction is explained by the mechanistic practices of retail pricing. The cash discount is not viewed as part of the invoice cost on which markups are figured. Instead, it is treated as a secret cushion against the shock of inadequate profit; a price concession equal in amount would not be nearly as acceptable to dealers.

2. Regulated F.O.B. price with freight absorption limited.
3. Unregulated F.O.B. price with freight absorption unrestricted.

Postage-Stamp Pricing

Postage-stamp pricing means delivered prices that are the same
for all buyers, regardless of location. This is a common pricing
practice when transportation cost is trivial and when it is desired
that the final retail price be the same everywhere. Examples include chewing gum, watches, magazines, and phonograph records.
But it is also used occasionally when transportation costs are important. For example, replacement engines for a popular car at
one time sold at the same price in Los Angeles as in Detroit.
Under these circumstances, the seller pays the freight and, in
effect, charges each buyer the average cost of freight for all shipments, so that the seller's net price at the factory is significantly
less for distant buyers than for near ones. This pricing practice gives all manufacturers in the industry access to all markets,
regardless of the seller's location. Market access is particularly
important when the products of rival firms are substantially the
same. The Supreme Court has construed a nation-wide uniform
delivered price as non-discriminatory in the legal sense, although
in the economic sense such a system entails discrimination to the
extent that transport costs vary among buyers.

Zone Pricing

Under zone pricing, delivered prices are uniform within specified areas (zones) and differ systematically among such areas. If
these zones conform to the areas for which transportation rates
from the seller's plant are the same, then zone pricing is equivalent
to uniform F.O.B. pricing (see below) and, hence, under present
interpretations, involves no legal hazards.

If price zones do not coincide with transport-rate zones, then
pricing within each zone has the properties of postage-stamp pricing. When the same price is charged all buyers throughout such
a price zone, they all presumably pay the average transportation
cost for the zone. The seller's mill-net is then greater for near
customers than for those located at distant edges of the zone.
Thus systematic geographic price discrimination in the economic
sense is involved. Under present interpretation there is consider-

able doubt as to the legality of such a pricing plan. It is particularly hazardous when all members of an industry, regardless of the location of their plants, use the same price zone boundaries.

Single-Basing-Point Pricing

Under single-basing-point systems, all plants, regardless of their location, calculate the delivered price of the product by adding to a base price the cost of rail transportation from a single pricing point. The classic example of a single-basing-point system is the "Pittsburgh Plus" plan formerly used in the steel industry. When producing points are located at points significantly distant from the single basing point, the geographical pattern of delivered prices involves discrimination, in that mill-net varies inversely with the distance of the customer from the basing point. "Phantom" freight appears when the freight charge from the basing point is more than the actual freight paid. If transport cost is important and plant locations scattered, a single-basing-point system is usually illegal under present interpretations.

Multiple-Basing-Point Pricing

Under multiple-basing-point pricing, a number of producing centers (though not all) are designated as basing points. The delivered price is computed by starting with the base price at the nearest basing point, and adding standard transportation cost (usually rail freight) from that basing point, regardless of the location of the plant from which the product is actually shipped. Under this pricing method, freight absorption is common and some phantom freight may be involved. Multiple-basing-point systems have been under attack by the Federal Trade Commission for many years, and recent decisions by the Supreme Court cast doubt on their legality.

Freight-Equalization Pricing

Full freight equalization differs from multiple-basing-point pricing in that all plants are pricing points. Delivered price is figured as the factory price at the nearest plant, plus standard transport cost to the buyer. A competitor whose location results in a transportation disadvantage in serving a particular customer, absorbs enough of the freight to equalize the delivered price from the nearest competitor's plant; thus there is a freight absorption but no phantom freight. The legality of systematic full freight equalization, when used by all or most members of an industry, was dubious after the Supreme Court decisions in the Cement Institute and Rigid Conduit cases.

F.O.B. Pricing

Under F.O.B. pricing, products are priced at the seller's plant and the buyer pays the actual freight and selects the method of transportation. If there is no freight absorption, the seller's mill-net is the same on all sales, regardless of the location of the buyer; and the delivered price varies spatially, depending on the location of the buyer in relation to his supplier.

Freight absorption, if it occurs in F.O.B. pricing, is presumed not to be systematic by geographical area. Instead, it takes the form of quoting varying mill-net prices on an individual basis, supposedly to meet competition on a particular transaction. Three kinds of F.O.B. pricing can be distinguished on the basis of freight absorption: (1) uniform mill-net (no freight absorption); (2) freight absorption limited by regulation; and (3) freight absorption unrestricted.

Uniform F.O.B. Pricing. F.O.B. pricing with no freight absorption allowed would cause drastic changes in the economic character of competition and in the relative strength of firms in industries that possess the following economic characteristics:

1. Industry demand that is inelastic in the short run, fluctuates violently over the cycle, and is also unstable geographically.

2. Products that are highly standardized, i.e., that have high cross-elasticity of demand.

3. Transportation costs that are large relative to mill prices.

4. Heavy fixed costs, with marginal costs considerably below average costs (except possibly at peak output rates).

5. Pronounced economies of scale, making high barriers to entry and an oligopoly industry structure.

6. A geographical distribution of plants not conforming closely to markets; hence, some areas with substantial surplus production and others with excess demand.

Under uniform F.O.B. mill pricing, if products of different plants are substantially the same and if freight cost is important, each producing point has an exclusive area in which the delivered price from this point is lower than from any other point. It also has border areas, where its delivered price is equal to that of rivals. Without freight absorption, the only way that a plant can extend its market area is by reducing prices in its entire market (relative to competitors' prices).

Advocates of F.O.B. pricing in such industries have hoped too much for it. Superficial changes in geographical pricing will not alter the basic economic characteristics of these industries and hence cannot change the fundamental nature and results of competition in these industries. Changing the pricing methods will not produce the pricing results of perfect competition.

It is doubtful whether price competition to push back the border of the exclusive trade areas would, in the long run, give consumers adequate protection against the enhanced power of locational monopoly. Not only would the number of sellers serving a single area be reduced, but a tendency toward fewer and larger firms in the industry as a whole can be expected.

Modified F.O.B. Pricing. The second variant of F.O.B. pricing is to permit some freight absorption, but to limit it by regulation. The regulation might take various forms: limits on distance of freight-absorbing sales, limits on the proportion of sales that involve absorption, limits on the total dollar amount of freight subsidy, and so forth. The effect of this plan would be to widen the border areas that are shared by several producing points and to permit competitive penetration of exclusive marketing areas.

The third variant of F.O.B. pricing is to permit individualized freight absorption without any restriction. If such freight absorption is widespread and on an area basis, then the geographical pricing results are probably not very different from those of full freight equalization. If freight absorption is really on an individual case basis and is trivial, then the results are quite similar to those of uniform F.O.B. pricing.

Selection of Geographical Price Structure

In formulating its policy on geographical pricing, a company must answer these questions: (1) What is legal? (2) What do competitors do? (3) How standardized is the product? (4) Where are competitors located in relation to the location of important customers? (5) How important are transportation costs? (6) What policy is to be adopted on resale price maintenance?

Legal Considerations

Recent court decisions in the three basing-point cases, namely, the Cement Case (F.T.C. v. The Cement Institute, 333 U.S. 683 1948); the Rigid Steel Conduit Case (Triangle Conduit and Cable Co. v. F.T.C., 168F 2nd 175, CCA 7th 1948); and the Glucose Case (Corn Produce Co. v. F.T.C., 324 U.S. 737, 1945), may profoundly affect geographical pricing methods. The trend of these cases indicates that freight absorption that is systematic, market-wide, and substantial is to be forbidden. Legal considerations may, therefore, eventually control geographical pricing policy, but at present much confusion and uncertainty exists. If this confusion is resolved by permissive legislation or by the slow process of individual adjudication, then considerable freedom of choice in geographical price structure will remain for some time for most firms. Other than legal considerations are, therefore, germane.

Competitive Considerations

In the past, the geographical price structure of competitors has been a major consideration, especially when the product is standardized and when transport costs are important. A study of the origin of the geographical pricing methods for hundreds of chemicals was made recently by a leading company. It reveals that in most instances the company adopted the geographical plan of competitors who made the same product, or of firms that made substitute products that the new chemical was designed to displace. New firms typically adopt the geographical price practices of the industries they enter. Thus custom plays a strong influence in formulating the practices of new entrants as well as in discouraging older firms from changing.

Product Uniformity

The degree of uniformity of products restricts discretion in geographical pricing. When products are markedly different, as in most types of machinery, for example, F.O.B. pricing is feasible even though competitors are scattered, since comparative prices are only one of many factors affecting choice among brands. The importance of transportation costs relative to sales price also affects the responsiveness of market share to differences in price related to freight charges. When transport costs are trivial, their effect on delivered price may be overridden by other demand factors—prompt delivery, quality, reliability, and friendship.

Location

The location of competing plants with respect to buyers and to the firm in question has an important effect on geographical pricing. In order to get access to markets barred by transportation cost, new plants have resorted to freight allowances, freight absorption, and freight equalization, which, by repercussion, have frequently transformed an F.O.B. pricing method into some variant of delivered pricing. We have seen that when sellers are few and when transportation costs are important, a scattered location of sellers of a standardized product makes F.O.B. pricing impractical because market areas are rigidly governed by the set of price differentials among plants. In industries where demand fluctuates badly and shifts from area to area rapidly, competitors are tempted to maintain production by granting price concessions that give them access to the richest markets. This practice in general results only in the most chaotic kind of price warfare and is intolerable to the industry. Some systematic scheme to permit all competitors access to the richest markets at all times is the usual way to avoid disastrous competition.

Price Maintenance

Resale price maintenance restricts the feasibilty of F.O.B. pricing, particularly when an advertised retail price is uniform over a broad area. If freight is an important cost, then the distributors' margins differ systematically with their location. An adequate margin at the market periphery results in excessive dealer margins nearer the plant.

Summary

1. Discount structures are general schedules of price variation along several dimensions of a product-service package. They are used to tailor net prices to the circumstances of an individual purchase; thus total revenue to the company depends on the kinds of buyers as well as on the product.

2. The use of discount structures raises complex legal questions of personal discrimination among buyers. There is no definitive economic concept of price discrimination that is useful

for detecting it in the real world, because the cost disparity test is hard to apply to the complicated cost situations in multiple-product firms. Whatever its legal status may be, price discrimination cannot be considered an unqualified social evil; it is widespread and in many forms receives much public approval. Price discrimination becomes important in practice when it is possible, by various means, to break the total market into segments with different price elasticities, so that each segment can be charged a price closely tuned to its own demand characteristics.

3. Discount structures have several purposes besides price discrimination: they are a selective device for getting the most desirable kinds of customer, for invading new markets, and for competitive adaptation.

4. Distributor discounts are the cost of floating the product down distribution channels to market. In setting their levels, the problem is what job each distributor is to do, and what profit margin is necessary to get him to do it. Variations in distributor costs and functions makes this a question of high marketing strategy and judgment. Distributor discounts are important in market segmentation, since distribution channels are often the method for dividing the market.

5. Quantity discount structures are used to prevent losses on small-order business. The controlling factor in designing them is the impact and net price for desired classes of customers relative to competitors' net prices. Quantity discounts have a complicated legal standing, and in general they can only be used when supported by good evidence of cost savings in handling and selling.

6. Cash discounts are used to expedite collections. They blur the real price level, since it is sometimes hard to tell how many buyers take advantage of them. Because they represent an exorbitant interest rate, they are useful not for reducing capital requirements, but for identifying bad customers.

7. Geographical discount structures are important when transportation costs are high relative to selling price. They take a variety of forms, and the best one to use depends on the location of markets and competitors, and on industry practice. All systems except F.O.B. mill pricing are under a legal cloud, since they are practical means for covert collusion. But some form of delivered prices may be essential for reaching a nation-wide market under some industry conditions.

Chapter 10

CAPITAL BUDGETING

I. INTRODUCTION
MEANING OF CAPITAL EXPENDITURE
NATURE OF BUDGETING PROBLEM
PLANNING PERIOD

II. DEMAND FOR CAPITAL
NATURE OF DEMAND FOR CAPITAL
DEMAND SCHEDULE FOR CAPITAL EXPENDITURES
TIME DIMENSIONS OF DEMAND FOR CAPITAL
PRINCIPLES OF MEASURING CAPITAL EARNINGS
Payout Period vs. Profitability Yield
Postponability vs. Productivity
Allowances for Uncertainty
STAGES OF REFINEMENT IN ESTIMATES
SUMMARY

III. SUPPLY OF CAPITAL
INTERNAL SOURCES
Depreciation
Plow-back Guides
EXTERNAL SOURCES
Role of Cost of Capital
Determination of Company's Cost of Capital
Market Values
Costs of Flotation
Capital Structure
COST OF CAPITAL FUNCTIONS
AVERSION TO EXTERNAL FINANCING
Social View of Autonomous Capital Formation
SUMMARY

IV. CAPITAL RATIONING
REJECTION RATES
FLUCTUATING EFFECTIVE RATE
Autonomous Capital Budgeting
External Financing
BASIC MINIMUM RATE
THE LONG-RUN CUT-OFF RATE
EXCEPTION RATES
ASSUMPTIONS OF THEORY
ALTERNATIVES TO RATE-OF-RETURN RATIONING
SUMMARY

V. CLASSIFICATION OF CAPITAL EXPENDITURES

A Multiple Classification Plan

Replacement Investments

Expansion Investments

Product Investments

Strategic Investments

Cyclical Investment Policies

Capital Budgeting

I. INTRODUCTION

IN THIS CHAPTER we are concerned with the economics of capital budgeting—that is, with the kind of thinking that is necessary to design and carry through a systematic program for investing stockholders' money. Planning and control of capital expenditures is the basic executive function, since management is originally hired to take control of stockholders' funds and to maximize their earning power. In a broad sense, therefore, the other chapters of this book are a discussion of subsidiary problems of administering management's trusteeship over capital.

The scale on which management spends investors' money is reflected in Chart 10–1, which shows total non-farm investment expenditures in durable plant and equipment. This chart understates the role of capital budgeting, since as we point out below, capital budgeting is not limited to outlays on durable plant. The other types of capital expenditure, e.g., building a dealer organization, are classified as expenses rather than capital assets in conventional accounts and are, in practice, hidden among the running expenses. Panels B and C taken together show that the visible investment outlays are much more volatile than gross national product, but considerably more stable than other private investment, such as house construction and inventory changes. We discuss briefly in Section V the economic factors pro and con capital budgeting aimed at damping these fluctuations in outlay. Private business investment is a more strategic factor in the level of business activity than its percentage of the national product would indicate. Investment decisions depend on more sophisticated and more long-run views of future prospects than consump-

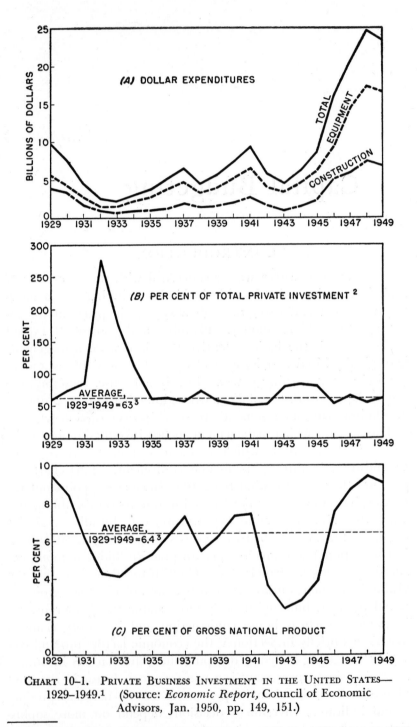

CHART 10–1. PRIVATE BUSINESS INVESTMENT IN THE UNITED STATES—
1929–1949.[1] (Source: *Economic Report,* Council of Economic
Advisors, Jan. 1950, pp. 149, 151.)

[1] Non-farm producers' plant and equipment expenditures. All data are gross
investment, before allowances for depreciation.

tion expenditures do, and are less closely tied to the current level of income. Hence, management in its capital budgeting is an independent source of demand for labor, and its decisions whether or not to spend have important consequences for general income levels.

Although capital budgeting is conceptually, at least, the universal business problem, encompassing all others, few executives are happy with their own solutions to it. Capital budget reviews take too much time, and without systematic rejection and acceptance criteria, the pivotal decision on the size of the total expenditure that should be authorized in a given year has no solid foundation. Allocation of funds among projects, moreover, is often determined by skill and persistence of persuasion rather than by objective indexes of company welfare.

This chapter is a broad-gauge view of a system for capital budgeting that highlights the economic issues, and may reduce the executive time and confusion involved in making decisions. The system is offered tentatively, because until recently capital budgeting has had little attention by economists, and there exists a no man's land between the pure theory of investment and management's decision to spend.

The managerial problem of planning and control of capital expenditure is examined from an economic standpoint. Accordingly, we shall be concerned primarily with principles and concepts, and only incidentally with procedures and problems of organization for capital budgeting.

The capital budgeting process takes different forms in different industries. For example, in the automobile industry, where demand is growing, where product improvements and innovations dominate capital outlays, and where competitors' innovations continually peril a company's market position, neat rate-of-return rationing of capital is not common. Prevailing uncertainties dictate that the process of winnowing investment proposals takes a different form, which is less formal but not necessarily less logical or thorough than the rate-of-return approach developed in this chapter. Executives don't think of a decision to develop a new engine as a rate-of-return problem. Instead, it is viewed as a

---

[2] Greater than 100% in 1932–1934 because of large inventory diminishment included in total investment.

[3] Ratio of the 21-year totals.

many-sided decision of operating policy calling for collective wisdom in reconciling research dreams, production feasibility, competitive pressures, and market acceptance.

These qualitative considerations are usually focused on earnings, but often in terms of what is needed to preserve or enhance the earning power of the division as a whole, rather than incrementally in terms of how much added profits will come from the added investment. Thus, a car may be thought of as needing a new engine when its earning power (or market share) slips, or is periled.

These various facets can be viewed as adding up to a rate-of-return estimate, but this economic structure is obscured by the heavy overlay of business judgment and grand strategy.

The theoretical and general aspects of capital budgeting are purposely emphasized in this chapter, which reflects the belief that the art of capital planning, i.e., judgment on imponderables, can be best developed and exercised against the background of a formal economic analysis that has "gone about as far as it can go," and maybe farther. The most that can be usefully learned from any book is the generic and abstract skeleton of judgment. Putting flesh on the bones is the job of experience.

Meaning of Capital Expenditure

A capital expenditure should be defined in terms of economic behavior, rather than in terms of accounting conventions or tax law. The criterion, then, is the flexibility of the commitment involved, that is, the rate of turnover into cash.[1] For instance, inventories and receivables, although assets on the balance sheet, turn over fast enough to make their level fairly adjustable to short-run changes in outlook. They are, therefore, excluded from the capital budget. Major replacements or additions to plant capacity, on the other hand, take several years to return their cash outlay. Their value to the company during this period is usually much above the amount they could be sold for—that is, they tie up capital inflexibly for long periods. They involve more uncertainty, forecasting judgment, and company-wide thinking than an inventory investment does, and justify a special procedure for management review. The same is largely true for

---

[1] In practice, an exception must be made for minute outlays, regardless of how slow to cash.

major research on new products and methods, and for advertising that has cumulative effects. It applies as well to costs of educating executives and developing dependable distribution connections.

Obviously, our definition of outlays that budget as capital expenditures does not correspond well to the accounting distinction between capitalized and expensed outlays. Although we include most items capitalized by accountants, we also include some important expenditures that are usually expensed by accountants, such as long-term advertising,[2] training, and research. The disparity hinges largely on the tangibility of an asset rather than its economic nature, and contrasts the need for controls and conventions in accounting with the economist's intellectual license.

Nature of Budgeting Problem

The capital budgeting problem consists broadly of three questions: (1) How much money will be needed for expenditures in the coming period? (2) How much money will be available? (3) How should the available money be doled out to candidate projects? The first question is that of demand for capital, and since the objective of capital expenditures is to make profits, "need" should be measured by prospective profitability. Thus this problem involves a survey of opportunities for profitable internal investment and implies some system of screening requests on the basis of prospective profitability. These problems are discussed in Section II.

The second question concerns capital supply. This problem has two parts: (a) How much can be raised internally from depreciation plus retained earnings? (b) How much will be obtained by outside financing? The policy decisions needed to answer these questions are discussed in Section III. The third question, how to ration funds, is the crux of the budgeting problem, the point where it becomes evident how much should be spent in total and where. The solution to this problem, both in general and for specific kinds of investment, is discussed in Sections IV and V. A final note is concerned with the problem of timing of investment and how far a company can go in stabilizing expenditures over the business cycle. Although stable invest-

---

2 Budgeting of advertising investments, because of distinctive features and importance, is discussed in Chapter 6, rather than here.

ment timing is an important goal of social policy, an individual company must view it in terms of the balance of added risks and gains that it entails.

Planning Period

A major question to face before getting deep into the budgeting job is how far into the future the plan should go. Ideally, capital expenditures should be planned for several years ahead for a number of reasons: (1) Long-term investments provide a framework for the future development of the company, which needs to be visualized in advance. (2) Big economies of plant size, for example, may make it desirable to build capacity in anticipation of growth of demand (e.g., hydro-electric dams). (3) There is usually a long gestation period between the time the project is planned and the time the plant goes into operation. (4) Sources of capital also usually require several months' advance planning. (5) Moreover, pronounced cyclical fluctuations occur in the amounts apparently needed (profitably investable) for capital expenditures. If any attempt is to be made to stabilize investment cyclically, long-term planning is needed. All these considerations underscore the desirability of projecting capital projects, at least in tentative terms, many years ahead.

Long-term capital investment programs that are integrated with company development plans are indeed not uncommon. In such cases, the capital expenditure budget starts with a comprehensive long-range plan for the company as a whole. Although the desirability of each individual capital expenditure should be tested by its prospective earnings, it must also be tested for consistency with this master plan. The probability that a given investment will produce the predicted profits depends in part on how it fits into the company's pattern of long-term development.[3] Capital expenditure plans of one of the building material companies, for example, were derived from a ten-year development program for expansion of product line and sales. A few firms have formulated a five-year budget for capital expenditures consisting of: (1) A cash inflow forecast, including all internal sources of cash less

---

[3] Capital expenditures must also be paced with development of executives. One large company recently decided to hold off on new investments because it had managerial indigestion. The men had not grown up to the job of getting full potentialities from the plant additions recently made.

dividends—annually for five years; (2) a cash requirement budget including both operating and capital outlays; (3) an estimate of the outside money needed to fill gaps, and where it will be obtained.

Dramatic and desirable though these brave dreams are, they exaggerate the precision with which a corporation can plan its capital life. The growth trend for established products in a growing industry can sometimes be projected ahead with precision, so that aggregate capacity that will be needed in some distant year can be foreseen. But expansion of competitors and other factors that influence market share are hard to predict far ahead. Other kinds of capital expenditures are even more intractable. They are a little like prospecting: there is no telling what opportunities for profitable investment may be dug up by the company's own research, or by dramatic technical advances in the equipment industry. Some companies who have tried five-year plans for capital budgeting have found that these projections are very tentative beyond two years. For all practical purposes, their capital budgeting is on an annual, or at most a two-year, basis, though they continue to look at a long range budget and sometimes ask whether current projects were foreseen when the budget was drawn up. There is an observed tendency to over-estimate capital expenditures in the near future and an offsetting tendency to underbudget for the later part of the planning period. Thus the projection for the second year is largely a conjecture— the best look the division can take down the road.[4]

To summarize, as a practical matter explicit capital budgeting is generally for only one year ahead, and the amount set is quite sensitive to changes in executive views (except when advance commitments to build or buy are necessary). The projects envisioned in longer-range capital planning are generally indefinite as to amount, timing, and estimated profitability. These distant projects, keyed to the company's long-range expansion program, are, so to speak, ghosts at the supper. Such projects may be

---

[4] In reality this may apply as well to the one-year budget. McGraw-Hill found in their 1950 survey of capital expenditure planning that 65 per cent of their sample companies review capital budgets monthly. There is thus much flexibility in budgeting over even the short run, and previously authorized projects are continuously subject to the axe if management's mood so decides. (*Business Week,* January 21, 1950.) For a statistical comparison of planned and realized investment, see Friend and Bronfenbrenner, "Business Investment Programs and Their Realization," *Survey of Current Business,* December, 1950, pp. 11–22.

screened on the basis of rough estimates of their prospective profitability, but there are limits on the precision that is worth striving for in rate-of-return estimates of distant capital expenditure. Before they are put into the short-range capital program, earnings are re-estimated more definitively.

II. DEMAND FOR CAPITAL

The usual starting point of a capital expenditure budget is a survey of the company's anticipated needs for capital. This inventory of internal investment opportunities is usually built up from the smallest operating units of the organization, often as an integral part of annual budgets or general development plans for a longer period. The catalogue of capital "needs," expressed in terms of specific individual assets, moves up the management hierarchy for supervisory review and for aggregation into larger managerial units.

This capital requirements survey is sometimes guided by advance notice of the general state of supply of funds [5] or even by specific "suggestions" on the minimum earnings rate that will be given serious consideration, or the aggregate amount of funds likely to be available (e.g., each operating unit will be limited to 90 per cent of its depreciation and depletion).

Behind the marshaling of investment proposals lies the discovery and creation of opportunities for capital expenditures. The backbone of a good capital budget is good projects—a surplus of opportunities to invest money internally at high rates of return, as compared with the amount of funds available. The worst that can happen from too many good opportunities is that the company may forego opportunities to invest profitably by not raising funds outside. On the other hand, a lack of good opportunities for internal investment may mean that misallocation of economic re-

---

[5] For example, in one company the president sends out a letter each year to the divisional vice-presidents requesting each division to have its individual units submit tentative capital expenditure plans by a specified date. The letter sets the general background for that year's capital expenditures by presenting the president's views on the economic outlook and the supply of funds. In this connection he sometimes points out that building projects should be deferred because he thinks building costs are coming down, or that since the supply of funds is this year quite limited, all postponable items should be deferred. On some occasions he has in general terms set minimum payout standards for a category of investment for which payouts can be easily estimated.

sources will result from a policy of plowing back earnings without regard to profit outlook: there may be more profitable opportunities for investors in other companies.

The discovery and development of good investment proposals usually require effort. Hence encouragement of an imaginative search for such opportunities is an important part of the program. Since these opportunities stem from continuing efforts to find better ways of doing things, they come rather automatically as a product of good management. More specifically, the activities of the research department create these opportunities in new products, in improved products, and in advanced technology. Similarly, the industrial engineering group's efforts to find ways of reducing costs generally produce opportunities for profitable investment.[6] Good projects also result from research and competition in the equipment industries whose business it is to promote their own sales by creating obsolescence.

Although long-range plans of company development are desirable, surveys of explicit capital requirements are, as we have seen, generally confined to one year, or at most two years, ahead. The capital projects themselves are hard to visualize in the distant future, since they depend upon unborn technical advances and long-range development of demand for the company's product. And even when projects are foreseeable their prospective earnings are highly uncertain, for they too depend upon unknown technical advances, market developments, and changes in relative prices.

Nature of Demand for Capital

Surveys of capital requirements are often phrased in terms of "need." How much new capital will a given plant or marketing district "need" to do a good job (i.e., attain some kind of planned development) during the planning period? "Need" is a meaningless concept for economic analysis, since it contains no objective measurement of intensity. "Demand" for capital, in contrast, can be made meaningful, since it can measure the intensity of need for capital by its earnings. Under most circumstances, the

---

[6] For example, a systematic survey of manufacturing operations in each plant of a large electrical company was made by a team of industrial engineers and other specialists. As a result, projects were developed for mechanization and for altered plant outlay which promised high productivity of capital.

underlying source of demand for capital expenditures is, or should be, prospective profitability.[7]

A company's investment proposals, when arrayed in a ladder of return on investment and cumulated, form its demand schedule for capital. This schedule shows the total amount that is demanded (i.e., that can be invested) at any given rate of return.

The first step in projecting demand for investment funds within a company should be a survey of what investments may be needed to keep the company competitive and progressive. The next step is to appraise these projects by estimating the rate of return on each capital proposal. Then the demand schedule for capital can be conceived as the total amount of money that can be invested to earn more than specified rates.

Demand Schedule for Capital Expenditures

To develop an empirical approximation to the company's demand schedule for capital for internal investment during a specified time period, it is necessary: (1) to marshal all individual "needs" for capital expenditures that can be discovered and foreseen throughout the company; (2) to estimate for each proposal its prospective productivity in the form of rate of return on the added investment; (3) to array projects in a ladder of rate of return (as illustrated by Table 10–1); and (4) to cumulate this ladder in the form of a schedule showing the amount of money that can be invested to equal or better each of a series of rates

TABLE 10–1

DEMAND SCHEDULE FOR CAPITAL

(a) Prospective Rate of Return	(b) Volume of Pro- posed Investments	(c) Cumulative Demand
Over 100%	2	2
50–100%	38	40
25– 50%	200	240
15– 25%	1200	1440
5– 15%	3400	4840

[7] This proposition is based upon the assumption that most firms try to make as much money as they can and that profits are their central objective. Our subsequent analysis of capital budgeting will take account of modifications of this profit-maximizing theory.

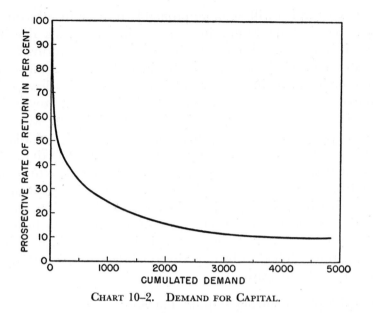

CHART 10–2. DEMAND FOR CAPITAL.

of return.   Chart 10–2 diagrams the resulting capital demand schedule.   (There are, to be sure, some types of investment that cannot be fitted into such a demand curve without an impossible degree of foresight.   These are discussed below in Sections IV and V.)

In tabular form, the company's demand schedule shows the relationship between yield and cumulative totals of proposals.   Consequently, it shows how much money can be invested at rates of return that will be better than the specified series.   In drawing such a schedule, the time span must be specified, and for simplicity we shall assume the common one-year capital planning period.

Time Dimensions of Demand for Capital

For simplicity, we have conceived the firm's demand schedule as including only capital projects to be initiated during the budget year.   That is to say, it includes only those investments whose productivity will never be higher than it is this year.   Those which will get better if postponed should go into future budgets.   Those which will deteriorate if postponed should be put into this year's demand curve.   This simple conception concentrates on rivalry with alternative investments to be made this year.   It ignores another dimension of rivalry, namely, with alternative investments which will be more profitable if made in subsequent years. To include future investments in this year's demand curve, it is necessary also to conceive of patterns for storing funds for later use. This storage can be in cash or in government bonds, or it can be in the form of investments which have high cash-to-cash turnover in spite of comparatively low prospective profitability.[8] The cost of maintaining liquidity, to whatever degree, is an offset to the improvement in profitability of a later-year investment over a present-year investment. Rejecting a 20 per cent return now to save money for a 40 per cent return two years from now involves carrying costs. Conceiving of demand for funds with this time dimension, therefore, requires an exploration of the alternative time patterns of investment in terms of requisite liquidity. It ties the capital budget intimately into the long-run cash budget by imposing dual standards, namely, productivity and cash payout.

Principles of Measuring Capital Earnings

The crucial estimate in analyzing demand for capital is the productivity (i.e., rate of return) of the proposed capital expenditure. Since capital productivity is the key factor in sound budgeting of internal investments, the care and precision with which it is estimated are likely to make the difference between good investment decisions and bad ones.

General principles for estimating capital productivity are summarized in this section. Application to different types of investment will be discussed later.

1. Recognition of the source of productivity of capital is essential to correct estimation of capital earnings. The source of earnings depends upon the nature of the investment. The most important direct sources are cost savings and sales expansion. Cost savings are the source for investments in replacement and modernization of equipment. Added sales volume (or more profitable volume) is the source for investments that involve new products or expansion of capacity to produce old ones. Earnings of many projects have more than one source.

2. Earnings must be estimated on an individual project basis. It is the prospective profitability of *individual units* of *added*

---

[8] Speculating on a fall in construction costs by getting along with temporary buildings is an illustration of this.

capital investment that is the key to their appraisal in allocating capital funds. Return on old, sunk investments has only historical interest and no relevance to decisions on new investments. And average return on old and new investments is badly misleading.

3. It is *future* profit on additional investment that is relevant. Thus, profit projections must be based on estimates of future prices, future costs, and so forth. The record of the past is useful only as a guide to estimates of the future.

4. Capital productivity estimates usually should involve comparison of future costs and profits with the *appropriate alternative*. An analysis of what will happen if no investment is made will reveal the proper alternative, i.e., the least-cost method without added capital. Pains must be taken to make sure the comparison is with the relevant alternative, for the kind of cost comparisons that are valid will differ according to the nature of the alternative.

5. Capital productivity should be measured by earnings over the whole life of the asset, even though in practice the view of the distant future is often browned out. Estimates of economic life are always inexact, but they are essential for measuring capital wastage costs. Earnings may be stated in terms of lifetime gross earnings, from which the cost of the investment (i.e., total capital wastage) is deducted, or in terms of net earnings after annual allowances for capital wastage. In either case, the result is a rate of return on investment. For comparability, the company should standardize on one method. Payout period—i.e., the number of years required for gross earnings (or cash savings) to pay back the capital investment—is a misleading measure of capital productivity. It is relevant solely for cash budgeting, and then only when confined to cash earnings (or savings).

6. Discounting the stream of capital earnings to take account of the diminishing value of distant earnings is an integral part of the theory of capital value. It introduces complications of measurement, however. When the economic life of assets is short or fairly uniform, when earnings estimates are necessarily rough, and when uncertainty rises steeply in the distant future, this refinement is not worth its complexity cost.

On the other hand, discounting has practical importance when there are distinctive time patterns of the income streams of different assets, and when the rate of discount (logically the firm's cost of capital) is high, e.g., 15 to 20 per cent.

7. The amount of investment to be used for comparison with earnings should be the average capital tied up in the asset over the period being considered. This period can be less than the full economic life of the asset. Property whose final value, in terms either of market value or of usefulness elsewhere in the company, will be less than initial cost, should be bought only if gross earnings will cover this loss in value as well as the required return on capital. Determining how much of gross earnings represents capital payback rather than profits is a problem in financial mathematics and depends on the time pattern of earnings. In view of the manifold uncertainties of forecasting, the conventional straight-line depreciation account may frequently be as good an estimate as any of capital payback.[9] In any case, the capital that has been liquidated by gross earnings is free to be invested elsewhere and is no longer dependent on the particular asset for its earnings. Thus an estimate of the average amount invested should be used, rather than the initial capital outlay.

8. Estimates of earnings (whether from cost savings or from added profits) should take account of the indirect effects of the proposed capital outlay upon the operation of existing facilities. Total company revenues and costs with the proposed investment should be compared with what they will be without it. Typically, estimates of these indirect earnings involve a high order of judgment and have wide error margins.[10]

9. In a self-adjusting competitive economy, there is a tendency for capital expenditures to destroy the economic opportunity that creates their profitability. Abnormal profits are indicators of the richest opportunities for more investment, and expenditures will flow in their direction until increasing costs or output tend to cause firms to overshoot the optimum outlay level. In the process, they destroy the abnormal profits. This risk of destroying

---

[9] However, when all the facts are known, the economic investment is usually seen to be different from the book investment. Accounting treatment, moreover, is properly governed by tax considerations and bookkeeping conventions, which should have no direct bearing on investment decisions.

[10] When equipment that is displaced by new is pushed downward in a cascade of demotions (e.g., successive levels of stand-by or successive grades of service of locomotives or trucks) then the productivity of the new equipment includes the aggregate cost savings (or other earnings) of all retained equipment in their new uses.

should be examined in connection with each profitability estimate.

10. Estimates of the productivity of capital expenditures will differ in inherent riskiness and in the width of error margins. Some systematic method for allowing for these differences in risk and for comparing investment proposals is desirable.

11. For some kinds of investments it is impractical to estimate a rate of return. The benefits are so diffused and conjectural (e.g., research laboratories and employee club houses) that they defy quantification. Earnings of others are so high and so apparent (e.g., replacing a washed-out railroad bridge) that estimating a return is an academic exercise. Earnings on other projects are patently too low to warrant return estimates. Capital productivity should be measured only when there is a factual foundation for estimates and for projects of borderline productivity.

These principles will be developed more fully in connection with their application to different kinds of capital expenditures. But first let's discuss some controversial matters that have general applicability, namely: (1) payout period vs. profitability yield; (2) postponability as an investment criterion; and (3) allowances for risk and uncertainty.

Payout Period vs. Profitability Yield

Payout period is the time required to pay back the investment from gross earnings (before allowance for capital wastage). It is a criterion commonly used in capital budgeting for appraising investment opportunities. It measures the rapidity with which the investment will replenish the capital fund. Payout period is essentially a cash concept, concerned solely with the cash budget, and designed to answer the very specific question, "How soon will this cash outlay be returned to the firm's treasury?"

Of itself, the payout period does not measure profitability in the sense of return on investment, and hence is not of much help in capital budgeting, as contrasted with cash budgeting. In limited-period investments, no fixed relationship exists between payout period and profitability.

Consider, for example, two alternative investment opportunities in machinery. Machine *A* costs $2,000 and will yield a gross earning (neglecting depreciation on new equipment) of $500 a year for six years. Machine *B* also costs $2,000, but will yield earnings of $500 a year for ten years. Thus, for both Machine *A* and Machine *B*, the payout period is four years:

$$\text{Payout period} = \frac{\$2,000}{\$500 \text{ per year}} = 4 \text{ years}$$

But at the end of the payout period, Machine *A* has only two more years of useful life, whereas Machine *B* will continue to yield annual revenues of $500 for six more years. Although their payout periods are equal, they are clearly not equally desirable investments.

The rate of return on the investment refers in theory to the rate of interest that will make the present value of future gross earnings just equal to the cost of the machine. In the above illustration, the rate of return on Machine *A* is about 13 per cent, since this is the interest rate that discounts a six-year annuity of $500 down to a present cost of $2,000. Machine *B* has a 21 per cent return, the discount rate that makes a ten-year annuity of $500 equal to $2,000 today. The comparative discount rates show that a dollar spent on *B* buys considerably more future income than a dollar spent on *A*.[11]

Profitability yield, i.e., the net return on investment, is the relevant criterion for developing a demand schedule for capital and for selection of projects. But in some situations payout period may be a valid subsidiary basis for ranking. When the firm's passion for cash is intense and it is unwilling (or unable) to borrow even for short terms, an investment that speedily returns the cash may be preferred to a more profitable one. In compromise situations, consideration must be given to speed of cash pay-back as well as to the underlying productivity of capital.

What explains the widespread use of payout period as a measure of profitability of capital outlays? To many it appears more simple, realistic, and safe than rate of return. It is somewhat simpler to compute, since capital wastage is not estimated. Ignoring these necessarily conjectural book costs confers on the pay-

---

[11] This kind of computation, though enlightening, is not feasible for common use. Actual estimates are made by approximations that, considering the degree of uncertainty, are probably quite good enough for choosing investments. We cannot go into them in detail here, but in essence the correct ones all compare total expected income with cost and are not limited to finding the period required to get the cash outlay back.

out method a halo of hardboiled realism that appeals to some but is nevertheless a delusion. Payout, in weighting the near years heavily, has built-in conservatism, by facing the possibility that the earnings of the new machine may be soon destroyed by obsolescence. A short minimum payback standard, e.g., two years, is one way of allowing for this uncertainty. But it does this captiously and crudely by counting only the earnings of the payout years. If it is clear that the cash will be returned before obsolescence or depression strikes, many companies are willing to take a gamble on profitability, which depends on what happens after the payout period. Rate of return, however, can be adjusted for uncertainty by methods that are more direct and flexible.

Postponability vs. Productivity

Another widely used standard for choosing among investment proposals is postponability, i.e., how long the project can be put off. If there is an excess of budget requests over available funds, many companies use postponability as a screen to reject projects that can be deferred, even though postponement would mean foregoing the profits made possible by an improved facility.

This method of selecting investments is not logical and is not likely to lead to allocation of investment that produces maximum profit. A large proportion of investments that would yield big savings and high profits could be put off almost indefinitely. For example, a service station purchase, which would be lost to a competitor if not accepted this month, may earn only 6 per cent, whereas a pipeline project, which could be postponed forever, would produce a 30 per cent return in the form of cost savings. Under those circumstances the company would be better off putting its money into the more postponable, rather than the less postponable, of the alternate projects.

The use of postponability as a criterion is likely to result in a stagnant operation. The postponability standard would tend to forestall expansion investment and technological advance. To be sure, certain high profitability items do happen to fall into the unpostponable class. But such projects are assured of acceptance through the comparison-of-profitability method, because the "must" items are high-profit items. "Must" items have high profitability automatically, because the alternative is catastrophe.

For example replacing a pumping station on a pipeline is enormously profitable, since, if it is not done, earnings of the whole line cease.

Allowances for Uncertainty

A dollar of estimated revenue several years hence is worth less than a dollar today, not only because of the interest cost of capital, but also because of uncertainty about the accuracy of estimates. Future conditions may destroy all revenue from the investment. Technological advance may make the asset obsolete and worthless. Future changes in wages, costs, prices, and operating volume may wipe out estimated revenues in future years.

Adjustments to allow for uncertainty may be challenged as nothing more than guesses. Perhaps they are. But even so, they are guesses that must be made, and will be made, either explicitly or implicitly. Failure to apply the probability adjustments does not enable management to avoid the problem; it merely transfers the guess element in a disguised form to some other stage of the decision-making process.[12]

Four different methods of allowing explicitly for differential uncertainty may be distinguished: (1) by informal judgment; (2) differential handicaps applied to unmodified return estimates; (3) modification of the return estimate itself by applying discount rates that differ with uncertainty for modifying the return estimate by adjusting the estimate of life expectancy for uncertainty; (4) modifying the estimate by probability multipliers applied to individual years.

The choice among these four methods depends upon the character of the uncertainty, and each of the four may be appropriate for different kinds of investments. For example, when the existence, rather than the amount of the estimated future revenues is uncertain, then the appropriate allowance is a probability multiplier which expresses the likelihood that the revenue in a particular year will occur at all. It may seem odd that even the existence of revenue should be uncertain, but these uncertainty characteristics are important when there is much obsolescence of methods or of style, or fickleness and obscurity of

---

12 When no modifications for uncertainty are incorporated in the earnings estimate, they may be taken into account in appraising investments—informally, or by differential standards of acceptable rate of return.

forecasting buyers' tastes, particularly in development of new and unknown product lines.

Stages of Refinement in Estimates

The method of applying these principles of measuring capital earnings will differ for different types of investment. Consequently, explicit application is discussed later for each main category. At this point we shall, however, mention an administrative requirement that applies to all categories of investment: the desirability of different stages of refinement in earnings estimates.

Certain stages of top-management approval parallel the progress of a capital project from a long-range plan to eventual fulfillment. Three stages may be distinguished: (1) Review of the general plan to see that it is consistent with a sensible general development program. Top-management concurrence in the long-range plan carries no commitment that funds will be made available. (2) Approval of definite projects as components of the one-year capital budget. But budget approval is not an authorization to spend money. (3) Specific authorization of funds for individual projects.[13]

As capital projects pass through these stages of evolution from nebulous notions to definite requests for final authorization, different degrees of refinement in the measurement of return are appropriate. Three degrees of estimating refinement, which parallel the three stages of approval, might be instituted: (1) Back-of-envelope estimates made roughly and rapidly by putting together already available knowledge. This estimate would merely feel out the economic feasibility and probe the survival chances of the project in a more rigorous capital productivity test. (2) Preliminary engineering estimates. These would be based upon considerable engineering analysis and rough forecasts of sales, prices, and other revenue factors. The estimates would be in terms of net return on capital and would be comprehensive enough to be submitted for the annual capital budget. (3) Final estimates. These would be the best projection of costs and

---

13 Specific project authorization added to long-range plan approval and capital budget approval enables management to take another look at each proposal on the basis of how the aggregate budget is shaping up as the year progresses; that is, how much money is coming in, how the economic situation is developing, and at what rate capital expenditure is being made.

revenues that the divisional staff could make, and would be reviewed and revised by a central financial staff and also by the capital expenditures group of top executives. These estimates would be the basis for the final authorization to spend the money.

Summary

1. The underlying requisite for effective capital expenditure planning is the opportunity to invest money internally at high rates of return. Such opportunities are in a sense a by-product of good management, but an imaginative search for them should be an integral part of capital budgeting.

2. A survey of the company's capital requirements built up from the roots of the smallest operating unit is usually the first step in capital budgeting. Ideally, capital expenditures should be planned for several years ahead as an integrated part of the company's long-term program. But, since projections become increasingly indefinite as they stretch into the future, as a practical matter it is usually necessary to budget capital expenditures over a one-year, or at most a two-year, planning period.

3. The demand for funds for investment within a company can be viewed as a schedule of relationship between the amount invested and the prospective rate of return. To develop such a schedule, individual investment proposals showing estimated yield should be arrayed in a ladder of capital productivity summarized on a company-wide basis for a specified planning period. The demand schedule thus derived shifts with changes in general business conditions and with the fortunes of the firm.

4. To get good and comparable estimates of return on investment, the company's measurement methods must be built upon certain basic principles of measuring capital earnings.

5. In applying these principles, the detailed methods differ for different types of capital projects, but a principle that applies quite generally is that different degrees of refinement in estimating the rate of return are appropriate at different stages in the development and review of a capital project.

III. SUPPLY OF CAPITAL

We have seen how a company can explore and measure its demand for capital funds. We now turn to problems of determining where the money will come from and how much will be available.

A useful distinction can be made between internal and external sources of capital funds. The chief internal sources are: (1) depreciation charges, and (2) retained earnings. External sources are principally sale of securities to insurance companies and to the public. (Term loans from financial institutions are not a permanent source of capital, since they must be paid off by either retained earnings or later security financing. They are a means for postponing the financing problem.) In the internal disposition of these funds no distinction should be made on the basis of sources of funds. In particular, the internal investment process should deal with gross rather than with net business savings—that is, with income before depreciation allowances. This gives a desirable fluidity of the internal investment process, where old, dying products can subsidize new ones by contributing funds that are not "earned" according to a "net" income concept. The barrier that depreciation charges set up against capital leakage from the firm may do more harm than good if they block flows of capital inside the firm. For example, the practice of allowing each of a company's divisions or plants to reinvest its own depreciation charges without central-office review carries division autonomy too far and undermines a major social and private advantage of multiple product firms. Cash earnings, rather than net earnings, should be pooled in a centrally administered supply of capital.

Internal Sources

The principal managerial problems in connection with internal sources are (1) to forecast how much cash will be generated internally, (2) to decide how much cash to pay out in dividends, and (3) to decide how much of the remainder may be tied up in long-term projects.

In modern corporate enterprise, current operations are the dominant source of capital funds. In some companies, capital expenditures are confined completely to the amount that can be obtained internally.[14] This may be a matter of choice or, in

---

[14] One study of capital budgeting practice emphasized that virtually every company interviewed made *realized* profits a first condition for capital expenditures. (*The Minneapolis Project,* Investors Diversified Services, Inc., Minneapolis, 1950, p. 17.) This attitude is the reverse of the economist's notion that *expected* profits from the expenditure are the motive for spending.

some sense, a matter of necessity because of the condition of the capital markets or the investment status of the firm.

Consequently, the projection of the amount that can be expected from accumulated depreciation and retained earnings is usually the most important part of capital expenditure budgeting. Some companies make elaborate five-year forecasts of the cash that will be generated and of its disposition for dividends and for liquid reserves. More commonly, such estimates are confined to a one-year or two-year period. Such projections are not only a matter of forecasting the level of sales prices and costs; they also involve management decisions on the adequacy of depreciation charges, the level of dividends, and the necessary degree of liquidity.

Depreciation

The adequacy of depreciation charges depends of course on their purposes, of which there are several, e.g., preserving dollar capital, physical capital, or earning power. If depreciation charges are intended to finance plant replacement, they should be adjusted for expected changes in equipment prices, but for this purpose, they are not different from retained earnings, and the significant problem is the amount of earnings plus depreciation that is not to be retained, i.e., paid out as dividends.

Occasionally, depreciation and depletion are used as criteria for the allocation of the capital budget among units in the company. It was, for example, fairly common during the great depression to confine each major operating unit to a capital budget that was no more than its depreciation and depletion, or some fraction thereof. In some instances this practice was carried down to regional marketing investments and to individual plants. Application of this criterion for allocation of capital funds among small units shows a blind faith in the status quo. Such a faith has little justification, particularly in periods of adversity.

Plow-back Guides

The importance of retained earnings as a source of capital funds makes plow-back policy an integral part of a firm's capital expenditure budgeting. How should a company decide how much of its earnings to plow back and how much to pay out?

One guide to plow-back policy is that outlined by the capital rationing theory set forth in Section IV of this chapter. If a company follows this plan faithfully, it retains earnings (up to the limit of stockholder rebellion) as long as they can be invested at a return higher than the firm's cost of capital (e.g., 15 per cent). It pays out earnings that cannot be invested internally (either now or in the future) to beat this cost-of-capital rate.

Another guide is suggested by the theory that dividends in the modern corporation are a kind of interest income (although more uncertain than contractual interest). If plow-back policy is determined by this theory (which is set forth in more detail in Chapter 1 ("Profits"), then retained earnings would be a highly volatile residual left after paying stable dividends out of fluctuating earnings.

A third guide to plow-back policy is found in the notion that a certain percentage of earnings should be held back for contingencies and for growth. This is a long-run view of an average minimum amount of plow-back that would rate a prior claim on earnings over an integral business cycle.[15]

The effects of plow-back policy upon the market price of the company's stock, and thus upon the firm's cost of capital, may modify these three approaches. There is some evidence to support the hypothesis that plowing back (as opposed to paying out) earnings depresses the price of a stock and thus raises cost of capital, at least temporarily. It would be logical to expect that from the standpoint of the effect of plow-backs upon market price and cost of capital there would be an optimum ratio of retained earnings. Paying all earnings out in dividends connotes impoverished opportunities for internal investment, no plans for growth, and inadequate contingency reserves. On the other hand, plowing back too much generally depresses stock values. The levels of these limits vary among companies and depend upon the prospects for profitable growth and the income-tax bracket of investors that hold the stock. But the question is important only when the company actually expects to go after outside capital.

---

[15] This consideration in plow-back policy is an allowance for uncertainty. Strictly, cash is one kind of capital investment, and thus an alternative use of plowed-back funds. But it is not usually thought of in this way. Hence, this factor of added liquidity as part of plow-back policy deals with uncertainty by non-rationing criteria.

External Sources

Historically, the capital markets have not been as large a source of investment funds as have earnings and depreciation charges, but apparently they are not losing their importance. During the thirties, when demand for capital was extremely low, new capital issues dropped to 18 per cent of their level during the twenties.[16] Although data are scarce, they do not indicate that any great secular changes have occurred in the importance of external sources of capital between the 1920's and 1940's. In the four-year period 1946–1949, net new corporate issues were about one-third the size of retained earnings and depreciation.

Role of Cost of Capital

When a company considers using outside sources to finance investment, a basic factor is the cost of capital, which for common stock is the ratio of prospective earnings per share to the selling price for new shares. By comparing the company's cost of capital with the prospective profits of new investments, we can measure the gain to present common shares to be derived from going after outside funds. Theoretically, there is no point in going outside unless present equity stands to gain. If a project promising a 25 per cent return is financed by sale of new shares to investors asking a 20 per cent return, the number of outstanding shares will be increased less percentage-wise than total earnings, and per-share earnings on existing shares will increase. But if the return appears to be 15 per cent, the number of shares increases more than total earnings, and per-share earnings fall.

In theory, the cost of capital plays another role: It shows the return that could be made by diverting cash out of the firm's business into alternative market investments. That is, it is the opportunity cost of retained earnings. Tax leakages blunt this measurement if capital is withdrawn in the form of dividends, which are taxable as income. To dodge the tax leak, it is possible to have a partial liquidation, which may be taxable only as a capital gain, or to have the company itself invest in securities of other companies, which postpones the tax question indefinitely. However, for a number of reasons (discussed in Chapter 1

---

[16] According to data published regularly in *Commercial and Financial Chronicle.*

"Profits"), this opportunity-cost principle is seldom marshaled to distribute capital by cost-of-capital signals.

For outside financing, on the other hand, cost of capital has much practical importance, at least in the negative decision not to invest when profit prospects are less than cost of capital. But, as we shall see, it does not always act positively to stimulate investments with profitability above the market rate. From a conceptual viewpoint, however, cost of capital is an important guide to capital budgeting and its level should be known.

Determination of Company's Cost of Capital

A company's cost of capital fluctuates with the company's fortunes and the condition of the security markets. It differs greatly among industries and companies. Nevertheless, the cost of capital can be estimated with sufficient accuracy to make it a useful capital budgeting tool if the foregoing philosophy of its role is accepted. As a practical problem, estimating cost of capital has three elements: (1) finding market values, (2) finding costs of flotation, (3) determining capital structure.

At some point, a decision must be made on the time period involved in the estimate. The choice lies among (1) a long-run average of past years, (2) a projection of long-term future costs, (3) current spot cost, computed continuously (or annually at capital-budget time), and (4) spot cost at the time flotation is contemplated. The four possibilities usually differ significantly.

In principle, the decision on where to cut off capital expenditures and when to supplement internal funds from external sources should be governed by current cost of capital.

Among the practical drawbacks are the fact that cost of capital fluctuates violently, and that stockholders have long memories and slight comprehension of these matters. Selling stock in bear markets to take advantage of internal investment opportunities that are rich (in relation to self-generated funds) apparently makes existing stockholders unhappy. Many, who are unable or unwilling to exercise rights, have the "birthright for pottage" illusion. Conversely, raising equity funds at the top of a market leaves a bad taste when the market sinks. Consequently, some managements try to hit the middle range, preferring to borrow temporarily or forego profitable investments in order to promote illogical stockholder happiness. Expected long-run future cost appears more practical from this standpoint. The best index of the future is usually an average past cost of capital.

Market Values

The first step in finding the company's cost of capital is to estimate for the relevant time period the market value of debt and equity securities of the type that the company plans to use. Estimates based on several companies with comparable risks can improve reliability. But the sample must be carefully selected to insure that it is homogeneous in the important long-run elements that determine market price.

Cost of debt capital raises few important problems, since bond prices depend on a fairly narrow range of factors and are dominated by the government bond markets. As a result, estimates of debt cost can be made highly precise in comparison to the uncertainties of estimating costs of equity capital, and when debt and equity are combined to find the total cost of capital, errors in interest cost estimates are negligible.

The cost of equity capital is a much more tenuous quantity, as the behavior of the stock market demonstrates. The basic difficulty is that stock prices are mere speculations about the future and depend on factors that have no statistical gauge. Any estimate of the cost of equity capital based on statistical analysis thus relies on broad assumptions of the relevance of measurable current and historical data to market expectations.

Estimates of cost of capital can frequently be made more economically by following market behavior directly instead of by analysis of such controlling factors as growth trends, sales volatility, and so forth. Thus, for an established company whose stock is well known and heavily traded, the practical problem is to forecast what the stock will sell for at the time the new issue is to be floated. Such a projection is often based on recent market value of the stock, since the new issue will not alter the investment character of the stock. For companies whose stock has no active market or no market at all, market value may be estimated by statistical analysis of comparable companies. For instance, the combined experience in price-earnings ratios of a large sample of companies of roughly similar size and similar products (e.g., groups as large as durable producer goods or processed foods) over the cycle gives some background information on long-run capital costs. Price-earnings behavior for a few highly similar companies may also be a good first approximation if the market's attitude on these few is well understood. Some investment bankers start from this point in the search for a "right" offering price on a new issue.

Costs of Flotation

The cost of capital in terms of trading prices for outstanding bonds and shares is only the first step in estimating the marginal cost of capital. The relevant figure for the company is the net proceeds from floating new securities in the market. These proceeds depend on the costs and inducements of security flotation, which are of three types: (1) underpricing—that is, the spread between the normal market price and the offering price required to dispose of a block of new shares; (2) commission and discount to underwriters as compensation for services in marketing the securities; (3) flotation expenses incurred by the issuing corporation in connection with the sale. For extreme differences in size of flotation, there are marked differences in aggregate costs of flotation that affect cost of capital. However, costs are flat over a wide range of size of issue.

Capital Structure

A company's cost of capital depends not only on the cost of debt capital and the cost of equity capital; it also depends on how much of each kind of capital it obtains. The debt ratio has a simple impact on combined cost of capital because debt is so much cheaper than equity capital. Nowadays, debt capital costs about 3 per cent, while equity capital costs 10 per cent or better in terms of current earnings. Clearly, a capital structure of two-thirds debt, which is characteristic of some electrical utilities, will be cheaper than a structure with no debt at all, which is found in many manufacturing companies.

But the capital structure itself affects the cost of equity capital. A high debt ratio (in relation to the volatility of earnings) not only increases the dangers of default on debt, but also heightens the risks of common stock ownership, and thus raises the cost of equity capital. This interrelationship makes the composition of the minimum cost package a question for technical advice, particularly since it changes with conditions of the security market.

A third factor relating capital structure to capital cost is the corporation income tax, which makes the unjustifiable distinction between interest as a deductible expense and dividends as taxable earnings. If the government takes, say, 50 per cent of earnings on equity capital, investments financed with stock must have gross (before-tax) profit prospects that are twice as high as debt-financed earnings in order to yield the investor a comparable return. Thus the over-all cost of capital in terms of earnings before tax depends on the mixture of non-taxable and taxable earnings. For example, assume that both bonds and stocks sell to yield the investor 5 per cent earnings, and that the tax rate is 50 per cent. A $1,000 investment financed entirely by debt need earn only $50; while if half of it comes from equity capital it must earn $75; and if it is wholly financed by stock it must be able to earn $100 to get the $1,000 from the market initially.

In principle, it is the prospective cost of additional permanent capital that is relevant for most capital budgeting problems.   But here, as in pricing problems, it is important to distinguish between short-run and long-run incremental costs.   Clearly, the cost of a credit line at the bank is not, for long-term capital projects, an appropriate concept of incremental cost of permanent capital.

Thus, since there is a considerable range of managerial discretion in balancing the added risks of more debt against its cheaper costs, the capital structure constitutes another dimension of management choice in determining the firm's cost of capital.

Cost of Capital Functions

The foregoing analysis indicates that a company's cost of capital is the function of several variables, many of which are, to a degree, within the control of its management.   Among these are: (1) plow-back policy, (2) capital structure, (3) level of the market at the time of issue, (4) size of issue, (5) amount of funds sought, and (6) market fame of the company.   The company's cost of capital has a wide band of managerial discretion, the width of which depends partly on the degree to which these variables are stabilized by the company's history.

These variables (plus others) affect the *level* of a company's cost of capital function.   Many of them also affect its shape—i.e., where it turns up as the amount of capital requested increases. As indicated previously, it is probable that the cost of capital function is flat over a wide range of investment. But at some point it rises, and probably precipitously.

Where this point is depends on the market conception of the ability of the company to put the added funds to profitable use. This conception shifts with the condition of the security markets and incorporates a large element of faith in the ability of management. Although large, established firms may be unaware of the rising phase of their supply curve, it is easy to find examples of firms which have experienced this abrupt limit on the amount the market "will absorb."

Whether a particular security flotation will encounter rising capital costs depends to a large extent upon the size of the company and its rate of growth. This relationship can be viewed as a migration of the company's supply schedule to the right as the firm develops along its long-term growth curve. The point of rising capital cost moves right and left with stock-market conditions, even at a fixed level of horizontal supply. There may even be a relationship between the amount that the company is willing to put up by plow-back and the amount that can be drawn in from outside at a given cost of capital.[17]

Perhaps the most important determinant of the marginal future cost of capital that is within the control of management is the timing of equity (and debt) flotation. The giant fluctuations of market prices create opportunities to keep the cost of outside capital low by picking the right time. Manipulating dividends and making short-term bank loans make it possible to ride through periods of high capital cost and to maintain a dividend policy that is optimum from the standpoint of cost of permanent capital. These practices also open opportunities to finance this year's outlays with future years' retained earnings, and time-rivalry in the supply of capital funds already encountered is brought into focus.

In private placements (i.e., sale to a single or to a few institutions) a different mechanism operates: typically, an insurance company offers to take $10 million in 3 per cent bonds, and per-

---

[17] Retaining earnings may, particularly in good times, indicate management's confidence and may thus influence outsiders' appraisal of these profit opportunities. In other periods, however, earnings are retained out of fear for the future, to increase the firm's liquidity.

haps another $5 million in a 4 per cent bond with rigid safety precautions.   It will take no more under any circumstances.   Here the supply curve, instead of rising continuously with size of flotation, has only one step and is vertical at $15 million.

These concepts of the cost of capital function will be directly applied in our examination of capital rationing theory in Section IV.   Before turning to this discussion, we shall make a digression to examine the aversion to external financing and the economic consequences of autonomous capital formation.

Aversion to External Financing

This whole problem of the cost of external capital is a matter of no concern to many companies, simply because they have no intention of ever using outside funds.[18]

For many firms it is a source of pride that they never resort to the banks for financing a new opportunity, no matter how profitable it appears.   They determine the amount of capital available for new schemes not on the basis of earning prospects but on the basis of availability of cash from retained earnings above the balance needed to meet the iron-clad standards for the current ratio.[19]

This behavior does not fit Schumpeter's picture of the entrepreneur who borrows all the capital he needs, pays its owners a competitive interest rate, and skims the cream off the top of the venture for himself.   (Chapter 1, "Profits," Section II.)   What are the reasons for this aversion to debt and this demand for liquidity among modern business managers?

First, debt financing for venture purposes cramps management's

---

18 In McGraw-Hill's 1950 "Survey of Capital Spending Plans," the companies were asked, "Would you boost 1950 spending if you could sell new common stock for 50 per cent more than its present market price?"   Only 7 per cent of the companies said Yes.   There were a number of reasons for this response, but it is significant, considering that a price increase of this magnitude would carry the Dow-Jones index 70 points higher than it has ever been, except during the 1929 boom.   (*Business Week*, Jan. 21, 1950.)

19 A sample statement: "It is traditional with Sun Oil Co. that capital funds for purposes of expansion must come from internal sources.   In this, we have followed a conservative practice, for we have permitted growth to take place only as fast as our company developed the internal ability to provide the means of growth. As a consequence, we believe that our company has maintained its characteristic qualities of independence and self-reliance, making it a stronger competitor in the oil industry and a more stable member of the business community than it would otherwise have been."   Statement of Robert Dunlop, President, Sun Oil Co.   Report of Joint Committee on the Economic Report on Profit Hearings, 80th Congress, 2nd Session, 1949, p. 104.

style. Most bank loans and bonds carry restrictions on the uses to be made of money, on future financing, on minimum levels of certain balance sheet items, and on dividend payments. They further put a fixed capital cost on the firm, since a periodic cash outlay sometimes extends into the unknown future, regardless of conditions or opportunities. Preferred stock, though legally different, is not, as a practical matter, much better in this respect. Furthermore, debt lowers the credit standing of the firm and smears the balance-sheet facade that is such a large part of management's reputation. This gives added attraction to getting capital by leasing assets instead of purchasing them, since in leaseholds neither the asset nor the liability is shown on the balance sheet. It would be interesting to see the balance sheet of the A & P or Safeway stores, with all of their lease liabilities written up.

Second, debt financing puts an asymmetrical risk on management. The men who make the decisions rarely regard the profit prospects as adequate to offset the threat to their personal security from general reorganization in bankruptcy. In many corporations, management's share in the profits of successful ventures (in the form of dividends on the stock they own) is an insignificant source of income compared with their salaries, which show admirable stability over the business cycle. Dividends are marginal income for management and are subject to steep marginal income tax rates.[20]

Executive bonuses based on profits reduce but do not cure this asymmetry. The profit bonuses of the individual executive are often not the result of initiating the slowly ripening profitable venture. Instead, they are the result of being there at the right

---

[20] This point was brought out in some empirical studies made during the thirties. R. A. Gordon found that in a sample of 161 executives, the median holding of stock in their own company in 1935 was $298,700, and the median dividend, $2,980, while median total compensation was $79,200. (*Business Leadership in the Large Corporation*, Washington, D. C., Brookings Institution, 1945, p. 298.) The SEC found the following picture of management holdings of securities in their own companies for the 200 largest non-financial corporations (*TNEC Monograph No. 29*, p. 60):

	Mean Holding	Median	Per Cent of Total Value of All Issues
Officers	$ 50,400	$ 9,300	0.1%
Officer-Directors	763,400	33,400	1.9
Directors	753,100	21,000	3.5
Total (Officers and Directors)	$616,000	$20,000	5.5%

phase of the cycle. Thus, despite stock-ownership and profit bonuses the personal interest of executives is usually toward conservatism. Who is to condemn (or even know), if management turns down a risky venture that could cost them their jobs.[21]

In the modern large corporation, equity financing of expansion (sale of new common shares) is free from debt restrictions and usually also from threats to control. With ownership widely scattered and passive, and with management in control of the proxy voting machinery, there is rarely a significant protest from stockholders about the uses that are made of their capital. On new offerings of common shares, stockholders are usually given rights to purchase their proportionate shares at the offering price, and this price can usually be put low enough to make rights valuable to them. For major expansions, equity financing thus provides a reasonably safe source of new capital (from management's point of view) for large corporations, even though SEC regulations now make security flotation a costly and time-consuming operation.[22]

But even new common stock is not without its perils to young and fast-growing industries, in which the need for new capital is greatest. In marketing a new and speculative security for a small company, it is never clear what the right price is and who the large buyers will be. In the early days of the electric power industry, General Electric and Westinghouse undertook to provide capital markets for the securities of the new and speculative utility companies, since the utilities were the principal market for electrical equipment. As a consequence, however, the small utilities soon found themselves buried in the holding company structures that proved to be the most expedient method for the

---

21 To be sure, a well-publicized *coup* can produce substantial gains in the market value of executives' stock (subject to the much lower capital gains tax rate), but such capital gains only create a pressure for short-run maximization of apparent profit prospects when executives want to sell stock. The importance of such manipulations for the sake of the insiders' capital gains has been greatly diminished by the SEC's new regulatory powers over management's stock transactions.

22 In the light of management's apparently impregnable position in equity financing, the reluctance of corporations to sell common stock in the bearish postwar markets is a mystery. The fact that stocks were being traded at prices far below management's estimate of their value in terms of profit prospects somehow made it seem "wrong" to sell new stock in such a market. The explanation of this attitude may lie deep in the moral code of business executives, or may again have some rational but hidden economic basis. Desire to maintain an established dividend rate could explain the aversion if management doubted that the net proceeds of the cheap stock could be invested profitably enough to cover the dividend comfortably.

manufacturers to sell to the public and to recover their own cash.[23] Similarly, AT & T had an office revolution in 1907 when it was bailed out of an unsuccessful offer of convertible bonds by the Morgan-Baker banking interests.

Social View of Autonomous Capital Formation

A serious criticism of autonomous capital formation by big business is that corporation management thereby evades an objective market test of the desirability of the capital expenditure as compared with all other uses of funds.

Profits have a dual role in capital formation. First, their reinvestment provides funds for capital formation. Second, the prospects of profits entice new money into the kind of economic activity that needs it, as judged by the criterion of demand and supply. If competition were fully effective and if profits were not the result of basic changes in the price level and the inadequacies of historical accounting, then profits would exist only when and where they were needed to induce capital formation. Profits are "exorbitant" when supply is inadequate to meet demand, and high profits entice new investment and lead to heavy plow-backs by existing firms in order to keep their market share. The resulting expansion of capacity tends to correct the supply deficiency. Prices come down, and exceptional profits disappear, having performed their salutary economic function.

Ideally, if a corporation paid out all its earnings in dividends, and then went to the capital markets for funds that it needed for internal investment, the flow of economic resources would be directed to the kinds of capital formation most needed, where "need" is measured by prospective profitability. When large corporations refuse this market test by retaining their earnings, there is at least the possibility that capital will go to the wrong places. Management's allocation of capital expenditure may be distorted as compared with the market's impartial allocation; sectors of the economy that need capital will suffer because sectors that have capital want to grow.

The allocation of capital inside a well managed, giant corporation may compensate by its efficiency for the lack of an impersonal

---

[23] Westinghouse itself had to go through the reorganization wringer in 1907, when utility financing undercut its working capital, even though it was basically a sound, going concern.

capital market test of the desirability of its internal investments. The rationing of capital inside such a company is likely to be cheaper, easier, and more expert than the rationing among companies performed by the capital market. Within the confines of the company's area of know-how, a good system of capital expenditure budgeting and control can perform the economic function of directing capital to its most profitable use (and presumably, therefore, to its highest economic service). Possibly the job will be done better than can reasonably be expected if funds were paid out in dividends (and chipped by the income tax) and then are brought back into the company by having each product division bid for funds against all other companies in the capital market, instead of merely against all other divisions within the same corporation.

When the capital expenditure proposals go beyond the firm's area of specialization, the superiority of internal rationing is more dubious. This superiority is, moreover, outweighed by the serious departure of the marginal rate of return from the company's external cost of capital over a long period. In this case, efficiency in rationing within the corporation cannot compensate for defeating the flow of funds throughout the economy by quasi-automatic regulators of profitability.[24]

The private consequences of a policy against outside financing will be examined in Section IV. For a company with this kind of policy, the cost of capital has in practice little usefulness, except when internal investment prospects are extremely low compared with other parts of the economy. A street railway company, for instance, may generate much more cash through depreciation charges than it can invest at a rate of return as high as an oil well promises. In the private interests of the stockholders, the best use of the money is probably a distribution to stockholders for investment elsewhere.

---

[24] Scattered returns indicate a great disparity in the prospective rates of return of the least profitable investments made by different corporations in different industries. Presumably this disparity indicates that distortion of resource allocation may be taking place. In defense of retained earnings, it should be recognized that the capital markets are not as perfect as envisaged by this theory and that high personal income taxes cause substantial leakage to the Federal Treasury when earnings are paid out in dividends.

Summary

1. A company's chief internal sources of supply of funds for capital expenditures are depreciation reserves and retained net profits. No distinction between these two should be made in the apportionment of internal investment.

2. The chief managerial problems in respect to internal sources are forecasting the amount of cash that will be generated and deciding how much earnings to pay in dividends and how much to plow back in capital expenditures.

3. Dramatic changes in price level throw doubt on the replacement adequacy of depreciation allowances based on historical cost. Extra-curricular allowances and outright increases in plow-back are needed to assure replacement.

4. Retained earnings are a major source of capital funds. Plowback policy is affected by many considerations: (a) opportunities for investment inside the company as opposed to outside, (b) regularity of stockholders' income, (c) reserves for contingencies and growth, and (d) the effect of plow-back on cost of capital from outside.

5. The pivotal consideration in external supply of funds is the cost of capital. It should signal dividend payouts that restrict internal supply and also signal when and how much recourse should be had to external supply.

6. Estimation of cost of capital involves determination of market values of securities, cost of flotation, and capital structure. Cost of capital is affected by many factors over which management has some control: (a) company policy on plow-backs, (b) capital structure, (c) the level of the market at time of issue, (d) size of issue, (e) amount raised, and (f) market fame of company. Projections of future costs of capital, therefore, have a wide band of control, its width depending partly on the stabilization of these variables by company policy.

7. Management's aversion to external financing, which is quite common, stems from distaste for possible restrictions and fear of upsetting the established organization. It cuts off a large reservoir of means for exploiting opportunities and puts narrow limits on sources of capital supply.

8. Autonomous capital formation raises questions of broad economic policy which have an important practical bearing upon the

pattern of business investment plow-back. The undoubted efficiency with which some big companies apportion funds within the fold may more than compensate for the fact that individual operating units do not have to meet the market test for funds. But it cannot be relied upon to overcome the injury to our resource allocation system when the corporation as a whole invests money internally at prospective rates of return that depart significantly from its external long-run cost of capital.

IV. CAPITAL RATIONING

In Section II we explored the company's demand for capital by translating an inventory of capital expenditure "needs" into a demand schedule for capital. We then sketched how this schedule could be approximated empirically by making an estimate of the capital productivity of each project and by arraying these estimates in a priority ladder of prospective rate of return. In Section III, we examined the supply of funds to a firm for capital expenditures. We surveyed the principal sources of funds, indicated some of the considerations that affect the amount to be obtained from each source, and sketched the theoretical relationship of the supply of capital to its price. We are now ready to put demand and supply together as an economic basis for appraising individual capital expenditure proposals in what may be called capital rationing.[25]

Rejection Rates

Practical rationing requires not only a ranking of projects according to a ladder of profitability, but also a rejection standard to separate projects that are not sufficiently profitable to merit funds from those that are. Theoretically, this cut-off rate of return is automatically determined by the intersection of the demand and supply schedules for capital. Thus, in theory, how much to invest and what the cut-off rate should be are two sides of the same coin. In practice, however, cut-off rates must be set by management if they are to be useful.

---

[25] Any system for rationing resources requires a criterion for comparing recipients. Normally, prices and incomes are the basis for rationing goods, although in war additional criteria of "war need" are set up for scarce and critical materials. The theory of capital rationing proposed here compares projects in terms of rate of return in contrast to capital budgeting that uses no systematic acceptance tests. Qualifications of the theory, however, make up a major part of this chapter.

The rejection rate has three uses in administrative control of capital budgeting. The first is to provide a tentative forecast of return expectancies for a next-year budgeting program. In this form, the rejection rate embodies a forecast of an uncertain and unknown demand schedule, and a projected internal supply schedule. Such forecasts of the rejection rate are necessary to top planning because time-lags and imperfect foresight make it impractical to wait until the relative profitability of individual projects has been determined, and until the resulting schedule has been compared with supply as determined by retainable earnings and cost of capital. Rough as it is, the resulting rejection rate provides some basis for immediate decisions on dividends, financing, and minor capital projects.

The second use of the rejection rate is to weed out projects that have too low a profitability to justify further attention at either divisional or top-management levels. It is thus a tool for economizing executive time.

The third use is to implement a long-run capital budgeting plan that seeks to avoid making marginal investments of low productivity in times of slack investment demand. For example, the cut-off rate for expenditures in all phases of the business cycle might be stabilized, regardless of short-run shifts in demand and supply. Funds thus preserved can be invested for higher returns when demand turns up again. In this form, the rejection rate is a rough substitute for budgeting that includes the rivalry of proposals to be made at different dates. (This method was sketched out in Section II.) It requires, however, a projection for an integral business cycle of both the total demand curve and the total internal supply curve. Making this projection is worth while only when the firm's capital sources for the cycle as a whole are so inadequate when compared with demand that the long-run cut-off point is far above the cost of capital.

Conceptually, four forms of rejection rate of return can be distinguished: (1) A fluctuating effective rate of return that may move up and down with phases of the cycle or with conditions of the treasury, and that will determine the cut-off point for normal projects at any one time. (2) A basic minimum rate of earnings that sets a normal floor for any projects in any phase of the cycle. (3) A stable long-run rate that is frozen as *the* cut-off rate for all phases of the business cycle. (4) Exception rates of return that differ for different kinds of investment to accommodate disparities in risks and the needs of grand strategy. Some circumstances may justify sheltering certain kinds of investment from the full rigors of competition with all alternative uses of capital funds on the basis of capital productivity.

The effective rate and the minimum rate can be used as a team for short-term budgeting. The long-term rate is an alternative to this team; it is a different system used for coping with cyclical fluctuations. Exception rates can be used in connection with either of these two types of rationing schemes, since such rates may take the form of handicapping differentials. The characteristics of these different rejection rates are discussed below.

Fluctuating Effective Rate

The flucuating effective rate of return is theoretically determined by the intersection of the forecasted demand and supply curves for capital, but in practice the rate for any one time is set at management's discretion as a means of regulating and timing the amount of capital expenditures. A major oil company, for example, has varied the effective rate from a five-year crude pay-out in the depths of depression, to a one-year pay-out during the postwar boom. Another company, which has a perennial minimum standard of 15 per cent, has at times raised the effective rate to as high as 50 per cent.

The underlying reasons for moving the effective rate up and down include: (1) variations in the supply of funds available to the company for capital expenditure; (2) speculations on price changes for capital equipment; (3) fear of general declines in business, which produce a high liquidity preference; and (4) informal deflation of earnings rate estimates.[26]

The fluctuations of the effective rate may in part be caused by a desire to hoard funds in anticipation of future demand for capital more favorable than today's demand. Better profit prospects

---

[26] During boom periods, anticipations concerning future earnings tend to become inflated, despite Herculean efforts top-side to keep middle management's feet on the ground across the business cycle. Some companies have informally deflated these over-sanguine boom-time earnings prospects by raising the effective rate. For example, one oil company has taken the position that declines in the price level of petroleum products will convert an apparent one-year pay-out proposal into a two-year pay-out proposal. Hence, the effective rate should be high when petroleum prices are high.

may come in the future from price changes, from improved productivity of specific projects that ripen with the passage of time, or from general economic changes that increase opportunities for capital investment. As we shall point out later, manipulation of the effective rate is not a precise instrument for coping with intertemporal rivalry of projects whose productivity improves if postponed, since it cannot coordinate their interactive relations.

In using the effective cut-off rate, two situations must be distinguished: (1) the autonomous firm that is determined to limit itself to internally generated funds only; and (2) the company that is willing to go outside for additional capital funds, either occasionally or regularly. The distinctive nature of the budgeting problem in these two cases stems from the shape and behavior of the supply curves.

Autonomous Capital Budgeting

The top panel of Chart 10–3 diagrams the situation for the company that is limited to plow-back earnings for its supply of capital. The demand schedule portrays for each prospective rate of return the amount of money that the firm can invest internally for earnings of at least that rate. At the point where the curve meets $S_A{}^1$, this firm can invest $10,000,000 at a rate of return of 20 per cent or better during the planning period. Drawing the function as a narrow line greatly overstates the precision possible in forecasting, and the error margin might properly be represented by a wide shaded band about the line. A smooth demand function is a simplifying extremity that abstracts from the fact that capital proposals are lumpy and discrete, usually causing the firm's statistical counterpart to descend in steps.

The curve D-2 is the demand function in conditions when "needs" for capital expenditures are extremely pressing and profitable, such as in the period immediately following World War II.

The supply curve in this case is the vertical line, $S_1{}^4$. Drawing it as a vertical line emphasizes that, as a practical matter, many companies' internal supply of funds seems to be unrelated to prospective profitability of investments. In Section III we saw that to maximize profits for stockholders, some measure of the cost of outside capital should be used as a floor for fluctuations in the cut-off rate. The effect of this rule is that when demand is so

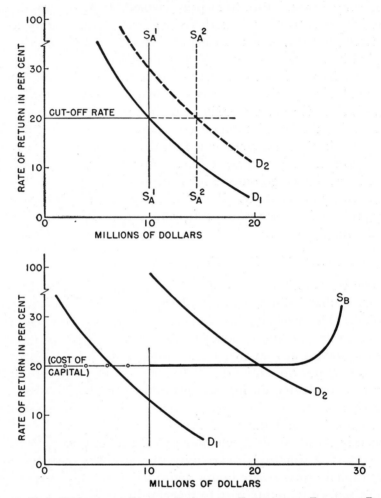

CHART 10–3. THEORY OF CAPITAL RATIONING: FLUCTUATING EFFECTIVE RATE

slack that marginal prospects are already down to the cost of capital, a further fall in demand produces a horizontal shift to the left in the supply curve. That is, the rule signals higher dividends and lower retained earnings.[27]

Viewing the business cycle as a whole, how does the cut-off rate for autonomous firms behave? Shifts in the demand curve

---

[27] This conjectural interrelationship is most easily viewed as a horizontal shifting of the supply curve rather than as a sloping supply curve, which would imply a high correlation between cost of capital, demand for capital, and the amount of retainable earnings.

are likely to be accompanied by parallel shifts in the supply curve, since the volume of investment prospects is related to current income.   This parallelism tends to reduce the fluctuations in the cut-off rate, as illustrated by the boom-time curves S_2^4 and D_2 in Chart 10–3, where, to illustrate the point by extremes, no change at all is shown.   It is clear from the diagram that, in general, nothing specific can be said about the relative level of the cut-off rate in boom and prosperity, since this level depends on the relative swing in the supply and demand curves.   When supply fluctuates more than demand, cut-off rates will be higher in depression than in prosperity.[28]

When demand is so slack that the cut-off rate limps along at the cost of capital (and this situation is conceivable in either high or low business activity), its fluctuations depend, of course, on conditions in the capital markets.

Although this theory portrays a company that under no circumstances is willing to use outside money, in practice a cut-off rate that goes much above the costs of capital will act powerfully to undercut this policy and induce the company to engage in some temporary borrowing.   How high this rate needs to be to send the company to the banks is a matter of surmise, but it is hard for a company with a 10 per cent cost of capital to reject a 50 per cent rate of return that must be externally financed.

External Financing

Panel 2 of Chart 10–2 illustrates the determination of the cut-off rate for a company that is willing to use outside money.   In contrast to the autonomous supply case, the whole supply function discussed in Section III is relevant here.   It extends to the right

---

[28] A case can reasonably be made that high cut-offs in depression are the usual situation.   Management's interests point toward stabilizing dividends and maintaining them, at least nominally, through depression.   Dividend stability increases the volatility of the supply curve, particularly when, in deficit years, dividends are paid out of past earnings.   But since demand for capital in depression is for cost-saving devices, industries with slow technical progress may have wide swings in the demand curve as well.

Whether the cut-off rate is higher or lower in boom than in depression may also depend on the nature of the boom.   The postwar boom rested on a demand for capital goods that had accumulated through a long depression and war.   Thus the demand curve was exceptionally high and tended to boost the cut-off rate.   With equipment shortages *per se* eliminated, demand shifts downward and reflects only routine replacement needs.   Receding backlogs of demand lower the cut-off rate of earnings as such a boom progresses, provided the supply curve is maintained far to the right.

from the limit of retainable earnings to the point where the market says "Enough!"

Here, again, depression shifts of the demand curve to the left that give a cut-off rate less than the cost of capital call for an increased dividend pay-out rather than for the use of funds for submarginal expenditures. As the demand curve shifts to the right, the cut-off rate will remain substantially horizontal to much higher levels of expenditure than most companies recently have been willing to venture. (That is, the supply of money seems to be much too elastic to raise the cost of capital in the relevant range of demand.) The whole supply curve may shift cyclically. Just how it shifts is a matter of speculation, but, in general, something like the behavior illustrated in Panel 2 of Chart 10–3 might be expected. Not only are the retainable earnings usually smaller in depression, but the securities market's estimate of prospects is gloomy enough to raise the cost of capital substantially.

A company's cost of capital should, according to this theory, call the signals that regulate supply of funds. When cost of capital is low (e.g., 10 per cent) as compared with the rate of return (adjusted for risk) on marginal internal investments (e.g., 15 per cent), then outside financing is indicated. When the least profitable investment that can be made from cash generated internally is below opportunity cost of capital, generous dividends are signaled. Thus cost of capital signals when dividends should restrict internal supply and when and how much recourse should be had to external supply.

Basic Minimum Rate

An important adjunct to the fluctuating effective cut-off rate is a basic minimum rate below which the effective rate shall not go, no matter how much internal supply exceeds demand for capital. Its purpose is to keep the company from making investments that cannot earn enough to pay their cost of capital. Hence this minimum rate should be set by anticipating future cost of capital. If the company is in a position to manipulate its short-term financing so as to raise permanent capital at low-cost times, then this floor rate will usually be lower than the current, or even a long-period average cost of capital.

But many companies don't know their cost of capital, and when no outside financing is in prospect, management may not see the relevance of capital markets to budgeting. Nevertheless, when such companies use supply-demand rationing of funds for capital budgeting, they recognize the need for some minimum return standard and understand fully that it is wrong to plow back earnings to the point where marginal profitability is zero.[29] When the cost of capital is eschewed, the minimum rate can be set by various standards.

The company's long-term average rate of earnings on past investment is sometimes used. This minimum is sometimes justified as follows: It represents an earnings rate with which stockholders have been satisfied in the past; it is functionally effective in an economic sense, since it seems to compensate for the risks of the enterprise and to have attracted capital needed for growth. Setting the minimum rate higher than this average would result in a refusal of investments earning rates that have in the past satisfied stockholders. It would probably also result in slowing down the rate of company growth as compared with what it would be if past earnings were the standard.

This kind of autonomous historical standard is, from the viewpoint of the economic system, unsatisfactory, unless it happens to coincide with the company's long-term cost of capital. If the average earnings rate is lower, capital is retained when it could be put to more productive use elsewhere. If the resulting minimum is higher than the firm's cost of capital, the firm invests at a slower rate than the vast impersonal forces of the capital market would allow if outside capital were sought in order to make the rejected submarginal investments.

Sometimes a company goal rate becomes the minimum standard. Some companies have a clear-cut notion of an adequate rate of earnings for the company as a whole. This rate is determined in part by the opportunity to make more than this, and by strategic limitations imposed by considerations of public, political, and labor relations.[30]

---

[29] The minimum argument for a cut-off rate is that earnings prospects should not be less than the discount factor for uncertainty that reflects the probability of out-of-pocket loss on the investment. (Uncertainty discount factors are discussed in Section II.)

[30] For example, one large company reported that its minimum rate-of-return standard of 30 per cent before taxes (at standard volume output) was its goal rate of return on net investment. This goal rate was evolved over the years as a "reasonable rate of return"; its origins are historic and rather indefinite.

The Long-Run Cut-Off Rate

The third major kind of rejection rate is the long-run rate that cuts across the cyclical swings in earnings prospects and is based on tentative guesses of demand and supply of funds in a five- or ten-year budget.   The purpose of this kind of cut-off rate is to avoid having to pass up high-profit projects in times of high demand because funds were squandered on low-return investments in times of low demand.   The long-run rate is different from the basic minimum rate both in purpose and level.   The basic minimum serves largely as insurance against major boners in investment, whereas the long-run rate tries to put the next ten years' investment opportunities on a single demand curve to compete for the ten-year supply of funds.[31]

The long-run rate is not a logically complete approach to long-run capital budgeting.   Investments made this year do not necessarily compete with investments to be made four years hence for the supply of funds, particularly if this year's investments have a high cash pay-out rate.   In its pure form, a long-run plan is a sequence of outlays and corresponding revenues that extends to the forecasting horizon.   Alternative plans embody different kinds of equipment or different dates for purchasing the equipment, and the best plan is the one with the greatest present value.   For instance, one plan might be to set up a system of regional warehouses this year, when materials are available but markets still undeveloped, with a prospective 30 per cent return.   An alternative might be to establish markets first and postpone warehouse outlays for three years, after which they would show a 40 per cent return unless costs had risen.   The funds could meanwhile be invested in projects with fast payouts—perhaps advertising—or even in liquid form such as marketable securities.

Obviously, the long-run cut-off rate cannot include this time

---

[31] We have seen in our discussion of demand for capital how difficult such a projection is.   With dynamic technology it is hard to foresee what kinds of opportunities may occur years hence, to say nothing of knowing how much money they will cost and what the return will be.   Although five-year forecasts of the cash-generating ability have been made, they depend for their accuracy upon projections of national economic activity over heroic distances into the future. The cost of capital from outside can be guessed for the long-term future on the basis of an average in the past only by assuming that the capricious stock market will follow historical patterns in the future.   Thus the empirical foundation for this kind of theoretical solution is frail.

dimension of competition for capital—that is, the same project at alternative dates. No project can enter the long-run demand curve more than once, presumably at the rate of return that corresponds to optimum timing of the expenditure. This demand curve therefore implies that a single plan has already been determined as the best, and that the long-run cut-off rate reflects previous planning decisions.

The long-run rate, therefore, cannot be the single tool for capital budgeting, since it stands on the shoulders of the decisions about the really big projects. Nevertheless, it often has much administrative value. Long-run planning in terms of alternative investment schedules, such as we mentioned above, must usually be limited to budgeting for the few grand schemes that dominate company ambitions. Planning for smaller projects is rapidly drowned in uncertainty as the planning period is extended. The alternatives are too numerous and interrelated to be plotted out in detail. It is here that the long-run cut-off rate can be brought into use, in the routine budgeting of these lesser proposals. If management has established a broad view of the company's future, the long-run rate can be made a time-saving device for tying the minor parts into an integrated scheme.

Exception Rates

The fourth kind of rejection rate is the special rate that includes a handicap allowance to give strategic investments a head start in the race for capital funds. For example, petroleum companies commonly have a concept of "balanced" investment in production, refining, transportation, and marketing capacities, that overrides profitability criteria on individual projects. A goal of eventually achieving production of 75 per cent of the crude that is marketed may be achieved by assigning well-drilling investments lower cut-off rates than service stations. Similarly, territories where coverage is inadequate or where earnings are below standard may get handicap rates.

Actually, of course, an exception rate is a confession of ignorance—the intangible benefits of such strategic investments are unmeasurable in dollars. The handicap allowance is a guess at the inadequacy of the profit estimate, and, being a guess, has little rational foundation.

Assumptions of Theory

Any economic theory is necessarily based on a set of simplifying assumptions. The assumptions that are most important to our theory of capital rationing are as follows:

(1) We assume, as usual in economic theory, that the objective of the enterprise is to maximize profits in a narrow and calculable sense of the word. But narrow profit maximization is not the only, or, in fact, the usual, goal of large corporate enterprise. (See Chapter 1, "Profits.")

(2) We assume what in reality is an impossible degree of foresight of all the opportunities for investing capital inside the company.

(3) We assume that the prospective rate of return on each capital proposal can be projected with precision. Accurate forecasts must be made of the amount of investment as well as of the added profits from the added capital outlay.

(4) We assume that the risks of all projects are either equal or have been accurately reduced to uniformity by a handicapping system that adjusts the rate of return for the proposal to a level that makes risks equal.

(5) We assume that the firm has access to the capital markets for raising equity money and debt money, and that the rates for each can be ascertained, so that, given a debt ratio, the combined cost of capital is determinate both currently and over the long run.

The emphasis of the theory, furthermore, is on what may be a more special case than the author thinks—namely, a situation in which the opportunities for profitable internal investment exceed the supply of funds the company is able or willing to devote to capital expenditures.

The justification for using this conceptual model is that it provides a simplified framework for practical analysis by showing what must be estimated; how, in general, estimates can be made; and how the results of the estimates can be logically fitted together. But it is only a starting point, since the theory overstates the degree to which capital budgeting can and should be mechanistic. Such formal systems will not take the place of good business judgment, but may channel and refine that judgment.

This capital rationing theory has greatest applicability to the middle size-range of investments. It is not very helpful in making large pivotal investments. These large investments are so important that they command protracted study from various viewpoints by top executives. The high command has more faith in its own judgment than in the comprehensiveness and accuracy of rate-of-return estimates made by staff people. On the other hand, it is not worth while to apply so elaborate a system to relatively small investments.

The coverage of this theory is incomplete in another way. The theory is dubiously applicable to investments where foresight is very imperfect, error margins are big, and strategy bulks large. It is wholly inapplicable to investments for which no rate of return can be estimated.[32]

Alternatives to Rate-of-Return Rationing

The approach to capital rationing sketched in this section is valid in principle, though limited in applicability. Other methods of capital budgeting can be appraised against this standard of reference.

A common method, which is the antithesis of a rate-of-return system, is to let the determination of the total amount of capital expenditure and its allocation among projects be governed solely by the judgment of top executives who "consider each project on its merits" and tailor the total as best they can to the company's purse. This intuitive approach, when applied in large companies, burdens top management with a multitude of decisions that must be made without objective criteria. Hence the appraisal of an investment proposal is influenced by top management's appraisal of the executive who proposes it, and by his persuasiveness and persistence in presenting it.

A similar approach, which is characteristic of public utilities, is to appraise projects not on the basis of prospective individual profitability, but on the basis of what is needed to provide ade-

---

32 Clearly, some kinds of investments cannot come into bare-knuckled rate-of-return rivalry, simply because their rate of return cannot be measured. Investments in research laboratories must be made largely on faith. Employee welfare investments, such as cafeterias and washroom facilities, also have an indeterminate productivity. Other kinds of investments may be held out because tests other than the rate-of-return test appear more appropriate. Some companies, for example, exclude replacement investments, such as the motor vehicle fleet, from any capital productivity standards, and, instead, use a routine replacement time schedule developed by a rule-of-thumb experience.

quate service.   An individual project return standard is presumably not necessary because demand is inelastic enough for rate adjustments to provide an adequate return for used and useful investment.   Thus rate-of-return neither governs the total nor guides its apportionment among projects.

Another method widely used in industry is to size up individual investment proposals against an ideal of company balance and growth goals.   For example, in the petroleum industry, a company might seek, as a long-run objective, a 50 per cent growth in a decade, and the attainment at the end of ten years of crude-oil production and refining facilities that equal its marketing demand.   Such a goal may provide a criterion for approving and rejecting investment proposals.   Whether it will be a more satisfactory criterion than the rate-of-return rationing plan outlined above is doubtful.   The effects of this kind of plan upon the company's long-run rate of return are difficult to determine, because this approach views the company as a monolithic strategic investment.   "Balance" usually means some form of vertical integration, and vertical integration has not proved universally profitable in all industries, nor is it sure to reduce the hazards of the enterprise.

Another device is postponability screening.   Sometimes both the total amount and the allocation among individual projects are determined by whether or not the proposed investment can be put off.   (An appraisal of postponability is found in Section II of this chapter.) [33]

Summary

1. Capital rationing is central in the planning and control of capital expenditures, since requests for funds normally exceed supply.   Screening proposals on the basis of their prospective rate of return (when measurable) puts capital rationing on an economically sound foundation and limits the degree to which

---

[33] A New York lawyer, innocent of any experience with chickens, bought a run-down chicken farm in southern New Jersey and hired a local yokel to run it. Every two months he toured his domain with the farmer, who invariably pointed out needs for capital expenditures—new chicken coops, fences, and so on. The lawyer's invariable reply to the first request for a project was, "Money is scarce; you will just have to fix it up and make it do." The second time the project came up. the same reply. If a project was requested a third time, it was granted. This was the criterion of capital rationing evolved by the lawyer to protect himself from his ignorance.

persistence and persuasiveness can influence the allocation of funds.

2. The theory of capital rationing, in its most rigorous form, is based on assumptions of unattainable foresight and accuracy in measurement of productivity and appraisal of risk. Constructively viewed, these assumptions set sights for empirical estimates and spur ingenuity in overcoming imperfections. Much of the practical framework of rejection rates and restricted coverage of rate-of-return rivalry represents this kind of positive application of perfectionistic theory.

3. The essence of the theory of rationing is to project, under assumed conditions, the rate of return at the point where the company's capital demand and supply curve will intersect. Theoretically, this cut-off rate is determined exogenously, but in practice rejection rates are, for administrative reasons, set by management. To a degree, they forecast the intersection rate; also, they serve to kill off unworthy projects at the roots of the organization and to help deal with rivalry of funds among time periods.

4. Four kinds of rejection rates can be differentiated: (a) the minimum rate, which is stable; (b) the effective rate, which fluctuates above the floor of the minimum; (c) the long-run rate, which is alternative to the plan that combines effective and minimum rates; and (d) the exception rates, which serve as differential handicaps for categories of investment that require unusual rejection standards because of differences in measurability of risks.

5. The minimum rate of return should be set on the basis of a projection of the future average cost of capital to the firm. When the error range of this projection is wide, substitute methods have merits.

6. The effective rate fluctuates with projections of the rate at which demand and supply curves will intersect. It is also manipulated for the purpose of regulating the firm's rate of investment to deal with temporary dearth of funds, speculation on changes in prices, anticipation of deterioration in the general economic situation, and informal deflation of the rosiness of boom-time estimates of capital productivity.

7. The long-run rejection rate differs from the basic minimum in purpose and level. It attempts to cope with cyclical fluctua-

tions and with rivalry among time periods by keeping the cut-off rate constant.

8. Exception rates are designed to compensate for differences in the accuracy of estimates of productivity in risks, and in strategic value. By supplying a set of handicap differentials, certain kinds of investments are sheltered from the full rigor of rate-of-return rivalry.

V. CLASSIFICATION OF CAPITAL EXPENDITURES

In the preceding analysis of principles of capital rationing, several kinds of rejection rates of return were examined in terms of their operating function. We recognized there that profitability standards might be different for different categories of investment. This relationship raises the problem of distinguishing between investments on a basis relevant to rate-of-return differentials.

In this section we shall first present the various ways in which investments can be classified. Next, we shall consider some alternative and simplifying classification schemes that are in use. Then we shall set up a classification that is convenient for our purpose and examine each of these investment categories to see how their productivity is measured, and how they should be treated in the capital expenditure budget.

Some kind of logical separation of the main categories of investments is needed, for three reasons: First, the methods for applying the general principles of measuring capital productivity will differ according to the nature of the productivity. Second, the accuracy of rate-of-return estimates varies widely among types of investment, and there are some types for which no estimate can be made at all. Third, certain overriding strategic considerations should shelter some kinds of investments from the full rigors of rate-of-return rivalry and give them preference in capital rationing. By grouping proposals in categories, the application of these differentiating considerations can be made easier and more systematic.

A Multiple Classification Plan

No definitive classification plan for investments is useful for all purposes. A capital outlay has too may facets to be described adequately by any one of them. Each facet is in effect a dimension of the outlay and a separate basis for distinguishing different types of investments. For purposes of capital budgeting, the important dimensions run somewhat as follows:

1. *Source of Earnings on Capital.* The objective of an investment is always increased capital productivity, and the source of the increase is an important basis of classification. In general, capital productivity arises from (a) cost reduction, (b) revenue expansion, (c) risk reduction, or (d) improvement of employee welfare.

2. *Competitive Orientation.* Most investments are either aggressive or defensive, depending on whether they cause competitive reactions, or are themselves reactions to competitors' moves.

3. *Form.* The distinctions here depend on the nature of the enterprise. For a manufacturer, a useful classification of investments might be (a) plant facilities, (b) product-line improvements, (c) operating methods and know-how, and (d) market positions. These classes naturally have any number of subdivisions, some of which themselves raise distinctive problems in capital budgeting. For instance, plant investments can be subdivided into replacements, expansions, and diversifications; product-line investments are roughly either new products or product improvements; and improvements in methods and know-how may involve investments in consulting services, technical education, or interoffice rapport. Market investments are the outlays needed to capture stable market shares, such as outlays for advertising or developing distributors.

4. *Relation to Technical Change.* Obsolescence is a major cause of investment. When it occurs in methods, cost-reducing replacement investments may result. Obsolescence of products is associated with investments for new or improved products. From a different viewpoint two kinds of investments related to technical change may be distinguished: (a) established, competitively mature products and methods, and (b) innovations—new ideas that are pushed into the arena by either the company or its competitors.

5. *Strategy Aspects.* By the "strategic" value of an investment, we mean its indirect benefits to other parts of the company. Some investments are entirely strategic—that is, they show no promise of profitability in themselves but shore up the rate of

return in other products or markets or contribute to the general strength of the company. Probably the most important strategic investments are the risk-reducers, but there are other kinds, as we shall see below.

As it stands, this multiple classification, with its five dimensions and the alternatives mentioned in each dimension, allows for over 250 different types of investment, and many more could be devised. Naturally, no management works with this array of distinctions. Rather, it picks and chooses according to importance in its company. Classification plans, when they exist at all, differ considerably from one company to another, but the groupings used by three companies will illustrate how management narrows the range of its budgeting problems.

An automobile manufacturer classifies capital expenditure proposals in the following four categories: (1) Replacement investments. (2) Expense-saving investments, generally in the form of equipment-obsolescence investments. (3) Expansion and new business investments, lumped together, even though they are recognized as somewhat different. (4) New-model investments, which are, for the most part, tools and dies whose economic life is as short-lived as that of the model.

A petroleum company, in contrast, uses the following classifications: (1) Essential investments, i.e., those required by law, by contractual obligations, or to meet competitive standards of product quality. Oil-drilling investments are put in this category because they are considered essential for the company's future. (2) Replacement investments, i.e., replacement of assets that wear out with other substantially similar ones (e.g., salesmen's cars and delivery trucks). These investments are also viewed as essential, since operations would break down without replacements. They do not meet profitability tests. (3) Profitability investments, which are of two main types, expense-saving and product upgrading (i.e., converting waste or low-value petroleum products into products of higher value). (4) Desirable investments, i.e., low pay-out investments and those for which no pay-out can be conveniently calculated.

Another classification plan, which is used by a building materials manufacturer, is the following: (1) Necessary replacement investments. (2) Cost-reducing investments. (3) Product-obsolescence investments. (4) New-products investments. (5) Expansion investments. (6) Working conditions improvement investments.[34]

An adequate discussion of investment types is beyond the scope of this chapter, but since we are concerned with investments from the point of view of rate-of-return budgeting, a brief word can be said about the comparative feasibility of using this criterion for different classes of project. For this purpose, the following classification is useful:

1. *Replacement Investments.* These include both like-for-like and obsolescence replacements, but only in the plant. Since the source of productivity is essentially cost savings, distinctive and somewhat controversial problems of profit estimates are raised.

2. *Expansion Investments.* The productivity here is increased revenue from doing more of the same thing. Profit estimates involve different factors from those involved in replacement decisions.

3. *Product-line Investments.* Expenditures on new products and improvement of old products combine features of replacement and expansion investments, but the kind of data available for profit estimates requires special treatment.

4. *Strategic Investments.* Although almost every investment yields benefits that seep into other parts of the company, there are some whose whole value seems to derive from such benefits.

As a comparison with the three company plans sketched above will indicate, there is nothing uniquely valid about this plan. It is designed for a discussion of profitability estimates rather than to fit the administrative convenience of an operating concern.

It should be noted, of course, that most capital expenditures have mixed objectives, forms, and competitive design, and thus do not fit neatly into any single category. For example, a new lithographic printing press may not only expand the capacity of a printing plant, but may also improve the quality of a printer's existing product, add new products to his line (e.g., four-color

---

34 This company investigated the way in which its capital expenditure dollar was split up among the various categories of investment. It found that during the first four postwar years, new and improved products took 27 per cent, expansion 24 per cent, cost reduction 24 per cent, replacement 18 per cent, and morale improvement 7 per cent. But, since expansion and replacement were large, the postwar period called for an abnormal allocation. As a longer-term goal, the company thinks in terms of about 40 to 50 per cent for cost-reduction and replacement investment, about 40 per cent for new and improved products, and about 10 per cent for welfare.

jobs), and reduce cost through lower maintenance costs and technological advances that save labor. In discussing each of these classes of investment, we shall nevertheless deal with the pure type, recognizing that the multiple-purpose character of many investments makes it necessary to classify them arbitrarily according to their main purpose and the chief method of attaining that purpose.[35]

Replacement Investments

A replacement investment is an investment for new equipment that will do the same job as discarded equipment. In its pure form, it is intended solely to produce cost savings. Two kinds of replacement investments can be distinguished: (1) like-for-like replacement, where the savings result primarily from operating inferiorities caused by physical wear and tear; and (2) obsolescence replacement where the savings are the result of technical progress. Thus for both types the source of earnings is prospective cost savings.

Replacement decisions, like all investment decisions, are inevitably forward-looking. The pivotal comparison is between the future costs of the old equipment and the future costs of the new, and the problem of estimating the return breaks down into cost forecasting focused upon ferreting out the differences in future costs between the two contemplated courses of action.

In this kind of calculation, comparison of future capital wastage costs (i.e., the rate of fall in value through time and use) presents unusual difficulties in both concept and measurement. Capital wastage for the existing equipment is the future decline in its disposal value. The original acquisition cost of the old machine is sunk, irrecoverable, and totally irrelevant. The depreciation charges shown on the books are similarly independent of the company's real future costs and future replacement earnings. These bookkeeping values, though useful for income measurement, have no significance for the replacement decision.

Capital wastage for the new machine over its lifetime is its prospective acquisition cost, less ultimate resale value. Since the investment commitment has not yet been made, this total decline

---

[35] A more complete analysis of managerial problems of controlling capital outlays for these various kinds of investment is contained in Joel Dean, *Capital Budgeting,* New York, Columbia University Press, 1951.

in value is relevant for the decision. The hard problem is to estimate the probable economic life of the new equipment which is essentially a guess as to when it, in turn, will become obsolete. This obsolescence guess lies at the heart of the replacement decision, even though most budgeting methods ignore it. Projection of other elements of cost for the new and the old equipment present no serious conceptual difficulties.

A capital earnings criterion of replacement is the essence of the method advocated here. The cost savings revealed by comparison of the future costs of keeping as opposed to replacing the machine must be high enough to produce a rate of return on the amount invested that will compare favorably with alternative investments and with the company's cost of capital. It is not enough that the new equipment be cheaper; it must be enough cheaper to justify tying up the capital.

For obsolescence replacements, the methods of estimating return are broadly similar to methods for identical replacements, but there are differences in emphasis. Two striking differences occur: labor-saving estimates and life expectancy estimates. Management runs the risk of being too optimistic about prospective labor savings from advanced technology because of inadequate allowance for informal slowdowns and for labor's bargaining power in taking a part of the gains, either in higher pay or lower exertion. Attainment of the full potential productivity of the new equipment often requires such concessions.

Guessing the probable economic life of the candidate equipment has wider error margins when the replacement stems from technical progress rather than aging. Hence more care must be given to projecting future life expectancies.

Obsolescence is, of course, not absolute. It depends upon the productivity of the equipment in the particular application, and also upon the company's standards of effective minimum return on investment. Hence a piece of equipment will be obsolete for some companies in some uses at some stages of the business cycle and not be obsolete for other companies, other uses, and other cyclical conditions.

Because their earnings are cost savings, obsolescence replacements lend themselves admirably to objective measurement of capital productivity and to rate-of-return rationing. The problem is only *how* to guess, not, as with other types, what to guess.

In practice, replacements are not commonly made by a profitability criterion. The usual method is to establish some arbitrary rule, such as replacement after x years or when average unit costs with the old machine are at a lifetime minimum. Although such rules are simple and time saving, their basic fallacy is neglecting the opportunity cost of replacement, that is, the competition for capital funds by projects in other parts of the company. Ignoring profitability aspects of replacement may keep high-return opportunities begging while circular flow in older activities hoards the cash.

Expansion Investments

The productivity of capital expenditures for plant enlargement and for invasion of new markets requires a different method of measurement from that of replacement investments. Both kinds of investment involve a comparison of alternatives. The alternatives for replacement investment are different ways of doing a job that is to be done by some means or other, and the source of earnings is cost savings. But for expansion investments the alternatives are between doing the job and not doing it. Consequently, the return on an expansion investment is the expected addition to profits that will result from making the investment as opposed to not making it. This added profit can be guessed at by projecting an income statement that shows the added revenue and added costs over the life of the investment. The return on the added investment is this increase in net revenue. This kind of projection involves appraisal of alternative ways of expanding volume without making the contemplated investment. Thus comparative costs enter even into this kind of rate-of-return estimate.

Economies of larger plants are often so great that it is desirable to build capacity ahead of sales growth. The problem is how far ahead. Production costs for various sizes of plant can usually be estimated with fair reliability at today's technology, but some guesses are usually necessary about tomorrow's technology. Production estimates, however, are not as tricky as the sales forecast, which is generally the biggest factor in determining the reliability of a rate of return on an expansion investment.

Because of the wide uncertainty bands of projections of both costs and sales, and because of strategic overtones in expansion investments, precise measurement and comparison of expansion investments on rate-of-return criteria is difficult.

Product Investments

Product investments are of two main types: improvements of existing products, and additions of new products. Strategic considerations in capital budgeting may be quite different for (1) defensive product-improvements—those required to bring the product up to a competitor's standard—and (2) aggressive improvements—those that push the product beyond competitive standards. A first-line competitor is usually under strong compulsion to make whatever investments are required for defensive improvements, and failure to keep a product abreast of rivals can cause deterioration of market share. The return on such investments, though difficult to quantify, can be catastrophically high.

In estimating the productivity of investments for adding products, it is desirable to construct what amounts to a long-term conjectural income statement, which involves forecasts of sales, prices, costs of market development and costs of production. In the early stages, such a projection is necessarily hazy. In deciding on an investment to add an established product, many large companies regard the long-run future size of the market as the pivotal estimate. Such a company is willing to take its chance on designing an acceptable product, getting its cost down to competitive levels, and obtaining an adequate market share. Consequently, precise estimates of prospective return are probably not controlling considerations, at least in the initial stages of investments made to add established products to the line.

For adding pioneering products, i.e., those new to the world as well as to the company, profit projections have such wide error ranges because of technical marketing and competitive uncertainties that forecasts of the rate of return give a false impression of precision. In making such investments, consequently, a high order of judgment is required in appraising the pivotal forecasts, and mechanical rate-of-return rivalry for such investments is hardly feasible.

Strategic considerations are likely to be dominant for investments to add either mature and pioneering products. New product investments may serve several kinds of strategic ends besides making money on the product itself. For example, they are used to meet full-line competition, or to stake out claims in new areas, like nucleonics, that promise a big future. The combination of big error-margins and strategic overtones makes the judgment of the high command the determining consideration and throws many new product investments out of the arena of rate-of-return rivalry.

Strategic Investments

There are two groups of investment that are almost entirely strategic in character—namely risk-reducing investments and welfare-improving investments. In both types, the benefits are spread over many phases of the company's activities and stretch into the distant future. Moreover, both present unusual difficulties in measuring their rate of return because benefits, though real, are often delayed, indirect, and imponderable.

Because of these characteristics, such investments must be sheltered from the full rigors of rate-of-return competition. This can be done by setting aside a certain proportion (say 5% per year) of planned capital expenditures for each kind of investment. But the size of the proportion is a critical question for which no objective competitive guides appear promising. An alternative is to make modified use of the objective rate-of-return criteria, supplemented by generous allowances for benefits and earnings that cannot be directly estimated. One technique is to apply handicapping percentages that reflect the judgment of the top executives concerning the benefits omitted from the earnings calculation. For example, defensive investments to assure quality or quantity of strategic raw materials could be given an advantage of plus 10 per cent in rate-of-return rivalry. Again, there is no clear indication of what is the right x per cent handicap.

Cyclical Investment Policies

The ordeal of the 1930's has made economists and businessmen acutely conscious of the desirability of stabilizing the rate of private capital formation in order to fill in the valleys of the business cycle. Although government has the will to stabilize activity and probably the ability (e.g., taxes, subsidies, public works), everyone agrees that to save economic flexibility, as much as possible should be done by private business acting in its own interest.

The feasibility of stabilization by a single company hinges on the relative importance of the gains (largely potential savings in acquisition costs) as opposed to the losses, costs, and uncertainties of long-range anticipation.

Whether it is wise to put off a capital expenditure because costs of construction or purchase are currently high, depends on: (1) guesses as to how soon and how much its costs will come down in the future; (2) estimates of how much earnings will be foregone by altering the timing disadvantageously; and (3) estimates of the costs and losses of shifting the funds used for capital expenditures to a different point in the cycle (carrying over the retained earnings or new outside capital of a boom into the next depression, or borrowing in depression in anticipation of longer-term funds from retained earnings or elsewhere).

It is impossible to avoid speculating on price level fluctuations in any effort to alter the cyclical timing of capital expenditures. Whatever gains come from successful speculation are at the expense of foregone earnings and savings during the period of postponement, carrying costs during the period of anticipation, increased risks from imperfect foresight, and sometimes lost strategic opportunities.

Shrinkage of the present value of a cyclically fluctuating stream of earnings is an underlying deterrent to stability. This deterrent is accentuated by heightened risks of obsolescence of processes and of products, by imperfect foresight concerning the amount and precise embodiment of demand, and by the perishability of certain kinds of strategic opportunities. The costs of carrying plant until needed and the higher supply price of funds in depression than in prosperity, coupled with shifts in affection for cash, supplement the other deterrents and tend to dwarf the savings in acquisition costs as an inducement for stable capital formation.

Cyclical changes in uncertainties and in management's appraisal and treatment of them are to a degree an autonomous cause of cyclical fluctuations, but it is impossible to separate real uncertainties from illusions born of the disasters of the great depression. Hence low visibility of future demand and technological shifts make management's propensity to capital expenditures highly volatile. This accentuates the fluctuations inherently caused by shifts in the firm's demand and supply schedules.

Thus, the causes of cyclical fluctuations in investment are deep-rooted: the gains from stability are relatively small and dubious as compared with the large and certain costs and risks of departure from the pattern dictated by the shifts in the firm's scheduled demand and supply of funds. Hence public exhortation to act for the social good seems to have dubious power, and if government is to induce private business to stabilize capital formation, the incentives and compulsions must be great indeed. If an individual firm is to do much without such changes in the rules of the game, sacrifices in earnings and loss of security will probably result.

Author Index

611

Subject Index

A

Accounting:
  allocation of common costs, 315–316
  approach to cost function, 280
  and business decisions, 25–26
  for internal control, 40
  measures of plant size, 308
  profit concept, 13–16
  profit measurement, 5, 12–28
  relation to cost analysis, 249–252
Adaptation:
  competitive, 515, 516
  of cost to output rate, 262, 273–278
Administration:
  internal control by profit standards, 39–43
  product-line policy, 120–121
Advertising:
  appropriation (see Advertising, budgets)
  budget, methods for determining, 363–375
    all-you-can-afford method, 366–368
    competitive parity approach, 372–374
    marginal approach, 355–363
    objective-and-task method, 370
    percentage-of-sales approach, 366
    return on investment approach, 368–369
  in capital budgeting, 555
  competition in, 354–355
  and competitive structure, 50–52
  contra-cyclical influence of, 376
  cost function, 356–359
  cyclical timing of, 375–385
  direct-mail, 362–363, 381–382
  economies of size and specialization in, 357
  informational, 353
  investment type, 368–369, 383
  keyed responses, 390–392
  measurement of effects of, 385–393
  national level of, 351
  nature of, 352–355

Advertising (Cont.):
  responsiveness of products, 353
  theories of, 355–363
Agricultural products, price elasticity of, 186
Allocation:
  of common costs, 313–324
  of resources by profit prospect, 583–584
Automobiles, demand for, 215, 220–229

B

Balance sheet, economic nature of, 13–16
Basing-point pricing, 74, 543
Brand, private, off-peak production, 493–494
Brand market vs. dumped market, 489
Break-even analysis, 326–341
  and short-run cost forecasting, 263
  usefulness of, 337
Budget (see also Capital budgeting):
  advertising (see Advertising, budget)
  cash, in capital budget planning, 556–557
  flexible, 327
  profit forcast, 324–325
Bulk:
  buying, 136
  selling, 135–136
Business cycles (see Cyclical)

C

Capacity:
  excess, 59–64
    relation to multiple products, 115–120
  measuring, 303–306
  cost of:
    measuring, 575–578
    shape of function, 578–580
Capital budgeting:
  demand:
    schedule of, 560–561
    survey of "needs," 558–559
    time dimension, 562–563
  nature of problem, 554–556